HISTORY OF AESTHETICS

Vol. I
ANCIENT AESTHETICS

WŁADYSŁAW TATARKIEWICZ

HISTORY OF AESTHETICS

Vol. I

ANCIENT AESTHETICS

edited by

J. HARRELL

1970
MOUTON
THE HAGUE · PARIS

PWN—POLISH SCIENTIFIC PUBLISHERS
WARSZAWA

Copyright © 1970
by
Państwowe Wydawnictwo Naukowe
(PWN—Polish Scientific Publishers)
Warszawa

No part of this book may be translated or reproduced in any form, by print, photoprint, microfilm,
or any other means, without written permission from the publishers

This is a translation from the original Polish
Historia Estetyki · Estetyka Starożytna
published in 1962 by "Ossolineum", Warszawa
translated by Adam and Ann Czerniawski

Printed in Poland
(DRP)

CONTENTS

TABLE OF ILLUSTRATIONS	vii
INTRODUCTION	1
Ancient Aesthetics	11
I. AESTHETICS OF THE ARCHAIC PERIOD	12
1. The Archaic Period	12
2. The Origins of Poetry	15
a. *Choreia*	15
b. Music	17
c. Poetry	20
3. The Origins of the Plastic Arts	22
4. The Common Aesthetic Assumptions of the Greeks	25
5. The Aesthetics of the Early Poets	30
A. Texts from Homer, Hesiod and Early Lyric Poets	34
II. AESTHETICS OF THE CLASSICAL PERIOD	41
1. The Classical Period	41
2. Literature	45
3. The Plastic Arts	48
B. Texts from the Classical Poets and Artists	75
4. Aesthetics and Philosophy	78
5. Pythagorean Aesthetics	80
C. Texts from the Pythagoreans and Heraclitus	85
6. The Aesthetics of Democritus	89
D. Texts from Democritus	93
7. The Aesthetics of the Sophists and of Socrates	95
E. Texts from the Sophists and about Socrates	104
8. Assessment of Pre-Platonic Aesthetics	111
9. The Aesthetics of Plato	112
F. Texts from Plato	127
10. The Aesthetics of Aristotle	138
G. Texts from Aristotle	155
11. The End of the Classical Period	166

III. Hellenistic Aesthetics 168
1. The Hellenistic Period 168
2. Aesthetics in Hellenistic Philosophy 171
3. The Aesthetics of the Epicureans 174
   H. Texts from the Epicureans 178
4. The Aesthetics of the Sceptics 180
   I. Texts from the Sceptics 184
5. The Aesthetics of the Stoics 185
   J. Texts from the Stoics 194
6. The Aesthetics of Cicero and the Eclectics 200
   K. Texts from Cicero 206
7. The Aesthetics of Music 215
   a. Hellenistic Music 215
   b. Musical Theory 217
   L. Texts on the Aesthetics of Music 226
8. Aesthetics of Poetry 231
   a. Hellenistic Poetry 231
   b. Poetics 235
   M. Texts on the Aesthetics of Poetry 247
9. The Aesthetics of Rhetoric 259
10. The Aesthetics of the Plastic Arts 265
    a. The Plastic Arts in Hellenistic Times 265
    b. Theory of Architecture 270
    N. Texts on the Aesthetics of Architecture 279
    c. The Theory of Painting and Sculpture 284
    O. Texts on the Aesthetics of the Plastic Arts 297
11. Classification of the Arts 307
    P. Texts on the Classification of the Arts 314
12. The Aesthetics of Plotinus 318
    R. Texts from Plotinus 325
13. An Assessment of Ancient Aesthetics 331

NAME INDEX 341
SUBJECT INDEX 349

TABLE OF ILLUSTRATIONS

1 and 2. Proportions of ancient temples 50
3. Orders in Greek architecture: Doric, Ionic and Corinthian 52
4. Geometrical plan of Roman theatres 53
5. Height and spacing of columns in Greek temples based on Pythagorean triangles 54
6. Rules followed by ancient architects in describing the helix 54
7. Rules for drawing the grooves in ancient columns 55
8. Circles and triangles as the guides for the Pantheon's proportions (based on O. Schubert) 56
9. Arrangement of acoustic vessels in ancient theatres 57
10. *Homo quadratus* (from the 1521 edition of Vitruvius) 58
11. A and B. Proportions of Greek vases (based on J. Hambidge and L. D. Caskey) 60
12. Varieties of Greek temples: pycnostylos, systylos, diastylos and areostylos 61
13. Diagram of the Parthenon's crowning (based on L. Niemojewski) . . 62
14. Modification by Greek architects of the thickness of columns depending on light or shade 64
15. Tilting of outer columns to counteract optical deformations 65
16. Reduction by ancient architects of the diameter of columns standing in shadow 66
17. Allowing for deformations of perspective in the shaping of temple architraves 67
18. Deforming the shapes of temples to achieve a proper optical effect (based on A. Choisy) 70
19. Proportions of Apollo Belvedere and Venus de Milo in correspondence to the golden section (based on A. Zholtovski) 73

Figures 1–7, 9, 12–17 are based on drawings made at the Department of the History of Architecture, Warsaw Polytechnic Institute, under the guidance of Professor P. Biegański.

INTRODUCTION

I

The study of aesthetics proceeds along many lines, containing both the theory of beauty and the theory of art, investigating both the theory of aesthetic objects and of aesthetic experiences, employing both description and prescription, both analysis and explanation.

1. THE STUDY OF BEAUTY AND THE STUDY OF ART. Aesthetics has been traditionally defined as the study of *beauty*. However some aestheticians, convinced that the notion of beauty is indeterminate and vague and therefore not suitable for investigation, have turned rather to an investigation of arts, defining aesthetics as a study of *art*. Others preferred to deal with both beauty and art; they separated these two fields of aesthetics, but investigated them both.

Each of these two concepts—of beauty and of art—undoubtedly has a different range. Beauty is not confined to art, while art is not solely the pursuit of beauty. In some periods of history, little or no connection was seen between beauty and art. The ancients studied beauty and studied art, but treated the two separately, seeing no reason to associate them.

But so many ideas about beauty have evolved from the study of art, and so many ideas about art from the study of beauty, that for modern thinkers it is impossible to dissociate the two fields. Antiquity has treated them separately, but later periods have brought them together, being interested primarily in artistic beauty and the aesthetic aspect of art. These two spheres—beauty and art—have the tendency to converge—this is in fact characteristic of the history of aesthetics. An aesthetician may interest himself in either beauty or art, but aesthetics as an entity is a twofold study, embracing both the study of beauty and the study of art. This is the first duality of aesthetics.

2. OBJECTIVE AND SUBJECTIVE AESTHETICS. Aesthetics is the study of aesthetic objects; it does however include the study of subjective aesthetic experiences. The examination of objective beauty and works of art has gradually led to subjective problems. There is probably not a single thing which someone somewhere has not regarded as beautiful nor anything whose beauty has not been denied. Everything or nothing may be beautiful, depending on the attitude one adopts. Thus, many aestheticians have reached the conclusion that the principle of their discipline is

neither beauty nor art, but the aesthetic experience, the aesthetic response to things—and that this is the proper concern of aesthetics. Some have even adopted the view that aesthetics is exclusively a study of aesthetic experience and can be a science only if it is psychological in approach. This is, however, too radical a solution: in aesthetics there is a place for both: for the study of the problems of subjective experience and of objective problems. Thus aesthetics has two lines of enquiry, this duality being as unavoidable as the first one concerning beauty and art.

This dual character of aesthetics may also be expressed through contrast between beauty conditioned by nature and beauty conditioned by man. Man is involved in aesthetics in several ways: he creates beauty and art, he evaluates them, he participates as an artist, as a receiver, and as a critic.

3. PSYCHOLOGICAL AND SOCIOLOGICAL AESTHETICS. Man's participation in art is a participation of the individual as well as of social groups. Aesthetics is, therefore, partly a study of the psychology of beauty and art, and partly of the sociology of beauty and art. This is the third duality of aesthetics.

4. DESCRIPTIVE AND PRESCRIPTIVE AESTHETICS. Many books in the field of aesthetics do no more than establish and generalize facts. They describe the properties of things which we consider beautiful, describe experiences which those beautiful things provoke in us. But other books on aesthetics go beyond establishing facts: they include recommendations on how to produce good art and real beauty, and on how to evaluate them properly. In other words: apart from descriptions aesthetics deals also with prescriptions. It is not exclusively an empirical, descriptive, psychological, social or historical science: its other aspects have a normative character. The French aesthetics of the seventeenth century was chiefly normative, the British aesthetics of the eighteenth century was descriptive. This is the fourth duality of aesthetics.

As they would be in other disciplines, prescriptions in aesthetics may be based on empirical investigations. In this case they are simple conclusions from descriptions. But they are not always so based. They are derived in part not from established facts but from postulates and standards of taste which are favoured at a particular moment. In this case the duality between descriptive and prescriptive aesthetics is at its most extreme.

5. PROPER AESTHETIC THEORY AND AESTHETIC POLITICS. This duality of aesthetics is akin to another one: to the duality of theory and politics. Establishment of facts serves the theory of art, while recommendations serve the politics of art. The theory tends to give an universal view of art and beauty, while politics defends one of many possible conceptions of art. When Democritus demonstrated that perspective alters the shapes and colours of things and that we therefore see shapes and colours not quite as they are, he contributed to the theory of art; but when Plato demanded that the artist, ignoring perspective, should present shapes and colours as they are and not as we see them, he was indulging in politics of art. In still other words, the propositions of aesthetics are partly an expression of knowledge and partly of taste.

6. AESTHETIC FACTS AND AESTHETIC EXPLANATION. Aesthetics, like every other discipline, attempts first of all to establish the properties of the objects of its studies; it investigates the properties of beauty and of art. But it also attempts to explain these properties, to say *why* beauty acts in certain way and why art has adopted certain forms and not others. There may be different kinds of explanation: aesthetics explains the impact of beauty psychologically and sometimes physiologically, it explains art-forms historically and sometimes sociologically. When Aristotle said that the beauty of things depends on their size, he was establishing a fact. But he offered an explanation of the fact when he said that things can be admired only if they are seen comfortably all at once, and too big things cannot be seen in this way. When he stated that art is imitation, Aristotle was (rightly or wrongly) establishing a fact, but he was explaining it when he said that man is naturally inclined to imitate. On the whole, ancient aesthetics was more concerned with establishing facts, while modern aesthetics lays greater stress on their explanation. This is the sixth duality that pervades aesthetics: the duality of establishing and explaining the facts and laws of beauty and art.

7. PHILOSOPHICAL AND PARTICULAR AESTHETICS. The most celebrated aesthetic theories have been inventions of philosophers: of Plato and Aristotle, Hume and Burke, Kant and Hegel, Croce and Dewey. But others are the work of artists, for instance of Leonardo, or the work of scientists, for instance that of Vitruvius or Vitelo. The Italian Renaissance possessed two great aestheticians: Ficino was a philosopher, Alberti an artist and a scholar.

All kinds of aesthetics may be empirical as well as aprioristic. There is, however, in philosophy a tendency towards apriority; and hundred years ago Fechner opposed philosophical aesthetics from *above* and scientific aesthetics from *below* (*von oben und von unten*). The historian is bound to be concerned with both.

8. AESTHETICS OF THE ARTS AND AESTHETICS OF LITERATURE. Aesthetics takes its material from the various arts; it is aesthetics of poetry, of painting, of music etc. These arts differ among themselves and their aesthetic theory moves along different lines. Actual contrasts divide *fine arts*, which appeal directly to the senses, from *poetry*, which is based on linguistic signs; and it is only natural that aesthetic theories and ideas differ from each other, because some are based on literature, some on fine arts, some emphasize sensuous images, and others intellectual symbols. A complete aesthetic theory must embrace both: sensuous and intellectual beauty, direct and symbolical art. It must be aesthetics of fine arts as well as aesthetics of literature.

Let us sum up. Every aesthetician moves in accordance with his predilections, along one of these several lines. He may 1. take more interest in beauty or more interest in art, 2. in aesthetic objects or in subjective aesthetic experiences, 3. he may provide either descriptions or prescriptions, 4. he may work in the field of psychology or sociology of beauty, 5. he may pursue the theory or the politics of art, 6. he may either establish facts or explain and interpret them, 7. he may base his views on literature or on fine arts. The aesthetician may choose between those lines of his discipline; but the historian wishing to present the development of his subject has to pursue all these lines.

The historian will find that aesthetic ideas and interests have very much changed during centuries. The gradual convergence of the ideas of art and beauty, the gradual transformation of the study of objective beauty into a study of subjective experience of it, the introduction of psychological and sociological investigations, the abandonment of prescriptions for descriptions are significant phenomena of the history of aesthetics.

II

The historian of aesthetics has not only to study the evolution of various kinds of aesthetics, but he has himself to apply various methods and points of view. In studying older ideas about aesthetics it is not enough to take into account only those which have been expressed under the name of aesthetics, or have belonged to the definite aesthetic discipline or have applied the terms "beauty" and "art". It is not sufficient to rely solely on explicit written or printed propositions. The historian will also have to draw on the taste he observes of a given period and refer to the works of arts it has produced. He will rely not only on theory, but also on practice, on works of sculpture and music, poetry and oratory.

A. If the history of aesthetics were to be limited to what has appeared under the name of aesthetics, it would have to start very late, for it was Alexander Baumgarten who in 1750 first used the term. The same problems were however discussed much earlier under other names. The term "aesthetics" is not important and even after it was coined not everybody adhered to it. Kant's great work on aesthetics though completed after Baumgarten's, was not called "aesthetics" but "critique of judgment", while the term "aesthetics" Kant employed for quite a different purpose, namely to denote a part of the theory of knowledge, the theory of space and time.

B. If the history of aesthetics were treated as the history of a particular discipline, it would not begin until the eighteenth century (Batteux, *Système des beaux arts*, 1747), and would cover merely two centuries. But beauty has been studied much earlier within other disciplines. In many instances the problems of beauty were merged with philosophy in general, as in the case of Plato. Even Aristotle did not deal with aesthetics as a separate discipline despite the fact that he has contributed a great deal to it.

C. The history of aesthetics would be very superficial in its method of selecting materials, if it were to include only thoughts uttered in treatises devoted specifically to beauty. The Pythagoreans, who exerted such a strong influence on the development of aesthetics, probably did not compose treatises of this kind; anyway, no such treatise is known. Plato admittedly did write a treatise on beauty, but he expounded his main ideas about it in other works. Aristotle did not write treatises on this subject.

Augustine wrote one, but he lost it. Thomas Aquinas not only did not write a treatise about beauty, he did not devote even a single chapter to it in any of his works; yet he said more on the subject in scattered remarks than others have said in books devoted entirely to the subject.

Thus, in its choice of material, the history of aesthetics cannot be guided by any exterior criterion, such as a particular name, or a particular area of study. It has to include *all* ideas which have a bearing on aesthetic problems and which use aesthetic concepts, even if they appear under different names and within other sciences.

If this course is adopted it will become clear that aesthetic investigation began in Europe over two thousand years before a special name was found for it and a separate area of study. Already in those early days problems were posed and resolved in a way similar to that done later under the name of "aesthetics".

1. THE HISTORY OF AESTHETIC IDEAS AND THE HISTORY OF TERMS. The historian, if he wants to describe the development of human ideas about beauty, cannot confine himself to the term "beauty", because such ideas have appeared also under other names. Particularly in ancient aesthetics more was said about harmony, *symmetria* and eurhythmy than about beauty. Conversely, the term "beauty" was used to mean something different from what we now understand by the word: in the ancient world it signified moral rather than aesthetic virtues.

Similarly, the term "art" signified in those days all kinds of skilled production and was by no means confined to fine arts. It is therefore necessary for a history of aesthetics to consider also those theories in which beauty is not called beauty and art is not called art. This creates an eighth duality: the history of aesthetics is not only a history of *ideas* of beauty and art, but also a history of the *terms* "beauty" and "art". The development of aesthetics consisted not only in the evolution of ideas, but also in the evolution of terminology, and the two evolutions were not concurrent.

2. HISTORY OF EXPLICIT AND OF IMPLICIT AESTHETICS. If the historian of aesthetics were to draw his information solely from learned aestheticians, he would fail to present a full record of what in the past was thought about beauty and art. He must also seek information among artists and must take into account the thoughts which have found expression not in learned books, but in the prevailing opinion and in the *vox populi*. Many aesthetic ideas have not immediately found verbal expression, but have first been embodied in works of art, have been expressed not in words, but in shape, colour and sound. Some works of art allow us to deduce aesthetic theses which without being explicitly stated are nevertheless revealed through them as the point of departure and the basis of these works. The history of aesthetics, when understood in its broadest sense, is composed not only of explicit aesthetic statements made by aestheticians, but also of those that are implicit in the prevailing taste or in the works of art. It should embrace not only aesthetic theory, but also the artistic practice which reveals that aesthetic theory. The historian may simply read some of the aesthetic ideas of the past in manuscripts and books, others however he must

glean from works of art, fashions and customs. This is yet another duality in aesthetics and its history, the duality of aesthetic truths conveyed explicitly in books and those contained implicitly in taste or works of art.

Progress in aesthetics has to a large extent been achieved by philosophers but it has also been achieved by psychologists and sociologists. Artists and poets, connoisseurs and critics too have revealed a number of truths about beauty and art. Their particular observations about poetry or music, painting or architecture have led to the discovery of general truths about art and beauty.

So far histories of aesthetics have confined themselves almost exlusively to the ideas of philosophers-aestheticians and to theories explicitly formulated. In any discussion of antiquity the ideas of Plato and Aristotle have been considered. But what about Pliny or Philostratus? They have their place not only in the history of artistic criticism but also in that of aesthetics. And Phidias? He belongs not only to the history of sculpture, but also to the history of aesthetics. And the Athenian attitude toward art? It too belongs to the history of taste and aesthetics. When Phidias gave to a statue which was to be placed on a high column a disproportionately large head and the Athenians objected to this, both he and they were expressing an opinion on an aesthetic problem, raised also by Plato: whether art should take account of the laws of human perception and alter nature to suit them. The Athenians' opinion was similar to Plato's, while Phidias expressed the opposite view. It is only natural that their opinions should be placed alongside Plato's and be included in the history of aesthetics with his.

3. THE EXPOSITORY AND THE EXPLANATORY HISTORY. Among aesthetic ideas born in past ages, some are quite natural and self-explanatory. The historian may do nothing more than state when and where they have appeared. On the contrary, others can be made clear only when the conditions are known which gave rise to them: i.e., the psychology of the artists, philosophers and connoisseurs who voiced them, contemporary views on art, and the social structure and taste of their time. An eleventh duality of the history of aesthetics appears.

(a) Some aesthetic ideas have arisen through the direct influence of social, economic and political conditions. They have depended upon the régime within which the exponents of these ideas lived and upon the social groups to which they belonged. Life in Imperial Rome tended to produce conceptions of beauty and art different from those of Athenian democracy and different again from those evolved in medieval monasteries. (b) Other ideas have depended only indirectly on social and political conditions, being more influenced by ideologies and philosophical theories. The aesthetics of the idealist Plato bore little resemblance to the relativistic aesthetics of the Sophists, though they lived in the same social and political conditions. (c) Aesthetic ideas have also been influenced by the contemporary art. Artists have on occasion relied on aestheticians, but the reverse is also true; theory has sometimes influenced artistic practice, but practice has also influenced aesthetic theory.

The historian of aesthetics must take account of this interdependence; when presenting the development of aesthetic ideas, he must time and again refer to the history of political systems, of philosophy, of art. This task is as necessary as it is difficult because political, artistic and philosophical influences on aesthetic theory have not only been various, but tangled often abscure and unexpected. Plato's evaluation of art, for example, was modelled on a political system. This system was not that of Athens, however, where he was born and spent his life, but of distant Sparta. His conception of beauty was dependent on philosophy, but (especially in later years) not so much on his own philosophy of Ideas, as on the Pythagorean philosophy of numbers. His ideal of art was based not on Greek art of his own times, but rather on the art of the archaic era.

4. THE HISTORY OF AESTHETIC DISCOVERIES AND THE HISTORY OF PREVAILING IDEAS. The historian of aesthetics is concerned primarily with the origin and development of notions about beauty and art, with the formation of theories of beauty, of art, artistic creation and artistic experience. His aim is to establish where, when, in what circumstances and through whom those notions and theories have arisen. He tries do discover who first defined the notions of beauty and art, who first distinguished between aesthetic and moral beauty, between art and craft, who first introduced the precise concepts of art, of creative imagination, and of aesthetic sense.

There is yet another question which the historian of aesthetics must consider important: which of the notions and theories discovered by aestheticians have found favour and response, which have been accepted and have dominated people's minds. It is significant that Greek thinkers and the Greeks in general for a long time did not regard poetry as an art, that they did not see any resemblance or connection between sculpture and music, that in the arts they laid greater stress on rules than on the free activity of the artist.

Because of this (twelfth) duality in the historian's interests, the history of aesthetics moves along two lines. It is, on the one hand, a history of discoveries and progress in aesthetic thought and, on the other, a history of its reception, which investigates aesthetic notions and theories which have been accepted by the majority of people and have prevailed for centuries.

Aesthetics has moved along many lines and the historian must follow all of them.

III

1. THE ORIGIN OF AESTHETIC HISTORY. When does the history of aesthetics begin? If we are to understand the term in its widest sense, so that it embraces the "implicit" aesthetics, then its origins are lost in the mists of time and can only be settled arbitrarily. At some point the historian must break the evolution and state: this is where I begin. The present history proceeds in this way. By deliberately limiting its task, it begins the history of aesthetics in Europe, or more specifically, in Greece. It does not deny that outside Europe, to the East, and particularly in Egypt, there probably

existed not only implicit, but also an explicitly stated aesthetics. This belonged, however, to a different historical cycle.

Although the present history does not include non-European aesthetics, it nevertheless draws attention to the relationship and the interdependence between non-European and European aesthetics. The first of these contacts appears at the very outset.

2. EGYPT AND GREECE. Diodorus Siculus wrote* that the Egyptians claimed the Greek sculptors as their pupils. By way of example they cited the two brothers who worked as sculptors in the early period and made a statue of Apollo for the island of Samos. As was often the case with Egyptian sculptors, the brothers divided their work between them. One of them completed his portion on Samos and the other completed his at Ephesus, and yet the two portions fitted together so exactly that they appeared to be the work of a single artist. Such a result was only possible where a certain method of work was adopted. Egyptian artists had a rigorously defined system of lines and proportions which they applied unvaryingly. They would divide the human body into 21 portions and would execute each member of the body in accordance with that module. Diodorus called this method *kataskeue*, which means "construction" or "fabrication".

Now Diodorus states that this method, very common in Egypt, "is not employed at all in Greece". The first Greek sculptors, like the creators of the Samian Apollo, had made use of the Egyptian method, but it is significant that their successors abandoned it. They abandoned not the measurements and canons, but the rigid systems. By doing this they not only introduced a different method, but a different conception of art.

The peoples of the ancient East, particularly the Egyptians, possessed an idea of perfect art and proportion, according to which they fixed their canons in architecture and sculpture.† They did not possess that kind of understanding of art which today we consider simpler and more natural. To judge by the surviving examples, they did not attach great importance to the representation of reality, to the expression of feelings or to giving pleasure to spectators. They linked their art with religion and the next world rather than with the world about them. They sought to embody in their works the essence of things rather than their appearance. They gave priority to schematized and geometric forms in preference to the organic forms of the world about them. The interpretation of the latter was left to the Greeks once they had broken with the East and set forth on an independent path which began a new era.

---

* Diodorus Siculus, I, 98.

† C. R. Lepsius, *Denkmäler aus Ägypten und Äthiopien* (1897). J. Lange, *Billedkunstens Fremstilling ar menneskeskikkelsen i den oeldste Periode*. W. Schäffer, *Von ägyptischer Kunst* (1930). E. Panofsky, "Die Entwicklung der Proportionslehre", *Monatshefte für Kunstwissenschaft*, IV (1921), p. 188. E. Iversen, *Canon and Proportions in Egyptian Art* (London, 1955). E. C. Keilland, *Geometry in Egyptian Art* (London, 1955). K. Michałowski, *Kanon w architekturze egipskiej* (1956).

Greek aesthetics was first embodied in Greek art before it received any verbal expression. The first writers to give such verbal expression to it were the poets Homer and Hesiod, who wrote on function and value of poetry. It was only later, in the fourth, or possibly the fifth century B.C., that this subject was taken up by scholars, chiefly those of the Pythagorean school.

3. PERIODS IN AESTHETIC HISTORY. European aesthetics has evolved from the time of the ancient Greeks and is still evolving. This evolution has been continuous, but not without crises, halts, retreats and turning-points. One of the most violent turning-points occurred after the fall of the Roman Empire, and another during the Renaissance. These two turning-points, which were the turning-points in the history of European culture as a whole, enable us to divide its history into three periods: the ancient, the medieval and the modern. This is a well established chronological division that has stood the test of time.

BIBLIOGRAPHY OF GENERAL HISTORIES OF AESTHETICS

R. Zimmermann, *Geschichte der Ästhetik als philosophischer Wissenschaft* (1858).—M. Schasler, *Kritische Geschichte der Ästhetik* (1872).—B. Bosanquet, *A History of Aesthetics* (3rd ed. 1910) (all three date from the last century and do not take account of more recent views and specialized studies).—B. Croce, *Estetica come scienza dell'espressione, e linquistica generale* (3rd ed., 1908) (ancient and medieval aesthetics treated briefly and superficially).—E. F. Carritt, *Philosophies of Beauty* (1931) (an anthology).—A. Baeumler, *Ästhetik* in: *Handbuch der Philosophie*, I (1954) (unfinished).—K. Gilbert and H. Kuhn, *A History of Aesthetics* (1939).—E. De Bruyne, *Geschiedenis van de Aesthetics*, 5 vols. (1951–3) (up to the Renaissance).—M. C. Beardsley, *Asthetics from Classical Greece to the Present* (1966).

General histories of philosophy, even the most exhaustive ones, have little or no information on aesthetics. The most recent work giving the fullest picture of our present state of knowledge is the Italian symposium *Momenti e problemi di storia dell'estetica* (Milan, 1959) (so far 2 vols., from antiquity to romanticism).

Among monographs on specialized problems relevant throughout history the following are particularly important: F. P. Chambers, *Cycles of Taste* (1928).—*History of Taste* (1932).—E. Cassirer, *Eidos und Eidolon* (1924).—E. Panofsky, *Idea* (1924).—P. O. Kristeller, "The Modern System of the Arts", *Journal of the History of Ideas* (1951).—H. Read, *Icon and Idea* (1954).

A history of the aesthetics of music: R. Schäfke, *Geschichte der Musikästhetik in Umrissen* (1934).—Also certain histories of music as such take account of the history of the aesthetics of music: J. Combarieu, *Histoire de la musique*, I (1924).—A. Einstein, *A Short History of Music* (2nd ed. 1953).

A history of the aesthetics of poetry: G. Saintsbury, *History of Criticism and Literary Taste*, 3 vols. (1902).

A history of the aesthetics of the plastic arts is L. Venturi, *Storia della critica d'arte* (1945).—An older, unfinished work is A. Dresdner's *Die Kunstkritik*, vol. I (1915).—J. Schlosser's *Die Kunstlitteratur* (1924) is in principle confined to modern times but includes an introduction about writings on art in the Middle Ages.

STUDIES OF ANCIENT AESTHETICS

E. Müller, *Geschichte der Theorie der Kunst bei den Alten*, 2 vols. (1834–7) (still valuable).—J. Walter, *Geschichte der Äesthetik im Altertum* (1893) (more of a monograph on the three chief Greek aestheticians than a true history).—K. Svoboda, *Vývoj antické estetiky* (1926) (a brief outline).—

W. Tatarkiewicz, "Art and Poetry, a Contribution to the History of Ancient Aesthetics", *Studia Philosophica*, Leopoli, II (1937).—C. Mezzantini, "L'estetica nel pensiero classico", *Grande Antologia Filosofica*, I, 2 (1954).—E. Utitz, *Bemerkungen zur altgriechischen Kunsttheorie* (1959).—A. Plebe, "Origini e problemi dell'estetica antica", *Momenti e problemi di storia dell'estetica*, I (1959).—C. Carpenter, The *Aesthetic Basis of Greek Art* (1959, 1st ed. 1921).—J. G. Warry, *Greek Aesthetic Theory* (1962).—E. Grassi, *Theorie des Schönen in der Antike* (1962).—J. Krueger, *Griechische Ästhetik* (1965) (an anthology).

On Plato's aesthetics: F. Jaffré, *Der Bergiff der techne bei Plato* (1922).—E. Cassirer, *Eidos und Eidolon* (1924).—G. M. A. Grube, "Plato's Theory of Beauty", *Monist* (1927).—P. M. Schuhl, *Platon et l'art de son temps* (1933).—L. Stefanini, *Il problema estetico in Platone* (1935).—W. J. Verdenius, *Mimesis: Plato's Doctrine of Artistic Imitation and its Meaning to Us* (Leiden, 1949).—C. Murely, "Plato and the Arts", *Classical Bulletin* (1950).—E. Huber-Abrahamowicz, *Das Problem der Kunst bei Plato* (Winterthur, 1954).—A. Plebe, *Plato, antologia di antica letteraria* (1955).—B. Schweitzer, *Platon und die bildende Kunst der Griechen* (1953).—R. C. Lodge, *Plato's Theory of Art* (1963).—Important earlier books: E. Zeller, *Philosophie der Griechen*, II Theil, 1 Abt., IV Aufl. (1889).—G. Finsler, *Platon und die aristotelische Poetik* (1900).—E. Frank, *Plato und die sogenannten Pythagoreer* (1923).

On Aristotle's aesthetics: G. Teichmüller, *Aristotelische Forschungen, II: Aristoteles' Philosophie der Kunst* (1869).—J. Bernays, *Zwei Abhandlungen über die aristotelische Theorie des Dramas* (1880).—Ch. Bénard, *L'esthétique d'Aristote* (1887).—J. Bywater, *Aristotle on the Art of Poetry* (1909).—S. H. Butcher, *Aristotle's Theory of Poetry and Fine Arts* (1923).—L. Cooper, *The Poetics of Aristotle, its Meaning and Influence* (1924).—K. Svoboda, *L'esthétique d'Aristote* (1927).—L. Cooper and A. Gudeman, *Bibliography of the Poetics of Aristotle* (1928).—E. Bignami, *La poetica di Aristotele e il concetto dell'arte presso gli antichi* (1932).—D. de Montmoulin, *La poétique d'Aristote* (Neufchatel, 1951).—R. Ingarden, "A Marginal Commentary on Aristotle's Poetics", *Journal of Aesthetics and Art Criticism* (1953).—H. House, *Aristotle's Poetics* (1956).—G. F. Else, *Aristotle's Poetics: the Argument* (1957).

ANCIENT AESTHETICS

The history of ancient aesthetics, which forms the origins and foundation of European aesthetics, covers nearly a thousand years. It begins in the fifth century B.C. (or even perhaps in the sixth) with a period that was still evolving as late as the third century A.D.

Ancient aesthetics was largely the work of the Greeks. At first it was exclusively their achievement, but later it was shared with other nations: we have in view this change when we say that aesthetics was at first "Hellenic" and then "Hellenistic". Because of this we can divide ancient aesthetics into two periods, Hellenic and Hellenistic, with the division occurring in the third century B.C.

Hellenic aesthetics may in turn be subdivided into two consecutive phases: the archaic period and the classical period. The archaic period of Greek aesthetics covered the sixth and the beginning of the fifth century B.C., while the classical period lasted from the late fifth and throughout the fourth century. If we combine the two divisions we obtain three periods in ancient aesthetics: the archaic, the classical and the Hellenistic.

The archaic period was still far from possessing a full aesthetic theory. It only produced disconnected reflections and ideas which were mostly concerned with particulars and dealt only with poetry rather than with art and beauty in general. One can treat this period as the prehistory of ancient aesthetics, its history being covered by the two later periods. But, even thus reduced, this history spans eight centuries.

I. AESTHETICS OF THE ARCHAIC PERIOD

1. The Archaic Period

1. ETHNIC CONDITIONS. When the Greeks first began to reflect on aesthetics their culture was no longer young but already had a long and complex history. As long ago as 2000 B.C. culture and art (called Minoan after the legendary king Minos) were flourishing in Crete. Then between the years 1600 and 1260 B.C. a new and different culture was created by the "proto-Hellenes" who arrived in Greece from the North. Their new culture and art, which combined features of the southern Minoan culture with the characteristics of a northern culture, had its centre in Mycenae on the Peloponese and is therefore known as Mycenaean. Its most splendid period was around the year 1400 B.C., but already in the thirteenth and twelfth centuries it had begun to decline as a result of its inability to defend itself against tribes coming from the North. These were the Dorian tribes, which until then had occupied lands to the north of Greece, but which under pressure from the Illyrians, who were moving from the Danube basin, had begun to move south. They conquered and destroyed the rich city of Mycenae and established their own rule and culture.

The period of Greek history from the Dorian conquest in the twelfth century to the fifth is known as "archaic". It embraces two distinct phases. During the first life was still primitive, but in the second—from the seventh to the beginning of the fifth century B.C.—the foundations of Greek culture, including government, learning and art, were laid. In this second phase one can find the first traces of aesthetic thought.

After the Dorian conquest Greece was inhabited by various tribes who had lived there before the invasion and by the invaders themselves. The older tribes, particularly the Ionians, had partially removed themselves from the Greek peninsula and settled on the nearby islands and along the shores of Asia Minor. Thus Ionian and Dorian territories and states in Greece bordered on each other, but the characters and the destinies of the inhabitants were different. The differences between Dorians and Ionians were not only ethnic and geographical, but embraced economy, state organization and ideology. The Dorians maintained aristocratic governments while the Ionians established democratic rule. The former were led by soldiers, while among the latter merchants soon took the lead. The Dorians venerated tradition while the Ionians were curious about novelties. Thus, at quite an early stage, the Greeks evolved two types of culture, the Dorian and the Ionian. The Ionians preserved more Mycenaean culture and also came under the influence of Cretan culture and the culture of the flourishing civilizations of the East in whose proximity they had settled. This duality between the Dorian and the Ionian culture dominated Greece for a considerable time and is discernible in her history, particularly in the history of her art and theory of art. The Greek search for constant norms in art and immutable laws governing beauty stemmed from the Dorian tradition, while their love of living reality and sensory perception stemmed from the Ionian tradition.

2. GEOGRAPHICAL CONDITIONS. Greek culture evolved with astonishing speed and splendour. This evolution is at least partly explained by the favourable natural conditions of the territories which the Greeks inhabited. The geographical situation of the peninsula and the islands, which possessed a developed coastline with suitable harbours surrounded by calm seas, facilitated travel, commerce and the exploitations of the riches of other countries. The warm healthy climate and the fertile soil ensured that the energies of the people were not wholly used up in the struggle for existence and the satisfaction of elementary human needs, but could be devoted to learning, poetry and art. On the other hand, the fertility and the natural riches of the country being only just adequate for them, the Greeks could not allow themselves to indulge in luxury or to dissipate their energies. The successful development of the country was also due to the social and political organization, and in particular to its division into a multitude of small states with numerous cities, which evolved many competing centres of life, work and culture.

The regular and harmonious structure of the landscape of Greece may have exercised a special influence on Greek artistic culture. This may have contributed to the fact that the Greek eye became used to regularity and harmony which, perhaps for that reason, the Greeks systematically applied in their art.

3. SOCIAL CONDITIONS. Over the centuries the Greeks greatly expanded their territories. With colonies established from Asia to Gibraltar they dominated the Mediterranean. The Ionians founded the eastern colonies in Asia Minor, while the Dorians founded colonies in the West in Italy, or so-called Greater Greece. By acquiring control of the Mediterranean, the Greeks evolved from a maritime nation into a seafaring nation and this in turn had further consequences.

Until the seventh century Greece was mainly an agricultural country with only a limited amount of industry. There were many products which the Greeks did not manufacture because they were bought from the Phoenicians in the East. This situation changed when the Greeks acquired colonies. Their production rose with the demand of their produce in the colonies outside Greece. From the colonies their products found their way to other countries. The Greeks possessed iron and copper ore as well as clay, while their numerous herds ensured a supply of wool. All these materials were in demand and could be exported. The export of manufactured goods followed the export of raw materials. Favourable terms of trade gave an impetus to industry, and industrial centres based on metallurgy, ceramics and weaving sprang up all over the country. Industry in turn stimulated trade and the Greeks themselves became middlemen and merchants. Trade centres were established in the Ionian colonies, particularly at Miletus, as well as in European Greece, particularly at Corinth, and later at Athens. Seafaring and trade not only increased the prosperity of the Greeks, but also their knowledge of the world and their aspirations to be no longer merely citizens of a small peninsula, but citizens of the world. Their great capacities, once they became linked with great aspirations, produced in a small nation artists and scientists of world stature.

The economic changes, most of which took place in the seventh and sixth centuries B.C., gave rise to demographic, social and political changes. Once they became established as economic centres, the cities attracted not only townspeople, but (at the foot of the Acropolis) villagers as well. They were not large centres—even Corinth and Athens in the sixth century had only about 25,000 inhabitants each—but there were many of them and they were in rivalry with each other. When industry and trade led to the rise of a prosperous middle class, a struggle with the nobility followed. As a result, the patriarchal kingdoms supported by the nobility fell and were superseded first by timocracy and then democracy, which rested not only on the people and the middle class, but also on an enlightened and prosperous nobility capable of adapting itself to new conditions. In this way a whole nation could and did take part in the creation of Greek culture.

The system was democratic but based on slavery; there were numerous slaves in Greece. In certain centres there were in fact more slaves than free citizens. Slaves relieved the free population of physical toil, enabling it to pursue its interests, which were primarily political but also included science, literature and art.

4. RELIGIOUS BELIEFS. Such, then, were the living conditions—moderately prosperous and affluent, partially industrialized, with a democratic system, though one based on slavery—which evolved in Greece during the seventh and sixth centuries. These conditions were responsible for the universally admired Greek culture. Centuries of travel and trade, of industrialization and evolution of democratic processes had to a great degree led Greece away from her early religious beliefs towards a mundane way of thinking in which the natural meant more than the supernatural. All the same, the Greeks had retained in their convictions and preferences, and, therefore, also in their arts and sciences, certain older elements—relics of other beliefs and relationships. In an enlightened, cosmopolitan community of industrialists and merchants there were regressive echoes of the dim past and an older way of thinking. This was particularly noticeable in religion and more so in the motherland of Greece than in the colonies removed from sacred sites and traditions.

Greek religion was not monolithic. The Olympian religion, which we know through Homer, Hesiod and the marble statues, was the product of new conditions and more enlightened times. It was a religion of lofty, happy, godlike supermen, it was human and anthropomorphic, full of light and serenity, without magic or superstitions, daemonism or mysteries.

However, side by side with this religion, there survived in the beliefs of the people a gloomy religion of underground deities common to the primitive peoples of Greece, while from outside, mainly from the East, the mysterious, mystical and ecstatic religion of Orphians and the cult of Dionysius infiltrated. This was a barbarous and wild cult, finding its outlet in mysteries and bacchanalia and providing an escape from the world and a means of release. Thus, two streams appeared in Greek religion; one of them embodying a spirit of order, clarity and naturalness, the other a spirit of mystery. The former brought out particular characteristics of the Greeks which in succeeding centuries have been regarded as typically Greek.

The Olympian religion, humanist and adaptable, conquered Greek poetry and sculpture. For a long time Greek poets sang the praise of the Olympian gods and Greek sculptors carved figures of gods before turning to the portrayal of human beings. This religion permeated the art of the Greeks; and aesthetics permeated their religion.

Mystical religion is less noticeable in Greek art, at least as far as poetry and sculpture are concerned. Music, however, served that religion and was therefore interpreted in accordance with its spirit. But Greek mystical religion was chiefly revealed in philosophy, and through philosophy it influenced aesthetics. While one stream of early aesthetics was an expression of philosophical enlightenment, the other was an expression of mystico-religious philosophy. This was the first clash in the history of aesthetics.

Philosophy emerged in Greece in the sixth century B.C., but its range was at first limited. The early philosophers concerned themselves with theories of nature rather than with theories of beauty and art. The latter make their first appearance in the works of poets. Their observations and aesthetic generalizations were modest in scope, but are important in the history of aesthetics: they show how the Greeks reacted to beauty at a time when they had already produced splendid works of art, but had not yet laid down any scientific propositions concerning beauty and art.

2. The Origins of Poetry

(a) *CHOREIA*

1. THE TRIUNE *Choreia*. Information about the original character and organization of the arts in Greece is indirect and hypothetical, but it is certain that their character as well as the organization were different from those in later ages. In fact the Greeks began with only two arts: an expressive art and a constructive art,* but each had

---

* Nietzsche with great insight observed the duality in Greek art, but he saw this as two currents of art, which he named "Apollonian" and "Dionysian", while indeed primarily for the Greeks they were two different arts.

numerous constituents. The first consisted of an amalgam of poetry, music and dance, while the second included architecture, sculpture and painting.

Architecture was the basis of constructive art; sculpture and painting complemented architecture in the building of temples. The dance formed the core of expressive art; it was accompanied by words and musical sounds. The dance, combined with music and poetry into a whole, formed what the eminent philologist T. Zieliński has described as the "triune *choreia*". This art expressed man's feelings and impulses through words and gestures, melody and rhythm. The term *choreia* underlines the crucial role of the dance; it is derived from *choros*, a chorus, which originally signified a group dance.

2. KATHARSIS. A later writer Aristides Quintilian, who flourished at the turn of the second century A.D., says of the archaic Greek art that it was above all an expression of feelings: "Already in ancient times people realized that some cultivate song and music when they are happily disposed, when they experience pleasure and joy, others indulge in them while experiencing melancholy and anxiety, and yet others when in a divine rapture and ecstasy". In this art of *choreia* people expressed their feelings expecting that this would bring relief. Aristides says that at a lower cultural level only those who actually participated in the dancing and singing experienced relief and satisfaction, while afterwards, on a higher intellectual level, this was also achieved by the spectators and listeners.

At first dance fulfilled the role which was later to be taken over by the theatre and by music. Dance was then the most important of the arts and had the most powerful stimulus. The experiences which were to be later available to the spectators and listeners, on the lower level of evolution had been available only to the participants, i.e., the dancers and singers. Originally the purifying art was performed within a framework of mysteries and cults, and Aristides adds that "Dionysian and similar sacrifices were justified because the dances and singing which were there performed had a soothing effect".

Aristides' testimony is important for several reasons. It shows that the early Greek *choreia* had an expressive character, that it expressed feelings rather than shaped things, that it stood for action rather than contemplation. Aristides shows that this art consisted of dancing, singing and music, and also that it was linked with cults and rituals, particularly those associated with Dionysus. It strove to soothe and pacify feelings or, to use a contemporary expression, to purge souls. Such purification the Greeks called *katharsis*, a term they employed quite early in relation to art.

3. MIMESIS. Aristides called this early expressive art "imitation", *mimesis*. Like *katharsis*, this term and concept appeared early and had a long career in Greek aesthetics. But while later it signified the representation of reality through art (in drama, painting and sculpture in particular), at the dawn of Greek culture it was applied to the dance and signified something quite different; namely, the expression of feelings and the manifestation of experiences through movement, sound and

words.* This original meaning was later changed. In early Greece *mimesis* signified imitation, but in the sense in which this term is applied to acting and not to copying. It probably made its first appearance in connection with the Dionysian cult where it signified mimicry and the ritual dances of the priests. In the Delian hymns and in Pindar the word *mimesis* means a dance. The early dances, particularly the ritual ones, were expressive, not imitative. They expressed feelings rather than imitating them. Later *mimesis* came to mean the actor's art, later still it was applied to music and even later to poetry and sculpture, and it was at this point that its primary meaning shifted.

The expressive cult dances which aimed at inducing a release of feelings and at purification were not peculiar to Greek culture, but were known to many primitive peoples. The Greeks, however, retained them even when they had reached the zenith of their culture.† They continued to hold sway over the Greek people, not merely as ritual, but as spectacle for the masses. At first these dances formed the basic art of the Greeks, who at that time had still not developed music as a separate entity divorced from movement and gesture. Neither did they have separate poetry. "There never was any archaic Greek poetry", says a student‡ of the subject. By this he means that it did not exist as a distinct art expressed only through words without the accompaniment of movement and gestures. Only in time did independent poetry and independent music develop out of this "triune *choreia*", this single art composed of movement, gesture and expression.

The primitive theory of art was based upon this primitive expressive art. The early Greeks interpreted poetry and music expressively and emotionally. By being associated with cult and magic, *choreia* paved the way for the later acceptance of the theory that poetry is an enchantment. Furthermore, because of its expressiveness, *choreia* gave substance to the evolution of the first theory of the origins of art, which stated that it is a natural expression of man, that it is for him a necessity and a symptom of his nature. This expressive art also contributed to the evolution in the consciousness of the Greeks of a duality between poetry and music on the one hand and the plastic arts on the other. For a long time the Greeks failed to see any connection between poetry and such arts as sculpture, because poetry for them was an expression and it did not occur to them to interpret sculpture in terms of expressiveness.

(b) MUSIC

1. ASSOCIATION WITH CULTS. Music, on the other hand, assumed quite early a special place in the primitive triune Greek *choreia* and gradually took over the

---

* H. Koller, *Die Mimesis in der Antike*. Dissertationes Bernenses (Bern, 1954).

† A. Delatte, *Les conceptions de l'enthousiasme chez les philosophes présocratiques* (1934).

‡ T. Georgiades, *Der griechische Rhythmus* (1949): "Altgriechische Dichtung hat es nie gegeben".

function of the dominant expressive art, the voicing of feelings.* At the same time it retained its links with religious cults. Its various forms evolved from cults connected with several deities. The pean was sung in praise of Apollo, the dithyramb, sung by the choir during spring rites, praised Dionysius, and the prosodies were sung during processions. Music was a feature of the mysteries, the singer Orpheus being regarded as its originator, just as he was regarded as the originator of the mysteries themselves. Music maintained its association with religion, although it spread to secular ceremonies both public and private. It was regarded as a special gift of the gods. Special attributes, such as magic powers, were ascribed to it. It was believed that incantation (*aoide*) exercised a power over man, depriving him of the freedom to act. Orphic sects assumed that the frenzied music which they used did at least temporarily snatch the soul from the bounds of flesh.

2. ASSOCIATION WITH THE DANCE. Even after it had moved away from the triune *choreia*, Greek music retained its association with the dance. The singers of dithyrambs dressed as satyrs were also dancers. The Greek word *choreuein* had two meanings: group dancing and group singing. The "orchestra", that is, the place in the theatre reserved for the singers, took its name from *orchesis*, dance. The singer himself played the lyre, while the chorus combined accompaniment with dancing. Arm movements were no less significant than leg movements. As in the case of Greek music, its essential feature was rhythm. It was a dance that did not require technical mastery, that was without solo performances, without rapid turns, without embraces, without women, without eroticism. It was an expressive art just as much as music was.

3. ASSOCIATION WITH POETRY. Early Greek music was also closely associated with poetry. Just as there was no poetry which was not sung, so all music was vocal music, the instruments serving merely as an accompaniment. The dithyramb (sung by a chorus to the rhythm of a trochaic pentameter) was a poetic as well as a musical form. Archilochus and Simonides were both poets and musicians to an equal degree, and their poems were sung. In the tragedies of Aeschylus sung parts (*mele*) predominated over spoken parts (*metra*).

Originally songs were not even accompanied. According to Plutarch, it was Archilochus who in the seventh century introduced accompaniment. Music without song was a later development. Solo playing on the cithara was a novelty introduced at the Pythian contests in 588 B.C. and remained something of an exception. The Greeks did not develop instrumental music of the type we know today.

Greek instruments emitted soft sounds, not very resonant and not particularly effective. This is easily understood if we consider that for a long time the instruments were used only for accompaniment. They gave no scope for virtuosity and could not be used in more complex compositions. The Greek did not use metal or leather

---

* R. Westphal, *Geschichte der alten und mittelalterlichen Musik* (1864). F. A. Gevaërt, *Histoire de la musique de l'antiquité*, 2 vols. (1875–81). K. v. Jan, *Musici auctores Graeci* (1895). H. Riemann, *Handbuch der Musikgeschichte*, Bd. I. J. Combarieu, *Histoire de la musique*, vol. I (1924).

instruments. Only the lyre and the cithara, an improved version of the lyre, were regarded by them as their own national instruments. They were so simple that anyone could play them.

From the East the Greeks borrowed wind instruments, particularly the *aulos*, which resembled the flute. Only this instrument was capable of replacing disconnected sounds with a continuous melody and, therefore, when it was first introduced it made a powerful impression on the ancient Greeks. It came to be regarded as an orgiastic stimulant and acquired a dominant position in the Dionysian cult comparable to that of the lyre in the cult of Apollo. It played the same role in drama and the dance as the lyre played in sacrifices, processions and general education. The Greeks regarded the two types of musical instruments as so different that they did not even include all instrumental music within one concept; Aristotle himself still treated "citharoetics" and "auletics" as quite distinct.

4. RHYTHM. Greek music, especially in early times, was simple. The accompaniment was always in unison and there was no question of having two parallel independent melodies. The Greeks did not know anything of polyphony. This simplicity was not, however, a symptom of primitivism and it arose not out of incompetence, but from certain theoretical assumptions, that is, from the theory of consonance (*symphonia*). The Greeks maintained that consonance between sounds is achieved when they intermingle to such an extent that they become indistinguishable, when, as they themselves put it, they fuse "like wine and honey". This, they thought, could only be achieved when the relationships between the sounds are the simplest possible.

In their music, rhythm took precedence over melody.* There was less melody in it than in modern music, but there was more rhythm. As Dionysius of Halicarnassus was later to write, "melodies please the ear, but it is rhythm which incites". This predominance of rhythm in Greek music is partly explained by the fact that music was linked with poetry and the dance.

5. NOMOS. The origins of Greek music go back to archaic times and were associated by the Greeks with Terpander, who lived in Sparta in the seventh century B.C. His achievement consisted of establishing musical norms. Thus the Greeks associated the origins of their music with the moment when its fixed norms were established. They used to describe Terpander's action as "the first fixing of norms", and the musical form which he fixed (on the basis of older liturgical chants) they called *nomos*, that is, law or order. Terpander's *nomos* was a monodic tune consisting of seven parts. Four times it achieved victory at Delphi and became in the end the obligatory form. It was an outline to which various texts were set. Certain modifications were later introduced by Thaletas the Cretan, who also flourished in Sparta and, according to Plutarch, was responsible for "the second fixing of norms". The norms changed, but neither then nor at any later time did Greek music cease to depend on them. They were most strictly observed during its golden age in the sixth

---

* H. Abert, "Die Stellung der Musik in der antiken Kultur", *Die Antike*, XII (1926), p. 136.

and fifth centuries B.C. The term *nomos* signified that in Greece the cultivation of music was regulated by compulsory norms. Even the late Greek musicologist Plutarch could write: "The highest and most proper characteristic in music is the maintenance of a suitable measure in all things".

Norms were the same for the composer and the performer. The modern distinction between the two was virtually unknown in antiquity. The composer merely supplied a skeleton of the work to be completed in detail by the performer. In a sense both were composers, but their freedom of composition was restricted by fixed norms.

(c) POETRY

1. EXCELLENCE. The great epic poetry of the Greeks probably dates from the eighth and seventh centuries B.C., the *Iliad* belonging to the eighth and the *Odyssey* to the seventh century. These were the first written poems in Europe, yet their excellence was unsurpassed. They had no antecedents since they were based on oral tradition, but in their final form were written down by poets of genius. Despite great resemblances, they were the work of two different men: the *Odyssey* embodied later attitudes and described a more southerly community. Just as in the following period Greece was to produce several tragedians of genius in succession, so now she produced two epic writers of genius of a calibre that was to remain unmatched for thousands of years to come. Thus at the time when Greece was taking the first steps in aesthetic thought, she already possessed great poetry.

This poetry soon became legendary. Its creators quickly lost their individuality and, as far as the Greeks were concerned, Homer became a synonym for a poet. He was revered as a demigod and his poetry came to be regarded as revelation. It was treated not only as art, but also as the highest wisdom, and this attitude left a mark on the Greeks' first thoughts about beauty and poetry.

The original aesthetic views of the Greeks derived from the character of Homeric poetry. Being full of myths and having divine as well as human heroes, this poetry not only consolidated but probably also to a large extent created Olympian religion. But in the divine and mythical world of Homeric poetry order reigned and everything happened in a rational and natural way. The gods were not miracle makers and their actions were subject to the forces of nature rather than of supernatural powers.

At the time when they began to think about beauty and art, the Greeks already possessed poetry of various kinds. Besides the Homeric poetry they had Hesiod's epic poetry, which praised not armed heroism, but the dignity of labour. They also had the lyric poetry of Archilochus and Anacreon, of Sappho and Pindar, and this lyric poetry was in its own way almost as perfect as Homer's epic. The excellence of this early poetry, which shows no trace of primitivism, naïveté or clumsiness, can only be explained by the fact that it had inherited a long tradition, that songs had lived and perfected themselves on the lips of the people before they were exploited by professional poets.

2. POETRY'S PUBLIC CHARACTER. This early and quite unexpected poetry of the Greeks preceded their prose. They then had no literary prose and even their philosophical treatises were in the form of poems. This poetry flourished in conjunction with music and had not completely broken away from the primitive *choreia*. Since it was associated with religion and cults, it was something more than art. Songs were a feature of processions, sacrifices and ritual. Even the great epinicia of Pindar, which praised achievements in sport, had a semi-religious atmosphere.

By being associated with ritual, Greek poetry possessed a public, social, communal and national character. Even the strict Spartans regarded it, together with music, singing and dancing, as an indispensable feature of ceremonies. They were much concerned with maintaining its artistic standard and invited the best artists to their country. Homer's epic, by its inclusion in the official programmes of state ceremonies in Sparta, Athens and other places, became the common property of the Greeks.

The cult and ceremonial poetry was intended for recitation and singing rather than individual reading. This applied to all poetry, and even the erotic lyric had more the character of a public banqueting song than a personal character. Anacreon's songs were performed at court while Sappho's songs were intended for banquets.

This communal and ritualistic poetry was an expression of public feelings and forces rather than of personal emotions. It was used as an instrument for social struggle, and some poets gave their talents to the service of democracy, while others chose to defend the past. The elegies of Solon were essentially political, Hesiod's poems were an expression of protest against social injustice, the lyrics of Alcaeus denounced tyrants, while those of Theognis voiced the complaints of nobles who had lost their status. Its ceremonious and public character, as well as its involvement in social problems, caused the poetry of the day to have a special appeal in the country.

Early Greek poetry was thus both committed to contemporary issues and had its links with the past. The links were there because of the inherited oral tradition, which had a long history. This inheritance of the past included myths, which became essential elements in poetry. These archaic, remote and mythical qualities were responsible for a gulf between the poetry and the people. This would transport the audience from mundane preoccupations into a realm of ideals. In so far as the *Iliad* and the *Odyssey* were concerned, the distance was further emphasized by their language, which was artificial, or at least no longer in use in classical Greece. This distance further enhanced their sublimity and monumentality.

3. A DOCUMENT AND A MODEL. This poetry of the Greeks—archaic yet distinguished, based on folk literature, yet full of literary accomplishment, topical, yet endowed with a remote grandeur, lyrical yet public—provides historians of aesthetics with a document reflecting the artistic understanding of an age which had yet to formulate its ideas explicitly. It shows that the age was not given to pure poetry and art for art's sake. On the contrary, it regarded poetry as being associated with religion

and ritual, as a communal and social activity capable of serving social, political and daily needs, while, at the same time, withdrawn from the world and speaking to men from a remote vantage point.

The early Greek aestheticians took this early poetry as a model, which they steadfastly kept in view when they formulated the first ideas and definitions regarding beauty and art. Yet they drew on this model only in part, noting only its superficial characteristics and missing the fundamental ones. This was so even in the case of observations made by the practitioners of verse themselves, because they too were still incapable of stating explicitly all that they had expressed in their poetry. It seems as though it was easier in those ancient times to be a good poet than a good aesthetician.

4. THE COMMON MEANS OF EXPRESSION. "There was a time", says Plutarch, "when poems, songs, chants were the common means of expression". Tacitus and Varro thought likewise. This was how the ancients accounted for the origins of poetry, music and the dance: they regarded them as archetypal, natural forms in which men expressed their feelings. But there came a time when their function and status changed. Plutarch continues: "Later, when a change came over man's life, fate and nature, things that could be got rid of were abandoned. People removed gold ornaments from their hair, discarded soft purple raiment, cut off their long locks and took off their high-heeled shoes because they had rightly become accustomed to taking pride in simplicity and to discovering in simple things the greatest ornament, splendour and brilliance. Speech, too, had changed its character with prose distinguishing truth from myth".

Perhaps there was once a time when poetry, music and the dance had been "the common means of expression" and perhaps that was the time when the arts began. But with the rise of the *theory* of poetry, music and the dance and the beginnings of ancient aesthetics that period drew to an end.

3. The Origins of the Plastic Arts

In the Greek mind there was a close association between architecture, sculpture and painting but these were regarded as totally unconnected with poetry, music and the dance. Their function was different: the former produced objects for viewing while the latter expressed feelings, the former were contemplative, the latter expressive. They did, nevertheless, all belong to the same country and the same period; and despite the differences which separated them, the historian can see that they possessed common characteristics which Greek artists themselves failed to notice.

1. ARCHITECTURE. The period spanning the eighth to the sixth centuries B.C., during which the first great Greek poetry appeared, also produced great architecture, which, like the poetry of Homer, rapidly reached such excellence that 25 centuries later modern architects, by-passing all later forms, have returned to the

models of Greek architecture in its archaic period. Thus the Greeks who first began investigating art and beauty had before them both architecture and poetry of the first quality.

Greek architecture derived certain elements from other countries, especially from Egypt (for example, the column and the colonnade) and from the North (the ridged temple roof). Nevertheless, taken as a whole, it was an original and unified creation. At a certain point in time it broke away from foreign influence and continued to develop independently in accordance with its own logic and came to be regarded by the Greeks as their own achievement.

Thus the Greeks were easily convinced that their architecture was a free creation established by them unhampered even by technical limitations and the demands of the material they used, and that it was they who had guided the technical means rather than vice versa. They had evolved such techniques as were necessary for their aims. Above all they had mastered the technique of working stone. From wood and soft limestone which they had originally employed, they had advanced, as early as the sixth century B.C., to precious materials, such as marble. Quite early they were able to undertake projects of enormous size: the Temple of Hera on the island of Samos, dating from the end of the sixth century, was a colossal building with 135 columns.

Greek architecture was as associated with religion and cults as was poetry. The efforts of the early Greek architects were devoted entirely to the creation of temples. The living quarters of the period had a wholly utilitarian character without any artistic pretensions.

2. SCULPTURE. Although it already played a significant role in archaic Greece, sculpture had not yet attained the same excellence as architecture, and was neither as independent nor as definitive in its forms. Nevertheless, it revealed some characteristics of the Greek attitude toward art and beauty even more emphatically than architecture.

Sculpture, too, was associated with cults. It confined itself to statues of the gods and temple decorations such as pediments and metopes. Only later did the Greeks begin to sculpt human forms: at first only the dead but in time also the distinguished living, particularly the winners of wrestling contests and games. This association between sculpture and religion accounts for the fact that its character was more complex than might be expected of early art. The artist was representing the world not of men, but of the gods.

Greek worship was anthropomorphic, as was Greek sculpture. It served the gods but portrayed men, it did not portray nature and had no other forms beside the human; it was anthropocentric.

But although it portrayed men, it did not represent individuals. Early Greek statues appear to have had a general character, with no attempt made to represent personality, and there was as yet no portraiture. The early sculptors treated faces schematically and did not try to impart expression to them. Indeed, it was the limbs rather than the faces which they endowed with expressiveness. In representing the human figure they were guided more by geometric invention than by observation of organic bodies and for this reason they altered, deformed and reduced the human figure to geometric patterns. They continued to arrange hair and draperies archaically in ornamental patterns with little regard for reality. In this they were not original: Greek artists were no more the inventors of geometric forms than of superhuman themes, for in both respects they were copying the East. Only when they came to repudiate these influences did the Greeks really find their own ground, but this did not occur until the classical period.

3. CONSCIOUS RESTRICTION. This early Greek art invariably relied on restricted themes and resorted to restricted forms. It laid no claim to variety, originality or novelty. It possessed a limited number of themes, types, iconographical motifs, patterns of composition, decorative forms and basic ideas and solutions. The only buildings were colonnaded temples with only minor variations allowed. Sculpture consisted of little more than the naked male figure and the draped female figure, always inflexibly symmetrical and presented frontally. Even such a simple motif as a head turned to one side or out of the perpendicular does not appear before the fifth century. But within these limits the artist had considerable freedom. Although they were subject to a set plan, temples could differ in the proportion of their parts, the number and height of columns and their disposition, the space between the columns and the weight of the entablature. Analogous variants were permissible in sculpture. But the stubborn rigidity of archaic art and its narrow limits also had positive results: by setting themselves the same task and employing the same scheme over and over again, artists were able to evolve the necessary techniques and mastery of form.

4. ARTISTIC CANONS. Greek artists treated their art as a matter of skill and obedience to general rules rather than of inspiration and imagination. They thus invested it with universal, impersonal and rational characteristics. Rationalism entered that concept of art which established itself in Greece and also became accepted by Greek philosophers. The rationality of art and its dependence on rules was the crucial point of the aesthetics implicit in archaic Greek art. These rules were absolute but were not based on *a priori* assumptions. They had been determined by structural needs, particularly in architecture. The forms of the columns and entablature of any temple, its triglyphs and metopes were dictated by statics and the nature of the building materials.

Despite its universality and rationality, Greek plastic art had a number of variants. It had two styles: the Doric and the Ionic. The Ionic displayed more freedom and imagination, while the Doric was more rigorous and subject to stricter rules. The two styles also differed in their proportions, those used in Ionic art being slimmer than those in Doric art. Both styles evolved simultaneously, but the Doric, which reached perfection earlier, became the characteristic form of the archaic period.

A famous nineteenth century architect said* that the sense of light gave the Greeks joys unknown to us. One may assume that they felt the harmony of shapes, as musically oriented people feel the harmony of sounds, that they had "perfect sight".

The Greeks saw isolated, specific objects rather than combinations of objects. Evidence of this may be observed in their art: the early group figures in the pediments of their temples are collections of separate statues.

At the close of the archaic period the Greeks already possessed a great art but had not produced any theories of art, or at least none that has come down to us in writing. The sciences of the period were concerned exclusively with nature, not with works of man, and therefore did not include aesthetics. Nevertheless, the Greeks possessed their own conception of beauty and art, which they did not record but which we can reconstruct from their artistic practice.

4. The Common Aesthetic Assumptions of the Greeks

The Greeks had to devise a language in which to think and talk about the art they created.† Some of their commonly employed concepts had been formed even before the philosophers came on the scene. They were adopted, at least in part, by the philosophers, who enlarged and transformed them. Yet they were very different from those which after centuries of learned discussion are in common use today. Even where the words employed were the same, their meaning was different.

1. THE CONCEPT OF BEAUTY. First of all, the word *kalon*, which the Greeks used and which we translate as "beauty", had a different meaning from that which this word commonly has today. It signified everything that pleases, attracts and arouses admiration. In other words, its range was wider than it is now. While it included that which pleases the eye and the ear, that which pleases by virtue of its shape, it also embraced a multitude of other things which please in different ways and for different reasons. It meant sights and sounds but also a quality of human mind and character in which we today see a value of a different order and which we only call "beautiful" with the realization that the word is being used metaphorically. The famous pronouncement of the Delphic oracle, "The most just is the most beautiful", demonstrates how the Greeks understood beauty. Out of this wide and general concept of beauty commonly used by the Greeks there emerged, but only gradually, the narrower, more specific concept of aesthetic beauty.

The Greeks first gave this narrower concept other names. Poets wrote about "charm", which "gives joy to mortals", hymns spoke of the "harmony" (*harmonia*)

---

* E. E. Viollet-le-Duc, *Dictionnaire d'architecture*: "Nous pouvons bien croire que les Grecs étaient capables de tout en fait d'art, qu'ils éprouvaient par le sens de la vue des jouissances que nous sommes trop grossiers pour jamais connaître."

† W. Tatarkiewicz, "Art and Poetry", *Studia Philosophica*, II (Lwów, 1939).

of the cosmos, sculptors referred to "symmetry" (*symmetria*), i.e., commensurateness or appropriate measure (from *syn*—together, and *metron*—measure), orators talked about eurhythmy (*eurhythmia*) that is, proper rhythm (from *eu*—well, and *rhythmos*—rhythm) and good proportion. But these terms did not become general until a later, more mature epoch. The mark of the Pythagorean philosophers is visible in such terms as harmony, symmetry and eurhythmy.

2. THE CONCEPT OF ART. The Greeks also gave a wider significance to the term *techne*,* which we translate as "art". For them it meant all skilful production and included the labours of carpenters and weavers as well as architects. They applied the term to every craft created by man (as opposed to nature) so long as it was productive (and not cognitive), relied on skill (rather than inspiration), and was consciously guided by general rules (and not just routine). They were convinced that in art, skill mattered most and for that reason held art (including the art of the carpenter and the weaver) to be a mental activity. They laid stress on the knowledge which art entails and valued it primarily on account of that knowledge.

Such a concept of art included the characteristics common not only to architecture, painting and sculpture, but also to carpentry and weaving. The Greeks did not possess a term to cover exclusively the fine arts, that is, architecture, painting and sculpture. Their wide concept of art (which we today would perhaps term "skill") survived to the end of antiquity and had a long career in European languages (which, when stressing the special features of painting or architecture, could not call them simply arts, but had to qualify them as "fine" arts). It was not until the nineteenth century that attempts were made to drop the descriptive adjective and the term "art" came to be regarded as synonymous with "fine arts". The evolution of the concept of art was similar to the evolution of the concept of beauty: it was first wider and was only gradually narrowed down to a specifically aesthetic concept.

3. DIVISION OF THE ARTS. As far as the Greeks were concerned, the arts which came later to be called fine arts did not even constitute a distinct group†. They did not divide art into fine arts and crafts. They thought that all art could be regarded as fine arts. They took it for granted that a craftsman (*demiourgos*) in any art could achieve perfection and become a master (*architekton*). The Greek attitude toward those who engaged in the arts was complex. They were valued for the knowledge they possessed, but at the same time they were despised for the fact that their work was on the same level as that of a skilled labourer and also provided a means of livelihood. The fact that *knowledge* was required for them caused the Greeks to ascribe to skills and crafts more value than we would, while the *toil* involved caused them to underrate art. This attitude had already developed in prephilosophical times, but the philosophers accepted and maintained it.

---

* R. Schaerer, Ἐπιστήμη τέχνη, *étude sur les notions de connaissance et d'art d'Homère à Platon* (Mâcon, 1930).

† W. Tatarkiewicz, *op. cit.*, pp. 15–16; P. O. Kristeller, *op. cit.*, pp. 498–506.

For the Greeks the most natural division of the arts was into those that were free and those that were servile, according to whether they demanded physical exertion or not. The free arts, which did not involve toil, were much more highly esteemed. What we term "fine" arts they categorized partly as free (as, for example, music) and partly as servile (as, for example, architecture and sculpture). Painting at first was considered servile; much later it was elevated to the higher category.

While the Greeks treated "art" in general very broadly, they had a very narrow conception of each particular art. As we have already remarked, they regarded "auletics" (the art of flute-playing) as separate from "citharoetics" (the art of playing the cithara) and only rarely did they combine the two under the concept of music. Nor did they place in the same class sculpture carved in stone and sculpture cast in bronze. Whenever different materials, tools and methods were used, or the work was executed by different types of people, two works of art were, as far as the Greeks were concerned, products of two different arts. In a similar way tragedy and comedy, epic and dithyramb were regarded as distinct types of creative activity and were only occasionally combined under the common concept of poetry. Such concepts as music or sculpture were used infrequently. More common was the much more general concept of art as a whole or such extremely specialized concepts as auletics, citharoetics, stone carving and bronze casting. Paradoxically, the Greeks created great sculpture and poetry, but in their conceptual vocabulary they did not possess generic terms covering these activities.

Greek vocabulary may lead us astray, because the same terms (such as poetry, music, architecture) were used then as now, but they meant something different to the Greeks centuries ago. *Poiesis* (deriving from *poiein*—to make) originally signified any type of production, and *poietes* meant any kind of producer, not only the producer of poems. The narrowing of the term came later. *Mousike* (derived from "Muses") signified every activity patronized by the Muses and not just the art of sound. The term *mousikos* was applied to every educated man. *Architekton* meant "senior foreman" and *architektonike* meant "major art" in a general sense. Only in time did these terms signifying "production", "education", and "major art" become narrowed down and begin to mean poetry, music and architecture respectively.

Greek ideas about art were formed in relation to the arts which the Greeks actually cultivated and these, particularly in the early stages, were different from ours. They had no poetry designed for reading; only verse for speaking, or rather for singing. They had vocal music but no purely instrumental music. Some of the arts which are today quite separate were practised by the Greeks in combination and, therefore, were treated as one art or at least as a group of related arts. It was thus with the theatre, music, and the dance. Because tragedy was staged together with songs and dances, it was, within the Greek system of ideas, closer to music and the dance than to (epic) poetry. The term "music", even when it was narrowed down to mean the art of sound, still included the dance. This gave rise to ideas which strike us as strange, as for instance, that music is superior to poetry because it acts on two senses (sound and sight), while poetry acts on one only (sound).

4. THE CONCEPT OF POETRY. While the Greek conception of art was broader, on the whole, than it is today, it was narrower in one important respect, namely in the case of poetry. The Greeks did not class poetry as art, because it did not fit the concept of art as material production based on skill and rules. Poetry they regarded as the product not of skill but of inspiration. In the plastic arts skill blinded them to the presence of inspiration while in poetry inspiration blinded them to the presence of skill, and for that reason they could see nothing in common between sculpture and poetry.

Because they could not see a relationship between poetry and the arts, they attempted to find for it a relationship with soothsaying. They placed sculptors among craftsmen, and poets among soothsayers. In their opinion, a sculptor was able to fulfil his tasks thanks to a skill (inherited from his ancestors) while a poet could do so thanks to inspiration (granted by heavenly powers). Art signified for them a production which could be learnt, and poetry that which could not. Poetry, thanks to divine intervention, gives knowledge of the highest order; it leads the soul, it educates men, it is capable of making them better. Art, on the other hand, does something quite different: it produces useful and sometimes perfect objects. It took a long time for the Greeks to realize that everything which they attributed to poetry lies within the aims and possibilities of the arts, for they too are subject to inspiration, they too guide the soul and all this shows how much in common there is between poetry and the arts.

While the Greeks of the early period failed to notice characteristics common to poetry and the plastic arts and could not find a unifying higher principle, they not only perceived poetry's relation to music, but exaggerated it so much that they treated the two as one and the same creative sphere. The explanation of this lies in the fact that they apprehended poetry acoustically and performed it simultaneously with music. Their poetry was sung and their music was vocal. Moreover, they noted that both led to a state of exultation. This served to link the two and to contrast them with the plastic arts. Sometimes they even apprehended music not as a separate art, but as an element of poetry and vice versa.

The role of the Muses was to express mythologically the ideas of the period. There were nine of them. Thalia represented comedy, Melpomene tragedy, Erato elegy, Polyhymnia lyric (sacred song?), Calliope oratory and heroic poetry, Euterpe music, Terpsichore the dance, Clio history, and Urania astronomy. There are three characteristic features of this group of nine: 1. the absence of a Muse presiding over the whole range of poetry: lyric, elegy, comedy and tragedy are not covered by a single concept since each of these literary categories has its own Muse; 2. the literary genres are related to music and the dance since these likewise are presided over by the Muses; 3. they are not, however, related to the visual arts, which have no Muses of their own. The Greeks considered poetry above the visual arts. They had Muses of history and astronomy but had no Muses of painting, sculpture or architecture.

5. THE CONCEPT OF CREATION. The early Greeks did not possess a concept of creation: they regarded art as a skill. They distinguished three elements in it: the material provided by nature, knowledge provided by tradition and the labour provided by the artist. They were quite oblivious of the fourth factor: the creative individual. They did not make any distinction between the work of a creative artist and the work done by an artisan. Nor did they attach any importance to originality. Novelty they placed lower than conformity with tradition, in which they discerned a guarantee of permanence, universality and perfection. In the early period artists were not even mentioned by name. Nothing appeared to the Greeks more important than the "canon", that is, the general rules which an artist should obey. They held that a good artist is one who has learnt the rules and applies them rather than one who tends to express his individuality.

6. THE CONCEPT OF CONTEMPLATION. The Greek view of aesthetic experience was analogous to that of artistic production. They did not consider it essentially different from any other type of human production, and similarly there is no indication that they regarded aesthetic experience as being *sui generis*. They did not have a special term for it. They did not distinguish between an aesthetic and a scientific attitude, and had the same word to describe both aesthetic contemplation and scientific enquiry, namely *theoria*, which meant viewing. In the contemplation of beautiful objects they saw nothing distinct from ordinary perception of objects. Admittedly, this contemplation was accompanied by pleasure, but then they thought this to be characteristic of all perception and cognition.

When in the fifth century Greek science reached maturity and psychologists appeared on the scene, they retained this old and commonly held view without putting forward any suggestion that the perception of beauty and of works of art may have a specific character. They took perception to be a kind of enquiry but, on the other hand, regarded enquiry as a kind of perception (*theoria*). They believed in the superiority of thought to perception and yet regarded thought as akin to perception, though to visual perception only. They regarded seeing as essentially different from hearing—not to mention the perceptions of other senses—and visual art as being totally different from art perceived by the ears. While admittedly they recognized that music was a great, sacred art, the only one capable of expressing the soul, only visual art would they call beautiful. Their concept of beauty was universal, embracing also moral beauty, but when they tried to confine it to sensual beauty they limited it to visual perception. Therefore, they built their narrower concept of beauty upon this one sense, defining it (at a later date) through shape and colour.

These, then, were the commonly accepted aesthetic ideas of the Greeks, upon which later aesthetic theories of their philosophers, critics and artists were based. These ideas were quite different from those which in modern times are employed by both laymen and philosophers. Their concept of art was wider, and they defined it differently than it is defined today. The same may be said of their concept of beauty. They divided and grouped the arts in a different way. They saw contrasts between poetry and visual arts which are unknown to modern thought. They possessed neither the idea of artistic creation nor that of aesthetic experience. In time the Greeks themselves gave up some of these specific ideas and supplied some of those that were missing, but the remainder of this task was not completed until modern times.

5. The Aesthetics of the Early Poets

1. POETS ON POETRY. Aesthetic pronouncements of poets preceded those of theorists; they were embodied not in treatises, but in poems. In the course of writing about a multitude of things, early poets incidentally would allude also to poetry, if not to art in general. We find commentary on poetry both in early epic writers, such as Homer and Hesiod, and in lyric and elegiac poets such as Archilochus, Solon, Anacreon, Pindar and Sappho. They posed simple questions which, nevertheless, were crucial to later aesthetics*. These were chiefly questions such as: What are the origins of poetry? What are its aims? How does it affect men? What is its subject-matter? What value has it? And finally, is what it says true?

2. THE PROBLEMS IN HOMER. The simplest and perhaps the most typical solutions of the period are to be found in Homer. 1. To the question: Where does poetry come from? he would answer simply that it was derived from the Muses,†[(1)] or, in a more general term, from the gods.[(2)] The singer of the *Odyssey* says, "the god has put into my heart all manner of my lays", although he adds, "none has taught me but myself".[(3)] 2. What is the aim of poetry? Here too Homer gives a simple answer. Its aim is to provide joy. "The god hath given minstrelsy to him to make men glad."[(4)]

Homer regarded the pleasure that poetry provides highly but not as something distinct from or higher than that provided by food and drink.[(5)] In listing the things he considered to be most pleasurable and most valuable he would mention feasts, dances, music, clothes, warm baths and relaxation.[(6)] He considered that the proper object of poetry was the embellishment of feasts and this was undoubtedly the popular view. "There is nothing more attractive than when ... those who take part in a feast sit in rows in the hall listening to bards: ... that seems to me to be the most beautiful thing in the world."[(7)] 3. What effect does poetry have on men? Homer expressed the thought that it spreads not only joy but charm as well. He spoke of

---

* K. Svoboda, "La conception de la poésie chez les plus anciens poètes grecs", *Charisteria Sinko* (1951). W. Kranz, "Das Verhältnis des Schöpfers zu seinem Werk in der althellenischen Literatur", *Neue Jahrbücher für das klassische Altertum*, XVII (1924). G. Lanata, "Il problema della tecnica poetica in Omero", *Antiquitas*, IX, 1–4 (1954). "La poetica dei lirici greci arcaici", *Miscellanea Paoli* (1955).

† Numerical references are to source material listed at the end of each chapter.

the spell of poetry when he described the Sirens' song.[8] He thus originated the idea of spellbinding through poetry, which was to play quite a considerable role in later Greek aesthetics. 4. What should be the subject of poetry? Homer's answer was that its subject should be famous deeds. Naturally, he had epic poetry in mind. 5. What makes poetry valuable? The fact that it is the voice of the gods speaking through poets,[9] but also the fact that it gives joy to men and preserves the memory of ancient deeds.

The general characteristic of Homer's thoughts on poetry is that they contain not a trace of the idea of its being an autonomous art. Poetry comes from the gods, its purpose is no different from that of wine, its subject no different from that of history, its value similar to that of divine voices, wine and history.

Nevertheless, Homer did value highly this gift of the gods and the inspired poet-bard[10] who is "like to the gods in voice".[11] In the group of people "useful to the country" (this was another meaning ascribed in the *Odyssey* to the term "demiurge"), next to the soothsayer, physician and artisan, Homer placed the bard; he is "welcome all over the wide earth".[12] It was quite obvious to him that the poet's skill, granted to him by the gods, was superhuman. Even if he had "ten tongues ... and ten mouths, and a voice unwearied, and a heart of bronze", he could not, without the aid of the Muses, do what he actually does.[13] This is because the profession of the poet demands knowledge, while the average man "hears only rumours and knows not anything"; only the Muses "know all things".

However, this is still not the highest praise that Homer bestows on poetry. In the *Iliad* Helen says that thanks to the song the heroes of the Trojan war will live among the "men that shall be hereafter".[14] Similarly, in the *Odyssey* we read that if the fame of Penelope's virtues is remembered, it will be thanks to song.[15] In other words, poetry is more durable than life. In order to survive in poetry it is worthwhile suffering the worst fates: the gods impose them "that there might be a song in the ears even in the folk of aftertime".[16] This is perhaps Homer's most striking statement about art.

Does poetry tell the truth, or does it invent? Homer thought it told the truth; and he valued poetry for this faithfulness. He praised the bard who sings about past events as if he himself had been present.[17] He valued equally faithfulness in sculpture and saw a "great marvel" of art in a shield which, though made of gold, resembled—thanks to the way in which it was engraved—the ploughed earth it was meant to represent.[18] But Homer also knew that art requires freedom. When Penelope asks a bard to sing in the accepted manner, her son pleads with her to let him sing in the way that his spirit will move him.[19]

These are the chief poetic problems raised by Homer. Others are only touched upon in passing, but even these are sometimes treated in a remarkable way, as, for example, the role of novelty as a means of achieving poetic effect. We read in the *Odyssey* that of all songs "men prize most (the one) which rings newest in their ears".[20]

3. THE SOURCE OF POETRY. Other early poets' views on poetry did not differ greatly from those of Homer. Regarding the source of poetry, Hesiod wrote of himself that the Muses had initiated him upon Helicon[21]. Pindar, like Homer, claimed that the gods can teach poets things which mortals are unable to discover.[22] On the other hand, Archilochus saw his poetry differently. He wrote that he was able to sing dithyrambs because "like a thunder, wine had struck his brain".[23] For him wine superseded the Muses.

4. THE AIM OF POETRY. Hesiod was in agreement with Homer that the aim of poetry was to give joy; he expressed this thought by saying that the Muses give joy to Zeus.[24] Hesiod differed, however, with respect to the kind of joy he thought poetry provided. He maintained that the Muses were created to bring relief and freedom from care. The aim he proposed was, therefore, negative but more human. Anacreon admittedly held to the traditional view of the poet as one who sings at feasts, but he wanted him to sing about other things besides conflicts and wars, and to arouse merriment in his listeners by combining the gifts of the Muses with those of Aphrodite. In the early period there was little variety in views on poetry. Anacreon's words were repeated almost unaltered by Solon when he wrote that he adored the joy-giving works of Aphrodite, Dionysus and the Muses, i.e., love, wine and poetry.[25] In this early period poetry had not yet incorporated didactic purposes. It was not to do so until the classical era when Aristophanes could say, "the poet is the teacher of adults".

5. THE EFFECTS OF POETRY. Hesiod described the effects of poetry in conformity with its aim: "Suppose one, ever drawing grief in his fresh-sorrowing spirit ... if a minstrel ... shall have chanted the glories of men of yore and the blessed gods ... quickly does he forget his melancholy, nor does he remember his care".[26] Sappho wrote: "It is not becoming that sadness should live in the homes of those who serve the Muses". Pindar wrote: "god sends a spell over songs", and elsewhere, "charm gives mortals everything that is joyful", and "awakens sweet smiles". The Greek word for "charm" is *charis* and the Graces were called Charites. These early ideas of the spell and of charm have to be emphasized in the history of aesthetics, for of all terms that were then in use, these were the closest to what we today call beauty. A slightly different idea of poetic effect appeared in the *Homeric Hymns*, where poetry is described as the "heart's serenity, love's longing and wakeful dreams".[27]

6. THE SUBJECT OF POETRY. On the subject of poetry Hesiod wrote that the Muses tell of what is, was and will be, that they constrain the poet to sing "of the past and the future". Hesiod's own poetry dealt with various topics. The *Theogony* treated of the gods, while *Works and Days* described everyday human life.

Pindar also expressed an opinion on the question whether inborn talent or acquired knowledge was more important for an artist. His reply was that talent was more important: An artist is one "who of his nature hath knowledge" and not one who has merely learnt what he has been taught.[28] His opinion was derived from the practice of poetry, and it is doubtful whether an early Greek would have applied it to sculpture or architecture, since he would have been convinced that these depended on rules.

7. THE VALUE OF POETRY. The early poets evaluated poetry realistically. Instead of begging the Muses for poetic gifts, Solon preferred to ask them for comfort, a good reputation, kindliness to friends and firmness towards enemies. In listing the representatives of various professions, he classed the poet with the merchant, peasant, craftsman, fortune-teller and physician. The poet was not placed lower than these, but neither was he treated as being above them. This was an estimate of poetry derived from the point of view of utility in everyday life.

Pindar is the author of the dictum that art is difficult.[29]

8. POETRY AND TRUTH. The Greeks also judged poetry in relation to another factor which they thought important. Here their judgment was rather unfavourable. Solon accused the bards of not telling the truth, of inventing[30] and, therefore, of lying. When at a later date philosophers arrived on the scene, their verdict on poets was similar. Pindar wrote that in defiance of truth poets deluded the souls of mortals through various inventions and by means of their sweet spell made it possible for the most unlikely things to be believed.[31] Hesiod was more circumspect. The Muses had told him that they could sing many fictions which resembled the truth, but could also, if they wished, tell "what was true".[32]

But Solon also said that he owed wisdom to the Muses.[33] To equate poetry with wisdom and the poet with the sage was the most complimentary opinion a Greek could express about poetry and poets. But wisdom (*sophia*) could have two meanings: on the one hand, it could mean cognition of the most profound truth and this was the wisdom poets sought and ascribed to themselves and, above all, to Homer. They claimed for themselves wisdom at a time when there were no philosophers or scientists.

But when Solon said he owed his wisdom to the Muses, he may also have meant, and doubtless did mean, practical wisdom, skill in writing, and art. Similarly, with Pindar *sophia* stood for "art", and *sophos* meant "artist". Wisdom in this sense did not imply truth.

There was yet another standpoint from which poets could see their work in the most favourable light. They would repeat after Homer that poetry, and poetry alone, guaranteed the survival of men and their deeds. Pindar in particular said that words outlast deeds[34]: "even deeds of might for lack of song fall into deep darkness".[35] He also said that the sufferings of Odysseus were worthwhile because, thanks to Homer, his fame would outweigh the sufferings.

To these early Greeks, poetry was something very different from art and skill. They did not even compare them. However, one archaic poet is credited with making a comparison between poetry and painting which the Greeks were to reiterate through the ages. Simonides is alleged to have said that painting is silent poetry and that poetry is spoken painting.[36]

9. BEAUTY. The words "beauty" and "beautiful" were only rarely employed by poets. Theognis wrote: "that which is beautiful is pleasant, that which is ugly is unpleasant".[37] In one of her poems, Sappho says; "A beautiful man is only so in appearance, while a good man will be beautiful as well".[38] These words meant that whatever enchants, attracts and arouses our admiration and approval (all of which the Greeks called beautiful) is also valuable and worthy to be treasured (and this they called good). Sappho's aphorism, which expressed the typically Greek association of beauty and goodness (*kalokagatia*), referred to beauty not only in its modern, purely aesthetic sense, although this sense was also included. Sappho's aphorism thus belongs to the history of aesthetics just as much as does that of Homer, who made no reference to beauty but undoubtedly had it in mind when he made the old men in the *Iliad* (III, 156) say of Helen that for such a woman it was worth waging war and risking all its discomforts.

10. MEASURE AND SUITABILITY. Hesiod formulated the following rule: "Observe moderation: in everything the fitting season is best",[39] and Theognis repeated it twice in almost the same words.[40] This rule was not intended to be an aesthetic principle, but rather to provide moral guidance. It was, however, especially characteristic of this early period not to treat beauty and art as independent, but to put them together with moral values and other aspects of life. Yet it is noteworthy that one early poet was already employing two terms ("measure" and "suitability") which were to become fundamental concepts in Greek aesthetics.

To sum up, the archaic poets saw the source of poetry as divine inspiration, its aim as the spreading of joy and enchantment as well as the glorification of the past, and its proper subject-matter as the fates of gods and men. The poets were convinced of its value, but did not realize that this was a distinct value peculiar to art. Their attitude was in some respects close to that which was later to be called romantic, and it was far removed from formalism. Had contemporary sculptors, painters, or architects recorded their views, these might have revealed a different character with more emphasis on form.

A. Texts from Homer, Hesiod and Early Lyric Poets*

ODYSSEY VIII 73.

1. Μοῦσ' ἄρ' ἀοιδὸν ἀνῆκεν
ἀειδέμεναι κλέα ἀνδρῶν.

ODYSSEY VIII 497.

2. αὐτίκ' ἐγὼ πᾶσιν μυθήσομαι
ἀνθρώποισιν,
ὡς ἄρα τοι πρόφρων θεὸς ὤπασε θέσπιν
ἀοιδήν.

SOURCES OF POETRY

1. The Muse stirred the minstrel to sing the songs of famous men.

2. So will I be thy witness among all men how the god of his grace hath given thee the gift of wondrous song.

---

* Excerpts from: *Odyssey*, tr. by S. H. Butcher and A. Lang; *Iliad*, tr. by A. Lang, W. Leaf and E. Myers; Hesiod, tr. by J. Banks; Pindar, tr. by E. Myers; Thucidides, tr. by B. Jowett; Solon, tr. by K. Freeman; *Homeric Hymns*, tr. by A. Lang.

ODYSSEY XXII 344.

3. γουνοῦμαί σ', Ὀδυσεῦ, σὺ δέ
[μ' αἴδεο καί μ' ἐλέησον.
αὐτῷ τοι μετόπισθ' ἄχος ἔσσεται, εἴ κεν
[ἀοιδὸν
πέφνῃς, ὅς τε θεοῖσι καὶ ἀνθρώποισιν
[ἀείδω.
αὐτοδίδακτος δ' εἰμί, θεὸς δέ μοι ἐν φρεσὶν
[οἴμας
παντοίας ἐνέφυσεν.

3. I entreat thee by thy knees, Odysseus, and do thou show mercy on me and have pity. It will be a sorrow to thyself in the aftertime if thou slayest me who am a minstrel, and sing before gods and men. Yea, none has taught me but myself and the god has put into my heart all manner of lays.

ODYSSEY VIII 43.

4. ... καλέσασθε δὲ θεῖον
[ἀοιδόν,
Δημόδοκον· τῷ γάρ ῥα θεὸς πέρι δῶκεν
[ἀοιδὴν
τέρπειν, ὅππῃ θυμὸς ἐποτρύνῃσιν ἀείδειν.

AIM OF POETRY

4. Moreover, bid hither the divine minstrel, Demodocos, for the god hath given minstrelsy to him as to none other to make men glad in what way soever his spirit stirs him to sing.

ODYSSEY I 150.

5. αὐτὰρ ἐπεὶ πόσιος καὶ ἐδητύος
[ἐξ ἔρον ἕντο
μνηστῆρες, τοῖσιν μὲν ἐνὶ φρεσὶν ἄλλα
[μεμήλει,
μολπή τ' ὀρχηστύς τε· τὰ γάρ τ' ἀναθή-
ματα δαιτός.

5. Now when the wooers had put from them the desire of meat and drink, they minded them of other things, even of song and dance: for these are the crown of the feast.

ODYSSEY VIII 248.

6. αἰεὶ δ' ἡμῖν δαίς τε φίλη κίθαρις
[τε χοροί τε
εἵματά τ' ἐξημοιβὰ λοετρά τε θερμὰ καὶ
[εὐναί.

6. ... and dear to us ever is the banquet, and the harp, and the dance, and changes of raiment and the warm bath, and love and sleep.

ODYSSEY IX 3.

7. Ἀλκίνοε κρεῖον, πάντων
[ἀριδείκετε λαῶν,
ἤτοι μὲν τόδε καλὸν ἀκουέμεν ἐστὶν
[ἀοιδοῦ
τοιοῦδ' οἷος ὅδ' ἐστί, θεοῖς ἐναλίγκιος
[αὐδήν.
οὐ γὰρ ἐγώ γέ τί φημι τέλος χαριέστερον
[εἶναι
ἢ ὅτ' ἐϋφροσύνη μὲν ἔχῃ κατὰ δῆμον
[ἅπαντα,
δαιτυμόνες δ' ἀνὰ δώματ' ἀκουάζωνται
[ἀοιδοῦ
ἥμενοι ἑξείης, παρὰ δὲ πλήθωσι τράπεζαι
σίτου καὶ κρειῶν, μέθυ δ' ἐκ κρητῆρος
[ἀφύσσων
οἰνοχόος φορέῃσι καὶ ἐγχείῃ δεπάεσσι·
τοῦτό τί μοι κάλλιστον ἐνὶ φρεσὶν εἴδεται
[εἶναι.

7. King Alcinous, most notable of all people, verily it is a good thing to listen to a minstrel such as this one, like to the gods in voice. Nay, as for me, I say that there is no more gracious or perfect delight than when a whole people makes merry, and the men sit orderly at the feast in the halls and listen to the singer, and the tables by them are laden with bread and flesh, and a wine bearer drawing the wine serves it round and pours it into cups. This seems to me well-nigh the fairest thing in the world.

ODYSSEY XII 41.

8. ὅς τις ἀϊδρείῃ πελάσῃ καὶ φθόγγον ἀκούσῃ
Σειρήνων, τῷ δ' οὔ τι γυνὴ καὶ νήπια τέκνα
οἴκαδε νοστήσαντι παρίσταται οὐδὲ γάνυνται,
ἀλλά τε Σειρῆνες λιγυρῇ θέλγουσιν ἀοιδῇ

THE EFFECTS OF SONG

8. Whoso draws nigh them unwittingly and hears the sound of the Siren's voice, never doth he see wife or babes stand by him on his return nor have they joy at his coming; the Sirens enchant him with their clear song.

ODYSSEY VIII 499.

9. ὃ δ' ὁρμηθεὶς θεοῦ ἄρχετο, φαῖνε δ' ἀοιδήν.

VALUE OF POETRY

9. The minstrel, being stirred by the god, began and showed forth his minstrelsy.

ODYSSEY VIII 479.

10. πᾶσι γὰρ ἀνθρώποισιν ἐπιχθονίοισιν
 [ἀοιδοί
τιμῆς ἔμμοροί εἰσι καὶ αἰδοῦς, οὕνεκ' ἄρα σφέας
οἴμας Μοῦσ' ἐδίδαξε, φίλησε δὲ φῦλον ἀοιδῶν.

10. For minstrels from all men on earth get their mead of honour and worship, inasmuch as the Muse teacheth them the paths of song and loveth the tribe of minstrels.

ODYSSEY I 369.

11. νῦν μὲν δαινύμενοι τερπώμεθα, μηδὲ
 [βοητὺς
ἔστω, ἐπεὶ τό γε καλὸν ἀκουέμεν ἐστὶν ἀοιδοῦ
τοιοῦδ' οἷος ὅδ' ἐστί, θεοῖς ἐναλίγκιος αὐδήν.

11. ...let us now feast and make merry and let there be no brawling; for, lo it is a good thing to listen to a minstrel such as him, like to the gods in voice.

ODYSSEY XVII 382.

12. τίς γὰρ δὴ ξεῖνον καλεῖ ἄλλοθεν
 [αὐτὸς ἐπελθὼν
ἄλλον γ', εἰ μὴ τῶν οἳ δημιοεργοὶ ἔασι,
μάντιν ἢ ἰητῆρα κακῶν ἢ τέκτονα δούρων,
ἢ καὶ θέσπιν ἀοιδόν, ὅ κεν τέρπῃσιν ἀείδων;
οὗτοι γὰρ κλητοί γε βροτῶν ἐπ' ἀπείρονα
 [γαῖα.

12. For whoever himself seeks out and bids to the feast a stranger from afar save only one of those that are craftsmen of the people, a prophet or a healer of ills, or a shipwright, or even a godlike minstrel who can delight all with his song? Nay, these men are welcome all over the wide earth.

ILIAD II 484.

13. ἔσπετε νῦν μοι, Μοῦσαι Ὀλύμπια
 [δώματ' ἔχουσαι,
ὑμεῖς γὰρ θεαί ἐστε, πάρεστέ τε, ἴστε τε
 [πάντα,
ἡμεῖς δὲ κλέος οἶον ἀκούομεν οὐδέ τι ἴδμεν...
πληθὺν δ' οὐκ ἂν ἐγὼ μυθήσομαι οὐδ'
 [ὀνομήνω,
οὐδ' εἴ μοι δέκα μὲν γλῶσσαι, δέκα δὲ στόματ'
 [εἶεν,
φωνὴ δ' ἄρρηκτος, χάλκεον δέ μοι ἦτορ ἐνείη,
εἰ μὴ Ὀλυμπιάδες Μοῦσαι...μνησαίαθ'...

DIVINITY OF POETRY

13. Tell me now, ye Muses that dwell in the mansions of Olympus, — seeing that ye are goddesses and are at hand and know all things, but we hear only a rumour and know not anything — ...But the common sort I could not number nor name, nay, not if ten tongues were mine and ten mouths, and a voice unwearied, and my heart of bronze within me, if the Muses of Olympus... did not put into my mind all that came to Ilios.

ILIAD VI 357.

14. οἷσιν ἐπὶ Ζεὺς θῆκε κακὸν μόρον,
[ὡς καὶ ὀπίσσω
ἀνθρώποισι πελώμεθ' ἀοίδιμοι ἐσσομένοισι.

ODYSSEY XXIV 196.

15. ... τῷ οἱ κλέος οὔ ποτ' ὀλεῖται
ἧς ἀρετῆς τεύξουσι δ'ἐπιχθονίοισιν ἀοιδὴν
ἀθάνατοι χαρίεσσαν ἐχέφρονι Πηνελοπείῃ.

ODYSSEY VIII 578.

16. ... Ἰλίου οἶτον...
τὸν δὲ θεοὶ μὲν τεῦξαν, ἐπεκλώσαντο
[δ' ὄλεθρον
ἀνθρώποις, ἵνα ᾖσι καὶ ἐσσομένοισιν ἀοιδή.

ODYSSEY VIII 489.

17. λίην γὰρ κατὰ κόσμον Ἀχαιῶν
[οἶτον ἀείδεις,
ὅσσ' ἔρξαν τ' ἔπαθόν τε καὶ ὅσσ' ἐμόγησαν
[Ἀχαιοί,
ὥς τέ που ἢ αὐτὸς παρεὼν ἢ ἄλλου ἀκούσας.

ILIAD XVIII 548.

18. ἡ δὲ μελαίνετ' ὄπισθεν, ἀρηρομένῃ
δὲ ἐῴκει,
χρυσείη περ ἐοῦσα· τὸ δὴ περὶ θαῦμα τέτυκτο.

ODYSSEY I 346.

19. τί τ' ἄρα φθονέεις ἐρίηρον ἀοιδὸν
τέρπειν ὅππῃ οἱ νόος ὄρνυται;

ODYSSEY I 351.

20. τὴν γὰρ ἀοιδὴν μᾶλλον ἐπικλείουσ'
[ἄνθρωποι,
ἥ τις ἀκουόντεσσι νεωτάτη ἀμφιπέληται.

HESIOD, Opera et dies 662.

21. Μοῦσαι γάρ μ' ἐδίδαξαν ἀθέσφατον
[ὕμνον ἀείδειν.

PINDAR, Paean VI 51 (ed. C. M. Bowra).

22. ταῦτα θεοῖσι μέν
πιθεῖν σοφοὺς δυνατόν,
βροτοῖσιν δ' ἀμάχανον εὑρέμεν.

ARCHILOCHUS, frg. 77 (ed. E. Diehl).

23. ὡς Διωνύσοι' ἄνακτος καλὸν
[ἐξάρξαι μέλος
οἶδα διθύραμβον οἴνῳ συγκεραυνωθεὶς φρένας.

PERMANENCE OF POETRY

14. ...on whom Zeus bringeth evil doom, that even in days to come we may be a song in the ears of men that shall be hereafter.

15. Wherefore the fame of her virtue shall never perish but the immortals will make a gracious song in the ears of men on earth to the fame of constant Penelope.

16. ...and the lay of Ilios... All this the gods have fashioned, and have woven the skein of death for men that there might be a song in the ears even in the folk of aftertime.

POETRY AND TRUTH

17. ...for rightly dost thou chant the faring of the Achaeans, even all they wrought and suffered, and all their travail, as if, methinks, thou hadst been present, or heard the tale from another.

18. And the field grew black behind and seemed as if it were aploughing, albeit of gold, for thus [the shield] was the great marvel of the work.

FREEDOM IN POETRY

19. Why then dost thou grudge the sweet minstrel to gladden us as his spirit moves him?

NOVELTY IN POETRY

20. ...for men always prize that song the most which rings newest in their ears.

SOURCE OF POETRY

21. ...for the Muses have taught me to sing the divine song.

22. Matters which the gods can teach the poets and which mortals are not able to discover.

23. When like a thunder wine strikes my brain, I am able to sing a beautiful song, a dithyramb, to the mighty Dionysus.

HESIOD, Theogonia 52.

24. Μοῦσαι Ὀλυμπιάδες... τὰς...
Κρονίδῃ τέκε πατρὶ μιγεῖσα Μνημοσύνη...
λησμοσύνην τε κακῶν ἄμπαυμά τε
[μερμηράων.

AIM OF POETRY

24. ...the Olympian Muses... the Muses, I say, whom Mnemosyne... bore to be a means of oblivion of ills and a rest from cares.

SOLON, frg. 20 (Diehl).

25. ἔργα δὲ Κυπρογενοῦς νῦν μοι φίλα
[καὶ Διονύσου
καὶ Μουσέων, ἃ τίθησ' ἀνδράσιν εὐφροσύνας.

25. The works of the Cyprus-born now are dear to me, and of Dionysus and the Muses, who give gladness to men.

HESIOD, Theogonia 96.

26. ὁ δ' ὄλβιος, ὅν τινα Μοῦσαι
φίλωνται· γλυκερή οἱ ἀπὸ στόματος ῥέει
[αὐδή.
εἰ γάρ τις καὶ πένθος ἔχων νεοκηδέι θυμῷ
ἄζηται κραδίην ἀκαχήμενος, αὐτὰρ ἀοιδὸς
Μουσάων θεράπων κλέεα προτέρων
[ἀνθρώπων
ὑμνήσῃ μάκαράς τε θεούς, οἳ Ὄλυμπον
[ἔχουσιν,
αἶψ' ὅ γε δυσφροσυνέων ἐπιλήθεται οὐδέ
[τι κηδέων
μέμνηται· ταχέως δέ παρέτραπε δῶρα θεάων.

THE EFFECTS OF POETRY

26. Yet happy he whomsoever the Muses shall have loved; sweet is the sound that flows from his mouth. For suppose one, ever drawing grief in his fresh—sorrowing spirit, pines away troubled at heart, yet if a minstrel, servant of the Muses, shall have chanted the glories of men of yore, and the blessed gods who hold Olympus, quickly does he forget his melancholy, nor does he remember his care and quickly have the gifts of the gods diverted them.

HOMERIC HYMNS, In Mercurium 439.

27. νῦν δ' ἄγε μοι τόδε εἰπέ,
[πολύτροπε Μαιάδος υἱέ,
ἦ σοι γ' ἐκ γενετῆς τάδ' ἅμ' ἕσπετο
[θαυματὰ ἔργα
ἠέ τις ἀθανάτων ἠὲ θνητῶν ἀνθρώπων
δῶρον ἀγαυὸν ἔδωκε καὶ ἔφρασε θέσπιν
[ἀοιδήν;...
τίς τέχνη, τίς μοῦσα ἀμηχανέων μελεδώνων,
τίς τρίβος· ἀτρεκέως γὰρ ἅμα τρία πάντα
[πάρεστιν,
εὐφροσύνην καὶ ἔρωτα καὶ ἥδυμον ὕπνον
[ἑλέσθαι.

27. But come now, tell me this, thou wily son of Maia, have these marvels been with thee even since thy birth, or is it that some immortal or some mortal man has given thee the glorious gift and shown thee song divine?...
What art is this, what charm against the threat of cares? What a path of song! For verily here is choice of all three things, joy, love and sweet sleep.

PINDAR, Olympia II 86 (Bowra).

28. σοφὸς ὁ πολλὰ εἰδὼς φυᾷ.
μαθόντες δὲ λάβροι
παγγλωσσίᾳ κόρακες ὣς
ἄκραντα γαρύετον.

28. His art is true who of his nature hath knowledge; they who have but learnt strong in the multitude of words, are as crows that chatter vain things in strife against the divine bird of Zeus.

PINDAR, Olympia IX 107 (Bowra).

29. σοφίαι μὲν
αἰπειναί.

29. Skill of all kinds is hard to attain unto.

SOLON, frg.21 (Diehl)

30. πολλὰ ψεύδονται ἀοιδοί.

PINDAR, Olympia I 28 (Bowra).

31. ἦ θαυματὰ πολλά, καί πού τι καὶ
 [βροτῶν
φάτιν ὑπὲρ τὸν ἀλαθῆ λόγον
δεδαιδαλμένοι ψεύδεσι ποικίλοις
ἐξαπατῶντι μῦθοι.
χάρις δ' ἅπερ ἅπαντα τεύχει τὰ μείλιχα
 [θνατοῖς
ἐπιφέροισα τιμὰν καὶ ἄπιστον ἐμήσατο πιστόν
 ἐμμέναι τὸ πολλάκις.

HESIOD, Theogonia 22.

32. αἵ νύ ποθ' Ἡσίοδον καλήν
 [ἐδίδαξαν ἀοιδήν...
τόνδε δέ με πρώτιστα θεαὶ πρὸς μῦθον
 [ἔειπον,
Μοῦσαι Ὀλυμπιάδες...
ἴδμεν ψεύδεα πολλὰ λέγειν ἐτύμοισιν ὁμοῖα
ἴδμεν δ', εὖτ' ἐθέλωμεν, ἀληθέα γηρύσασθαι.

THUCYDIDES, II 41 (Pericles' speech)

οὐδὲν προσδεόμενοι οὔτε
Ὁμήρου ἐπαινέτου οὔτε ὅστις ἔπεσι μὲν
τὸ αὐτίκα τέρψει, τῶν δ' ἔργων τὴν
ὑπόνοιαν ἡ ἀλήθεια βλάψει.

SOLON, frg. 1 w. 49 (Diehl).

33. ἄλλος Ἀθηναίης τε καὶ
 [Ἡφαίστου πολυτέχνεω
ἔργα δαεὶς χειροῖν ξυλλέγεται βίοτον,
ἄλλος Ὀλυμπιάδων Μουσέων πάρα δῶρα
 [διδαχθείς,
ἱμερτῆς σοφίης μέτρον ἐπιστάμενος.

PINDAR, Nemea IV 6 (Bowra).

34. Ῥῆμα δ' ἐργμάτων χρονιώτερον
 [βιοτεύει
ὅτι κε σὺν χαρίτων τύχᾳ
γλῶσσα φρενὸς ἐξέλοι βαθείας.

PINDAR, Nemea VII 12 (Bowra).

35. καὶ μεγάλαι γὰρ ἀλκαὶ
σκότον πολὺν ὕμνων ἔχοντι δεόμεναι·
ἔργοις δὲ καλοῖς ἔσοπτρον ἴσαμεν ἑνὶ σὺν
 [τρόπῳ,
εἰ Μναμοσύνας ἕκατι λιπαράμπυκος

POETRY AND TRUTH

30. Minstrels tell many falsehoods.

31. Verily many things are wondrous, and sometimes men's speech goes beyond the truth. We are deceived by fables embellished with colourful fictions. For grace who makes all sweet things for mortal men, by lending honour unto such maketh oft the unbelievable thing to be believed.

32. ...they [earth, ocean, dark night, the Immortals etc.] once taught Hesiod a lovely song... But first of all the goddesses, the Olympian Muses, daughters of Aegis-bearing Jove, addressed me in a speech such as this: ...we know to sing many fictions like to truths, and we know, when we will, to speak what is true.

We shall not need the praises of Homer or any other panegyrist whose poetry may please for a moment, although his representation of the facts will not bear the light of day.

VALUE OF POETRY

33. Another, skilled in the work of Athene and Hephaestos, the able craftsman, collects a living by means of his two hands. Another, trained in the gifts of the Olympian Muses, has knowledge of lovely verses' measure.

34. For speech is longer lived than act, whensoever by favour of the Graces the tongue hath drawn it forth out of the depth of the heart.

SURVIVAL THROUGH POETRY

35. For even deeds of might for lack of song fall into deep darkness, and in but one way have we knowledge of a mirror of fair deeds, if by the grace of Mnemosyne... they

εὕρηται ἄποινα μόχθων κλυταῖς ἐπέων
[ἀοιδαῖς...
ἀφνεὸς πενιχρός τε θανάτου πέρας
ἅμα νέονται. ἐγὼ δὲ πλέον' ἔλπομαι
λόγον Ὀδυσσέος ἢ πάθαν διὰ τὸν ἁδυεπῆ
[γενέσθ' Ὅμηρον.
ἐπεὶ ψεύδεσί οἱ ποτανᾷ τε μαχανᾷ
σεμνὸν ἔπεστί τι· σοφία δὲ κλέπτει
[παράγοισα μύθοις·

attain unto a recompense of toil by the sound of voice and verse...

Rich and poor alike move in even step towards death which ends everything. Now I have suspicion that the fame of Odysseus is become greater than his toil through the sweet lays that Homer sang; for over the feigning of his winged craft something of majesty abideth, and the excellence of his skill persuadeth us to his fables unaware.

PINDAR, frg. 106 b (Bowra).

... πρέπει δ' ἐσθλοῖσιν ὑμνεῖθαι
... καλλίσταις ἀοιδαῖς.
τοῦτο γὰρ ἀθανάτοις τιμαῖς ποτιψαύει μόνον
θνᾴσκει δὲ σιγαθὲν καλὸν ἔργον ⟨ἅπαν⟩.

...it is worthy to describe the noble ones in the most beautiful songs, only this will make it equal to the privileges of the immortals, while every noble deed dies when it sinks into oblivion.

PLUTARCH, De gloria Atheniensium 3.

36. ὁ Σιμωνίδης τὴν μὲν ζωγραφίαν ποίησιν σιωπῶσαν προσαγορεύει, τὴν δὲ ποίησιν ζωγραφίαν λαλοῦσαν.

PAINTING AND POETRY

36. Simonides calls painting silent poetry, and poetry articulate painting.

THEOGNIS 15.

37. Μοῦσαι καὶ Χάριτες, κοῦραι Διός...
... καλὸν ἀείσατ' ἔπος·
«ὅττι καλόν, φίλον ἐστί· τὸ δ' οὐ καλὸν οὐ
[φίλον ἐστίν».

BEAUTY

37. The Muses and the Graces, the daughters of Zeus... sang beautiful words: "That which is beautiful is pleasant, that which is ugly is unpleasant".

SAPPHO, frg. 49 (Diehl).

38. ὁ μὲν γὰρ κάλος, ὅσσον ἴδην,
[πέλεται ⟨ἄγαθος⟩,
ὁ δὲ κἄγαθος αὔτικα καὶ κάλος ἔσσεται.

38. A beautiful man is only so in appearance, while a good man will be beautiful as well.

HESIOD, Opera et dies 694.

39. μέτρα φυλάσσεσθαι· καιρὸς δ' ἐπὶ
[πᾶσιν ἄριστος.

MEASURE

39. Observe moderation: in everything the fitting season is best.

THEOGNIS 401.

40. μηδὲν ἄγαν σπεύδειν· καιρὸς δ' ἐπὶ
[πᾶσιν
ἄριστος ἔργμασιν ἀνθρώπων.

40. Not to desire anything too much; in all human actions *kairos* is best.

II. AESTHETICS OF THE CLASSICAL PERIOD

1. The Classical Period

1. THE ATHENIAN PERIOD. The second period of Greek history was the most splendid: it was a period of military conquests, social progress, of increasing prosperity and great works of art and learning. Having conquered Persia, the only other great power at that time, the Greeks became a nation without rivals. After their military victory over the Persians, the Greeks ousted them and the Phoenicians from the centres of trade, and in this sphere, too, they became supreme. The speed of growth in the fifth century was breath-taking: conquest succeeded conquest and political reform, scientific discoveries and masterpieces of art followed each other in rapid succession.

This period of splendour was by no means peaceful. On the contrary, it was a time of ceaseless wars and internal struggles among the different Greek states and between social classes, factions and leaders. The Greeks did not live peacefully, but in a state of tension. Battles against invaders aroused patriotic fervour and consolidated the feeling of power and national unity.

In a country boasting numerous political, industrial and trading centres and seats of learning, one region now gained predominance: this was Attica, and, in particular, Athens. Attica had a good geographical location and quite considerable natural resources. Already in the sixth century Pisistratus had developed Athens as a sea power, organized its crafts and trade, and established patronage over literature and the arts. Up to the middle of the fifth century, Athens granted citizenship liberally, but outsiders, too, were free to carry on trade there. By the middle of the fifth century, Athenian wealth and the size of its population eclipsed even that of Syracuse. Its prestige was raised both by military victories and cultural expansion. The Delian League was established under Athenian leadership and the treasury was moved from Delos to Athens. The peak of Athenian greatness was reached in the time of Pericles, towards the middle of the fifth century. Ever since, that period has been called "Attic" or "Athenian".

As late as the beginning of the fifth century, Greek culture was evolving along two lines, the one pursued by the Dorians and the other by the Ionians. Both elements, however, appeared in Athenian society and were intertwined in Athenian culture. The Doric and the Ionic ceased to be the styles of two provinces and became two styles of one country. Next to the Doric Parthenon on the Acropolis stood the Erechtheum, Ionic in style. A similar situation prevailed in the sciences, especially in aesthetics: Athenian Sophists followed the Ionian empirical style, while Plato maintained the tradition of the Dorian rationalistic approach.

2. THE DEMOCRATIC PERIOD. Evolution in Athens tended towards social progress and the democratization of life. Reform had already begun under Solon in the sixth century and expanded greatly in the fifth century under Cleisthenes, when citizens' rights were made uniform and everyone was allowed to participate in government. The Areopagus, the last undemocratic institution, lost its power in 464. The establishment of paid offices under Pericles enabled even the poorest to take part in government. Positions were filled not by vote but by drawing lots. In accordance with the constitution, the People's Ecclesia met at least three times a month. Even current affairs were settled collectively by the Council of Five Hundred. Every Athenian took part in public affairs and did so continuously. Every Athenian, that is, except the slaves, who laboured so that the citizens might govern and devote themselves to learning and the arts.

Never had art been more closely associated with the life of the nation. Tragedies and comedies served politics by praising or denouncing economic and political programmes.

3. THE ATHENIAN PEOPLE. It would be a mistake to regard the Athenian people who ruled the state during its most splendid period as a team of enlightened citizens, models of progress and virtue. On the contrary, they were not particularly enthusiastic about enlightenment, as is shown by their having condemned to death Socrates, an advocate for enlightenment. Xenophon, speaking through Socrates, observes that the People's Ecclesia consisted of those who traded in the market place and thought only of how to buy cheaper and sell dearer. We know about the Athenians' negative qualities: their greed, envy, vanity and affectation. But their great merits are also beyond doubt. They were excitable, sensitive, highly imaginative and, unlike the dour Spartans, serene and gay. They were free men unable to exist without freedom, they admired beauty, had innate good taste and appreciation for good art, they combined a natural sensuality with a love of abstract ideas. They loved the carefree life of leisure, but were capable of sacrifice and heroism when required. They were self-seeking but also ambitious, and this ambition made them magnanimous. They were all-rounders who divided their time between professional work, social affairs and amusements. Furthermore, as the eminent philologist T. Sinko has pointed out, "each citizen was also either a reservist or a veteran".

It would be a mistake to imagine the Athenians' life as rich, sumptuous and comfortable. Thucydides has preserved the words of Pericles: "We love beauty in moderation, we love wisdom without falling into weakness". They demanded little for themselves: their public buildings were splendid, but their private dwellings were not. They did not boast of their riches, nor did they disguise their poverty. Because they were satisfied with little, many of them were free of material worries and could, if not create art, at least enjoy it. Isocrates looking back to the time of Pericles could say, "each day was a festival", and, despite the bustle of the Athenian period, it was at that time that Anaxagoras is supposed to have said in reply to the question why he preferred to be rather than not to be, "In order to gaze at the sky and the harmony of the universe".

4. THE END OF THE PERIOD. Favourable political conditions in Greece did not last long. Towards the end of the fifth century, the concord among the Greek states was broken by dissensions and rivalries, and the long drawn-out Peloponesian War in particular led to the impoverishment of the land. Athens especially suffered heavy blows: sieges, plagues, intensified internecine strife, frequent political upheavals, restrictions imposed upon the political system, and fruitless attempts by the Athenians to regain their hegemony. Meanwhile, with the fourth century came the era of Macedonian and Chaeronean supremacy. Politically Athens was in decline. From the political point of view, there might be grounds for confining the classical period to the fifth century, but this demarcation cannot be applied to intellectual life. In this respect the fourth century brought no significant change, and Athens remained the capital of letters, oratory, art and science. The Greek state was in decadence, but their culture flourished so magnificently that it was able to become a universal culture dominating the world. The political and social achievements of the Greeks have proved ephemeral, but their art has survived for centuries as has their knowledge of art.

5. CLASSICISM. The term "classicism" is applied to the short-lived but supreme period of Greek culture, and its art and literature are called "classical".* However, this term is ambiguous.

A. In one sense, we call classical that which is the most mature, most excellent product of a culture. Thus the fifth and fourth centuries B.C. in Greece, and particularly the age of Pericles, may be called classical because this was its period of greatest perfection, its culmination. But we must remember that in this sense of the word other cultures, quite unlike that of Periclean Greece, may be described as classical. The Gothic culture of the thirteenth century, dissimilar though it is, is from this point of view also classical, because it is the mature expression of the Middle Ages, just as the other is an expression of antiquity. When we describe a culture in this way as classical, we define its value, but not its character. Classical periods

---

* G. Rodenwaldt, "Zum Begriff und geschichtlichen Bedeutung des Klassischen in der bildenden Kunst", *Zeitschrift für Ästhetik u. allg. Kunstwissenschaft*, XI (1916). *Das Problem des Klassischen in der Kunst, acht Vorträge*, ed. W. Jaeger (1931) (the works of B. Schweitzer, J. Stroux, H. Kuhn and others). A. Körte, "Der Begriff des Klassischen in der Antike", *Berichte über Verhandlungen der Sächsischen Akademie der Wissenschaften*, Phil.-hist. Klasse, CXXXVI, 3 (1934). H. Rose, *Klassik als künstlerische Denkform des Abendlandes* (1937). Volume of *Recherches*, II (1946) (works by W. Deonna, P. Fierens, L. Hautecoeur and others). W. Tatarkiewicz, "Les quatre significations du mot 'classique' ", *Revue Internationale de Philosophie*, 43 (1958).

usually last for a very short time. No sooner do culture, art and poetry reach their zenith than they begin to decline, for it is difficult to remain on the summit. In Greece the indisputably classical period was the brief Periclean age and only in a looser sense can it be extended to cover two centuries.

The opposite of classical art and poetry is in this sense simply less perfect and less mature art and poetry. More precisely, the opposite of classicism is, on the one hand, "archaism" or "primitivism", when art has not yet reached maturity, and on the other, art that has become decadent. In the past, decadent art used to be called "baroque", but today we are inclined to the view that baroque is a type of art in its own right with its own classical and decadent periods.

B. The term "classical" has yet another meaning: it denotes culture, art, poetry, with certain characteristics, namely moderation, restraint, harmony, balance between parts. Greek art and poetry of the fifth and fourth centuries B.C. were classical also in this sense; they even became a model for all succeeding periods which aimed at restraint, harmony and balance.

In this sense we can no longer speak of "the classicism of the thirteenth century" or about "classical Gothic", because Gothic art makes no claims to restraint. So also baroque and romantic art are not classical, since they pursue ends other than moderation. While in the first meaning "classical" is a concept of valuation (as it distinguishes classicism on the basis of its perfection), in the second one it is a descriptive concept.

The art, literature and culture of the Age of Pericles (and even of the whole of the fifth and fourth centuries B.C.) were classical in both senses. The term "classical" is sometimes stretched to describe the whole of antiquity, but that use of the term corresponds to neither of the two meanings of this term: antiquity was not mature from the beginning, nor was it characterized by restraint and balance right to the end. It also had its baroque and romantic periods; its classical age spanned only the fifth and the fourth centuries.

Though this was the prototypic classical age, it was not the only classical period in history. In later antiquity, in the Middle Ages and in modern times we find periods of excellence and restraint. It was so in Roman times under Augustus, in France under Charlemagne and in Florence under the Medicis. In the Paris of Louis XIV and of Napoleon, attempts were made to achieve not only a classical art, but an art identical with that of the Greeks: instead of original classical forms being sought, old ones were imitated. In the nineteenth century such imitative classical art was called "pseudo-classical" and today is called "classicist" or "neoclassical". The theatre of Sophocles is classical, that of Racine neoclassical; the sculpture of Phidias is classical, that of Canova neoclassical.

The Periclean Age was not only a *kat exochen* classical period, but also a prototype of other classical periods and a model for the neoclassical ones.

2. Literature

1. TRAGEDY. The classical age in Greece did not produce any great new epics or lyrical works, but the poetry of Homer and the early lyrical poets continued to have a vital importance. Homer was still regarded not only as the greatest poet but also as a sage, a fount not only of beauty but of wisdom also. In the eyes of the earliest aestheticians the poetry of the first great poets was already far in the past but was surrounded with a halo imposed by time.

But the classical age also possessed its own great poetry: the major Greek tragedies. The following features of Greek tragedy are especially important in the history of aesthetics.*

(*a*) Greek tragedy grew out of ritual which belonged to religious cults and was more closely linked with them than was the Greek epic or lyric. It originated in traditional *choreia*, dances and songs but attained greatness because of its thought and subject-matter that concerned the great problems of life and human fate.

(*b*) Visually, it was more like modern opera than modern tragedy. At first the chorus played the leading role. There was only one actor, and it was Aeschylus who introduced a second. There were choral declamations, but these were really songs. Music and the dance were a continuation of the primitive triune *choreia*, which relied upon speech, sound and movement in equal measure. It was more like a sound performance than a spectacle. Especially at the beginning, decor was of secondary importance.

(*c*) At first tragedy had nothing in common with realism. In its early period it was concerned not with human affairs, but with the borderline between the human and the divine. Aeschylus' tragedies were close to dithyrambic cantatas. Their themes were mythical, their plots simple, and they dealt with the relationship between men and gods, between freedom and necessity; they unrolled in a miraculous, supernatural atmosphere, without making any attempt at differentiation of characters or at representation of reality. In their design these dramas were more like the archaic sculpture of Olympia than the classical sculpture of the Parthenon.

(*d*) It was an art for all. From the time of Pericles every Athenian citizen received money from the State for theatre tickets. Five official judges chose the plays but they were guided by the taste of a mass audience.

(*e*) It was the product of a single individual and not the composite work of poet, composer and producer. At first the author not only wrote the script but composed the music and the songs, arranged the dances, and was also the producer, actor and even business manager.

(*f*) According to the consensus of opinion in later ages this tragedy reached heights which have not since been surpassed. In accordance with the strange "law of series" three great Greek tragedians appeared in close succession: Aeschylus (525–456),

---

* E. Egger, *L'histoire de la critique chez les Grecs* (1887). J. W. H. Atkins, *Literary Criticism in Antiquity* (1934). The two books do not contribute a great deal to the history of aesthetics.

Sophocles (496–406), and Euripides (480–406/5). The eldest was still writing when the youngest one began.

Greek tragedy developed at a breath-takingly swift pace. Aeschylus reduced the size of the chorus, developed dialogue, introduced more sumptuous decor, and dressed the actors in flowing robes and higher cothurni. Sophocles discarded the archaism still evident in Aeschylus, and his tragedies are more complex, more intricate in design, more realistic and human, but also harmonized and idealized. He maintained that he showed men "as they ought to be".[1] The final stage was reached by Euripides, who depicted men "as they are", and was a realist, who made the transition from divine to human tragedy.

(g) The great tragedians were concerned with social actualities. Sophocles represented the ideology of the right and was opposed to the radical enlightenment of the Sophists, while Euripides was associated with the Sophists. In the writings of these two dramatists the conflict between tradition and innovation, between conservative and progressive tendencies, was introduced into art and soon passed into the theory of art as well.

2. AESTHETIC OPINIONS OF THE TRAGEDIANS AND OF EPICHARMUS. It is difficult to find statements on aesthetics in the texts of the tragedians. They were more inclined to express themselves on ethical problems because they were more concerned with subject-matter than with form. Nevertheless, we do find in Sophocles allusions to the utility and pleasure provided by plays; in Euripides we read that love makes man a poet[2] and also find a repetition of the statement by Theognis: "that which is beautiful is pleasant".[3]

More comprehensive remarks on aesthetics are to be found in Epicharmus, the chief representative of the Sicilian realistic and nonritual drama. Epicharmus was a contemporary of Aeschylus and may even have been older than him. His remarks are fuller because he was a philosopher and a scholar as well as a dramatist. Diogenes Laertius informs us that his works included treatises on physics and medicine as well as a collection of aphorisms. His treatise *On Nature* was known in antiquity, although some philologists question his authorship of it, and it is in this work that his observations on aesthetics are to be found. He used to be classified as a Pythagorean, but the fragments which have come down to us (including those on aesthetics), far from confirming this, show him to have been close to the other pole of philosophy of the time, that is, to the empirical and relativistic idea of the Sophists.

One fragment attributed to him speaks of the relativity of artistic forms, of their dependence on man. Another states that the most important thing in art is the artist's talent granted him by nature.[4] In the third we read, that "mind has sight and mind has hearing".[5] This is a concise formulation of Greek intellectualism, stating that our knowledge derives from thought even when it seems to come from our eyes and ears. This view was also significant for the theory of beauty and art, and it is remarkable that it should have been a poet who gave it such a radical expression.

3. THE END OF TRAGEDY; ARISTOPHANES. The great period of drama was brief and did not survive beyond the fifth century: Athenian tragedy came to an end with the death of Sophocles and Euripides. In the fourth century works for the theatre continued to appear; indeed, production in fact increased, many authors wrote for the stage and some were extremely prolific. Astidamus of Athens composed 240 tragedies and satirical dramas and Carcinus of Acragas 160, Antiphanes of Athens wrote 245 comedies and Alexis of Thurii 280. But the standard was not high, and in the fourth century eminent minds turned rather to prose. Admittedly, audiences were in love with the theatre and stars of the stage toured Greece, but the theatrical cult was chiefly a cult of the actor. Aristophanes tells us that in his time the actor meant more than a poet.

In 406, after the deaths of Sophocles and Euripides, Aristophanes summed up the stage of Athenian tragedy in his comedy *The Frogs*. He concluded, not unjustly, that tragedy had come to an end, and blamed the last tragedian (Euripides) for this. He ascribed this misfortune to Euripides' modernist and enlightened views, which he considered were ruining the country. The underlying cause was that Euripides had fallen under the influence of Socrates and been swayed by philosophy, and that he had exchanged sublimity for sobriety. This judgment was accurate to the extent that Socrates and the Sophists, philosophy and enlightenment, did bring about a change in Greek culture. In the fourth century prose became more important than poetry. Philosophy took over from poetry the dominant role in Greek intellectual life. The great problems of human existence which had given birth to tragedy now caused its eclipse, because it came to be generally considered that it was more satisfactory to pose these questions elsewhere and in a different way and that they were better dealt with by philosophers than by poets. Indirectly, this had a beneficial outcome for art, because it led philosophers to construct a theory of poetry and art.

Aristophanes was not a theorist, but he influenced theory by originating the idea of criticizing art in accordance with the moral and political needs of society and insisting that this consideration should guide art.[6] He was not the only one to think thus, but he was the first to enunciate the principle. He did so in a poetical composition, but this moralizing principle was soon adopted by philosophers.*

He also initiated another motif in the theory of art. In one of his comedies he says: "What we do not have in reality comes to us from imitation (in poetry)".[7] This was a fresh restatement of the old concept of imitation-mimesis. The philosophers were soon to develop it.

4. PROSE. Prose, which constitutes one of the fourth century's principal achievements, was the prose of the great historians Herodotus and Thucydides, and of orators like Isocrates and, later, Demosthenes. The Athenian system of government encouraged the development of oratory which, like the Greek epic and tragedy,

---

* B. Snell, "Aristophanes und die Ästhetik", *Die Antike*, XIII (1937), p. 249ff. G. Ugolini, "L'evoluzione della critica letteraria d'Aristofane", *Studi italiani di filologia classica* (1923).

has not been surpassed since. But these works of oratory have posed a problem for theoreticians of art, for although they were works of art, their object was so practical that they seem not to belong to the sphere of art at all.

The founders of Greek prose also included Gorgias and Plato, who founded the theory of art. Later on, Philostratus, another Greek, was to compare Gorgias' services to artistic prose with Aeschylus' services to tragedy. Plato evolved his own literary form, a combination of learned dissertation and drama, as well as his own language and style. As Wilamowitz remarks, his prose should be read aloud, so that its beauties may be revealed, for it is something which "human speech has not surpassed and is incapable of surpassing". As for Aristotle, he provided a model of simple, businesslike scientific prose, whose greatest adornment is precisely its lack of adornment.

3. The Plastic Arts

1. ARTISTS ON ART. We know the fifth- and fourth-century architecture of the Greeks chiefly from ruins, their classical sculpture chiefly from copies, and their painting only from descriptions; but these ruins, these copies and these descriptions suffice to convince us that Greek classical art was a great art. Later ages have produced a different art, but according to the general opinion formed over the centuries, have never produced a more excellent one.

Artistic theory developed side by side with this great art. There were even personal connections between the two. Many of the artists of the day not only built, sculpted and painted, but wrote about art as well. Their treatises consisted not only of technical information and ideas based on practical experience, but also of general discussions about "laws and symmetry" and "canons of art", and contained aesthetic principles which provided a guide for contemporary artists.[8]

Among architects of the classical period who wrote about their art, we find Silenus, the author of a book called *On Dorian Symmetry*, Ictinus, the creator of the Parthenon, and many others. The great Polyclitus wrote about sculpture as did Euphranor. The famous painter, Parrhasius, has left us a treatise, *On Painting*, and so has the painter Nicias. The painter Agatharchus wrote about painting for the stage which, due to its *trompe d'oeil* effect, aroused great discussion at the time. As Philostratus tells us, "the sages of earlier days wrote about symmetry in painting", and by "sages" he meant artists.

All these theoretical writings are lost, but some classical works of art have survived, and it is from them that the historian has to discover the aesthetic views of the period. He will find that (a) in principle, they conformed to canons, that (b) they, however, may consciously deviate from them, and that (c) they abandoned the traditional rather schematic patterns in favour of organic forms. These three features of classical art, since they have general aesthetic significance, must here be discussed in turn.

2. THE CANON. The classical art of the Greeks assumed that in the case of every work there exists a canon (*kanon*), i.e., a form by which the artist is bound. The term *kanon* was the equivalent in the plastic arts of the term *nomos* in music; ultimately both terms carried the same meaning. Just as Greek musicians established their *nomos*, or law, so Greek plastic artists fixed their *kanon*, or measure: they sought it, were convinced they had found it, and applied it to their works.

The history of art distinguishes between "canonical" and "noncanonical" periods. This means that in some periods artists seek and observe a canon, as a guarantee of perfection, while in others they shun it as a danger to art, a restriction of its freedom. Greek art of the classical period was canonical.

Most canons known to history had either liturgical or social origin and justification, but some prescribed artistic norms only because they were the most perfect: they were justified on aesthetic grounds. The Greek canons in fact had an aesthetic justification. This is their main feature. Another is their elasticity: they were sought rather than fixed and were subjected to revision and correction. Their third feature was that they concerned proportions and could be expressed in numbers. They postulated by how much the base of a perfect column should exceed in volume its capital, and by how much the body in a perfect statue should be larger than the head. The philosophical assumption behind the canon was that there was one single proportion which was the most perfect of all.

3. CANON IN ARCHITECTURE. Architects were the first among Greek artists to establish canonical forms. By the fifth century they were applying them to temples and setting them down in treatises;* the remains dating from this period prove that the canon was then already generally applied. It was applied comprehensively to buildings as a whole, as well as to parts of them, such as columns, capitals, cornices, friezes and gables. The permanent, canonical forms of Greek architecture made it appear objective, impersonal and inevitable. Sources rarely give names of the artists, as if the artist was not a creator but rather the executor, and as if architectural works followed eternal laws independent of the individual and of time.

The canon of classical Greek architecture was mathematical in character. The Roman Vitruvius, who continued the tradition of classical Greek architects, wrote: "Composition depends on symmetry, whose laws architects should observe strictly. Symmetry is created through proportions ... the proportions of a building we call the calculations relative to its parts as well as to the whole, in accordance with an established module". (Archaeologists differ over whether the module of a Doric

---

* G. Dehio, *Ein Proportionsgesetz der antiken Baukunst* (1896). A. Thiersch, "Die Proportionen in der Architektur", *Handbuch der Archäologie*, IV, 1 (1904). O. Wolff, *Tempelmasse, das Gesetz der Proportionen in den antiken und altchristlichen Sakralbauten* (1912). E. Mössel, *Die Proportion in der Antike und Mittelalter* (1926). Th. Fischer, *Zwei Vorträge über Proportionen* (1955).

Fig. 1–2. These drawings show the constant proportions of ancient temples. According to Vitruvius, these were determined in such a way that the width of both a four- and six-column portico measured 27 modules, a module being equal half the width of a column measured at its base.

temple was the triglyph or half-the-bottom width of a column, but both assumptions make the reconstruction of the whole temple possible.)

In a Greek temple each detail had its due proportion. If we take half the width of a column as a module, then the Athenian Thesaeum has a six-column façade of 27 modules: the six columns measure 12 modules, the three middle aisles cover 3.2 modules, the two side aisles 2.7 each — 27 in all. The relation of a column to the middle aisle is thus $2:3.2$, or $5:8$. The triglyph is one module wide and the metope is 1.6 of this, so their relation is again $5:8$. The same numbers are to be found in many Doric temples (Figs. 1 and 2).

Vitruvius wrote: "The module is the basis of all calculations. The diameter of a column should equal 2 modules, the height of column, including the capital, 14 modules. The height of the capital should equal one module, its width $2^1/_6$ ... The architrave together with the tenia and the drops should be 1 module in height ... Above the architrave should be placed the triglyphs and the metopes; the triglyphs should be $1^1/_2$ modules high and 1 module wide". He described other elements of the order in a similar way. To the historian of aesthetics the detailed figures are of small interest compared with the supremely important fact that all the elements were numerically determined (Fig. 3).

In antiquity the canon was chiefly applied to temples, but the construction of theatres* (Fig. 4) was also subjected to it. Vitruvius wrote: "The shape of a theatre should be planned in the following manner: the point of a compass should be placed in the centre of the projected circumference of the lower section of the theatre, and a circle drawn. Within the circle there should be inscribed four equilateral triangles, the apexes touching the circumference at equal intervals". This geometrical lay-out of theatres was used in Greece from classical times: we find it already in the Athenian theatre of Dionysus, the oldest known stone-built theatre. (Architects who designed theatres also maintained a constant proportion between the height of the stage and its distance from the audience. Where in later constructions the height was diminished, the auditorium was proportionately closer.)

The architectural canon also covered such details as columns (Fig. 5), the entablature and even the helices of capitals and the grooves in the columns. With the help of mathematical methods architects applied the canon to all these details accurately and meticulously. The canon prescribed helices in Ionic capitals, and the architects would plot the line of the curve of this helix geometrically (Fig. 6). The canon decreed not only the number of flutes in a column (20 in Doric ones, 24 in Ionic) but also their depth (Fig. 7). In the Doric order the depth was determined by taking the radius from the intersection of the diagonals of a square constructed on the chord of the groove. In the Ionic order it was arrived at with the aid of the so-called Pythagorean triangle, which the Greeks held to be an especially perfect geometric figure. The circle was of course also regarded as a perfect figure (Fig. 8).

---

* W. Lepik-Kopaczyńska, "Mathematical Planning of Ancient Theatres", *Prace Wrocławskiego Towarzystwa Naukowego*, A. 22 (1949).

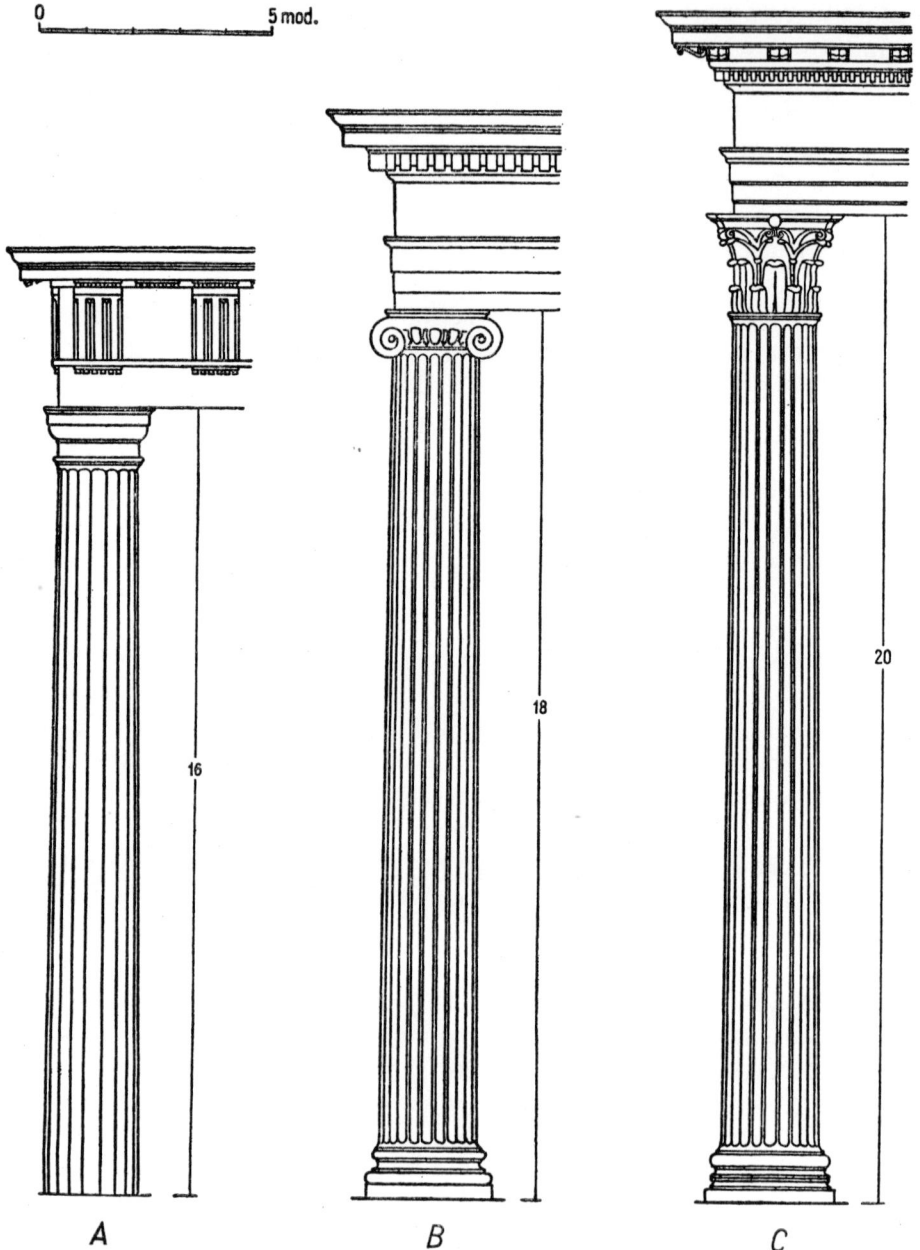

Fig. 3. Greek architecture was governed by a general canon which defined the proportions of its various elements, but within the framework of this canon there were at least three "orders": the Doric (*A*), the Ionic (*B*) and the Corinthian (*C*), these proportions being either heavier or lighter, displaying either a more disciplined or a more relaxed effect.

THE PLASTIC ARTS 53

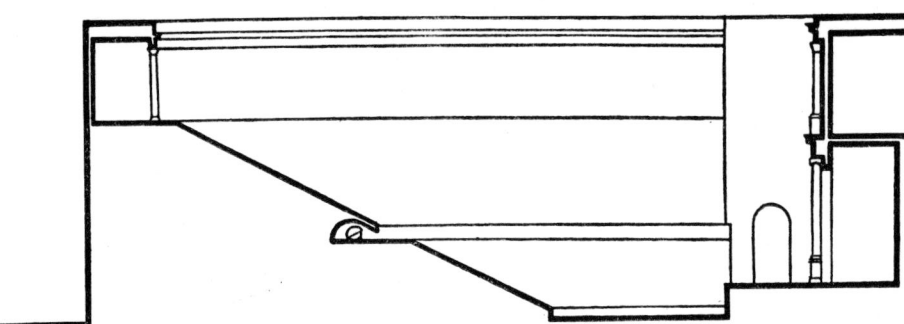

Fig. 4. A theatre constructed on geometrical principles: "Draw a circle with its centre in the middle of the projected circumference of the lower section of the theatre; inside the circle inscribe four equilateral triangles, their apexes touching the circumference at equal intervals. The side of that triangle which is nearest to the stage, at the point where it intersects the circumference, marks the line of the front of the stage" (Vitruvius). This is the principle upon which Roman theatres were constructed; the Greek principle is similar except that it is based on squares instead of triangles.

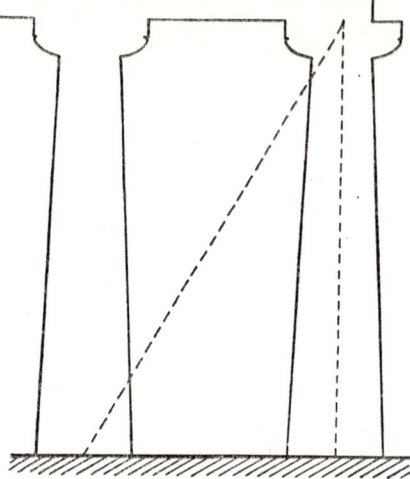

Fig. 5. The height and the disposition of columns in Greek temples were generally in accordance with the so-called Pythagorean triangles, whose sides were in proportion of 3:4:5.

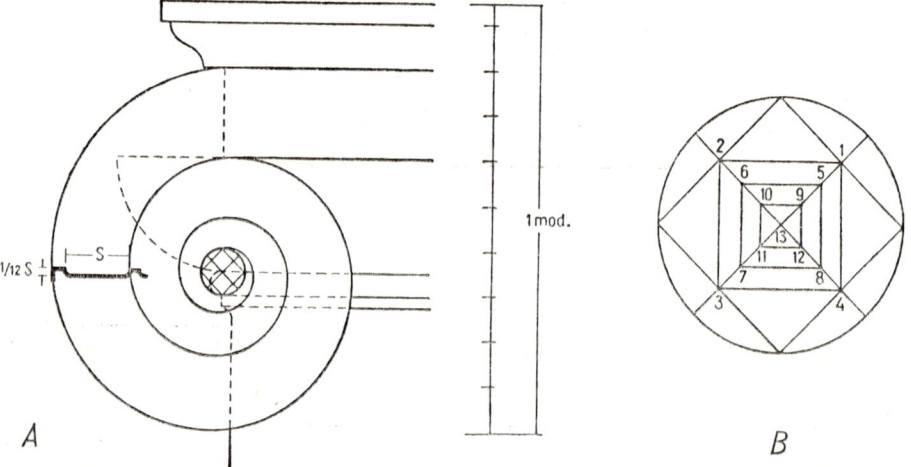

Fig. 6. The drawings illustrate the way architects in antiquity drew a helix: the curve was determined geometrically with reference to points derived from squares inscribed in a circle. These were the so-called "Platonic" squares displaying a specific relation one to the other.

In certain circumstances, the architectural canon of antiquity was intended to serve the ear as well as the eye. The theatrical canon not only defined the shape of the building but also the methods by which good acoustics could be achieved. Acoustical vessels were deployed in theatres in a specific way designed not only to amplify the force of the voice, but also to give it the required tone (Fig. 9).

4. CANON OF SCULPTURE. Greek sculptors also attempted to establish a canon for their art. It is known that Polyclitus was the most successful in this respect.

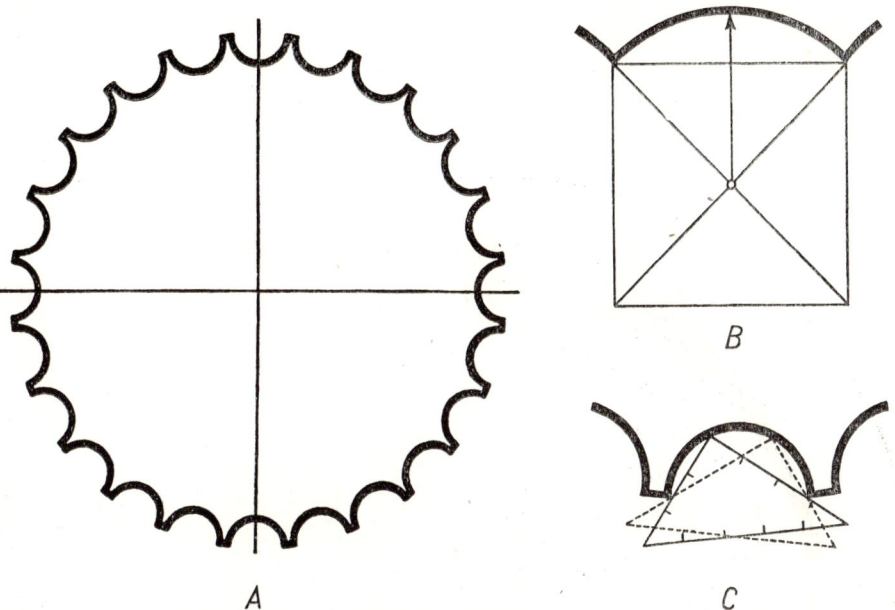

Fig. 7. The Greek canon was chiefly concerned with defining the number of grooves in a column (*A*), but it also laid down what the depth of the grooves should be. In the Doric order (*B*) this was done by constructing a square on the groove's arc: the depth of the groove was then determined by an arc of a circle with its centre in the middle of the square. In the Ionic order this depth was also determined geometrically though not in quite the same way (*C*). Triangles with sides in the proportion of 3:4:5, which the ancients regarded as one of the most perfect geometrical figures, were employed instead.

The canon of sculpture was also numerical and depended on a fixed proportion. As Galen[9] informs us, beauty resides "in the proportions ... of the parts, that is to say, of finger to finger and of all the fingers to the palm and wrist, and of these to the forearm, and of the forearm to the upper arm, and of all the parts to each other, as set forth in the *Canon* of Polykleitos". Vitruvius urges in a similar vein: "Nature has so designed the human body that the skull, from the chin to the upper part of the forehead and the roots of the hair, should equal one-tenth of the length of the body", and he goes on to define numerically the proportions of the various parts of the human body. This canon was strictly observed by the classical sculptors. The only extant fragment of Polyclitus' treatise states that in a work of art "perfection (*to eu*) depends on many numerical relations, and small variants are decisive".[10]

The sculptors' canon was really concerned with nature, not art. It measured the proportions appearing in nature, particularly in a well-built man, rather than the proportions which should appear in a statue. It was, therefore, as Panofsky* called

---

* E. Panofsky, "Die Entwicklung der Proportionslehre als Abbild der Stilentwicklung", *Monatsheft für Kunstwissenschaft*, IV (1921).

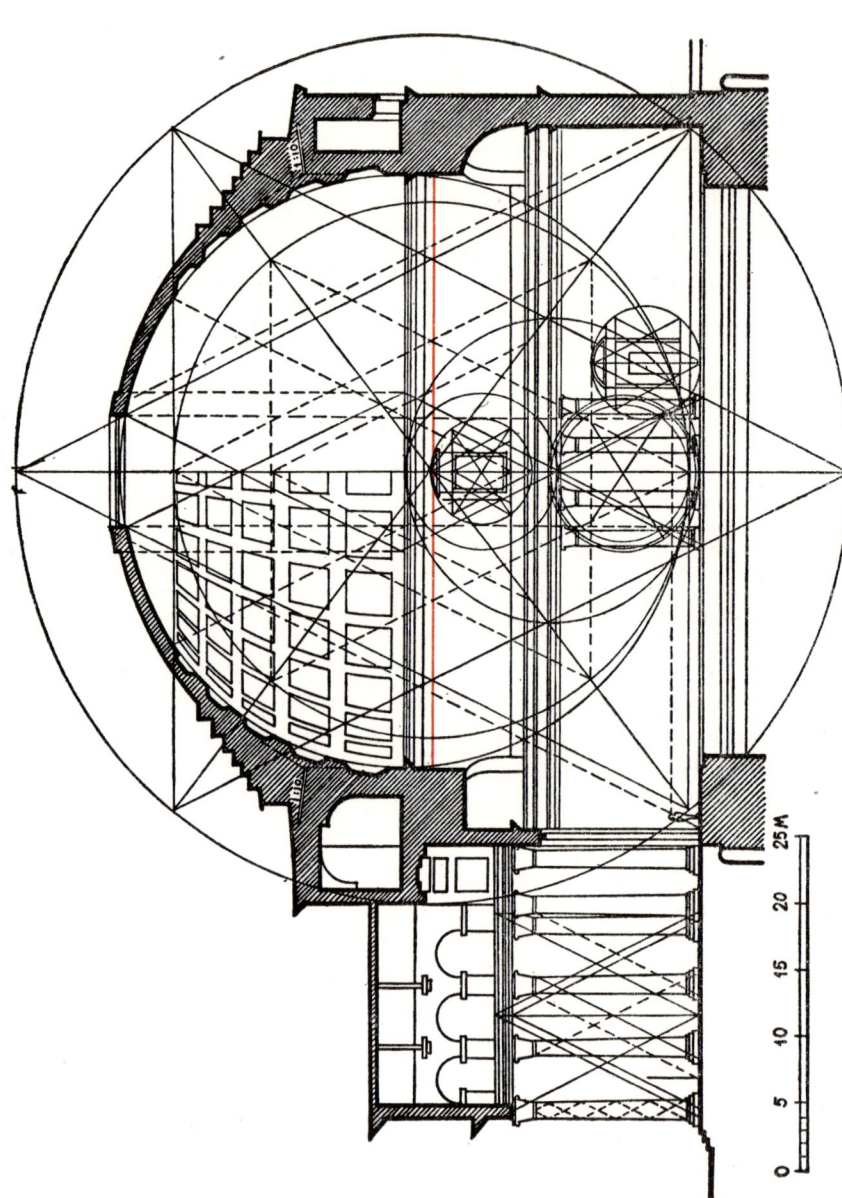

Fig. 8. The internal proportions of Rome's Pantheon show that some proportions of ancient architecture were related to the circumference of a circle. The diameter of the circle (shown in red) marks the fundamental division of the building between its walls and the cupola. The drawing (based on O. Schubert) shows also many other circles and triangles determining the Pantheon's proportions.

it, an "anthropometric" canon. As such, it laid down no principles as to whether a sculptor had the right to introduce corrections in anatomy and perspective in order to improve upon nature. However, the fact that Greek sculptors took an

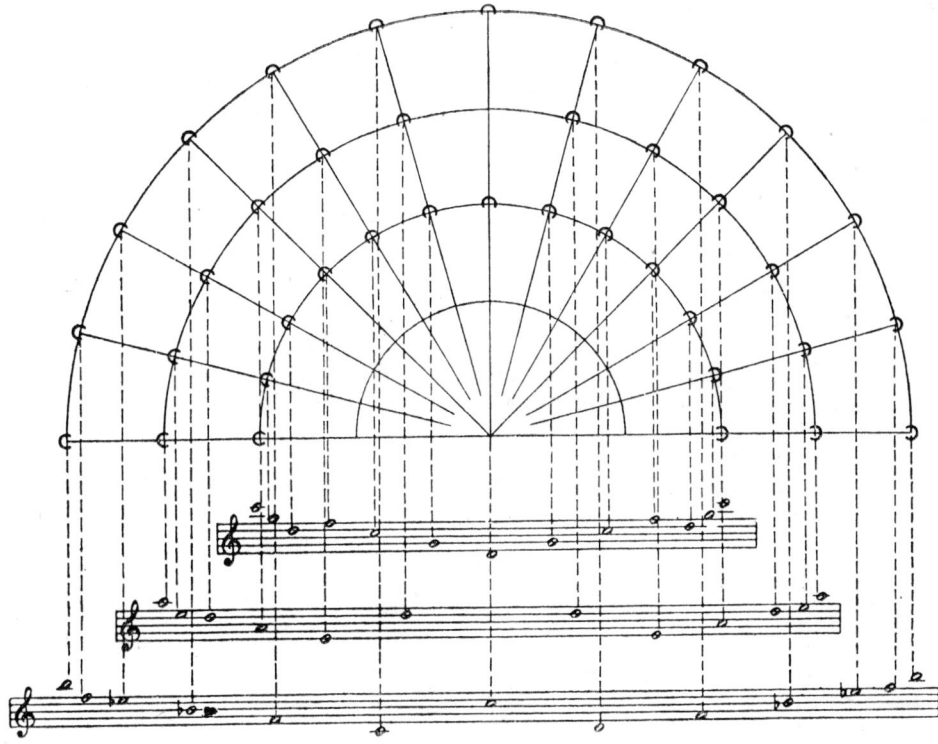

Fig. 9. This drawing shows how ancient architects deployed acoustic vessels in theatres. They were selected and arranged in order not only to amplify the voice, but also to give it suitable timbre.

interest in the canon of nature and made use of it in their art proves that they regarded it as binding art as well. Vitruvius goes on: "Painters and famous sculptors exploited their knowledge of these proportions (which in reality are the properties of a well-built man) and gained for themselves great and perpetual fame". (The Greeks took it for granted that nature, and the human body in particular, displays mathematically defined proportions and inferred from this that representations of nature in art must show similar proportions.)

The sculptors' canon covered not only the proportions of the body as a whole, but also of its parts, particularly the proportions of the face.* They divided the face into three parts: the forehead, the nose, and the lips including the chin. Here, however, as detailed measurements have revealed, the canon was subject to variation.

---

* A. Kalkman, "Die Proportionen des Gesichts in der griechischen Kunst", 53 Programm der archäolog. Gesellschaft in Berlin (1893).

The sculpture of a particular period in the fifth century shows a low forehead and an elongated lower part of the face. Polyclitus returned to the division of the face into three equal sections, while Euphranor moved slightly away from this division. During the classical period the taste of the Greeks fluctuated in some way and, despite their striving after an objective art, proportions in sculpture shifted in accordance with prevailing taste.

During the Greek classical period the idea was also established that the body of an ideally built man could be contained within the simple geometric figures of the circle and the square. "If we lay a man on his back with his legs and arms outstretched

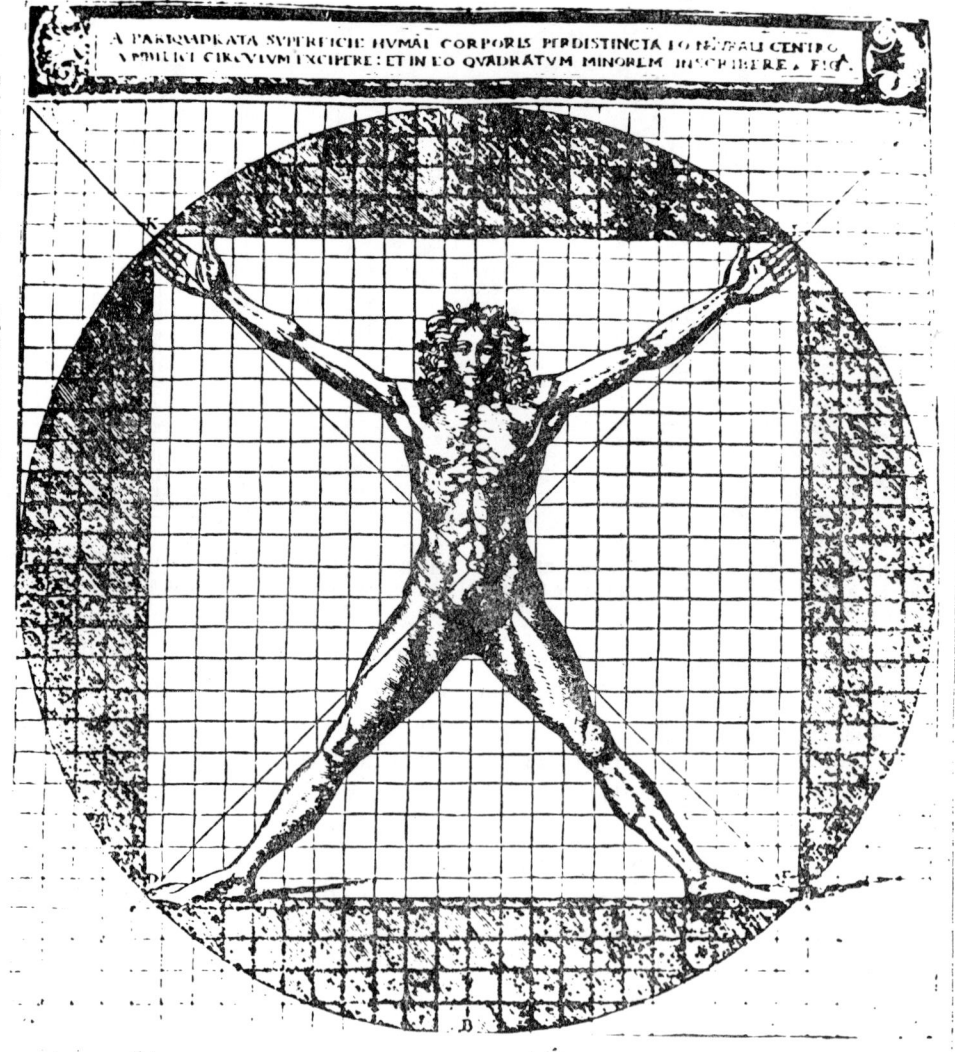

Fig. 10. *Homo quadratus*: the drawing follows the 1521 edition of Vitruvius.

and draw a circle with its centre in the man's navel, the circumference of the circle will touch the tips of the man's fingers and his toes". The Greeks thought that in a similar way the human body can be inscribed within a square, and this gave rise to the idea of the square man (in Greek *aner tetragonos*, in Latin *homo quadratus*) which survived in art anatomy until modern times (Fig. 10).

5. THE CANON IN VASES. A canon may also be distinguished in the development of the minor Greek art of vase making. Two American scholars, Hambidge and Caskey,* have established that Greek vases have fixed proportions, that some of these proportions are very simple, for example the proportions of a square, but that most of them cannot be expressed in natural numbers, being $1:\sqrt{2}$ or $1:\sqrt{3}$ or $1:\sqrt{5}$. The authors call these numbers "geometric", as opposed to arithmetic. The proportion of the "golden section" is also to be found in the vases (Fig. 11).

Speaking very generally, the Greeks held that the perfect forms of beauty were the simplest geometrical figures, namely the triangle, the square and the circle. And the simplest numerical relations seemed to them to determine the beauty of a shape (just as they did in the harmony of sounds). The triangles which they regarded as perfect were the equilateral and the "Pythagorean", whose sides have the ratio of $3:4:5$.

6. THE COGNITIVE ASPIRATIONS OF ART. We may assume that this faith in a mathematical canon did not arise in Greek art quite spontaneously: it derived not only from the artists themselves but also from philosophers. In particular from the Pythagoreans and Platonists. Later, the Greeks came to think that the term *kanon* (which originally meant a builder's rule) owed its metaphorical sense to the philosopher Pythagoras.† In its aesthetic sense it was first used in connection with building but was later also employed in music and sculpture. It owed its currency to Polyclitus.

Greek artists were convinced that in their works they were applying and revealing the laws which govern Nature, that they were representing not only the appearance of things, but also their eternal structure. Their basic concept of *symmetria* signified proportions which are not invented by artists but are a property of Nature. Seen in this light, art was a species of knowledge. Especially the Sicyonian school of sculptors regarded their art as knowledge. This view was a pendant to the view widely held, in Greece, that poets, Homer in particular, were "teachers of wisdom". Pliny tells us that the painter Pamphilus, teacher of the great Apelles, was a distinguished mathematician who claimed that no one could be a good artist without arithmetic and geometry. Many Greek artists not only sculpted and painted, but also explored the theory of their art. They regarded canon in art as a discovery and not as an invention; they regarded it as an objective truth rather than a human device.

---

* L. D. Caskey, *Geometry of Greek Vases* (Boston, 1922).
† H. Oppel, "Kanon", Suppl.-Bd. des *Philologus*, XXX, 4 (1937).

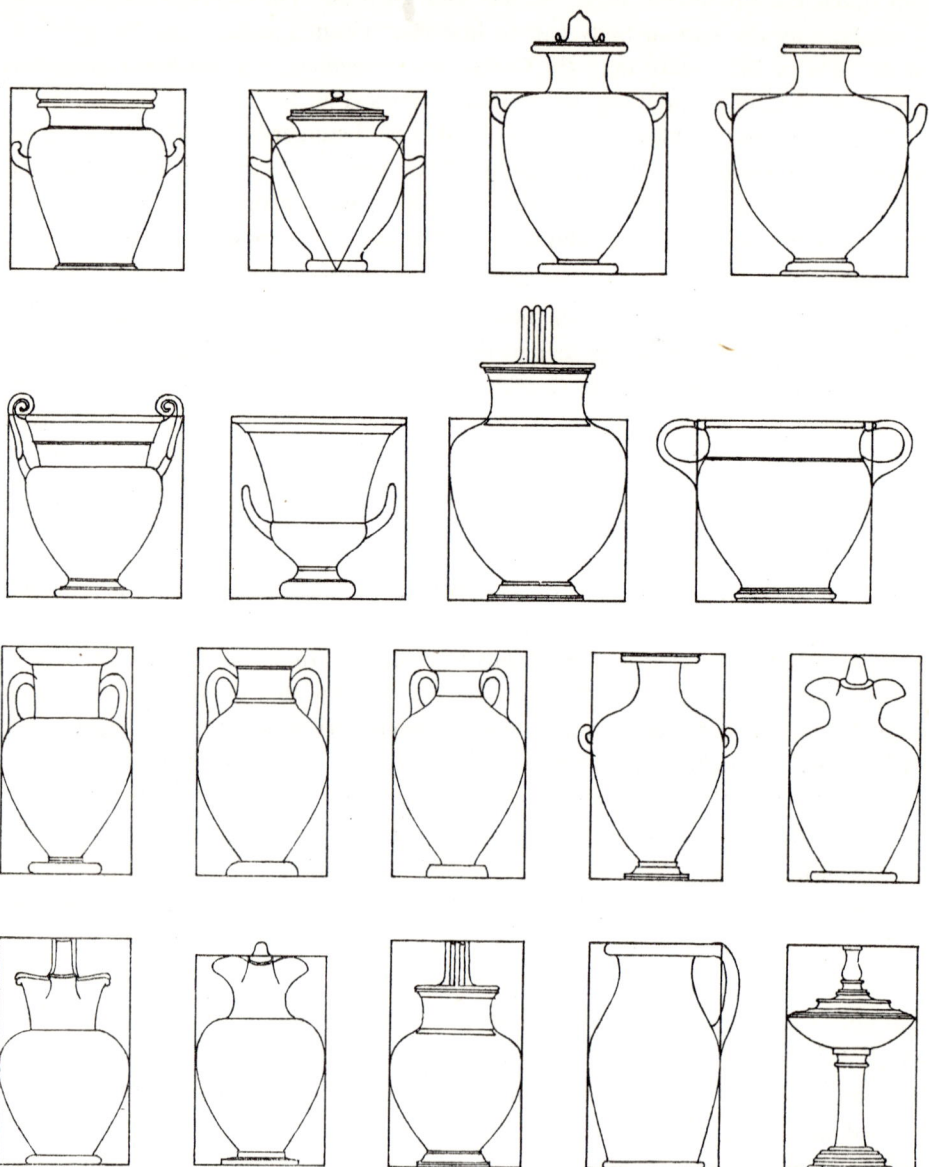

Fig. 11. Greek vases, like Greek buildings, display constant geometrical proportions. The first group of eight vases (the two upper rows) is based on the principle of a square, that is, on a relation of height to width of 1:1. The second group of ten vases (the two lower rows) has a height to width relationship of $1:\dfrac{\sqrt{5}-1}{2}$, that is, 1:0.618. These reproductions follow the calculations of J. Hambidge and the publications of L. D. Caskey.

THE PLASTIC ARTS

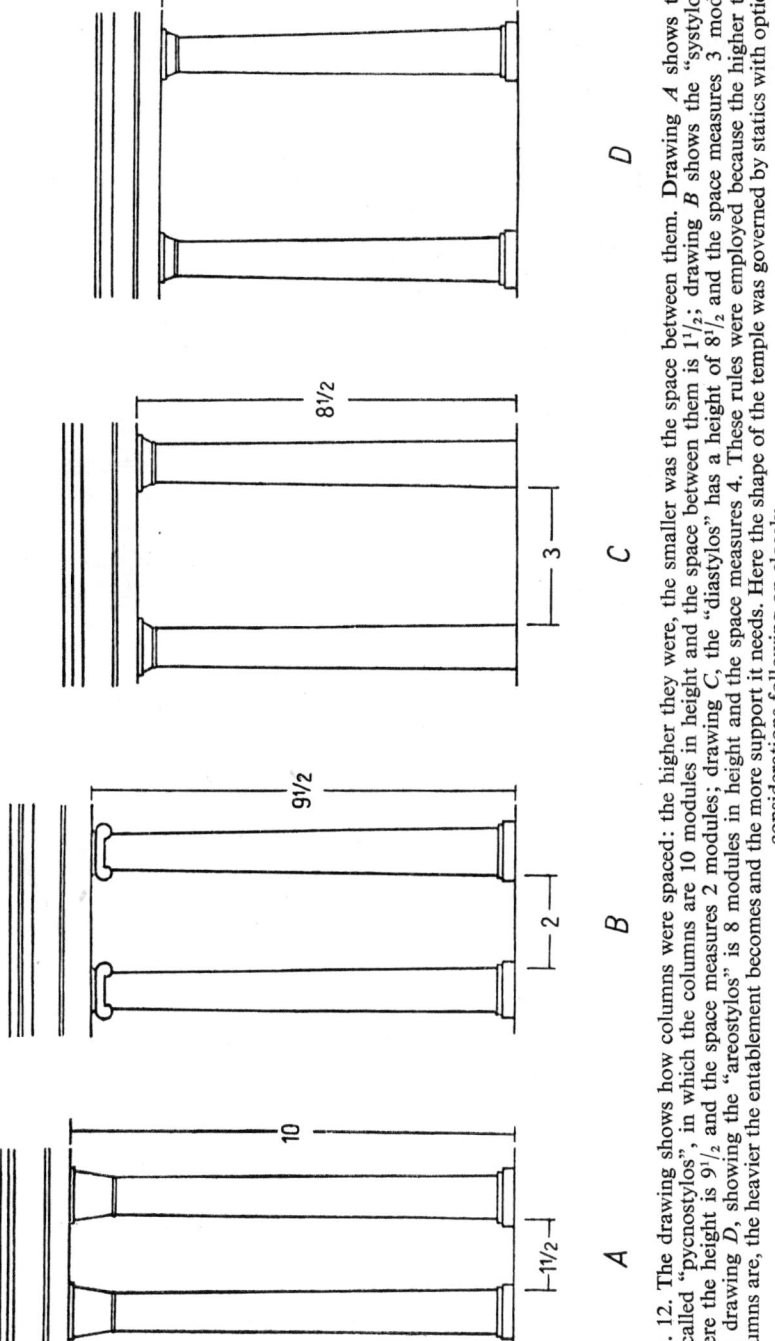

Fig. 12. The drawing shows how columns were spaced: the higher they were, the smaller was the space between them. Drawing *A* shows the so-called "pycnostylos", in which the columns are 10 modules in height and the space between them is $1^1/_2$; drawing *B* shows the "systylos" where the height is $9^1/_2$ and the space measures 2 modules; drawing *C*, the "diastylos" has a height of $8^1/_2$ and the space measures 3 modules; drawing *D*, showing the "areostylos" is 8 modules in height and the space measures 4. These rules were employed because the higher the columns are, the heavier the entablement becomes and the more support it needs. Here the shape of the temple was governed by statics with optical considerations following on closely.

62   AESTHETICS OF CLASSICAL PERIOD

7. THREEFOLD BASIS OF THE CANONS. The Greeks relied on several criteria in fixing their canons:

(*a*) First of all, there was the general *philosophical* basis. The Greeks were persuaded that cosmic proportions were perfect, so that human artefacts would have to abide by them. Vitruvius wrote: "Since Nature so created the body that its members are proportional to the whole frame, the principle of the ancients was that in buildings also the relationship of the parts should correspond to the whole".

(*b*) Another basis of the canons lay in the observation of *organic* bodies. This played a decisive role in sculpture and its anthropometric canon.

(*c*) A third basis, which was significant in architecture, was supplied by the knowledge of the laws of *statics*. The higher the columns were, the heavier was the entablature and the more support it required; therefore, Greek columns were spaced

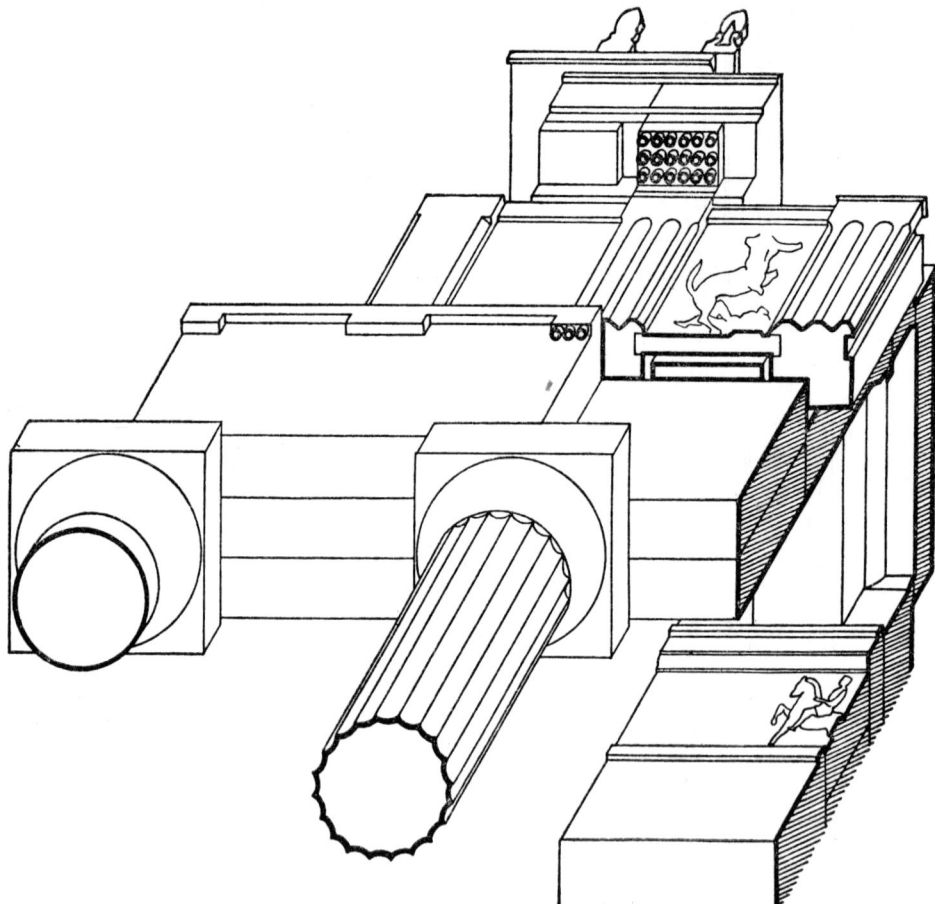

Fig. 13. Using the Parthenon as an example, the drawing (by L. Niemojewski), demonstrates the principle of crowning ancient temples. It is a static principle: the mutual correlation of the parts has produced forms and proportions which we feel to be perfect.

in various ways, depending on their height (Fig. 12). The forms of a Greek temple were the fruit of technical expertness and of familiarity with the properties of materials. These factors were to a large degree responsible for those forms and proportions which the Greeks felt and we feel to be perfect (Fig. 13).

II

8. ART AND VISUAL REQUIREMENTS. Although the Greeks composed their works in accordance with mathematical proportions and geometric forms, they did, in certain instances, depart from them. There is too much consistency in these irregularities for them not to have been conscious and deliberate. They were made with a clear aesthetic intention. The purpose of some of them was the accommodation of shapes to the demands of human sight. Diodorus Siculus writes that in this particular respect Greek art differed from the art of the Egyptians, who worked out these proportions without reference to the demands of sight. The way the Greeks took account of this phenomenon was by attempting to counter optical deformations. They gave irregular shapes to painted and sculpted figures, knowing that precisely this method would ensure that they appeared regular.

Similar methods were used in painting, particularly theatrical painting. Since theatrical decorations were meant to be seen from a distance, they had to employ a specific technique taking account of perspective. This was the reason why eventually all perspective painting was called *skenographia*.*†

Analogous methods were also used in figurative sculpture if it was either very large or placed very high. We have already mentioned the statue of Athene, whose shape Phidias deliberately deformed as it was to be placed on top of a column.‡ The inscription on a temple in Priene consisted of letters which were of unequal size, those higher up being larger.

Architects worked in the same manner, and with them these correctives assumed special importance. Doric temples built from the middle of the fifth century onwards had their middle parts widened.[11] In the porticos the side columns were spaced more widely. These columns were slightly inclined inwards, because in this way they would give the appearance of being straight. Since lighted columns appear thinner than those standing in the shade, this illusion was corrected by suitable adjustments of the thicknesses of the appropriate columns (Figs. 14–16). Architects resorted to these methods because, as Vitruvius was to remark later, "the illusion of the eyes must be rectified by calculations". As a Polish scholar§ has put it, they

---

* P. M. Schuhl, *Platon et l'art de son temps* (1933).

† From the fifth century, the Greek painting became impressionistic: it disposed light and shadow in such a way that it might give an illusion of reality, though when seen at close quarters, they were no more than shapeless stains, as Plato reproached the painters. This impressionistic painting, the Greeks used to term *skiagraphia* (from *skia*—shadow).

‡ Tzetzes, *Historiarum variarum chiliades*, VII, 353–69, ed. T. Kiesling (1826), pp. 295–6.

§ J. Stuliński, "Proporcje architektury klasycznej w świetle teorii denominatorów", *Meander*, XIII (1958).

applied proportions which were not linear but angular. For them the fixed measure was not the column or the entablature, but the angles at which the column and the entablature were observed. And if this was so, then the size of the column and the entablature had to undergo change when placed higher or further away (Fig. 17).

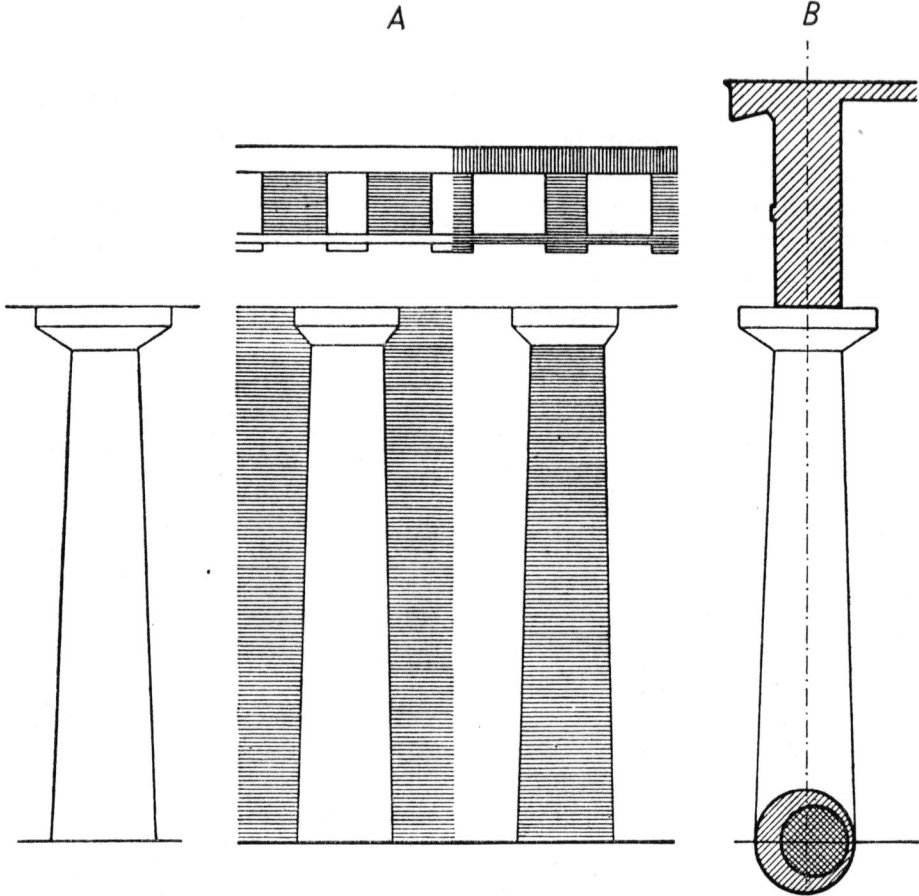

Fig. 14. Drawing *A* shows that a column standing in full light appears thinner than one standing in the shade. Since they wished all columns to appear identical, they would make the outer columns standing in the light thicker, and the inner columns standing in the shade thinner. This was one of many ways ancient architects employed to counteract optical deformations. A similar procedure is illustrated in drawing *B*: the outer columns are tilted towards the centre, so that they would appear to be standing straight, otherwise they would have made the impression of tilting away from the centre.

9. DEVIATIONS. Greek architects went even further in deviating from straight lines. They curved lines which one would expect to be straight. In classical architecture, the outlines of socles, cornices and columns, as well as horizontal and vertical lines, are slightly curved. It is true of the finest classical buildings, such as the Parthenon and the temples of Paestum. These deviations from straight lines are slight and

Fig. 15. The principle of tilting outer columns to counteract optical deformations.

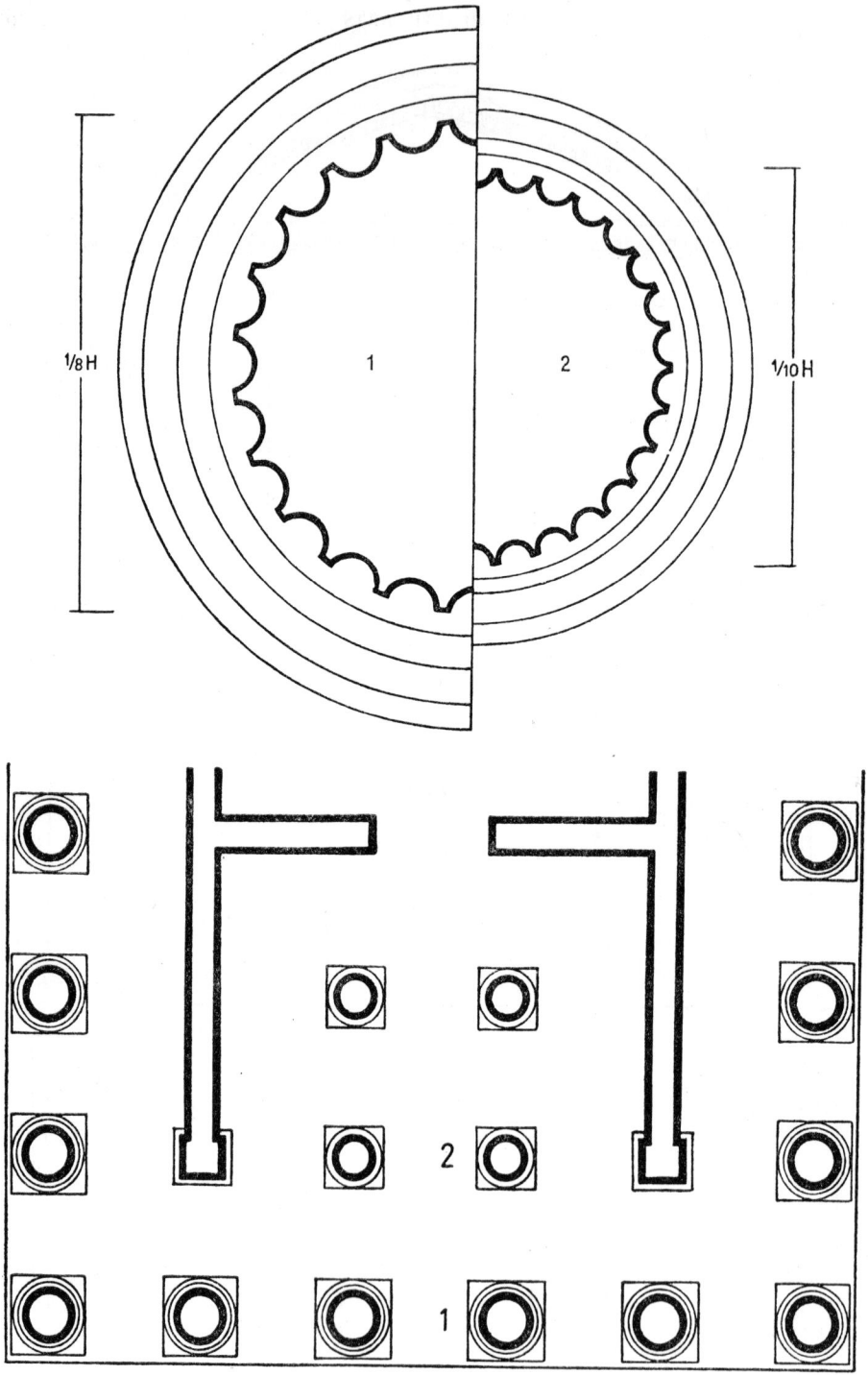

Fig. 16. These two drawings show that the inner columns of Greek temples, being in the shade, had a smaller diameter than the outer ones. The relation between the diameters was 8:10 (the inner ones were $1/10$ of the height, while the outer ones were $1/8$ of the height), because this proportion created the illusion that they were equal. The thinness of the shafts of the inner columns was compensated by an increased number of grooves, the relation being 30:24 (Vitruvius, IV, 4, 1).

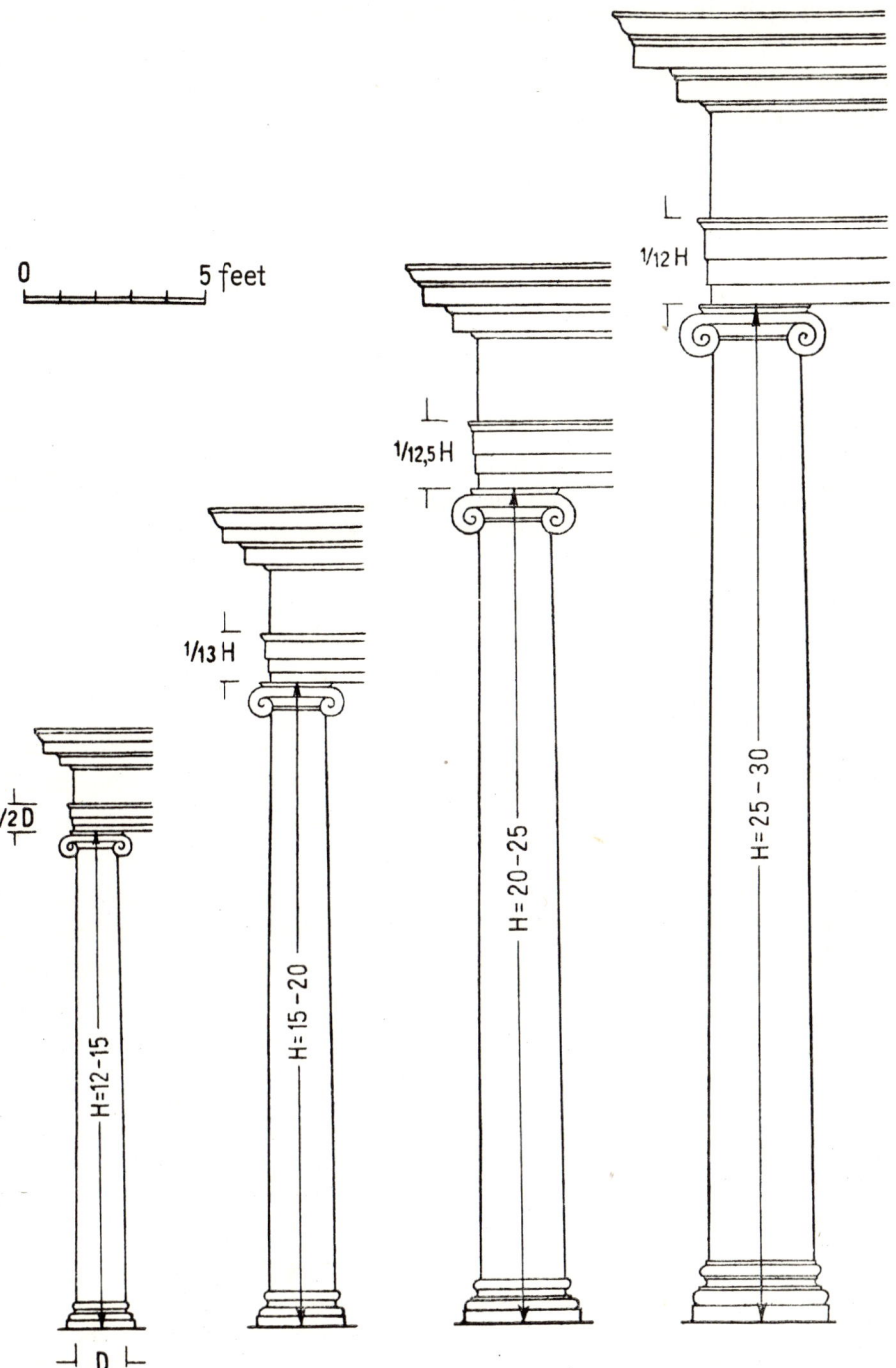

Fig. 17. This drawing illustrates one more characteristic of ancient architecture conditioned by the demands of perception. The higher the columns, the higher were the architraves resting on them.

have only quite recently been discovered. The discovery was first made in 1837 but was not published until 1851.* At first received with incredulity, it is now seen to be an indisputable fact, although the explanation for it is still in doubt.

Can these deviations also be explained as attempts to correct optical deformations? Figure 18 demonstrates that they can. This must have been the case where the situation of certain buildings determined the point from which they would be seen, particularly when, as in the case of the Parthenon, this point was on a different level from that of the building itself.

There was also another reason for deviations from straight lines in Greek architecture: the same reason as when a painter paints rectilinear objects and curved lines without the aid of ruler and compass. Despite the insistence on regularity, the aim was to convey an impression of freedom and to avoid rigidity.

Vitruvius commented later: "The eye seeks a pleasant view; if we are not going to satisfy it by the employment of proportions and by rectifications of the modules, we shall leave the onlooker with an unpleasant sight lacking in charm". These "rectifications of the modules" to which Greek artists resorted served to counterbalance deformations of our vision, but also to allow a certain freedom in the outlines of buildings. The American archaeologist who has made the most detailed study of these "refinements" explains that they were designed to give pleasure to the eye by the avoidance of monotony and mathematical precision which is unartistic and inadmissible in good art.

Deviations from straight lines and right angles in Greek buildings doubtless served the two aims: avoiding optical deformation as well as rigidity. Double aims are apparent particularly in the case of vertical lines: ancient architects inclined external columns towards the center because otherwise an optical illusion would give the impression that the columns were inclined away from the center. However, they must also have resorted to this refinement to strengthen in the buildings the impression of solidity and firm support. On the whole, they were probably better at building than at explaining why their buildings were excellent. They had formed their skill in practice, empirically and intuitively, rather than on the basis of scien-

---

* Irregularities in classical Greek architecture were observed by the Englishman J. Pennethorne about 1837. The same observation was made simultaneously by J. Hoffer, a German architect in the service of the Greek king. The fullest and most exhaustive compilation of facts and figures so far to appear is in F. C. Penrose's *An Investigation of the Principles of Athenian Architecture* (1851). Supplementary information is available in G. Hauck's *Subjective Perspective of the Horizontal Curves of the Doric Style* (1879); G. Giovannoni, *La curvatura della linee nel tempio d'Ercole a Cori* (1908). A synthesis of the problem is contained in W. H. Goodyear: *Greek Refinements* (1912). The vertical deviations are more noticeable and had been observed and described earlier: the "enthasis" by Cockerell in 1810, the declinature of the columns in 1829 by Donaldson and in 1830 by Jenkins. Analogous curvatures appear in Egyptian architecture and were noticed by Pennethorne as early as 1833, but his findings were not published until 1878 in *The Geometry and Optics of the Ancients*.

tific premises. However, they constructed a theory to support the practice: this was the Greek method of behaviour.

10. THE ELASTICITY OF CANONS. While it is a fact that Greek architects possessed a canon and obeyed simple proportions, it is also true that no two Greek temples are alike. Had the canon been remorselessly applied, they would have been. Their variety is explained by the fact that architects allowed themselves a certain latitude in applying the canons and proportions. They did not follow them slavishly, they regarded them as pointers rather than as precepts. The canon was general but deviations were not only permitted but widely applied. These deviations from straight lines and plumb lines, the curvatures and inclinations gave rise to minute variants, which though slight, were nevertheless sufficient to give the buildings freedom and individuality and to make the severe Greek art free as well.

Classical art proves that its creators were conscious of the aesthetic importance of regularity as well as of freedom and individuality.

III

11. ORGANIC VERSUS SCHEMATIC FORMS. There was a third important feature, which manifested itself in the classical art of the Greeks. It found its expression particularly in classical sculpture.

While in representing living forms archaic sculpture approximated them to schematic, geometric ones, classical sculpture relied on organic forms. It thus came closer to nature, thereby moving away from Oriental and archaic tradition. This was a tremendous change: some historians judge it the greatest in the history of art. Greek art moved from schematic to real forms, from artificial to living forms, from invented to observed forms, from those which drew attention because they were symbols to those which were attractive intrinsically.

Greek art mastered organic forms with almost incredible speed. The process began in the fifth century B.C. and was complete half way through it. Myron, the first great sculptor of the century, only began to free sculpture from archaic schema and to bring it closer to nature, whereas Polyclitus, who followed him, established its canon, already based on the observation of organic nature. And soon Phidias, another fifth-century sculptor, reached the peak of perfection, according to the consensus of Greek opinion.

Classical sculptors represented the *living* shapes of the human body, but sought to find its *constant* proportions. This combination was the most characteristic feature of their art: they represented not copies but a synthesis of live bodies. If they made the bodies seven times the length of the face and the face three times the length of the nose, this was because they discerned in these numerical relations the synthesis of human proportions. They represented vital reality but they sought in it common, typical shapes. They were as far removed from naturalism as they were from abstraction. One may say of Periclean sculptors what Sophocles used to say of himself:

70   AESTHETICS OF CLASSICAL PERIOD

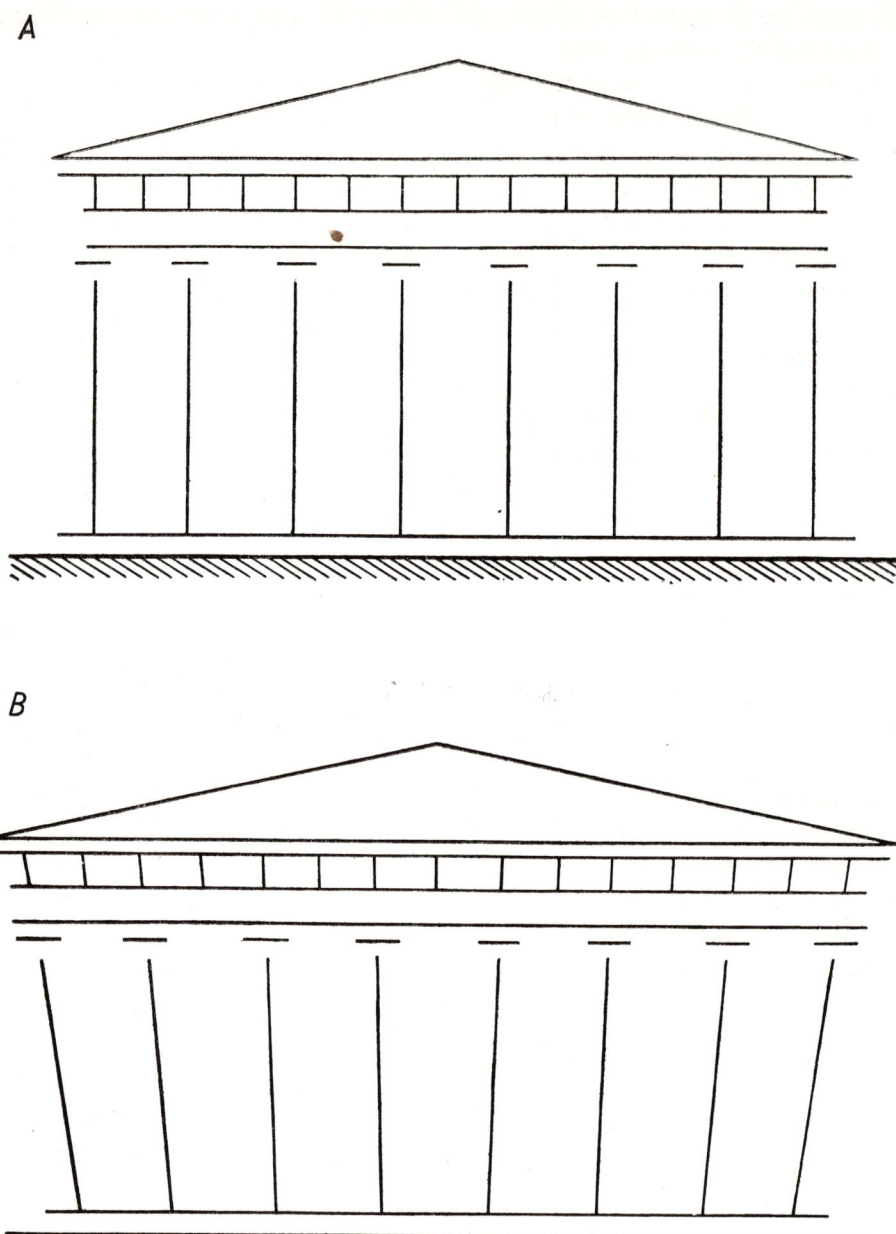

Fig. 18. Drawing *A* shows how a temple ought to look: it ought to give the impression of an oblong. But Greek architects observed that if they were in fact to construct it as an oblong, then, the mode of our perception being what it is, it would appear to us that the vertical lines of the oblong diverge in the way shown in drawing *B*, while the horizontal lines sag as shown in drawing *C*. Thus, in order to counteract the deformations of *B* and *C* and to achieve effect *A*, the architects of antiquity built in the manner shown in drawing *D*. That is, they deformed shapes so that they would produce the effect of not being deformed. These drawings, which follow A. Choisy, deliberately magnify the deformations, whereas in reality both the optical deviations and the adjustments introduced by the Greeks are in comparison minimal.

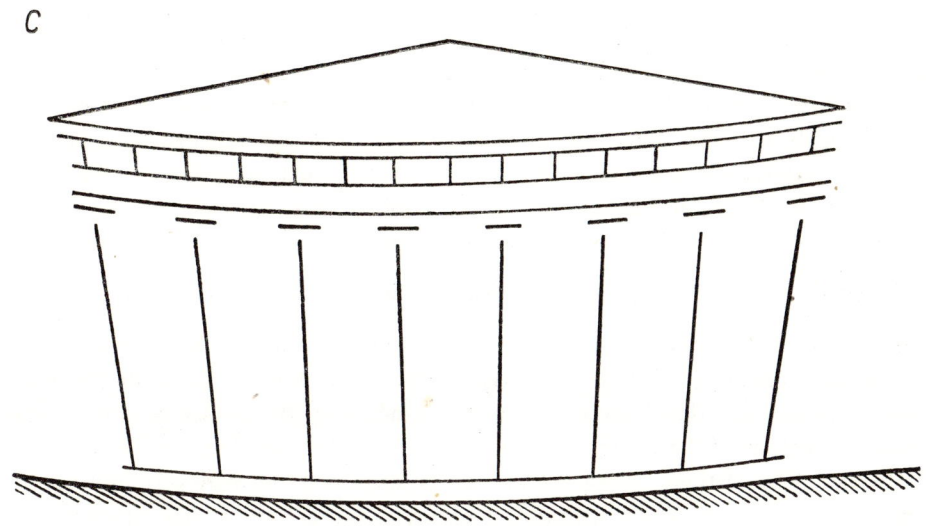

Fig. 18 (*cont.*)

that they represented men as they should be. Reality was idealized in their works, and this may have given them the feeling that their works were permanent and would not pass away. Asked why he painted so slowly, Zeuxis replied: "Because I paint eternity".

12. MAN AS MEASURE. The canon of the proportions of Greek sculpture and classical buildings is attested by sources. From these we know that the façade of a temple had to have 27 modules and the length of the human body 7. Moreover, measurements of Greek ruins have revealed an even more general regularity, namely that both the statues and the buildings were constructed according to the same proportion of the golden section. This is the name given to the division of a line in which the smaller part is to the greater as the greater is to the whole. Expressed mathematically, $\frac{\sqrt{5}+1}{2} = 1 : \frac{\sqrt{5}-1}{2}$. The golden section divides the line into parts of which the approximate relation is 0.618:0.382. The finest temples, like the Parthenon, and the most celebrated statues as the Apollo Belvedere and the Venus de Milo are constructed in every detail according to the principle of the golden section or the so-called function of the golden section, i.e., 0.528:0.472 (see Fig. 19).

The exactness of these measurements can be disputed, but there certainly occurs a general conformity. Both sculpture and architecture had similar proportions, and those of sculpture were intended by the Greeks to be the synthetic proportions of living people: it follows that the proportions which the Greeks of the classical era applied, in architecture as well as in sculpture, were their own proportions: all proportions they used were on a human scale.

During certain periods of culture man regards his own scale of proportion as the most beautiful and models his works accordingly. This is characteristic of "classical" periods: they are typified by a preference for natural human proportions, by the shaping of things to human scale. However, there are also other periods which consciously shun these forms and proportions, seeking objects greater than the human and proportions more perfect than the organic ones. Thus taste, proportions, art and aesthetics are subject to fluctuation. Classical Greek art was the product of an aesthetics which equated perfect forms with natural forms and perfect proportions with organic proportions. It gave direct expression to this aesthetics in sculpture, but indirectly also in architecture. Classical Greek sculpture represented gods but in human shape; classical Greek architecture produced temples for gods, but their scale was based on human proportions.

13. PAINTING. Greek sculpture has survived at least in fragments, but the paintings have perished and have been overshadowed, therefore, in the memories of posterity by sculpture. Yet painting had an important place in classical art. Before the classical era, painters knew neither the third dimension nor chiaroscuro and only occasionally stepped beyond monochrome. Even the pictures of Polygnotus were outline drawings coloured with four local pigments. However, a couple of

THE PLASTIC ARTS 73

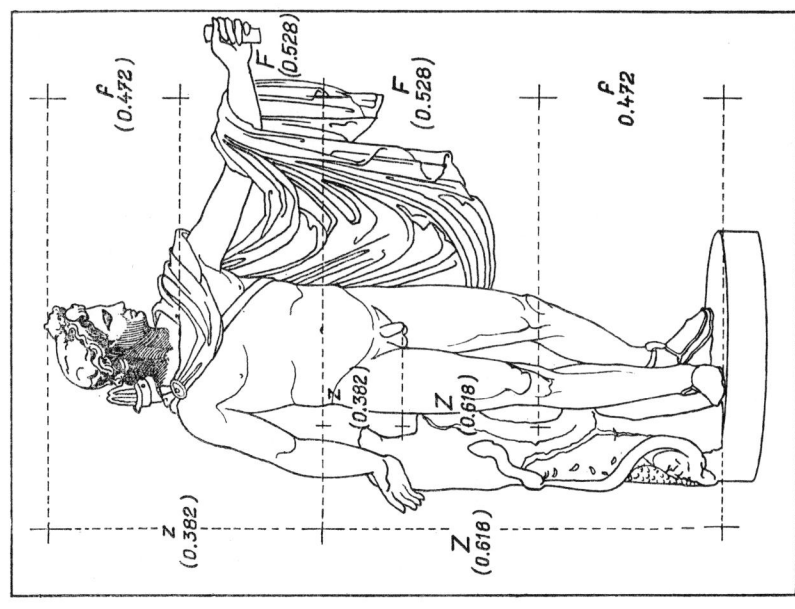

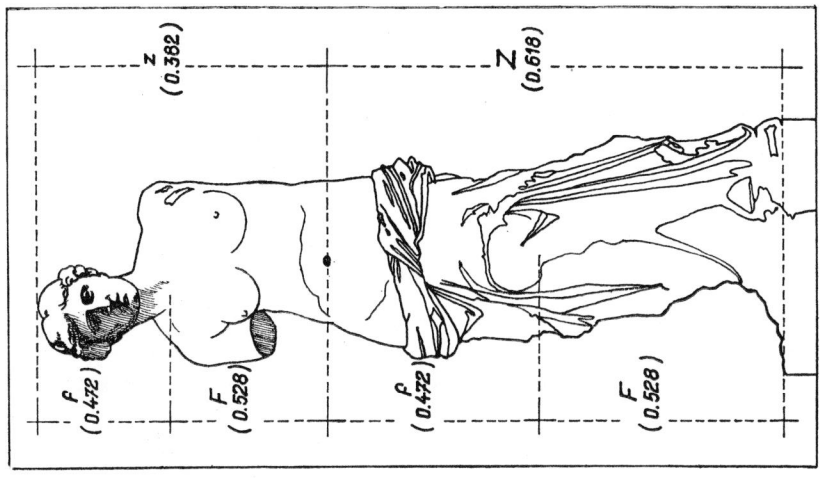

Fig. 19. In the sculpture of antiquity we may discover proportions of the human body equivalent to the golden section (Z, z) approximately 0.618:0.382, and to the function of the golden section (F, f), approximately 0.528:0.472. The statues here used to demonstrate these measurements are Apollo Belvedere and Venus de Milo. The calculations are by the Soviet architect Zholtovski.

generations in the fifth century B.C. sufficed to turn this primitive painting into a mature art.

The painting of the fifth century, like contemporary sculpture, was an expression of the classical attitude and was characterized by organic forms and human scale. Yet in some respects, its character was different from that of contemporary sculpture. It tackled much more various and complicated subjects: Parrhasius attempted to paint the personification of the Athenian people with their virtues and faults, Euphranor painted a cavalry battle and Odysseus simulating madness; Nicias painted animals, Antiphilus the reflection of flames on a human face, while Aristides of Thebes, according to an ancient writer, "was the first to paint the soul and characters". Dionysius of Colophon was the only one who confined himself to painting human beings and was therefore called "anthropographer". Pamphilus even painted thunder and lightening and generally, as Pliny remarked, "painted that which cannot be painted" (*pinxit et quae pingi non possunt*). This shows that, despite its unity, classical art offered wide possibilities.

Though the Greeks did not then possess the terms "form" and "content", their art, particularly painting, posed the problem of form and content. Zeuxis was indignant with the public for admiring the "matter" of a painting in preference to its execution, while Nicias emphasized the importance of weighty themes against those who squandered their art on such trivialities as "birds or flowers".[12]

14. THE AESTHETICS OF CLASSICAL ART. To summarize, we can say that the aesthetics implied in classical Greek art was, first, an aesthetics of *canonical* forms. It was based on the conviction that objective beauty and objectively perfect proportions existed. It apprehended these proportions mathematically, and rested upon the conviction that objective beauty depended on number and measure. Yet, despite its objective and mathematical character, this aesthetics left sufficient *freedom* for an artist to express his art individually.

Secondly, it was an aesthetics characterized by a preference for *organic* forms. It was based on the conviction that the greatest beauty appeared in the forms, the proportions, and the scale of human beings. Classical art maintained a balance between mathematical and organic elements. The canon of Polyclitus was a canon of organic forms expressed in numbers.

Thirdly, the aesthetics of classical art was *realistic* in the sense that it relied on the belief that art draws its beauty from nature; it neither can nor is required to oppose the beauty of nature to a different artistic beauty.

Fourthly, it was a *static* aesthetics, giving highest place to the beauty of forms arrested in movement, of forms poised and at rest. It was also an aesthetics valuing *simplicity* more highly than richness.

Fifthly, it was an aesthetics of *psychophysical* beauty, a beauty both spiritual and physical, embracing both form and content. This beauty lay, above all, in the unity and harmony of the soul and the body.

This aesthetics, embodied in classical art, had a counterpart in the aesthetics formulated by contemporary philosophers: its mathematical principles found expression in the Pythagorean philosophy, and its psychophysical principles in the philosophy of Socrates and of Aristotle as well.

Certain features of this aesthetics remained in the art and in the art theory of the Greeks. Others, however, vanished together with the classical era. This was true especially of the aesthetics of repose and simplicity: "quiet greatness and noble simplicity" did not remain an ideal of art for long, and artists soon began to set themselves the task of presenting, on the contrary, rich life and forceful expression. The same thing happened with the objectivist aspirations: both artists and students of aesthetics began to realize the subjective conditioning of beauty and to move away from the tenet of objective "symmetry" to that of subjective "eurhythmy".

15. EVOLUTION OF CLASSICAL ART AND INTIMATIONS OF A NEW ART. The fifth and fourth centuries B.C. are usually considered together as constituting the classical period, but the differences between them were great. In the fourth century, priority was given to proportions. In architecture the finer Ionic order took precedence over the Doric order, while in sculpture the canon of Polyclitus came to be regarded as too heavy and Euphranor introduced a different canon.

Secondly, in the fourth century there developed a love for richness, colour, lights, shapes and movements in all their variety, which the Greeks called *poikilia*. In the plastic arts there was also an increase in psychic dynamism, in emotional tension and pathos.

The third change was, from the aesthetic point of view, the most important. Lysippus expressed it in the following words: "Until now men have been represented as they are, but I represent them as they seem to be". This was a transition from the representation of the objective forms of things to the representation of the artist's subjective impressions of them; in other words, it was a transition from the quest for forms beautiful in themselves to those which seem beautiful because they conform to the conditions of human sight.

The painting of stage scenery (*skenographia*), which was the first to adopt illusionism, influenced easel painting, and all painting began to apply the perspective deformations (*skiagraphia*). The Greeks had learned to look at paintings from a distance: "Stand back, as would a painter", says Euripides. People in those days became impressed by the fact that painting gives an illusion of reality precisely when it departs from reality. Plato criticized illusionist painting as an unwarrantable deceit, "unclear and delusive", but the conservative theorist did not succeed in preventing art from evolving towards subjectivism and impressionism.

B. Texts from the Classical Poets and Artists

SOPHOCLES (Aristotle, Poët. 1460b 36).

IDEALIZATION AND REALISM

1. Σοφοκλῆς ἔφη αὐτὸς μὲν οἵους δεῖ ποιεῖν, Εὐριπίδην δὲ οἷοι εἰσι.

1. ...Sophocles... said that he drew men as they ought to be, and Euripides as they were.

tr. W. D. Ross

EURIPIDES (Plut., De Pyth. orac. 405 F).

POETRY AND EROS

2. ... ὁ δ' Εὐριπίδης εἰπών, ὡς «ἔρως ποιητὴν διδάσκει, κἂν ἄμουσος ᾖ τοπρίν» ἐνενόησεν, ὅτι ποιητικὴν καὶ μουσικὴν ἔρως δύναμιν οὐκ ἐντίθησιν, ἐνυπάρχουσαν δὲ κινεῖ, καὶ ἀναθερμαίνει λανθάνουσαν καὶ ἀργοῦσαν.

2. When Euripides said "Love doth the poet teach, even though he knew naught of the Muse before", his thought was that Love does not implant in one the poetical or musical faculty, but when it is already existent in one, Love stirs it to activity and makes it fervent, while before it was unnoticed and idle.

tr. F. C. Babbit

PLATO, Convivium 196 E.

πᾶς γοῦν ποιητὴς γίγνεται, κἂν ἄμουσος ᾖ τὸ πρίν, οὗ ἂν Ἔρως ἅψηται.

And at the touch of him [Love] everyone becomes a poet, even though he had no music in him before.

tr. B. Jowett

EURIPIDES, Bacchae 881.

3. ὅ τι καλὸν φίλον ἀεί.

3. What is noble is always precious.

tr. J. C. B. Lowe

EPICHARMUS (Stob. Eclog. II 31, 625; frg. B 40 Diels).

TALENT AND LEARNING

4. φύσιν ἔχειν ἄριστόν ἐστι, δεύτερον δὲ ⟨μανθάνειν⟩.

4. To have natural endowment is best, and second best is to learn.

tr. K. Freeman

EPICHARMUS (Plut., De fort. Alex. 336b; frg. B 12, Diels).

THE UNDERSTANDING

5. νοῦς ὁρῇ καὶ νοῦς ἀκούει· τἆλλα κωφὰ καὶ τυφλά.

5. Mind has sight and Mind has hearing; All things else are deaf and blind.

tr. F. C. Babbit

ARISTOPHANES, Ranae 1008.

ART TO SERVE MORAL ENDS

6. ἀπόκριναί μοι, τίνος οὕνεκα χρὴ
[θαυμάζειν ἄνδρα ποιητήν;
δεξιότητος καὶ νουθεσίας, ὅτι βελτίους τε
[ποιοῦμεν
τοὺς ἀνθρώπους ἐν ταῖς πόλεσιν.

6. Answer me, for what reasons ought one to admire a poet? For ability and advice, because we make the inhabitants of the various cities better men.

tr. F. G. Plaistowe

ARISTOPHANES, Ranae 1053–1056.

ἀλλὰ ἀποκρύπτειν χρὴ τὸ πονηρὸν τόν γε
[ποιητήν,
καὶ μὴ παράγειν μηδὲ διδάσκειν. τοῖς μὲν
[γὰρ παιδαρίοισιν
ἔστι διδάσκαλος ὅστις φράζει, τοῖς ἡβῶσιν
[δὲ ποιηταί.
πάνυ δὴ δεῖ χρηστὰ λέγειν ἡμᾶς...

But a poet at any rate ought to conceal what is base and not bring it forward and put it on the stage. For mere boys have a schoolmaster to instruct them, grown men have poets. From every point of view it is our duty to speak of good things.

tr. F. G. Plaistowe

ARISTOPHANES, Thesm. 156.

7. ἃ δ' οὐ κεκτήμεθα μίμησις ἤδη ταῦτα συνθηρεύεται.

PHILOSTRATUS THE YOUNGER, Imagines, Proem. (p. 4, ed. Schenkl-Reisch).

8. δοκοῦσι δέ μοι παλαιοί τε καὶ σοφοὶ ἄνδρες πολλὰ ὑπὲρ συμμετρίας τῆς ἐν γραφικῇ γράψαι.

LAERTIUS DIOGENES, VIII 47.

Πυθαγόραν... πρῶτον δοκοῦντα ῥυθμοῦ καὶ συμμετρίας ἐστοχάσθαι.

POLYCLITUS (Galen, De plac. Hipp. et Plat. V, Müll. 425; frg. A 3, Diels).

9. [Χρύσιππος]... τὸ δὲ κάλλος οὐκ ἐν τῇ τῶν στοιχείων, ἀλλὰ ἐν τῇ τῶν μορίων συμμετρίᾳ συνίστασθαι νομίζει, δακτύλου πρὸς δάκτυλον δηλονότι καὶ συμπάντων αὐτῶν πρός τε μετακάρπιον καὶ καρπὸν καὶ τούτων πρός πῆχυν καὶ πήχεως πρὸς βραχίονα καὶ πάντων πρὸς πάντα, καθάπερ ἐν τῷ Πολυκλείτου Κανόνι γέγραπται. Πάσας γὰρ ἐκδιδάξας ἡμᾶς ἐν ἐκείνῳ τῷ συγγράμματι τὰς συμμετρίας τοῦ σώματος ὁ Πολύκλειτος ἔργῳ τὸν λόγον ἐβεβαίωσε δημιουργήσας ἀνδριάντα κατὰ τὰ τοῦ λόγου προστάγματα καὶ καλέσας δὴ καὶ αὐτὸν τὸν ἀνδριάντα καθάπερ καὶ τὸ σύγγραμμα Κανόνα.

POLYCLITUS (Galen, De temper. I g, Helm 42, 26; frg. A 3, Diels).

οὕτω γοῦν καὶ πλάσται καὶ γραφεῖς ἀνδριαντοποιοί τε καὶ ὅλως ἀγαλματοποιοὶ τὰ κάλλιστα γράφουσι καὶ πλάττουσι καθ' ἕκαστον εἶδος, οἷον ἄνθρωπον εὐμορφότατον ἢ ἵππον ἢ βοῦν ἢ λέοντα, τὸ μέσον ἐν ἐκείνῳ τῷ γένει σκοποῦντες. καὶ πού τις ἐπαινεῖται Πολυκλείτου Κανὼν ὀνομαζόμενος ἐκ τοῦ πάντων τῶν μορίων ἀκριβῆ τὴν πρὸς ἄλληλα συμμετρίαν ἔχειν ὀνόματος τοιούτου τυχών.

POLYCLITUS (Philon, Mechan. IV, 1 p. 49, 20, R. Schöne; frg. B 2, Diels).

10. τὸ εὖ παρὰ μικρὸν διὰ πολλῶν ἀριθμῶν γίνεται.

MIMESIS

7. What we do not have in reality comes to us from imitation [in poetry].

SYMMETRIA

8. Learned men of olden times have written much, I believe, about symmetry in painting.
tr. A. Fairbanks

Pythagoras [of Rhegium, a sculptor] appears to have been the first to aim at rhythm and symmetry.

CANON

9. Chrysippus holds beauty to consist in the proportions not of the elements but of the parts, that is to say, of finger to finger and of all the fingers to the palm and wrist, and of these to the forearm, and of the forearm to the upper arm, and of all the parts to each other, as they are set forth in the *Canon* of Polyclitus. For Polyclitus, when he had taught us all the proportions of the human figure by means of that treatise, confirmed his theory by a practical illustration and made a statue according to the dictates of the theory, and called the statue, like the treatise, his Canon.
tr. W. H. S. Jones

Painters, makers of statues, and sculptors create the most beautiful paintings and sculpture of the various kinds, that is, they create the best shaped man, horse, bull or lion by turning their attention to what is general in each kind. After all, the statue by Polyclitus called Canon acquired that name because it possesses typical proportions in so far as the mutual relations of all parts of the body are concerned.

BEAUTY AND NUMERICAL RELATIONS

10. Perfection depends on many numerical relations, and small variants are decisive.

HERON (Th.-H. Martin, p. 420).

11. οὕτω γοῦν τὸν μὲν κύλινδρον κίονα, ἐπεὶ κατεαγότα ἔμελλε θεωρήσειν καὶ μέσα πρὸς ὄψιν στενούμενον, εὐρύτερον κατὰ ταῦτα ποιεῖ.

NICIAS (Demetrius, De eloc. 76).

12. Νικίας δ' ὁ ζωγράφος καὶ τοῦτο εὐθὺς ἔλεγεν εἶναι τῆς γραφικῆς τέχνης οὐ μικρὸν μέρος τὸ λαβόντα ὕλην εὐμεγέθη γράφειν, καὶ μὴ κατακερματίζειν τὴν τέχνην εἰς μικρά, οἷον ὀρνίθια ἢ ἄνθη, ἀλλ' ἱππομαχίας καὶ ναυμαχίας... ᾤετο γὰρ καὶ τὴν ὑπόθεσιν αὐτὴν μέρος εἶναι τῆς ζωγραφικῆς τέχνης, ὥσπερ τοὺς μύθους τῶν ποιητῶν. οὐδὲν οὖν θαυμαστόν, εἰ καὶ τοῖς λόγοις καὶ ἐκ πραγμάτων μεγάλων μεγαλοπρέπεια γένηται.

OPTICAL ILLUSIONS

11. Because a cylindrical column would appear to the eye to be narrower towards the middle, [the architect] makes that part thicker.

WEIGHTY SUBJECT

12. The painter Nicias used to maintain that no small part of the artistic faculty was shown in the painter's choosing at the outset a theme of some amplitude, instead of whittling down his art into small things, little birds [for example] or flowers. The right subjects, he said, were such as naval battles and cavalry engagements... His view was that the subject itself was a part of the painter's art, just as the ancient legends were a part of the art of poetry. So it need awaken no surprise that, in prose writings also, elevation results from the choice of a great subject.

tr. W. R. Roberts

4. Aesthetics and Philosophy

1. THE FIRST PHILOSOPHERS-AESTHETICIANS. Philosophy, born earlier in Greece, during the classical period widened its range to include problems of aesthetics*. Until then aesthetics had belonged to no particular discipline and lay within the competence of every citizen who might see and listen to works of art. There was no branch of knowledge in whose sphere of interests it might be contained. What early Greeks thought about art and beauty can be learned only from the works of art themselves and from random observations by poets. For the classical period, works of art and observations of poets continued to be a source of aesthetic ideas, but they were neither the only nor the most important source, for by then philosophers had become the spokesmen for aesthetic ideas.

At first concerned with problems of nature, they did not express themselves on aesthetic matters. The earliest to do so were the Dorian philosophers of the Pythagorean school; but even this was probably not until the fifth century. What is more, they only partly considered aesthetic problems from a scientific point of view, and partly continued to rely on religious traditions. The Ionian philosophers were at that time still completely occupied with the philosophy of nature; it was only Democritus, the last and the most illustrious of them, who gave wider consideration to

---

* All the source material on the origins of the philosophical aesthetics of the Pythagoreans, of Democritus, Heraclitus, the Sophists and Gorgias, is collected in H. Diels, *Fragmente der Vorsokratiker* (4th ed., 1922), but it is not distinguished from material on other matters.

aesthetic problems, which he tackled in the empirical way characteristic of the Ionian philosophers.

Democritus already belonged to the next generation of philosophers: that of Socrates and the famous Sophists. In this generation humanist problems became as important as those of nature; Athens became the centre of philosophy; the opposition between the Dorian and the Ionian thought diminished and even synthesized in the form of Attic culture and philosophy. This synthetic philosophy was given expression in the two following generations—the generations of Plato and of Aristotle. The works of these philosophers represent the twin peaks of classical aesthetics and even of the aesthetics of antiquity as a whole.

2. CONSEQUENCES OF MERGING AESTHETICS WITH PHILOSOPHY. Since the beginning of the classical period, most aesthetic thought was carried out within the framework of philosophy. This fact had two consequences, one positive and one negative. For, on the one hand, aesthetics developed not in isolation but in conjunction with man's other major quests. But on the other hand, some of its needs remained unsatisfied, philosophical speculation tending to relegate specialist studies to second place. Other disciplines, the humanities in particular, were at first in a similar situation, but they were quicker to gain independence and break away from philosophy.

From the very beginning, the philosophers' treatment of aesthetics was twofold. On the one hand, they analysed phenomena and concepts: there are many of these analyses in Democritus, in the Sophists and in Socrates. But on the other hand, philosophers formed aesthetic phenomena and concepts according to their systems. The Sophists were responsible for introducing into aesthetics a minimalist philosophy, while Plato introduced a maximalist one, together with the doctrine of eternal ideas and absolute values. The philosophy of this period had many systems, applied many points of view, was engaged in internal disputes and bequeathed them to aesthetics.

The attitude of the philosophers toward art was also twofold. Some drew on the experiences of artists and formulated theories of art on the basis of their practice, as with the theory that art both represents and idealizes nature. Here theory followed practice. Others, on the contrary, themselves initiated theories of art which influenced the artists. Here the theory of philosophers guided the practice of artists. For example, the application by architects and sculptors of canons and mathematical calculations had one of its sources in Pythagorean philosophy.

This survey of the aesthetics of the classical period had to start with the poetry and art which the philosophers were familiar with when they constructed their aesthetic theories. This poetry and art implied aesthetic judgments: sculpture implied a mathematical understanding of beauty, and poetry a moralistic one. However, the most crucial part of classical aesthetics is to be found in the aesthetics of philosophers. This spanned at least four generations: in the first the Dorian aesthetics of the Pythagoreans, in the second the Ionian aesthetics of Democritus and the

Attic aesthetics of the Sophists and of Socrates, in the third the aesthetics of Plato, and in the fourth that of Aristotle. It contained a wealth of great ideas and detailed studies, ranging from still archaic attempts to fully developed problems and solutions.

5. Pythagorean Aesthetics

1. THE PYTHAGOREAN IDEA OF PROPORTION AND MEASURE. The Pythagoreans formed a group whose character was chiefly moral and religious, but they also carried out scientific investigations, mainly in mathematics. They originated in the Dorian colonies in Italy and their founder was Pythagoras, who lived in the sixth century B.C. The scientific achievements of the school were not due to him, however, but to his successors in the fifth and fourth centuries. The dual character of the Pythagorean movement (i.e., partly religious and partly scientific) was reflected in its aesthetics.*

One philosophical concept of the Pythagoreans was of fundamental importance to aesthetics: namely, that the world is constructed mathematically. Aristotle wrote of them that they were so absorbed by mathematics that "they thought its principles were the principles of all things".[1] In particular, they established a mathematical order in acoustics because they observed that strings sound harmoniously or otherwise, according to their length. They sound harmoniously if their lengths reflect direct numerical relations. In the relation 1 : 2 they produce an octave, in 2 : 3 a fifth, and, when their lengths are in the proportion of 1 : 2/3 : 1/2, this produces the chord C-G-c which they called the "harmonious" chord. Thus they explained the puzzling phenomenon of harmony in terms of proportion, measure and number, and considered that harmony depended on a mathematical relation of parts. This was an important discovery. Thanks to it music became an art: an art in the Greek meaning of the word.

The Pythagoreans had no thought of pursuing aesthetics as an independent science. To them harmony was a property of the cosmos, and they contemplated it within the framework of cosmology. They did not use the term "beauty", but employed rather the term "harmony", which they probably invented themselves. The Pythagorean Philolaus wrote: "Harmony is a Unity of many mixed elements and an agreement between disagreeing elements".[2] Etymologically, harmony meant the same as attunement and unification, and signified the concord and unity of the constituent parts. It was mainly because of this unity that harmony was for the Pythagoreans something positive and beautiful in the wide, Greek sense of the word. Philolaus wrote that things which are "unlike and unrelated and unequally arranged are necessarily fastened together by such a harmony".[3] The harmony of sounds they regarded merely as a manifestation of a deeper harmony, as an expression of an inner order in the very structure of things.

---

* A. Delatte, *Études sur la littérature pythagoricienne* (1915).

An essential feature of Pythagorean theory was that they regarded[4] harmony and just proportion (*symmetria*) not only as valuable, beautiful and useful, but also as objectively determined, as an *objective* property of things. Another of their tenets was that the property which determines the harmony of things is their *regularity* and order. Thirdly, harmony is not a property of a particular object, but the correct arrangement of many objects. Pythagorean theory went even further and maintained, fourthly, that harmony is a mathematical, a *numerical* disposition, depending on *number*, *measure*, and *proportion*. This thesis constituted the particular Pythagorean doctrine, derived from their mathematical philosophy and based on their discoveries in acoustics. It laid the foundations of the future aesthetics of the Greeks and became its basic feature. It also influenced Greek art, in particular music,[5] but also, indirectly, architecture and sculpture.[6] Pythagorean philosophy strengthened the Greek conviction that regularity is a guarantee of harmony and beauty. The mathematical interpretation of music was the achievement of the Pythagorean school: but also the canons of the visual arts, with their arithmetic calculations and geometric constructions, were in no small measure the result of Pythagorean ideas.

The Greeks regarded beauty as a property of the visible world, but their theory of beauty was mainly influenced not by the visual arts, but by music, which was what first gave rise to the belief that beauty is a question of proportions, measure and number.

2. THE HARMONY OF THE COSMOS. Since they were convinced that the universe is constructed harmoniously, the Pythagoreans gave it the name of *kosmos*, that is, "order". They thereby introduced an aesthetic feature into cosmology and into the term employed to describe it. On the subject of cosmic harmony they indulged in far-reaching speculations. Assuming that every regular movement makes a harmonious sound,[7] they thought that the whole universe produced a "music of the spheres", a symphony which we do not hear only because it sounds continuously. Proceeding from this premise they inferred that the shape of the world must also be regular and harmonious: the sphere is such a shape and therefore they assumed that the world must be spherical. Their psychology was also imbued with their aesthetics: taking souls to be analogous to bodies, they assumed that those souls are perfect which are harmoniously constructed, that is, those which have a proper proportion of parts.

The aesthetic principle of the Pythagoreans was adopted generally in Greece, though only in the looser sense that beauty is a matter of order and of regularity in the disposition of parts. In that sense it became, one might say, an axiom of ancient aesthetics. The narrower sense of beauty as a matter of number, of numerical order, remained the tenet of some trends in art and theory of art. For beauty in the first sense the Greeks retained the Pythagorean term *harmonia*, while to describe beauty in the second sense they normally used the term *symmetria*.

3. THE ETHOS OF MUSIC. There is another theory by which the Pythagoreans are remembered in the history of aesthetics. This too was connected with music but

had an entirely different character. The first theory claimed that music is based on proportion, while the second declared it to be a power acting on the soul. The first concerned the essence of art; the second, its effect on men.

This theory was a counterpart of the expressive arts of the Greeks, of the "triune *choreia*", which was realized through words, gesture and music. Originally the Greeks thought that the *choreia* acted exclusively on the feelings of the dancer or singer himself. But the Pythagoreans noticed that the art of the dance and of music has a similar effect on the spectator and the listener. They saw that it acts not only through movement but also through watching movement; that a cultured man, in order to experience intense feelings, does not need to perform orgiastic dances, as it is enough for him to watch them. A later Greek historian of music, Aristides Quintilian, informs us that this idea was already current among "ancient" theorists of music: he must have had the Pythagoreans in mind, for they sought to explain the powerful effect of art in terms of the relationship between movements, sounds and feelings. Movements and sounds express feelings and, conversely, they evoke feelings. Sounds find an echo in the soul, which resounds in harmony with them. It is as with a pair of lyres: when we strike one, the other standing nearby will respond.

From this the conclusion follows that music can act on the soul: good music may improve it, and, on the other hand, bad music may corrupt it. The Greeks here used the term *psychagogia*, that is, "guidance of souls", so that the dance, and more particularly, music, had, according to them, a "psychagogic" power. It can, as they put it, lead the soul into a good or a bad "ethos" (state of mind). Against this background there grew up a study of the ethos of music, that is, of its psychagogic and educational effects, and this became a permanent feature of the Greeks' view of music, even more popular than the mathematical interpretation. In accordance with this teaching, the Pythagoreans, and later those who inherited their ideas, placed great stress on differentiating between good and bad music. They demanded that good music should be legally protected, and that—in a matter so morally and socially important—freedom and its attendant risks should not be allowed.[8]

4. THE ORPHIC ELEMENT: PURIFICATION THROUGH ART. The Pythagorean principle concerning the power of music had its main source in Greek religion, or, to be precise, in Orphic beliefs. The essence of these beliefs was that the soul is imprisoned in the body for its sins, that it would be liberated when it was purified and that this purification and liberation was the most significant aim of man. This aim was served by the Orphic mysteries, which made use of the dance and of music. The Pythagoreans, however, introduced the idea that music more than anything else serves to purify the soul. They saw in music not only a psychagogic, but also a purifying power (a "cathartic" power), which was not only ethical, but also religious. "The Pythagoreans", according to Aristoxenus, "employed medicine to purge the body, and music to purge the soul".[9] From the giddiness which they observed resulting from Bacchic music, they drew the conclusion that under its influence the soul could liberate itself and momentarily leave the body. Because of the connection

between this idea and the Orphic mysteries, we may call it the Orphic element in the theory of the arts.

5. MUSIC, AN ART UNLIKE OTHER ARTS. The Pythagoreans did not ascribe an expressive and psychagogic power to all the arts, but exclusively to music. They held that the efficient way to affect the soul is by means of hearing, and not through any other senses. Thus they regarded music as an exceptional art,[10] a special gift of the gods. They held that music is not the product of man, but "of nature"; rhythms belong to nature and are innate in man: man cannot arbitrarily invent them, he can only conform to them. By its very nature the soul expresses itself in music; this art is its natural expression. They said that rhythms were "likenesses" (*homoiomata*) of the psyche, the "signs" or expressions of character.

The Pythagorean theory of purification through music consisted of a whole cluster of propositions: 1. that music is the expression of the soul, its character, temper and ethos; 2. that it is a "natural" expression, unique of its kind; 3. that music is either good or bad, depending on the character it expresses; 4. that, thanks to the connection of the soul with music, it is possible to act on the soul through music, either to improve or to deprave it; 5. that, therefore, the aim of music is not by any means solely to provide pleasure, but to form character, as Athenaeus was to write later: "the aim of music is not pleasure but the service of virtue"; 6. that through good music the "purification" and liberation of the soul from the bonds of the flesh is achieved, and 7. that therefore music is something exceptional, unique, unlike the other arts.

6. CONTEMPLATION. The Pythagoreans conceived yet another concept important to aesthetics, namely the concept of contemplation.[11] They contrasted contemplation with activity, i.e., the position of the onlooker with that of the doer. According to Diogenes Laertius, Pythagoras compared life with games to which some come in order to participate in the contests, others to buy and sell, and others still only to watch. This last position he regarded as the loftiest because it is adopted not out of concern for fame or gain, but solely in order to acquire knowledge. This concept of contemplation embraced the viewing of both beauty and truth. Only later on was it differentiated into epistemological contemplation of truth, and aesthetic contemplation of beauty.

7. DAMON'S DOCTRINE. While the religious interpretation of music remained a specifically Pythagorean and Orphic idea, its psychological, ethical, and educational interpretation gained widespread recognition among the Greeks. It spread beyond the Pythagorean school and the Pythagorean association, even beyond the Dorian states. True, it was attacked by the empirical Ionian thinkers, to whom it appeared too mystical, but their attacks in turn provoked a counter defence in fifth-century Athens. There the most impressive defender of the Pythagorean theory was Damon.* At this stage the question lost some of its theoretical significance, gaining a political and social one instead.

---
* K. Jander, *Oratorum et rhetorum Graecorum nova fragmenta nuper reperta* (Rome, 1913).

Damon flourished in the middle of the fifth century B.C. His writings have not survived, but we know the contents of his *Envoi* to the members of the Areopagus, in which he warned them against innovations in music because of their social and educational dangers. Basing himself on the Pythagorean theory, he demonstrated the connection between music and the human soul, and its consequent value in the service of public education. Proper rhythm is a sign of an orderly spiritual life and teaches spiritual harmony (*eunomia*). Singing and playing teach the young not only courage and moderation but also, he maintained, justice. He held that any change in the forms of music would have such profound effects that it inevitably would cause a change in the system of government. These ideas about the politico-social role of music we may regard as Damon's own doctrine.

We know of Damon largely through Plato, who shared his views and who has probably done most to spread them. It was also thanks to Plato that the Pythagorean conception of music left its mark on the whole Greek theory of art. Through him this theory evolved, on the one hand, under the banner of proportion, measure and number, and on the other, under the banner of perfecting and "purifying" the soul. This early aesthetico-philosophical idea of the Greeks proved their most enduring concept. It left a particularly strong mark on the theory of music: it was responsible for the fact that music was treated in Greece as an exceptional art, different from all the other arts, and the only one with expressive and therapeutic qualities. Music was believed to have epistemological significance—because it reveals the laws governing the world—as well as moral and soteriological significance; whereas the aesthetic consideration of music was relegated to a subordinate place.

8. THE HERACLITEAN DOCTRINE. Damon and Plato were the Attic sympathizers of Pythagoreanism. But at the same time they were representatives of the different and antagonistic Ionian culture and philosophy. They had taken over from the Pythagoreans only one important idea, that of harmony. Many years before Plato this idea had spread east to Ionia: it was taken up by Heraclitus of Ephesus, who was active at the beginning of the fifth century B.C. and must have come into contact with representatives of the Pythagorean school. This philosopher, who chiefly stressed multiplicity, change and opposition in the world, also saw, however, its unity and harmony.

Four of his fragments on harmony have survived. One says that harmony is most beautiful when it is derived from various sounds.[12] Another even goes so far as to say that harmony arises out of opposing forces.[13] As examples of harmony, Heraclitus cited the bow and the lyre: the greater their tension, that is, the more divergent are the forces acting upon them, the more effectively the bow shoots and the lyre sounds. He concluded that harmony may arise also out of opposing, divergent elements. According to the third Heraclitean fragment, "hidden" harmony,[14] is supposed to be "stronger" than the visible one (but by "hidden" harmony he probably meant the harmony which arises out of opposites). Finally, the fourth fragment states that out of opposites there arises a symphony not only in nature, but also in art, which thereby imitates nature.⁽¹⁵⁾

Harmony played as great a part in his view of the world as in that of the Pythagoreans. But there is nothing to suggest that he ascribed a mathematical character to it: he had in mind rather a harmony in a looser, qualitative sense, and emphasized the fact that it arises out of opposites. The doctrine of harmony issuing out of opposites was the special Heraclitean contribution to aesthetics.

The concept of harmony took root: it was employed not only by Heraclitus but by all later Ionian philosophers. Empedocles wrote that harmony determines the unity of nature, Democritus that it determines human happiness. It was, however, a cosmological or an ethical concept rather than an aesthetic one; at best we can only say that it introduced an aesthetic element into cosmology and ethics.

9. ORDER AND CHAOS. The Greek concepts of harmony and of its opposite, disharmony, were based on even wider concepts: order and chaos. Only things which are calculable, regular and lucid and which embody order and regularity, did the Greeks regard as comprehensible. Only the comprehensible was regarded as reasonable, and only the reasonable as good and beautiful. Therefore, in the Greek view, the reasonable, the good and the beautiful were identified with what is ordered, regular and finite, while things irregular and unlimited were regarded as chaos, incomprehensible and irrational, which can be neither good nor beautiful. This conviction was from the earliest days embodied in the art of the Greeks and stated in their philosophy. It was first formulated by philosophers, namely the Pythagoreans, but it must have accorded with the natural disposition of the Greeks, for otherwise it would never have been adopted so widely, would not have been for many centuries a principle of their art and an axiom of their aesthetics.

C. Texts from the Pythagoreans and Heraclitus

PYTHAGOREANS (Aristotle, Metaph. A 5, 985b 23).

1. οἱ καλούμενοι Πυθαγόρειοι τῶν μαθημάτων ἀψάμενοι πρῶτοι ταῦτα προήγαγον καὶ ἐντραφέντες ἐν αὐτοῖς τὰς τούτων ἀρχὰς τῶν ὄντων ἀρχὰς ᾠήθησαν εἶναι πάντων... ἐπειδὴ τὰ μὲν ἄλλα τοῖς ἀριθμοῖς ἐφαίνετο τὴν φύσιν ἀφωμοιῶσθαι πᾶσαν, οἱ δ' ἀριθμοὶ πάσης τῆς φύσεως πρῶτοι, τὰ τῶν ἀριθμῶν στοιχεῖα τῶν ὄντων στοιχεῖα πάντων ὑπέλαβον εἶναι, καὶ τὸν ὅλον οὐρανὸν ἁρμονίαν εἶναι καὶ ἀριθμόν.

SYMMETRIA AND HARMONY

1. The Pythagoreans, as they are called, devoted themselves to mathematics; they were the first to advance this study, and having been brought up in it they thought its principles were the principles of all things... Since, then, all other things seemed in their whole nature to be modelled after numbers, and numbers seemed to be the first things in the whole of nature, they supposed the elements of numbers to be the elements of all things, and the whole heaven to be a musical scale and a number.

tr. W. D. Ross

PHILOLAUS (Nicomachus, Arithm. II 19, p. 115, 2; frg. B 10, Diels).

2. ἔστι γὰρ ἁρμονία πολυμιγέων ἕνωσις καὶ δίχα φρονεόντων συμφρόνησις.

2. Harmony is a Unity of many mixed [elements], and an agreement between disagreeing [elements].
   tr. K. Freeman

PHILOLAUS (Stobaeus, Ecl. I 21, 7d; frg. B 6, Diels).

3. τὰ μὲν ὦν ὁμοῖα καὶ ὁμόφυλα ἁρμονίας οὐδὲν ἐπεδέοντο, τὰ δὲ ἀνόμοια μηδὲ ὁμόφυλα μηδὲ ἰσοταγῆ ἀνάγκα τᾷ τοιαύτᾳ ἁρμονίᾳ συγκεκλεῖσθαι, οἵᾳ μέλλοντι ἐν κόσμῳ κατέχεσθαι.

3. Now the things which were like and related needed no harmony; but the things which were unlike and unrelated and unequally arranged are necessarily fastened together by such a harmony through which they are destined to endure in the universe.
   tr. K. Freeman

PYTHAGOREANS (Stobaeus IV 1, 40 H.; frg. D 4, Diels).

4. ἡ μὲν τάξις καὶ συμμετρία καλὰ καὶ σύμφορα, ἡ δ' ἀταξία καὶ ἀσυμμετρία αἰσχρά τε καὶ ἀσύμφορα.
(Alike Jambl. Vita Pyth. 203)

4. Order and proportion are beautiful and useful, while disorder and lack of proportion are ugly and useless.

PHILOLAUS (Stobaeus, Ecl. I, proem. cor. 3; frg. B 11, Diels).

5. ἴδοις δέ καὶ οὐ μόνον ἐν τοῖς δαιμονίοις καὶ θείοις πράγμασι τὰν τῶ ἀριθμῶ φύσιν καὶ τὰν δύναμιν ἰσχύουσαν, ἀλλὰ καὶ ἐν τοῖς ἀνθρωπικοῖς ἔργοις καὶ λόγοις πᾶσι παντᾷ καὶ κατὰ τὰς δημιουργίας τὰς τεχνικὰς πάσας καὶ κατὰ τὰν μουσικάν. ψεῦδος δὲ οὐδὲν δέχεται ἁ τῶ ἀριθμῶ φύσις οὐδὲ ἁρμονία.

5. And you may see the nature of Number and its power at work not only in supernatural and divine existences, but also in all human activities and words everywhere, both throughout all technical production and also in music. The nature of Number and Harmony admits of no Falsehood.
   tr. K. Freeman

PYTHAGOREANS (Sextus Emp., Adv. mathem. VII 106).

6. πᾶσά γε μὴν τέχνη οὐ χωρὶς ἀναλογίας συνέστε· ἀναλογία δ' ἐν ἀριθμῷ κεῖται. πᾶσα ἄρα τέχνη δι' ἀριθμοῦ συνέστη... ὥστε ἀναλογία τις ἐστιν ἐν πλαστικῇ, ὁμοίως δὲ καὶ ἐν ζωγραφίᾳ, δι' ἣν ὁμοιότητα καὶ ἀπαραλλαξίαν κατορθοῦνται. κοινῷ δὲ λόγῳ πᾶσα τέχνη ἐστὶ σύστημα ἐκ καταλήψεων, τὸ δὲ σύστημα ἀριθμός. τοίνυν ὑγιὲς τὸ ἀριθμῷ δέ πάντ' ἐπέοικε τουτέστι τῷ κρίνοντι λόγῳ καὶ ὁμοιογενεῖ τοῖς τὰ πάντα συνεστακόσιν ἀριθμοῖς. ταῦτα μὲν οἱ Πυθαγορικοί.

6. No art comes about without proportion, and proportion resides in number. All art therefore arises through number... So there is a certain proportion in sculpture and also in painting. Thanks to this proportion they achieve complete propriety. Generally speaking, every art is a system of perceptions, and system is number, one can therefore justly say "things look beautiful by virtue of number", which means thanks to a mind capable of judgment and related to numbers which are the principle of all things. This is what the Pythagoreans assert.

PYTHAGOREANS (Aristotle,
De coelo B 9. 290b 12).

7. γίνεσθαι φερομένων ⟨τῶν ἄστρων⟩ ἁρμονίαν, ὡς συμφώνων γινομένων τῶν ψόφων... ὑποθέμενοι δὲ ταῦτα καὶ τὰς ταχυτῆτας ἐκ τῶν ἀποστάσεων ἔχειν τοὺς τῶν συμφωνιῶν λόγους, ἐναρμόνιόν φασι γίγνεσθαι τὴν φωνὴν φερομένων κύκλῳ τῶν ἄστρων.

7. ...the theory that the movement of the stars produces harmony, i.e., that the sounds they make are concordant... Starting from this argument and from the description of their speeds, as measured by their distances, are in the same ratios as musical concordances, they assert that the sound given forth by the circular movement of the stars is a harmony.

tr. W. D. Ross

PYTHAGOREANS (Aristides
Quintilian II 6, Jahn 42).

8. ταῦτ' οὖν ὁρῶντες ἐκ παίδων ἠνάγκαζον διὰ βίου μουσικὴν ἀσκεῖν καὶ μέλεσι καὶ ῥυθμοῖς καὶ χορείαις ἐχρῶντο δεδοκιμασμέναις, ἔν τε ταῖς ἰδιωτικαῖς εὐφροσύναις καὶ ταῖς δημοσίαις θείαις ἑορταῖς συνήθη μέλη τινὰ νομοθετήσαντες, ἃ καὶ νόμους προσηγόρευον, μηχανήν τινα εἶναι τῆς βεβαιότητος αὐτῶν τὴν ἱερουργίαν ποιησάμενοι καὶ μένειν δὲ ἀκίνητα διὰ τῆς προσηγορίας ἐπεφήμισαν.

EFFECTS OF MUSIC

8. Observing these [effects of music], they concluded that it was indispensable for everyone to cultivate music from childhood onwards, and to this end they employed well-tested melodies, rhythms and dances. They decreed which melodies are to be used for public ceremonies, and these they called "laws", and which for private amusement. By introducing them into ritual they ensured their permanent form and by the name they gave them they underlined their immutability.

PYTHAGOREANS (Iamblichus,
Vita Pyth. 169).

9. χρῆσθαι δὲ καὶ ταῖς ἐπῳδαῖς πρὸς ἔνια τῶν ἀρρωστημάτων. ὑπελάμβανον δὲ καὶ τὴν μουσικὴν μεγάλα συμβάλλεσθαι πρὸς ὑγιείαν, ἄν τις αὐτῇ χρῆται κατὰ τοὺς προσήκοντας τρόπους. ἐχρῶντο δὲ καὶ Ὁμήρου καὶ Ἡσιόδου λέξεσιν ἐξειλεγμέναις πρὸς ἐπανόρθωσιν ψυχῶν.

9. It is said they employed incantations against certain illnesses; they assumed that music also has a great influence on health if it is used in a proper way. They also used the words of Homer and Hesiod to repair the soul.

PYTHAGOREANS (Cramer, Anecd.
Par. I 172).

ὅτι οἱ Πυθαγορικοί, ὡς ἔφη Ἀριστόξενος, καθάρσει ἐχρῶντο τοῦ μὲν σώματος διὰ τῆς ἰατρικῆς, τῆς δὲ ψυχῆς διὰ τῆς μουσικῆς.

The Pythagoreans, according to Aristoxenus, employed medicine to purge the body, and music to purge the soul.

THEON OF SMYRNA, Mathematica I
(Hiller, p. 12).

καὶ οἱ Πυθαγορικοὶ δέ, οἷς πολλαχῇ ἕπεται Πλάτων, τὴν μουσικήν φασιν ἐναντίων συναρμογὴν καὶ τῶν πολλῶν ἕνωσιν καὶ τῶν δίχα φρονούντων συμφρόνησιν· οὐ γὰρ ῥυθμῶν μόνον καὶ μέλους συντακτικήν, ἀλλ' ἁπλῶς παντὸς συστήματος· τέλος γὰρ αὐτῆς τὸ

The Pythagoreans, whom Plato follows in many respects, call music the harmonization of opposites, the unification of disparate things and the conciliation of warring elements. For they claim that not only rhythms and melody but in fact the whole system [of the world] de-

ἐνοῦν τε καί συναρμόζειν. καί γάρ ὁ θεὸς συναρμοστής τῶν διαφωνούντων, καί τοῦτο μέγιστον ἔργον θεοῦ κατά μουσικήν τε καί κατά ἰατρικήν τά ἐχθρά φίλα ποιεῖν. ἐν μουσικῇ, φασίν, ἡ ὁμόνοια τῶν πραγμάτων, ἔτι καί ἀριστοκρατία τοῦ παντός καί γάρ αὕτη ἐν κόσμῳ μὲν ἁρμονία, ἐν πόλει δ' εὐνομία, ἐν οἴκοις δὲ σωφροσύνη γίνεσθαι πέφυκε· συστατική γάρ ἐστι καί ἐνωτική τῶν πολλῶν· ἡ δὲ ἐνέργεια καί ἡ χρῆσις, φησί, τῆς ἐπιστήμης ταύτης ἐπί τεσσάρων γίνεται τῶν ἀνθρωπίνων, ψυχῆς, σώματος, οἴκου, πόλεως· προσδεῖται γάρ ταῦτα τά τέσσαρα συναρμογῆς καί συντάξεως.

pends on music, whose object is unity and harmony. God harmonizes warring elements and this in fact is his greatest aim in music and the art of medicine, namely that he reconciles things which are hostile. Music, as they say, is the basis of agreement among things in nature and of the best government in the universe. As a rule it assumes the guise of harmony in the universe, of lawful government in a state, and of a sensible way of life in the home. It brings together and unites. They say that the effects and application of [musical] knowledge reveal themselves in four human spheres: in the soul, in the body, in the home and in the state. For it is these things that require to be harmonized and unified.

PYTHAGOREANS (Strabo, X 3, 10).

10. Καί διά τοῦτο μουσικήν ἐκάλεσε Πλάτων καί ἔτι πρότερον οἱ Πυθαγόρειοι τήν φιλοσοφίαν, καί καθ' ἁρμονίαν τόν κόσμον συνεστάναι φασί, πᾶν τό μουσικόν εἶδος θεῶν ἔργον ὑπολαμβάνοντες· οὕτω δὲ καί αἱ Μοῦσαι θεαί καί Ἀπόλλων Μουσαγέτης καί ἡ ποιητική πᾶσα ὑμνητική.

10. And on this account Plato, and even before his time the Pythagoreans, called philosophy music; and they say that the universe is constituted in accordance with harmony, assuming that every form of music is the work of the gods. And in this sense, also, the Muses are goddesses, and Apollo is leader of the Muses, and poetry as a whole is laudatory of the gods.

tr. H. L. Jones

PYTHAGORAS (Laërt. Diog. VIII 8).

11. Καί τόν βίον ἐοικέναι πανηγύρει. ὡς οὖν εἰς ταύτην οἱ μὲν ἀγωνιούμενοι, οἱ δὲ κατ' ἐμπορίαν, οἱ δέ γε βέλτιστοι ἔρχονται θεαταί, οὕτως ἐν τῷ βίῳ οἱ μὲν ἀνδραπόδωδεις, ἔφη, φύονται δόξης καί πλεονεξίας θηραταί, οἱ δὲ φιλόσοφοι τῆς ἀληθείας.

THE CONCEPT OF CONTEMPLATION

11. Life, he said, is like a sporting event. Some go there as competitors, some to do business, but the best come as spectators; and similarly in life people with slave mentality seek fame or profit, but those who are philosophically minded seek truth.

HERACLITUS (Aristotle, Eth. Nic. 1155b 4; frg. B 8 Diels).

12. τό ἀντίξουν συμφέρον καί ἐκ τῶν διαφερόντων καλλίστην ἁρμονίαν καί πάντα κατ' ἔριν γίνεσθαι.

HARMONY OF OPPOSITES

12. That which is in opposition is in concert, and from things that differ comes the most beautiful harmony.

tr. K. Freeman

HERACLITUS (Hippolytus, Refut. IX g; B 51 Diels).

13. οὐ ξυνιᾶσιν ὅκως διαφερόμενον ἑωυτῷ ὁμολογέει· παλίντροπος ἁρμονίη ὅκωσπερ τόξου καί λύρης.

13. [People] do not understand how that which differs with itself is in agreement: harmony consists of opposing tension, like that of the bow and the lyre.

tr. K. Freeman

HERACLITUS (Hippolytus, Refut. IX g;
    frg. B 54 Diels).

14. ἁρμονίη ἀφανὴς φανερῆς κρείττων.

14. The hidden harmony is stronger [or "better"] than the visible.

tr. K. Freeman

HERACLITUS (Pseudo-Aristotle,
    De mundo, 396b 7).

15. Ἴσως δὲ τῶν ἐναντίων ἡ φύσις γλίχεται καὶ ἐκ τούτων ἀποτελεῖ τὸ σύμφωνον, οὐκ ἐκ τῶν ὁμοίων·... ἔοικε δὲ καὶ ἡ τέχνη τὴν φύσιν μιμουμένη τοῦτο ποιεῖν.

15. But perhaps nature actually has a liking for opposites; perhaps it is from them that she creates harmony, and not from similar things... It seems too that art does this in imitation of nature.

tr. D. J. Finley

6. The Aesthetics of Democritus

1. THE AESTHETIC WRITINGS OF DEMOCRITUS. The Ionian philosophers, of whom Democritus was one, formed the first philosophical school in Greece, but Democritus represented its last days and neither chronologically nor substantially was he an archaic philosopher. The dates of his life are disputed, but it is known that he was still alive at the beginning of the fourth century, that he had outlived Protagoras and Socrates and had been a contemporary of Plato at the height of his powers.

Among the Ionian philosophers, with their leanings towards materialism, determinism and empiricism, he was the most convinced materialist, determinist and empiricist. This is also evident in his ideas about art.

He was not only a philosopher but also a polymath, writing on a variety of subjects and initiating or developing scientific studies in many fields. One of the subjects he considered was the theory of poetry and art. In the tetralogical arrangement of his writings compiled later by Thrasyllus, this occupied the tenth and half the eleventh tetralogy. The text in which he considered it were *On Rhythms and Harmony, On Poetry, On the Beauty of Words, On Well and Ill Sounding Letters, On Homer,* and *On Singing*. All these writings have perished, and only their titles and small fragments have survived; but these demonstrate that, as well as the theory of poetry, he studied the theory of the fine arts. Later Greek historians regarded him as the scholar who originated aesthetics. At all events he originated certain detailed studies concerned not so much with beauty as with the arts. From his extensive work in this field we know only those few ideas which have by chance been preserved.

2. ART AND NATURE. One of Democritus' general ideas about art concerned its dependence on nature. He wrote: "We have been the pupils [of the animals] in matters of fundamental importance, of the spider in weaving and mending, of the swallow in home-building, of the sweet-voiced swan and nightingale in our

imitation of their song".[1] Democritus here talks of the "imitation" of nature by art and uses the term *mimesis*; however, he does it not in the sense which this word had in *choreia*, not in the sense of an actor's imitation of feelings, but as following nature in its methods of action. This second Greek conception of imitation was quite different from the first: the earlier was imitation in dance and music, the later one in building and weaving. The third conception, that of imitation of appearances in painting and words, which was soón to become the most common, was as yet unknown to the Greeks.

Democritus was probably not the first to conceive the idea of art imitating the ways of nature. It was doubtless known to Heraclitus, for it appears in the treatise *On the Diet*, which originated in his circle. The Greeks took to it and would also illustrate it by the example of culinary art by which food is prepared through a process imitating the digestion of nourishment by organisms. It was this that they had in mind when they wrote, "art performs its task by imitating nature". In Heraclitus occurs the parallel idea, "the arts are... like the nature of man".[2]

Democritus also drew attention to yet another connection between beauty and nature. He considered that the fact that certain people are competent at beauty and seek it, is also a gift of nature.[3]

3. THE JOYS OF ART. Another idea of Democritus concerned the effect of art: he maintained, "great joys are derived from beholding beautiful works".[4] This statement contains the earliest known conjunction of the ideas of *beauty*, *beholding* (contemplation), and *joy*. It is not surprising that it should have been written by Democritus, who was a hedonist and regarded all things, and therefore art and beauty as well, from the point of view of the joys they provide.

4. INSPIRATION. His next idea was concerned with the *origins* of creative art and in particular of poetry. He maintained, as Cicero and Horace confirm: "No man can be a good poet who is not on fire with passion".[5] And more vividly: "No one can be a great poet without being in a state of frenzy (*furor*)";[6] from Helicon will be barred "poets in their sober senses".[7] These statements prove that he considered poetic creativity to be derived from a special state of mind, different from the normal one.

This idea of Democritus was later often invoked and variously interpreted. Clement of Alexandria, one of the early fathers of the Church, wrote that, according to Democritus, poetic creation was guided by a supernatural "divine inspiration".[8] But it is this very interpretation which conflicts with Democritus' philosophy, since he only recognized natural events and regarded them as purely mechanistic. Perception he interpreted mechanistically as the outcome of the mechanical action of things upon the senses. And, as Aristotle records, he applied the same interpretation to poetic images arising in the poet's mind. Thus, he did not see poetic creation as guided by supernatural forces but, quite the contrary, sought to present it as subject to mechanical forces. It was precisely this new attitude which broke away from the traditional belief that poets derived their creativity from the inspiration of the Muses.

Thus, creation, like every other occurrence in the world, was for him a mechanical process, which, however, only took place in exceptional circumstances. These circumstances were not, it is true, supernatural but were at least supernormal. He was the first to deny that poets need to be inspired by the gods, but he did not conclude from this that they did not need inspiration at all. He held that inspiration could also be regarded as something natural. He was equally against the supernatural and the intellectual conception of poetry. He thought that poetry was possible only when "the spirit was inflamed". In this he was at one with Plato, with whom he was otherwise almost completely at variance.

There is, however, no trace of his having explained the plastic arts in a similar way, i.e., in terms of inspiration, "enthusiasm", and the "inflaming of the spirit". He belonged to an epoch which saw differences between poetry and art more clearly than similarities. For him, as for other Greeks of the period, poetry, just because it was a matter of inspiration, was not an art at all.

5. DEFORMATION IN ART. There was another concept which Democritus applied to art. This was linked with the schools of painting of the time, particularly stage painting. Since in the Greek theatre spectators saw the decorations from a distance, they appeared to them deformed in perspective, and Democritus pondered how to correct these deformations and render them harmless. Vitruvius tells us that he investigated how in accordance with the laws of nature rays are diffused and affect sight and how to turn indistinctly painted architectural scenery into distinct pictures and to make two-dimensional figures appear in relief.[9]

Democritus' philosophy found this problem particularly appealing because it regarded sensory qualities as subjective reactions of the senses and, in particular, treated colours as the reactions of the eye. In contrast with the traditionalists he regarded the deformations of painter-scenographers as justified because they endeavoured to make spectators see things just as they are in reality. In any case, in conformity with his whole philosophical outlook, Democritus did not instruct artists as to the aims they should pursue, but only as to the means they have to apply in order to achieve their aims. He is the prototype of those aestheticians who wish to analyse art rather than legislate about it; Plato was to emerge as the prototype of the opposite school.

6. PRIMARY COLOURS. Some other of Democritus' ideas that have come down to us concerned painting; he devoted his studies to discovering the primary colours to which all the colours we see may be reduced. This problem, which he posed himself, suited the general tendency of his philosophy, which reduced the multifariousness of things to a few types of atoms.

But he was not the only scholar of the time interested in this problem: it was discussed also by the Pythagoreans and by Empedocles. As a problem it belonged mainly to optics but it impinged upon the theory of art. Democritus, like Empedocles, distinguished four primary colours: white, black, red and yellow.⁽¹⁰⁾ His list conformed with the palette of contemporary painters.

7. MUSIC A MATTER OF LUXURY. Democritus also expressed views on music and these were, as though in reaction against the mystical attitude of most Greeks, negative. Philodemus wrote: "Democritus, who was not only the most scientifically minded among all the old philosophers, but was also active in historical research, says that music is a recent development and supports his claim by saying that it is the outcome not of necessity but of luxury".⁽¹¹⁾ This means, firstly, that according to Democritus music was not one of man's primordial activities and, secondly, that it arose not out of necessity but out of luxury. Using the language of the times, we may say that it was not a product of nature but of human invention. Both the immediate and the more remote disciples of Democritus steadfastly defended this sober view of music in direct conflict with the Greek tradition.

8. MEASURE, THE HEART AND SIMPLICITY. The doctrine of "just measure", which had for a long time been in the forefront of Greek thought, also made its appearance in Democritus. In this respect there was agreement even between the poets and the sober philosopher because this was a doctrine common among the Greeks. Democritus, like other Greeks, valued moderation in all human activities and products including art and beauty.⁽¹²⁾ But in this instance too he gave his ideas a hedonistic colouring which was characteristic of his philosophy: "If anyone oversteps the measure, the most pleasurable things become most unpleasant".⁽¹³⁾

The surviving fragments of Democritus' writings bear witness to the catholicity of his attitude. He acknowledged both spiritual and corporal beauty and wrote that without an element of intelligence corporal beauty is merely animal beauty.⁽¹⁴⁾ In beauty he acknowledged an emotional element beside the rational one, holding that beauty is incomplete if it appeals only to the senses or the mind and not the emotions but is, as he put it, "empty of heart".⁽¹⁵⁾

The surviving fragments of his works give us an inkling of his taste. One of them states: "In decorations simplicity is beautiful". It was, however, not only his own taste, but the taste of the period, and this fragment of Democritus could serve as a motto for Greek art in the classical period.⁽¹⁶⁾

9. SUMMARY. Although the writings of Democritus have perished and only isolated fragments have survived, it is possible, thanks to quotations and summaries by later writers, to acquire a general idea of his views on aesthetics. 1. His position was that of an empiricist and materialist and it manifested itself firstly in the fact that he concerned himself with the theory of art rather than with beauty. 2. So far as art was concerned he was more interested in description than prescription and in the establishment of facts than in the formation of concepts. 3. He regarded the arts as the achievement of man's natural abilities. He was convinced that they arose independently of divine inspiration, that nature was their model and pleasure their aim, that, moreover, this applied to all the arts, including music, which the Greeks treated as an exceptional art.

The position which Democritus adopted in aesthetics was new and different from the archaic position adopted by the poets and people in general. It was also different from the Pythagorean position, because it was neither mathematical nor mystical. It was an expression of Enlightenment, the first one in the history of aesthetics. But almost simultaneously another aspect of Enlightenment was to be revealed by the Sophists. The careful and restrained aesthetics of Democritus tended to eschew general theories, but the Sophists came forward with minimalistic theories of art.

D. Texts from Democritus

DEMOCRITUS (Plutarch, De sollert. anim. 20, 974 A.).

1. ἀποφαίνει μαθητὰς ἐν τοῖς μεγίστοις γεγονότας ἡμᾶς· ἀράχνης ἐν ὑφαντικῇ καὶ ἀκεστικῇ, χελιδόνος ἐν οἰκοδομίᾳ καὶ τῶν λιγυρῶν, κύκνου καὶ ἀηδόνος ἐν ᾠδῇ κατὰ μίμησιν.

ART AND NATURE

1. ...we have been the pupils [of the animals] in matters of fundamental importance, of the spider in weaving and mending, of the swallow in home-building, of the sweet-voiced swan and nightingale in our imitation of their song.

tr. H. F. Cherniss and W. C. Helmbold

HERACLITEAN SCHOOL (Hippocrates, De victu I 11).

2. οἱ δὲ ἄνθρωποι ἐκ τῶν φανερῶν τὰ ἀφανέα σκέπτεσθαι οὐκ ἐπίστανται. τέχνῃσι γὰρ χρεόμενοι ὁμοίῃσιν ἀνθρωπίνῃ φύσει οὐ γινώσκουσιν.

2. But men do not understand how to observe the invisible through the visible. For though the arts they employ are like the nature of man, yet they know it not.

tr. W. H. S. Jones

DEMOCRITUS (Democrates, Sent. 22; frg. B 56 Diels).

3. τὰ καλὰ γνωρίζουσι καὶ ζηλοῦσιν οἱ εὐφυέες πρὸς αὐτά.

3. Noble deeds are recognized and emulated by those of natural good disposition.

tr. K. Freeman

DEMOCRITUS (Stobaeus, Flor. III 3, 46; frg. B 194 Diels).

4. αἱ μεγάλαι τέρψεις ἀπὸ τοῦ θεᾶσθαι τὰ καλὰ τῶν ἔργων γίνονται.

JOY OF ART

4. The great pleasures come from the contemplation of noble works.

tr. K. Freeman

DEMOCRITUS (Cicero, De orat. II 46, 194).

5. Saepe enim audivi poëtam bonum neminem (id quod a Democrito et Platone in scriptis relictum esse dicunt) sine inflammatione animorum exsistere posse et sine quodam adflatu quasi furoris.

INSPIRATION

5. For I have often heard that—as they say Democritus and Plato have left on record—no man can be a good poet who is not on fire with passion, and inspired by something very like frenzy.

tr. E. W. Sutton and H. Rackham

DEMOCRITUS (Cicero, De divin. I 38, 80).

6. Negat enim sine furore Democritus quemquam poëtam magnum esse posse, quod idem dicit Plato.

6. Democritus says that no one can be a great poet without being in a state of frenzy, and Plato says the same thing.
tr. W. A. Falconer

DEMOCRITUS (Horace, De art. poët. 295).

7. Ingenium misera quia fortunatius arte Credit et excludit sanos Helicone poëtas Democritus.

7. Democritus believes that native talent is a greater boon than wretched art, and shuts out from Helicon poets in their sober senses.
tr. H. R. Fairclough

DEMOCRITUS (Clement of Alex., Strom. VI 168; frg. B 18 Diels).

8. Καὶ ὁ Δημόκριτος ὁμοίως· «ποιητὴς δὲ ἄσσα μὲν ἂν γράφῃ μετ' ἐνθουσιασμοῦ καὶ ἱεροῦ πνεύματος, καλὰ κάρτα ἐστίν».

8. What a poet writes with enthusiasm and divine inspiration is most beautiful.
tr. K. Freeman

DEMOCRITUS ET ANAXAGORAS (Vitruvius, De architectura VII pr. 11).

9. Primum Agatharchus Athenis Aeschylo docente tragoediam scaenam fecit et de ea commentarium reliquit. Ex eo moniti Democritus et Anaxagoras de eadem re scripserunt quemadmodum oporteat ad aciem oculorum radiorumque extentionem certo loco centro constituto lineas ratione naturali respondere, uti de certa re certae imagines aedificiorum in scaenarum picturis redderent speciem et quae in directis planisque frontibus sint figurata, alia abscedentia, alia prominentia esse videantur.

OPTICAL DEFORMATIONS

9. ...to begin with: Agatharchus at Athens, when Aeschylus was presenting a tragedy, was in control of the stage and wrote a commentary about it. Following his suggestions, Democritus and Anaxagoras wrote upon the same topic, in order to show how, if a fixed centre is taken for the outward glance of the eyes and the projection of the radii, we must follow these lines in accordance with a natural law, such that from an uncertain object, uncertain images may give the appearance of buildings in the scenery of the stage, and how what is figured upon vertical and plane surfaces can seem to recede in one part and project in another.
tr. F. Granger

DEMOCRITUS (Theophrastus, De sens. 73; frg. B 135 Diels³, 46).

10. τῶν δὲ χρωμάτων ἁπλᾶ μὲν λέγει τέτταρα.

PRIMARY COLOURS

10. The simple colours, he says, are four.
tr. G. M. Stratton

EMPEDOCLES (Aëtius, Plac. I 15, 3; frg. A 92 Diels).

Ἐμπεδοκλῆς χρῶμα εἶναι ἀπεφαίνετο τὸ τοῖς πόροις τῆς ὄψεως ἐναρμόττον. τέτταρα δὲ τοῖς στοιχείοις ἰσάριθμα, λευκὸν, μέλαν, ἐρυθρὸν, ὠχρόν.

Empedocles maintained that colour is what corresponds to the pores of the eye: there are four colours corresponding to the number of the elements: white, black, red and yellow.

DEMOCRITUS (Philodemus, De musica, Kemke 108, 29).

MUSIC

11. Δημόκριτος μὲν τοίνυν, ἀνὴρ οὐ φυσιολογώτατος μόνον τῶν ἀρχαίων, ἀλλὰ καὶ τῶν ἱστορουμένων οὐδενὸς ἧττον πολυπράγμων, μουσικήν φησι νεωτέραν εἶναι καὶ τὴν αἰτίαν ἀποδίδωσι λέγων μὴ ἀποκρῖναι τἀναγκαῖον, ἀλλὰ ἐκ τοῦ περιεῦντος ἤδη γενέσθαι.

11. Democritus, who was not only the most scientifically minded among all the old philosophers, but was also active in historical research, says that music is a recent development and supports his claim by saying that it is the outcome not of necessity but of luxury.

DEMOCRITUS (Democrates, Sent. 68; frg. B 102 Diels).

MODERATION

12. καλὸν ἐν παντὶ τὸ ἴσον· ὑπερβολὴ δὲ καὶ ἔλλειψις οὔ μοι δοκεῖ.

12. In all things equality is fair, excess and deficiency not so in my opinion.

tr. K. Freeman

DEMOCRITUS (Stobaeus, Flor. III 17, 38; frg. B 23 Diels).

13. εἰ τις ὑπερβάλλοι τὸ μέτριον, τὰ ἐπιτερπέστατα ἀτερπέστατα ἂν γίγνοιτο.

13. If anyone oversteps the measure, the most pleasurable things become most unpleasant.

tr. K. Freeman

DEMOCRITUS (Democrates, Sent. 71; frg. B 105 Diels).

INTELLECTUAL BEAUTY

14. σώματος κάλλος ζῳῶδες, ἢν μὴ νοῦς ὑπῇ.

14. Physical beauty is [merely] animal unless intelligence be present.

tr. K. Freeman

DEMOCRITUS (Stobaeus, Flor. III 4, 69; frg. B 195 Diels).

BEAUTY AND EMOTION

15. εἴδωλα ἐσθῆτι καὶ κόσμῳ διαπρεπέα πρὸς θεωρίην, ἀλλὰ καρδίης κενέα.

15. Images conspicuous for their dress and ornament, empty of heart.

tr. K. Freeman

DEMOCRITUS (Stobaeus, Flor. IV 23, 38; frg. B 274 Diels).

BEAUTY OF SIMPLICITY

16. καλόν δὲ καὶ κόσμου λιτότης.

16. Paucity of adornment is also beautiful.

tr. K. Freeman

7. The Aesthetics of the Sophists and of Socrates

I

1. THE SOPHISTS. In the middle of the fifth century B.C., the scientific studies of the Greeks moved beyond nature, to which they had been at first confined, and came to include man together with his functions and products. The chief agents

of this change were the Sophists in Athens. This was the name given to a group of people who were teachers of adults by profession and social philosophers by vocation.* The most philosophical mind among them was Protagoras (481–411?) and their main ideas derived from him. Similar ideas were formulated by Gorgias, who was not a Sophist by profession but shared the views of their circle, and the same may be said of Isocrates, professional orator.†

The Sophists concerned themselves mainly with questions of morality, law and religion, but also with questions of art. Their investigations were distinguished not only by their subject-matter but also by the empirical manner in which they were conducted. If the first characteristic of the Sophists' activity was a shift in philosophical interests from nature to human culture, that is towards a *humanization* of philosophy, the second one was the shift from general affirmations to more detailed observations, to a *particularization* of philosophy. A third feature of their activity was the *relativist* character of their results: having included in their studies the products of men they could not overlook the fact that these products were relative and dependent on many factors. This relativism also appeared in their theory of art and beauty, where they originated a relativistic stream.

Of the writings of the Sophists, and of their leader Protagoras in particular, only a few fragments have survived; the only slightly more extensive work to have reached us being that of an unknown Sophist entitled *Dialexeis* or *Dissoi logoi*. We also possess a longer text about art by Gorgias, known under the title *The Defence of Helen*. We know the opinions of Isocrates on oratory. The dialogues of Plato in their polemical sections may also serve as source of information about the aesthetic views of the Sophists.

The nature of the Sophists' interests was responsible for the fact that their views covered the theory of art rather than beauty. In this field they threw up many conceptual distinctions, mostly new and often significant, such as art versus nature, useful arts versus pleasurable arts, form versus content, talent versus education. They also produced their own theories of beauty and art: a relativistic theory of beauty and an illusionistic theory of art.

2. NATURE VERSUS ART. Protagoras himself was undoubtedly responsible for opposing the notions of art, nature and chance.[1] This opposition covered the whole range of art in its wide Greek sense, that is to say, it covered more than just the fine arts. It was natural for the concept of art to be contrasted with that of nature, because art was seen as a product of man, while nature exists independently of him. But the full meaning of the concept of art was revealed only when it was contrasted with chance. For not every product of man is a work of art; a work of art is not created by chance but deliberately accomplished in accordance with general principles. For the Greek conception of art this second distinction was no less important:

---

* M. Untersteiner, *Sofisti, testimonianze e frammenti* (1949).

† E. Mikkola, *Isokrates, seine Anschauungen im Lichte seiner Schriften*, (Helsinki, 1954).

art was for them the product of a purposeful activity which excluded arbitrariness and chance. The Sophists saw chance in nature rather than in art. According to one of Plato's dialogues, Protagoras equated nature with chance, contrasted it with art and by means of this double relation defined art.

3. USEFUL ARTS VERSUS PLEASURABLE ARTS. The Sophists employed another significant contrast, that between pleasure and utility, and applied it in art. The Sophist Alcidamas said[2] that statues give us joy but are not useful. Another member of the group said the same of poetry. Other Sophists, however, held: "Poets write their works ... to give pleasure to men".[3]

Taking up this antithesis, the orator Isocrates, who was close to the Sophists' circle, distinguished two types of human product: the useful and the pleasurable.[4] This was a natural distinction (its origins can be found in the poets Theognis and Simonides, and later in Sophocles), but it was the Sophists who applied it to art. The straightforward distinction between two types of art, the useful and the pleasurable, could have served as a provisional means of distinguishing the (pleasurable) fine arts from the great mass of the (useful) arts. But for the time being this idea did not meet with much response among the Greeks.

4. A HEDONISTIC DEFINITION OF BEAUTY. There was, however, yet another way in which the Sophists employed the concept of pleasure: they made use of it to define beauty. Most probably the following definition of beauty came from them: "the beautiful is that which gives pleasure through hearing and sight".[5] This was the aesthetic expression of the sensualism and hedonism to which the Sophists adhered. It was a move towards narrowing the idea of beauty and of differentiating aesthetic beauty, since it had no application to moral beauty. Both Plato and Aristotle mention this definition and both reject it; they do not give its source, but who could have thought it up if not one of the Sophists? Thus, we may assume that the Sophists were the first to formulate a hedonistic conception of beauty and of art.[6]

5. A RELATIVISTIC DOCTRINE OF BEAUTY. The belief in the relativity of beauty and art resulted from the general assumptions of the Sophists no less than the hedonist conceptions of beauty and art. Since they regarded laws, political systems and religion as relative and conventional, it is only natural that they should have treated art in a similar way. Since they regarded goodness and truth as relative, it is natural that they should have regarded beauty in a similar light. This was a consequence of their basic conviction: "Man is the measure of all things". The matter is discussed in the treatise known as *Dialexeis*: the whole of the second part of this little work deals with "beauty and ugliness".[7] The relativity of beauty is here demonstrated by examples: it is beautiful when women adorn and paint themselves, but it is ugly when men do so; in Trace tattooing is regarded as an "ornament", but in other countries it is a punishment for convicts.

This doctrine of relativity of art and beauty was closely associated with the general philosophy of the Sophists; but it was not their exclusive possession. It also appeared in Xenophanes, one of the earliest philosophers. He wrote as follows:

"If oxen [and horses] and lions had hands or could draw with hands and create works of art like those made by men, horses would draw pictures of gods like horses, and oxen of gods like oxen, and they would make the bodies [of their gods] in accordance with the form that each species itself possesses".[8] With these words Xenophanes was primarily attacking the absolute character of religion but he was also expressing a conviction about the relativity of art.

Epicharmus, the philosophizing dramatist, similarly wrote that it was no wonder that we admired ourselves and thought we were handsomely built. "For dog, too, seems very handsome to dog, and ox to ox ... and even pig to pig".[9] In this fragment there is something more than the usual aesthetic relativism: it embodies an aesthetic counterpart of the epistemological thesis of Protagoras: "Man is the measure of all things". Epicharmus says less succinctly but more generally that for every creature the measure of beauty is the species to which it belongs.

6. SUITABILITY. From observations of the variety and diversity of beauty, a thinker of the fifth century, probably Protagoras, drew the conclusion that beauty is relative, while another one, Gorgias or Socrates, drew another conclusion that a thing is beautiful when it is adapted to its purpose, nature, time and conditions, i.e. when it is suitable (*prepon*, as the Greeks were later to call it). Beauty, in fact, is suitability: this was the new opinion of the fifth century. This conclusion, no less than the conclusion of the relativists, was aimed against the original aesthetic standpoint of the Greeks. Just as the one conclusion attacked its absolutism, so the other attacked its universalism. Whereas the early Greeks had been inclined to assume that a form which had proved beautiful for one thing would also apply to other things, now the idea of aesthetic suitability made it necessary to assume that each beautiful thing is beautiful in its own way.

The doctrine of "suitability" and of aesthetic individualism won acceptance among the Greeks. From then on their aesthetics evolved along two antithetical lines, the one holding that beauty depended on an accord with eternal laws, the other that it depended on adjustment to individual conditions.

7. FORM VERSUS CONTENT. In the Platonic dialogue bearing his name, Protagoras says that in the poetry of Homer, Hesiod and Simonides the words are only a vessel for wisdom, and this is the proper subject of poetry. It would appear from this that the leading Sophist denied any aesthetic significance to poetry, since he discerned its true meaning in wisdom, that is in its cognitive aspect. One may, however, suspect that Plato, as was often his wont, here was putting his own ideas into someone else's mouth, because we know from other sources that the Sophists took exactly the opposite view, namely that the verses themselves and the rhythm of the words were the essential elements of poetry. This view was certainly held by writers such as Gorgias and Isocrates, who were close to the Sophists.[10] Perhaps the Sophists combined the two ideas: both accorded with their position and, in the last resort, could be satisfactorily merged. One way or the other, they discussed the question whether the essence of poetry lay in the sound of the words or in the wisdom which

it contained, or, to put the important question in a more modern way and in terms which the Greeks of the day did not possess, whether form or content was the essential element in poetry. They might have been uncertain how to answer it; but the posing of the question, in this case, may be regarded as no less important than the answer.

8. TALENT VERSUS EDUCATION. Another question which was discussed among the Sophists was whether talent or education was more important for an artist. Alcidamas distinguished these two elements without deciding which one was more important. Isocrates held that talent is more important[11] and should be trained.[12] Protagoras considered that both art and training are necessary,[13] that art is nothing without training and training nothing without art.[14] This problem was discussed at the time; but—like the problem of form and content—discussed rather than solved.

9. GORGIAS' DOCTRINE: ILLUSIONISM. Gorgias, ideologically close to the Sophists, was a rhetorician by profession, the first of those many rhetoricians who played a part in the history of aesthetics. Philosophically, he was allied to the Eleatic school, combining its extreme and paradoxical method of thinking with the relativism of the Sophists. His three famous ontologico-epistemological theses were: that nothing exists; that if anything did exist we could not know it; and that if we did know anything we could not communicate it. His main aesthetic thesis appears, however, to be almost the antithesis of his third epistemological thesis.

Elaborated in the treatise *Enkomion Helenes* (*The Defence of Helen*) it claimed no less than that everything can be expressed in words.[15] Words can convince of anything, can make the listener believe anything, even that which is nonexistent. Words are a "mighty potentate", they have quasi-magical and daemonic power. Some sadden, some gladden, some terrify, some give courage. Through them a theatre audience is in turn moved by terror, pity, admiration or sadness and can experience the problems of others as if they were their own.* Words are capable of poisoning the soul just as some substances poison the body. They enchant it, throw a spell and a charm (*goeteia*) over it. They deceive it, lead it into a state of hallucination or as we would say today, delusion.† This state of deception, hallucination and delusion the Greeks called *apate*.‡ It was particularly beneficial in the theatre; Gorgias, therefore, said of tragedy:" [it is] a deception in which the deceiver is more honest than the non-deceiver, and the deceived is wiser than the non-deceived".[16]

This illusionistic or apatetic (to use the term derived from the root word) theory which seems to be in all respects modern, yet was an invention of the ancients. Not only do we find it in the writings of the Sophists, in *Dialexeis*[17] and *Peri*

---

* E. Howard, "Eine vorplatonische Kunsttheorie", *Hermes*, LIV (1919).

† M. Pohlenz, "Die Anfänge der griechischen Poetik", *Nachrichten v.d. Königl. Gesellschaft der Wissenschaften zu Göttingen* (1920). O. Immisch, *Gorgiae Helena* (1927).

‡ Q. Cataudella, "Sopra alcuni concetti della poetica antica", I. "ἀπάτη", *Rivista di filologia classica*, IX, N.S. (1931). S. W. Melikova-Tolstoi, "Μίμησις und ἀπάτη bei Gorgias-Platon, Aristoteles", *Recueil Gebeler* (1926).

diaites,⁽¹⁸⁾ which have come down to us as anonymous works, but its echoes are still audible in Polybius,⁽¹⁹⁾ Horace and Epictetus. However, its originator was Gorgias.

Gorgias applied his theory chiefly to tragedy and comedy, but also to oratory. What is more, he seems to have perceived an analogous phenomenon in the visual arts, particularly in painting, when writing: "Painters delight the eye by making one body, one figure out of many colours and bodies". This remark might have had a link with Athenian painting, particularly with stage scenery with its impressionism, its illusionism, and its deliberate deformations, which had also engaged the attention of other contemporary philosophers, Democritus and Anaxagoras.

The apatetic theory harmonized with the Sophists' views on beauty and art, with their sensualism, hedonism, relativism and subjectivism. On the other hand, it was a position diametrically opposed to the objectivist and rationalist views of the Pythagoreans. This was the great antithesis of early aesthetics.

The art produced by the Greeks of the classical era, and in particular their search for ideal shapes, justifies the conclusion that the artists of the day were closer to the Pythagoreans and that, if they drew their theory from philosophy, it must have been from Pythagorean philosophy. What we know about the contemporary public indicates that it did not sympathize with the Sophists either. The subjectivist Sophists were in a minority and comprised the opposition, voicing new ideas which did not immediately find a response in the wider circles of the public of ancient Greece.

The Sophists' achievement in aesthetics, particularly if we class Gorgias as one of their number, is considerable and includes: 1. a definition of beauty, 2. a definition of art (by contrasting it with nature and chance), 3. pertinent comments on the purpose and the effects of the arts, and 4. the first attempts to differentiate beauty and art in the narrower, properly aesthetic sense. But the achievement of their antagonist Socrates was no smaller.

II

10. SOCRATES AS AN AESTHETICIAN. The recognized difficulty over establishing what were Socrates' views lies in the fact that he did not write anything and that those who wrote about him—Xenophon and Plato—convey conflicting information about his views. Now this problem is less acute where his aesthetic ideas are concerned because here we have really only one informer, Xenophon, in his *Memorabilia* (book III, chapters 9 and 10). What Plato says through the mouth of Socrates about beauty is probably Plato's own view, while everything suggests that the conversations with artists recorded by Xenophon are authentic.

Socrates (469–399) posed humanist problems similar to those raised by the Sophists, but the position he adopted was different from theirs. In logic and ethics the Sophists were relativists, while Socrates was opposed to relativism; but this was not so in the case of aesthetics. Socrates' fundamental assumptions about life did not allow him to deny absolute goodness and absolute truth but they did not prevent him from recognizing relativist elements in art. Socrates opposed the Sophists in ethics, but he did not do so in aesthetics. On the contrary, here their ideas and observations moved in similar directions.

Socrates is known chiefly for his ethics and logic, but he also deserves a place in the history of aesthetics. His thoughts on art, as transmitted by Xenophon, were novel, just and significant. But what if, as some maintain, they were not his own, but merely ascribed to him by Xenophon? That would change the authorship but it would still remain true that these thoughts arose in Athens at the turn of the fifth century B.C., and it is this fact that is most important in the history of aesthetics.

11. REPRESENTATIONAL ARTS. According to Xenophon's notes, Socrates attempted above all to establish the purpose of the work of an artist, a painter or a sculptor. In the course of doing this he provided some explanation as to how such arts as painting or sculpture differ from other human efforts, or—to use modern terminology—what is the feature which distinguishes "fine arts" from other arts. This undoubtedly was one of the earliest attempts to think along these lines. Socrates' explanation was that while other arts, such as that of the smith or the shoemaker, made things which nature did not make, painting and sculpture repeated and imitated those that she had made. That is to say, he thought they had an imitative and representational character distinguishing them from other arts.[20] "Surely, painting is the representation of that which we see", Socrates told Parrhasius, the painter. In these words he formulated the theory of imitation of nature by art. To the Greeks this idea was natural, because it matched their belief in the passive nature of the mind as a whole. It therefore met with acceptance and became the foundation of the first great systems of aesthetics, those of Plato and Aristotle. The conversation between Socrates and Parrhasius is an illustration of how this idea first came into being: in it both the philosopher and the artist still use an undetermined terminology and employ a variety of terms (*eikasia, apeikasia, apsomoiosis, ekmimesis*, and *apomimesis*) to denote representation; the noun form *mimesis*, which later gained acceptance, was still not available.

12. SOCRATIC DOCTRINE: IDEALIZATION IN ART. Socrates' second idea about art was linked with the first. He said to Parrhasius: "You wish to represent a human figure without blemish, and as it is difficult to find a figure free from all blemish, you draw on many models, taking the best each has to give, in order to form in this way an ideal whole". In these words he formulated the theory of idealization of nature by art. This supplemented the theory of the representation of nature through art. From the time when the representational idea of art first originated among the Greeks it had always contained this proviso. It was not confined to philosophers, but was recognized by artists and appeared not only in the theory but in artistic practice as well. "Indeed, we do as you say", Parrhasius agreed with Socrates. The classical art of the Greeks represented reality but contained an element of

idealization. Thus, the theory of art as idealization and selection did not conflict in the minds of the Greeks with the theory of art as representation, because the latter left room for idealization. With Socrates and other Greeks the selective imitation of nature was, however, an imitation.

Socrates' second thesis was no less successful with the Greeks than the first. Later writers of antiquity frequently enlarged upon it. They saw the best way of idealizing nature in selecting and multiplying her own beauties. They usually illustrated it with the story about the painter Zeuxis, who for a single likeness of Helen in the temple of Hera in Croton chose as many as five models from among the most beautiful girls of the city. As it was a thesis particularly characteristic of Socrates, so it is reasonable to call it a Socratic doctrine.

13. SPIRITUAL BEAUTY. His third aesthetic thesis (and here he had sculpture particularly in mind) was that art represented not only bodies but souls as well, and "this was the most interesting, most attractive and wonderful thing". Parrhasius in a conversation with Socrates (also reported by Xenophon) at first expressed doubts at these propositions and wondered whether they did not go beyond the possibilities of art, since the soul has neither *symmetria* nor colour, upon which art relies. He was, however, finally convinced by Socrates' arguments and agreed that in a statue the eyes in particular can be expressive of the soul: kindly or hostile, drunk with success or depressed by misfortune, expressing "magnificence and nobility, baseness and meanness, restraint and wisdom, impertinence and crudeness". This was a second modification of the purely representational conception of art. It was a new idea, not immediately accepted by the Greeks, though it had a basis in the contemporary art. It is not difficult to observe its connection with the activity of the sculptors Scopas and Praxiteles, who began to make statues conceived more individualistically and in particular with an individual expression of the eyes.

Socrates' idea of spiritual beauty marked a departure from the exclusively formalist Pythagorean conception of beauty. There beauty depended on *proportion*, here on the *expression* of the soul as well. This idea bound beauty more closely to man than the Pythagorean conception, which sought beauty in the cosmos rather than in man. The concept of spiritual beauty did not emerge until the classical period of Greek culture. In the later aesthetic systems of Greece both concepts—the beauty of form and the beauty of spirit—became equally strong and vital.

14. BEAUTY AND THE ADJUSTMENT TO ENDS. Socrates' other ideas on beauty have been preserved in a conversation with Aristippus, which Xenophon also recorded. To the question whether he knows any beautiful things, Socrates replies to Aristippus that beautiful things are very diverse, no two being alike. A beautiful runner is unlike a beautiful wrestler and a beautiful shield is unlike a beautiful javelin, and it cannot be otherwise because a shield is beautiful when it provides good protection, and a javelin when it is capable of being thrown swiftly. Each thing is beautiful when it serves its purpose well: "Even a golden shield is ugly and a rubbish bin beautiful if the former is badly and the latter well fitted to its purpose". "For all

things are good and beautiful in relation to those purposes for which they are well adapted, bad and ugly in relation to those for which they are ill adapted".[21]

In these words Socrates said about beauty what he was constantly saying about goodness. When Aristippus reminded him of this he replied that what is good must surely be beautiful. To the Greeks this identification was natural because for them a thing was good if it performed its function and beautiful if it aroused admiration. Socrates was convinced that nothing was admired save that which performed its function. This idea that the beauty of a thing lay in its purposefulness Socrates applied with particular force to architecture. "A house can justly be regarded as most pleasant and most beautiful if at all times its owner can find in it the most congenial shelter for himself and the safest shelter for his possessions, no matter what the paintings and the sculpture are like".

Socrates' thesis sounds as relativist as that of the Sophists, but there is a fundamental difference. He thought a shield was beautiful when it was suitable for its purpose, while the Sophists thought it could be regarded as such when it corresponded to the taste of the person looking at it. Socrates' view was functional, while that of the Sophists was relativist and subjective.

15. EURHYTHMY. No less important a concept came to the fore in Socrates' conversation with the armourer Pistias. Suits of armour, the armourer said, have good proportion when they fit the body of the wearer. But what about armour for someone whose body has bad proportions? Or, in the language of the day, how can one make eurhythmical armour for someone who is not eurhythmically built? Should the armourer in this instance also consider fitness for the body or should he, in spite of it, seek good proportions? Pistias was of the opinion that in this case also the armour should be made to fit the body because it is on this that its good proportions depend. There was a paradox here, and its solution probably lay in the fact that different principles apply to good proportions of armour from those which apply to good proportions of the human body. But in the solution he proposed, Socrates introduced yet another valid distinction: Pistias is talking not of proportions which are beautiful in themselves (*eurhythmon kat heauton*), but of those which may be beautiful for a particular person. There is a distinction here between the beauty of a thing in itself and its beauty for the person who uses it (*eurhythmon pros ton chromenon*).[22] This distinction was an amplification and a correction of the conversation with Aristippus: while this conversation assumed one kind of eurhythmy, in fact there are two kinds of it: two kinds of good proportions. Only one of these types of beauty consists in suitability and purposefulness.

This Socratic distinction, which undoubtedly is significant for aesthetics, gained acceptance and was employed by many writers in Greece and later by Roman writers. Purposeful beauty Socrates called *harmotton* (which derives from the same source as *harmonia*), and the later Greeks called it *prepon*. The Romans translated the term as *decorum* or *aptum* and distinguished two types of beauty: *pulchrum* and *decorum*, that is, things which are beautiful because of their form and those which are beautiful because of their purpose and utility.

The aesthetic vocabulary of Socrates already contained terms which were to be extensively employed by later Greeks. These included the expression "rhythm" and its derivatives. He would say that good proportions were characterized by "measure and rhythm". Good proportions he called "eurhythmical" and their opposites, "arhythmical". The term "eurhythmy" the Greeks came to regard as the chief term, alongside "harmony" and *symmetria*, to describe beauty, that is beauty in the narrower, specifically aesthetic sense.

Socrates' tentative analysis of art resembled the Sophists' analysis and, if in other fields of philosophy he and they represented two hostile camps, there was no significant divergence between them in their conception of aesthetics and art.

16. XENOPHON. Such information as we have about Socrates' aesthetics has been transmitted to us by his pupil Xenophon, who himself made pronouncements on similar subjects and even along similar lines. But the similarity is only apparent because Xenophon was not really interested in art and aesthetic beauty. In the *Symposium* he did admittedly state in conformity with his master that the beauty of things depends on their adjustment to the purpose which they serve, and that the bodies of animals and men were beautiful if nature had constructed them appropriately,[23] but he supplied surprising examples to support his argument. Bulging eyes are the most beautiful, he wrote, because they see best, and huge lips are best because they are the most practical for eating with, so that Socrates with his bulging eyes and huge mouth was more beautiful than Critobulus, who was renowned for his good looks. This peculiar example is no longer paradoxical, however, if we assume that Xenophon was using the term "beautiful" in the old Greek sense in which it could be synonymous with "useful".

In the *Oeconomicus*, however, he was using the term in its aesthetic sense as well as in its daily, practical sense when he recommended the preservation of "order" in the construction of a house and when he wrote that things which have order in them "are worth looking at and listening to".

E. Texts from the Sophists and about Socrates

SOPHISTS (Plato, Leges X 889 A).

1. Ἔοικε, φασί, τὰ μὲν μέγιστα αὐτῶν καὶ κάλλιστα ἀπεργάζεσθαι φύσιν καὶ τύχην, τὰ δὲ σμικρότερα τέχνην.

NATURE AND ART

1. They say that the greatest and fairest things are the work of nature and chance, the lesser of art.

tr. B. Jowett

ALCIDAMAS, Oratio de sophistis 10.

2. ταῦτα μιμήματα τῶν ἀληθινῶν σωμάτων ἐστί, καὶ τέρψιν μὲν ἐπὶ τῆς θεωρίας ἔχει, χρῆσιν δ' οὐδεμίαν τῷ τῶν ἀνθρώπων βίῳ παραδίδωσι.

ARTS SERVING PLEASURE

2. [Statues] are imitations of real bodies; they give joy to the beholder, but they serve no useful purpose.

DIALEXEIS 3, 17.

3. τέχνας δὲ ἐπάγονται, ἐν αἷς οὐκ ἔστι τὸ δίκαιον καὶ τὸ ἄδικον. καὶ τοὶ ποιηταὶ οὔ [το] ποτ' ἀλάθειαν, ἀλλὰ ποτὶ τὰς ἀδονὰς τῶν ἀνθρώπων τὰ ποιήματα ποιέοντι.

ISOCRATES, Panegyricus 40.

4. καὶ μὲν δὴ καὶ τῶν τεχνῶν τάς τε πρὸς τἀναγκαῖα τοῦ βίου χρησίμας καὶ τὰς πρὸς ἡδονὴν μεμηχανημένας, τὰς μὲν εὑροῦσα, τὰς δὲ δοκιμάσασα χρῆσθαι τοῖς λοιποῖς παρέδωκεν.

SOPHISTS (Plato, Hippias maior 298 A).

5. τὸ καλόν ἐστι τὸ δι' ἀκοῆς τε καὶ ὄψεως ἡδύ.

(This view is also quoted by Aristotle, Topica 146 a 21).

GORGIAS, Helena 18 (frg. B 11 Diels).

6. ἀλλὰ μὴν οἱ γραφεῖς ὅταν ἐκ πολλῶν χρωμάτων καὶ σωμάτων ἓν σῶμα καὶ σχῆμα τελείως ἀπεργάσωνται, τέρπουσι τὴν ὄψιν· ἡ δὲ τῶν ἀνδριάντων ποίησις καὶ ἡ τῶν ἀγαλμάτων ἐργασία θέαν ἡδεῖαν παρέσχετο τοῖς ὄμμασιν.

DIALEXEIS 2, 8.

7. οἶμαι δ', αἴ τις τὰ αἰσχρὰ ἐς ἓν κελεύοι συνενεῖκαι πάντας ἀνθρώπως, ἃ ἕκαστοι νομίζοντι, καὶ πάλιν ἐξ ἀθρόων τούτων τὰ καλὰ λαβέν, ἃ ἕκαστοι ἄγηνται, οὐδὲ ἕν ⟨κα⟩ καλλειφθῆμεν, ἀλλὰ πάντας πάντα διαλαβέν. οὐ γὰρ πάντες ταὐτὰ νομίζοντι. παρεξοῦμαι δὲ καὶ ποίημά τι·
    καὶ γὰρ τὸν ἄλλον ὧδε θνητοῖσιν νόμον
    ὄψῃ διαιρῶν· οὐδὲν ἦν πάντῃ καλόν,
    οὐδ' αἰσχρόν, ἀλλὰ ταῦτ' ἐποίησην λαβὼν
    ὁ καιρὸς αἰσχρὰ καὶ διαλλάξας καλά.
ὡς δὲ τὸ σύνολον εἶπαι, πάντα καιρῷ μὲν καλά ἐστι, ἀκαιρίᾳ δ' αἰσχρά.

XENOPHANES (Clement of Alex., Strom. V 110; frg. B 15 Diels).

8. ἀλλ' εἰ χεῖρας ἔχον βόες ⟨ἵπποι τ'⟩ ἠὲ λέοντες ἢ γράψαι χείρεσσι καὶ ἔργα τελεῖν

3. They invoke the arts in which there is neither justice nor injustice, because poets write their works not for the sake of truth but in order to give pleasure to men.

4. ...the arts also, both those which are useful in producing the necessities of life and those which have been devised to give us pleasure, she [Athens] has either invented or stamped with her approval, and has then presented them to the rest of the world to enjoy.

tr. G. Norlin

5. The beautiful is that which gives pleasure through hearing and sight.

tr. J. C. B. Lowe

6. Painters give pleasure to the eye when, from many colours and bodies, they create one body and one shape; and the making of human and divine statues affords pleasure to sight.

RELATIVITY OF BEAUTY

7. If all men were told to throw on a pile all things which they judge to be ugly and to remove from the pile all things which they consider beautiful, I believe that nothing would be left on the pile because all people differ in their opinions. I will also call to witness a certain poem:

"For, if you reflect, you will see a different law for mortals. Nothing was either wholly beautiful or wholly ugly; it was merely *kairos* which seized them and divided them, making some ugly, some beautiful."

In general, then, everything is beautiful thanks to *kairos*, and everything that lacks it is ugly.

8. But if oxen [and horses] and lions had hands or could draw with hands and create

ἅπερ ἄνδρες, ἵπποι μέν θ' ἵπποισι βόες δέ τε
βουσὶν ὁμοίας καὶ ⟨κε⟩ θεῶν ἰδέας ἔγραφον
καὶ σώματ' ἐποίουν τοιαῦθ' οἷόν περ καὐτοὶ
δέμας εἶχον ⟨ἕκαστοι⟩.

works of art like those made by men, horses
would draw pictures of gods like horses, and
oxen of gods like oxen, and they would make
the bodies [of their gods] in accordance with
the form that each species itself possesses.

tr. K. Freeman

EPICHARMUS (Laërt. Diog. III 16; frg. B 5 Diels).

9. θαυμαστὸν οὐδὲν ἁμὲ ταῦθ' οὕτω [λέγειν, καὶ ἀνδάνειν αὐτοῖσιν αὐτοὺς καὶ δοκεῖν καλῶς πεφύκειν· καὶ γὰρ ἁ κύων κυνὶ κάλλιστον εἶμεν φαίνεται, καὶ βοῦς βοΐ, ὄνος δὲ ὄνῳ κάλλιστον, ὗς δέ θην ὑΐ.

9. It is not at all remarkable that we should speak thus of these things and should afford pleasure to ourselves and think ourselves well-endowed by nature. For dog, too, seems very handsome to dog, and ox to ox, and donkey very handsome to donkey, and even pig to pig.

tr. K. Freeman

ISOCRATES, Euagoras 10.

10. πρὸς δὲ τούτοις οἱ ⟨ποιηταὶ⟩ μὲν μετὰ μέτρων καὶ ῥυθμῶν ἅπαντα ποιοῦσιν, οἱ δ' οὐδενὸς τούτων κοινωνοῦσιν· ἃ τοσαύτην ἔχει χάριν, ὥστ' ἂν καὶ τῇ λέξει καὶ τοῖς ἐνθυμήμασιν ἔχῃ κακῶς, ὅμως αὐταῖς ταῖς εὐρυθμίαις καὶ ταῖς συμμετρίαις ψυχαγωγοῦσι τοὺς ἀκούοντας.

RHYTHM

10. Besides, the poets compose all their works with metre and rhythm, while the orators do not share in any of these advantages; and these lend such charm that even though the poets may be deficient in style and thoughts, yet by the very spell of their rhythm and harmony they bewitch their listeners.

tr. L. van Hook

ISOCRATES, Philippus 27.

ταῖς περὶ τὴν λέξιν εὐρυθμίαις καὶ ποικιλίαις... δι' ὧν τοὺς λόγους ἡδίους ἂν ἅμα καὶ πιστοτέρους ποιοῖεν.

...with the rhythmic flow and manifold graces of style... as a means by which they might make their oratory more pleasing and at the same time more convincing.

tr. G. Norlin

ISOCRATES, De permutatione 189.

11. ταῦτα μὲν οὖν ἐστίν, ἃ κατὰ πασῶν λέγομεν τῶν τεχνῶν... τὸ τῆς φύσεως ἀνυπέρβλητόν ἐστι καὶ πολὺ πάντων διαφέρει.

TALENT AND EXERCISE

11. Now these observations apply to any and all of the arts... natural ability is paramount and comes before all else.

tr. G. Norlin

ISOCRATES, Contra sophistas 17.

12. δεῖν τὸν μὲν μαθητὴν πρὸς τῷ τὴν φύσιν ἔχειν οἵαν χρή, τὰ μὲν εἴδη τὰ τῶν λόγων μαθεῖν, περὶ δὲ τὰς χρήσεις αὐτῶν γυμνασθῆναι.

12. For this the student must not only have the requisite aptitude but he must learn the different kinds of discourse and practise himself in their use.

tr. G. Norlin

PROTAGORAS (Cramer, Anecd. Par. I 171).

13. φύσεως καὶ ἀσκήσεως διδασκαλία δεῖται.

13. Teaching needs endowment and practice.

tr. K. Freeman

PROTAGORAS (Stobaeus, Flor. III. 29, 80).

14. ἔλεγε μηδὲν εἶναι μήτε τέχνην ἄνευ μελέτης μήτε μελέτην ἄνευ τέχνης.

14. [He said] art without practice and practice without art are nothing.

tr. K. Freeman

GORGIAS, Helena 8
(frg. B 11 Diels).

ART AND DECEPTION

15. λόγος δυνάστης μέγας ἐστίν, ὃς σμικροτάτῳ σώματι καὶ ἀφανεστάτῳ θειότατα ἔργα ἀποτελεῖ· δύναται γὰρ καὶ φόβον παῦσαι καὶ λύπην ἀφελεῖν καὶ χαρὰν ἐνεργάσασθαι καὶ ἔλεον ἐπαυξῆσαι. ταῦτα δὲ ὡς οὕτως ἔχει δείξω· δεῖ δὲ καὶ δόξῃ δεῖξαι τοῖς ἀκούουσι· τὴν ποίησιν ἅπασαν καὶ νομίζω καὶ ὀνομάζω λόγον ἔχοντα μέτρον· ἧς τοὺς ἀκούοντας εἰσῆλθε καὶ φρίκη περίφοβος καὶ ἔλεος πολύδακρυς καὶ πόθος φιλοπενθής, ἐπ' ἀλλοτρίων τε πραγμάτων καὶ σωμάτων εὐτυχίαις καὶ δυσπραγίαις ἴδιόν τι πάθημα διὰ τῶν λόγων ἔπαθεν ἡ ψυχή. φέρε δὴ πρὸς ἄλλον ἀπ' ἄλλου μεταστῶ λόγον. αἱ γὰρ ἔνθεοι διὰ λόγων ἐπῳδαὶ ἐπαγωγοὶ ἡδονῆς, ἀπαγωγοὶ λύπης γίνονται. συγγινομένη γὰρ τῇ δόξῃ τῆς ψυχῆς ἡ δύναμις τῆς ἐπῳδῆς ἔθελξε καὶ ἔπεισε καὶ μετέστησεν αὐτὴν γοητείᾳ. γοητείας δὲ καὶ μαγείας δισσαὶ τέχναι εὕρηνται, αἵ εἰσι ψυχῆς ἁμαρτήματα καὶ δόξης ἀπατήματα.

15. Speech is a great power, which achieves the most divine works by means of the smallest and least visible form; for it can even put a stop to fear, remove grief, create joy, and increase pity. This I shall now prove: it needs to be demonstrated to the hearers.

All poetry can be called speech in metre. Its hearers shudder with terror, shed tears of pity, and yearn with sad longing; the soul, affected by the words, feels as its own, an emotion aroused by the good and ill fortunes of other people's actions and lives. Now from this argument let me proceed to another.

The inspired incantations of words can induce pleasure and avert grief; for the power of the incantations, uniting with the feeling in the soul, soothes and persuades and transports by means of its wizardry. Two types of wizardry and magic have been invented, which are errors in the soul and deceptions in the mind.

tr. K. Freeman

GORGIAS (Plutarch, De glor. Ath. 5, 348 c; frg. B 23 Diels).

16. ἡ τραγῳδία... παρασχοῦσα τοῖς μύθοις καὶ τοῖς πάθεσιν ἀπάτην, ὡς Γοργίας φησίν, ἣν ὅ τε ἀπατήσας δικαιότερος τοῦ μὴ ἀπατήσαντος καὶ ὁ ἀπατηθεὶς σοφώτερος τοῦ μὴ ἀπατηθέντος.

16. Tragedy, by means of legends and emotions, creates a deception in which the deceiver is more honest than the non-deceiver, and the deceived is wiser than the non-deceived.

tr. K. Freeman

DIALEXEIS 3, 10.

17. ἐν γὰρ τραγῳδοποιίᾳ καὶ ζωγραφίᾳ ὅστις ⟨κα⟩ πλεῖστα ἐξαπατῇ ὅμοια τοῖς ἀληθινοῖς ποιέων, οὗτος ἄριστος.

17. In tragedy and in painting those are best who are best at leading into error by creating things which resemble real things.

HERACLITUS (Hippocrates, De victu I 24).

18. ὑποκριτικὴ ἐξαπατᾷ εἰδότας. ἄλλα λέγουσιν καὶ ἄλλα φρονέουσιν· οἱ αὐτοὶ ἐσέρπουσι καὶ ἐξέρπουσι καὶ οὐχ οἱ αὐτοί.

18. The actor's art deceives those who know. They say one thing and think another; they come on and go off, the same persons yet not the same.

tr. W. H. S. Jones

EPHORUS OF CYME (Polybius IV 20).

19. Οὐ γὰρ ἡγητέον μουσικήν, ὡς Ἔφορός φησιν ἐν τῷ προοιμίῳ τῆς ὅλης πραγματείας, οὐδαμῶς ἁρμόζοντα λόγον αὐτῷ ῥίψας, ἐπ' ἀπάτῃ καὶ γοητείᾳ παρεισῆχθαι τοῖς ἀνθρώποις.

19. For we must not suppose as Ephorus, in the Preface to his History, making a hasty assertion quite unworthy of him, says, that music was introduced by men for the purpose of deception and delusion.

tr. W. R. Paton

XENOPHON, Commentarii III 10, 1.

20. εἰσελθὼν μὲν γάρ ποτε πρὸς Παρράσιον τὸν ζωγράφον καὶ διαλεγόμενος αὐτῷ· Ἆρα, ἔφη, ὦ Παρράσιε, ἡ γραφική ἐστιν εἰκασία τῶν ὁρωμένων; τὰ γοῦν κοῖλα καὶ τὰ ὑψηλὰ καὶ τὰ σκοτεινὰ καὶ τὰ φωτεινὰ καὶ τὰ σκληρὰ καὶ τὰ μαλακὰ καὶ τὰ τραχέα καὶ τὰ λεῖα καὶ τὰ νέα καὶ τὰ παλαιὰ σώματα διὰ τῶν χρωμάτων ἀπεικάζοντες ἐκμιμεῖσθε. Ἀληθῆ λέγεις, ἔφη. Καὶ μὴν τά γε καλὰ εἴδη ἀφομοιοῦντες, ἐπειδὴ οὐ ῥᾴδιον ἑνὶ ἀνθρώπῳ περιτυχεῖν ἄμεμπτα πάντα ἔχοντι, ἐκ πολλῶν συνάγοντες τὰ ἐξ ἑκάστου κάλλιστα οὕτως ὅλα τὰ σώματα καλὰ ποιεῖτε φαίνεσθαι. Ποιοῦμεν γάρ, ἔφη, οὕτω. Τί γάρ; ἔφη, τὸ πιθανώτατον καὶ ἥδιστον καὶ φιλικώτατον καὶ ποθεινότατον καὶ ἐρασμιώτατον ἀπομιμεῖσθε τῆς ψυχῆς ἦθος; ἢ οὐδὲ μιμητόν ἐστι τοῦτο; Πῶς γὰρ ἄν, ἔφη, μιμητὸν εἴη, ὦ Σώκρατες, ὃ μήτε συμμετρίαν μήτε χρῶμα μήτε ὧν σὺ εἶπας ἄρτι μηδὲν ἔχει μηδὲ ὅλως ὁρατόν ἐστιν; Ἆρ' οὖν, ἔφη, γίγνεται ἐν ἀνθρώπῳ τό τε φιλοφρόνως καὶ τὸ ἐχθρῶς βλέπειν πρός τινας; Ἔμοιγε δοκεῖ, ἔφη. Οὐκοῦν τοῦτό γε μιμητὸν ἐν τοῖς ὄμμασι; Καὶ μάλα, ἔφη. Ἐπὶ δὲ τοῖς τῶν φίλων ἀγαθοῖς καὶ τοῖς κακοῖς ὁμοίως σοι δοκοῦσιν ἔχειν τὰ πρόσωπα οἵ τε φροντίζοντες καὶ οἱ μή; Μὰ Δί' οὐ δῆτα, ἔφη· ἐπὶ μὲν γὰρ τοῖς ἀγαθοῖς φαιδροί, ἐπὶ δὲ τοῖς κακοῖς σκυθρωποὶ γίγνονται. Οὐκοῦν, ἔφη, καὶ ταῦτα δυνατὸν ἀπεικάζειν; Καὶ μάλα, ἔφη. Ἀλλὰ μὴν καὶ τὸ μεγαλοπρεπές τε καὶ ἐλευθέριον καὶ τὸ ταπεινόν τε καὶ ἀνελεύθερον καὶ τὸ σωφρονικόν τε καὶ φρόνιμον καὶ τὸ ὑβριστικόν τε καὶ ἀπειρόκαλον καὶ διὰ τοῦ προσώπου καὶ διὰ τῶν σχημάτων καὶ ἑστώτων καὶ κινουμένων ἀνθρώπων διαφαίνει. Ἀληθῆ λέγεις, ἔφη. Οὐκοῦν καὶ ταῦτα μιμητά.

REPRESENTATIONAL ART

20. Thus, on entering the house of Parrhasius the painter one day, he asked in the course of a conversation with him: "Is painting a representation of things seen, Parrhasius? Anyhow, you, painters, with your colours, represent and reproduce figures high and low, in light and in shadow, hard and soft, rough and smooth, young and old."

"True".

"And further, when you copy types of beauty, it is so difficult to find a perfect model that you combine the most beautiful details of several, and thus contrive to make the whole figure look beautiful."

"Yes, we do!"

"Well now, do you also reproduce the character of the soul, the character that is in the highest degree captivating, delightful, friendly, fascinating, loveable? Or is it impossible to imitate that?"

"Oh no, Socrates; for how could one imitate that which has neither shape nor colour nor any of the qualities you mentioned just now, and is not even visible?"

"Do human beings commonly express the feelings of sympathy and aversion by their looks?"

"I think so."

"Then cannot thus much be imitated in the eyes?"

"Undoubtedly."

"Do you think that the joys and sorrows of their friends produce the same expression on men's faces, whether they really care or not?"

"Oh no, of course not: they look radiant at their joys, downcast at their sorrows."

"Then is it possible to represent these looks too?"

"Undoubtedly."

"Moreover, nobility and dignity, self-abasement and servility, prudence and understanding, insolence and vulgarity, are reflected in the face and in the attitudes of the body whether still or in motion."

"True."

"Then these, too, can be imitated, can they not?"

"Undoubtedly."

tr. E. C. Marchant

XENOPHON, Commentarii III 8, 4.

21. Πάλιν δὲ τοῦ ᾿Αριστίππου ἐρωτῶντος αὐτόν, εἴ τι εἰδείη καλόν· Καὶ πολλά, ἔφη. ῏Αρ᾿ οὖν, ἔφη, πάντα ὅμοια ἀλλήλοις; Ὡς οἷόν τε μὲν οὖν, ἔφη, ἀνομοιότατα ἔνια. Πῶς οὖν, ἔφη, τὸ τῷ καλῷ ἀνόμοιον καλὸν ἂν εἴη; ὅτι νὴ Δί᾿, ἔφη, ἔστι μὲν τῷ καλῷ πρὸς δρόμον ἀνθρώπῳ ἄλλος ἀνόμοιος καλὸς πρὸς πάλην, ἔστι δὲ ἀσπὶς καλὴ πρὸς τὸ προβάλλεσθαι ὡς ἔνι ἀνομοιοτάτη τῷ ἀκοντίῳ καλῷ πρὸς τὸ σφόδρα τε καὶ ταχὺ φέρεσθαι. Οὐδὲν διαφερόντως, ἔφη, ἀποκρίνει μοι ἢ ὅτε σε ἐρώτησα, εἴ τι ἀγαθὸν εἰδείης. Σὺ δ᾿ οἴει, ἔφη, ἄλλο μὲν ἀγαθόν, ἄλλο δὲ καλὸν εἶναι; οὐκ οἶσθ᾿ ὅτι πρὸς ταὐτὰ πάντα καλά τε κἀγαθά ἐστι; πρῶτον μὲν γὰρ ἡ ἀρετὴ οὐ πρὸς ἄλλα μὲν ἀγαθόν, πρὸς ἄλλα δὲ καλόν ἐστιν, ἔπειτα οἱ ἄνθρωποι τὸ αὐτό τε καὶ πρὸς τὰ αὐτὰ καλοί τε κἀγαθοὶ λέγονται, πρὸς τὰ αὐτὰ δὲ καὶ τὰ σώματα τῶν ἀνθρώπων καλά τε κἀγαθὰ φαίνεται, πρὸς ταὐτὰ δὲ καὶ τἆλλα πάντα, οἷς ἄνθρωποι χρῶνται, καλά τε κἀγαθὰ νομίζεται, πρὸς ἅπερ ἂν εὔχρηστα ᾖ. ῏Αρ᾿ οὖν, ἔφη, καὶ κόφινος κοπροφόρος καλόν ἐστι; Νὴ Δί᾿, ἔφη, καὶ χρυσῆ γε ἀσπὶς αἰσχρόν, ἐὰν πρὸς τὰ ἑαυτῶν ἔργα ὁ μὲν καλῶς πεποιημένος ᾖ, ἡ δὲ κακῶς. Λέγεις σύ, ἔφη, καλά τε καὶ αἰσχρὰ τὰ αὐτὰ εἶναι; καὶ νὴ Δι᾿ ἔγωγε, ἔφη, ἀγαθά τε καὶ κακά· [...] πολλάκις δὲ τὸ μέν πρὸς δρόμον καλὸν πρὸς πάλην αἰσχρόν, τὸ δὲ πρὸς πάλην καλὸν πρὸς δρόμον αἰσχρόν· πάντα γὰρ ἀγαθὰ μὲν καὶ καλά ἐστι πρὸς ἃ ἂν εὖ ἔχῃ, κακὰ δὲ καὶ αἰσχρὰ πρὸς ἃ ἂν κακῶς.

BEAUTY AND FITTINGNESS

21. Again Aristippus asked him whether he knew of anything beautiful: "Yes, many things", [Socrates] replied.

"All like one another?"

"On the contrary, some are as unlike as they can be."

"How, then, can that which is unlike the beautiful be beautiful?"

"The reason, of course, is that a beautiful wrestler is unlike a beautiful runner, a shield beautiful for defence is utterly unlike a javelin beautiful for swift and powerful hurling."

"That is the same answer as you gave to my question whether you knew of anything good."

"You think, do you, that good is one thing and beautiful another? Don't you know that all things are both beautiful and good in relation to the same things? In the first place, Virtue is not a good thing in relation to some things and a beautiful thing in relation to others. Men, again, are called "beautiful and good" in the same respect and in relation to the same things: it is in relation to the same things that men's bodies look beautiful and good and that all other things men use are thought beautiful and good, namely, in relation to those things for which they are useful."

"Is a dung basket beautiful then?"

"Of course, and a golden shield is ugly, if the one is well made for its special work and the other badly."

"Do you mean that the same things are both beautiful and ugly?"

"Of course—and both good and bad... what is beautiful for running is often ugly for wrestling, and what is beautiful for wrestling is ugly for running. For all things are good and beautiful in relation to those purposes for which they are well adapted, bad and ugly in relation to those for which they are ill adapted."

tr. E. C. Marchant

XENOPHON, Commentarii III 10, 10.

RELATIVE BEAUTY

22. ἀτάρ, ἔφη, λέξον μοι, ὦ Πιστία, διὰ τί οὔτ' ἰσχυροτέρους οὔτε πολυτελεστέρους τῶν ἄλλων ποιῶν τοὺς θώρακας πλείονος πωλεῖς; Ὅτι, ἔφη, ὦ Σώκρατες, εὐρυθμοτέρους ποιῶ. Τὸν δὲ ῥυθμόν, ἔφη, πότερα μέτρῳ ἢ σταθμῷ ἀποδεικνύων πλείονος τιμᾷ; οὐ γὰρ δὴ ἴσους γε πάντας οὐδὲ ὁμοίους οἶμαί σε ποιεῖν, εἴ γε ἁρμόττοντας ποιεῖς. Ἀλλὰ νὴ Δί', ἔφη, ποιῶ· οὐδὲν γὰρ ὄφελός ἐστι θώρακος ἄνευ τούτου. Οὐκοῦν, ἔφη, σώματά γε ἀνθρώπων τὰ μὲν εὔρυθμά ἐστι, τὰ δὲ ἄρρυθμα; Πάνυ μὲν οὖν, ἔφη. Πῶς οὖν, ἔφη, τῷ ἀρρύθμῳ σώματι ἁρμόττοντα τὸν θώρακα εὔρυθμον ποιεῖς; Ὥσπερ καὶ ἁρμόττοντα, ἔφη· ὁ ἁρμόττων γάρ ἐστιν εὔρυθμος. Δοκεῖς μοι, ἔφη ὁ Σωκράτης, τὸ εὔρυθμον οὐ καθ' ἑαυτὸ λέγειν, ἀλλὰ πρὸς τὸν χρώμενον.

22. "But tell me, Pistias," he added, "why do you charge me more for your breast-plates than any other maker, though they are no stronger and cost no more to make?"

"Because the proportions of mine are better, Socrates."

"And how do you show their proportions when you ask a higher price—by weight or measure? For I presume you don't make them all of the same weight or the same size, that is, if you make them to fit."

"Fit? Why, of course! a breast-plate is of no use without that!"

"Then are not some human bodies well, others ill proportioned?"

"Certainly."

"Then if a breast-plate is to fit an ill-proportioned body, how do you make it well-proportioned?"

"By making it fit; for if it is a good fit, it is well-proportioned."

"Apparently you mean well-proportioned not absolutely, but in relation to the wearer..."

tr. E. C. Marchant

XENOPHON, Convivium V, 3.

RANGE OF BEAUTY

23. Πότερον οὖν ἐν ἀνθρώπῳ μόνον νομίζεις τὸ καλὸν εἶναι ἢ καὶ ἐν ἄλλῳ τινί; Ἐγὼ μὲν ναὶ μὰ Δί', ἔφη, καὶ ἐν ἵππῳ καὶ βοῒ καὶ ἐν ἀψύχοις πολλοῖς· οἶδα γοῦν οὖσαν καὶ ἀσπίδα καλὴν καὶ ξίφος καὶ δόρυ. Καὶ πῶς, ἔφη, οἷόν τε ταῦτα μηδὲν ὅμοια ὄντα ἀλλήλοις πάντα καλὰ εἶναι; Ἢν νὴ Δί', ἔφη, πρὸς τὰ ἔργα, ὧν ἕνεκα ἕκαστα κτώμεθα, εὖ εἰργασμένα ᾖ ἢ εὖ πεφυκότα πρὸς ἃ ἂν δεώμεθα, καὶ ταῦτ', ἔφη ὁ Κριτόβουλος, καλά.

23. "Do you hold, then, that beauty is to be found only in man, or is it also in other objects?"

CRITOBULUS: "In faith, my opinion is that beauty is to be found quite as well in a horse or an ox or in any number of inanimate things. I know, at any rate, that a shield may be beautiful, or a sword, or a spear."

SOCRATES: "How can it be that all these things are beautiful when they are entirely dissimilar?"

"Why, they are beautiful and fine", answered Critobulus, "if they are well made for the respective functions for which we obtain them, or if they are naturally well constituted to serve our needs."

tr. O. J. Todd

XENOPHON, Oeconomicus VIII, 3.

24. ἔστι δ' οὐδὲν οὕτως, ὦ γύναι, οὔτ' εὔχρηστον οὔτε καλὸν ἀνθρώποις ὡς τάξις. καὶ γὰρ χορὸς ἐξ ἀνθρώπων συγκείμενός ἐστιν· ἀλλ' ὅταν μὲν ποιῶσιν ὅ, τι ἂν τύχῃ ἕκαστος, ταραχή τις φαίνεται καὶ θεᾶσθαι ἀτερπές, ὅταν δὲ τεταγμένως ποιῶσι καὶ φθέγγωνται, ἅμα οἱ αὐτοὶ οὗτοι καὶ ἀξιοθέατοι δοκοῦσιν εἶναι καὶ ἀξιάκουστοι.

ORDER

24. ...there is nothing so convenient or so good for human beings as order. Thus, a chorus is a combination of human beings; but when the members of it do as they choose, it becomes mere confusion, and there is no pleasure in watching it; but when they act and chant in an orderly fashion, then those same men at once seem worth seeing and worth hearing.
tr. E. C. Marchant

8. Assessment of Pre-Platonic Aesthetics

If we summarize what was achieved in aesthetics by the Pythagoreans, Heraclitus and Democritus, and by the Sophists, Gorgias and Socrates, we see that a considerable advance was made in the fifth century B.C. Although these philosophers belonged to different schools, they shared common aesthetic doctrines, or at least showed interest in similar problems. Harmony was discussed not only by the Pythagoreans in Italy, but also by Heraclitus in Ephesus; Democritus had also written a work on harmony. Measure was the fundamental concept, not only of Pythagorean aesthetics, but also of Heraclitus and Democritus. Another conception of it, namely the conception of order, appears in Socrates and Xenophon. Empedocles as well as Democritus concerned himself with primary colours and like Democritus, Anaxagoras, and Agatharchus studied deformations caused by perspective. Both Democritus and Socrates looked for an expression of the spirit in the beauty of the body. Socrates and Gorgias alike spoke of the idealization of reality in art. The relativity of beauty was a subject treated by the Eleatic Xenophanes and Epicharmus, the writers with philosophical tastes, as well as by the Sophists. Several Sophists pronounced on the relationship between art and beauty and between pleasure and utility. The relationship between talent and art was discussed both by the Sophists and by Democritus. Canons were a topic which chiefly interested the artists but philosophers were also drawn to them. While contemporary theories of existence and knowledge were rent by the most profound contradictions, in the field of aesthetics there was a large measure of agreement.

The problems tackled by the philosophers of the fifth century went far beyond anything that had been raised earlier by poets. Yet there was a thread linking the poets' belief in initiation by the Muses with Democritus' theory of inspiration; what Hesiod and Pindar wrote about truth in poetry was connected with the philosophers' theory of *mimesis* and deception, and what these same poets had to say about the effects of poetry was not unlike Gorgias' conviction about its seductive charms. Early pre-Platonic aesthetics was something more than a kaleidoscope of ideas—there was a certain agreement in its theories and a certain continuity in its development.

It gave rise to no less than *three theories about beauty*: the mathematical theory of the Pythagoreans (that beauty depends on measure, proportion, order and harmony); the subjectivist theory of the Sophists (that it depends on the pleasures of eye and ear); and the functional theory of Socrates (that the beauty of things resides in their suitability for the tasks they are to perform). Already in this early period aestheticians were contrasting bodily with spiritual beauty and absolute with relative beauty, the Pythagoreans putting forward an absolutist theory and the Sophists a relativist one.

The early aesthetic ideas of the Greeks also included *three theories* regarding *aesthetic experiences*: the cathartic one of the Pythagoreans, the illusionist one of Gorgias, and the mimetic one of Socrates. According to the first, these experiences are the result of a purging of the mind, according to the second, they are due to the creation of an illusion in the mind, while the third one stated that they arise when similarities are discovered between the products of artists and their models in nature.

No less remarkable were the views on *art* formulated by pre-Platonic philosophers. The Sophists explained arts, contrasting them with chance, and opposing arts "pleasant to the eye and ear" to useful arts. Socrates formed the idea that art represents reality but idealizes it. Discussion began on the proper relationship between form and content in a work of art and between talent and education in an artist.

This early period also saw the development of various *conceptions of the artist*. He was thought either to express characters, or (according to the Pythagoreans, for whom the artist was a kind of scientist) to discover the laws of nature. Some Sophists saw him as a man of action, transforming nature, while Gorgias thought of the artist as a type of magician, creating illusion and enchantment. It is remarkable that in this early period relatively little attention was paid to the apparently simple naturalistic theory of art as the representation of reality. The two spheres of beauty and art were still independent; their convergence was gradual and slow.

The investigations of the pre-Platonic period were concerned not so much with art in general as with sculpture (Socrates), painting (Democritus) and tragedy (Gorgias). But in these narrower fields they found solutions applicable to the whole range of beauty and the arts.

The conception of the artist as the man who expresses feelings had its origin in the theory of dance. The conception of the artist as the reproducer of reality derived from visual arts, as a scientist—from music, as a magician—from poetry.

9. The Aesthetics of Plato

1. PLATO'S WRITINGS ON AESTHETICS. Zeller, the famous historian of Greek philosophy, said of Plato (427–347 B.C.), the great Athenian philosopher of the classical period, that he did not mention aesthetics; and that the theory of art lay outside

the field of his enquiries. This is true, but only to the extent that we can say his predecessors and contemporaries did not treat of aesthetics either. That is to say, Plato did not work out a systemic compilation of aesthetic problems and postulates, yet he dealt in his writings with all the problems of aesthetics. His interests, qualifications and original ideas in the field of aesthetics ranged very widely. He returned to the problems of beauty and art again and again, particularly in his two great works, the *Republic* and the *Laws*. In the *Symposium* he gave an exposition of an idealist theory of beauty, in the *Ion* of a spiritualist theory of poetry; and in the *Philebus* he analysed the aesthetic experience. In the *Hippias Major* (whose authenticity has been unjustly questioned) he demonstrated the difficulties of defining beauty.

There has never been a more wide-ranging philosopher than Plato: he was an aesthetician, a metaphysician, a logician and a master of ethics. In his mind aesthetic problems became intertwined with other problems, with metaphysics and ethics in particular. His metaphysical and ethical theories influenced his aesthetic theories; his idealistic theory of existence and his aprioristic theory of knowledge were reflected in his concept of beauty, while his spiritualist theory of man and his moralist theory of life were reflected in his concept of art.

For the first time, the concepts of beauty and art were drawn into a great philosophical system. This system was idealist, spiritualist and moralist in character. It is only possible to understand Plato's aesthetics in conjunction with his theories of Ideas, souls and Ideal state. But independently of his system, Plato's works also contain a number of considerations about aesthetics, though these are chiefly to be found in the form of allusions, summaries, hints and similes.

Plato's work span half a century, and in his constant search for better solutions he changed his views several times. His ideas on aesthetics were caught up in these fluctuations and led him to a different understanding and evaluation of art. Nevertheless, the existence of certain recurrent features of his thought makes it possible to present Plato's aesthetics as a unity.

2. THE CONCEPT OF BEAUTY. Plato wrote in the *Symposium* that "if there is anything worth living for, it is to behold beauty". And the whole of that dialogue consists of enthusiastic praise of beauty as the highest value. This is doubtless the first such praise known in literature.

But when he praised beauty, Plato was praising something different from what is today understood by the term. Shapes, colours and melodies were, as far as he and the Greeks in general were concerned, only a portion of the full scope of beauty. Within this term they included not only physical objects, but also psychological and social ones, characters and political systems, virtues and truths. They included not only things which are a joy to behold and hear, but everything which causes admiration, which arouses delight, appreciation and enjoyment.

In the *Hippias Major* Plato attempted to define this concept. The protagonists are Socrates and the Sophist Hippias, both making attempts to clarify the essence of beauty. The first examples they give—beautiful girls, horses, musical instruments and vases—seem to provide an indication that they are concerned with beauty in the narrower, purely aesthetic sense. Subsequent sections of the dialogue also treat of beautiful persons, colourful designs, pictures, melodies and sculpture. Nevertheless, this does not exhaust the list of examples. Socrates and Hippias also took into account beautiful occupations, beautiful laws, beauty in politics and the state. They mention "beautiful laws" alongside "beautiful bodies". The utilitarian Hippias was convinced that "the most beautiful thing is to make a fortune, enjoy a good health, win fame among the Hellenes and live to a ripe old age", while the moralist Socrates held that "of all things wisdom is the most beautiful".

In other dialogues too, Plato expressed a similar conception of beauty. He mentioned not only the beauty of women, the beauty of Aphrodite, but also the beauty of justice and prudence, of good customs, of learning and of virtue, and the beauty of a soul. There is therefore no doubt that Plato's notion of beauty was very broad. He included in it not only the values we call "aesthetic", but also moral and cognitive values. Indeed, his concept of beauty differed little from a broadly understood concept of the good. Plato could, and did, use the terms interchangeably. His *Symposium* carries the subtitle "On the Good", but treats of beauty. What it says there about the idea of beauty coincides with what his other dialogues say about the idea of the good.

This was not Plato's personal idea, but the generally accepted view of the ancients. They took as much interest in beauty as is taken in modern times, but in a slightly different sense. In modern times the concept of beauty is usually restricted to aesthetic values. In antiquity, however, the concept was wider and brought together things having relatively little similarity. Such a broad concept was not particularly useful where more exact formulations were called for; on the other hand, it could help in formulating very general ideas of philosophical aesthetics.

Thus, when we read Plato's praise of beauty in the *Symposium*, we have to remember that he was praising not only the aesthetic beauty of the forms. Plato's remark that "beauty is the only thing worth living for" has often in modern times been invoked whenever attempts have been made to give precedence to aesthetic values. This was, however, precisely what Plato did not do. He appreciated the beauty of truth and goodness still more than aesthetic beauty. In this case the posterity has made more use of his authority than of his actual thoughts.

3. TRUTH, GOODNESS AND BEAUTY. Plato was the author of the famous triad of "truth, goodness and beauty", which epitomizes the highest human values. He placed beauty on a level with other supreme values, not above them. Plato referred to this triad several times: in the *Phaedrus*[1] and also, in a slightly different form, in the *Philebus*. Later times continued to invoke this triad, however in a different sense. The references to truth, goodness and beauty are in Plato usually followed by the phrase "and all similar things", and this shows that he did not regard the triad as a complete epitome. More important, in this context, "beauty" had the

Greek meaning, which was not exclusively aesthetic. Plato's triad has been adopted by later centuries, but with a greater emphasis on aesthetic values than he envisaged.

4. AGAINST A HEDONISTIC AND FUNCTIONAL UNDERSTANDING OF BEAUTY. It is certain that Plato attached value to beauty, but how did he understand it? In the *Hippias Major* he examined as many as five definitions: beauty as suitability, beauty as efficacy, beauty as utility (that is, as something efficacious in promoting the good), beauty as pleasure for the eyes and ears, and beauty as pleasurable utility. These definitions can effectively be reduced to two: beauty as *suitability* (since efficacy and utility can be regarded as variants of suitability), and beauty as *pleasure for the eyes and ears*.

What was Plato's attitude to these definitions? In the *Gorgias*, one of his early dialogues, he appears inclined to accept both definitions simultaneously, for he wrote that the beauty of a body depends either on its being useful for its purpose, or on its being pleasant to look at.[2] Diogenes Laertius confirms this when he relates that, according to Plato, beauty depended either on its purposefulness and utility, or upon a shape pleasing to the eye.[3] This account, however, is in so far inaccurate, since although Plato considered both definitions, he did not accept either of them.

A. Both definitions were used in pre-Platonic philosophy. The first—"beauty is suitability"—belonged to Socrates. When discussing it, Plato relied on the same examples as Socrates, repeating after him that some bodies are "beautiful for running" and others "beautiful for fighting". Socrates illustrated his idea by saying that a suitable waste bin is more beautiful than a golden shield which is useless for defence, while Plato maintained that a wooden spoon, because it is more suitable, is more beautiful than a golden one.

Plato raised two objections to this definition. Firstly, suitable things being a means to good ends, need not themselves be good, whereas beauty is always good. This Plato regarded as an axiom and would not accept any definition which did not agree with it. Secondly, among beautiful bodies, shapes, colours and sounds there are indeed those that we value for their suitability, but there are also those that we value in themselves and they are not included in the definition of Socrates. Indeed Socrates himself did distinguish things which are beautiful in themselves from those which are beautiful because of their suitability.

B. The second definition, one which derived from the Sophists, was that beauty consists of "what we enjoy through our senses of hearing and sight".[4] This Plato also rejected. Beauty cannot be defined in visible terms because there is beauty for the ear. Nor can it be defined in audible terms because there is also beauty for the eye. The Sophists' definition stated that beauty is something common to the eye and ear, but said nothing about what this common thing might be.

The definition of the Sophists narrowed the Greek concept of beauty, confining it to the beauty of appearances and forms. Plato, however, clung to the former Greek idea that beauty is everything that arouses admiration. Beauty cannot be confined to beauty for eyes and ears. It also includes wisdom, virtue, noble deeds and good laws.

5. AN OBJECTIVE UNDERSTANDING OF BEAUTY. Plato condemned the Sophists' definition also because it interpreted beauty subjectively: causing pleasure is not an objective property of beautiful things, but a subjective reaction to them. "I am not concerned", he wrote, "with what appears beautiful to the people, but with what it is". In this he was not an innovator, but was following the traditional Greek view; it was the Sophists who represented the new dissident outlook.

Plato's understanding of beauty differed in many ways from that of Sophists. He said, firstly, that beauty is not confined to sensuous objects; secondly, that it is an objective property, a property inherent in beautiful things, and not man's subjective reaction to beauty; thirdly, that its test is an inborn sense of beauty, and not a transient feeling of pleasure; and, fourthly, that not everything we like is truly beautiful.

In the *Republic* Plato contrasted lovers of real beauty with those who simply desire to see and hear, and who take pleasure in sounds, colours and shapes.[5] He was probably the first to draw the significant distinction between real and apparent beauty. It is not surprising that this should have been the achievement of Plato, who also distinguished between real and apparent virtue.

Plato broke with the principle that a thing which is liked is beautiful; and this break had far-reaching consequences. On the one hand, it paved the way for aesthetic criticism and the distinction between proper and improper aesthetic judgments; and on the other, it opened the way for speculation on the nature of "true" beauty and drew many aestheticians away from empirical studies. We can thus regard Plato as the originator of both artistic criticism and aesthetic speculation.

In the *Hippias* he rejected all accepted definitions of beauty, but did not discover a better one; neither did his later writings produce a formal definition. In fact there were two concepts which he employed: one of Pythagorean origin, the other his own. Plato's own concept was developed in the dialogues of his mature years, in the *Republic* and the *Symposium*, but in the last works, in the *Laws*, he adopted the Pythagorean concept.

6. BEAUTY AS ORDER AND MEASURE. According to the Pythagorean concept, which Plato adopted and developed, the essence of beauty lay in order (*taxis*), measure, proportion (*symmetria*), consonance and harmony. That is, it was understood first as a property dependent on arrangement (disposition, harmony) between parts, and second, as a numerical property capable of expression in numbers (measure, proportion).

Plato ended the *Philebus* by saying that "measure (*metriotes*) and proportion (*symmetria*) are ... beauty and virtue".[6] This dialogue contended that the essence of beauty, as of all good, lies in measure and proportion. The same thought is found in another dialogue, the *Sophist*, complemented by a negative one to the effect that "the quality of disproportion... is always ugly".[7] In the *Timaeus*, one of his last works, Plato also spoke of the connection between beauty and measure, and declared in general terms, that "all that is good is beautiful, and what is good cannot lack proportion";[8] he explained that measure determines the beauty of things because it gives them unity.[9] The dialogue *Politicus* makes it clear that in some cases "measure" is to be understood as number and in others as moderation and suitability.[10]

This Pythagorean doctrine of measure and proportion appeared comparatively late in Plato's philosophy, but once it did, it became its permanent feature. It provided the last word of Platonic aesthetics appearing in the *Laws*, the great work of Plato's old age. Plato maintained that the sense of beauty, similar to the sense of order, measure, proportion and harmony, specific to man,[11] is an expression of his "relationship with the gods". Upon this he also based his appreciation of art. He admired the Egyptians because they understood that in art order and measure are the most important things, that once the proper measure has been discovered one should abide by it and not search for new forms. He denounced contemporary Athenian art for abandoning measure and succumbing to the temptations of "disorderly pleasures". He contrasted good art based on measure with bad art, which relied on people's sensual and emotional reactions. He reproached contemporary musicians with placing the judgment of the ear higher than that of the mind. Judgment of the senses, he said, was an improper criterion of beauty and art.

Plato not only claimed that beauty is a matter of fitting measure. He also attempted to discover what this measure was. In the dialogue *Meno* he singled out two squares whose relationship is such that a side of the one is equal to half the diagonal of the other. It would seem that he regarded this as ideal proportion. Taking his word as authority, architects for many centuries based their structures on the relationship of these squares.

In the *Timaeus* Plato singled out other proportions. He made use of the view of contemporary mathematicians that there are only five regular three-dimensional figures which, because of their regularity, are "perfect bodies". To these five figures with the most perfect proportions, he ascribed cosmological significance, maintaining that the world was founded on them, since God was incapable of employing imperfect proportions in constructing it. These same proportions he recommended to art. In particular, he recommended equilateral and Pythagorean triangles, which he regarded as being elements of those perfect bodies. He thought that only these were perfect forms really beautiful. He was responsible for the fact that the triangles of *Timaeus*—in addition to the squares of *Meno*—became the ideal of artists and particularly architects; first Greek, then Roman, and later still mediaeval buildings were for centuries planned on the principle of triangles and squares. Thus geometry supplied the fundamentals of aesthetics.

In his aesthetic theory of measure, order and proportion Plato did not by any means advocate formalism. He did, it is true, allow form a decisive role in beauty and art, but only in the sense of "arrangement of parts" and not form understood as the "appearance of things". He praised beauty of the appearance, but also that of the content. He stressed their interrelations when writing: "whoever dances and sings beautifully (*kalos*), dances and sings something beautiful (*ta kala*)".

7. THE IDEA OF BEAUTY. Plato's other concept of beauty, advocated in his middle years, stemmed from his own philosophical beliefs, which were spiritualistic and idealistic. He acknowledged the existence not only of bodies, but also of souls, not only of sensory phenomena, but also of eternal Ideas. Souls were to Plato more perfect than bodies, while Ideas were more perfect than either bodies or souls. From these beliefs follow certain consequences with a bearing on aesthetics. Beauty is not, as Plato saw it, confined to bodies, but also characterizes souls and Ideas, whose beauty is superior to that of bodies. The outcome of Plato's philosophical premises was a spiritualization and an idealization of beauty, and consequently a shift in aesthetics from experience to construction.

Plato did not deny that men find pleasure in beautiful bodies, but he considered thoughts and actions to be more beautiful than bodies. Spiritual beauty is a higher beauty, though not the highest. That resides in the "Idea", which alone is "pure beauty". When a man succeeds in doing something beautiful he is modelling himself on the Idea.[12] If bodies and souls are beautiful, they are so because of the fact that they resemble the Idea of Beauty.[13] Their beauty is transient, while only the Idea of Beauty is eternal: "When you perceive it, gold, diamond and the most beautiful boys and youths will appear as nothing in comparison".

In the *Symposium*[14] Plato employed the highest terms to describe everlasting beauty: it neither comes into being nor passes away, neither waxes nor wanes; next, it is not beautiful in part and ugly in part, nor beautiful at one time and ugly at another, nor beautiful here and ugly there, nor beautiful to one and ugly to another; it is not like the beauty of a face or of hands or anything else corporal, or like the beauty of a thought or a science, or like the beauty of a living creature or the earth or the sky or anything else whatever; but it is absolute, existing alone with itself, unique, eternal, and all other beautiful things which come into being and pass away partake of it.

When he conceived the Idea of Beauty as surpassing all understanding, Plato departed from the conviction of the Greeks. This was his personal concept, which was not merely a novelty but marked a revolution. It moved beauty to a transcendent plane.

The revolution was threefold. 1. First, the already wide compass of the Greek concept of beauty was widened still further, so that it now also included abstract objects beyond experience. 2. Second, a new evaluation was introduced: real beauty was now devalued in favour of the ideal beauty. 3. Third, a new measure of beauty was introduced: the measure of beauty of real things now depended on their distance or proximity to the Idea of Beauty.

Up to this time philosophers had introduced three measures of beauty. The Sophists' measure resided in subjective aesthetic experience, in the degree of pleasure it contained. For the Pythagoreans the measure was objective regularity and harmony. Socrates saw the measure of beauty in the degree to which it was attuned to the task it was meant to perform. Now Plato came forward with a fourth measure: the perfect Idea of Beauty which we have in our mind and against which we measure the beauty of things. Consonance with an ideal was assuredly a different measure of beauty from the pleasure which beauty gives, the form it has, or the task it fulfils.

Plato's concept contrasted sharply with that of the Sophists, and did not accord with the Socratic view; but it did agree with the Pythagorean concept; indeed, the two were even complementary, for in what could the Idea of beauty consist, if not in correctness and harmony? In his later years Plato laid even greater stress on the Pythagorean concept than on his own. He thus bequeathed to following generations mathematical as well as metaphysical aesthetics.

Plato's philosophical views gave an *idealistic* colouring to his aesthetics, but also gave it a *moralist* colouring. The Greeks appreciated moral as well as aesthetic beauty; but in the classical era they were especially attracted by the beauty of the visible world, by the theatrical spectacles, sculptures, temples, music and the dance. Moral beauty for Plato acquired a dominant position. He maintained the Greek identification of goodness with beauty, but reversed the emphasis. For the average Greek the most certain fact was that there are beautiful things which are *eo ipso* good. For Plato, on the contrary, the most certain fact was that there are things which are good, and being so, they arouse admiration and are considered as beautiful.

8. GREAT BEAUTY AND THE BEAUTY OF MODERATION; RELATIVE AND ABSOLUTE BEAUTY. Plato was an artist and a lover of art, but he was also a philosopher distrustful of art. His *general* concept of beauty and art was derived from his philosophy, but his artistry and connoisseurship were responsible for many of his *specific* observations, thoughts, analyses and distinctions.

In the *Laws* Plato distinguished between great (*megaloprepes*) art and the art of moderation (*cosmion*), between serious and light beauty. He saw this duality in poetry and the theatre, as well as in music and the dance. The distinction he drew became the origin of the distinction between sublimity and beauty, which was to be important in the eighteenth century.[15]

In our times another of Plato's distinctions seems still more significant and contemporary. In the *Philebus* he distinguished between the beauty of real things (and their representation in paintings) on the one hand, and the beauty of abstract forms, of straight lines or circles, of planes and solids on the other.[16] The first beauty, he thought, was relative, and only the second did he regard as "beautiful always and for its own sake". He preferred the beauty of simple abstract shapes, and also of pure colours, which, he thought, in themselves are "beautiful and delectable". We can assume that if he had known abstract art, he would have approved of it. His attitude toward visual art was analogous to the Pythagorean attitude toward music. He thought that beautiful simple shapes, colours and sounds gave special pleasure.[17] Those pleasures were exceptional in that they were not mixed with pain. By this one could distinguish aesthetic experiences from other experiences.

These specific observations of Plato, even the most profound and significant ones, were much less influential than his general concept of art. The latter exercised an influence for centuries after and proved to be his true aesthetic legacy, despite the fact that it was much more questionable than his specific observations.

9. THE CONCEPT OF ART; POETRY VERSUS ART. The connection between Plato's theory of art and his theory of beauty was rather loose. He saw the greatest beauty not in art, but in the universe. He was using the broad Greek conception of art which also embraced crafts; for him, as for other Greeks, not only painting or music, but everything that man produces purposefully and skilfully was art. He said that man had discovered art because nature did not adequately provide for him and he needed protection. In saying this Plato was naturally thinking of weaving and building and not of painting and sculpture.

Plato's conception of art included crafts; but it seemed not to include poetry, which he regarded as a matter of inspiration and not of skill. Developing the Greek view of poetry, he thought of it as prophetic and irrational. "The authors of those great poems we admire", he wrote in the *Ion*, "do not attain to excellence through the rules of any art, but they utter their beautiful melodies of verse in a state of inspiration, and, as it were, possessed by a spirit not their own ... [creating] in a state of divine insanity".[18] "Poets ... are the interpreters of divinities—each being possessed by some one deity".[19] In the *Phaedrus*, also, Plato described *poetry as* a lofty *madness* (*mania*). When the Muses bring inspiration, "the soul overflows with songs and other forms of artistic creation". "But if any man comes to the gates of poetry without the madness of the Muses, persuaded that skill alone will make him a good poet, then shall he and his works of sanity ... be brought to nought by the poetry of madness".[20] This statement stresses the important opposition of inspiration to craftsmanship. Plato was not alone in ascribing poetry to inspiration: Democritus thought likewise. The idealist and the materialist both regarded poetry as psychologically exceptional. It was characteristic of the early epoch to see inspiration solely in poetry and to classify the arts together with crafts.

Plato went furthest in stressing the contrast between poetry and art; but at the same time he himself undermined this contrast. He had observed that not all poetry is inspiration, for there are writers who rely on routine. There is a "mania" poetry born of poetic ecstasy,[21] and there is also "technical" poetry produced by skill in writing. These two types of poetry are not of equal value: the first type Plato regarded as man's highest activity, the second, as an art like any other. In the hierarchy of men which he presented in the *Phaedrus*, he assigned two different places to the poets: some were assigned a low place in the company of craftsmen and farmers, while others, those "chosen by the Muses", were given the first place together with philosophers. Similarly, in the *Symposium*, he contrasted the bard, "the divine man", the mediator between gods and men, with "those who know a certain art or craft" and are only simple "workers". He recognized this bard-craftsman duality among poets, but not among artists; for, in his view, painters and sculptors were nothing more than craftsmen.

10. DIVISION OF ART; IMITATIVE ARTS. The extensive domain of art, which included both painting and sculpture, as well as weaving and shoe-making, called for classification. This Plato attempted on a number of occasions. In the *Republic* he divided the arts in three classes:[22] arts which utilize things, which produce them and which imitate them. A similar but more complicated division appeared in the *Sophist*,[23] where he distinguished between "ctetics", that is, the art of making use of what exists in Nature, and "poetics", that is, the art of producing what Nature lacks (the term "poetics" was here used in a wide sense and was not confined to the art of the word). In ctetics he included such arts as hunting and fishing. Poetics was further subdivided into that which serves man directly, that which serves man indirectly (tool-making) and that which imitates.

Most important in this classification for aesthetics was the separation of the arts which reproduce things from those that produce them, the distinction of the *productive* and *imitative* arts. Plato, however, did neither provide a list of imitative arts, nor define the term exactly, so that the range of "mimetic" arts remained fluid. At one time he would contrast poetry with them, at another he would include it among them; once he included music in poetry (in the *Symposium*) and on another occasion (in the *Republic*) he included poetry in music. He took only the first step to a theory of imitative arts.

Nevertheless, Plato had a decisive influence on the evolution of this theory. The notion that the art imitates or represents reality was not of course alien to the earlier Greeks. They easily realized that the *Odyssey* represented the adventures of Odysseus, and that a statue on the Acropolis represented a human body; but they showed relatively little interest in this function of art. They devoted more thought to such art as music and the dance, which express something. But, even in the case of such representative arts as sculpture and painting, the Greeks were interested rather in the fact that the arts differ from reality, that, as Gorgias argued, they create illusions. This lack of interest for representative art may be explained by the fact that before the middle of the fifth century B.C. the Greek visual arts had indeed little resemblance to reality, and the representations of human figures had more geometry than reality in them. Apart from Socrates' conversation with Parrhasius, recorded by Xenophon, it is difficult to find anything in pre-Platonic writers about the representation of reality through art.

The term used to denote representation through art was not fixed. In his conversations Socrates used a variety of terms, including some close to *mimesis*, but never *mimesis* itself, which the Greeks of the period used to mean expression of character and the acting of a part, not imitation of reality. The term *mimesis* was used to describe the ritual activities of priests in connection with music and dance, but not to describe the visual arts. Democritus and the school of Heraclitus used the term to mean "following Nature", but not in the sense of "repeating the appearance of things". It was Plato who first introduced the new application of the old term.

In Plato's day, sculpture abandoned the geometrical style and began to portray real living people, and painting showed an analogous change. Plato could observe that the arts which "serve the Muses" turned representation of reality into a living issue. He referred to this new phenomenon under the old name *mimesis* and in doing so he inevitably changed the meaning of the term. He continued the practice of applying it to music[24] and dance,[25] but he also applied it—though not until Book X of the *Republic*—to the visual arts.[26] He still applied it to representation of character and feelings, but he also used it to denote the representation of the appearance of things. At first, following tradition, he called "imitative" only those arts in which the artist himself acts as the tool,[27] as in the case of an actor or dancer; but later he extended the term to embrace other arts as well. In the *Republic* he confined "imitative" poetry to that in which the heroes themselves speak, as in tragedy; but in the *Laws* he extended the term to include epic, where heroes are described by the poet. In the *Laws* all "musical" art, i.e., that which serves the Muses, is called "representational and imitative".

Plato was concerned with the truthfulness with which art represented reality. In the *Cratylus* he wrote that a faithful copy is superfluous, as it is merely a replica of the original. But on the other hand, an unfaithful imitation is a lie. Therefore Plato doubted whether imitation is even desirable in the arts.[28]

11. IMAGE-CREATING ARTS. When painters or sculptors "imitate" a man, they do not, of course, make another man similar to the first, but only an *image* of him; and the image of a human being belongs to a different order from a real human being. Despite similarities, it has other properties. Plato realized this, and his concept of "mimesis"—imitation had therefore two aspects: firstly, the artist creates an image of the reality, and, secondly, this image is unreal.[29] Works of art which are "imitations" are "phantasms". "Imitative arts", which create images and phantasms, Plato contrasted with those "that create things". For him the essential characteristic of the imitative arts, of painting and sculpture, of poetry and music, was not only their imitativeness, but also the *unreality* of their products.

Having in the *Sophist* divided the arts into those that produce things (vessels or utensils) and those which produce only images, Plato proceeded to subdivide the latter into those arts that in portraying things preserve their proper proportions and colours and those that alter them.[30] This second category is composed, in fact, not of "imitations", but of "illusions". In introducing this division, Plato was influenced by contemporary art with its illusionism and its deliberate deformation of shapes and colours. He wrote that "today, artists take no account of truth and endow their works with proportions which *seem* beautiful and not with those that *are* beautiful". He wrote that illusionistic painting attempted "wonders" and "sorceries" and was the art of "delusion". He detected in it the same properties as Gorgias had, but, while Gorgias appreciated highly this seductive magic, Plato regarded it as a deviation and vice. It was the illusionism of art rather than its representational character that persuaded Plato to give a negative account of it. But he did not consider illusionism to be a necessary characteristic of art; on the contrary, he believed that when divested of illusionism, art performs its proper function.

12. FUNCTIONS OF ART: MORAL UTILITY AND RIGHTNESS. What then did Plato believe to be the function of art? Its first function was utility. By this Plato meant *moral* utility, being the only true utility. Art has to be a means of moulding character and of forming an ideal state.

Secondly and most importantly, in order to fulfil its function art must follow the laws governing the world, must penetrate the divine plan of the cosmos and shape things in accordance with it. Therefore, truthfulness or rightness (*orthotes*)[31] is the second fundamental function of art. The things it produces must be "suitable, accurate and just, without deviations". Every deviation from the laws governing the world is a fault and a mistake.

Only calculation and measure can give art a guarantee of rightness: this component of the Platonic theory of art was a Pythagorean inheritance. Only art employing calculation and measure (in contrast with art guided simply by experience and intuition) is capable of discharging its function reliably. Architecture is an example. The "rightness" of a work of art depends, first of all, upon a proper arrangement of parts, an internal order and good structure. It has to have an adequate "beginning, middle and end", to be similar to a living being, to an organism, which cannot be without "either head or feet; it must have a middle and extremities so composed as to suit each other and the whole work".[32] Only by representing rightly each part can a painter create a beautiful whole.[33] In order to achieve this the artist must know and apply the eternal laws governing the world.

These then are the criteria of good art: "rightness" in the sense of accordance with the laws of the world, and "utility", in the sense of the capacity to form moral character. Pleasure in art can at best be no more than a supplement to it. Pleasure is not its goal, nor a criterion of its value, as the Sophists claimed. Art which aims at providing pleasure is bad art. Since the criterion of art resides in rightness, the guiding principle must be reason and not emotion.

And what of beauty? Plato was too much an artist himself to remain insensitive to beauty in art, but his philosophy made divergent demands. His eyes were sensitive, but, as it has been observed, "his inward eye gradually veiled his outward vision". To be sure, he wrote that service to the Muses should "end... in the love of beauty".[34] But he meant "beauty" in a wide sense, which embraced primarily moral beauty. Beauty so understood did not differ from moral utility and rightness.

But is not the *internal* truth of a work of art a criterion of its value? Plato's *Republic* contains the following sentence: "Suppose a painter had drawn an ideally beautiful figure complete to the last touch, would you think any the worse of him, if he could not show that a person as beautiful as that could exist?".[35] This sentence seems to say that the value of a work of art is decided by its internal rather than by any external truth. It has been taken to signify Plato's recognition of a specific "artistic truth". However, Plato can only have had an inkling of this idea: he mentioned it once never to return to it. His whole theory of art is, in fact, incompatible with the idea of a distinctive artistic truth: with exceptional determination he applied to art the criterion of literally understood truth and of conformity with what it portrays. His axiom was that art should portray things in their proper, inherent proportions. Otherwise it would be untrue, and untrue art is bad art. For that reason he condemned contemporary impressionistic painting because it altered the proportions and colours of things even though this made the spectator *see* the *proper* proportions and colours.

Plato's view was that art should *not* enjoy autonomy. Art should even be doubly non-autonomous: in relation to real existence, which it is to represent, and also in relation to the moral order, which it is to serve.

We are thus left with the conclusion that Plato demanded from art two things: that it should mould its works in accordance with the laws of the cosmos and should shape characters in accordance with the Idea of the Good. Arising out of this there could be only two criteria of good art: rightness and moral utility.

Can art really fulfil these ideal demands? Plato thought that it could, and that it had done so both in the archaic art of the earlier Greeks and especially in the art of the Egyptians.

13. ART CONDEMNED. Plato's attitude toward the art of his own day, however, was one of condemnation. He disapproved of this art for aiming at novelty and variety, for producing illusions and distorting proportions. His purpose was to defend art from being overwhelmed by subjectivism and untruth. His criticism of contemporary art was so generally formulated that Plato appeared to be an enemy of all art.

More precisely, Plato assessed art negatively because he thought it did not fulfil either of his two criteria. Art is neither right nor useful. First, it gives a false picture of reality and, second, it corrupts people. It deforms things. Even on occasion when it does not deform things, it only represents their surface, their superficial appearance. According to Plato, external sensuous appearance of reality is not only superficial, but is also a false image.[36-40]

According to Plato's philosophy, art corrupts because it acts on emotions and inflames them at a time when man should be guided solely by reason. By affecting the emotions, art weakens character and lulls men's moral and social vigilance. Plato's first argument against art was concerned primarily with visual arts, and the second chiefly with poetry and music.

Plato's first argument against art was drawn from a theory of knowledge and metaphysics, and the second from ethics. Plato drew nothing from aesthetics. This was not the first time that poetry had been judged from a moral viewpoint and condemned. Aristophanes had done so prior to Plato. Plato was, however, the first to introduce this viewpoint into the general philosophy of art. He provoked a split between the philosophy of art and art itself. This was probably the first split of this kind in the European history. The views of pre-Platonic theoreticians conformed to contemporary artistic practice. Plato, on the contrary, wished art to conform with *his* views. He laid down *prescriptions* as to what art should be like. And his prescriptions happened to move in the opposite directions from that taken by contemporary art. The split was unavoidable.

Dissatisfied with the art of his day, he wanted art to abide by tradition. He has been called "the first classicist" because he was the first known thinker to advocate return to art of the past .

Platonic arguments had a limited persuasive power. Unconvinced, Greek artists paid no attention to Plato and continued to develop their art independently. Plato's arguments are based upon his own personal assumptions: that the perceptible properties of things do not accord with the true properties of being, and that there was only *one* right method of producing art and educating citizens. His criticism was *not* an *aesthetic* evaluation of art and at best demonstrated that, from a cognitive and moral point of view, art was harmful. In Plato's view, however, lower values had to be completely subordinated to higher ones, and beauty stood below truth and virtue. Furthermore, his arguments did not condemn art as a whole, because not every art deforms reality and not every art weakens character. His arguments were of interest only to those who accepted his axioms that art should conform rigidly to the objective truths, that it should agree with reason and should approach the world of ideal Forms. Plato himself did not always follow his own arguments. His dialogues contain passages praising the arts and a declaration that poets are the "interpreters of the gods".

Plato's final judgment on art, however, was negative. Even where Plato did not condemn art, he belittled it. "All imitative arts", he wrote in the *Politician*, "are merely playthings (*paignia*); they contain nothing serious and are nothing but entertainments". Imitation is only a game, though no doubt a charming one. It is a frivolous occupation dragging men away from their sublime duties. Plato contrasted the art of the painter, who works with images and not real things, with "serious" arts which "co-operate with Nature", arts like medicine, farming, gymnastics or politics. Nothing perhaps characterizes Plato's position so well as his contention that art is a game, while beauty is a very serious and difficult thing: *chalepa ta kala*.

Yet Plato did not simply identify shortcomings of art. On the contrary, he tried to remedy those shortcomings, which, he thought, were not inevitable. There is bad art, but there can be also good art. Good art requires guidance and control. Plato wrote about "compelling poets".[41] He wanted to prevent new ideas and revolutions in music, fearing the social and political consequences of such upheavals.[42] He demanded that the law-givers should "persuade or, if persuasion fails, impel [the poet] to compose as he ought".[43] He called art a "plaything", but he must have discerned its power: since he wrote that "there never occurs a change of style in music without a revolution in political laws".

14. THE CONFLICT BETWEEN PHILOSOPHY AND ART. Plato liked art and was associated with many artists. He himself painted and composed poems, and his own dialogues were works of art. Yet, in spite of this, Plato assessed art negatively. On closer observation, Plato's negative attitude toward art does not appear to be solely a result of his personal views. It reflected Greek thinking and the "immemorial conflict" between philosophy and poetry.[44] The origin of this conflict lay in the claim that Greek poetry instructed people in the same way as philosophy. Homer and Hesiod were responsible for what the Greeks thought of their gods, while Aeschylus was responsible for what they thought of the destiny of man. To the question why should poets be respected, Aristophanes replied: "for the *teaching* they provide".

As soon as philosophy appeared, its conflict with poetry was inevitable. Philosophers with relativistic approach might tolerate poetry as another source of knowledge. But not Plato, the believer in the oneness of truth. He was convinced that only philosophy can approach the truth. In the *Apology* he wrote: "Poets are like seers and oracles, they do not know what they say; but I have also observed that on account of their poetry they regard themselves as learned in matters in which they are not learned at all". Here was a conflict between science and poetry, into which the arts were also drawn as poetry's natural ally.

15. SUMMARY. Very briefly, Plato's position on the subject of aesthetics was as follows. Being constructed according to eternal forms and governed by immutable laws, the world is perfect in its order and measure. Every single thing is a particle of that order, and in this resides its beauty. The mind can apprehend this beauty, while the senses register merely its distant, uncertain and accidental reflections.

In view of this there is only one thing for the artist to do, and that is to discover and represent the unique perfect shapes of different things. Every deviation from them is a fault, a falsification and a vice; and many artists are at fault, as they only create illusion. In theory, the function of art is lofty and useful, but in practice it errs and causes harm.

Never have there been more extreme statements regarding beauty and art than Plato's statements that beauty is a property of reality and not of human invention, that art can be based only on knowledge, that there is no place in it for freedom, for individuality, originality or creativity, and that, in comparison with the perfection of reality, the possibilities of art are negligible.

The derivation of this doctrine is clear. Plato based it on the cosmological conviction of the Pythagoreans that the world is one of mathematical order and harmony. He combined this theory both with that of Socrates (that moral value is supreme) and the theory of Aristophanes (that art should be guided by morals). Neither the Pythagoreans nor Socrates envisaged the conclusions that were drawn by Plato from their theories. It was he who initiated the idealist interpretation of beauty and the mimetic and moralistic interpretation of art. Both interpretations were based upon his metaphysical views, and stand or fall together with them.

Plato appears rather isolated in his views. His transcendent concept of beauty seems foreign to a classical period appreciating the immanent beauty of this world. He was in particularly marked contrast to the relativistically minded Sophists who were his contemporaries. He was a metaphysician and a spiritualist, while they stood in the vanguard of enlightenment. Yet the classical Greek culture was characterized by variety; it had a moralist attitude as well as an aesthetic one; it gave rise to the ideology of idealism as well as to ideology of enlightenment. The Sophists represented one ideological extreme and Plato another.

F. Texts from Plato

PLATO, Phaedrus 246 E.

1. τὸ δὲ θεῖον καλόν, σοφόν, ἀγαθόν, καὶ πᾶν ὅ τι τοιοῦτον.

BEAUTY, TRUTH, GOODNESS

1. The divine nature, which is fair, wise and good, and possessed of all other such excellences.

PLATO, Gorgias 474 D.

2. τὰ καλὰ πάντα, οἷον καὶ σώματα καὶ χρώματα καὶ σχήματα καὶ φωνὰς καὶ ἐπιτηδεύματα, εἰς οὐδὲν ἀποβλέπων καλεῖς ἑκάστοτε καλά; οἷον πρῶτον τὰ σώματα τὰ καλὰ οὐχὶ ἤτοι κατὰ τὴν χρείαν λέγεις καλὰ εἶναι, πρὸς ὃ ἂν ἕκαστον χρήσιμον ᾖ, πρὸς τοῦτο, ἢ κατὰ ἡδονήν τινα, ἐὰν ἐν τῷ θεωρεῖσθαι χαίρειν ποιῇ τοὺς θεωροῦντας;

BEAUTY, UTILITY, PLEASURE

2. All fair things, like bodies and colours and figures and sounds and observances—is it according to no standard that you call these fair in each case? Thus, in the first place, when you say that fair bodies are fair, it must be either in view of their use for some particular purpose that each may serve, or in respect of some pleasure arising when, in the art of beholding them, they cause delight to the beholder.

tr. W. R. M. Lamb

LAERTIUS DIOGENES III, 55
(on Plato).

3. Τὸ κάλλος διαιρεῖται εἰς τρία· ἓν μὲν γὰρ αὐτοῦ ἔστιν ἐπαινετόν, οἷον ἡ διὰ τῆς ὄψεως εὐμορφία· ἄλλο δὲ χρηστικόν, οἷον ὄργανον καὶ οἰκία καὶ τὰ τοιαῦτα πρὸς χρῆσιν εἰσι καλά· τὰ δὲ πρὸς νόμους καὶ ἐπιτηδεύματα καὶ τὰ τοιαῦτα πρὸς ὠφέλειάν εἰσι καλά. τοῦ ἄρα κάλλους τὸ μέν ἐστι πρὸς ἔπαινον, τὸ δὲ πρὸς χρῆσιν, τὸ δὲ πρὸς ὠφέλειαν.

THREEFOLD CONCEPTION OF BEAUTY

3. Beauty has three divisions. The first is the object of praise, as of form fair to see. Another is serviceable; thus an instrument, a house and the like are beautiful for use. Other things again which relate to customs and pursuits and the like are beautiful because beneficial. Of beauty, then, one kind is matter for praise, another is for use, and another for the benefit it procures.

tr. R. D. Hicks

PLATO, Hippias maior 297 E.

4. εἰ ὃ ἂν χαίρειν ἡμᾶς ποιῇ, μήτι πάσας τὰς ἡδονάς, ἀλλ' ὃ ἂν διὰ τῆς ἀκοῆς καὶ τῆς ὄψεως, τοῦτο φαῖμεν εἶναι καλόν, πῶς τι ἄρ'

BEAUTY FOR THE EYE AND THE EAR

4. If we were to say that whatever we enjoy—I do not mean to include all pleasures, but only what we enjoy through our senses of hearing

ἂν ἀγωνιζοίμεθα; οἵ τέ γέ που καλοὶ ἄνθρωποι, ὦ Ἱππία, καὶ τὰ ποικίλματα πάντα καὶ ζωγραφήματα καὶ τὰ πλάσματα τέρπει ἡμᾶς ὁρῶντας, ἃ ἂν καλὰ ᾖ· καὶ οἱ φθόγγοι οἱ καλοὶ καὶ ἡ μουσικὴ ξύμπασα καὶ οἱ λόγοι καὶ αἱ μυθολογίαι ταὐτὸν τοῦτο ἐργάζονται, ... τὸ καλόν ἐστι τὸ δι' ἀκοῆς τε καὶ ὄψεως ἡδύ.

and sight—if we were to say that this is beautiful, how should we fare in our struggle? Surely, beautiful human beings, and all decorative work, and pictures, and plastic art, delight us when we see them if they are beautiful; and beautiful sounds, and music as a whole, and discourses, and tales of imagination, have the same effect. ...beauty is the pleasant which comes through the senses of hearing and sight.

tr. B. Jowett

PLATO, Respublica 476 B.

5. Οἱ μέν που... φιλήκοοι καὶ φιλοθεάμονες τάς τε καλὰς φωνὰς ἀσπάζονται καὶ χρόας καὶ σχήματα καὶ πάντα τὰ ἐκ τῶν τοιούτων δημιουργούμενα, αὐτοῦ δὲ τοῦ καλοῦ ἀδύνατος αὐτῶν ἡ διάνοια τὴν φύσιν ἰδεῖν τε καὶ ἀσπάσασθαι.

TRUE BEAUTY

5. Your lovers of sights and sounds delight in beautiful tones and colours and shapes and in all the works of art into which these enter; but they have not the power of thought to behold and to take delight in the nature of Beauty itself.

tr. F. M. Cornford

PLATO, Philebus 64 E.

6. μετριότης γὰρ καὶ συμμετρία κάλλος δήπου καὶ ἀρετὴ πανταχοῦ ξυμβαίνει γίγνεσθαι... Οὐκοῦν εἰ μὴ μιᾷ δυνάμεθα ἰδέᾳ τὸ ἀγαθὸν θηρεῦσαι, σὺν τρισὶ λαβόντες, κάλλει καὶ ξυμμετρίᾳ καὶ ἀληθείᾳ.

BEAUTY AND MEASURE

6. ...for measure and proportion are everywhere identified with beauty and virtue... Then, if we cannot catch the good with the aid of one idea, let us run it down with three—beauty, proportion and truth.

tr. H. N. Fowler

PLATO, Sophista 228 A.

7. ἀλλ' αἶσχος ἄλλο τι πλὴν τὸ τῆς ἀμετρίας πανταχοῦ δυσειδὲς ὂν γένος;

7. But is deformity anything else than the presence of the quality of disproportion, which is always ugly?

tr. H. N. Fowler

PLATO, Timaeus 87 C.

8. πᾶν δὲ τὸ ἀγαθὸν καλόν, τὸ δὲ καλὸν οὐκ ἄμετρον· καὶ ζῷον οὖν τὸ τοιοῦτον ἐσόμενον ξύμμετρον θετέον· ... οὐδεμία ξυμμετρία καὶ ἀμετρία μείζων ἢ ψυχῆς αὐτῆς πρὸς σῶμα αὐτό.

8. All that is good is beautiful, and what is beautiful cannot lack proportion. In the case of a living creature, too, such proportion is necessary... No proportion or disproportion is more important than that between the soul itself and the body itself.

PLATO, Timaeus 31 C.

9. Δύο δὲ μόνω καλῶς συνίστασθαι τρίτου χωρὶς οὐ δυνατόν· δεσμὸν γὰρ ἐν μέσῳ δεῖ τινα ἀμφοῖν ξυναγωγὸν γίγνεσθαι· δεσμῶν δὲ κάλλιστος ὃς ἂν αὑτόν τε καὶ τὰ ξυνδούμενα ὅ τι μάλιστα ἓν ποιῇ. τοῦτο δὲ πέφυκεν ἀναλογία κάλλιστα ἀποτελεῖν.

9. Now two terms cannot be fairly wrought together without a third; there must be a bond between them to bring them together. The fairest of all bonds is that which makes itself and the terms it binds together most utterly one, and this is most perfectly effected by a proportion.

tr. A. E. Taylor

PLATO, Politicus 284 E.

10. Δῆλον ὅτι διαιροῖμεν ἂν τὴν μετρητικήν, καθάπερ ἐρρήθη, ταύτῃ δίχα τέμνοντες, ἓν μὲν τιθέντες αὐτῆς μόριον ξυμπάσας τέχνας, ὁπόσαι τὸν ἀριθμὸν καὶ μήκη καὶ βάθη καὶ πλάτη καὶ παχύτητας πρὸς τοὐναντίον μετροῦσι· τὸ δὲ ἕτερον, ὁπόσαι πρὸς τὸ μέτριον καὶ τὸ πρέπον καὶ τὸν καιρὸν καὶ τὸ δέον καὶ πάνθ' ὁπόσα εἰς τὸ μέσον ἀπῳκίσθη τῶν ἐσχάτων.

10. We should evidently divide the science of measurement into two parts in accordance with what has been said. One part comprises all the arts which measure number, length, depth, breadth and thickness in relation to their opposites; the other comprises those which measure them in relation to the moderate, the fitting, the opposite, the needful and all the other standards that are situated in the mean between the extremes.

tr. H. N. Fowler

PLATO, Leges 653 E.

11. τὰ μὲν οὖν ἄλλα ζῷα οὐκ ἔχειν αἴσθησιν τῶν ἐν ταῖς κινήσεσι τάξεων οὐδὲ ἀταξιῶν, οἷς δὴ ῥυθμὸς ὄνομα καὶ ἁρμονία· ἡμῖν δὲ οὓς εἴπομεν τοὺς θεοὺς συγχορευτὰς δεδόσθαι, τούτους εἶναι καὶ τοὺς δεδωκότας τὴν ἔνρυθμόν τε καὶ ἐναρμόνιον αἴσθησιν μεθ' ἡδονῆς.

MAN AND HARMONY AND RHYTHM

11. Now animals at large have no perception of the order or disorder in these motions, no sense of what we call rhythm or melody. But in our case the gods... have likewise given us the power to perceive and enjoy rhythm and melody.

tr. A. E. Taylor

PLATO, Timaeus 28 A.

12. ὅτου μὲν οὖν ὁ δημιουργὸς πρὸς τὸ κατὰ ταὐτὰ ἔχον βλέπων ἀεί, τοιούτῳ τινὶ προσχρώμενος παραδείγματι, τὴν ἰδέαν καὶ δύναμιν αὐτοῦ ἀπεργάζηται, καλὸν ἐξ ἀνάγκης οὕτως ἀποτελεῖσθαι πᾶν· οὗ δ' ἂν εἰς τὸ γεγονός, γεννητῷ παραδείγματι προσχρώμενος οὐ καλόν.

THE IDEA OF BEAUTY

12. Now when the maker of anything fixes his gaze upon the ever selfsame and takes it for his model in the fashioning of form and quality, the thing thus fashioned is necessarily always beautiful; if his gaze is upon that which has come to be and his model a thing that comes to be, his work is not beautiful.

tr. A. E. Taylor

PLATO, Timaeus 29 A.

13. εἰ μὲν δὴ καλός ἐστιν ὅδε ὁ κόσμος ὅ τε δημιουργὸς ἀγαθός, δῆλον ὡς πρὸς τὸ ἀΐδιον ἔβλεπεν.

13. For if this world is a thing of beauty and its maker good, manifestly his gaze was upon the eternal.

tr. A. E. Taylor

PLATO, Convivium 210 E—211 D.

14. Ὃς γὰρ ἂν μέχρι ἐνταῦθα πρὸς τὰ ἐρωτικὰ παιδαγωγηθῇ, θεώμενος ἐφεξῆς τε καὶ ὀρθῶς τὰ καλά, πρὸς τέλος ἤδη ἰὼν τῶν ἐρωτικῶν ἐξαίφνης κατόψεταί τι θαυμαστὸν τὴν φύσιν καλόν, τοῦτο ἐκεῖνο, ὦ Σώκρατες, οὗ δὴ ἕνεκεν καὶ οἱ ἔμπροσθεν πάντες πόνοι ἦσαν, πρῶτον μὲν ἀεὶ ὂν καὶ οὔτε γιγνόμενον οὔτε ἀπολλύμενον, οὔτε αὐξανόμενον οὔτε φθῖνον, ἔπειτα οὐ τῇ μὲν καλόν, τῇ δ' αἰσχρόν, οὐδὲ τοτὲ μέν, τοτὲ δ' οὔ, οὐδὲ πρὸς μὲν τὸ

14. He who has been instructed thus far in the things of love and who has learned to see the beautiful in due order and succession, when he comes towards the end, will suddenly perceive a nature of wondrous beauty (and this, Socrates, is the final cause of all our former toils)—a nature which in the first place is everlasting, knowing not birth or death, growth or decay; secondly, not fair in one point of view and foul in another, or at one time or

καλόν, πρὸς δὲ τό αἰσχρόν, οὐδ' ἔνθα μὲν καλὸν ἔνθα δὲ αἰσχρόν, ὡς τισὶ μὲν ὂν καλόν, τισὶ δὲ αἰσχρόν· οὐδ' αὖ φαντασθήσεται αὐτῷ τὸ καλὸν οἷον πρόσωπόν τι οὐδὲ χεῖρες οὐδὲ ἄλλο οὐδὲν ὧν σῶμα μετέχει, οὐδέ τις λόγος οὐδέ τις ἐπιστήμη, οὐδέ που ὂν ἐν ἑτέρῳ τινί, οἷον ἐν ζῴῳ ἢ ἐν γῇ ἢ ἐν οὐρανῷ ἢ ἐν τῷ ἄλλῳ, ἀλλὰ αὐτὸ καθ' αὑτὸ μεθ' αὑτοῦ μονοειδὲς ἀεὶ ὄν, τὰ δὲ ἄλλα πάντα καλὰ ἐκείνου μετέχοντα τρόπον τινὰ τοιοῦτον, οἷον γιγνομένων τε τῶν ἄλλων καὶ ἀπολλυμένων μηδὲν ἐκεῖνο μήτε τι πλέον μήτε ἔλαττον γίγνεσθαι μηδὲ πάσχειν μηδέν. ὅταν δή τις ἀπὸ τῶνδε διὰ τὸ ὀρθῶς παιδεραστεῖν ἐπανιὼν ἐκεῖνο τὸ καλὸν ἄρχηται καθορᾶν, σχεδὸν ἄν τι ἅπτοιτο τοῦ τέλους. τοῦτο γὰρ δή ἐστι τὸ ὀρθῶς ἐπὶ τὰ ἐρωτικὰ ἰέναι ἢ ὑπ' ἄλλου ἄγεσθαι, ἀρχόμενον ἀπὸ τῶνδε τῶν καλῶν ἐκείνου ἕνεκα τοῦ καλοῦ ἀεὶ ἐπανιέναι, ὥσπερ ἐπαναβαθμοῖς χρώμενον, ἀπὸ ἑνὸς ἐπὶ δύο καὶ ἀπὸ δυεῖν ἐπὶ πάντα τὰ καλὰ σώματα, καὶ ἀπὸ τῶν καλῶν σωμάτων ἐπὶ τὰ καλὰ ἐπιτηδεύματα, καὶ ἀπὸ τῶν καλῶν ἐπιτηδευμάτων ἐπὶ τὰ καλὰ μαθήματα, ἕως ἀπὸ τῶν μαθημάτων ἐπ' ἐκεῖνο τὸ μάθημα τελευτήσῃ, ὅ ἐστιν οὐκ ἄλλου ἢ αὐτοῦ ἐκείνου τοῦ καλοῦ μάθημα, καὶ γνῷ αὐτὸ τελευτῶν ὅ ἔστι καλόν. ἐνταῦθα τοῦ βίου... εἴπερ που ἄλλοθι, βιωτὸν ἀνθρώπῳ, θεωμένῳ αὐτὸ τὸ καλόν.

in one relation or at one place fair, at another time or in another relation or at another place foul; as if fair to some and foul to others, or in the likeness of a face or hands or any other parts of the bodily frame, or in any form of speech or knowledge, or existing in any individual being, as for example, in a living creature, whether in heaven, or in earth or anywhere else; but beauty absolute, separate, simple, and everlasting, which is imparted to the ever growing and perishing beauties of all other beautiful things, without itself suffering diminution, or increase, or any change. He who ascending from these earthly things under the influence of true love, begins to perceive that beauty, is not far from the end. And the true order of going, or being led by another to the things of love, is to begin from the beauties of the earth and mount upwards for the sake of that other beauty, using these as steps only, and from one going on to two, and from two to all fair bodily forms, and from fair bodily forms to fair practices, and from fair practices to fair sciences, until from fair sciences he arrives at the science of which I have spoken, the science which has no other object than absolute beauty, and at last knows that which is beautiful by itself alone. This... is that life above all others which man should live, in the contemplation of beauty absolute.

tr. B. Jowett

PLATO, Leges 802 D.

15. Ἔτι δὲ θηλείαις τε πρεπούσας ᾠδὰς ἄρρεσί τε χωρίσαι που δέον ἂν εἴη τύπῳ τινὶ διορισάμενον, καὶ ἁρμονίαισι δὴ καὶ ῥυθμοῖς προσαρμόττειν ἀναγκαῖον·... ἀναγκαῖον δὴ καὶ τούτων τὰ σχήματά γε νομοθετεῖν... τὸ δὴ μεγαλοπρεπὲς οὖν καὶ τὸ πρὸς τὴν ἀνδρείαν ῥέπον ἀρρενωπὸν φατέον εἶναι, τὸ δὲ πρὸς τὸ κόσμιον καὶ σῶφρον μᾶλλον ἀποκλῖνον θηλυγενέστερον ὡς ὂν παραδοτέον ἔν τε τῷ νόμῳ καὶ λόγῳ.

BEAUTY OF SIZE AND MODERATION

15. It will further be necessary to make a rough general distinction between two types of song, those suited for females and those suited for males, and so we shall have to provide both with their appropriate scales and rhythms... so we shall further have to legislate on these points, at any rate in general outline... Accordingly, we shall pronounce the majestic and whatever tends to valour masculine, while it will be the tradition of our law and our theory alike that what makes rather for order and purity is peculiarly feminine.

tr. A. E. Taylor

PLATO, Philebus 51 B.

16. Πάνυ μὲν οὖν οὐκ εὐθὺς δῆλά ἐστιν ἃ λέγω, πειρατέον μὴν δηλοῦν. σχημάτων τε γὰρ κάλλος οὐχ ὅπερ ἂν ὑπολάβοιεν οἱ πολλοὶ

BEAUTY ABSOLUTE AND RELATIVE

16. My meaning is certainly not clear at the first glance and I must try to make it so. For when I say: beauty of form, I am trying

πειρῶμαι νῦν λέγειν, ἢ ζώων ἤ τινων ζωγραφημάτων, ἀλλ' εὐθύ τι λέγω, φησὶν ὁ λόγος, καὶ περιφερὲς καὶ ἀπὸ τούτων δὴ τά τε τοῖς τόρνοις γιγνόμενα ἐπίπεδά τε καὶ στερεὰ κα τὰ τοῖς κανόσι καὶ γωνίαις, εἴ μου μανθάνεις. ταῦτα γὰρ οὐκ εἶναι πρός τι καλὰ λέγω, καθάπερ ἄλλα, ἀλλ' ἀεὶ καλὰ καθ' αὑτὰ πεφυκέναι καὶ τινας ἡδονὰς οἰκείας ἔχειν,... καὶ χρώματα δὴ τοῦτον τὸν τύπον ἔχοντα καλὰ καὶ ἡδονάς.

to express, not what most people would understand by the words such as the beauty of animals or of paintings, but I mean, says the argument, the straight line and the circle and the plane and solid figures formed from these by turning-lathes and rules and patterns formed of angles; perhaps you understand. For I assert that the beauty of these is not relative, like that of other things, but they are always absolutely beautiful by nature and give peculiar pleasures. ...and these are colours which possess beauty and give pleasures of this character.

tr. H. N. Fowler

PLATO, Philebus 51 A.

17. ΠΡΩ. Ἀληθεῖς δ' αὖ τίνας (ἡδονάς), ὦ Σώκρατες, ὑπολαμβάνων ὀρθῶς τις διανοοῖτ' ἄν;
ΣΩ. Τὰς περί τε τὰ καλὰ λεγόμενα χρώματα καὶ περὶ τὰ σχήματα καὶ τῶν ὀσμῶν τὰς πλείστας καὶ τὰς τῶν φθόγγων καὶ ὅσα τὰς ἐνδείας ἀναισθήτους ἔχοντα καὶ ἀλύπους τὰς πληρώσεις αἰσθητὰς καὶ ἡδείας, καθαρὰς λυπῶν παραδίδωσιν.

AESTHETIC DELIGHT

17. PROTARCHOS: But what pleasures, Socrates, may rightly be considered true?
SOCRATES: Those arising from what are called beautiful colours or from forms, most of those that arise from odours and sounds, in short all those the want of which is unfelt and painless, whereas the satisfaction furnished by them is felt by the senses, pleasant, and unmixed with pain.

tr. H. N. Fowler

PLATO, Io 533 E.

18. πάντες γὰρ οἵ τε τῶν ἐπῶν ποιηταὶ οἱ ἀγαθοὶ οὐκ ἐκ τέχνης ἀλλ' ἔνθεοι ὄντες καὶ κατεχόμενοι πάντα ταῦτα τὰ καλὰ λέγουσι ποιήματα, καὶ οἱ μελοποιοὶ οἱ ἀγαθοὶ ὡσαύτως... καὶ οὐ πρότερον οἷός τε ποιεῖν, πρὶν ἂν ἔνθεός τε γένηται καὶ ἔκφρων καὶ ὁ νοῦς μηκέτι ἐν αὐτῷ ἐνῇ.

MADNESS OF THE MUSES

18. For the authors of those great poems which we admire, do not attain to excellence through the rules of any art, but they utter their beautiful melodies of verse in a state of inspiration, and, as it were, possessed by a spirit not their own. Thus the composers of lyrical poetry create those admired songs of theirs in a state of divine insanity. [Nor can a poet] compose anything worth calling poetry until he becomes inspired, and, as it were, mad, or whilst any reason remains in him.

tr. B. P. Shelley

PLATO, Io 534 C.

19. ὁ θεὸς ἐξαιρούμενος τούτων τὸν νοῦν τούτοις χρῆται ὑπηρέταις καὶ τοῖς χρησμῳδοῖς καὶ τοῖς μάντεσι τοῖς θείοις, ἵνα ἡμεῖς οἱ ἀκούοντες εἰδῶμεν, ὅτι οὐχ οὗτοί εἰσιν οἱ ταῦτα λέγοντες οὕτω πολλοῦ ἄξια, οἷς νοῦς μὴ πάρεστιν, ἀλλ' ὁ θεὸς αὐτός ἐστιν ὁ λέγων, διὰ τούτων δὲ φθέγγεται πρὸς ἡμᾶς. ... οὐκ ἀνθρώπινά ἐστι τὰ καλὰ ταῦτα ποιήματα οὐδὲ ἀνθρώπων, ἀλλὰ θεῖα καὶ θεῶν, οἱ δὲ ποιηταὶ

19. The God seems purposely to have deprived all poets, prophets and soothsayers of every particle of reason and understanding, the better to adapt them to their employment as his ministers and interpreters; and that we, their auditors, may acknowledge that those who write so beautifully, are possessed, and address us, inspired by the God... And, thus, it appears to me that the God proves beyond

οὐδὲν ἀλλ' ἢ ἑρμηνεῖς εἰσὶ τῶν θεῶν, κατεχόμενοι ἐξ ὅτου ἂν ἕκαστος κατέχηται.

doubt, that these transcendent poems are not human as the work of men, but divine as coming from the God. Poets, then, are the interpreters of the divinities—each being possessed by some one deity...

tr. B. P. Shelley

PLATO, Phaedrus 245 A.

20. ῞Ος δ' ἂν ἄνευ μανίας Μουσῶν ἐπὶ ποιητικὰς θύρας ἀφίκηται, πεισθεὶς ὡς ἄρα ἐκ τέχνης ἱκανὸς ποιητὴς ἐσόμενος, ἀτελὴς αὐτός τε καὶ ἡ ποίησις ὑπὸ τῆς τῶν μαινομένων ἡ τοῦ σωφρονοῦντος ἠφανίσθη.

20. But if any man comes to the gates of poetry without the madness of the Muses, persuaded that skill alone will make him a good poet, then shall he and his works of sanity with him be brought to nought by the poetry of madness and behold, their place is nowhere to be found.

tr. R. Hackforth

PLATO, Phaedrus 249 D.

21. ῎Εστι δὴ οὖν δεῦρο ὁ πᾶς ἥκων λόγος περὶ τῆς τετάρτης μανίας, ἣν ὅταν τὸ τῇδέ τις ὁρῶν κάλλος, τοῦ ἀληθοῦς ἀναμιμνησκόμενος, πτερῶταί τε καὶ ἀναπτερούμενος προθυμούμενος ἀναπτέσθαι, ἀδυνατῶν δέ, ὄρνιθος δίκην βλέπων ἄνω, τῶν κάτω δὲ ἀμελῶν, αἰτίαν ἔχει ὡς μανικῶς διακείμενος· ὡς ἄρα αὕτη πασῶν τῶν ἐνθουσιάσεων ἀρίστη.

IDEAL BEAUTY

21. Mark therefore the sum and substance of all our discourse touching the fourth sort of madness..., such as one, as soon as he beholds the beauty of this world, is reminded of true beauty, and his wings begin to grow; then is he fain to lift his wings and fly upward; yet he has not the power, but inasmuch as he gazes upward like a bird, and cares nothing for the world beneath, men charge it upon him that he is demented. Of all frenzies this is the best.

tr. R. Hackforth

PLATO, Respublica 601 D.

22. περὶ ἕκαστον ταύτας τινὰς τρεῖς τέχνας εἶναι, χρησομένην, ποιήσουσαν, μιμησομένην.

DIVISION OF THE ARTS

22. ...there are three arts concerned with any object—the art of using it, the art of making it, and the art of representing it.

tr. F. M. Cornford

PLATO, Sophista 219 A.

23. Ἀλλὰ μὴν τῶν γε τεχνῶν πασῶν σχεδὸν εἴδη δύο... γεωργία μὲν καὶ ὅση περὶ τὸ θνητὸν πᾶν σῶμα θεραπεία, τό τε αὖ περὶ τὸ ξύνθετον καὶ πλαστόν, ὃ δὴ σκεῦος ὠνομάκαμεν, ἥ τε μιμητική, ξύμπαντα ταῦτα δικαιότατ' ἑνὶ προσαγορεύοιτ' ἂν ὀνόματι.

23. But of all arts there are, speaking generally, two kinds... Agriculture and all kinds of care of any living beings, and that which has to do with things which are put together or moulded (utensils we call them) and the art of imitation—all these might properly be called by one name.

tr. H. N. Fowler

PLATO, Leges 798 D.

24. ἐλέγομεν, ὡς τὰ περὶ τοὺς ῥυθμοὺς καὶ πᾶσαν μουσικήν ἐστι τρόπων μιμήματα βελτιόνων καὶ χειρόνων ἀνθρώπων.

IMITATIVE ART

24. When we said that rhythms and music generally are a reproduction expressing the moods of better or worse men.

tr. A. E. Taylor

PLATO, Leges 655 D.

25. ἐπειδὴ μιμήματα τρόπων ἐστὶ τὰ περὶ τὰς χορείας, ἐν πράξεσί τε παντοδαπαῖς γιγνόμενα καὶ τύχαις καὶ ἤθεσι μιμήσεσι διεξιόντων ἑκάστων οἷς μὲν ἂν πρὸς τρόπου τὰ ῥηθέντα ἢ μελῳδηθέντα ἢ καὶ ὁπωσοῦν χορευθέντα ᾖ... τούτους μὲν καὶ τούτοις χαίρειν.

25. A choric exhibition is mimic presentation of manners with all variety of action and circumstances, enacted by performers who depend on characterization and impersonation. Hence those who... find words, melodies or other presentations of the choir to their taste cannot but enjoy... the performance.

tr. A. E. Taylor

PLATO, Respublica 597 D.

26. Ἦ καὶ τὸν ζωγράφον προσαγορεύωμεν δημιουργὸν καὶ ποιητὴν τοῦ τοιούτου; Οὐδαμῶς... Τοῦτο, ἔμοιγε δοκεῖ μετριώτατ' ἂν προσαγορεύεσθαι μιμητὴς οὗ ἐκεῖνοι δημιουργοί... Τοῦτ' ἄρα ἔσται καὶ ὁ τραγῳδιοποιός, εἴπερ μιμητής ἐστι.

26. Can we also call the painter a performer and maker?
Certainly not...
I think it would be fairest to describe him as the artist who represents the things which the other two make...
The tragic poet, too, is an artist who represents things...

tr. F. M. Cornford

PLATO, Sophista 267 A.

27. Τὸ τοίνυν φανταστικὸν αὖθις διορίζωμεν δίχα... Τὸ μὲν δι' ὀργάνων γιγνόμενον, τὸ δὲ αὐτοῦ παρέχοντος ἑαυτὸν ὄργανον τοῦ ποιοῦντος τὸ φάντασμα... Ὅταν, οἶμαι, τὸ σὸν σχῆμά τις τῷ ἑαυτοῦ χρώμενος σώματι προσόμοιον ἢ φωνὴν φαίνεσθαι ποιῇ, μίμησις τοῦτο τῆς φανταστικῆς μάλιστα κέκληταί που.

27. Let us, then, again bisect the fantastic art... One kind is that produced by instruments, the other that in which the producer of the appearance offers himself as the instrument... When anyone, by employing his own person as his instrument, makes his own figure or voice seem similar to yours, that kind of fantastic art is called mimetic.

tr. H. N. Fowler

PLATO, Respublica 606 D.

28. ποιητικὴ μίμησις... τρέφει γὰρ ταῦτα ἄρδουσα, δέον αὐχμεῖν, καὶ ἄρχοντα ἡμῖν καθίστησι, δέον ἄρχεσθαι αὐτά, ἵνα βελτίους τε καὶ εὐδαιμονέστεροι ἀντὶ χειρόνων καὶ ἀθλιωτέρων γιγνώμεθα.

28. ...poetic representation... waters the growth of passions which should be allowed to wither away and sets them up in control, although the goodness and happiness of our lives depend on their being held in subjection.

tr. F. M. Cornford

PLATO, Sophista 265 B.

29. ἡ ... μίμησις ποίησις τίς ἐστιν, εἰδώλων μέντοι.

MIMESIS

29. Imitative art is a kind of production—of images... not of real things.

tr. H. N. Fowler

PLATO, Sophista 235 D—236 C.

30. ΞΕ. φαίνομαι δύο καθορᾶν εἴδη τῆς μιμητικῆς... Μίαν μὲν τὴν εἰκαστικὴν ὁρῶν ἐν αὐτῇ τέχνην. ἔστι δ' αὕτη μάλιστα, ὁπόταν

30. STRANGER: I think I see this time also two classes of imitation... I see the likeness-making art as one part of imitation. This

κατὰ τὰς τοῦ παραδείγματος συμμετρίας τις ἐν μήκει καὶ πλάτει καὶ βάθει, καὶ πρὸς τούτοις ἔτι χρώματα ἀποδιδοὺς τὰ προσήκοντα ἑκάστοις, τὴν τοῦ μιμήματος γένεσιν ἀπεργάζηται.

ΘΕΑΙ. Τί δ'; οὐ πάντες οἱ μιμούμενοί τι τοῦτ' ἐπιχειροῦσι δρᾶν;
ΞΕ. Οὔκουν ὅσοι γε τῶν μεγάλων πού τι πλάττουσιν ἔργων ἢ γράφουσιν. εἰ γὰρ ἀποδιδοῖεν τὴν τῶν καλῶν ἀληθινὴν συμμετρίαν, οἶσθ' ὅτι σμικρότερα μὲν τοῦ δέοντος τὰ ἄνω, μείζω δὲ τὰ κάτω φαίνοιτ' ἂν διὰ τὸ τὰ μὲν πόρρωθεν, τὰ δ' ἐγγύθεν ὑφ' ἡμῶν ὁρᾶσθαι. ἆρ' οὖν οὐ χαίρειν τὸ ἀληθὲς ἐάσαντες οἱ δημιουργοὶ νῦν οὐ τὰς οὔσας συμμετρίας, ἀλλὰ τὰς δοξούσας εἶναι καλὰς τοῖς εἰδώλοις ἐναπεργάζονται;

ΘΕΑΙ. Πάνυ μὲν οὖν.
ΞΕ. Τὸ μὲν ἄρα ἕτερον οὐ δίκαιον, εἰκὸς γε ὄν, εἰκόνα καλεῖν;

ΘΕΑΙ. Ναί.
ΞΕ. Καὶ τῆς γε μιμητικῆς τὸ ἐπὶ τούτῳ μέρος κλητέον, ὅπερ εἴπομεν ἐν τῷ πρόσθεν, εἰκαστικήν;

ΘΕΑΙ. Κλητέον.
ΞΕ. Τί δέ; τὸ φαινόμενον μὲν διὰ τὴν ἀκολουθίαν ἐοικέναι τῷ καλῷ, δύναμιν δὲ εἴ τις λάβοι τὰ τηλικαῦτα ἱκανῶς ὁρᾶν, μηδ' ἐοικὸς ᾧ φησὶν ἐοικέναι, τί καλοῦμεν; ἆρ' οὐκ', ἐπείπερ φαίνεται μέν, ἔοικε δὲ οὔ, φάντασμα;

ΘΕΑΙ. Τί μήν;
ΞΕ. Οὐκοῦν πάμπολυ καὶ κατὰ τὴν ζωγραφίαν τοῦτο τὸ μέρος ἐστὶ καὶ κατὰ ξύμπασαν μιμητικήν;

ΘΕΑΙ. Πῶς δ' οὔ;
ΞΕ. Τὴν δὴ φάντασμα ἀλλ' οὐκ εἰκόνα ἀπεργαζομένην τέχνην ἆρ' οὐ φανταστικὴν ὀρθότατ' ἂν προσαγορεύοιμεν;

ΘΕΑΙ. Πολύ γε.
ΞΕ. Τούτω τοίνυν τὼ δύο ἔλεγον εἴδη τῆς εἰδωλοποιϊκῆς, εἰκαστικὴν καὶ φανταστικήν.

ΘΕΑΙ. Ὀρθῶς.

is met with, as a rule, whenever anyone produces imitation by following the proportions of the original in length, breadth, and depth, and giving, besides, the appropriate colours to each part.

THEAETETUS: Yes, but do not all imitators try to do this?
STR: Not those who produce some large work of sculpture or painting. For if they reproduced the true proportions of beautiful forms, the upper parts, as you know, would seem smaller and the lower parts larger than they ought, because we see the former from a distance, the latter from near at hand. Is it not the case, therefore, that makers do not care about truth and give their images not those proportions which actually exist but those which will seem beautiful?

THEAET: Certainly.
STR: That, then, which is other, but like, we may fairly call a likeness, may we not?

THEAET: Yes.
STR: And the part of imitation which is concerned with such things, is to be called, as we called it before, likeness-making?

THEAET: It is to be so called.
STR: Now then, what shall we call that which appears, because it is seen from an unfavourable position, to be like the beautiful, but which would not even be likely to resemble that which it claims to be like, if a person were able to see such large works adequately? Shall we not call it, since it appears, but is not like, an appearance?

THEAET: Certainly.
STR: And to the art which produces appearance, but not likeness, the most correct name we could give would be "fantastic art", would it not?

THEAET: By all means.
STR: These, then, are the two forms of the image-making art that I meant, the likeness-making and the fantastic.

THEAET: You are right.

tr. H. N. Fowler

PLATO, Respublica 601 D.

31. Οὐκοῦν ἀρετὴ καὶ κάλλος καὶ ὀρθότης ἑκάστου σκεύους καὶ ζώου καὶ πράξεως οὐ πρὸς ἄλλο τι ἢ τὴν χρείαν ἐστί, πρὸς ἣν ἂν ἕκαστον ᾖ πεποιημένον ἢ πεφυκός;

ORTHOTES

31. May we not say... that the excellence or beauty or rightness of any implement or living creature or action has reference to the use for which it is made or designed by nature? Yes.

tr. F. M. Cornford

PLATO, Phaedrus 264 C.

32. δεῖν πάντα λόγον ὥσπερ ζῷον συνεστάναι σῶμά τι ἔχοντα αὐτὸν αὑτοῦ, ὥστε μήτε ἀκέφαλον εἶναι μήτε ἄπουν. ἀλλὰ μέσα τε ἔχειν καὶ ἄκρα, πρέποντ' ἀλλήλοις καὶ τῷ ὅλῳ γεγραμμένα.

32. ...any discourse ought to be constructed like a living creature, with its own body, as it were; it must not lack either head or feet; it must have a middle and extremities so composed as to suit each other and the whole work.

tr. R. Hackforth

PLATO, Respublica 420 D.

33. μὴ οἴου δεῖν ἡμᾶς οὕτω καλοὺς ὀφθαλμοὺς γράφειν, ὥστε μηδὲ ὀφθαλμοὺς φαίνεσθαι, μηδ' αὖ τἆλλα μέρη, ἀλλ' ἄθρει εἰ τὰ προσήκοντα ἑκάστοις ἀποδιδόντες τὸ ὅλον καλὸν ποιοῦμεν.

33. Really, you must not expect us to paint eyes so handsome as not to look like eyes at all. This applies to all the parts: the question is whether by giving each its proper colour, we make the whole beautiful.

tr. F. M. Cornford

PLATO, Respublica 403 C.

34. δεῖ δέ που τελευτᾶν τὰ μουσικὰ εἰς τὰ τοῦ καλοῦ ἐρωτικά.

ART AND BEAUTY

34. Then is not our account of education in poetry and music now complete? It has ended where it ought to end, in the love of beauty.

tr. F. M. Cornford

PLATO, Respublica 472 D.

35. Οἴει ἂν οὖν ἧττόν τι ἀγαθὸν ζωγράφον εἶναι, ὃς ἂν γράψας παράδειγμα, οἷον ἂν εἴη ὁ κάλλιστος ἄνθρωπος, καὶ πάντα εἰς τὸ γράμμα ἱκανῶς ἀποδοὺς μὴ ἔχῃ ἀποδεῖξαι, ὡς καὶ δυνατὸν γενέσθαι τοιοῦτον ἄνδρα;

ART NOT NECESSARILY IMITATIVE

35. Then suppose a painter had drawn an ideally beautiful figure complete to the last touch, would you think any the worse of him, if he could not show that a person as beautiful as that could exist?

tr. F. M. Cornford

PLATO, Politicus 288 C.

36. τὸ περὶ τὸν κόσμον καὶ γραφικὴν ... καὶ ὅσα ταύτῃ προσχρώμενα καὶ μουσικῇ μιμήματα τελεῖται, πρὸς τὰς ἡδονὰς μόνον ἡμῶν ἀπειργασμένα, δικαίως δ' ἂν ὀνόματι περιληφθέντα ἑνί... παίγνιόν πού τι λέγεται... τοῦτο τοίνυν τούτοις ἓν ὄνομα ἅπασι πρέψει προσαγορευθέν· οὐ γὰρ σπουδῆς οὐδὲν αὐτῶν χάριν, ἀλλὰ παιδιᾶς ἕνεκα πάντα δρᾶται.

ART AS AMUSEMENT

36. ...that [concerning] ornamentation and painting and all the imitations created by the use of painting and music solely for our pleasure and properly included under one name... is called by some such name as plaything... So this one name will properly be applied to all the members of this class; for none of them is practised for any serious purpose, but all of them merely for play.

tr. H. N. Fowler

PLATO, Respublica 598 A.

37. κλίνη, ἐάν τε ἐκ πλαγίου αὐτὴν θεᾷ ἐάν τε καταντικρὺ ἢ ὁπῃοῦν, μή τι διαφέρει αὐτὴ ἑαυτῆς... φαίνεται δὲ ἀλλοία; καὶ τἆλλα ὡσαύτως; ... πρὸς πότερον ἡ γραφικὴ πεποίηται περὶ ἕκαστον; πότερα πρὸς τὸ ὄν, ὡς ἔχει, μιμήσασθαι, ἢ πρὸς τὸ φαινόμενον, ὡς φαίνεται, φαντάσματος ἢ ἀληθείας οὖσα μίμησις; Φαντάσματος... Πόρρω ἄρα που τοῦ ἀληθοῦς ἡ μιμητική ἐστι.

CONDEMNATION OF THE ARTS

37. ...you may look at a bed... from straight in front or slantwise or at any angle. Is there then any difference in the bed itself, or does it merely look different?
It only looks different.
Well, that is the point. Does painting aim at reproducing any actual object as it is, or the appearance of it as it looks? In other words, is it a representation of the truth or of a semblance?
Of a semblance.
The art of representation, then, is a long way from reality...
tr. F. M. Cornford

PLATO, Respublica 603 A.

38. ἡ γραφικὴ καὶ ὅλως ἡ μιμητικὴ πόρρω μὲν τῆς ἀληθείας ὂν τὸ αὑτῆς ἔργον ἀπεργάζεται, πόρρω δ' αὖ φρονήσεως ὄντι τῷ ἐν ἡμῖν προσομιλεῖ τε καὶ ἑταίρα καὶ φίλη ἐστὶν ἐπ' οὐδενὶ ὑγιεῖ οὐδ' ἀληθεῖ... Φαύλη ἄρα φαύλῳ ξυγγιγνομένη φαῦλα γεννᾷ ἡ μιμητική... Πότερον... ἡ κατὰ τὴν ὄψιν μόνον, ἢ καὶ κατὰ τὴν ἀκοήν, ἣν δὴ ποίησιν ὀνομάζομεν;

38. Paintings and works of art in general are far removed from reality, and the element in our nature which is accessible to art and responds to its advances is equally far from wisdom. The offspring of a connexion thus formed on no true or sound basis must be as inferior as the parents. This will be true not only of visual art, but of art addressed to the ear, poetry as we call it.
tr. F. M. Cornford

PLATO, Respublica 605 A.

39. Ὁ δὲ μιμητικὸς ποιητὴς ... καὶ τιθεῖμεν ἀντίστροφον αὐτὸν τῷ ζωγράφῳ; καὶ γὰρ ... καὶ τῷ πρὸς ἕτερον τοιοῦτον ὁμιλεῖν τῆς ψυχῆς, ἀλλὰ μὴ πρὸς τὸ βέλτιστον, καὶ ταύτῃ ὡμοίωται· καὶ οὕτως ἤδη ἂν ἐν δίκῃ οὐ παραδεχοίμεθα εἰς μέλλουσαν εὐνομεῖσθαι πόλιν ... ταὐτὸν καὶ τὸν μιμητικὸν ποιητὴν φήσομεν κακὴν πολιτείαν ἰδίᾳ ἑκάστου τῇ ψυχῇ ἐμποιεῖν, τῷ ἀνοήτῳ αὐτῆς χαριζόμενον καὶ οὔτε τὰ μείζω οὔτε τὰ ἐλάττω διαγιγνώσκοντι, ἀλλὰ τὰ αὐτὰ τοτὲ μὲν μεγάλα ἡγουμένῳ, τοτὲ δὲ σμικρά, εἴδωλα εἰδωλοποιοῦντα, τοῦ δὲ ἀληθοῦς πόρρω πάνυ ἀφεστῶτα.

39. We have, then, a fair case against the poet and we may set him down as the counterpart of the painter, whom he resembles in two ways: his creations are poor things by the standard of truth and reality, and his appeal is not to the highest part of the soul, but to one which is equally inferior. So we shall be justified in not admitting him into a well-ordered commonwealth, because he stimulates and strengthens an element which threatens to undermine the reason. As a country may be given over into the power of its worst citizens while the better sort are ruined, so, we shall say, the dramatic poet sets us a vicious form of government in the individual soul: he gratifies that senseless part which cannot distinguish great and small, but regards the same things as now one, now the other; and he is an image-maker whose images are phantoms far removed from reality.
tr. F. M. Cornford

PLATO, Leges 889 A.

40. Ἔοικε, φασί, τὰ μὲν μέγιστα αὐτῶν καὶ κάλλιστα ἀπεργάζεσθαι φύσιν καὶ τύχην, τὰ δὲ σμικρότερα τέχνην, ἣν δὴ παρὰ φύσεως λαμβάνουσαν τὴν τῶν μεγάλων καὶ πρώτων γένεσιν ἔργων πλάττειν καὶ τεκταίνεσθαι πάντα τὰ σμικρότερα, ἃ δὴ τεχνικὰ πάντες προσαγορεύομεν. ... τέχνην δὲ ὕστερον ἐκ τούτων ὑστέραν γενομένην, αὐτὴν θνητὴν ἐκ θνητῶν, ὕστερα γεγεννηκέναι παιδιάς τινας ἀληθείας οὐ σφόδρα μετεχούσας, ἀλλὰ εἴδωλ' ἄττα ξυγγενῆ ἑαυτῶν, οἷ' ἡ γραφικὴ γεννᾷ καὶ μουσικὴ καὶ ὅσαι ταύταις εἰσὶ συνέριθοι τέχναι· αἱ δέ τι καὶ σπουδαῖον ἄρα γεννῶσι τῶν τεχνῶν, εἶναι ταύτας, ὁπόσαι τῇ φύσει ἐκοίνωσαν τὴν αὐτῶν δύναμιν, οἷον αὖ ἰατρικὴ καὶ γεωργικὴ καὶ γυμναστική.

40. Evidently so they say all the grandest and fairest of things are products of nature and chance, and only the more insignificant of art. Art takes over the grand primary works from the hands of nature, already formed, and then models and fashions the more insignificant, and this is the very reason why we call them "artificial"... Art, the subsequent late-born product of these causes, herself as perishable as her creators, has since given birth to toys with little real substance in them; simulacra as shadowy as the arts themselves, such as those which spring from painting, music and the other fellow crafts. Or if they are arts which really produce anything of genuine worth, they are those which lend their aid to nature like medicine, husbandry, gymnastic.

tr. A. E. Taylor

PLATO, Respublica 401 B.

CONTROL OF THE ARTS

41. Ἆρ' οὖν τοῖς ποιηταῖς ἡμῖν μόνον ἐπιστατητέον καὶ προσαναγκαστέον τὴν τοῦ ἀγαθοῦ εἰκόνα ἤθους ἐμποιεῖν τοῖς ποιήμασιν ἢ μὴ παρ' ἡμῖν ποιεῖν;

41. Then we must... compel our poets, on pain of expulsion, to make their poetry the express image of noble character...

tr. F. M. Cornford

PLATO, Respublica 424 B.

42. παρὰ πάντα αὐτὸ φυλάττωσι, τὸ μὴ νεωτερίζειν περὶ γυμναστικήν τε καὶ μουσικὴν παρὰ τὴν τάξιν. ... εἶδος γὰρ καινὸν μουσικῆς μεταβάλλειν εὐλαβητέον ὡς ἐν ὅλῳ κινδυνεύοντα· οὐδαμοῦ γὰρ κινοῦνται μουσικῆς τρόποι ἄνευ πολιτικῶν νόμων τῶν μεγίστων... Ἡ γοῦν παρανομία... ῥᾳδίως αὕτη λανθάνει παραδυμένη... ὡς ἐν παιδιᾶς γε μέρει καὶ ὡς κακὸν οὐδὲν ἐργαζομένη. ... ἠρέμα ὑπορρεῖ πρὸς τὰ ἤθη τε καὶ τὰ ἐπιτηδεύματα.

42. In short, then, those who keep watch over our commonwealth must take the greatest care not to overlook the least infraction of the rule against any innovation upon the established system of education either of the body or of the mind. ...such innovation is not to be commended, nor should the poet be so understood. The introduction of novel fashions in music is a thing to beware of as endangering the whole fabric of society, whose most important conventions are unsettled by any revolution in that quarter.

tr. F. M. Cornford

PLATO, Leges 660 A.

43. τὸν ποιητικὸν ὁ ὀρθὸς νομοθέτης ἐν τοῖς καλοῖς ῥήμασι καὶ ἐπαινετοῖς πείσει τε καὶ ἀναγκάσει μὴ πείθων, τὰ τῶν σωφρόνων τε καὶ ἀνδρείων καὶ πάντως ἀγαθῶν ἀνδρῶν ἔν τε ῥυθμοῖς σχήματα καὶ ἐν ἁρμονίαις μέλη ποιοῦντα ὀρθῶς ποιεῖν.

43. A true law-giver likewise will persuade or, if persuasion fails, will compel the man of poetic gifts to compose as he ought, to employ his noble and fine-filed phrases to represent by their rhythms the bearing and by their melodies the strains of men who are pure, valiant and, in a word, good.

ΚΛ. Νῦν οὖν οὕτω δοκοῦσί σοι, πρὸς Διός, ὦ ξένε, ἐν ταῖς ἄλλαις πόλεσι ποιεῖν; ἐγὼ μὲν γὰρ καθ' ὅσον αἰσθάνομαι, πλὴν παρ' ἡμῖν ἢ παρὰ Λακεδαιμονίοις, ἃ σὺ νῦν λέγεις, οὐκ οἶδα πραττόμενα, καινὰ δὲ ἄττα ἀεὶ γιγνόμενα περί τε τὰς ὀρχήσεις καὶ περὶ τὴν ἄλλην μουσικὴν ξύμπασαν, οὐχ ὑπὸ νόμων μεταβαλλόμενα ἀλλ' ὑπό τινων ἀτάκτων ἡδονῶν, πολλοῦ δεουσῶν τῶν αὐτῶν εἶναι καὶ κατὰ ταὐτά, ὡς σὺ κατ' Αἴγυπτον ἀφερμηνεύεις, ἀλλ' οὐδέποτε τῶν αὐτῶν.

CLIN: Great God! Sir, do you imagine that is how poetry is actually produced in other cities? As far as my own observation goes, I know of no such practice as you recommend, except here at home, or in Lacedaemon; elsewhere I notice endless innovations in dancing and all branches of music generally, constant change, inspired not by the laws but by a sort of unregulated taste which is so far from being fixed and permanent, as is the case of Egypt by your account, that it never shows any constancy.

tr. A. E. Taylor

PLATO, Respublica 607 B.

44. παλαιὰ μέν τις διαφορὰ φιλοσοφίᾳ τε καὶ ποιητικῇ· ... ὡς ξύνισμέν γε ἡμῖν αὐτοῖς κηλουμένοις ὑπ' αὐτῆς· ἀλλὰ γὰρ τὸ δοκοῦν ἀληθὲς οὐχ ὅσιον προδιδόναι.

ART AND PHILOSOPHY

44. ...there is a long-standing quarrel between poetry and philosophy... we for our part should welcome it [poetry] back, being ourselves conscious of its charm; only it would be a sin to betray what we believe to be the truth.

tr. F. M. Cornford

10. The Aesthetics of Aristotle

1. ARISTOTLE'S WRITINGS ON AESTHETICS. Ancient bibliographies list several treatises on the theory of art by the great Aristotle (384–323): *On Poets, Homeric Questions, On Beauty, On Music* and *Questions Concerning Poetics*. These, however, are lost and only the *Poetics* survives. Even this is probably incomplete. Old bibliographies speak of two books. Only one of these remains, however, a rather short book which, apart from a general introduction, contains only a theory of tragedy.

In spite of our incomplete legacy, Aristotle's *Poetics* has a special place in the history of aesthetics. It is the oldest surviving treatise of any significant length. It is a professional treatise dealing with very specialized problems of plot and poetic language, but it also contains general observations on aesthetics. It was probably intended to be delivered as a series of lectures and was a draft of another dissertation no longer extant. The *Poetics* was not published in Aristotle's lifetime.

Apart from the *Poetics* Aristotle also commented on aesthetics in works devoted to other subjects. The most numerous comments are found in Book III of the *Rhetoric*, where problems of style are discussed, and in Book VIII of the *Politics*, where in chapters 3–7 Aristotle presents his views on music in the course of drawing up a programme of education. Books I and III of the *Politics* also touch on aesthetic questions. Some chapters of the *Problems* are devoted to the aesthetics of music. This work is not by Aristotle himself however, but by his disciples. His remarks on beauty and art in the *Physics* and *Metaphysics* are mostly scattered in single sentences, but these are full of significance. The two *Ethics*, particularly the *Eudemian Ethics*, speak of aesthetic experience.

In Aristotle's aesthetic works detailed special discussions predominate over general philosophical discussions. They deal with tragedy or music, rather than with beauty or poetry in general. Still, some of the theses which Aristotle applied only to tragedy or only to music, have later proved to be general truths applying to art as a whole.

2. PRECURSORS. Aristotle's precursors in aesthetic studies were, on the one hand, philosophers (Gorgias, Democritus and Plato) and, on the other, artists (who formulated working rules on the object of their art). But not one before Aristotle investigated aesthetics so systematically. It was he who led aesthetics, to use a Kantian phrase, onto a secure path of knowledge. The development of a science is a constant process, and it is dangerous to name one particular time as the point where the science began. However, the history of aesthetics may be divided into "prehistory" and "history". Aristotle may be located between these because he replaced more or less loose inquiries with a coherent discipline.

Aristotle's closest and most important precursor and teacher was Plato, and it is only natural that there should have been similarities in their perspectives. It has even been said that Aristotle's aesthetics contains nothing that is not already in Plato. This is not true. Aristotle broke away from the metaphysical framework which was the basis of Plato's aesthetics. He partly systematized, partly changed Plato's aesthetic ideas, and partly developed what in Plato were only allusions and outlines.

Aristotle based his aesthetic ideas on the poetry and art of his country and his age: on the poetry of Sophocles and Euripides, on the painting of Polygnotus and Zeuxis. However, the sculptors whom he most esteemed, Phidias and Polyclitus, were both of a slightly older generation than Aristotle's own. This was also true of the great painters whom he valued most and the great tragedians on whose works he based his *Poetics*. Thus Aristotle's aesthetics was influenced by this contemporary art which had already gained general acceptance. It was the same art and poetry which Plato knew, but Aristotle's attitude toward it was different from Plato's. Whereas Plato condemned art and poetry because they did not fit into his ideology, Aristotle adapted his aesthetics to the established practice.

3. THE CONCEPT OF ART. Aesthetic investigation may be centred either in the concept of beauty or the concept of art. While Plato gave priority to the concept of beauty, Aristotle, according to Zeller, "at the beginning of his *Poetics* has put aside the concept of beauty and launched upon the study of art". The relatively concrete and explicit fact of art attracted him more than the rather vague concept of beauty.

Aristotle's concept of art—*techne*—was not new. But although he maintained the concept then generally in use, he defined it precisely. Art was primarily characterized as a *human* activity. Aristotle formulated this principle thus: "from art proceed the things of which the form is in the soul"[1] and "has its efficient cause in the maker and not in itself".[2] Hence its products are capable "of either being or not being", while the products of Nature come about of necessity.

More precisely, human activities are threefold in character: they are either investigation, or action, or production. As production, art differs from both investigation and action chiefly because it leaves behind a product. A picture is the product of painting, and a statue is the product of sculpting. More specifically still, all art is production, but not all production is art. According to Aristotle's formulation, the latter is so only when "production is conscious and based on knowledge". Thus the *genus* to which art belongs is that of *production*, and its *differentia* is its basis in knowledge and general rules. Since this knowledge uses rules, art may also be defined as a conscious production. It follows from this definition that production based solely on instinct, on experience or practice, is *not* art since it lacks rules and a conscious application of means to ends. Only he who knows the means and the ends of his production masters art. It follows also that the arts are not limited to those which have been later called fine arts. This Aristotelian concept of art was consonant with the Greek tradition. It acquired classical status and survived for centuries.

It was not only the production itself which Aristotle called "art", but the *ability* to produce. The ability of the artist is based on *knowledge* and a familiarity with the rules of production, and this knowledge, because it is the basis of production, Aristotle called "art" as well. Later this term was also applied to the *product* of the artist's activity, but Aristotle did not use it in this sense. Production, productive ability, the knowledge necessary to production, and the thing produced were all linked together, and the meaning of the term "art" shifted easily from one to the other. The ambiguity of the Greek term *techne* was inherited by the Latin *ars* and the corresponding words in modern languages. But while for Aristotle the chief meaning of *techne* was the ability of the producer, the main reference of the mediaeval *ars* was his knowledge, and that of modern "art" his product.

Aristotle's concept of art has several characteristic features: (*a*) First, he interpreted art dynamically. He was familiar with biological studies, and as a student of living organisms, he tended to see in nature processes rather than objects. His concept of art was similarly dynamic, stressing production more than the end product. (*b*) He also emphasized the intellectual factor in art, the necessary knowledge and reasoning. There is no art without general rules. "Art arises", he wrote, "when from many notions gained by experience one universal judgment about a class of objects is produced".[3] (*c*) Furthermore, he conceived art as a psycho-physical process; though art originates in the mind of the artist, it is directed towards a natural product. (*d*) Aristotle opposed art and nature, but he drew no sharp distinction between them because both follow one aim. The purposefulness of art and nature draws them together.[3a]

In defining art as an ability, Aristotle merged it with science. He did, it is true, establish a formula to distinguish the two, saying that science has to do with being and art with becoming.[4] This formula was less influential, however, than his concept of art as an ability and as knowledge. This concept blurred the distinction between art and science to the extent that in antiquity and the Middle Ages geometry and astronomy were classified as arts.

Aristotle's concept of art survived for nearly two thousand years. Only in modern times has it undergone a change, and a change that is radical. First, "art" has acquired the narrower sense of "fine art"; second, it has come to be thought of as a product rather than as an ability or an activity; third, knowledge and rules of art have ceased to be emphasized as they were in antiquity.

A significant feature of Aristotle's method was that he did not confine himself to general deductions, but studied particular phenomena attempting to explore all their elements, constituents and variants. This was his approach to the theory of art. Though his detailed analyses belong to the history of artistic theories rather than of general aesthetics, two examples at least should be cited, the relationship between art and its material, and the conditions of art.

(*a*) Material is always necessary to art but is used in different ways. Aristotle distinguished five:[5] art either alters the shape of the material (as in the case of casting statues in bronze), or it adds material, or removes it (as in the case of statues carved in stone), or it arranges the material (as in building), or it alters it qualitatively.

(*b*) Knowledge, efficiency and inborn talent are for Aristotle three principal conditions of art. The knowledge which art requires must be general and include rules of conduct. The efficiency which the artist needs is achieved through practice. Like most Greeks, Aristotle regarded practice as an essential element in art and believed art can and should be learned. But learning will not help where there is no inborn talent, since that too is an equally essential factor of art. Aristotle's particular stress on knowledge and general rules was thus tempered by his recognition of the importance of efficiency and talent in art.

4. IMITATIVE ARTS. Aristotle was a master of classification. In classifying arts, however, he did not make what seems to be the most important distinction in the history of aesthetics, the distinction, made later, of "fine arts". Nowhere does he mention "fine arts", though it must be noted that under another name he came close to the subsequent separation of "fine arts" from "crafts".

How, then, did Aristotle divide the arts? He did not accept the Sophists' division of the arts into the useful and the pleasurable, because arts such as poetry, sculpture or music are both useful and pleasurable. They are neither exclusively one nor the other. In his classification of the arts he developed Plato's idea, pointing out first the relation between the arts and Nature. In a famous formulation, he stated that the arts either *complement* Nature with what she is unable to do, or *imitate* her in what she has done.[6] These last he called "imitative arts" (the mimetic arts) and included among them painting, sculpture, poetry and partly music, that is, the arts which later came to be described as "fine arts".

In imitation Aristotle discovered the essential feature of these arts. Imitation is not only their means, but also their aim. A painter or poet does not simply imitate reality in order to create beautiful works. His end itself is imitation. It is *mimesis* alone, Aristotle insisted, that makes a poet a poet. He even wrote that "the poet should speak as little as possible in his own person, for it is not this that makes him an imitator".[7] "Imitation" is one of the dominant concepts of Aristotle's theory. Upon it he based both the division of the arts and his definition of the particular arts. Aristotle's definition of tragedy is the classic example of this. He was convinced that imitation is a natural, inborn function of man, and therefore a cause of his activity and of his satisfaction. This explains why in art pleasure is aroused even when it imitates things which do not please in Nature.

5. THE CONCEPT OF IMITATION IN ART. What did Aristotle **mean by** "imitation"? Nowhere did he define the term. However, a definition is implicit in his works: he clearly did not mean faithful copying. He maintained first that, in imitation, artists may present reality not only as it is, but also as uglier or more beautiful. They may represent men just as they are in real life, as worse than they are, or as better than they are. In painting, Aristotle observed, Polygnotus depicted men as nobler than they are, Pauson as less noble, and Dionysius drew them true to life.[8] In another passage he wrote that since the poet is an imitator, like a painter, or any other artist he must choose one of three ways of imitating things: "as they were or are... as they are said or thought to be, or... as they ought to be".[9] Aristotle also quoted Sophocles, who said that he himself represented people as they ought to be, while Euripides presented them as they were. Aristotle held that Zeuxis was unjustifiably blamed for wanting to make his painting more perfect than his models. As Socrates had already observed, a painting may be more beautiful than Nature if it brings together her scattered charms.[10] It may be impossible, Aristotle wrote, that there should be men such as Zeuxis painted; he embellished them; but he was right to do so, because "the ideal type must surpass the reality".[11] It is possible for art to present things better (or worse) than they are; and this is different from copying.

Secondly, Aristotle's theory of imitation also departed from naturalism in that it demanded of art that it should present only those things and events which have a general significance, i.e., which are typical. In a well-known aphorism, Aristotle says that poetry is more philosophical and more profound than history because it presents what is general, while history presents what is individual.[12]

Thirdly, Aristotle held that art has to represent things and events which are necessary. "The poet's task is to speak not of what actually happened, but of what might have happened and this depends on probability and necessity." On the other hand, the artist is entitled to introduce even impossible things into his work if the goal which he has set himself demands it. Aristotle applied the concept of imitation mainly to tragedies, which were peopled by mythical heroes and took place somewhere between the human world and the divine. Here there could hardly be any question of representing reality.

Fourthly, what matters in a work of art are not particular things and events, colours and shapes, but rather their composition and harmony. Aristotle wrote that "the most beautiful colours, laid on confusedly, will not give as much pleasure as the chalk outline of a portrait".[13] This could be applied to tragedy as well. In the *Politics* he wrote: "A painter would not let his animal have its foot of disproportionately large size, even though it was an exceptionally beautiful foot..., nor yet will a trainer of choruses allow a man who sings louder and more beautifully than the whole band to be a member of it".[14] It is not the particular object which an artist imitates that matters in a work of art, but the new whole which he forms out of them.

All this indicates that Aristotle's idea of *mimesis* cannot be taken in the literal modern sense of imitation. He spoke of *mimesis* mostly in connection with his theory of tragedy, and saw it as the activity of a "mime", that is, an actor. To pretend, to create fictions and act them, is the essence of this activity, though of course it can also draw on reality and use it as a model.

Many of Aristotle's statements confirm that this is the sense in which he really understood *mimesis*. First, there is the statement that in art impossible things may be represented. Aristotle says that poetry may contain impossible things "if these are necessary to its goal". The goal then must be something other than the representation of reality. He also says elsewhere that plausible impossibilities are to be preferred in art to implausible possibilities.[15] Secondly, in discussing the "modes of imitation", Aristotle singled out rhythm, melody and language[16]—in other words, three things which are exactly what distinguishes poetry from reality. Thirdly, though Aristotle called poets imitators, he thought of them as creators. He wrote that "even if he chances to take an historical subject, he is none the less a poet".[17] And he regarded the activity of the artists as similar to that of a poet. He saw this "imitative" activity as creation, an invention of the artist who may draw upon reality, but who need not do so if he produces a work which is convincing, possible and likely.

Aristotle's *Poetics* closed the complex history of the Greek idea of imitation and of the term *mimesis*. Recall that *mimesis* meant to the Pythagoreans the expression of inner "character". Its chief domain was music. According to Democritus, it meant taking example by the workings of Nature, and was applicable to all arts, not just to the imitative ones. It was through Plato, however, that *mimesis* began to mean imitation of external things in poetry, painting and sculpture. The Pythagoreans understood "imitation" in the sense in which an actor imitates; Democritus understood it in the sense in which a pupil imitates a master. Only Plato understood *mimesis* in the sense in which a copyist imitates a model. Plato's understanding of the term left its mark on Aristotle, as can be seen in his remark that imitation pleases us because we recognize its original.⁽¹⁸⁾ On the whole, however, Aristotle remained faithful to the older meaning of imitation as the expression and presentation of characters. He cited epic and tragedy, poetry and the arts of the theatre as imitative in the same sense that music was. His understanding of imitation, different from that of modern thinkers, had two aspects: *mimesis* is the representation of reality on the one hand, and, on the other, its free expression. When speaking of *mimesis*, Plato thought of the first meaning, the Pythagoreans of the second, while Aristotle had both in mind.

In what way do imitative arts differ from other arts? Or, more specifically, in what way does poetry differ from what is not poetry? If both use similar language, how does a poem differ from a treatise? Gorgias had previously answered the question by stating that the difference lies in the metrical form of the poetry. But Aristotle knew that metric form will not turn a scientific treatise into poetry. He therefore gave a different answer; poetry is distinguished by the fact that it "imitates". He meant by this that the essential feature of poetry is expression and performance. It is both an expression of feelings and a representation of reality, though representation is here only a means and can assume various guises ranging from faithful repetition to a quite free adaptation.

A modern aesthetician would be inclined to ask what is the relation of the imitative arts to form and content. Are these arts concerned with what is imitated or with how the imitation is performed? Aristotle would probably have regarded this as an improperly posed question. He wrote that "a poet should create plot rather than verse", in other words, that poetry is concerned with *content*; but he also described poetry as diction, rhythm and melody. These constitute its *form*. It never occurred to him, any more than it did to the majority of his countrymen, that a conflict could exist between form and content, and that a choice might have to be made between the two.⁽¹⁹⁾ He did not distinguish between them.

6. ART VERSUS POETRY. Aristotle considered the following arts as "imitative": epic and tragedy, comedy and dithyrambic poetry, the flute and the cithara playing. Today we would simply refer to these as poetry and music. But Aristotle lacked these more general terms and so gave a more detailed enumeration. Although his conceptual tools were far ahead of anything his predecessors had used, there were still many that he lacked. He himself observed that he had no term to cover literary art as a whole. In Greek the term "poet" meant either every maker (in accordance with etymology), or only the maker of poems excluding prose writers. As a result of these inadequacies, Aristotle was forced to list tragedy, comedy, epic, dithyramb, etc. separately. He also lacked generic terms for music and the visual arts, and so again listed their particulars. The visual arts fitted less well into Aristotle's concept of imitative arts than did poetry and music, but the analogy proved sufficient. The list of imitative arts with which Aristotle begins his *Poetics* does not include painting or sculpture, but his other works indicate that he thought of them as belonging

to the same category. According to him, imitative arts embraced poetry, music and the visual arts.

The most significant point to notice about Aristotle's classification is that he changed the established Greek separation of art and poetry. They were separated because art was production and poetry was soothsaying. Aristotle integrated poetry with the arts. Even Plato had not counted poetry among the arts, since he thought art arose from skill and poetry arose out of "divine madness". Aristotle, however, had no faith in "divine madness". He had no patience with it even in poetry. He held that poetry is "a matter of inborn gifts rather than madness". Good poetry comes about in the same way as any other good art, through talent, skill and exercise, and is subject to rules no less than other arts. Because of this it can be the subject of a scientific study: this study is called "poetics".

Through this approach Aristotle was able to bring together poetry and the visual arts. He made it possible to include them under a single concept of art, or, more precisely, under the concept of imitative art. The old opposition of poetry and art (inspiration versus skill) was reduced by Aristotle to a distinction of two types of poets and artists: those who are guided by skill, and those who write under the spell of inspiration. Aristotle was inclined to prefer the former, since the latter easily lost control of their work.[20]

7. DIFFERENCES BETWEEN THE ARTS. Aristotle identified in a classic manner the different types of imitative arts. He showed that they differ either on account of the means employed, or on account of their objects, or on account of their methods of "imitating".

A. Rhythms, speech and melody are the *means* employed both by poetry and music, and these means are used either together or separately. For example, instrumental music employs both melody and rhythm, while the dance uses rhythms without melody. By means of rhythmical movements of the body, dance portrays characters, feelings and actions. Some arts, such as tragedy, comedy and dithyramb, employ all three means.

B. As far as the *objects* imitated were concerned, the most important division for Aristotle was the one already cited, namely that some art portrays people as they commonly are and others either worse or better than they are. In Aristotle's time, however, art portraying average people was so insignificant that he thought of art as divided into only two extreme types: the noble and the vulgar, represented respectively by tragedy and comedy.

C. In considering the *methods* of imitation peculiar to the literary art, Aristotle stressed two: that the author either speaks directly or makes his heroes speak. He considered this duality to be represented by *epic* and *dramatic* art respectively.

8. PURGATION THROUGH ART. Aristotle's view of imitative art finds succinct expression in his famous definition of tragedy: "Tragedy, then, is an imitation of an action that is serious, complete, and of a certain magnitude; in language embellished with each kind of artistic ornament, the several kinds being found in separate

parts of the play; in the form of action, not narrative; through pity and fear effecting the proper purgation of these emotions".[21] We can distinguish eight elements in this definition. 1. Tragedy is imitative portrayal, 2. employs speech, 3. uses ornate speech, 4. has as its object a serious action, 5. imitates by means of the utterances of people in action, 6. must have a certain magnitude, 7. acts in such a way as to arouse pity and fear and 8. brings about the purging of these emotions.

Aristotle's *Poetics* also included a theory of comedy but this section of it has not survived. However, an early mediaeval MS, the so-called *Tractatus Coislinianus** of the tenth century, contains a definition of comedy which is a counterpart of Aristotle's definition of tragedy and is derived from it. The gist of it is as follows: "Comedy is the imitative portrayal of a comic and imperfect action... which through pleasure and laughter brings about the purging of these passions".

Some elements of these definitions concern only poetics, but "purging" (*katharsis*) and "imitation" (*mimesis*) have a general application in aesthetics, since they define the aim and effects of art. In his definition, however, Aristotle mentioned "purging" only briefly and obscurely, never returning to it again. His meagre statement on this significant matter has led to extended dispute.

The primary point of dispute has been whether by "purging" Aristotle meant the purification *of* the emotions or the purging of the mind *from* those emotions. Did he refer to a sublimation or a discharge of emotions, to their improvement or to emancipation from them? The first interpretation was accepted for a long time, but today historians agree that the second meaning of "purging" is the one intended in the *Poetics*. Aristotle did not mean that tragedy ennobles and perfects the spectator's emotions, but that it discharges them. Through it the spectator rids himself of the excess of those emotions which trouble him and gains internal peace. Only this interpretation can be historically justified.

Historians have also debated whether Aristotle drew his concept of "purging" from religious cults or from medicine. There is no doubt that he took a close personal interest in medicine; however, his idea of *katharsis* as well as of *mimesis*, his views of purging as well as of imitation, derived from religious ritual and Pythagorean views. Aristotle had taken over a traditional doctrine and given it a different interpretation: he saw the purging of emotions as discharging, as a natural psychological and biological process.

According to Orphic and Pythagorean ideas, *katharsis* was induced by music. Aristotle endorsed this view. He divided the modes of music into ethical, practical and enthusiastic, and invested the last with the ability to release emotions and purge souls. But it was above all in poetry that he saw *katharsis* in operation. He

---

* The *Tractatus Coislinianus* is a précis of Aristotle's *Poetics*, based on a text which is fuller than the one we know, but which included some pseudo-Aristotelian passages. Its definition of comedy is just such a later work, being modelled on Aristotle's definition of tragedy, but, in the opinion of the editor of the *Tractatus*, clumsily (*inscite*) constructed. G. Kaibel, *Comicorum Graecorum fragmenta*, I, 50.

never claimed, however, that the visual arts could produce similar results. *Katharsis* was for him an effect of some, but not all, imitative arts. He distinguished a "cathartic" group among the "imitative arts"; he included in this group poetry, music and the dance. The visual arts formed another group.

9. THE AIM OF ART. We use "aim" to mean either the artist's *intention* or the *effect* of his works. One can perhaps say that Aristotle did not regard art as having an aim in the first sense, because "imitation" is a natural human impulse and is itself an aim serving no other aims. In the second sense, however, art possesses not one, but many aims.

The Pythagoreans adopted a view of art as *katharsis*; the Sophists held a hedonist view; Plato maintained that art can and should be moralistic; while Aristotle in typically conciliatory and pluralistic fashion saw some truth in all of these solutions. Art not only brings about a purging of the emotions, it also provides pleasure and entertainment. It contributes towards moral perfection. It also arouses emotions: "The aim of poetry", he wrote, "is to make things more moving". Its effects, however, go still further and deeper.

According to Aristotle, art contributes to the achievement of man's highest aim, which is *happiness*. It contributes to it through what he called *schole*, which may be best translated as "leisure".[22] Aristotle had in mind the kind of life in which man is free of mundane worries and the wearisome demands of life and can devote himself to things which are truly worthy of man, things which can be regarded not merely as means, but as ends in life. Leisure should not be wasted on common entertainment, but should be spent on *diagoge*—noble entertainment — which combines pleasure with moral beauty. The activities of the learned fall within this category: philosophy and pure knowledge are not a necessity in life, but are part of leisure and are entertainment in the noblest sense of the word. The same applies to art, which is also appropriate to leisure and which achieves that totally satisfying state in life which we call happiness.[23]

Despite all the similarities which Aristotle saw between art and nature, he realized that each yielded a different kind of pleasure. The chief reason for this is that in nature it is the objects themselves which affect us, whereas in art—representational art, that is—it is their likenesses (*eikones*). The pleasure derived from likenesses springs not only from our recognition of their resemblance to their originals but also from our appreciation of the artistry of the painter or sculptor.[24]

The question of whether children should be taught music caused Aristotle considerable difficulty. In the chapter in which he considered this problem he indicated multiple aims and effects of art. Different points of view on the teaching of music led to different conclusions. Aristotle was undecided about whether a man who could choose his occupation, should perform himself or listen to the performances of professionals.[25–25a] Although he recognized value in music, like all Greeks he scorned professional performances of it. His solution was one of compromise. One should study music in early life, he decided, but leave its later performance to professionals. In contrast with earlier, one-sided views of music, Aristotle based his opinion on the conviction that music has more than one aim.[26] He held that music contributes to the purging and therapy of the emotions, to moral improvement, the education of the mind, relaxation, ordinary entertainment and pleasure, and, last but not least, to leisure. It thus promotes a life which is both happy and worthy of man.

Although he recognized pleasure as an important element in art, Aristotle did not agree with the Sophists who thought the effects of art were confined to pleasure. The pleasures which art provides are varied—discharge of the emotions, skilful imitation, excellent execution, beautiful colours and sounds. These pleasures are intellectual as well as sensory. Because each art "creates the kind of pleasure that is proper to it", the type of pleasure produced depends on the type of art. Intellectual pleasures predominate in poetry, and sensory ones in music and visual arts. Man draws pleasure not only from that which suits him but also from that which is in itself worthy of love.

Aristotle followed Plato in distinguishing two types of beauty—the "great" and the "pleasant". The second type has, he thought, no other aim than pleasure. He observed the same duality in art. Not every art is great, and art can be good without being great.

10. THE AUTONOMY OF ART AND ARTISTIC TRUTH. Aristotle regarded art as important and serious and not the plaything Plato took it to be. He saw more mental elements in it than did Plato.

Aristotle distinguished four types of life, devoted respectively to indulgence, the acquisition of gain, politics, and contemplation. He did not list the artistic life separately, but evidently included it in the meaning of *theoria*. The Greek concept of *theoria* or the contemplative life included the life of artists and poets as much as that of philosophers and scientists. Aristotle did not think that artistic life, in the passive sense of enjoying art, could independently complete human existence, and therefore did not regard it as a separate type of life. It could, however, be a component of any of the above-mentioned four types.

In contrast with the majority of the Greeks, and in particular Plato, Aristotle admitted that art, especially poetry, is autonomous and that it is so in two ways, both in relation to moral and natural laws, both in relation to virtue and truth.

First, he wrote that different standards of correctness apply to poetry and to politics.[27] And for Aristotle rules in politics were moral rules. This shows that Aristotle believed artistic poetic truth to be different from moral truth. Second, poetry, "even when it errs may yet be right", that is, although it may err as far as reality is concerned (by not representing it faithfully), yet in its own right it may be correct. Elsewhere he wrote: "The poet who is criticized for presenting something not in accordance with the truth may reply that nevertheless he represented it in proper manner". If he gives an incorrect or impossible description, for example of a horse raising both right legs at once, he commits "a mistake which does not concern the essence of poetic art". This statement makes it clear that Aristotle believed that there are two types of error and two types of truth, or, in other words, there is an *artistic truth* different from *cognitive truth*. In the past, historians found the concept of artistic truth in Plato where in fact there was none. It is, on the contrary, found in Aristotle.

Aristotle made an even more striking statement in one of his treatises on logic: "Not all propositions are judgments", he wrote, "but only those that have truth or falsity in them. For instance, an expression of a desire is a sentence, but has neither truth nor falsity". Such forms of speech, he added, "morepro perly belong to the province of rhetoric or poetics".[28] The idea here seems to be that poetry deals with propositions which, from a cognitive point of view, are neither true nor false and whose function is other than cognition. The musical and visual arts have even less to do with truth and falsehood, since they do not employ propositions. One cannot speak, therefore, of justness and error, or of truth and falsehood in art, in a cognitive sense.

11. CRITERIA OF ART. Aristotle wrote that one may criticize poetic works under five heads. One may say that it is 1. impossible in its subject-matter, 2. contrary to reason (*alogos*), 3. pernicious, 4. contradictory, or 5. against the rules of art. These five kinds of criticism can, it seems, be reduced to three: incompatibility with 1. reason, 2. moral laws, and 3. artistic laws. Aristotle applied these criticisms only to poetic works, but they can be applied to all works of art.

The above three types of criticism correspond to the three criteria by which the value of a work of art may be judged: *logical, ethical* and specifically *artistic*. A work of art should accord with the canons of logic, with moral canons, and with its own artistic canons. Such a position demanded that the canons of logic and morality should be observed, but also assumed that every art is subject to its particular canons. The particular principle of imitative art entails whatever is necessary to make it persuasive and moving.

These three criteria of art were not, however, in Aristotle's view all of equal value. He regarded the logical criterion as relative in art and only the aesthetic criterion as absolute. Aristotle considered the demands of art should be fulfilled in all circumstances, but the demands of logic only in so far as they are not at variance with demands of art. It is a mistake to portray something which is impossible, but such an error becomes justified if the aim of the work demands it. He wrote that it is better not to commit logical errors in a work of poetry, adding however: "if this is possible". This is the most extreme statement in all classical aesthetics on the subject of the autonomy of art.

Aristotle thought of art as *universal* in two senses: first, art deals with general problems, and second, it does so in a manner accessible to everyone. Plato made similar demands on art, but thought that it does not fulfil these demands and only produces singular interpretations of individual things. Aristotle, on the other hand, valued art because he was convinced that it can have general significance, that it is not exclusively the personal vision of the artist. Although the functions of science differ from those of art, the two are linked by their universality.

Because of its universal character, art can and should be subject to rules. However, rules are no substitute for the judgments of the experienced individual. Such judgments must be taken into account in moral actions and still more in art. Not everyone is a suitable judge of art, but only those who are wise in it. Aristotle noted that artists err when they take too much account of mass audiences.

Aristotle distinguished three possible attitudes towards art: he did this in a discussion of the art of medicine, but his distinctions are applicable to all arts, including the "imitative" arts. In art, one man is a craftsman, another an artist, and a third a connoisseur.[29] This observation is remarkable both in its distinction between artists and craftsmen, and in its recognition of expertise as relevant to the understanding of art.

Aristotle did not emphasize beauty in art, though when discussing the genesis[30] of poetry he maintained that it sprang from two causes immanent in human nature: imitation, "inherent in man since childhood", and "a sense of harmony and rhythm". What Aristotle called "a sense of harmony and rhythm" was later called a sense of beauty. He himself did not express it this way because in Greek the word "beauty" had too general a meaning. Nor did he talk of creativity in art because this word and this concept were still unknown to the Greeks. However, Aristotle's comments on the genesis of art suggest that he linked with art the two ideas: of *creativity* and *beauty*. What he called "imitation" was creativity, and what he called "harmony and rhythm" was beauty.

12. A CONCEPT OF BEAUTY. Aristotle's theory of art has for a long time formed the most popular chapter in the history of aesthetics. His theory of beauty has been obscure, however, because his remarks on the subject are occasional and elliptical, and the historian is forced to reconstruct the theory from fragmentary references.

Aristotle's definition of beauty appears in the *Rhetoric*. This rather involved[31] definition can be simplified as follows: beauty is that which in itself *is valuable* and at the same time *gives pleasure*. Aristotle thus based his definition of beauty on two of its properties. First, he interpreted beauty as that whose value lies in itself and not in its effects. Second, he interpreted it as that which supplies pleasure, that is, as that which not only possesses value, but which thereby causes enjoyment or admiration. The first property ("valuable in itself") formed the *genus*, the second ("pleasurable") the *differentia* of beauty. Aristotle's definition accorded with the commonly accepted Greek idea of beauty. Aristotle did for the idea of beauty, however, what he did for that of art: he turned a more or less loose idea into a concept, and replaced older reference to intuitive apprehension by a definition. Aristotle's definition of beauty was more inclusive than the modern concept. In its universality it remained traditionally Greek. It included aesthetic beauty, but was not confined to it. This explains why appearance or form were not mentioned, but only value and pleasure.

Aristotle's thought may be also expressed thus: all beauty is goodness, but not all goodness is beauty; all beauty is pleasure, but not all pleasure is beauty; beauty is only that which is both goodness and pleasure. It is no wonder then, that Aristotle held beauty in high esteem.

Beauty is associated with pleasure but differs from utility because the value of beauty is intrinsic while the value of utility derives from results.[32-33] Some human acts, Aristotle wrote, aim to achieve the useful, but others aim exclusively at the beautiful. Men fight in order to have peace, work in order to have rest; they seek things that are necessary and indispensable, but in the last resort they act for the sake of beauty. He added: "One ought to be capable of doing what is necessary and useful, yet beauty stands higher than these".

13. ORDER, PROPORTION AND SIZE. What properties necessarily fall within Aristotle's definition of beauty? Aristotle supplied various answers to this question, but most often the old Pythagorean-Platonic one.

Both in the *Poetics*[34] and the *Politics* he wrote that beauty depends upon *taxis* and *megethos*. The first of these terms may be translated as "order" and the second as "size". In the *Methaphysics* he added a third general property of beauty, when he wrote that beauty also depended on *symmetria* (proportion).[35] According to Aristotle, then, beauty depended on size, order and proportion. But he tended to equate proportion with order, leaving only two main properties of beauty: order (or proportion) and size.

A. What he called *order*, or the most suitable arrangement, was later commonly termed "form". Although it was Aristotle who introduced the term "form" into science, he did not use it in aesthetics, because by form he understood conceptual form, that is to say, the essence of things rather than the arrangement of parts. It was not until later that the meaning of the term changed so that it could be introduced into aesthetics and even become basic to its vocabulary. Aristotle gave a quite new shade of meaning to the older concepts of order and proportion by equating them with *moderation*. This idea was known to earlier Greek philosophers, but while they applied it to morals, Aristotle applied it to beauty.

Aristotle's theory of beauty, based on the concepts of order and proportion, has a Pythagorean cast. This is not surprising: Pythagorean philosophy reached him through Plato. It suited him more than the philosophy of the Sophists,[36] although the latter was equally popular at the time. Aristotle even thought of widening the Pythagoreans mathematical explanation of the harmony of sounds to include the harmony of colours.

Nevertheless, Aristotle's view was not truly Pythagorean. He added to the doctrine of proportion the doctrine of suitability, and he emphasized the latter. He held that if certain proportions make things beautiful, they do so not because they are in themselves perfect, but because they are suitable, because they accord with the nature of things. The doctrine of proportion was Pythagorean, but the doctrine of suitability came from Socrates. Though Aristotle's writings concerning order and proportion have a Pythagorean flavour, their essential reference is closer to Socrates.

B. The idea that beauty depends on *size* was Aristotle's own. By this he meant suitable size or dimensions suitable to the given objects. He thought that larger objects please more than smaller ones. People of small build, he wrote, may have charm, but they are not beautiful.[37] On the other hand, he held that objects cannot be beautiful if they are too big: this is the consequence of the nature of human perception.

14. BEAUTY AND PERCEPTIBILITY. Here lies Aristotle's more personal tenet: only what is easily perceptible can be beautiful. When in his *Metaphysics* he discussed the properties which determine an object's beauty, he mentioned limitation (*horismenon*) along with order and proportion. Only objects of limited size can be comfortably perceived and can please the senses and the mind. In the *Poetics* and *Rhetoric* he used a special word, *eusynopton*, by which he meant that which can be well grasped by the eye.[38] This applied to all kinds of beauty, to the beauty of poetry as much as to the beauty of visible objects. "Just as objects and live creatures have to have a suitable size easily apprehended at one glance in order to be beautiful, similarly the plot of a tragedy must be of such length as can be retained in the memory." Every object, if it is to give pleasure, must be suited to the capacity of senses, imagination and memory. Trendelenburg, the nineteenth-century Aristotelian, even maintained that Aristotle introduced this new concept of perceptibility to replace the previous basic aesthetic concept of *symmetria*. Such a contention is too sweeping. Aristotle retained *symmetria* alongside perceptibility—the objective condition of beauty alongside the subjective condition. Nevertheless, he shifted the stress in aesthetics from concern with the properties of perceived things to that of the properties of perception.

Perceptibility is a condition of *unity* in a work of art. Aristotle was convinced, as were most Greeks, that unity is the source of greatest satisfaction in art. He stressed unity not only in his theory of tragedy, but also in his views on visual arts. No other element of Aristotle's theory of the arts has had until modern times such a strong influence.

15. THE RANGE AND THE CHARACTER OF BEAUTY. Aristotle saw the range of beauty as extending very widely to embrace God and man, human bodies and social bodies, things and acts, terrestrial Nature and art. And his view as to how beauty is apportioned between the two was typically Greek. First, he did not think that art had a special claim to beauty; rather, he saw beauty in Nature, because there everything has suitable proportion and size, while man, the creator of art, may easily go astray. Secondly, he saw beauty in isolated objects rather than in complicated wholes. He spoke of the beauty of human bodies, never of the beauty of landscapes. This may be connected with the Greek conviction that beauty springs from proportion and accordance, both of which are harder to find in a landscape than in a single live creature, a statue or building. This was also an expression of a specific

taste. While the Romantics preferred landscape arrangements, those of the classical period preferred isolated objects whose limit more clearly revealed their proportions, measure and unity.

Aristotle emphasized the fact that beauty is manifold and changeable. For example, the beauty of a man depends on his age. It is different in a young man and in a mature man, and different again in an old man.[38a] It cannot be otherwise if beauty resides in suitable shape. This was by no means a relativist view. Like most of the Greeks, Aristotle held beauty to be an intrinsic property of certain things. The value (*to eu*) of works of art, he wrote, lies in themselves: "let it possess a certain quality, and this is all we ask of it".[39]

Why do we value beauty? There is no explicit answer to this question in Aristotle's writings, but Diogenes Laertius, biographer of the Greek philosophers, has recorded the following statement of Aristotle: Only a blind man can ask why we try to commune with what is beautiful.[40] There can be no doubt as to the meaning of this statement. Since beauty (*ex definitione*) includes goodness as well as pleasure, it must be appreciated. No explanation is necessary. Aristotle, accordingly, did not labour the point. He observed a division, more clearly than other philosophers, between propositions which can and should be proved and explained, and propositions which are self-evident or which represent a limit of proof and explanation. He did not doubt that the value of beauty is self-evident.

16. AESTHETIC EXPERIENCE. Most references to beauty in Aristotle's writings are not simply concerned with aesthetic beauty, but with beauty in the wider Greek sense. Aristotle had no separate term for aesthetic beauty. He had such a reference in mind, however, when he wrote in the *Ethics* of delight at the sight of the beauty of men, animals, statues, colours, shapes, at the sound of singing and instrumental music, at watching actors performing, and at the fragrance of fruits, flowers and incense.[41] He also clearly stated that this delight was provoked by harmony and beauty.

It was not in the *Poetics*, but in the *Ethics*, particularly the *Eudemian Ethics*,[42] that Aristotle characterized aesthetic experience, though here too he had no specific term to denote the idea. He meant 1. a state of intensive delight, and 2. a passive state. He who experiences it feels as if he were spellbound, like one "charmed by the Sirens". 3. This experience may also have appropriate strength, but even if it is excessive, nobody objects. 4. It is an experience proper only to man. Other creatures draw their pleasures from taste and touch rather than from sight and hearing and their harmony. 5. This experience derives from the senses but does not depend on their acuteness, since the senses of other living creatures are more acute than those of man. 6. Its delight arises from the sensations themselves and not, as we would say today, from what we associate with them. For example, we enjoy smells of flowers "for their own sake", while the smells of dishes and drinks are enjoyed because they promise the pleasure of eating and drinking. There is an analogous duality in the pleasures of the eyes and the ears. This analysis indicates that, though Aristotle did not refer to it by a single term, he was aware of "aesthetic" experience.

17. SUMMARY. I. Aristotle significantly advanced the theory of art. Some of his thoughts about beauty and art were new formulations of old ideas, others were original. Among the first group were the definitions of beauty and art, the division of the arts into representational and productive, and the concepts of imitation, of the purging of emotions, and of suitable proportions.

In the second group we find the following tenets: A. The recognition of various sources of art: art arises as much out of imitation as out of harmony. B. The recognition of various aims of art, naming as most important the worthy realization of man's leisure. C. The classification, contrary to Greek tradition, of poetry as an art. D. The separation of imitative arts from the mass of other arts. E. The defence of the autonomy of art in relation both to morality and truth. (This was a break with dominant opinions in antiquity.) F. The view that beauty depends on proportion, order and good arrangement, with the addition that it depends on "perceptibility", i.e., on the capacity of a beautiful object to be apprehended at sight or in memory. G. The assertion that the value of beauty and art is intrinsic. H. The approach to a concept of "aesthetic beauty".

These tenets of Aristotle were new in his day. But they strike us, more in their content than in their formulation, as also modern. This is especially the case with tenets concerned with subjective elements in beauty, the autonomy of art, its inner truth, and with specific aesthetic satisfaction.

In his observations that subsequently led to the concept of the "fine arts", Aristotle made a major contribution to aesthetics. This he obtained through his distinction of "imitative" arts as those arts which represent life freely, render it in a general, harmonious, moving and satisfying way, and create it anew out of material supplied by reality.

II. These thoughts dominate Aristotle's aesthetics: imitation as the function of art, the purging of emotions as its effect, and the idea of suitable proportion as the source of beauty. These ideas were partly inherited and partly original. Aristotle treated them more systematically than anyone had before. He also gave them an original interpretation. He interpreted *mimesis* actively, *katharsis* biologically, and measure as moderation. But he also established a unified theory of art as a whole, in which poetry had an equal place with the visual arts and with music. And he investigated not only the general properties of art, but also the great diversity of its particular forms. Above all, he gave precision and definition to what had been hitherto only dimly sensed.

Aristotle took the majority of his problems, ideas and tenets from Plato, but in doing so he gave them an empirical and analytical meaning and turned Plato's allusions into defined propositions. He differed from Plato in his interests: he devoted more attention to art than to beauty, and he arrived at different conclusions than his great predecessor. Unlike Plato, he did not condemn art. His aesthetics did not make use of the "Idea of Beauty". It lacked Plato's intellectual and moral extremism. These two aestheticians had so much in common and differed so widely that the most conflicting conclusions about their relationship are possible. According to Finsler, for example, Aristotle owed everything to Plato and, according to Gudeman, he owed him nothing.

III. The survival of early thinkers other than Aristotle seems to have depended on the extreme and paradoxical character of their writings. Aristotle was perhaps the only aesthetician of antiquity who survived without being either extreme or paradoxical. His works, in contrast, were moderate and reasonable. In this sense Aristotle was not a spectacular thinker. It may be said, too, that he was the only restrained thinker of the period, and restrained in the sense that he was deeply conscientious and just.

One can say of certain parts of the *Poetics* that "it forms a closely-knit structure in which there is nothing to question and in which in fact no one has ever questioned anything" (Finsler). In the history of ideas, which is torn by disputes, this is an exceptional state of affairs.

IV. Aristotle's influence has been extensive. It has been said, not without justice, that one can learn more about him from his influence on the thought of others than from the fragmentary remains of his own works. The principal tenets of Aristotle's theory of art have become in time so well known that they seem obvious and therefore of little interest. Yet his thought is so rich that, despite his remarkable popularity, many of his ideas have hardly been noticed. When we discover them anew, they are strikingly fresh and excellent.

While Plato's greatest influence was in his philosophy of beauty, Aristotle's greatest influence lay in his study of art, especially through his *Poetics*. In latter antiquity and the Middle Ages, Plato was more influential than Aristotle. In modern times the balance has been corrected. Most of Aristotle's ideas have had a positive influence on the development of the theory of art and art itself. One, however, had a negative effect. This was partly due to Aristotle himself, and partly to those who adopted his ideas centuries later. Aristotle was convinced that every development has its end and that this also applies to the evolution of art and poetry. He took Greek epic and tragedy to be definitive masterpieces and regarded the theories which he based upon them as universally and eternally valid. This led his later followers to imagine that there existed eternal and unalterable forms of art; and this contributed to the inhibition of literary theory and even of literature itself.

G. Texts from Aristotle

ARISTOTLE, Metaphysica 1032b 1.

1. ἀπὸ τέχνης δὲ γίγνεται ὅσων τὸ εἶδος ἐν τῇ ψυχῇ.

CONCEPT OF ART

1. ...from art proceed the things of which the form is in the soul of the artist.

tr. J. A. Smith and W. D. Ross

ARISTOTLE, Ethica
Nicomach. 1140a 9.

2. Ταὐτὸν ἂν εἴη τέχνη καὶ ἕξις μετὰ λόγου ἀληθοῦς ποιητική. ἔστι δὲ τέχνη πᾶσα περὶ γένεσιν, καὶ τὸ τεχνάζειν, καὶ θεωρεῖν ὅπως ἂν γένηταί τι τῶν ἐνδεχομένων καὶ εἶναι καὶ μὴ εἶναι, καὶ ὧν ἡ ἀρχὴ ἐν τῷ ποιοῦντι ἀλλὰ μὴ ἐν τῷ ποιουμένῳ· οὔτε γὰρ τῶν ἐξ ἀνάγκης ὄντων ἢ γινομένων ἡ τέχνη ἐστίν, οὔτε τῶν κατὰ φύσιν.

2. It follows that an art is nothing more or less than a productive quality exercised in combination with true reason. The business of every art is to bring something into existence, and the practice of an art involves the study of how to bring into existence something which is capable of having such an existence and has its efficient cause in the maker and not in itself. This condition must be present, because the arts are not concerned with things that exist or come into existence from necessity or according to Nature...

tr. J. A. K. Thomson

ARISTOTLE, Metaphysica 981a 5.

3. γίνεται δὲ τέχνη, ὅταν ἐκ πολλῶν τῆς ἐμπειρίας ἐννοημάτων μία καθόλου γένηται περὶ τῶν ὁμοίων ὑπόληψις.

3. ...art arises, when from many notions gained by experience one universal judgment about a class of objects is produced.

tr. J. A. Smith and W. D. Ross

ARISTOTLE, Physica II 8, 199.

3a. οἷον εἰ οἰκία τῶν φύσει γινομένων ἦν οὕτως ἂν ἐγίνετο ὡς νῦν ὑπὸ τῆς τέχνης· εἰ δὲ τὰ φύσει μὴ μόνον φύσει, ἀλλὰ καὶ τέχνῃ γίγνοιτο, ὡσαύτως ἂν γίνοιτο ᾗ πέφυκεν ἕνεκα ἄρα θατέρου θάτερον.

SIMILARITY OF ART AND NATURE

3a. Had, for example, a house been a product of nature, it would be constructed in just the same way as it now is by art; and had natural objects been the products of art, they would appear as though made by nature. For in both instances every link in the chain is there for the sake of the succeeding link.

ARISTOTLE, Analytica
posteriora 100a 6.

4. ἐκ δ' ἐμπειρίας ἢ ἐκ παντὸς ἠρεμήσαντος τοῦ καθόλου ἐν τῇ ψυχῇ, τοῦ ἑνὸς παρὰ τὰ πολλά, ὃ ἂν ἐν ἅπασιν ἓν ἐνῇ ἐκείνοις τὸ αὐτό, τέχνης ἀρχὴ καὶ ἐπιστήμης, ἐὰν μὲν περὶ γένεσιν, τέχνης, ἐὰν δὲ περὶ τὸ ὄν, ἐπιστήμης.

SCIENCE AND ART

4. And experience, that is, the universal, when established as a whole in the soul—the One that corresponds to the Many, the unity that is identically present in them all—provides the starting-point of art and science: art in the world of process and science in the world of facts.

tr. H. Tredennick

ARISTOTLE, Physica 190b 5.

5. γίγνεται δὲ τὰ γιγνόμενα ἁπλῶς τὰ μὲν μετασχηματίσει, οἷον ἀνδριὰς ἐκ χαλκοῦ, τὰ δὲ προσθέσει, οἷον τὰ αὐξανόμενα, τὰ δ' ἀφαιρέσει, οἷον ἐκ τοῦ λίθου ὁ Ἑρμῆς, τὰ δὲ συνθέσει, οἷον οἰκία, τὰ δ' ἀλλοιώσει, οἷον τὰ τρεπόμενα κατὰ τὴν ὕλην.

ART AND ITS MEDIUM

5. The processes by which things "come into existence" in this absolute sense may be divided into (1) change of shape, as with the statue made of bronze, or (2) additions, as in things that grow, or (3) substractions, as when a block of marble is chipped into a Hermes,

ARISTOTLE, Physica 199a 15.

6. ὅλως τε ἡ τέχνη τὰ μὲν ἐπιτελεῖ ἃ ἡ φύσις ἀδυνατεῖ ἀπεργάσασθαι, τὰ δὲ μιμεῖται.

ARISTOTLE, Poëtica 1460a 7.

7. αὐτὸν ... δεῖ τὸν ποιητὴν ἐλάχιστα λέγειν· οὐ γάρ ἐστι κατὰ ταῦτα μιμητής.

ARISTOTLE, Poëtica 1448a, 1.

8. Ἐπεὶ δὲ μιμοῦνται οἱ μιμούμενοι πράττοντας, ἀνάγκη δὲ τούτους ἢ σπουδαίους ἢ φαύλους εἶναι... ἤτοι βελτίονας ἢ καθ' ἡμᾶς ἢ χείρονας ἢ καὶ τοιούτους, ὥσπερ οἱ γραφεῖς· Πολύγνωτος μὲν γὰρ κρείττους, Παύσων δὲ χείρους, Διονύσιος δὲ ὁμοίους εἴκαζεν... καὶ γὰρ ἐν ὀρχήσει καὶ αὐλήσει καὶ κιθαρίσει ἔστι γενέσθαι ταύτας τὰς ἀνομοιότητας, καὶ τῷ περὶ τοὺς λόγους δὲ καὶ τὴν ψιλομετρίαν, οἷον Ὅμηρος μὲν βελτίους, Κλεοφῶν δὲ ὁμοίους, Ἡγήμων δὲ ὁ Θάσιος ⟨ὁ⟩ τὰς παρῳδίας ποιήσας πρῶτος καὶ Νικοχάρης ὁ τὴν Δηλιάδα χείρους [...] ἐν ταύτῃ δὲ τῇ διαφορᾷ καὶ ἡ τραγῳδία πρὸς τὴν κωμῳδίαν διέστηκεν· ἡ μὲν γὰρ χείρους ἡ δὲ βελτίους μιμεῖσθαι βούλεται τῶν νῦν.

ARISTOTLE, Poëtica 1460b 8.

9. ἐπεὶ γάρ ἐστι μιμητὴς ὁ ποιητὴς ὡσπερανεὶ ζωγράφος ἤ τις ἄλλος εἰκονοποιός, ἀνάγκη μιμεῖσθαι τριῶν ὄντων τὸν ἀριθμὸν ἕν τι ἀεί· ἢ γὰρ οἷα ἦν ἢ ἔστιν, ἢ οἷά φασιν καὶ δοκεῖ, ἢ οἷα εἶναι δεῖ.

ARISTOTLE, Politica 1281b 10.

10. τῶν μὴ καλῶν τοὺς καλοὺς φασί [διαφέρειν] καὶ τὰ γεγραμμένα διὰ τέχνης τῶν ἀληθινῶν, τῷ συνῆχθαι τὰ διεσπαρμένα χωρὶς

or (4) combination, as in building a house, or (5) such modifications as affect the properties of the material itself.

tr. F. M. Cornford and P. H. Wicksteed

DIVISION OF THE ARTS

6. ...the arts either, on the basis of Nature, carry things further than Nature can, or they imitate Nature.

tr. F. M. Cornford and P. H. Wicksteed

IMITATIVE ARTS

7. The poet should speak as little as possible in his own person, for it is not this that makes him an imitator.

tr. S. H. Butcher

8. Since the objects of imitation are men in action, and these men must be either of a higher or lower type..., we must represent men either as better than in real life, or as worse, or as they are. It is the same in painting. Polygnotus depicted men as nobler than they are, Pauson as less noble, Dionysius drew them true to life. (...) Such diversities may be found even in dancing, flute-playing, and lyre-playing. So again in language, whether prose or verse unaccompanied by music. Homer, for example, makes men better than they are; Cleophon as they are; Hegemon the Thasian, the inventor of parodies, and Nicochares, the author of the Deiliad, worse than they are. (...) The same distinction marks off Tragedy from Comedy; for Comedy aims at representing men as worse, Tragedy as better than in actual life.

tr. S. H. Butcher

9. The poet being an imitator, like a painter or any other artist, must of necessity imitate one of three objects—things as they were or are, things as they are said or thought to be, or things as they ought to be.

tr. S. H. Butcher

ART MORE BEAUTIFUL THAN REALITY

10. ...the superiority... of handsome men, so it is said, over plain men and of the works of the painter's art over the real objects, really

εἰς ἕν, ἐπεὶ κεχωρισμένων γε κάλλιον ἔχειν τοῦ γεγραμμένου τουδὶ μὲν τὸν ὀφθαλμόν, ἑτέρου δέ τινος ἕτερον μόριον.

consists in this, that a number of scattered good points have been collected together into one example; since if the features be taken separately, the eye of one real person is more beautiful than that of the man in the picture, and some other feature of somebody else.

tr. H. Rackham

ARISTOTLE, Poëtica 1461b 12.

11. ⟨καὶ ἴσως ἀδύνατον⟩ τοιούτους εἶναι οἵους Ζεῦξις ἔγραφεν, ἀλλὰ βέλτιον· τὸ γὰρ παράδειγμα δεῖ ὑπερέχειν.

11. ...it may be impossible that there should be men such as Zeuxis painted. "Yes", we say, "but the impossible is the higher thing; for the ideal type must surpass the reality".

THE NECESSITY AND UNIVERSALITY OF ART

ARISTOTLE, Poëtica 1451a 36.

12. οὐ τὸ τὰ γενόμενα λέγειν, τοῦτο ποιητοῦ ἔργον ἐστίν, ἀλλ᾽ οἷα ἂν γένοιτο καὶ τὰ δυνατὰ κατὰ τὸ εἰκὸς ἢ τὸ ἀναγκαῖον. ὁ γὰρ ἱστορικὸς καὶ ὁ ποιητὴς οὐ τῷ ἢ ἔμμετρα λέγειν ἢ ἄμετρα διαφέρουσιν (εἴη γὰρ ἂν τὰ Ἡροδότου εἰς μέτρα τεθῆναι καὶ οὐδὲν ἧττον ἂν εἴη ἱστορία τις μετὰ μέτρου ἢ ἄνευ μέτρων). ἀλλὰ τούτῳ διαφέρει τῷ τὸ μὲν τὰ γενόμενα λέγειν, τὸν δὲ οἷα ἂν γένοιτο. διὸ καὶ φιλοσοφώτερον καὶ σπουδαιότερον ποίησις ἱστορίας ἐστίν· ἡ μὲν γὰρ ποίησις μᾶλλον τὰ καθόλου, ἡ δ᾽ ἱστορία τὰ καθ᾽ ἕκαστον λέγει.

12. ...it is not the function of the poet to relate what has happened, but what may happen, what is possible according to the law of probability or necessity. The poet and the historian differ not by writing in verse or in prose. The work of Herodotus might be put into verse, and it would still be a species of history, with metre no less than without it. The true difference is that one relates what has happened, the other what may happen. Poetry, therefore, is a more philosophical and a higher thing than history: for poetry tends to express the universal, history the particular.

tr. S. H. Butcher

ARISTOTLE, Poëtica 1450a 39.

13. παραπλήσιον γάρ ἐστι καὶ ἐπὶ τῆς γραφικῆς· εἰ γάρ τις ἐναλείψειε τοῖς καλλίστοις φαρμάκοις χύδην, οὐκ ἂν ὁμοίως εὐφράνειεν καὶ λευκογραφήσας εἰκόνα.

THE ROLE OF COMPOSITION IN ART

13. A similar fact is seen in painting. The most beautiful colours, laid on confusedly, will not give as much pleasure as the chalk outline of a portrait.

tr. S. H. Butcher

ARISTOTLE, Politica 1284b 8.

14. οὔτε γὰρ γραφεὺς ἐάσειεν ἂν τὸν ὑπερβάλλοντα πόδα τῆς συμμετρίας ἔχειν τὸ ζῷον, οὐδ᾽ εἰ διαφέροι τὸ κάλλος, οὔτε ναυπηγὸς πρύμναν ἢ τῶν ἄλλων τι μορίων τῶν τῆς νεώς· οὐδὲ δὴ χοροδιδάσκαλος τὸν μεῖζον καὶ κάλλιον τοῦ παντὸς χοροῦ φθεγγόμενον ἐάσει συγχορεύειν.

14. ...a painter would not let his animal have its foot of disproportionately large size, even though it was an exceptionally beautiful foot, nor would a ship-builder make the stern or some other part of a ship disproportionately big, nor yet will a trainer of choruses allow a man who sings louder and more beautifully than the whole band to be a member of it.

tr. H. Rackham

ARISTOTLE, Poëtica 1461b 11.

15. πρός τε γὰρ τὴν ποίησιν αἱρετώτερον πιθανὸν ἀδύνατον ἢ ἀπίθανον καὶ δυνατόν.

15. With respect to the requirements of art, a probable impossibility is to be preferred to a thing improbable and yet possible.

tr. S. H. Butcher

ARISTOTLE, Poëtica 1447a 13.

16. ἐποποιία δὴ καὶ ἡ τῆς τραγῳδίας ποίησις, ἔτι δὲ κωμῳδία καὶ ἡ διθυραμβοποιητικὴ καὶ τῆς αὐλητικῆς ἡ πλείστη καὶ κιθαριστικῆς, πᾶσαι τυγχάνουσιν οὖσαι μιμήσεις τὸ σύνολον· διαφέρουσι δὲ ἀλλήλων τρισίν, ἢ γὰρ τῷ γένει ἑτέροις μιμεῖσθαι ἢ τῷ ἕτερα ἢ τῷ ἑτέρως καὶ μὴ τὸν αὐτὸν τρόπον. ὥσπερ γὰρ καὶ χρώμασι καὶ σχήμασι πολλὰ μιμοῦνταί τινες ἀπεικάζοντες (οἱ μὲν διὰ τέχνης οἱ δὲ διὰ συνηθείας), ἕτεροι δὲ διὰ τῆς φωνῆς, οὕτω κἀν ταῖς εἰρημέναις τέχναις ἅπασαι μὲν ποιοῦνται τὴν μίμησιν ἐν ῥυθμῷ καὶ λόγῳ καὶ ἁρμονίᾳ τούτοις δ' ἢ χωρὶς ἢ μεμιγμένοις.

TYPES OF IMITATIVE ARTS

16. Epic poetry and Tragedy, Comedy also and Dithyrambic poetry, and the music of the flute and of the lyre in most of their forms, are all in their general conception modes of imitation. They differ, however, from one another in three respects—the medium, the objects, the manner or mode of imitation, being in each case distinct.

For as there are persons who, by conscious art or mere habit, imitate and represent various objects through the medium of colour and form, or again by the voice; so in the arts above mentioned, taken as a whole, the imitation is produced by rhythm, language, or "harmony", either singly or combined.

tr. S. H. Butcher

ARISTOTLE, Poëtica 1451b 27.

17. δῆλον οὖν ἐκ τούτων ὅτι τὸν ποιητὴν μᾶλλον τῶν μύθων εἶναι δεῖ ποιητὴν ἢ τῶν μέτρων, ὅσῳ ποιητής κατὰ τὴν μίμησίν ἐστιν, μιμεῖται δὲ τὰς πράξεις. κἂν ἄρα συμβῇ γενόμενα ποιεῖν, οὐδὲν ἧττον ποιητής ἐστιν· τῶν γὰρ γενομένων ἔνια οὐδὲν κωλύει τοιαῦτα εἶναι οἷα ἂν εἰκὸς γενέσθαι καὶ δυνατὰ γενέσθαι, καθ' ὃ ἐκεῖνος αὐτῶν ποιητής ἐστιν.

THE IMITATOR IS A CREATOR

17. It clearly follows that the poet or "maker" should be the maker of plots rather than of verses; since he is a poet because he imitates, and what he imitates are actions. And even if he chances to take an historical subject, he is none the less a poet; for there is no reason why some events that have actually happened should not conform to the law of the probable and possible, and in virtue of that quality in them he is their poet or maker.

tr. J. H. Freese

ARISTOTLE, Rhetorica 1371b 4.

18. ἐπεὶ δὲ τὸ μανθάνειν τε ἡδύ καὶ τὸ θαυμάζειν, καὶ τὰ τοιάδε ἀνάγκη ἡδέα εἶναι οἷον τό τε μιμητικόν ὥσπερ γραφικὴ καὶ ἀνδριαντοποιία καὶ ποιητικὴ καὶ πᾶν ὃ ἂν εὖ μεμιμημένον ᾖ, κἂν ᾖ μὴ ἡδὺ αὐτὸ τὸ μεμιμημένον· οὐ γὰρ ἐπὶ τούτῳ χαίρει, ἀλλὰ συλλογισμός ἐστιν, ὅτι τοῦτο ἐκεῖνο, ὥστε μανθάνειν τι συμβαίνει.

18. Again, since learning and admiring are pleasant, it follows that pleasure is given by acts of imitation, such as painting, sculpture, poetry, and by every skilful copy, even though the original be unpleasant; for one's joy is not in the thing itself; rather, there is a syllogism—"This is that", and so it comes that one learns something.

tr. R. C. Jebb

ARISTOTLE, Rhetorica 1405b 6.

19. κάλλος δὲ ὀνόματος τὸ μέν, ὥσπερ Λικύμνιος λέγει, ἐν τοῖς ψόφοις ἢ τῷ σημαινομένῳ, καὶ αἶσχος δὲ ὡσαύτως.

FORM AND CONTENT

19. ...the beauty or ugliness of a word consisting, as Likymnios says, either in the sound or in the sense.

tr. R. C. Jebb

ARISTOTLE, Poëtica 1455a 30.

20. πιθανώτατοι γὰρ ἀπὸ τῆς αὐτῆς φύσεως οἱ ἐν τοῖς πάθεσίν εἰσιν, καὶ χειμαίνει ὁ χειμαζόμενος καὶ χαλεπαίνει ὁ ὀργιζόμενος ἀληθινώτατα. διὸ εὐφυοῦς ἡ ποιητική ἐστιν ⟨μᾶλλον⟩ ἢ μανικοῦ· τούτων γὰρ οἱ μὲν εὔπλαστοι, οἱ δὲ ἐκστατικοί εἰσιν.

TWO TYPES OF POETS

20. Again, the poet should work out his play, to the best of his power, with appropriate gestures; for those who feel emotion are most convincing through natural sympathy with the characters they represent; and one who is agitated storms, one who is angry rages, with the most lifelike reality. Hence poetry implies either a happy gift of nature or a strain of madness. In the one case a man can take the mould of any character; in the other, he is lifted out of his proper self.

tr. S. H. Butcher

ARISTOTLE, Poëtica 1449b 24.

21. ἔστιν οὖν τραγῳδία μίμησις πράξεως σπουδαίας καὶ τελείας, μέγεθος ἐχούσης, ἡδυσμένῳ λόγῳ χωρὶς ἑκάστῳ τῶν εἰδῶν ἐν τοῖς μορίοις, δρώντων καὶ οὐ δι' ἀπαγγελίας, δι' ἐλέου καὶ φόβου περαίνουσα τὴν τῶν τοιούτων παθημάτων κάθαρσιν.

DEFINITION OF TRAGEDY

21. Tragedy, then, is an imitation of an action that is serious, complete, and of a certain magnitude; in language embellished with each kind of artistic ornament, the several kinds being found in separate parts of the play; in the form of action, not narrative; through pity and fear effecting the proper purgation of these emotions.

tr. S. H. Butcher

ARISTOTLE, Politica 1338a 13.

22. διὸ καὶ τὴν μουσικὴν οἱ πρότερον εἰς παιδείαν ἔταξαν οὐχ ὡς ἀναγκαῖον (οὐδὲν γὰρ ἔχει τοιοῦτον) οὐδ' ὡς χρήσιμον, ὥσπερ τὰ γράμματα... πρὸς πολιτικὰς πράξεις πολλάς· λείπεται τοίνυν πρὸς τὴν ἐν τῇ σχολῇ διαγωγήν, εἰς ὅπερ καὶ φαίνονται παράγοντες αὐτήν· ἣν γὰρ οἴονται διαγωγὴν εἶναι τῶν ἐλευθέρων, ἐν ταύτῃ τάττουσιν.

EFFECTS OF ART

22. Hence our predecessors included music in education not as a necessity (for there is nothing necessary about it), nor as useful (in the way in which reading and writing are useful... for many pursuits of civil life)... It remains, therefore, that it is useful as a pastime in leisure, which is evidently the purpose for which people actually introduce it, for they rank it as a form of pastime that they think proper for free men.

tr. H. Rackham

ARISTOTLE, Ethica
Nicomach. 1177b 1.

23. δόξαι τ' ἂν αὐτὴ μόνη (τέχνη θεωρητική) δι' αὑτὴν ἀγαπᾶσθαι· οὐδὲν γὰρ ἀπ' αὐτῆς γίνεται παρὰ τὸ θεωρῆσαι, ἀπὸ δὲ τῶν

CONTEMPLATION

23. Finally it may well be thought that the activity of contemplation is the only one that is praised on its own account, because nothing

πρακτῶν ἢ πλεῖον ἢ ἔλαττον περιποιούμεθα παρὰ τὴν πρᾶξιν. δοκεῖ τε ἡ εὐδαιμονία ἐν τῇ σχολῇ εἶναι· ἀσχολούμεθα γὰρ ἵνα σχολάζωμεν καὶ πολεμοῦμεν ἵν' εἰρήνην ἄγωμεν.

comes of it beyond the act of contemplation, whereas from practical activities we count on gaining something more or less over and above the mere action. Again, it is commonly believed that, to have happiness, one must have leisure; we occupy ourselves in order that we may have leisure, just as we make war for the sake of peace.

tr. J. A. K. Thomson

ARISTOTLE, De partibus animalium I 5

24. ἄτοπον, εἰ τὰς μὲν εἰκόνας αὐτῶν θεωροῦντες συνθεωροῦμεν, οἷον τὴν γραφικὴν ἢ τὴν πλαστικήν, αὐτῶν δὲ τῶν φύσει συνεστώτων μὴ μᾶλλον ἀγαπῶμεν τὴν θεωρίαν δυνάμενοί γε τὰς αἰτίας καθορᾶν... ἐν πᾶσι γὰρ τοῖς φυσικοῖς ἔνεστί τι θαυμαστόν.

THE PLEASURE OF BEHOLDING OBJECTS AS OPPOSED TO THEIR LIKENESSES

24. Likenesses of objects we behold with pleasure because at the same time we see the art which has created them, e.g. painting or sculpture; but do we not behold with greater pleasure the natural objects themselves in which we can discern causes?... Something miraculous inheres in every creation of nature.

ARISTOTLE, Politica 1339a 23.

25. καὶ τὸ ἦθος ποιόν τι ποιεῖν, ἐθίζουσαν δύνασθαι χαίρειν ὀρθῶς, ἢ πρὸς διαγωγήν τι συμβάλλεται καὶ πρὸς φρόνησιν· καὶ γὰρ τοῦτο τρίτον θετέον τῶν εἰρημένων.

THE AIM OF ART

25. [Music] has the power of giving a tone to our character by habituating us to feel pleasure in the right sort of way. There is still a third possible view—that music has some contribution to make to the cultivation of our minds and to the growth of moral wisdom.

tr. E. Barker

ARISTOTLE, Politica 1339b 4.

25a. ὁ δ' αὐτὸς λόγος κἂν εἰ πρὸς εὐημερίαν καὶ διαγωγὴν ἐλευθέριον χρηστέον αὐτῇ· τί δεῖ μανθάνειν αὐτούς, ἀλλ' οὐχ ἑτέρων χρωμένων ἀπολαύειν; ... καὶ βαναύσους καλοῦμεν τοὺς τοιούτους καὶ τὸ πράττειν οὐκ ἀνδρὸς μὴ μεθύοντος ἢ παίζοντος. ... ἡ δὲ πρώτη ζήτησίς ἐστι πότερον οὐ θετέον εἰς παιδείαν τὴν μουσικὴν ἢ θετέον, καὶ τί δύναται τῶν διαπορηθέντων τριῶν, πότερον παιδείαν ἢ παιδιὰν ἢ διαγωγήν. εὐλόγως δ' εἰς πάντα τάττεται καὶ φαίνεται μετέχειν. ἥ τε γὰρ παιδιὰ χάριν ἀναπαύσεώς ἐστι, τὴν δ' ἀνάπαυσιν ἀναγκαῖον ἡδεῖαν εἶναι (τῆς γὰρ διὰ τῶν πόνων λύπης ἰατρεία τίς ἐστιν)· καὶ τὴν διαγωγὴν ὁμολογουμένως δεῖ μὴ μόνον ἔχειν τὸ καλὸν ἀλλὰ καὶ τὴν ἡδονήν· τὸ γὰρ εὐδαιμονεῖν ἐξ ἀμφοτέρων τούτων ἐστίν. τὴν δὲ μουσικὴν πάντες εἶναι φαμεν τῶν ἡδίστων, καὶ ψιλὴν οὖσαν καὶ μετὰ μελῳδίας.

25a. And the same argument applies also if music is to be employed for refined enjoyment and entertainment; why need people learn to perform themselves instead of enjoying music played by others?... But professional musicians we speak of as vulgar people, and indeed we think it not manly to perform music, except when drunk or for fun... Our first enquiry is whether music ought not or ought to be included in education, and what is its efficacy among the three uses of it that have been discussed—does it serve for amusement or entertainment? It is reasonable to reckon it under all of these heads, and it appears to participate in them all. Amusement is for the sake of relaxation, and relaxation must necessarily be pleasant, for it is a way of curing the pain due to laborious work; also entertainment ought admittedly to be not only honourable but also pleasant, for happiness is derived from both honour and pleasure; but we all pronounce music to be one of the pleasantest things, whether instrumental or instrumental and vocal music together...

tr. H. Rackham

ARISTOTLE, Politica 1341b 38.

26. φαμὲν δ' οὐ μιᾶς ἕνεκεν ὠφελείας τῇ μουσικῇ χρῆσθαι δεῖν ἀλλὰ καὶ πλειόνων χάριν — καὶ γὰρ παιδείας ἕνεκεν καὶ καθάρσεως ... τρίτον δὲ πρὸς διαγωγήν, πρὸς ἄνεσίν τε καὶ πρὸς τὴν τῆς συντονίας ἀνάπαυσιν.

MULTIPLICITY OF AIMS IN ART

26. On the other hand, we hold that music should not be pursued for any single benefit which it can give, but for the sake of several. One is education; a second is release of emotion...; a third is the benefit of cultivation, with which may be linked that of recreation and relaxation of strain.

tr. E. Barker

ARISTOTLE, Poëtica 1460b 13.

27. οὐχ ἡ αὐτὴ ὀρθότης ἐστὶν τῆς πολιτικῆς καὶ τῆς ποιητικῆς οὐδὲ ἄλλης τέχνης καὶ ποιητικῆς. αὐτῆς δὲ τῆς ποιητικῆς διττὴ ἁμαρτία, ἡ μὲν γὰρ καθ' αὑτήν, ἡ δὲ κατὰ συμβεβηκός. εἰ μὲν γὰρ προείλετό τι μιμήσασθαι δι' ἀδυναμίαν, αὐτῆς ἡ ἁμαρτία· εἰ δὲ τῷ προελέσθαι μὴ ὀρθῶς, ἀλλὰ τὸν ἵππον ἄμφω τὰ δεξιὰ προβεβληκότα, ἢ τὸ καθ' ἑκάστην τέχνην ἁμάρτημα οἷον τὸ κατ' ἰατρικὴν ἢ ἄλλην τέχνην ἢ ἀδύνατα πεποίηται ὁποῖ' ἂν οὖν, οὐ καθ' ἑαυτήν ... πρῶτον μὲν τὰ πρὸς αὐτὴν τὴν τέχνην· ⟨εἰ⟩ ἀδύνατα πεποίηται, ἡμάρτηται· ἀλλ' ὀρθῶς ἔχει, εἰ τυγχάνει τοῦ τέλους τοῦ αὑτῆς... εἰ οὕτως ἐκπληκτικώτερον ἢ αὐτὸ ἢ ἄλλο ποιεῖ μέρος.

AUTONOMY OF ART

27. Add to this, that the standard of correctness is not the same in poetry and politics, any more than in poetry and any other art. Within the art of poetry itself there are two kinds of faults, — those which touch its essence, and those which are accidental. If a poet has chosen to imitate something, but has imitated incorrectly through want of capacity, the error is inherent in the poetry. But if the failure is due to a wrong choice—if he has represented a horse as throwing out both his off legs at once, or introduced technical inaccuracies in medicine, for example, or in any other art—the error is not essential to the poetry. (...) First as to matters which concern the poet's own art. If he describes the impossible, he is guilty of an error; but the error may be justified, if the end of the art be thereby attained (...) if, that is, the effect of this or any other part of the poem is thus rendered more striking.

tr. S. H. Butcher

ARISTOTLE, De interpretatione 17a 2.

28. ἀποφαντικὸς δὲ οὐ πᾶς, ἀλλ' ἐν ᾧ τὸ ἀληθεύειν ἢ ψεύδεσθαι ὑπάρχει, οὐκ ἐν ἅπασι δὲ ὑπάρχει. οἷον ἡ εὐχὴ λόγος μὲν ἀλλ' οὔτε ἀληθὴς, οὔτε ψευδής. [...] ῥητορικῆς γὰρ' ἢ ποιητικῆς οἰκειοτέρα ἡ σκέψις.

28. We call propositions those only that have truth or falsity in them. A prayer is, for instance, a sentence but neither has truth nor falsity. ...their study more properly belongs to the province of rhetoric or poetics.

tr. H. P. Cooke

ARISTOTLE, Politica 1282a 3.

29. ἰατρὸς δ' ὅ τε δημιουργὸς καὶ ὁ ἀρχιτεκτονικὸς καὶ τρίτος ὁ πεπαιδευμένος περὶ τὴν τέχνην. εἰσὶ γὰρ τινες τοιοῦτοι καὶ περὶ πάσας ὡς εἰπεῖν τὰς τέχνας.

CRAFTSMAN, ARTIST AND CONNOISSEUR

29. [The term "doctor"] is applied to the ordinary practitioner; it is applied also to the specialist who directs the course of treatment; and it is applied to the man who has some general knowledge of the art of medicine. There are men of this last type to be found in connexion with nearly all the arts...)

tr. E. Barker

ARISTOTLE, Poëtica 1448b 4.

30. ἐοίκασι δὲ γεννῆσαι μὲν ὅλως τὴν ποιητικὴν αἰτίαι δύο τινὲς καὶ αὗται φυσικαί· τό τε γὰρ μιμεῖσθαι σύμφυτον τοῖς ἀνθρώποις ἐκ παίδων ἐστὶ καὶ τούτῳ διαφέρουσι τῶν ἄλλων ζῴων ὅτι μιμητικώτατόν ἐστι καὶ τὰς μαθήσεις ποιεῖται διὰ μιμήσεως τὰς πρώτας, καὶ τὸ χαίρειν τοῖς μιμήμασι πάντας. σημεῖον δὲ τούτου τὸ συμβαῖνον ἐπὶ τῶν ἔργων. ἃ γὰρ αὐτὰ λυπηρῶς ὁρῶμεν, τούτων τὰς εἰκόνας τὰς μάλιστα ἠκριβωμένας χαίρομεν θεωροῦντες οἷον θηρίων τε μορφὰς τῶν ἀτιμοτάτων καὶ νεκρῶν... ἐπεὶ ἐὰν μὴ τύχῃ προεωρακώς, οὐχὶ μίμημα ποιήσει τὴν ἡδονήν, ἀλλὰ διὰ τὴν ἀπεργασίαν ἢ τὴν χροιὰν ἢ διὰ τοιαύτην τινὰ ἄλλην αἰτίαν.

GENESIS OF IMITATIVE ARTS

30. Poetry in general seems to have sprung from two causes, each of them lying deep in our nature. First, the instinct of imitation is implanted in man from childhood, one difference between him and other animals being that he is the most imitative of living creatures, and through imitation learns his earliest lessons; and no less universal is the pleasure felt in things imitated. We have evidence of this in the facts of experience. Objects which in themselves we view with pain, we delight to contemplate when reproduced with minute fidelity: such as the forms of the most ignoble animals and of dead bodies. (...) For if you happen not to have seen the original, the pleasure will be due not to the imitation as such, but to the execution, the colouring, or some such other cause.

tr. S. H. Butcher

ARISTOTLE, Rhetorica 1366a 33.

31. καλὸν μὲν οὖν ἐστίν, ὃ ἂν δι' αὑτὸ αἱρετὸν ὂν ἐπαινετὸν ᾖ, ἢ ὃ ἂν ἀγαθὸν ὂν ἡδὺ ᾖ, ὅτι ἀγαθόν.

DEFINITION OF BEAUTY

31. That, then, is Morally Beautiful or Noble, which being desirable for its own sake, is also laudable or which being good, is pleasant because good.

tr. R. C. Jebb

ARISTOTLE, Politica 1338a 40.

32. ὁμοίως δὲ καὶ τὴν γραφικὴν δεῖ παιδεύεσθαι... μᾶλλον ὅτι ποιεῖ θεωρητικὸν τοῦ περὶ τὰ σώματα κάλλους. τὸ δὲ ζητεῖν πανταχοῦ τὸ χρήσιμον ἥκιστα ἁρμόττει τοῖς μεγαλοψύχοις καὶ τοῖς ἐλευθέροις.

BEAUTY AND UTILITY

32. Similarly, the object of instruction in drawing is... rather to give them an observant eye for beauty of form and figure. To aim at utility everywhere is utterly unbecoming to high-minded and liberal spirits.

tr. E. Barker

ARISTOTLE, Politica 1338b 29.

33. τὸ καλὸν ἀλλ' οὐ τὸ θηριῶδες δεῖ πρωταγωνιστεῖν.

33. Consequently, honour and not animal ferocity should play the first part.

tr. H. Rackham

ARISTOTLE, Poëtica 1450b 38.

34. τὸ γὰρ καλὸν ἐν μεγέθει καὶ τάξει ἐστί, διὸ οὔτε πάμμικρον ἄν τι γένοιτο καλὸν ζῷον, συγχεῖται γὰρ ἡ θεωρία ἐγγὺς τοῦ ἀναισθήτου χρόνῳ γινομένη οὔτε παμμεγέθες, οὐ γὰρ ἅμα ἡ θεωρία γίνεται ἀλλ' οἴχεται τοῖς θεωροῦσι τὸ ἓν καὶ τὸ ὅλον ἐκ τῆς θεωρίας οἷον εἰ μυρίων σταδίων εἴη ζῷον· ὥστε δεῖ καθάπερ ἐπὶ τῶν συστημάτων καὶ ἐπὶ τῶν ζῴων ἔχειν μὲν μέγεθος, τοῦτο δὲ εὐσύνοπτον εἶναι, οὕτω καὶ ἐπὶ τῶν μύθων ἔχειν μὲν μῆκος, τοῦτο δὲ εὐμνημόνευτον εἶναι.

ORDER AND SIZE

34. ...for beauty consists in magnitude and ordered arrangement. From which it follows that neither would a very small creature be beautiful—for our view of it is almost instantaneous and therefore confused—nor a very large one, since being unable to view it all at once, we lose the effect of a single whole; for instance, suppose a creature 1000 miles long. As then creatures and other organic structures must have a certain magnitude and yet be easily taken in by the eye, so too with plots: they must have length but must easily be taken in by the memory.

tr. W. H. Fyfe

ARISTOTLE, Metaphysica 1078a 31.

35. ἐπεὶ δὲ τὸ ἀγαθὸν καὶ τὸ καλὸν ἕτερον (τὸ μὲν γὰρ ἀεὶ ἐν πράξει, τὸ δὲ καλὸν καὶ ἐν τοῖς ἀκινήτοις)... τοῦ δὲ καλοῦ μέγιστα εἴδη τάξις καὶ συμμετρία καὶ τὸ ὡρισμένον, ἃ μάλιστα δεικνύουσιν αἱ μαθηματικαὶ ἐπιστῆμαι.

35. Now since the good and the beautiful differ inasmuch as the former always implies action while the latter is found in unchangeable things also [those who hold that mathematics says nothing of the beautiful or of the good are wrong]... The main species of beauty are order, symmetry, and definiteness, which are revealed in particular by mathematics.

tr. J. Warrington

ARISTOTLE, Topica 146a 21.

36. ἔτι ἐὰν πρὸς δύο τὸς ὁρισμὸν ἀποδῷ καθ' ἑκάτερον, οἷον τὸ καλὸν τὸ δι' ὄψεως ἢ τὸ δι' ἀκοῆς ἡδύ ... ἅμα ταὐτὸν καλόν τε καὶ οὐ καλὸν ἔσται... εἰ οὖν τί ἐστι δι' ὄψεως μὲν ἡδὺ δι' ἀκοῆς δὲ μή, καλόν τε καὶ οὐ καλὸν ἔσται.

CRITICISM OF SENSUALISM

36. If "the beautiful" [is defined] as "what is pleasant to the sight or to the hearing" ... then the same thing will be both beautiful and not beautiful... If a thing is pleasant to the sight but not to the hearing, it will be both beautiful and not beautiful.

tr. E. S. Forster

ARISTOTLE, Ethica Nicomach. 1123b 6.

37. ἐν μεγέθει γὰρ ἡ μεγαλοψυχία, ὥσπερ καὶ τὸ κάλλος ἐν μεγάλῳ σώματι, οἱ μικροὶ δ' ἀστεῖοι καὶ σύμμετροι, καλοὶ δ' οὔ.

BEAUTY OF SIZE

37. ...for that kind of superiority must rest on greatness, just as personal beauty requires that one should be tall; little people may have charm and elegance, but beauty—no.

tr. J. A. K. Thomson

ARISTOTLE, Rhetorica 1409a 35.

38. λέγω δὲ περίοδον λέξιν ἔχουσαν ἀρχὴν καὶ τελευτὴν αὐτὴν καθ' αὑτὴν καὶ μέγεθος εὐσύνοπτον. ἡδεῖα δ' ἡ τοιαύτη καὶ εὐμαθής, ἡδεῖα μὲν διὰ τὸ ἐναντίως ἔχειν τῷ ἀπεράντῳ

BEAUTY AND PALPABILITY

38. ...by a period I mean a sentence that has a beginning and end in itself and a magnitude that can be easily grasped. What is written in this style is pleasant and easy to learn,

καὶ ὅτι ἀεί τι οἴεται ἔχειν ὁ ἀκροατὴς καὶ πεπεράνθαι τι αὐτῷ· τὸ δὲ μηδὲν προνοεῖν εἶναι μηδὲ ἀνύειν ἀηδές. εὐμαθὴς δέ, ὅτι εὐμνημόνευτος. τοῦτο δέ, ὅτι ἀριθμὸν ἔχει ἡ ἐν περιόδοις λέξις, ὃ πάντων εὐμνημονευτότατον.

pleasant because it is the opposite of that which is unlimited, because the hearer at every moment thinks he is securing something for himself and that some conclusion has been reached; whereas it is unpleasant neither to forsee nor to get to the end of anything. It is easy to learn, because it can be easily retained in the memory. The reason is that the periodic style has number, which of all things is the easiest to remember...

tr. J. H. Freese

ARISTOTLE, Rhetorica 1361b 5.

38a. κάλλος δὲ ἕτερον καθ' ἑκάστην ἡλικίαν ἐστίν.

RELATIVITY OF BEAUTY

38a. Beauty varies with each age.

tr. J. H. Freese

ARISTOTLE, Ethica Nicomach. 1105a 27.

39. τὰ μὲν γὰρ ὑπὸ τῶν τεχνῶν γινόμενα τὸ εὖ ἔχει ἐν αὑτοῖς, ἀρκεῖ οὖν ταῦτά πως ἔχοντα γενέσθαι.

VALUE OF ART AND BEAUTY

39. A work of art is good or bad in itself—let it possess a certain quality, and this is all we ask of it.

tr. J. A. K. Thomson

LAERTIUS DIOGENES (V 1, 20) (on Aristotle).

40. πρὸς τὸν πυθόμενον διὰ τί τοῖς καλοῖς πολὺν χρόνον ὁμιλοῦμεν, «Τυφλοῦ», ἔφη, «τὸ ἐρώτημα».

40. When someone inquired why we spend much time with the beautiful, "That", he said, "is a blind man's question".

tr. R. D. Hicks

ARISTOTLE, Ethica Nicomach, 1118a 2.

41. οἱ γὰρ χαίροντες τοῖς διὰ τῆς ὄψεως, οἷον χρώμασι καὶ σχέμασι καὶ γραφῇ, οὔτε σώφρονες οὔτε ἀκόλαστοι λέγονται· καίτοι δόξειεν ἂν εἶναι καὶ ὡς δεῖ χαίρειν καὶ τούτοις, καὶ καθ' ὑπερβολὴν καὶ ἔλλειψιν. ὁμοίως δὲ καὶ ἐν τοῖς περὶ τὴν ἀκοήν· τοὺς γὰρ ὑπερβεβλημένως χαίροντας μέλεσιν ἢ ὑποκρίσει οὐδεὶς ἀκολάστους λέγει, οὐδὲ τοὺς ὡς δεῖ σώφρονας. οὐδὲ τοὺς περὶ τὴν ὀσμήν, πλὴν κατὰ συμβεβηκός. τοὺς γὰρ χαίροντας μήλων ἢ ῥόδων ἢ θυμιαμάτων ὀσμαῖς οὐ λέγομεν ἀκολάστους, ἀλλὰ μᾶλλον τοὺς μύρων καὶ ὄψων.

AESTHETIC EXPERIENCES

41. The people who find pleasure in looking at things like colours and forms and pictures are not called temperate or intemperate. At the same time we must suppose that pleasure in these things can be felt too much or too little or in due measure. It is so with the pleasures of listening. A man may take inordinate delight in music or acting. But nobody is prepared to call him intemperate on that account; nor, if he takes neither too much nor too little, do we think of describing him as temperate. It is the same with the pleasures of smell, except when some association comes in. A man is not called intemperate if he happens to like the smell of apples or roses or incense. Yet he may be, if he inhales essences or the emanations of the cuisine...

tr. J. A. K. Thomson

ARISTOTLE, Ethica
Eudem. 1230b 31.

42. εἰ γοῦν τις ἢ καλὸν ἀνδριάντα θεώμενος ἢ ἵππον ἢ ἄνθρωπον, ἢ ἀκροώμενος ᾄδοντος, μὴ βούλοιτο μήτε ἐσθίειν μήτε πίνειν μήτε ἀφροδισιάζειν, ἀλλὰ τὰ μὲν καλὰ θεωρεῖν τῶν ᾀδόντων δ' ἀκούειν, οὐκ ἂν δόξειεν ἀκόλαστος εἶναι ὥσπερ οὐδ' οἱ κηλούμενοι παρὰ ταῖς Σειρῆσιν. ἀλλὰ περὶ τὰ δύο τῶν αἰσθητῶν ταῦτα, περὶ ἅπερ καὶ τἆλλα θηρία μόνα τυγχάνει αἰσθητικῶς ἔχοντα καὶ χαίροντα καὶ λυπούμενα περὶ τὰ γευστὰ καὶ ἁπτά. περὶ δὲ τὰ τῶν ἄλλων αἰσθήσεων ἡδέα σχεδὸν ὁμοίως ἅπαντα φαίνεται ἀναισθήτως διακείμενα, οἷον περὶ εὐαρμοστίαν ἢ κάλλος· οὐδὲν γάρ, ὅ τι καὶ ἄξιον λόγου, φαίνεται πάσχοντα αὐτῇ τῇ θεωρίᾳ τῶν καλῶν ἢ τῇ ἀκροάσει τῶν εὐαρμόστων, εἰ μή τί που συμβέβηκε τερατῶδες. ἀλλ' οὐδὲ πρὸς τὰ εὐώδη ἢ δυσώδη· καίτοι γὰρ τάς γε αἰσθήσεις ὀξυτέρας ἔχουσι πάσας. ἀλλὰ καὶ τῶν ὀσμῶν· ταύταις χαίρουσιν ὅσαι κατὰ συμβεβηκὸς εὐφραίνουσιν, ἀλλὰ μὴ καθ' αὑτάς. λέγω δὲ μὴ καθ' αὑτάς, αἷς ἐλπίζοντες χαίρομεν ἢ μεμνημένοι, οἷον ὄψων καὶ ποτῶν· δι' ἑτέραν γὰρ ἡδονὴν ταύταις χαίρομεν, τὴν τοῦ φαγεῖν ἢ πιεῖν. καθ' αὑτὰς δέ, οἷαι αἱ τῶν ἀνθῶν εἰσίν. διὸ ἐμμελῶς ἔφη Στρατόνικος τὰς μὲν καλὸν ὄζειν, τὰς δὲ ἡδύ.

42. ...a man would not be considered profligate if when looking at a beautiful statue or horse or person, or listening to someone singing, he did not wish for food or drink or sexual indulgence but only wished to look at the beautiful objects or listen to the music—any more than the persons held spellbound in the abode of the Sirens. Temperance and profligacy have to do with those two sorts of sensory objects in relation to which alone the lower animals also happen to be sensitive and to feel pleasure and pain—the objects of taste and of touch, whereas about virtually all the pleasures of the other senses alike animals are clearly so constituted as to be insensitive—e.g. harmonious sound or beauty; for clearly they are not affected in any degree worth speaking of by the mere sight of beautiful objects or by listening to musical sounds, except possibly in the case of some miraculous occurrences. Nor yet are they sensitive to good or bad smells, although it is true that all their senses are keener than man's; but even the smells they enjoy are those that have agreeable associations, and are not intrinsically agreeable. By smells not intrinsically agreeable I mean those that we enjoy because of either anticipation or recollection, for example the smell of things to eat or drink, for we enjoy these scents on account of a different pleasure, that of eating or drinking; by intrinsically agreeable I mean scents such as those of flowers (this is the reason for Stratonicus's neat remark that the scent for flowers is beautiful but that of things to eat and drink sweet).

tr. H. Rackham

11. The End of the Classical Period

With Aristotle we come to the end of the classical period of ancient aesthetics. His aesthetics is a summary of its achievement, though in some important respects it reaches beyond it to a new era.

The archaic and classical aesthetics of the Greeks was not only unlike our own but also unlike what we would expect to emerge at the dawn of history. Theirs was the first system of aesthetics, at least in Europe, to comprise a written theory of art, and yet this was neither simple nor what later ages would regard as natural and primitive.

First, this system barely mentioned beauty. When the Greeks referred to it, they did so almost exclusively in the ethical rather than the aesthetic sense. This is remarkable since this aesthetics arose at a time and in a country which had created so much beauty, yet saw a closer connection of art with goodness, truth and utility than with beauty. The idea of "fine" arts did not exist.

Secondly, this theory took little interest in the representation of Nature through art. This was also remarkable since it was the theory of a time and a country, whose art had abandoned abstract symbols in favour of natural forms. It is even more remarkable that it should have been the theory of the Greeks, who saw the human mind as passive and who thought that everything that man does comes not from within himself but from an external model; in every human activity, in art and poetry as well as in science, the Greeks regarded truth as the most significant element. Before Socrates and Plato we find few references to representations of Nature by painters, sculptors and poets. The term *mimesis* was used, but it originally meant play-acting and spectacle and not representation of the external world. It was applied to the dance, music and the actor's art but not to sculpture, painting and epic poetry. When applied to Nature it meant imitation of her methods rather than her appearances. According to Democritus, men learned to build by imitating swallows and to sing by imitating the nightingale and the swan.

Thirdly, classical theory did not connect art with creativity and this was particularly curious in a nation whose creative abilities were so great. The Greeks paid little attention to the creative element in their art and did not value it. The reason for this lay in their conviction that the world was ruled by eternal laws and that art should discover the forms appropriate to things rather than try to invent them. Hence they did not value novelty in art, although they introduced a great deal that was new to it. They held that whatever is good and proper in art (and in life in general) is eternal; therefore, the employment of new, idiosyncratic and original forms is a sign that art has taken a wrong turn.

Fourthly, from its very beginning with Pythagorean ideas, the Greek theory of art was a mathematical theory. It penetrated also the visual arts. Sculptors, led by Polyclitus, set themselves the task of discovering a canon for the human body, that is, a mathematical formula for its proportions. It is especially noteworthy that this aesthetics arose just at the time when Greek art passed from geometrical to organic forms.

It was only after the transition from Hellenic to Hellenistic culture that the tenets of classical aesthetics began to make room for new ones which came closer to our own. It was then that the idea of creativity in art was given a dominant emphasis and the connection between art and beauty became to understood. There were also other changes: a shift in the theory of art from thought to imagination, from experiences to ideas, and from rules to the artist's personal abilities.

III. HELLENISTIC AESTHETICS

1. The Hellenistic Period

1. DEMARCATION LINES. Extremely significant political events occurred during the six centuries between the beginning of the third century B.C. and the end of the third century A.D. Greece collapsed, the kingdoms of the Diadochi rose and fell, the West Roman Empire came into being, achieved supremacy and began to crumble. The economic, political and cultural structure of the world changed beyond recognition. But it was quite otherwise with the ideas about beauty and art. During that period they did not undergo any significant change. Ideas formulated in the Greek language, first in Athens and then in Alexandria, were still, six centuries later, upheld in Latin in Rome with only comparatively minor changes. For this reason these six centuries may be treated as a single chapter in the history of aesthetics, although it covers two great epochs of economic and political history: the Hellenistic epoch of the last three centuries B.C. and the epoch of the Roman Empire of the first centuries A.D.

2. THE STATES OF THE DIADOCHI. It is common to contrast Hellenistic culture with Hellenic culture. The name *Hellenic* is given to the culture which the Greeks evolved at the time when they lived in comparative isolation, neither significantly influencing, nor being influenced by other nations. Their culture was at that time uniform and pure but had a limited range. By *Hellenistic* we mean that culture of the Greeks which from the third century began to spread to other countries. In so doing it reached a wider area but lost its uniformity. The reign of Alexander the Great marks the dividing line between the Hellenic and the Hellenistic era; Hellenism begins with Alexander.

The old Greece was now a small weak country, particularly in comparison with the kingdom of Alexander and the Diadochi. It ceased to be an important cultural centre or a political force and quickly dwindled into a poor and remote province. It still consisted of numerous tiny states, which tried to save themselves by forming leagues like the Aetolian or the Achaean league. At first the intellectual life of this politically weak country remained intensive, at least in Athens, where according to Lucian, "a most philosophical climate prevailed and was best suited to those who thought best". From there intellectual life radiated out to the states of the Diadochi and later to the Roman Empire. However, Greece could not long withstand intellectual and political competition and it gave way to the states of the Diadochi.

There were four great states of the Diadochi. Of these Macedonia, which remained in the hands of the heirs of Antigonus, was comparatively the least important culturally, while the most important was Egypt, ruled by the heirs of Ptolemy, with its capital in Alexandria. Syria under the reign of the Seleucids and with the capital in Antioch, was also important. Similarly, the kingdom of Pergamum under the Attalids, which arose later, had great possibilities and aspirations in the cultural field.

In the Hellenistic period, as early as the third century B.C., the way of life changed in many respects. Absolute monarchies, states comprising vast territories and populations running into millions replaced the one typical Athenian democratic republic, the small Greek *polis*. This was bound to have an influence on art, which was no longer a commodity of the people but of the courts and the ruling classes. The meagre resources of a Greek democratic republic were nothing compared with those of Hellenistic monarchies. From the economic point of view Alexander's conquest of the East may be compared with the discovery of America. The immense wealth of the Persians and vast areas of fertile land were conquered. Trade reached an unprecedented scale. Ships sailed laden with luxuries as well as basic utilities—purple, silks, glass, bronze, ivory, fine woods and precious stones. Descriptions of contemporary ceremonies speak of the display of riches, of innumerable objects of gold and silver. Hellenistic splendour was in great contrast to Hellenic frugality. This contrast is discernible in art as well as in culture as a whole. The royal riches of Egypt, Syria or Pergamum, drawn from estates, monopolies and taxes, could support huge cultural establishments, both scientific and artistic. Art acquired unprecedented material value: Pliny mentions sums running into millions paid by the Hellenistic kings and the wealthy for paintings.

3. GREEK ÉMIGRÉS. The old Greece was ravaged by wars and depopulated, the old cities and temples fell into ruins. Unable to find scope in their own country for their energies, the Greek people emigrated to the states of the Diadochi, where, although few in number, they constituted the most active and cultured section of the multilingual and multiracial populations. Among the Greek émigrés there were, on the one hand, highly sought after and privileged men of letters, artists and scientists, and on the other, merchants and businessmen, who with their Greek industriousness and energy outstripped the apathetic peoples of the East. They owed their prosperity and position to sheer hard work as well as to initiative, for in agriculture and industry, particularly in Egypt, little use was made of slaves. These Greek émigrés spread Greek language and culture over wide areas and the known world became Hellenistic, even though it did not become Hellenic. Having once left their small homelands of Athens or Thebes, these Athenians and Thebans became simply Greeks. They shed their regional traits in favour of universal Greek ones and this was reflected in the disappearance of local dialects and their replacement by a Pan-Hellenic *koiné*. While the old Greece was an enclosed country relying on its own resources, the Hellenistic world witnessed an exchange of in-

fluences, talents, customs and cultures. Greek taste influenced the people of the East but in the process came under their influence so that Oriental taste also made a mark upon the Greeks. In Greek rhetoric Asian style found a place alongside the Attician. A great wave of Hellenization followed in the wake of the conquests of Alexander the Great, but 150 years later came a similar wave of Orientalization and submission to Eastern tastes and predilections.

4. ROME. Meanwhile, in the West, republican Rome was developing upon quite different foundations. Intellectual pursuits had only a subordinate place there and almost everything in the field of sciences that the Romans possessed was acquired from the Hellenistic world. The first states to fall were Macedonia and Greece in the year 146 and the last Egypt in 30 B.C. Thus, even before the beginning of our era, the whole "habitable world" (*oikoumene*), to use an expression of those times, was united by the Romans.

A new chapter in the history of the world had now begun. Rome had conquered the world and at the same time had ceased to be a republic and became an empire. It became the capital of the world, replacing the numerous capitals that had existed not long before. It lay in the West and not in the East. Latin succeeded Greek as the language of the rulers and not long after as the language of literature also. Rome resembled the Hellenistic kingdoms in its possession of vast territories and vast material means, but the scale of these was even greater, since the riches derived not from industry and trade, but from plunder, and there was also a greater inequality in their distribution.

Rome's attitude to art and beauty was peculiar.* The vast majority of the population consisted of slaves and serfs who had no opportunity to enjoy the benefits of art. These were also denied to a considerable number of Romans in the military profession, who passed their lives in fortified camps and marching on foot. But even the wealthiest members of the population could not enjoy art because they were so engrossed in struggles for power and position that they lacked what is (as Aristotle had already taught) essential for the cultivation and enjoyment of arts: a mind free from the preoccupations of a life of affairs†. Although some free and wealthy Romans living under the Empire acquired a love of art, this was confined to enjoyment and did not include creation. Greece remained the source of art and the authority on artistic matters and when the Romans made use of art it was chiefly with a view to embellishing their dwellings or winning over the masses for whom they built theatres and baths.

The attributes of the Roman character and the conditions of Roman life explain certain aspects of Roman art, such as the gigantic scale of its architecture, the sumptuousness of its decoration, the realism of the visual arts and the derivative nature of the majority of the works of art that embellished Rome. Burckhardt states in his *Die Zeit Konstantins* that "various ancient and modern nations were

---

* H. Jucker, *Vom Verhältnis der Römer zur bildenden Kunst der Griechen* (1950).

† Ch. Bénard, *L'esthétique d'Aristote* (1887), Part II: "L'esthétique d'après Aristote", pp. 159–369.

capable of building on a colossal scale but Rome of those days will remain unique for all time because the love of beauty aroused by Greek art will never again be linked with such material resources and such a need to be surrounded by magnificence". But at the same time the immensity, the magnificence and might of Rome was mingled with a feeling of dependence and inferiority. After praising the Greeks Seneca adds: "To us they appear so great because we ourselves are so small".

Conditions in Rome explain also certain characteristics of the Roman theory of art and aesthetics. The first Roman men of learning appeared in the first century and some of them concerned themselves with theories of art. They were mostly specialists in one narrow field such as, for example, oratory and were scholars rather than creators, remaining content to pass on the ideas of Greek theoreticians rather than attempting to develop them. This is true of Vitruvius, to whom we owe our knowledge of ancient ideas about painting and sculpture, and of Cicero, whose work provides us with our knowledge of the ancient theory of oratory and also the theory of art in general.

5. GREATNESS AND FREEDOM. The treatise *On the Sublime* by Pseudo-Longinus, written in the first century A.D., one of the ancient treatises on aesthetics which has survived, poses in its final chapter the question why that age had not produced any great man. "It surprises me, and doubtless surprises many others, why it is that though our century has produced men endowed with the greatest power of speech and political abilities, possessed of keen and active natures..., truly sublime natures rising above the average are very rare indeed. In this respect there is a great dearth throughout the whole world".

Pseudo-Longinus produces a twofold explanation. First, invoking an unidentified philosopher, he asserts that there were no great men because life was devoid of freedom. "We, men of this age, have been nourished on despotism since childhood... and we do not drink from the most beautiful and the most bountiful fountain, that of liberty. Every despotism, however just it may be, is like a cage and a universal prison".

The second explanation, the author's own, is that there are no great men because there is no inner freedom. Men are overcome by passions and desires, above all by greed and the desire for riches. "Greed, from which we all suffer without satisfying it, and a craving for indulgence make us all slaves".

2. Aesthetics in Hellenistic Philosophy

1. HELLENISTIC PHILOSOPHY. Philosophy of the Hellenistic era changed its character. The urge to acquire a good understanding of the world and of life was superseded by the urge to discover a means of living well and happily in this world. This had repercussions in aesthetics. When philosophers discussed it, their main concern was not only to ask what beauty and art are, but also, whether they are *conducive to happiness*.

Hellenistic philosophers solved these new and fundamental problems early, in the first generation of the Hellenistic age. Not many years after Aristotle's death they added three new solutions to these which Plato and Aristotle had proposed: one hedonistic, another moralistic and the third sceptical. These claimed that happiness in life was achieved respectively by pleasure, virtue and abstention from life's difficulties and doubts.

These solutions became slogans of philosophical schools. Philosophers now ceased to act singly and formed groups. This too was characteristic of the philosophy of the period. Three new schools developed in addition to Plato's Academy and Aristotle's Peripatetic school.

The first slogan, that of hedonism, was taken up by the Epicurean school, which evolved a materialistic, mechanistic, and sensualist philosophy. The second slogan, that of moralism, was defended by the Stoic school, while around the third slogan the school of the Sceptics created a negative philosophy, regarding all judgments as uncertain and all important problems as insoluble. This school opposed the remaining four, considering them as dogmatic; it came relatively nearer to the school of Epicurus. Of the dogmatic schools, the materialistic school of Epicurus and the idealistic Academy of Plato represented the two extremes. The Peripatetic school of Aristotle and the Stoic school occupied intermediate positions, but both rather approached the idealist Platonic extreme. Because of certain similarities between these three trends, a fourth one came into being in due course: this was the Eclectic school, which united the doctrines of all three, with the purpose of combining everything which in ancient philosophy was neither scepticism nor materialism.

All these schools survived for centuries. The greatest changes occurred among the Platonists, whose philosophy even approached the philosophy of the Sceptics for a time. However, by the end of antiquity they had in the system known as Neo-Platonism reinforced the speculative, ecstatic and transcendent elements of their philosophy, moving furthest from the sober principles of Epicurus and the Sceptics.

The Hellenistic systems were many-sided: they contained a theory of cognition, a theory of being and practical conclusions about life as well. They also found a place for aesthetics, though not a very prominent one. In a philosophy mainly concerned with practical, moral and bio-technical problems, aesthetic problems naturally took second place. Since they were worked out in philosophical schools they had the merits and defects of a collective undertaking: they were systematical and schematic. Nevertheless, this era also produced personalities who influenced the history of aesthetics. These were Cicero and Plotinus.

2. ATHENS AND ROME. The philosophical schools of Hellenism arose in Athens, where, even when the city was in political and economic decline, philosophers from various parts of the "inhabited world" were still drawn. The Athenian philosophy found followers outside Athens, but there were only a few creative spirits. Alexandria was a scientific, not a philosophical centre. Imperial Rome took more interest in

philosophy, but preferred to import rather than actively develop it. The subtle arguments of the Sceptics and the lofty Platonic idealism did not find favour with the Romans, who, on the contrary, produced a distinguished exponent of Epicureanism in Lucretius, and several excellent Stoics, among whom Seneca took a particular interest in aesthetics. Whereas in Greece the various schools were in conflict with each other, the Romans aimed at reconciling them and preserving what was common to them all; the Eclectic school was therefore most successful in Rome, where its chief exponent, Cicero, resided.

The general features of Hellenistic philosophy appeared also in aesthetics. Aesthetic investigations did not play an important part in the programme of the Alexandrian "grammarians"; but Athens and Rome distinguished themselves in this sphere. Athens was more prolific in new ideas, while Romans excelled in digests. But only a little of the Athenian contribution has survived, and most of what we know about the aesthetics of this period comes from the writings of Roman scholars.

During the long Hellenistico-Roman period aesthetic ideas underwent little change. The principal tenets had become established as early as the third century B.C. and were later developed rather than modified. A certain revival in aesthetics occurred in the first century B.C. as a result of the activity of several philosophers: of the Eclectic academician Antiochus and the Stoics Panaetius and Posidonius. Soon afterwards a similar revival took place in Rome. To this and the following century belong the Latin compilations and monographs which are our richest source of information about Hellenistic and Roman aesthetics.

During the centuries that followed, a transcendent and mystical strain in philosophy began to gain ground and to find expression in aesthetics. A late but magnificent manifestation of this was the aesthetics of Plotinus in the third century A.D.

3. WRITINGS ON AESTHETICS. We possess various Hellenistic texts on aesthetics, although in relation to what was actually written these are very few. The original works were doomed to be lost. Only subsequent commentaries survive. Pliny's books on painting and sculpture have survived, but the works of Xenocrates, Antigonus, Pasiteles and Varro, on which Pliny drew, have perished. We have the work of Vitruvius on architecture, but not the writings of the architect Hermogenes and others which were the sources of Vitruvius. We have Cicero's and Seneca's treatises on aesthetics but not those of Panaetius and Posidonius which preceded and inspired them. It is however probable that the most important aesthetic ideas have survived. Those which were not recorded by any contemporary digests and doxographers must have been of little importance.

4. PHILOSOPHERS AND ARTISTS. The aesthetics of the Hellenistico-Roman period was not exclusively the achievement of philosophers, but also of scholars and artists. There even occurred a reversal of the roles played by philosophers and specialists: while in the classical period the former had been the leading aestheticians, the latter became so in the Hellenistico-Roman period.

174 HELLENISTIC AESTHETICS

One of the reason for this lay within the philosophy itself. Its three new streams, that is, Epicureanism, Stoicism and Scepticism, adopted an unfavourable attitude towards beauty and art, considering that beauty and art did not serve either moralistic or hedonistic aims. Despite this, stoicism at least contributed to the development of aesthetics more than might have been expected. Of the two older schools of philosophy, the Aristotelians were occupied rather with special problems, while the Platonic school was entering a period of decline. For this reason the three negatively inclined schools present a more typical picture of the attitude of Hellenistic philosophy towards aesthetics.

A specialized theory was first evolved for music, and a little later for the visual arts. Aristotle had already paved the way for poetics. There was an intensive study of rhetoric, the theory of oratory, which was greatly prized in antiquity. Our knowledge of the Hellenistic theory of music comes from the extant fragments by Aristoxenus (an Aristotelian of the third century B.C.), the theory of poetry has been preserved by Horace, the theory of oratory by Cicero and Quintilian (an orator who flourished at the turn of the first century A.D.), the theory of architecture has come down to us through the work of Vitruvius (who was active in the first century B.C.), and the theory of painting and sculpture has survived thanks to the encyclopaedic work of Pliny written in the first century A.D.

We shall here first discuss the ideas of the philosophical schools in the following order: 1. The aesthetics of the Epicureans (chiefly Lucretius). 2. The aesthetics of the Sceptics (chiefly as presented by Sextus Empiricus). 3. The aesthetics of the Stoics (chiefly Seneca) 4. The aesthetics of the Eclectics (chiefly Cicero). We shall then turn to the specialized theories: 5. The aesthetics of music (chiefly Aristoxenus). 6. Poetics (chiefly Horace). 7. Rhetoric (chiefly Quintilian). 8. The aesthetics of architecture (chiefly based on Vitruvius). 9. The aesthetics of painting and sculpture.

Finally we shall have to return to philosophy, because the last word of the period belongs to Neo-Platonic philosophy, in which aesthetics occupied an important position and which was different in character from the philosophies current in the earlier stages of Hellenism.

3. The Aesthetics of the Epicureans

1. EPICUREAN WRITINGS ON ART. The writings of Epicurus (340–271), the founder of the school which bears his name, included works on the arts entitled *On Music* and *On Oratory**, but these represented only a very small part of his achievement and have, in any case, perished. Diogenes Laertius, who transmitted much information about Epicurus, is silent on the subject of his aesthetic views and other chroniclers have little to add. We can draw our conclusions only from tiny fragments and indi-

---

* H. Usener, *Epicurea* (1887).

rect sources. It is, however, plain that aesthetics occupied a very low place among Epicurus' interests.

A little more material on the subject of aesthetics is available in *On the Nature of Things* (*De Rerum Natura*), the philosophical poem of the Roman Epicurean Lucretius (95–55 B.C.), which has been preserved in full. But the theme of the poem is cosmological and ethical in character, with discussion of aesthetics introduced only marginally. Certain other members of the school, notably Horace, the author of the well-known poetics, showed more interest in the subject. Philodemus of Gadara, who flourished in the first century B.C., was another Epicurean and large fragments of his *On Poetical Works** and *On Music* have survived† in the papyri of Herculaneum. These fragments contain both the aesthetic ideas of the Epicureans and their criticism of other schools and are therefore our main source regarding the aesthetics of the Hellenistic philosophers.

2. MATERIALISM, HEDONISM AND SENSUALISM. Epicurean philosophy gave a materialistic interpretation of existence, a hedonistic interpretation of action and a sensualist interpretation of knowledge. Such interpretations had a bearing on aesthetics. The materialism of the Epicureans was responsible for the fact that they took little interest in "spiritual" beauty, to which classical aestheticians had paid considerable attention. As a result of their hedonism, the Epicureans saw the value of beauty and art in terms of the pleasure they provided. As a consequence of their sensualism, they linked pleasure, and therefore beauty also, with sensual experiences. For them beauty meant "that which is pleasurable to the eye and ear". All this stands in sharp contrast to the aesthetics of Aristotle and even more to that of Plato, while it appears to be close to the aesthetics of the Sophists. However, this similarity is confined to certain assumptions and does not extend to their consequences. Closely allied assumptions gave rise to the Sophists' sympathetic and the Epicureans' hostile attitude towards beauty and art.

3. NEGATIVE ATTITUDE TOWARDS BEAUTY AND ART. There were two variants of Epicurus' hedonistic attitude towards beauty. One proclaimed that beauty is identical with pleasure, that there is no beauty without pleasure and that the amount of beauty corresponds to the amount of pleasure. The difference between beauty and pleasure was seen as a purely linguistic one: when you speak of beauty, he says, you speak of pleasure, since beauty would not be beauty if it were not pleasurable.[1] The second variant associated beauty with pleasure but did not equate the two. Beauty was only considered valuable when it provided pleasure;[2] then and only then was it worthwhile.[3] Here Epicurus expressed himself even more forcibly, saying that he scorned beauty which provided no pleasure and scorned men who vainly admired such beauty.[4] Both variants are connected with hedonism but differ from each other in one vital respect. According to the first, all beauty depends

---

* Ch. Jensen, *Philodemos über die Gedichte*, fünftes Buch (1923).
† *Philodemi de musica librorum quae extant*, ed. by I. Kemke (1884).

on pleasure and all beauty has value, while according to the second, there also exists beauty which does not give pleasure and has no value. It is difficult to tell whether this discrepancy is to be ascribed to our source (Athenaeus and Maximus of Tyre) or to Epicurus himself, who, caring little about beauty, was not concerned to examine it. A similar conflict in Epicurus and his school appears in their evaluation of art. They claimed either that art is the production of pleasurable and useful things or that art can be justified only if it produces pleasurable and useful things.

With such propositions the Epicurean school could have produced a hedonistic aesthetics in the spirit of the Sophists or of Democritus, whom the Epicureans followed in so many respects. And yet this did not happen because they saw no pleasure in art and beauty. Their first tenet was that art has value in so far as it causes pleasure, but their other tenet was that art does not cause true pleasure. It is, therefore, worthless and does not merit attention.

According to Epicurus, everything that man does arises out of some need. However, he did not consider all needs to be indispensable and he did not regard beauty as belonging to the category of absolutely necessary things. Art too was expendable in his view for, as his disciples held, it had arisen at a late stage in man's history. Man had been able to do without it for a long time before. Art does not even have the virtue of being independent, but, on the contrary, everything in it derives from nature. Man, being in himself quite ignorant, has to learn everything from nature. It is not surprising therefore that the Epicureans did not value art. The founder of the school described music and poetry as "noise".[5] His pupils, so Cicero tells us, were not disposed to waste time reading poets who can offer nothing "solid and useful".[6] Epicurus even went so far as to regard poetry as pernicious because it creates myths.[7] Therefore, like Plato, he thought poets should be removed from the state, although he based his argument on different premises.[8] He conceded that in the last resort a wise man might frequent the theatre but only on condition that he treated it as entertainment and not as anything of any consequences. As far as music was concerned, the Epicureans were wont to quote from a little poem which said that it brings about "indolence, inebriation and ruin."

4. ABSENCE OF AUTONOMY IN ART. The Epicureans adopted an exclusively practical attitude towards aesthetics. They judged beauty and art solely by utilitarian standards and maintained that value consisted in utility and utility in pleasure. They did not allow the possibility that art might have its own principles. Poets should conform with the general aims of mankind. The Epicureans held to the dubious thesis that poetry must not express anything the truth of which science has not confirmed and Epicurus himself went further than Plato in his condemnation of poets for their mendacious fantasies. He claimed that "only the wise man will be able to converse correctly about music and poetry".[9] Lucretius ascribed a servile role to poetry, saying that "art is philosophy's handmaiden", *ars ancilla philosophiae*. So far as the Epicureans were concerned, art did not possess any aims, criteria or standards of its own. They pushed their denial of the autonomy of art to its

furthest limit by maintaining that it lacks autonomy both in relation to daily life and in relation to science.

5. Two AESTHETIC DOCTRINES. The attitude toward beauty and art initiated by Epicurus survived among his disciples in the generations immediately following, but was later somewhat modified. Even then, however, the School showed little enthusiasm for beauty and art. However, in the first century B.C. the School included among its members philosophers such as Lucretius and humanists such as Philodemus who treated aesthetics more seriously. From the very beginning Epicurean philosophy subscribed to two doctrines, one of which saw everything exclusively from the point of view of utilitarian interests and was unfavourable to aesthetics. Formulated as a thesis on the uselessness of beauty and art, this became a fundamental element of the Epicureans' doctrine. It was a Cynical doctrine. It resembled Plato's condemnation of uselessness. It did not extend to beauty, and did not even cover art outside the Epicureans' own time. This doctrine caused the Epicureans to neglect the study of beauty, and this in turn led them to an incompetent and conservative attitude towards it.

The other Epicurean doctrine originated with Democritus. This doctrine proclaimed naturalism and empiricism and was opposed to all versions of idealism and mysticism. It was a later development in Epicurean aesthetics and had a much more positive significance. Both Lucretius and Philodemus subscribed to it.

6. LUCRETIUS. One of the characteristic ideas of Lucretius was that the forms of art are derived from Nature, which provides their model. By imitating the songs of birds men created their own songs. The wind whistling in the reeds suggested the pipes. Mankind owed the origins of poetry to birds and the origins of music to winds.[10] At first, art was nothing but a game and a relaxation, but later it was developed to the "topmost pinnacles" in all its spheres, in music, painting and sculpture. This, Lucretius thought, occurred slowly, gradually, step by step, in a rational and utilitarian manner, through "the inventiveness of the eager mind" and under the guidance of practice.[11]

7. PHILODEMUS. Philodemus set himself a different task. He rejected the exaggerated and unjustifiably mystical conception which the Greeks had of art. "Music", he said, "was *not* invented by a god who handed it to mankind". Man himself invented music and there was, in his view, no analogy between it and atmospheric phenomena. Man was its measure and controlling agent. There was nothing exceptional about it and it acted like any other human product. "Songs resemble smells and tastes in their effects". Contrary to the opinion of the majority, music was irrational and precisely for this reason its effects on men were limited. The "theory of ethos", in particular, had no foundation, since music does not portray characters and its connection with spiritual life is not greater than that of the culinary art.[12]

Following the general tendency of his school, Philodemus condemned formal interpretations of poetry and argued that "even if a poem has a beautiful form, it is bad if the thoughts embodied in it are bad". But when writing about music*, he took account of its different character as an art which he thought justified a formalist approach. Here he demonstrated his adherence to the school on different grounds, this time by combating the idea that music had a special influence on the soul. The emphasis which the Epicurean Philodemus placed on content in poetry is explained by the school's practical, utilitarian and educational outlook, while his emphasis on form in music was due to his distrust of the mystical interpretation, which was so popular in Greece. To champions of enlightenment, such as the Epicureans were, mysticism was more dangerous than formalism. In art they valued content more than form, but, given the choice, they preferred form to mystical content.

8. THE MINIMALIST CAMP. Philodemus devoted more attention to a specialized theory of the arts than to general aesthetics and was more concerned with combating the theories of others than with developing his own. We shall, therefore, have to return to his writings in discussing the ideas of other schools and the specialized theory of art current in his time, particularly in relation to the theories of music and poetry.

The attitude of the Epicureans towards aesthetics (i.e., both their original condemnation of beauty and art and their subsequent naturalistic interpretation of them) reflected the view of only a minority of the Hellens. The majority, including both Platonists and Peripatetics and even Stoics, admired beauty and art and tended to interpret them spiritualistically. In aesthetics as well as in other fields of philosophy, the Epicureans moved away from those schools and found themselves in the same camp as the Sceptics. Together these two groups formed in aesthetics a minimalist camp in opposition to the maximalists.

H. Texts from the Epicureans

EPICURUS (Maximus of Tyre, or. XXXII 5, Hobein 272).

BEAUTY AND PLEASURE

1. κἂν γὰρ τὸ καλὸν εἴπῃς, ἡδονὴν λέγεις· σχολῇ γὰρ ἂν εἴη τὸ κάλλος κάλλος, εἰ μὴ ἥδιστον εἴη.

1. Even if you speak of the beautiful you are speaking of pleasure; for beauty would hardly be beauty if it were not pleasurable.

EPICURUS (Athenaeus, XII, 546e).

2. οὐ γὰρ ἔγωγε δύναμαι νοῆσαι τἀγαθόν, ἀφαιρῶν μὲν τὰς διὰ χυλῶν ἡδονάς, ἀφαιρῶν δὲ τὰς δι' ἀφροδισίων, ἀφαιρῶν δὲ

2. As for myself, I cannot conceive the Good if I exclude the pleasures derived from taste, or those derived from sexual intercourse, or those

---

* A. Rastagni, "Filodemo contra l'estetica classica", *Rivista di filosofia* (1923). C. Benvenga, *Per la critica e l'estetica classica* (1951). A. J. Neubecker, *Die Bewertung der Musik bei Stoikern und Epikureern, Eine Analyse von Philodemus Schrift, "De musica"* (1956). A. Plebe, "Philodemo e la musica", *Filosofia*, VIII, 4 (1957).

τὰς δι' ἀκροαμάτων, ἀφαιρῶν δὲ καὶ τὰς διὰ μορφῆς κατ' ὄψιν ἡδείας κινήσεις.

derived from entertainments to which we listen, or those derived from the motions of a figure delightful to the eye.

tr. C. B. Onlick

EPICURUS (Athenaeus, XII 546f).

3. τιμητέον τὸ καλὸν καὶ τὰς ἀρετὰς καὶ τὰ τοιουτότροπα, ἐὰν ἡδονὴν παρασκευάζῃ· ἐὰν δὲ μὴ παρασκευάζῃ, χαίρειν ἐατέον.

3. We should prize the beautiful and the virtues and such things as that, provided they give us pleasure; but if they do not give pleasure, we should renounce them.

tr. C. B. Onlick

EPICURUS (Athenaeus, XII 547a).

4. προσπτύω τῷ καλῷ καὶ τοῖς κενῶς αὐτὸ θαυμάζουσιν, ὅταν μηδεμίαν ἡδονὴν ποιῇ.

4. I spit upon beauty and those who fruitlessly admire it, whensoever it causes no pleasure.

tr. C. B. Onlick

EPICURUS (Plutarch, Non posse suaviter vivi 2, 1086f).

5. 'Ηρακλείδης οὖν ... γραμματικὸς ὢν ἀντὶ τῆς ποιητικῆς τύρβης, ὡς ἐκεῖνοι λέγουσι, καὶ τῶν Ὁμήρου μωρολογημάτων ἀποτίνει ταύτας 'Επικούρῳ χάριτας.

NEGATIVE ATTITUDE TO ART

5. The grammarian Heracleides repays Epicurus in kind because the Epicurean school dared to talk about "poetical noise" and talked nonsense about Homer.

EPICURUS (Cicero, De fin. I 21, 71).

6. Nullam eruditionem esse duxit nisi quae beatae vitae disciplinam iuvaret. An ille tempus aut in poëtis evolvendis ... consumeret, in quibus nulla solida utilitas omnisque puerilis est delectatio?

6. ...he refused to consider any education worth the name that did not help to school us in happiness. Was he to spend his time... in perusing poets who give us nothing solid and useful, but merely childish amusement?

tr. H. Rackham

HERACLITUS, Quaest. Homer. 4 et 75.

7. ἅπασαν ὁμοῦ ποιητικὴν ὥσπερ ὀλέθριον μύθων δέλεαρ ἀφοσιούμενος... ὁ πᾶσαν ποιητικὴν ἄστροις σημηνάμενος, οὐκ ἐξαιρέτως μόνον Ὅμηρον.

7. He dismissed not only Homer but all poetry; he would have nothing to do with it because he assumed it to be merely a pernicious decoy for myths.

ATHENAEUS, V 187c.

8. ἀλλ' ὅμως τοιαῦτα γράφοντες ('Επίκουρος καὶ Πλάτων) τὸν Ὅμηρον ἐκβάλλουσι τῶν πόλεων.

8. Nevertheless, while writing that kind of stuff, they [Epicurus and Plato] banish Homer from their states.

tr. C. B. Onlick

LAËRTIUS DIOGENES, X 121.

9. μόνον τε τὸν σοφὸν ὀρθῶς ἂν περί τε μουσικῆς καὶ ποιητικῆς διαλέξεσθαι.

THE WISE MAN AS JUDGE OF ART

9. Only the wise man will be able to converse correctly about music and poetry.

tr. R. D. Hicks

LUCRETIUS, De rerum natura V 1379.

10. At liquidas avium voces imitarier ore
ante fuit multo quam levia carmina cantu
concelebrare homines possent aurisque iuvare.
et zephyri cava per calamorum sibila primum
agrestis docuere cavas inflare cicutas.
inde minutatim dulcis didicere querellas.

NATURE AS MODEL FOR ART

10. But imitating with the mouth the liquid notes of birds came long before men were able to repeat smooth songs in melody and please the ear. And the whistling of the zephyr through hollows of reeds first taught the men of the countryside to breathe into hollowed hemlock-stalks. Then little by little they learned the sweet lament...

tr. C. Bailey

LUCRETIUS, De rerum natura V 1448

11. Navigia atque agri culturas moenia
[leges
arma vias vestes et cetera de genere horum
praemia, delicias quoque vitae funditus omnis,
carmina, picturas et daedala signa polita,
usus et impigrae simul experientia mentis
paulatim docuit pedetemptim progredientis.
sic unum quicquid paulatim protrahit aetas
in medium ratioque in luminis erigit oras;
namque alid ex alio clarescere corde videbant
atribus ad summum donec venere cacumen.

EVOLUTION OF THE ARTS

11. Ships and the tilling of the land, walls, laws, weapons, roads, dress, and all things of this kind, all the prizes and the luxuries of life, one and all, songs and pictures and the quaintly wrought polished statues, practice and therewith the inventiveness of the eager mind taught them little by little as they went forward step by step. So, little by little, time brings out each thing into view and reason raises it up into the coasts of light. For they saw one thing after another grow clear in their mind, until by their arts they reached the topmost pinnacle.

tr. C. Bailey

12. The texts from Philodemus are given in the chapters concerning poetry and music (L and M, pp. 229-230, 248, 251, 256-258).

4. The Aesthetics of the Sceptics

1. AESTHETICS IN THE WRITINGS OF THE SCEPTICS. The basic philosophical conviction of the Sceptics was that certainty is unattainable. Early Sceptics applied it only to truth and goodness and not to beauty. It does not seem that either Pyrrhon, the founder of the school, or his immediate successors expressed themselves on the subject of beauty and art. The matter is, however, discussed by a late representative of the school, Sextus Empiricus; a large portion of his work has survived. This physician and philosopher, who flourished towards the end of the second century A.D., compiled the problems and arguments of the Sceptics. The arguments concerning aesthetics are discussed in *Against the Professors* (*Adversus mathematicos*), while the fullest discussion of music occurs in book VI of *Against the Musicians* (vol. II, 238-261) and of the problems of poetry in *Against the Grammarians*, chap. XIII (vol. II, 274-277).

In accordance with their general philosophy, the Sceptics emphasized the discords and the contradictions of all judgments about beauty and art. So long as the Greeks lived in isolation and had little contact with foreigners, so long as they were acquainted only with their own art and their own taste, they could see few divergences of opinion. When, however, from the days of Alexander the Great, they began to be confronted with other, non-Greek, types of art and judgments on beauty, they realized the existence of contradictory aesthetic views. The Sceptics utilized these contradictions as an argument in support of their aesthetic scepticism.

If earlier Greek philosophers condemned aesthetics, they did so because they distrusted either art or beauty or aesthetics itself. Plato was condemning art, the Epicureans were condemning beauty, and the Sceptics attacked aesthetics; they did so for its claim to be a science. Though beauty and art exist, there can be no true knowledge about them, they maintained. In particular, they attacked the theories of literature and music. A theory of visual art had not yet developed. So far no claim had been made that it was a science.

2. AGAINST LITERARY THEORY. The Sceptics held that poetry has little use and is even harmful, because its fictions confuse the mind. At best, poetry gives pleasure. It lacks objective beauty. It does not teach happiness or virtue. In contrast to what the Greeks believed, poetry lacks philosophical content: from a philosophical point of view poetry is either trivial or false. The opinion of the Sceptics on poetical theory was even more hostile than on poetry itself.

In Hellenistic times the theory of literature was termed "grammar" and the theoreticians "grammarians" (from *gramma*—"letter"; our term "man of letters" comes from the latin equivalent). The Sceptics' objections to "grammar" were threefold; they considered it impossible, as well as unnecessary and harmful.

(*a*) A theory of literature is *impossible*. Since the Sceptics set out to prove that no science, not even mathematics or physics, could fulfil the demands we should make on science, it was easy for them to prove that the study of literature cannot fulfil them, that indeed no such science could exist or be possible. They reasoned[1] that the theory of literature is either knowledge of all literary works or of some. If it were knowledge of all works, then it must be knowledge of an infinite number of works, and since infinity is beyond our comprehension, such a science is an impossibility. And a science concerned with only certain works is not a science.

Another similar argument employed by the Sceptics was as follows: theory of literature is either knowledge of things which literary works describe, or of the words which these works employ. But knowledge of things is the province of the physicists and not of literary theorists. And a knowledge of words is impossible because there is an infinite number of words, and because everyone uses them in a different way.

(*b*) A literary theory is *unnecessary*. It is true that certain literary works of a reflective or educational character can be useful to some degree, but these are lucid in expression and do not require explanations by theoreticians. And literary works which need elucidation, serve no useful purpose.⁽²⁾ Evaluation of literary works is useful but it can only be provided by philosophy and serious study, not by literary theory.⁽³⁾ It might even be that literary theory is useful for the state; but it does not therefore follow that it is useful to man. It would be so only if it made man happy.⁽⁴⁾

(c) A literary theory may even be *harmful*. Among literary works some are perverse, demoralizing and harmful; any theory which is concerned with such works, which tries to elucidate or propagate them, must also cause harm.

3. AGAINST MUSIC. The Sceptics attacked musical theory with equal force. Since the ancients did not distinguish between music and musical theory, because they regarded music as being merely the application of theory, the Sceptics' attack was aimed at both music and its theory. They thought that its value and potentialities were overrated. They attacked it in two ways: the first argument was similar to that of the Epicurean school, and the second was their own; the former being moderate, the latter radical.

The first line of argument was directed against the widely disseminated Greek theory of the special psychological effects of music. The Pythagoreans, as well as Platonists and the Stoics, attributed a positively magical power to music, believing that it strengthened soldiers' courage in battle, soothed anger, gave enjoyment to the contented and brought relief to the suffering. It was thus seen as a potent and useful force.

To the Sceptics all this force was an illusion since there are men and beasts on whom it has no effect or whom it affects differently. If there are people who under the influence of its sound cease to be angry, afraid or sad, this is not because it arouses better emotions in them but because it temporarily distracts their attention. When it ceases, the unhealed mind lapses back into fear, anger or sorrow. Trumpets and drums do not increase an army's courage, but merely drown its fear momentarily. It is true that music affects men, but its effect is no different from that of sleep or wine—it is either soothing like sleep, or exciting like wine.

Other arguments, too, which the Greeks were wont to employ to show the force and value of music, were in turn rejected by Sextus. (a) According to one argument, the musical sense is a source of pleasure. To this Sextus replied that the non-musical do not miss⁽⁵⁾ this pleasure. A trained musician may be better able to judge a competition than a layman, but his pleasure is not therefore greater. (b) The defenders of music claimed that musicality is proof of education and, therefore, of the excellence of the mind. But, Sextus rejoined, music affects also those who have no education. Melodies lull children to sleep and even animals succumb to the magic of the flute. (c) The advocates of music claimed that melodies, some in particular, have an ennobling effect, but Sextus reminded the readers that this assertion had been questioned on many sides. For there were Greeks who, as we know, held that it was music which brings about sloth, inebriation and ruin. (d) The Pythagoreans said that music is constructed upon the same principles as philosophy, which is the highest activity of man. To this the Sceptics replied that this was obviously false. (e) The Pythagoreans also claimed that the harmony of music is an echo of cosmic harmony, to which the Sceptics retorted that cosmic harmony does not exist.[6]

The conclusion of this argument was that music possesses no special power, has no utility, does not bring happiness, and does not refine. Contrary assertions are based on prejudices, dogmas, superstitions and mistakes.

4. THE ALLEGED PROPERTIES OF MUSIC. If there were no sounds, Sextus said, there would be no music. And, in fact, there are no sounds: this follows from the work of eminent philosophers such as the Cyrenaics, Plato and Democritus. According to the Cyrenaics, nothing but sensations exist, and since sound is not sensation but that which evokes sensations, then there are no sounds. The same may be inferred from Plato, for whom only Ideas existed, and from Democritus, for whom only atoms existed, and sounds are neither Ideas nor atoms. And if the sounds do not exist, then neither does music.

The conclusion of the argument that music does not exist sounds paradoxical, but its meaning is simply that music does not exist independently of man and his sensations, though it does of course exist as a human experience. If this is so and if music is only an experience, then it has no objective, fixed properties. This is the meaning of the statement that "there is no music". It means, in particular, that music has no objective capability of affecting the emotions, of soothing or refining them, and that the effect depends as much on man as on music.

If music has no objective properties, then there can be no science of music, or, to use a modern terminology, there is no theory of music, but only a psychology of music. The Sceptics' conclusions, even when expressed in this less radical form, were painful to the Greeks, because they struck at their deep-seated conviction that they possessed an exact science of music and its effect on the human soul.

From Sextus' arguments against poetry and music can be deduced the Sceptics' view on art in general. If we ignore their deliberately paradoxical formulations, this view is as follows: general truths stated about art, its effect and value are only alleged truths, in reality they are false, unjustified generalizations. Moreover, they treat subjective human reactions to art as if those were objective properties of art.[7] This applies particularly to two assertions about art to which the Greeks attached particular importance, namely, assertions concerning its cognitive and ethical values. The Sceptics denied both, maintaining that art neither educates men nor improves them morally. Sometimes they asserted that its effect on man is negative, morally depraving,[8] but on the whole they were sceptical about its effect, whether positive or negative.

This view was not entirely new; it had been adumbrated by the Sophists when they preached the relativity and subjectivity of culture. In aesthetics their activity was important as a warning against dogmatism and hasty generalizations.

I. Texts from the Sceptics

SEXTUS EMPIRICUS,
Adv. mathem. I 66.

1. ὅταν οὖν λέγωσιν αὐτὴν [γραμματικὴν] ἐμπειρίαν κατὰ τὸ πλεῖστον τῶν παρὰ ποιηταῖς καὶ συγγραφεῦσι λεγομένων, φασὶ πάντων ἢ τινῶν. καὶ εἰ πάντων ... τῶν δὲ ἀπείρων οὐκ ἔστιν ἐμπειρία. διόπερ οὐδὲ γραμματική τις γενήσεται. εἰ δὲ τινῶν, ἐπεὶ καὶ οἱ ἰδιῶταί τινα τῶν παρὰ ποιηταῖς καὶ συγγραφεῦσι λεγομένων εἰδότες οὐκ ἔχουσι γραμματικὴν ἐμπειρίαν, οὐδὲ ταύτῃ εἶναι λεκτέον γραμματικήν.

LEARNING ABOUT LITERATURE IMPOSSIBLE

1. Now when they describe it as "expertness regarding most of the speech of the poets and composers", they mean either all or some of it. And if they mean "all", then, in the first place, it is no longer "regarding most of their speech" but all of it, and if all, then endless (for their speech is endless): but of the endless there is no experience: hence no Art of Grammar will exist. But if they mean "some", then, since even ordinary folk understand some of the speech of the poets and composers though they possess no grammatical expertness, neither in this case can one say that an Art of Grammar exists.

tr. R. G. Bury

SEXTUS EMPIRICUS,
Adv. mathem. I 278, 280.

2. πρόδηλόν ἐστιν, ὅτι ὁπόσα μὲν βιωφελῆ καὶ ἀναγκαῖα εὑρίσκεται παρὰ ποιηταῖς, οἷά ἐστι τὰ γνωμικὰ καὶ παραινετικά, ταῦτα σαφῶς αὐτοῖς πέφρασται καὶ οὐ δεῖται γραμματικῆς, ⟨ὁπόσα δὲ δεῖται γραμματικῆς⟩... ταῦτ' ἔστιν ἄχρηστα... χρειώδης γίνεται οὐχ ἡ γραμματική, ἀλλ' ἡ διακρίνειν δυναμένη φιλοσοφία.

LEARNING ABOUT LITERATURE VALUELESS

2. It is certainly plain that all the sayings in the poets which are found useful for life and necessary—such as those of a gnomic and hortatory character—are expressed by them clearly and have no need of grammar; [and those which need it]... are useless...What is useful is not grammar but that which is capable of making the distinction, namely philosophy.

tr. R. G. Bury

SEXTUS EMPIRICUS,
Adv. mathem. I 313, 314.

3. Οὐκοῦν τὰ μὲν πράγματα οὐ νοοῦσιν οἱ γραμματικοί. λείπεται τοίνυν τὰ ὀνόματα νοεῖν αὐτούς. ὃ πάλιν ἐστὶ ληρῶδες. πρῶτον μὲν γὰρ οὐδὲν ἔχουσι τεχνικὸν εἰς τὸ λέξιν γινώσκειν. ... εἶτα καὶ τοῦτ' ἀδύνατόν ἐστιν ἀπείρων οὐσῶν λέξεων καὶ ἄλλως παρ' ἄλλοις ὀνοματοποιηθεισῶν.

3. So then, the Grammarians do not understand the objects (behind the words). It only remains, then, that they understand the words. And that again is nonsense. For, firstly, they have no technical means for getting to know terms... And secondly, even this is impossible, as words are infinite in number and are constructed differently by different people...

tr. R. G. Bury

SEXTUS EMPIRICUS,
Adv. mathem. I 294.

4. ἄλλο μέν ἐστι τὸ πόλει χρήσιμον. ἄλλο δὲ τὸ ἡμῖν αὐτοῖς. σκυτοτομικὴ γοῦν καὶ χαλκευτικὴ πόλει μέν ἐστιν ἀναγκαῖον, ἡμῖν δὲ χαλκεῦσι γενέσθαι καὶ σκυτοτόμοις πρὸς

4. Moreover, usefulness for the State is one thing, usefulness for ourselves another thing. Thus the arts of the cobbler and the coppersmith are necessary to the State, but it is not

εὐδαιμονίαν οὐκ ἀναγκαῖον, διόπερ καὶ ἡ γραμματικὴ οὔκ, ἐπεὶ πόλει χρησίμη καθέστηκεν, ἐξ ἀνάγκης καὶ ἡμῖν ἐστὶν [ἡ] τοιαύτη.

necessary for our happiness that we should become copper-smiths and cobblers. Hence, the Art of Grammar is not necessarily useful to the State.

tr. R. G. Bury

SEXTUS EMPIRICUS,
Adv. mathem. VI 33.

5. ...Καὶ διὰ τοῦτο μή ποτε, ὃν τρόπον χωρὶς ὀψαρτυτικῆς καὶ οἰνογευστικῆς ἐδόμεθα ὄψου ἢ οἴνου γευσάμενοι, ὧδε καὶ χωρὶς μουσικῆς ἡσθείεμεν ἂν τερπνοῦ μέλους ἀκούσαντες, τοῦ μὲν ὅτι τεχνικῶς γίνεται, τοῦ τεχνίτου μᾶλλον παρὰ τὸν ἰδιώτην ἀντιλαμβανομένου, τοῦ δὲ πλεῖον ἡστικοῦ πάθους μηδὲν κερδαίνοντος.

MUSICAL KNOWLEDGE IS NOT A SOURCE OF PLEASURE

5. And for this reason it may be that, just as we enjoy tasting food or wine though without the art of cooking food or that of wine-tasting, so also, though without the art of music, we take pleasure in hearing a delightful melody; for though the expert musician understands that it is artistically performed better than the ordinary man, he gets from it no greater feeling of pleasure.

tr. R. G. Bury

SEXTUS EMPIRICUS,
Adv. mathem. VI 37.

6. τὸ δὲ κατὰ ἁρμονίαν διοικεῖσθαι τὸν κόσμον ποικίλως δείκνυται ψεῦδος, εἶτα καὶ ἂν ἀληθὲς ὑπάρχῃ, οὐδὲν τοιοῦτον δύναται πρὸς μακαριότητα, καθάπερ οὐδὲ ἡ ἐν τοῖς ὀργάνοις ἁρμονία.

THE WORLD IS NOT CONSTRUCTED HARMONIOUSLY

6. ...and that the Universe is ordered according to harmony is shown to be false by a variety of proofs; and further, even if it be true, a thing of this kind can be of no help towards felicity, just as the harmony in instruments is of no help.

tr. R. G. Bury

SEXTUS EMPIRICUS,
Adv. mathem. VI 20.

7. τῶν κατὰ μουσικὴν μελῶν οὐ φύσει τὰ μὲν τοῖά ἐστι, τὰ δὲ τοῖα, ἀλλ' ὑφ' ἡμῶν προσδοξάζεται.

SUBJECTIVITY OF JUDGMENTS ABOUT MUSIC

7. ... in the case of musical tunes it is not by nature that some are of this kind and others of that kind, but it is we ourselves who suppose them to be such.

tr. R. G. Bury

SEXTUS EMPIRICUS,
Adv. mathem. VI 34.

8. ἀνάπαλιν γὰρ ἀντικόπτει καὶ ἀντιβαίνει πρὸς τὸ τῆς ἀρετῆς ἐφίεσθαι, εὐαγώγους εἰς ἀκολασίαν καὶ λαγνείαν παρασκευάζουσα τοὺς νέους.

MORAL HARM OF MUSIC

8. [Music] resists and opposes the striving after virtue, making young people easily led into incontinence and debauchery...

tr. R. G. Bury

5. The Aesthetics of the Stoics

1. THE STOICS' WORKS ON AESTHETICS. The history of Stoicism* spans several centuries and may be divided into three periods. The first period covers the early

---

* J. ab Arnim, *Stoicorum veterum fragmenta,* 3 vols. (1903–5). M. Pohlenz, *Die Stoa, Geschichte einer geistigen Bewegung* (1948), esp. vol. II, p. 216 ff.

Stoicism of the third century B.C. and includes the work of Zeno, Cleanthes and Chrysippus, the founders of the school. This is followed by the middle period of Stoicism from the late second to early first century. Prominent in this period were Philon of Larissa, Panaetius and Posidonius. Finally comes the late Stoicism of the Roman Empire.

Ariston of Chios, a pupil of Zeno in the third century B.C., also belonged to the old school. We know his poetics from Philodemus. In a similarly indirect way we know that Diogenes the Babylonian (middle of the second century B.C.) had an interest in aesthetics. He was a pupil of Chrysippus and the teacher of Panaetius, and he thus provided a link between the old and the middle school. Although we do not have any direct knowledge of Ariston's or Diogenes' views, we do know that their achievement lay in the field of aesthetics.

Our knowledge of the aesthetics of Panaetius (c.185–110) and Posidonius (c.135–c.50), the leaders of the middle school, is also fragmentary, but it shows that their interest in aesthetics was wider than that of older Stoics.

There were two types of Stoics. There were the so-called *panu stoikoi*, that is, the complete, extreme and uncompromising thinkers, who preached the absolute subordination of beauty to virtue and allowed little space to aesthetics in their studies. This, however, does not apply to other members of the school such as Ariston or Posidonius.

The later Roman Stoics such as Epictetus and Marcus Aurelius paid little attention to beauty and art. Seneca (d.65. A.D.) wrote somewhat more on the subject. His *Letters* (*Epistolae Morales ad Lucilium*) are a fairly substantial source of Stoic aesthetics*, which he adopted to Roman taste and simplified. Cicero was not a Stoic, but several features of Stoic aesthetics found their way into the writings of this most distinguished of Roman aestheticians.

2. THE PHILOSOPHICAL FOUNDATIONS OF STOIC AESTHETICS. Stoicism found itself in a special position both during the Hellenistic and the Roman era. Platonism appeared too vague, Aristotelianism too professional, and Scepticism too negative. Epicurus had little sympathy for art and took no interest in aesthetics. This turned out to be advantageous for the aesthetics of the Stoics. Although it was of little importance to the Stoics themselves, paradoxically it enjoyed wide popularity in the Hellenistic world.

The aesthetics of the Stoics was circumscribed by the general assumptions of their system: by their ethics and ontology. It was characterized by Stoic moralism, by the belief that aesthetic values should be subordinated to moral values. On the other hand, the aesthetics of the Stoics was based on their theory of the Logos, which constrained the Stoics to regard the world as being imbued with reason. They ascribed to the real world the reason, perfection and beauty, which Plato had perceived only in ideal Forms.

---

* K. Svoboda, "Les idées esthétiques de Sénèque", *Mélanges Marouzeau* (1948), p. 537.

Thus, while the Stoics' ethical assumptions meant that their aesthetics approximated the non-autonomous aesthetics of the Epicureans, their cosmological assumptions approximated Platonic and Aristotelian theory. This gave rise to two variants of Stoic aesthetics: a negative one, with Cynical features, and a positive one, which rejected Cynical elements in favour of Platonic ones.

3. MORAL VERSUS AESTHETIC BEAUTY. The Stoics adopted the traditional wide concept of beauty, which included both mental (moral) and sensory (bodily) beauty. But as they valued moral beauty more highly than bodily beauty, they distinguished the two more sharply than it had ever been done before. They thus brought about an isolation of mental beauty on the one hand and of sensory beauty on the other.

This is how Philon describes the ideas of the Stoics: „For beauty of body lies in well-proportioned parts, in a fine complexion [*euchroia*] and good condition of flesh [*eusarkia*], ... beauty of mind lies in harmony of creed, in concert [*symphonia*] of virtue".[1] Similar statements occur in Stobaeus,[2] Cicero and others.* All of them regarded spiritual and moral beauty, the beauty of the mind, as almost identical with moral good and quite distinct from beauty in an aesthetic sense. On the contrary, what they regarded as physical and sensory beauty was in fact aesthetic beauty.

The Stoics, however, attributed little value to aesthetic beauty, the true beauty being moral beauty. In their aesthetic moralism they surpassed even Plato. They wrote that beauty and goodness are either synonymous with virtue or have a connection with it.[3] Zeno, the founder of the Stoic school, claimed that the function of art is to serve useful ends, which in his opinion could only be moral ends. Since, in turn, the Stoics equated virtue with wisdom, they proclaimed paradoxically that a sage "is most handsome even when he is repulsive", that he is morally beautiful even though physically ugly.[4]

Replying to the question "what is goodness?" Cleanthes supplied 31 adjectives; one of these, but only one of these 31 was the adjective "beautiful". In speaking of beauty, Seneca must chiefly have had moral beauty in mind, since he held that there is nothing more beautiful than virtue, beside which all other beauty pales. It is, on the contrary, virtue that gives the body its true beauty and "consecrates it" (*corpus suum consecrat*). Epictetus wrote: "Human beauty is not physical beauty. Your body, your hair, is not beautiful, but your mind and your will may be beautiful. Make them beautiful and you will be beautiful". Seneca would not even accept Virgil's statement that "virtue is more appealing in a beautiful body". Virtue "is an embellishment unto itself and quite a considerable one at that". Physical beauty

---

* A number of the Stoics' propositions regarding aesthetics achieved wide acceptance in antiquity and were constantly quoted by writers, through whom they have been handed down to us. Among these is the Stoic definition of art which we find formulated in similar terms not only in Philon and Stobaeus, but also in Lucian's *De paras.*, c. 4, in Sextus Empiricus' *Adv. math.*, II, 10, and *Pyrrh. Hipot.*, III, 188, 241, 251, in the *Scholia ad Dionysium*, 659 and 721, and in Latin in Quintilian and in Cicero *Acad. Pr.*, II, 22; *De Fin.*, III, 13, and *De nat. deor.*, II, 148.

may even be harmful to man depending on the use he makes of it and it is in this that it differs from spiritual beauty, which is always good. If the Stoic moralists were less reluctant to talk about beauty than the Epicureans, it was because they were thinking primarily of moral beauty.

The Stoics' moralism constrained them to seek beauty in virtue, that is, in man. Their moralism, however, represented only a part of their aesthetics. Pantheism and optimism impelled them to discover beauty also in nature and the universe.

4. BEAUTY OF THE WORLD. The Stoics claimed that "Nature is the greatest artist" and held that, in Cicero's words, "there in nothing better or more beautiful than the world". They followed the Pythagoreans in saying that order rules the world and Heraclitus in saying that harmony rules it; they followed Plato in saying that the world is constructed organically, and Aristotle in believing it has a teleological end. Their achievement was to lay greater stress on these ideas and to attain a theory about the universality of beauty in the world; employing a Greek term, we might call it *pankalia*. The concept of *pankalia*, which we know best from later aesthetics, particularly the religious aesthetics of the Christians, originated with the Stoics and was characteristic of their doctrine.

Posidonius wrote: "The world is beautiful. This is clear from its shape, colour and rich array of stars".[5] It has the shape of a sphere, the most beautiful shape. Thanks to its homogeneity—or, as we would say, organic character—it is as beautiful as an animal or a tree. In describing the Stoics' ideas Cicero said[6] that the world has no deficiency, that it is perfect in all its proportions and parts.

The Stoics discerned beauty not only in the world as a whole, but also in its separate parts, in particular objects and particular living things. The later *kalodicea* of the Christians was more circumspect. It defended the beauty of the world as a whole, but would not commit itself regarding the beauty of its parts. The Stoics even claimed that beauty is the *raison d'être* of some objects, because Nature "loves beauty and takes delight in richness of colours and shapes".[7] Thanks to the miraculous guidance of nature, the vine not only brings useful fruit but is also capable of embellishing its trunk.[8] Chrysippus maintained that peacocks came into being solely because of their beauty, though as a moralist he condemned those who reared them. The Stoics did not deny the existence of ugly things in the world, but argued that they exist because they are needed to provide a contrast with beauty and make it more distinguishable from them. They saw nature as art's model and tutor (*magister*) but, on the other hand, they regarded it both as an art and as an "artist". Cicero records Zeno's view as *omnia natura artificiosa est*,[9] while Chrysippus wrote that the universe is the most excellent of all works of art.[10-11]

5. ESSENCE OF BEAUTY. To the question of what beauty depends on, the Stoics gave a unanimous reply in line with the main tradition of Greek aesthetics and declared that beauty depends on measure and proportion. They retained both the traditional concept and the traditional term *symmetria*. One of the definitions of beauty put forward by the early Stoics described it as that which is "ideally pro-

portional" (*to teleios symmetron*). According to Galen's description[12] of the Stoics' view, *symmetria* and *asymmetria*, or proportion and lack of proportion are the decisive factors in beauty and ugliness, while in another place he says that the Stoics saw beauty as being like health because in a similar way it depends on the *symmetria* of parts.[13] They also applied the concept of *symmetria* to spiritual beauty. Chrysippus drew a parallel between the beauty of the body and the beauty of the soul, treating them as two kinds of *symmetria*. Stobaeus described the Stoics' outlook thus: "The beauty of the body is the just proportion of parts in their mutual relation and in relation to the whole. So, similarly, the beauty of the soul is a just proportion of the mind, of its parts in relation to the whole and to each other". Diogenes Laertius gives the following Stoic definitions of beauty: 1. that which is ideally proportioned, 2. that which is adapted to its purpose, 3. that which adorns. However, the first of these was their fundamental definition.[14]

The Stoic school assimilated this broad definition of beauty and art, which was traditional in Greece and which, through their influence, became disseminated even more widely. But by applying the concept of *symmetria* to spiritual beauty, the Stoics had to abandon its mathematical basis and treat the idea in a more general sense. In addition to this definition, the Stoic school originated another narrower definition which applied exclusively to physical beauty. According to this definition, beauty depends not only on proportion, but also on colour. Cicero says: "What we call beauty in a body is some suitable appearance of parts (*apta figura membrorum*) combined with a certain pleasurableness of colour (*cum coloris quadam suavitate*). This definition gained acceptance in the Hellenistic period when the description of beauty was often based on the two characteristics of proportion and colour. This was a shift of considerable significance, for it meant a narrowing of the concept of beauty to the merely sensuous or even exclusively visual. In this way it anticipated the modern concept. It is remarkable also that the concept should have originated with the Stoics, who primarily valued non-sensuous beauty.

6. DECORUM. The Stoics employed yet another very general concept, which was also inherited but to which they added more independent thought that they did to the concept of beauty. The Greek term was *prepon* and the Latin *decorum*.* In Latin there were the variants *decens* and *quod decet* and the synonyms *aptus* and *conveniens*. All these expressions meant that which is proper, fitting and just. These terms denoted beauty, but a beauty of a special kind, different from *symmetria*. *Decorum* embodied the concern for the adjustment of parts to the whole, while *symmetria* was concerned with the agreement of parts among themselves. There was a further, more essential difference: in *decorum* the ancients saw individual beauty, adjusted to fit the specific character of each object, human being or situation, while *symmetria* signified an accord with the general laws of beauty. They sought

---

* M. Pohlenz, "Τό πρέπον", *Nachrichten von der Gesellschaft der Wissenschaften zu Göttingen*, Philol.-hist. Klasse, Bd. 1, p. 90 ff.

symmetria primarily in nature and *decorum* primarily in human artefacts, which, however, included not only art but also ways of life and customs. The concept was thus not only aesthetic in character but also ethical, or, more correctly, it was originally ethical, and only later came to include beauty and art. It was applied specially to those arts that have to do with man and his ethos, that is to poetics and oratory. The concept of *decorum* was basic to poetics and oratory, but was much less relevant to the theory of the visual arts.

Since *decorum* ruled human actions, it seemed particularly important. Cicero advised "adherence to and observance of what is proper", while Quintilian recommended that "one should abide by what is proper" and Dionysius called *decorum* "the highest virtue". Since, however, *decorum* was individual in character and did not depend on conformity to rules, it had on each occasion to be fixed anew and thus presented special difficulties. Cicero wrote that "there is nothing more difficult than to discover what is fitting; the Greeks call it *prepon* while we call it *decorum*".[15]

The concept of *decorum* occupied a worthy place in the general framework of ancient aesthetics. If the theory of *symmetria* represented one of its main doctrines, the theory of *decorum* represented another, complementary to it, and on occasion even predominant. The one was motivated by the idea of general and absolute beauty, the other by human, individual, relative beauty. The former was Pythagoreo-Platonic, while the other was decisively anti-Platonic and had already its spokesmen in Gorgias and the Sophists. The one was an expression of archaic art, the other of the later, more individualistic art initiated by Euripides and the fifth-century sculptors. To the latter belonged the Socratic idea that beauty depends on conformity with a goal. Aristotle divided his sympathies between these two doctrines of ancient aesthetics and the same was true of the Stoics, who recognized beauty both as *symmetria* and as *decorum*.

Symmetria was absolute beauty, but *decorum* was relative. According to the Stoics, it was relative only with respect to the subject (*to pragmati*).[16] Each object they believed had its *decorum* dependent upon its nature, and not upon time. The Sophists had thought otherwise, and in later times also some writers, among them Quintilian, argued that *decorum* alters with each person, time, place and cause (*pro persona, tempore, loco, causa*).

The ancients regarded the discovery of *symmetria* as a task involving thought, understanding and calculation. The discovery of *decorum*, however, required feeling and talent. It was the Stoics, in particular, who emphasized this sensuous and irrational element in aesthetics. This had further consequences, which we shall describe below.

7. VALUE OF BEAUTY. Like Plato and Aristotle, the Stoics held beauty is valuable in itself. Chrysippus said that "beautiful things are praiseworthy".[17] Unlike the Epicureans, the Stoics were convinced that we value things for their own sake and not for their utility. Although they may be useful, this usefulness is a product and not an aim: *sequitur, non antecedit*. Cicero tells us that the Stoics thought things in

art and nature were valuable for their own sake because they bore the stamp of reason. The Stoics, he says, did not think these things valuable because of their utility, nor exclusively because of the pleasure they provide. Such pleasure, too, is a product and not an aim. The Romans classed beauty as *honestum*, by which, Cicero explains, they understood that which is precious and praiseworthy independently of its usefulness or the rewards and fruits it would bring. To use modern terms, beauty had for the Stoics an objective value. Only moral beauty had a high value, however. Aesthetic beauty was objective, but possessed relatively low value. For this reason beauty could not be an ultimate goal and art could not be autonomous. There was, however, no contradiction between the Stoic belief in the objectivity of beauty and their view that art had no autonomy.

8. IMAGINATION. The Stoics also made a contribution to the history of the psychology of beauty. This they achieved by supplementing the original Greek psychology, which by and large relied on the two basic concepts: of thought and the senses. For a long time these were the only concepts employed to explain how a work of art is formed in the artist's mind and how it affects the spectator or the listener. During the Hellenistic era a third concept, that of imagination, appeared. This was a contribution of Stoics, who took a greater interest in psychology than other philosophical schools and had arrived at much finer distinctions. The Stoics also coined the term *phantasia*.[18] Their contribution soon became common property. Though at first it had a general psychological character, it soon came to be employed specifically in the psychology of art, where it acquired a dominant position and began to supersede the old concept of "imitation". Thus, towards the end of antiquity Philostratus could write that "the imagination is a wiser artist than imitation".

9. ART. The Stoics took comparatively less interest in art than in beauty, since they regarded its beauty as inferior to that of nature. They employed the broad traditional idea, which embraced not only the fine arts, but the whole range of skilled human production. They defined and developed this concept independently, however, by likening art to a "road". As a road is assigned by its goal, so is art; and it must be subordinated to its goal. This idea originated with Zeno[19] and Cleanthes, and later was expressed by Quintilian.[20]

In defining art the Stoics also employed the term "system" (*systema*), meaning a closely knit cluster. They spoke of art as being "a cluster and a collection of observations",[21] or, more precisely, as "a cluster of observations tested by experience and serving a useful purpose in life".[22–22a]

They classified arts in the most ordinary way. Just as they contrasted physical with spiritual life, so they divided the arts into *vulgares* and *liberales*, that is, "common" arts, which demanded physical toil, and "free" arts, which did not. In this sense, skills, rather than art in the modern meaning of the term, were free. From Posidonius onwards two further categories were added: the "recreational" (*ludicrae*) and "educational" (*pueriles*) arts.[23] This fourfold classification appears in Seneca, Quintilian and Plutarch. The arts in the modern sense did not constitute a distinct group but were, on the contrary, completely divided. Painting and sculpture were classed as recreational, architecture was seen as a craft, while music and poetry belonged to the educational and free arts.

10. THE STOIC VIEW OF POETRY. The philosophical bias of the Stoics inclined them in their treatment of the arts to give much attention to poetry and to value it principally for its content. For them a poem was beautiful when it "contained a wise thought".[24] Rhythmical utterance and poetical form were to them no more than a means of presenting wise thoughts either more emphatically or more pleasantly. Old Cleanthes compared poetic form with a musical instrument, a trumpet, which makes the player's breath more resonant.[25] Posidonius' definition of poetry, which enjoyed the greatest esteem in the Hellenistic era, retained this original Stoic view and stated that poetry was "words charged with meaning, representing divine or human things" and distinguished by a metrical and rhythmical form.

In his interpretation the task of poetry was hardly different from that of knowledge. Such a view had been adopted by the early Greeks, but their descendants saw fundamental difference between poetry and knowledge and tried to define it, while the Stoics went back to the original conception. Cleanthes even held that melodies and rhythms may better reveal the truth about divine things than philosophical argument.[26] One could say that he ascribed to poetry extraordinary functions and did not pay much attention to its ordinary ones. Normally, however, the Stoics did not go so far as this, but saw in poetry only a propaedeutic philosophy, teaching the same things as philosophy but in a pleasant and accessible manner. The object of poetry, as of philosophy and science in general, was thought to be the conveyance of truth. Poetry, however, had to be stated allegorically so that the fiction would fall away and only the truth would be left. Thus, the Stoics became champions of an allegorical interpretation of poetry. In the light of this view they insisted that those who judge poetry and art should have special qualifications and that these qualifications[27] are possessed only by few.

The Stoics did not value poets who only "flatter the ear" (*aures oblectant*) and worry about the beauty of their poems instead of fulfilling their task of speaking the truth and acting morally.[28] In a similar way, Seneca rebuked musicians for striving towards a harmony of sounds instead of a harmony of the soul. He did not count painting and sculpture among the liberal arts.[29] Of all the arts, the Stoics valued least those which we call fine arts, because they believed them to be least well suited for the utterance of truth and for moral action. They expressed their negative attitude toward them by saying that they were invented by men, whereas Nature taught the other arts. They valued beauty only so long as it was spiritual and did not value art if it concerned itself with the sensuous beauty of shapes, colours and sounds.

11. DIRECT INTUITION OF BEAUTY. During a period of six centuries there were many Stoics and their school harboured many streams and groups. This variety was also reflected in their aesthetics. One stream was that of philosopher-moralists

and intellectuals. It began with Zeno and Chrysippus and ended with Marcus Aurelius and Seneca. Here we find the views which have been described above, namely that truth and moral action are the criteria of good art. There is, however, another line which can be traced from Ariston and Diogenes the Babylonian, who drew upon the Academician Speusippus. The representatives of this line laid stress on the sensuous elements of beauty and art* and developed the concepts of suitability and fantasy. They also produced a different evaluation of art and a different description of its nature and effect; contrary to the Pythagoreans, they stated that art is not rational and does not act on the mind. Contrary to the Epicureans, they thought that art is not a matter of feeling and subjective pleasure, since it affects sensuous impressions (*aisthesis*). It is judged by the ears and eyes and not the mind, and man reacts towards it in a natural way without any rationalization; his judgment of it is individualistic, not general. The Stoics doubtless based this idea on Ariston, who, having distinguished two cognitive faculties (the rational and the sensuous), connected poetry as well as music with the senses, seeing their value in harmonious sound and the criterion by which they should be judged in their auditory effect.

This point of view was elaborated by Diogenes,[30] who accepted the idea that in man there exists a congenital irrational impression (*aisthesis autophues*) but at the same time thought that this may be developed by training and education (*epistemonike*). Such training and education becomes the surest criterion of measure, harmony and beauty. This was a valuable idea, a middle course between the usual extremes of the Greeks, their extreme intellectualism on the one hand and their extreme sensualism and emotionalism on the other. Diogenes drew a distinction between impressions and feelings with their attendant pleasures and pains, maintaining that these feelings are subjective but not the impressions. "Educated" impressions are sensuous but they are also objective and so may serve as basis of scientific knowledge.

Diogenes' idea was taken up by his pupil Panaetius, who was also convinced of man's direct experience of beauty. Thanks to him this second line pursued by the Stoics became dominant in their middle period. The idea of direct experience of beauty appeared about that time in several quarters but it would seem that the Stoics contributed most to its formulation and consolidation.

12. SUMMARY. Although their philosophical principles were not suited to make aestheticians of them and, on the whole, impeded their investigations into aesthetics, the Stoics had some successes in this field. They perfected the definitions of beauty, art and poetry, they introduced a sharper distinction between spiritual and physical beauty, they developed the concept of *decorum*, and they grasped the role of the imagination and the direct experience of beauty. They also originated the idea of the beauty of the world.

---

* Cf. Neubecker, *op. cit.* and Plebe, *op. cit.*

The aesthetic ideas of the Stoics were the most influential in the Hellenistic period. At the beginning of the period aesthetics benefited most from the detailed investigations of the Aristotelians, and at its close from the final synthesis of the Neo-Platonic Plotinus; the middle centuries of this long period, however, were dominated by the aesthetic ideas of the Stoics. Their views about beauty and art gained a general acceptance which persisted for a long time. In this sense it may be said that the aesthetics of the Stoics was the aesthetics of Hellenism. Cicero, the most distinguished Roman aesthetician, was indeed an eclectic, but he paid more attention to the doctrines of the Stoics than to those of any other school.

J. Texts from the Stoics

STOICS (Philon, De Moyse III, vol. II. Mang. 156).

1. τὸ μὲν γὰρ τοῦ σώματος [scil. κάλλος] ἐν συμμετρίᾳ μερῶν εὐχροίᾳ τε καὶ εὐσαρκίᾳ κεῖται, ... τὸ δὲ τῆς διανοίας ἐν ἁρμονίᾳ δογμάτων καὶ ἀρετῶν συμφωνίᾳ.

BODILY AND HEAVENLY BEAUTY

1. For beauty of body lies in well-proportioned parts, in a fine complexion and good condition of flesh... But beauty of mind lies in harmony of creed, in concert (*sic*) of virtue.

tr. F. H. Colson

STOICS (Stobaeus, Ecl. II 62, 15 W.).

2. τὸ κάλλος τοῦ σώματός ἐστι συμμετρία τῶν μελῶν καθεστώτων αὐτῷ πρὸς ἄλληλά τε καὶ πρὸς τὸ ὅλον, οὕτω καὶ τὸ τῆς ψυχῆς κάλλος ἐστὶ συμμετρία τοῦ λόγου καὶ τῶν μερῶν αὐτοῦ πρὸς τὸ ὅλον τε αὐτῆς καὶ πρὸς ἄλληλα.

2. Bodily beauty is the proportion of limbs in their mutual relation and in relation to the whole; similarly the beauty of the soul is a proportion of the mind, of its parts in relation to the whole and to each other.

CHRYSIPPUS (in Stobaeus, Ecl. II 77, 16 W.).

3. δῆλον ... ὅτι ἰσοδυναμεῖ «τὸ κατὰ φύσιν ζῆν» καὶ «τὸ καλῶς ζῆν» καὶ πάλιν «τὸ καλὸν κἀγαθόν» καὶ «ἡ ἀρετὴ καὶ τὸ μετόχον ἀρετῆς».

MORAL BEAUTY

3. It is clear that the expressions "to live in accordance with nature", "to live beautifully", mean the same, and that "beautiful" and "good" means the same as "virtue or that which is connected with virtue".

STOICS (Acro, Ad Hor. Serm. I 3, 124).

4. Dicunt Stoici sapientem divitem esse, si mendicet, et nobilem esse, si servus sit, et pulcherrimum esse, etiamsi sit sordidissimus.

4. The Stoics say the wise man is rich even when he begs, is of noble birth even when he is a slave, and is most handsome even when he is repulsive.

POSIDONIUS (Aëtius, Plac. I 6).

5. καλὸς δὲ ὁ κόσμος· δῆλον δὲ ἐκ τοῦ σχήματος καὶ τοῦ χρώματος καὶ τῆς περὶ τὸν κόσμον τῶν ἀστέρων ποικιλίας· σφαιροειδὴς

BEAUTY OF THE WORLD

5. The world is beautiful. This is clear from its shape, colour and rich array of stars. For it has the shape of a sphere which surpasses

γὰρ ὁ κόσμος, ὃ πάντων σχημάτων πρωτεύει ... καὶ τὸ χρῶμα δὲ καλόν ... καὶ ἐκ τοῦ μεγέθους καλός. πάντων γὰρ τῶν ὁμογενῶν τὸ περιέχον καλὸν ὡς ζῷον καὶ δένδρον. ἐπιτελεῖ τὸ κάλλος τοῦ κόσμου καὶ ταῦτα τὰ φαινόμενα.

all other shapes... Its hue is also beautiful. Further, it is beautiful on account of its great size. Because it embraces related objects, it is as beautiful as living creatures and trees. These phenomena add to the world's beauty.

STOICS (Cicero, De nat. deor. II 13, 37).

6. Neque enim est quicquam aliud praeter mundum quoi nihil absit quodque undique aptum atque perfectum expletumque sit omnibus suis numeris et partibus.

6. In fact there is nothing else beside the world that has nothing wanting, but is fully equipped and complete and perfect in all its details and parts.

tr. H. Rackham

CHRYSIPPUS (Plutarch, De Stoic. repugn. 21, 1044c.).

BEAUTY OF LIVING THINGS

7. Γράψας τοίνυν ἐν τοῖς περὶ Φύσεως ὅτι «πολλὰ τῶν ζῴων ἕνεκα κάλλους ἡ φύ σι ἐνήνοχε, φιλοκαλοῦσα καὶ χαίρουσα τῇ ποικιλίᾳ» καὶ λόγον ἐπειπὼν παραλογώτατον ὡς «ὁ ταὼς ἕνεκα τῆς οὐρᾶς γέγονε, διὰ τὸ κάλλος αὐτῆς».

7. [Chrysippus] has written in his treatise on nature: "Nature brings forth many living creatures for the sake of beauty because it loves beauty and takes delight in richness of colours and shapes", and he added a most strange observation: "The peacock was created on account of its tail, on account of the beauty of the tail".

CHRYSIPPUS (Philon, De animalibus, Aucher, 163).

8. Certe omnino per mirabilem operique praesidentem naturam par fuit non solum utilissimo fructui ferendo, verum etiam adornando trunco decore (sc. vitis).

8. Surely it was due to the miraculous guidance of nature that [the vine] has not only brought forth a useful fruit, but was also able to decorate its trunk.

ZENO (Cicero, De nat. deor. II 22, 57).

NATURE AS ARTIST

9. Censet enim [Zeno] artis maxime proprium esse creare et gignere; quodque in operibus nostrarum artium manus efficiat, id multo artificiosius naturam efficere, id est, ut dixi, ignem artificiosum, magistrum artium reliquarum. Atque hac quidem ratione omnis natura artificiosa est, quod habet quasi viam quandam et sectam, quam sequatur.

9. [According to Zeno] to create and to give birth is the characteristic of art, but everything that our hand does is done far more artistically by nature; as I have said, the creative fire is the teacher of other arts. For this reason nature in all its manifestations is an artist, because it has its ways and means to which it adheres.

CHRYSIPPUS (Philon, De monarchia I 216M.)

10. Ἀεὶ τοίνυν γνωρίσματα τῶν δημιουργῶν πέφυκέ πως εἶναι τὰ δημιουργηθέντα· τίς γὰρ ἀνδριάντας ἢ γραφὰς θεασάμενος οὐκ εὐθὺς ἐνόησεν ἀνδριαντοποιὸν ἢ ζωγράφον; τίς δ' ἐσθῆτας ἢ ναῦς ἢ οἰκίας ἰδὼν οὐκ ἔννοιαν ἔλαβεν ὑφάντου καὶ ναυπηγοῦ καὶ

10. An artefact is always in some way an expression of its creator: for who, seeing a statue or a painting will not at once think of the sculptor or the painter? Who, seeing a robe, a ship or a house will not think of the weaver, the shipwright, the architect?... No

οἰκοδόμου. [...] Οὐδὲν γὰρ τῶν τεχνικῶν ἔργων ἀπαυτοματίζεται· τεχνικώτατος δὲ καὶ ὁ κόσμος, ὡς ὑπό τινος τὴν ἐπιστήμην ἀγαθοῦ καὶ τελειοτάτου πάντως δεδημιουργῆσθαι. Cf. Aëtius, Plac. I 6.

work of art arises out of itself. And the greatest work of art is the universe—so is it not the work of someone of excellent wisdom and most perfect in every respect?

STOICS (Cicero, De nat. deor. II 13, 35).

11. Ut pictura et fabrica ceteraeque artes habent quendam absoluti operis effectum, sic in omni natura, ac multo etiam magis, necesse est absolvi aliquid ac perfici.

11. Just as painting, handicraft and other arts result in a finished product, so in the whole of nature there must, even more so, arise something finished and final.

CHRYSIPPUS (Galen, De placitis Hipp. et Plat. V 2 (158) Müll. 416).

12. ἡ ἐν θερμοῖς καὶ ψυχροῖς καὶ ὑγροῖς καὶ ξηροῖς γενομένη συμμετρία ἢ ἀσυμμετρία ἐστὶν ὑγίεια ἢ νόσος, ἡ δ' ἐν νεύροις συμμετρία ἢ ἀσυμμετρία ἰσχὺς ἢ ἀσθένεια καὶ εὐτονία ἢ ἀτονία, ἡ δ' ἐν τοῖς μέλεσι συμμετρία ἢ ἀσυμμετρία κάλλος ἢ αἶσχος.

CONCEPT OF BEAUTY

12. Just as proportion and the lack of it in warmth and cold or in dampness and dryness affect health and illness, just as proportion and the lack of it in muscles result in strength or weakness, in resilience or atrophy, so proportion or the lack of it in the limbs result in beauty or ugliness.

CHRYSIPPUS (Galen, De placitis Hipp. et Plat. V 3 (161) Müll. 425).

13. τὴν μὲν ὑγίειαν ἐν τῇ τῶν στοιχείων συμμετρίᾳ θέμενος, τὸ δὲ κάλλος ἐν τῇ τῶν μορίων.

ESSENCE OF BEAUTY

13. He claimed that health depends on the just proportion of the elements while beauty depends on the just proportion of the parts.

STOICS (Laert. Diog., VII 100).

14. καλὸν δὲ λέγουσι τὸ τέλειον ἀγαθὸν παρὰ τὸ πάντας ἀπέχειν τοὺς ἐπιζητουμένους ἀριθμοὺς ὑπὸ τῆς φύσεως ἢ τὸ τελείως σύμμετρον. εἴδη δὲ εἶναι τοῦ καλοῦ τέτταρα, δίκαιον, ἀνδρεῖον, κόσμιον, ἐπιστημονικόν· ἐν γὰρ τοῖσδε τὰς καλὰς πράξεις συντελεῖσθαι. ... ἑτέρως δὲ τὸ εὖ πεφυκὸς πρὸς τὸ ἴδιον ἔργον· ἄλλως δὲ τὸ ἐπικοσμοῦν, ὅταν λέγωμεν μόνον τὸν σοφὸν ἀγαθὸν καὶ καλὸν εἶναι.

VARIOUS MEANINGS OF "BEAUTY"

14. The reason why they characterize the perfect good as beautiful is that it has in full all the "factors" required by nature or has perfect proportion. Of the beautiful there are four species, namely what is just, courageous, orderly and wise; for it is under these forms that fair deeds are accomplished... though in another sense it signifies a good aptitude for one's proper function; while in yet another sense the beautiful is that which lends new grace to anything, as when we say of the wise man that he alone is good and beautiful.
tr. R. D. Hicks

CICERO, Orator 21, 70.

15. Ut enim in vita, sic in oratione nihil est difficilius quam quid deceat videre. Πρέπον appellant hoc Graeci; nos dicamus sane decorum. De quo praeclare et multa praecipiuntur

DECORUM

15. In oratory, as much as in life, there is nothing more difficult than to discover what is fitting; the Greeks call it "prepon" while we call it "decorum". There are many excellent

et res est cognitione dignissima; huius ignoratione non modo in vita, sed saepissime et in poëmatis et in oratione peccatur.

rules concerning this and the whole matter is well worth studying. When we lack this knowledge, we lose our way in life as well as very often in poetry and oratory.

DIOGENES THE BABYLONIAN
(v. Arnim, frg. 24).

16. πρέπον ... ἐστὶ λέξις οἰκεία τῷ πράγματι.

16. Fittingness ... is style proper to the subject.
tr. J. C. B. Lowe

PLUTARCH, De aud. poët. 18d.

οὐ γάρ ἐστι ταὐτὸ τὸ καλόν τι καὶ καλῶς τι μιμεῖσθαι· καλῶς γάρ ἐστι τὸ πρεπόντως καὶ οἰκείως, οἰκεῖα δὲ καὶ πρέποντα τοῖς αἰσχροῖς τὰ αἰσχρά.

For it is not the same thing at all to imitate something beautiful and something beautifully. Since beautifully means "fittingly and properly" and ugly things are "fitting and proper" for the ugly.
tr. F. C. Babbit

CHRYSIPPUS (Alexander of Aphr., De fato 37, Bruns 210).

17. τὰ μὲν καλὰ ἐπαινετά.

PRAISE OF BEAUTY

17. Beautiful things are praiseworthy.
tr. J. C. B. Lowe

MARCUS AURELIUS,
Ad se ipsum IV 20.

17a. πᾶν τὸ καὶ ὁπωσοῦν καλόν ἐστι καὶ ἐφ' ἑαυτὸ καταλήγει οὐκ ἔχον μέρος ἑαυτοῦ τὸν ἔπαινον· οὔτε γοῦν χεῖρον ἢ κρεῖττον γίνεται τὸ ἐπαινούμενον. τοῦτό φημι καὶ ἐπὶ τῶν κοινότερον καλῶν λεγομένων, οἷον ἐπὶ τῶν ὑλικῶν καὶ ἐπὶ τῶν τεχνικῶν κατασκευασμάτων· τό γε δὴ ὄντως καλὸν τίνος χρείαν ἔχει; οὐ μᾶλλον ἢ νόμος, οὐ μᾶλλον ἢ ἀλήθεια, οὐ μᾶλλον ἢ εὔνοια ἢ αἰδώς.

17a. Anything in any wise, beautiful or noble, owes the beauty to itself, and with itself its beauty ends; praise forms no part of it; for praise does not make its object worse or better. This is true of the commoner forms of beauty—material objects, for instance, and works of art—no less than of the ideal. True beauty needs no addition, any more than law, or truth, or kindness, or self-respect.
tr. G. H. Randall

CICERO (on Zeno), Acad. Post. I 11, 40.

18. [Zeno] de sensibus ipsis quaedam dixit nova, quos iunctos esse censuit e quadam quasi impulsione oblata extrinsecus, quam ille φαντασίαν, nos visum appellemus licet. ...Visis non omnibus adiungebat fidem.

FANTASY

18. He made some new pronouncements about sensation itself, which he held to be a combination of a sort of impact offered from outside (which he called "phantasia" and we may call a presentation...). He held that not all presentations are trustworthy.
tr. H. Rackham

ZENO (Schol. ad Dionys. Thracis Gramm. Bekk. Anecd. Gr. p. 663, 16).

19. ὡς δηλοῖ καὶ ὁ Ζήνων λέγων «τέχνη ἐστὶν ἕξις ὁδοποιητική», τουτέστι δι' ὁδοῦ καὶ μεθόδου ποιοῦσά τι.

DEFINITION OF ART

19. Zeno, too, points to this by defining: "art is an ability which points the way", which means that it creates its works along a sure way and with the aid of a method.

CLEANTHES (Quintilian, Inst. Or. II 17, 41).

20. Ut Cleanthes voluit, ars est potestas viam, id est ordinem, efficiens.

20. As Cleanthes maintained, an art is a power working its effect by a course, that is, by method.

tr. J. S. Watson

CHRYSIPPUS (Sextus Emp., Adv. mathem. VII 372).

21. τέχνη σύστημα γὰρ ἦν καὶ ἄθροισμα καταλήψεων.

21. [According to Chrysippus] art is a cluster and a collection of observations.

ZENO (Olympiodor, In Plat. Gorg. p. 53. Jahn 239 sq.).

22. Ζήνων δέ φησιν ὅτι τέχνη ἐστὶ σύστημα ἐκ καταλήψεων συγγεγυμνασμένων πρός τι τέλος εὔχρηστον τῶν τῷ βίῳ.

22. While Zeno says that art is a cluster of observations tested by experience and serving a useful purpose in life.

SENECA, Epistulae ad Lucilium 29, 3.

22a. Non est ars quae ad effectum casu venit.

22a. A work which comes about by chance is not true art.

POSIDONIUS (Seneca, Epist. 88, 21).

23. Quatuor ait esse artium Posidonius genera: sunt volgares et sordidae, sunt ludicrae, sunt pueriles, sunt liberales: volgares opificum, quae manu constant et ad instruendam vitam occupatae sunt, in quibus nulla decoris, nulla honesti simulatio est. Ludicrae sunt, quae ad voluptatem oculorum atque aurium tendunt... Pueriles sunt et aliquid habentes liberalibus simile hae artes, quas ἐγκυκλίους Graeci, nostri has liberales vocant. Solae autem liberales sunt, imo, ut dicam verius, liberae, quibus curae virtus est.

DIVISION OF THE ARTS

23. Posidonius says there are four kinds of arts—the workaday—mercenary, the scenic, the pupillary and the liberal. The workaday are those of the artisan, manual crafts engaged in catering for life and making no pretence of any aesthetic or moral ideals. The scenic are those which aim at the diversion of eye and ear... The pupillary (which aren't altogether unlike the really liberal) are those arts which the Greeks call ἐγκυκλίους—"encyclic"—and our own writers "liberal". But the only liberal arts or rather, to speak more truly, arts of liberty are those which concern themselves with virtue.

tr. E. P. Barker

STOICS (Philodemus, De poëm. V, Jensen, 132).

24. οἱ φήσαντες πόημα καλὸν εἶναι τὸ σοφὴν διάνοιαν περιέχον.

BEAUTY OF POETRY DEPENDS ON ITS CONTENT

24. Those who said that a poem was beautiful which contained wise thought.

tr. J. C. B. Lowe

CLEANTHES (Seneca, Epist. 108, 10).

25. Nam, ut dicebat Cleanthes, quemadmodum spiritus noster clariorem sonum reddit, cum illum tuba per longi canalis angustias tractum patentiore novissimo exitu effudit, sic sensus nostros clariores carminis arta necessitas efficit.

ROLE OF FORM IN POETRY

25. In fact, to use Cleanthes' "simile", as our breath gives a clearer note when coursing through the long narrow tube of a trumpet it in discharged at last from a bell mouth, so our meanings are clarified by the narrow restrictions of the verse form.

tr. E. P. Barker

CLEANTHES (Philodemus, De musica, col. 28, 1, Kemke, 79).

26. εἰ μ[ὴ τὸ π]αρὰ Κλεάν[θ]ει λέγειν [τάχ]α θελήσουσ[ι]ν, ὅς φησιν ἀμείνο[νά] τε εἶναι τὰ ποιητικὰ καὶ μ[ουσ]ικὰ παραδείγματα καὶ, τοῦ [λόγ]ου τοῦ τῆς φιλοσοφίας ἱκανῶ[ς] μὲν ἐξαγ[γ]έλλειν δυναμένου τὰ θε[ῖ]α καὶ ἀ[ν]θ[ρ]ώ[πινα], μὴ ἔχον[τ]ος δὲ ψειλοῦ τῶν θείων μεγεθῶν λέξεις οἰκείας, τὰ μέτρ[α] καὶ τὰ μέλη καὶ τοὺς ῥυθμοὺς ὡς μάλιστα προσικνεῖσθαι πρὸς τὴν ἀλήθειαν τῆς τῶν θείων θ[ε]ωρίας.

POETRY AND PHILOSOPHY

26. Cleanthes says that poetic and musical forms are better: that a philosophical treatise may, it is true, well express divine and human matters, yet it lacks the proper words to express divine greatness. For this reason, melodies and rhythms are incomparably better at arriving at the truth about divine matters.

CHRYSIPPUS (Diocles Magnes. in Laërt. Diog., VII 51).

27. ἔτι τῶν φαντασιῶν... αἱ μέν εἰσι τεχνικαί, αἱ δὲ ἄτεχνοι· ἄλλως γοῦν θεωρεῖται ὑπὸ τεχνίτου εἰκὼν καὶ ἄλλως ὑπὸ ἀτέχνου.

JUDGMENTS BY CONNOISSEUR AND LAYMAN

27. Certain imaginings are based on a knowledge of art and others are not. Also, an artist sees a painting differently from one who is ignorant about art.

STOICS (Clement of Alex., Strom. V 3, 17, 655 P.).

οὐ γὰρ πλῆθος ἔχει συνετὴν κρίσιν,
[οὔτε δικαίαν
οὔτε καλήν, ὀλίγοις δὲ παρ' ἀνδράσι
[τοῦτό κεν εὕροις.

A crowd is not capable of judgment which is either wise or just or beautiful; only a few are capable of such judgment.

CICERO, Tusc. disp. II, 11, 27.

28. Sed videsne, poëtae quid mali adferant? Lamentantis inducunt fortissimos viros, molliunt animos nostros, ita sunt deinde dulces, ut non legantur modo, sed etiam ediscantur. Sic ad malam domesticam disciplinam vitamque umbratilem et delicatam cum acces- serunt etiam poëtae, nervos omnis virtutis

CRITICISM OF POETRY

28. But do you note the harm which poets do? They represent brave men wailing, they enervate our souls, and besides this they do it with such charm that they are not merely read, but learnt by heart. Thus when the influence of the poets is combined with bad family discipline and a life passed in the shade

elidunt. Recte igitur a Platone eiciuntur ex ea civitate, quam finxit ille, cum optimos mores et optimum rei publicae statum exquireret.

of effeminate seclusion, the strength of manliness is completely sapped. Plato was right then in turning them out of his imaginary state, when he was trying to find the highest morality and the best conditions for the community.

tr. J. E. King

CHRYSIPPUS (Chalcidius, Ad Timaeum 167).

Pictores quoque et fictores, nonne rapiunt animos ad suavitatem ab industria?

CRITICISM OF THE ARTS

Do not painters and sculptors also divert men's minds from industry to pleasure?

tr. J. C. B. Lowe

SENECA, Epist. 88, 18.

29. In illo feras me necesse est non per praescriptum euntem: non enim adducor, ut in numerum liberalium artium pictores recipiam, non magis quam statuarios aut marmorarios aut ceteros luxuriae ministros.

29. Now follows a point on which you must forgive my forsaking the beaten track. The fact is I firmly refuse to admit painters into the precinct of the liberal accomplishments, any more than sculptors, marble-masons and other servants of sumptuousness.

tr. E. P. Barker

DIOGENES THE BABYLONIAN
(Philodemus, De musica, Kemke 11).

30. συνωμολογηκέναι δ' αὐτῷ, τὰ μὲν αὐτοφυοῦς αἰσθήσεως δεῖσθαι, τὰ δ' ἐπιστημονικῆς, τὰ θερμὰ μὲν καὶ τὰ ψυχρὰ τῆς αὐτοφυοῦς, τὸ δ' ἡρμοσμένον καὶ ἀνάρμοστον τῆς ἐπιστημονικῆς· ἑτέραν δὲ τῇ τοιαύτῃ συνεζευγμένην καὶ παρακολουθοῦσαν ὡς ἐπὶ τὸ πολύ, δι' ἧς δεχόμεθα τὴν παρεπομένην ἑκάστῳ τῶν αἰσθητῶν ἡδονήν τε καὶ λύπην, οὖσαν οὐ πᾶσι τὴν αὐτήν. οὐ γὰρ ἂν ἀναμειχθῶσιν δύο αἰσθήσεις, περὶ μὲν τὸ ὑποκείμενον συμφωνεῖν οἷον ὅτι ... ηγον ἢ αὐστηρόν, περὶ δὲ τὴν παρεπομένην ἡδονήν τε καὶ λύπην διαφωνεῖν ἐναργῶς.

EDUCATED IMPRESSIONS

30. The perception of some qualities depends on innate sensibilities, while the perception of others depends on educated ones: thus perception of warmth and cold depends on the former, and the perception of harmony and disharmony on the latter. These educated sensibilities are linked with innate ones and normally accompany them; this leads to pleasure or pain connected with each impression, but not in the same measure in each case. For where the two types of impression are mixed, there we have agreement that a particular object is, say, bitter or sharp, but there follows a clear divergence over the accompanying pleasure or pain.

6. The Aesthetics of Cicero and the Eclectics

1. ECLECTICISM. Originally philosophical schools adopted quite distinct positions which were hostile to one another, but toward the end of the second century and particularly in the first century B.C. attempts were made in Athens and Rome to reach an understanding between them. The Stoic school under Panaetius and Posidonius emerged from its isolation, abandoned its intransigent attitudes and drew close to the Peripatetic school and even closer to the Platonic School. It became

the "Platonizing Stoa". The Academy of Plato under the leadership of Philo of Larissa and Antiochus of Ascalon made an even more decisive move toward Eclecticism by affirming agreement between Plato and Aristotle. This trend proved beneficial.

Three theories, those of Plato, Aristotle and of the Stoics, combined to form the aesthetics of Eclecticism, whose creed, as formulated by Quintilian, was: *eligere ex omnibus optima* (to choose the best in everything). Eclectic aesthetics, thanks to Cicero's great authority, had a wide influence and became typical of late Hellenism and classical Rome. Apart from the Eclectic school, only two were now left—the Sceptic and the Epicurean—which denounced rather than pursued aesthetic studies.

2. CICERO. In his youth M. Tullius Cicero* (106–43) studied and practised philosophy, then led an active life as a politician and leading orator, and finally, towards the end of his life, returned to philosophy. His main philosophical works belong to the last three years of his life. None of them is exclusively concerned with aesthetics, but all of them contain numerous obervations on the subject. This is particularly true of his *Academic Disputations* (*Academica*), *Tusculan Disputations* (*Tusculanae disputationes*), *On Duties* (*De officiis*), *On the Orator* (*De oratore*) and *The Orator* (*Orator*).

He was "a statesman and at the same time the best educated man, the most excellent stylist and the ablest writer in Rome". There were very good reasons why he should have become an Eclectic. During his studies in Athens and on the Rhodos he heard the Eclectic Academicians Philon and Antiochus, the accomodating Stoic Posidonius, as well as the Epicureans. He regarded himself as a supporter of the Academy but he was equally imbued with elements of Stoicism. He was a Roman with a Greek education. He was also in an excellent position to make a comprehensive study of aesthetics, being both a thinker and an artist. He modelled his aesthetics chiefly on the art of the word, as was quite natural in a speaker and a writer. His new aesthetic ideas may have been borrowed from writers whose works have perished. However that may be, we do not find them in any earlier writing. Those new ideas came surprisingly close to modern aesthetics. Thus, Cicero's works offer the historian of aesthetics two types of material. On the one hand, they help to form a picture of the Eclectic aesthetics which came into existence at the close of antiquity, and on the other, they show us the new ideas that came to the fore at that time. Cicero's Eclectic aesthetics was a summary of old ideas of the classical era, yet his new ideas opened a new era.

3. BEAUTY. *A.* The main aesthetic problems presented no difficulty to Eclectic philosophers, since the related philosophical schools were here in agreement. On the problem of defining beauty all the schools had agreed that beauty depends on order and measure, on suitable arrangement of parts. Cicero followed them by

---

* G. C. Finke, "Cicero's *De oratore* and Horace's *Ars poetica*", *University of Wisconsin Studies in Language and Literature* (1927). K. Svoboda, "Les idées esthétiques de Cicéron", *Acta Sessionis Ciceronianae* (Warsaw, 1960).

describing beauty as *ordo*, that is, order, and *convenientia partium*, that is, agreement of parts. But here already he adopted a fresh point of view by saying that beauty "affects by its appearance" (*sua specie commovet*), "stimulates the eyes" (*movet oculos*), depends upon a beautiful "aspect" (*aspectus*). Linking beauty with appearance and aspect, he thus conceived a notion of sensuous beauty, narrower than the traditional notion of beauty.

Despite analogies between intellectual and sensuous beauty, Cicero insisted on the difference which separated them;[1] while the first is the beauty of characters, customs and actions, the other is something quite different, a beauty of appearance. The first is both a moral and an aesthetic concept, the second is purely aesthetic. He considered the basic characteristic of moral beauty to be suitability which he called *decorum*. Moral beauty he defined as that which "is decent" (*quod decet*), while he defined sensuous and aesthetic beauty as that which "stimulates the eyes" (*movet oculos*).[2]

B. Cicero also retained the Socratic view that beauty depends on utility and purpose and that the most useful objects have the most dignity and pulchritude.[3] This he applied to nature as well as art; animals or plants have properties which keep them alive and at the same time are beautiful. Similarly buildings erected out of necessity have as much splendour as they have utility. But while every thing that is useful is also beautiful, the converse is not true because there are objects whose beauty has nothing in common with utility but is, as in the case of the plumage of a peacock or a dove, pure ornament (*ornatus*).

Beauty may be thus divided in several ways—into beauty of nature and beauty of art; into *pulchritudo* and *decorum*, aesthetic and moral beauty; and into useful and ornamental beauty.

C. To these three classifications Cicero added a fourth one which was based upon an idea of Plato. He distinguished two types of beauty: *dignitas* and *venustas*, that is, dignity and good looks.[4] Cicero called the first "masculine" and the second "feminine". In addition to *dignitas*, he also employed the term *gravitas*, gravity, and to *venustas* he added the term *suavitas*, sweetness. *Venustas* was the equivalent of the Greek *charis*, charm. This was one more attempt to differentiate the excessively broad concept of beauty.

D. The Platonic, the Peripatetic and the Stoic schools all agreed that beauty is an objective property of certain things, so it was natural that this view should enter into Eclectic aesthetics. Cicero wrote that we admire beauty in itself (*per se nobis placet*),[5] that it moves our minds by its very nature and shape and that by itself it is worthy of recognition and praise.

This thesis had two implications. Firstly, it implied that beauty is independent of the attitude of the mind. It was, therefore, opposed to the subjectivist aesthetics of the Epicureans. Here the two hostile camps of Hellenistic aesthetics confronted each other. But, secondly, the thesis that beauty is admired for itself meant that things, at least certain things, are beautiful and praiseworthy independently of their utility (*detracta omni utilitate ... iure laudari potest*).⁽⁶⁾ This does not contradict the fact that beauty of some things may coincide with their utility.

4. ART. Eclectic philosophy found it equally easy to define the concept of art, because here, even more than with the concept of beauty, a consensus of opinion existed among the schools. When Cicero called art everything that people made with their hands, *in faciendo, agendo, moliendo*, he was merely offering a variant of the traditional definition; so he was also when he wrote that art is to be found where knowledge is.⁽⁷⁾

However, he introduced a new point of view. While the ancients had bestowed the name of art in equal measure upon both production and the knowledge which guides production, Cicero distinguished two types of art: those arts (e.g., sculpture) which produce things and those (e.g., geometry) which merely investigate them—*rem animo cernunt*.⁽⁸⁾

Cicero took interest in the classification of the arts. Employing the traditional classifications, he divided the arts into liberal and servile⁽⁹⁾ (he also called the latter *sordidae*, unclean). But he radically altered the concept of the liberal arts because he did not define them negatively as those which do not require physical effort. Instead, he based his definition on the greater mental effort they demanded (*prudentia maior*) and their greater utility (*non mediocris utilitas*). This approach altered the meaning of the traditional classification and made it possible to classify all the "fine" arts, including architecture, as liberal arts.

Employing another time-honoured classification of the arts, Cicero divided them into those which are necessary in life and those which promote pleasure (*partim ad usum vitae, partim ad oblectationem*).⁽¹⁰⁾ And to these classifications which were current, Cicero added one of his own. This was a limited classification confined to the liberal and imitative arts. He distinguished two groups: arts of the ear and arts of the eye, or, in other words, the verbal arts and the mute arts.⁽¹¹⁾ In the first group he included poetry, oratory and music. Cicero the orator placed oratory higher than poetry because it serves truth, whereas poetry indulges in fictions; oratory attempts to persuade men while poetry merely expects to be liked. And he placed all verbal arts above mute arts because they represent both souls and bodies, whereas he thought that the mute ones represent only bodies.

5. INHERITED AND NEW IDEAS. While Cicero's basic conceptions of beauty and art were thus in accordance with the general Greek tradition, his other aesthetic views were more closely linked with Stoicism, especially with the "Middle School" of Panaetius and Posidonius. But they could easily be reconciled with Plato and Aristotle.

A. Cicero thought that the world is so beautiful that it is impossible to think of anything more beautiful.⁽¹²⁾ Beauty can be found both in art and nature. Certain shapes and colours, not only in art but also in nature, serve only beauty and adornment (*ornatus*).

B. His view on the relationship between art and nature was that works of art, being produced by men, cannot be as excellent as the works of nature;[13] but they can be gradually improved by selecting the beauties of nature.[14]

C. Concerning the conditions of art, Cicero thought[15] that art is by definition a matter of rules, but also of free impulses (*liber motus*). Art requires skill as well as talent. It is guided by reason but owes its greatness to inspiration (*adflatus*).[16]

Cicero adopted earlier ideas, but refined them and gave them more precision: he drew a distinction between beauty and utility, between dignified beauty and charm, between art and skill, between verbal and visual arts. Moreover, his aesthetic ideas were not limited to these; he had more original ideas, particularly on the creative process and the aesthetic experience.

6. IDEAS IN THE ARTIST'S MIND. Every ancient aesthetician had to express an opinion regarding imitation in art and Cicero also speaks about *imitatio*. He wrote this peculiar sentence on the subject: there is no doubt that truth conquers imitation (*sine dubio ... vincit imitationem veritas*).[17] Thus, imitation was with him not only different from truth but in some way opposed to it. This sentence of Cicero shows us once more that the ancients did not regard imitation as the faithful copying of reality, but as its free representation. Cicero also wrote that the most typical imitators among artists were orators, and orators can imitate only characters and not things.

If art, Cicero said, contained only truth it would be unnecessary. Following Aristotle he stressed the fictiveness of poetry: "What can be so unreal as poetry, the theatre, or stage plays?"[18] If the artist represents what he sees in reality, he does so on a selective basis. What is more, he draws his forms not only from the world but also from within himself. He fashions his works not only in the likeness of what he sees before his eyes but also in the likeness of ideas he has in his mind.[19] When Phidias sculpted his Zeus he must have been guided by a model of beauty (*species pulchritudinis*) appearing in his mind (*ipsius in mente*).

There are elements of reality in art, but besides these there are ideal elements; art has an external pattern but also an internal one in the artist's mind. Plato noticed chiefly the similarities between the external pattern and the work of art; Aristotle noticed rather the differences. Cicero stressed what in art is derived from the artist's mind; in doing this, he spoke for a new age.

The forms in the artist's mind Cicero called "Ideas". He took his theory of Ideas of course, and the term itself, from Plato ("the great writer and teacher", as he called him) and also from Plato's Academy and, in particular, from his teacher, Antiochus. But in adopting Plato's theory to the needs of aesthetics, he altered it radically. For Plato "Ideas" stood for abstract mental forms, whereas for Cicero they stood for concrete perceptible forms. To understand art, which after all makes use of concrete images, abstract ideas were of little value; and therefore Plato in his theory of art did not employ them. He applied the concept of Idea to the theory of being but not to his theory of art. The founder of idealism was thus not an idealist in his understanding of art; he held that man is guided by Ideas in his scientific knowledge and his moral actions, but not in art; art is modelled upon real objects, not upon Ideas. On the other hand, Cicero's concrete ideas could be applied in artistic theory. They offered a basis for a new understanding of artistic creation, for a fuller elucidation of a work of art by taking account of its internal patterns. Whereas Plato conceived the artist's attitude as imitative and passive, Cicero noticed its active element.

7. THE AESTHETIC SENSE. Cicero noticed an active element not only in creators of art but also in its recipients, not only in the psychology of the artist, but also in the psychology of the spectator and the listener. He expressed this by saying that man possesses a special sense (*sensus*) of beauty and art.[20] By means of this sense man comprehends and evaluates art and is capable of determining what is proper in art and what is false (*recta et prava dijudicare*). This view contained new thoughts: that man is capable of evaluating art and beauty,[21] that this is a separate ability, a kind of innate sense.[22]

This view that aesthetic experience is based on an innate "sense" was the corollary of the view that artistic creation is based on an equally innate "idea" of beauty. Both views removed the element of passivity from artistic creation and aesthetic experience; both anticipated modern theories of the "artistic sense" and the "sense of beauty", together with their merits and defects.

Like a number of writers before him, Cicero attributed the ability to recognize beauty and evaluate art exclusively to man. He alone of all living creatures, "perceives the beauty, charm and harmony". But Cicero went further by saying that man was born for the purpose of seeing and imitating the world (*homo ortus est ad mundum contemplandum et imitandum*).[23] Before Cicero only Aristotle might have approved of this opinion.

8. IN PRAISE OF HUMAN EYES, EARS AND HANDS. Cicero has ascribed aesthetic abilities solely to human beings, but to all of them, even to the *vulgus imperitorum*. These abilities which make art possible are various: they include the abilities of the soul and the body, of the mind and the senses. As was quite common in antiquity, Cicero not only praised the human mind, but he also praised ears and eyes.[24] The eyes judge the harmony and beauty of colours and shapes. The ears, too, must possess astonishing abilities, since they apprehend the various intervals and modalities produced by songs and musical instruments. Furthermore, Cicero also praised the human hand,[25] which has the skill "to paint, to model, to carve, and to draw forth the notes of the lyre and the flute". To it we owe the possesion of "cities, fortifications, houses and temples".

9. PLURALISM. Pluralism was a characteristic feature of Cicero's theory of art; he was aware that in art there are almost numberless shapes, which are, each in their own way, worthy of praise. "Things of so diversified a nature can never be formed into an art by the same percepts".[26-27] Myron, Polyclitus and Lysippus, all sculpted in a different manner. Their talents were unlike, but we would not wish any one of them to be other than he in fact was. Zeuxis, Aglaophon and Apelles painted in different ways and yet none of them can be faulted.

This pluralistic view, normal in modern times, took a long time to establish itself. In antiquity the tendency was to seek some single principle which would be common to all artists, all art and all beauty. This was particularly true of the main line of ancient aesthetics stemming from the Pythagoreans and Plato. It was opposed by the relativist view running from the Sophists to the Sceptics. The middle, pluralist approach did not appear until Aristotle and was intensified in Cicero.

10. EVOLUTIONARY AND SOCIAL FACTOR IN ART. Antiquity favoured either an ethico-metaphysical approach to art or a purely descriptive one. More rare was the psychological approach, and rarer still was the sociological, historical, or epistemological approach. These other points of view are, however, apparent in Cicero.

He saw the development and progress of the arts with the eye of an historian. He concluded that scattered forms and ideas were gradually welded into a unified art.[28] With a sociologist's eye he saw the influence of social conditions upon the circumstances of art and wrote that recognition and social success is art's nourishment (*honos alit artes*).[29]

With an epistemologist's eye he saw that it is easier to comprehend beauty than to explain it (*comprehendi quam explanari*).[30] For instance the beautiful may be separated from the good only in thought and not in reality (*cogitatione magis quam re separari*).[31]

11. PHILOSOPHERS AND ART THEORISTS. Cicero's views, based on Platonic, Stoic and Peripatetic ideas, were the last formulation of philosophical aesthetics in antiquity before Plotinus. From then on philosophical aesthetics underwent no major changes. New ideas were localized rather in the special theory of art, in the theory of music, in poetics and rhetoric, in the theory of architecture, of sculpture and of painting.

It is nevertheless true that art theorists of the time belonged to philosophical schools. Among those who distinguished themselves in the aesthetics of music, Aristoxenus was a Peripatetic, Heraclides Ponticus was a member of the Academy, Diogenes the Babylonian was a Stoic, and Philodemus was an Epicurean. As for those who contributed to the theory of the visual arts and those who were concerned with poetics, Maximus of Tyre and Plutarch of Chaeronea were Platonic Eclectics, Galen was an Aristotelian, Panaetius and Posidonius were Stoics, Philostratus was a Platonist with Pythagorean characteristics, Horace was an Epicurean, and Lucian was a Cynic and an Epicurean.

K. Texts from Cicero

CICERO, Tusc. disp. IV 13, 30.

BODILY AND SPIRITUAL BEAUTY

1. Sunt enim in corpore praecipua, valetudo, pulchritudo, vires, firmitas, velocitas, sunt item in animo... Et ut corporis est quaedam apta figura membrorum cum coloris quadam

1. For the chief blessings of the body are beauty, strength, health, vigour, agility; so are they of the soul... And as in the body a certain symmetrical shape of the limbs combined with

suavitate eaque dicitur pulchritudo, sic in animo opinionum iudiciorumque aequabilitas et constantia cum firmitate quadam et stabilitate virtutem subsequens aut virtutis vim ipsam continens pulchritudo vocatur.

a certain charm of colouring is described as beauty; so in the soul the name of beauty is given to an equipoise and consistency of beliefs and judgments, combined with a certain steadiness and stability following upon virtue or comprising the true essence of virtue.

tr. J. E. King

CICERO, De officiis I 28, 98.

2. Ut enim pulchritudo corporis apta compositione membrorum movet oculos et delectat hoc ipso, quod inter se omnes partes cum quodam lepore consentiunt, sic hoc decorum, quod elucet in vita, movet adprobationem eorum, quibuscum vivitur, ordine et constantia et moderatione dictorum omnium atque factorum.

PULCHRITUDO AND *DECORUM*

2. For, as physical beauty with harmonious symmetry of the limbs engages the attention and delights the eye, for the very reason that all the parts combine in harmony and grace, so this propriety, which shines out in our conduct, engages the approbation of our fellow-men by the order, consistency, and self-control it imposes upon every word and deed.

tr. W. Miller

CICERO, De finibus III 5, 18.

3. Iam membrorum, id est partium corporis, alia videntur propter eorum usum a natura esse donata, ut manus, crura, pedes, ut ea, quae sunt intus in corpore, quorum utilitas quanta sit, a medicis etiam disputatur, alia autem nullam ob utilitatem quasi ad quendam ornatum, ut cauda pavoni, plumae versicolores columbis, viris mammae atque barba.

BEAUTY AND UTILITY

3. Now of the limbs, that is to say, of the parts of the body, some appear to have been given to us by nature because of the use which they are to us, as, for instance, the hands, legs, feet, and also those internal organs of the body of which I may leave it to physicians to explain the exceeding usefulness; but others with no view to utility, but for ornament as it were, as the tail is given to the peacock, plumage of many colours to the dove, breasts and a beard to man.

tr. C. D. Younge

CICERO, De oratore III 45, 179.

Haec tantam habent vim, paulum ut immutata cohaerere non possint, tantam pulchritudinem, ut nulla species ne cogitari quidem possit ornatior. Referte nunc animum ad hominum vel etiam ceterarum animantium formam et figuram. Nullam partem corporis sine aliqua necessitate affictam totamque formam quasi perfectam reperietis arte, non casu. Quid in arboribus? In quibus non truncus, non rami, non folia sunt denique nisi ad suam retinendam conservandamque naturam, nusquam tamen est ulla pars nisi venusta. Linquamus naturam artesque videamus... Columnae et templa et porticus sustinent; tamen habent non plus utilitatis quam dignitatis.

This order of things has such force that, if there were the least alteration in it, they could not possibly subsist together, and such beauty, that no fairer appearance of nature could even be imagined. Turn your thoughts now to the shape and figure of man, or even that of other animals; you will find no part of the body fashioned without some necessary use, and the whole frame perfected as it were by art, not by chance. How is it with regard to trees of which neither the trunk nor the boughs nor even the leaves are formed otherwise than to maintain and preserve their own nature, yet in which there is no part that is not beautiful. Or let us turn from natural objects and cast our eyes on those of art... Pillars support temples and porticos, and yet have not more utility than dignity.

tr. J. S. Watson

CICERO, De officiis I 36, 130.

4. Cum autem pulchritudinis duo genera sint, quorum in altero venustas sit, in altero dignitas, venustatem muliebrem ducere debemus, dignitatem virilem.

BEAUTY AND DIGNITY

4. Again, there are two orders of beauty: in the one, loveliness predominates; in the other, dignity; of these, we ought to regard loveliness as the attribute of women, and dignity as the attribute of man.

tr. Walter Miller

CICERO, De oratore III 45, 178.

Sed ut in plerisque rebus incredibiliter hoc natura est ipsa fabricata, sic in oratione, ut ea, quae maximam utilitatem in se continerent, plurimum eadem haberent vel dignitatis vel saepe venustatis.

But as in most things, so in language, Nature herself has wonderfully continued, that what carries in it the greatest utility, should have at the same time either the most dignity, or, as it often happens, the most beauty.

tr. J. S. Watson

CICERO, De officiis II 9, 32.

5. Illud ipsum quod honestum decorumque dicimus, quia per se placet animosque omnium natura et specie sua commovet.

OBJECTIVE VALUES

5. ...that very quality which we term moral goodness and propriety is pleasing to us by and of itself and touches all our hearts both by its inward essence and its outward aspect...

tr. Walter Miller

CICERO, De finibus II 14, 45.

6. Honestum igitur id intellegimus, quod tale est, ut detracta omni utilitate sine ullis praemiis fructibusve per se ipsum possit iure laudari.

6. By moral worth, then, we understand that which is of such a nature that, though devoid of all utility, it can justly be commended in and for itself, apart from any profit or reward.

tr. H. Rackham

CICERO, De oratore II 7, 30.

7. Ars enim earum rerum est, quae sciuntur.

DEFINITION OF ART

7. Art is concerned with the things that are known.

tr. C. D. Younge

CICERO, Academica II 7, 22.

8. Artium aliud eius modi genus sit, ut tantum modo animo rem cernat, aliud, ut moliatur aliquid et faciat.

TYPES OF THE ARTS

8. ...one class of sciences is of such a nature as only to envisage facts mentally, and another such as to do or to make something...

tr. H. Rackham

CICERO, De officiis I 42, 150–151.

9. Iam de artificiis et quaestibus, qui liberales habendi, qui sordidi sint, haec fere accepimus. Primum improbantur ii quaestus, qui in odia hominum incurrunt, ut portitorum, ut faeneratorum. Inliberales autem et sordidi quaestus mercennariorum omnium, quorum operae, non quorum artes emuntur; est enim in illis ipsa merces auctoramentum servitutis. Sordidi etiam putandi, qui mercantur a mercatoribus, quod statim vendant; nihil enim proficiant, nisi admodum mentiantur, nec vero est quicquam turpius vanitate. Opificesque omnes in sordida arte versantur; nec enim quicquam ingenuum habere potest officina. Minimeque artes eae probandae, quae ministrae sunt voluptatum: "cetarii, lanii, coqui, fartores, piscatores", ut ait Terentius. Adde huc, si placet, unguentarios, saltatores totumque ludum talarium. Quibus autem artibus aut prudentia maior inest aut non mediocris utilitas quaeritur, ut medicina, ut architectura, ut doctrina rerum honestarum, eae sunt iis, quorum ordini conveniunt, honestae.

LIBERAL AND COMMON ARTS

9. Now in regard to trades and other means of livelihood, which ones are to be considered becoming to a gentleman and which ones are vulgar, we have been taught, in general, as follows. First, those means of livelihood are rejected as undesirable which incur people's ill-will, as those of tax-gatherers and usurers. Unbecoming to a gentleman, too, and vulgar are the means of livelihood of all hired workmen whom we pay for mere manual labour, not for artistic skill; for in their case the very wage they receive is a pledge of their slavery. Vulgar we must consider those also who buy from wholesale merchants to retail immediately; for they would get no profits without a great deal of downright lying; and verily, there is no action that is meaner than misrepresentation. And all mechanics are engaged in vulgar trades; for a workshop cannot have anything liberal about it. Least respectable of all are those trades which cater for sensual pleasures "Fishmongers, butchers, cooks, and poulterers, and fishermen", as Terence says. Add to these, if you please, the performers, dancers, and the whole *corps de ballet*.

But the profession in which either a higher degree of intelligence is required or from which no small benefit to society is derived—medicine and architecture, for example, and teaching—these are proper for those whose social position they become.

tr. Walter Miller

CICERO, De natura deorum II 59, 148.

10. Artes quoque efficimus partim ad usum vitae, partim ad oblectationem necessarias.

USEFUL AND ENTERTAINING ARTS

10. ...we create the arts that serve either practical necessities or the purpose of amusement.

tr. H. Rackham

CICERO, De oratore III 7, 26.

11. Et si hoc in quasi mutis artibus est mirandum et tamen verum, quanto admirabilius in oratione et in lingua.

MUTE AND VERBAL ARTS

11. And if this be wonderful, and yet true, in these, as it were, mute arts, how much more wonderful is it in language and speech?

tr. J. S. Watson

CICERO, De natura deorum II 7, 18.

12. Atqui certe nihil omnium rerum melius est mundo, nihil praestabilius, nihil pulchrius.

BEAUTY OF THE WORLD

12. Yet, beyond question, nothing exists among all things that is superior to the world, nothing that is more excellent or more beautiful.

tr. H. Rackham

CICERO, De natura deorum I 33, 92.

13. Nulla ars imitari sollertiam naturae potest.

ib. II 32, 81.

[Naturae] sollertiam nulla ars, nulla manus, nemo opifex consequi possit imitando.

NATURE SUPERIOR TO ART

13. ...no art can imitate the cunning of nature's handiwork.

[Nature is] possessed of a skill that no handiwork of artist or craftsman can rival or reproduce.

tr. H. Rackham

ART SELECTS BEAUTY FROM NATURE
(an anecdote on Zeuxis)

CICERO, De inventione II 1, 2-3.

14. "Praebete igitur mihi, quaeso, inquit, ex istis virginibus formosissimas, dum pingo id, quod pollicitus sum vobis, ut mutum in simulacrum ex animali exemplo veritas transferatur". Tum Crotoniatae publico de consilio virgines unum in locum conduxerunt et pictori, quam vellet, eligendi potestatem dederunt. Ille autem quinque delegit; quarum nomina multi poëtae memoriae prodiderunt, quod eius essent iudicio probatae, qui pulchritudinis habere verissimum iudicium debuisset. Neque enim putavit omnia, quae quaereret ad venustatem, in corpore uno se reperire posse ideo, quod nihil simplici in genere omnibus ex partibus perfectum natura expolivit.

14. "Please send me, then, the most beautiful of these girls, while I am painting the picture that I have promised, so that the true beauty may be transferred from the living model to the mute likeness." Then the citizens of Croton by a public decree assembled the girls in one place and allowed the painter to choose whom he wished. He selected five, whose names many poets recorded because they were approved by the judgment of him who must have been the supreme judge of beauty. He chose five because he did not think all the qualities which he sought to combine in a portrayal of beauty could be found in one person, because in no single case has Nature made anything perfect and finished in every part.

tr. H. M. Hubbell

CICERO, De oratore II 35, 150.

15. Inter ingenium quidem et diligentiam perpaullulum loci reliquum est arti. Ars demonstrat tantum, ubi quaeras atque ubi sit illud, quod studeas invenire; reliqua sunt in cura, attentione animi, cogitatione, vigilantia, assiduitate, labore, complectar uno verbo... diligentia; qua una virtute omnes virtutes reliquae continentur.

ART AND DILIGENCE

15. Indeed, between talent and painstaking there is very little room left for art. Art merely points out where to search, and the locality of what you are anxious to find: all else depends on carefulness, mental concentration, reflection, watchfulness, persistence and hard work; I shall sum up these in the single word I have often used already, painstaking to wit, on which single virtue all other virtues are dependent.

tr. C. D. Younge

CICERO, Tusc. disp. I 26, 64.

16. Mihi vero ne haec quidem notiora et illustriora carere vi divina videntur, ut ego aut poëtam grave plenumque carmen sine caelesti aliquo mentis instinctu putem fundere aut eloquentiam sine maiore quadam vi fluere

INSPIRATION

16. To my mind, even better known and more famous fields of labour do not seem unmoved from divine influence, or suffer me to think that the poet pours out his solemn, swelling strain without heavenly inspiration, or

abundantem sonantibus verbis uberibusque sententiis.

that eloquence flows in a copious stream of echoing words and fruitful thoughts without some higher influence.

tr. H. Rackham

CICERO, De natura deorum II 66, 167.

Nemo igitur vir magnus sine aliquo adflatu divino umquam fuit.

No one was ever great without some kind of divine inspiration.

tr. H. Rackham

TRUTH IN ART

CICERO, De oratore III 57, 215.

17. Ac sine dubio in omni re vincit imitationem veritas. Sed ea si satis in actione efficeret ipsa per sese, arte profecto non egeremus.

17. And in everything, without a doubt, truth has the advantage over imitation; and if truth were efficient enough in delivery of itself, we should certainly have no need of the aid of art.

tr. J. S. Watson

FICTIVENESS OF ART

CICERO, De oratore II 46, 193.

18. Quid potest esse tam fictum quam versus, quam scaena, quam fabulae?

18. What can be so unreal as poetry, the theatre, or stage plays?

tr. C. D. Younge

IDEA IN THE ARTIST'S MIND

CICERO, Orator 2, 8.

19. Sed ego sic statuo nihil esse in ullo genere tam pulchrum, quo non pulchrius id sit, unde illud ut ex ore aliquo quasi imago exprimatur, quod neque oculis neque auribus neque ullo sensu percipi potest, cogitatione tantum et mente complectimur. Itaque et Phidiae simulacris, quibus nihil in illo genere perfectius videmus, et iis picturis, quas nominavi, cogitare tamen possumus pulchriora. Nec vero ille artifex, cum faceret Iovis formam aut Minervae, contemplabatur aliquem, e quo similitudinem duceret, sed ipsius in mente insidebat species pulchritudinis eximia quaedam, quam intuens in eaque defixus ad illius similitudinem artem et manum dirigebat. Ut igitur in formis et figuris est aliquid perfectum et excellens, cuius ad cogitatam speciem imitando referentur ea, quae sub oculos ipsa ⟨non⟩ cadunt, sic perfectae eloquentiae speciem animo videmus, effigiem auribus quaerimus. Has rerum formas appellat ἰδέας ille non intelligendi solum, sed etiam dicendi gravissimus auctor et magister, Plato, easque gigni negat et ait semper esse ac ratione et intelligentia contineri.

19. But I am firmly of the opinion that nothing of any kind is so beautiful as not to be excelled in beauty by that of which it is a copy, as a mask is a copy of a face. This ideal cannot be perceived by the eye or ear, nor by any of the senses, but we can, nevertheless, grasp it by the mind and the imagination. For example, in the case of the statues of Phidias, the most perfect of their kind that we have ever seen, and in the case of the paintings I have mentioned, we can, in spite of their beauty, imagine something more beautiful. Surely, that great sculptor, while making the image of Jupiter or Minerva, did not look at any person whom he was using as a model, but in his own mind there dwelt a surpassing vision of beauty; at this he gazed and, all intent on this, he guided his artist's hand to produce the likeness of the god. Accordingly, as there is something perfect and surpassing in the case of sculpture and painting—an intellectual ideal by reference to which the artist represents those objects which do not themselves appear to the eye, so with our minds we conceive the ideal of perfect eloquence, but with our minds

we catch only the copy. These patterns of things are called "ideai" or ideas by Plato, that eminent master and teacher both of style and of thought; these, he says, do not "become"; they exist forever, and depend on intellect and reason.

tr. H. M. Hubbell

CICERO, De oratore III 50, 195.

20. Omnes enim tacito quodam sensu sine ulla arte aut ratione, quae sint in artibus ac rationibus recta ac prava, diiudicant; idque cum faciunt in picturis et in signis et in aliis operibus, ad quorum intellegentiam a natura minus habent instrumenti, tum multo ostendunt magis in verborum, numerorum vocumque iudicio, quod ea sunt in communibus infixa sensibus nec earum rerum quemquam funditus natura esse voluit expertem.

AESTHETIC SENSE

20. For all men, by a kind of tacit sense, without any art or reasoning, can form a judgment of what is right and wrong in art and reasoning, and as they do this with regard to pictures and statues and other works, for understanding which they have less assistance from nature, so they display this faculty much more in criticizing words, numbers, and sounds of language, because these powers are inherent in our common senses, nor has nature intended that any person should be utterly destitute of judgment in these particulars.

tr. J. S. Watson

CICERO, De officiis I 4, 14.

21. Nec vero illa parva vis naturae est rationisque, quod unum hoc animal sentit, quid sit ordo, quid sit quod deceat in factis dictisque, qui modus. Itaque eorum ipsorum, quae aspectu sentiuntur, nullum aliud animal pulchritudinem, venustatem, convenientiam partium sentit; quam similitudinem natura ratioque ab oculis ad animum transferens multo etiam magis pulchritudinem, constantiam, ordinem in consiliis factisque conservanda putat.

21. And it is no mean manifestation of Nature and Reason that man is the only animal that has a feeling for order, for propriety, for moderation in word and deed. And so no other animal has a sense of beauty, loveliness, harmony in the visible world; and Nature and Reason, extending the analogy of this from the world of sense to the world of spirit, find that beauty, consistency, order, are far more to be maintained in thought and deed...

tr. Walter Miller

CICERO, Orator 55, 183.

22. Esse ergo in oratione numerum quendam non est difficile cognoscere. Iudicat enim sensus... Neque enim ipse versus ratione est cognitus, sed natura atque sensu, quem dimensa ratio docuit, quod acciderit. Ita notatio naturae et animadversio peperit artem.

THE SENSES AND THE MIND

22. It is, then, not hard to recognize that there is a certain rhythm in prose. For the decision is given by our senses... Verse itself, as a matter of fact, is not recognized by abstract reason, but by our natural feeling: later on theory measured the verse and showed us what happened. The art of poetry, therefore, arose from observation and investigation of a phenomenon of nature.

CICERO, Orator 60, 203.

In versibus...modum notat ars, sed aures ipsae tacito sensu eum sine arte definiunt.

...in verse theory sets down the exact measure... but without theory the ear marks their limits with unconscious intuition.

CICERO, Orator 49, 162.

Sed quia rerum verborumque iudicium in prudentia est, vocum autem et numerorum aures sunt iudices, et quod illa ad intellegentiam referuntur, haec ad voluptatem, in illis ratio invenit, in his sensus artem.

...the decision as to subject-matter and words to express it belongs to the intellect, but in the choice of sounds and rhythms the ear is the judge; the former are dependent on the understanding, the latter on pleasure; therefore, reason determines the rules of art in the former case, and sensation in the latter.

CICERO, Orator 53, 178.

Poëticae versus inventus est terminatione aurium, observatione prudentium.

...in the realm of poetry, verse was discovered by the test of the ear and the observation of thoughtful men.

tr. H. M. Hubbell

CICERO, De natura deorum II 14, 37.

23. Ipse autem homo ortus est ad mundum contemplandum et imitandum.

23. ...man himself, however, came into existence for the purpose of contemplating and imitating the world...

tr. H. Rackham

CICERO, De natura deorum II 48, 145.

24. Omnisque sensus hominum multo antecellit sensibus bestiarum. Primum enim oculi in iis artibus, quarum iudicium est oculorum, in pictis, fictis caelatisque formis, in corporum etiam motione atque gestu multa cernunt subtilius; colorum etiam et figurarum [tum] venustatem atque ordinem et, ut ita dicam, decentiam oculi iudicant, atque etiam alia maiora. Nam et virtutes et vitia cognoscunt; iratum propitium, laetantem, dolentem, fortem ignavum, audacem timidumque cognoscunt. Auriumque item est admirabile quoddam artificiosumque iudicium, quo iudicatur et in vocis et in tibiarum nervorumque cantibus varietas sonorum, intervalla, distinctio et vocis genera permulta: canorum fuscum, leve asperum, grave acutum, flexibile durum, quae hominum solum auribus iudicantur.

IN PRAISE OF EYES AND EARS

24. And all the senses of man far excel those of the lower animals. In the first place, our eyes have a finer perception of many things in the arts which appeal to the sense of sight: in painting, modelling and sculpture, and also in bodily movements and gestures; since the eyes judge beauty and arrangement and, so to speak, propriety of colour and shape; and also other more important matters, for they also recognize virtues and vices, the angry and the friendly, the joyful and the sad, the brave man and the coward, the bold and the craven. The ears are likewise marvellously skilful organs of discrimination; they judge differences of tone, of pitch and of key in the music of the voice and of wind and stringed instruments, and many different qualities of voice, sonorous and dull, smooth and rough, bass and treble, flexible and hard, distinctions discriminated by the human ear alone.

tr. H. Rackham

CICERO, De natura deorum II 60, 150.

25. Itaque ad pingendum, ad fingendum, ad scalpendum, ad nervorum eliciendos sonos ac tibiarum apta manus est admotione digitorum. Atque haec oblectationis; illa necessi-

IN PRAISE OF HANDS

25. Thus, by the manipulation of the fingers, the hand is enabled to paint, to model, to carve, and to draw forth the notes of the lyre and of the flute. And beside these arts of recreation

tatis, cultus dico agrorum extructionesque tectorum, tegumenta corporum vel texta vel suta omnemque fabricam aeris et ferri; ex quo intellegitur ad inventa animo, percepta sensibus adhibitis opificum manibus omnia nos consecutos, ut tecti, ut vestiti, ut salvi esse possemus, urbes, muros, domicilia, delubra haberemus.

there are those of utility, I mean agriculture and building, the weaving and stitching of garments, and the various modes of working bronze and iron; hence we realize that it was by applying the hand of the artificer to the discoveries of thought and observations of the senses that all our conveniences were attained, and we were enabled to have shelter, clothing and protection, and possessed cities, fortifications, houses and temples.

tr. H. Rackham

CICERO, De oratore III 9, 34.

26. Nonne fore, ut, quot oratores, totidem paene reperiantur genera dicendi? Ex qua mea disputatione forsitan occurrat illud, si paene innumerabiles sint quasi formae figuraeque dicendi, specie dispares, genere laudabiles, non posse ea, quae inter se discrepant, iisdem praeceptis atque una institutione formari.

VARIETY OF FORMS IN ART

26. Would it not happen that almost as many kinds of eloquence as of orators would be found? But from this observation of mine, it may perhaps occur to you, that if there be almost innumerable varieties and characters of eloquence, dissimilar in species yet laudable in their kind, things of so diversified a nature can never be formed into an art by the same precepts and one single method of instruction.

tr. J. S. Watson

CICERO, Pro Archia poëta I, 2.

26a. Omnes artes, quae ad humanitatem pertinent, habent quoddam commune vinclum et quasi cognatione quadam inter se continentur.

26a. Indeed, the subtle bond of a mutual relationship links together all arts which have a bearing upon the common life of mankind.

tr. N. H. Watts

CICERO, De oratore III 7, 26.

27. At hoc idem, quod est in naturis rerum, transferri potest etiam ad artes. Una fingendi est ars, in qua praestantes fuerunt Myro, Polyclitus, Lysippus; qui omnes inter se dissimiles fuerunt, sed ita tamen, ut neminem sui velis esse dissimilem. Una est ars ratioque picturae, dissimilimique tamen inter se Zeuxis, Aglaophon, Apelles; neque eorum quisquam est, cui quidquam in arte sua deesse videatur.

27. But the same observation which is to be made in regard to nature may be applied also to the different kinds of art. Sculpture is a single art in which Myro, Polyclitus and Lysippus excelled all of whom, differed one from another, but so that you would not wish anyone of them to be unlike himself. The art and science of painting is one, yet Zeuxis, Aglaophon, Apelles are quite unlike one another in themselves, though to none of them does anything seem wanting in his peculiar style.

tr. J. S. Watson

CICERO, De oratore I 42, 187.

28. Omnia fere, quae sunt conclusa nunc artibus, dispersa et dissipata quondam fuerunt; ut in musicis numeri et voces et modi; ...in grammaticis poëtarum pertractatio, historiarum

PROGRESS IN ART

28. Nearly all elements, now forming the content of arts, were once without order or correlation: in music, for example, rhythms, sounds and measures; ...in literature the study

cognitio, verborum interpretatio, pronuntiandi quidam sonus; in hac denique ipsa ratione dicendi excogitare, ornare, disponere, meminisse, agere ignota quondam omnibus et diffusa late videbantur.

of poets, the learning of histories, the explanation of words and proper intonation in speaking them; and lastly in this very theory of oratory, invention, style, arrangement, memory and delivery, once seemed to all men things unknown and widely separated one from another.

tr. C. D. Younge

CICERO, Tusc. disp. I 2, 4.

SOCIAL CONDITIONS OF ART

29. Honos alit artes, omnesque incenduntur ad studia gloria, iacentque ea semper, quae apud quosque improbantur.

29. Public esteem is the muse of the arts, and all men are fired to application by fame, whilst these pursuits which meet with general disapproval, always lie neglected.

tr. J. E. King

CICERO, De officiis I 27, 94.

METHODOLOGICAL REMARKS

30. Qualis autem differentia sit honesti et decori, facilius intellegi quam explanari potest.

30. The nature of the difference between morality and propriety can be more easily felt than expressed.

tr. Walter Miller

CICERO, De officiis I 27, 95.

31. Est enim quiddam, idque intellegitur in omni virtute, quod deceat; quod cogitatione magis a virtute potest quam re separari. Ut venustas et pulchritudo corporis secerni non potest a valetudine, sic hoc, de quo loquimur, decorum totum illud quidem est cum virtute confusum, sed mente et cogitatione distinguitur.

31. For there is a certain element of propriety perceptible in every act of moral rectitude; and this can be separated from virtue theoretically better than it can be practically. As comeliness and beauty of person are inseparable from the notion of health, so this propriety of which we are speaking, while in fact completely blended with virtue, is mentally and theoretically distinguishable from it.

tr. Walter Miller

7. The Aesthetics of Music

(a) HELLENISTIC MUSIC

I. Archaic Greek art was based upon binding though unwritten rules. It was rational and objective. It sought neither richness nor originality, but only perfection. Plato had insisted that such art should be pursued always to the exclusion of all other art and that artists should confine themselves to creating variations upon this theme without introducing new principles or forms. But already in his lifetime painting and sculpture had moved into the quite different realm of impressionism and subjectivism. This change has also taken place in poetry, as it is evident from the tragedies of Euripides. Even music, despite its ritualistic nature and consequent conservatism, underwent alteration as early as the middle of the fifth century. Both

Plutarch and Plato regarded this early date as marking the beginning of "the fall of music".

The Greeks associated the turning-point in music* with the names of Melanippides, the cithara-player Phrynis of Mytilene (middle of the fifth century) and his pupil Timotheus of Miletus, active chiefly in Athens in the fifth and fourth centuries B.C. These musicians had abandoned the simplicity of the old school of Terpander[1] and had adopted a new type of composition in which melody took precedence over rhythm,[2] in which tonality and rhythm varied, and which made use of unexpected effects, striking contrasts, refined modulations, ample use of chromaticism and choral executions of the *nomos*. The music historian Abert has compared Timotheus with Richard Wagner. The changes which he introduced into Greek music were far-reaching. He abandoned old rules and immutable forms and inaugurated personal composition. The anonymous character of art thus came to an end and artists began to be distinguished by their individual styles. The reaction of audiences also changed and musical compositions now, for the first time, provoked applause.

In the fifth century music moved from canonical to individualist forms and from very simple to more complex forms. With particular reference to flute-playing Plutarch wrote that it evolved from "simple to rich forms". At the same time music evolved towards free forms. Dionysius of Halicarnassus said of musicians that "by mixing in one and the same composition the Dorian, the Phrygian and the Lydian modes, and the diatonic, chromatic and enharmonic scales, they indulged in inadmissible freedom in art".

At the same time there occurred in music a shift in emphasis from vocal to instrumental music. Traditionalists complained that "flute-players are no longer prepared to yield the leading role to the choruses, as used to happen in the past", and asserted that after all "the Muse has granted command to the chorus, so let the flute remain in the background, because it has a subservient role". This change had a result of considerable significance. When music became associated with instruments, it broke away from poetry and two arts came to replace what had formerly been one art. On the one hand, purely instrumental music came into being, and on the other, equally unknown in the past, poetry designed for reading and not for singing or recitation and listening. "The poet's song" became merely a metaphorical expression.

II. The Romans were neither particularly fond of music nor did they have any particular talent for it. They were not attracted to melody without words or spectacle. Under the name of song (*canticum*) they composed theatrical recitations and pantomime. This was the situation in the early Roman period, but later a change took

---

* In addition to those mentioned above, there are the following histories of ancient music: R. Westphal, *Harmonik und Melopoie der Griechen* (1863); *Geschichte der alten u. der mittelalterlichen Musik* (1864); Th. Gerold, *La musique des origines à nos jours* (1936); *The New Oxford History of Music*, vol. I: *Ancient and Oriental Music* (1955); F. A. Gevaërt, *Histoire et théorie de la musique dans l'antiquité,* vol. 2 (1875–81); cf. K. v. Jan, *Musici auctores Graeci* (1895).

place and Rome succumbed to the influences not only of Greek, but even of Eastern music. Livy tells us that in 187 B.C. Rome was invaded by Eastern music and that this was resisted by the conservatives, who in 115 brought about an official ban of all instruments other than the Roman tibia. However, nobody heeded the ban and life continued as before. Cicero was inclined to see a connection between the new musical forms and the decline of morals and therefore condemned the musical sophistication which became widespread during his lifetime.

Under the Caesars music became much more important in the public and private life of the Romans and performances rapidly assumed colossal proportions. The same was true of Alexandria, where concerts were given by huge choirs and orchestras. Under Ptolemy Philadelphus 300 singers and 300 citharas took part in Dionysian processions. But Rome surpassed even Alexandria. There, choirs several hundred strong would perform in the theatres and hundreds of performers would give concerts for tens of thousands of listeners.

While formerly the Romans had confined themselves to watching the dances of slaves and had not themselves taken part, from the time of the Gracchi dancing and singing schools appeared, despite the protests of the traditionalists. The Caesars, whose tastes brought them closer to the people than to the aristocracy, supported music and a number of them could themselves sing and play. The ability to sing and to play musical instruments came to be regarded as embellishments of a woman's personality. From Greece came the fashion of playing music at meals.

Star-performers were lionized and made tours throughout the empire. Many of them were maintained by the imperial court, and were not only lavishly remunerated, but also had statues erected in their honour. Nero gave a palace to the cithara-player Menecrates, while Anaxenous received from Marcus Aurelius the tributes of four conquered cities and had a guard of honour placed in front of his house. Strabo says of him that his own city bestowed upon him a religious title and erected a tablet with an inscription in which he was compared with the gods. We have to confine ourselves to this sociological information about music in Rome because, despite their love of it, the Romans made no contribution to its development.

Even in Greece, however, music made little progress in later centuries. Yet, although musical creativity made such small headway, musical theory developed very considerably. The same is true of the history of music. All that we know about the earlier creative Hellenic period we owe to the historians of the Hellenistic age, when love of scholarship supplanted creative work.

(b) MUSICAL THEORY

1. VARIOUS MEANINGS OF THE WORD "MUSIC". Etymologically derived from the Muses, the word "music" originally signified all the activities and crafts falling under their patronage. However, at an early stage its meaning became restricted to the art of sounds. By Hellenistic times the original wide meaning was already used only metaphorically.

The word *mousike* was an abbreviation of *mousike techne*, meaning the art of music, and retained permanently the ambiguity of the Greek term "art", which embraced both theory and practice. The word *mousike* meant not only music in the modern sense, but also musical theory, not only the ability to produce rhythms, but also the process of production itself.

Thus Sextus Empiricus wrote that in antiquity the word "music" had a threefold meaning.[3] Firstly, it signified a science, the science concerned with sounds and rhythms (i.e., what we would call today musical theory). Secondly, it meant proficiency in singing or playing a musical instrument, in the production of sounds and rhythms, but also the product of that proficiency, that is to say, the work of music itself. Thirdly, the word "music" signified in its original meaning every work of art in the widest sense, including painting and poetry, though it later ceased to be used in this sense.

2. COMPASS OF MUSICAL THEORY. The ancients' knowledge of music was extensive, particularly since they also included in it its mathematical and optical foundations, as well as the theory of the dance and, to some extent, the theory of poetry. The work of Aristoxenus* shows that already at the beginning of the Hellenistic age in the third century B.C. this knowledge covered a great variety of subjects.

Thus, knowledge of music had a theoretical and a practical aspect. The theoretical aspect consisted of the scientific bases and their technical application. These bases lay partly in arithmetic and partly in physics, while their application covered harmonics, eurhythmics and metrics. The practical aspect was both educational and productive. Composition could in turn be of one of three kinds: either musical

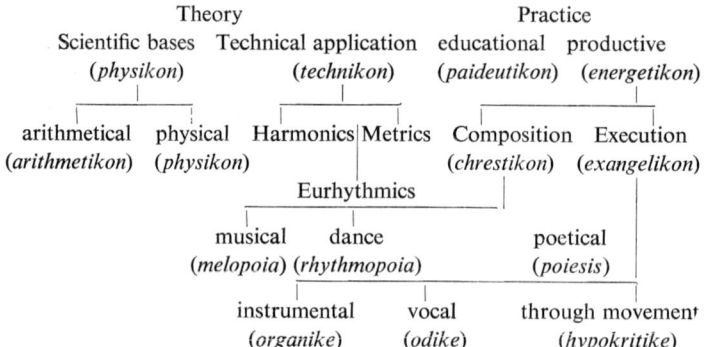

in our modern sense, or concerned with the dance or with poetry. Execution was similarly divisible: execution by instruments, execution by the human voice and execution through bodily movements as in the case of an actor or of a dancer.†

---

* *Die harmonischen Fragmente des Aristoxenos,* ed. P. Marquardt (1868).

† Aristoxenus was familiar with all these various aspects of musical knowledge. These were tabulated by P. Marquardt, who edited his works almost a hundred years ago.

3. THE TRADITION OF THE PYTHAGOREANS, PLATO AND ARISTOTLE. The Greeks were most strongly influenced in their attitude to music by those who had first studied its theory, namely the Pythagoreans.* Their understanding of music had two special features. Firstly, they interpreted it *mathematically*. From their observations on mathematics and acoustics they arrived at the conclusion that harmony is a matter of proportions and numbers. Plutarch was to describe this method as follows: "Pythagoras in his judgment about music rejected the testimony of experience;... the value of that art has to be apprehended with the mind".[4]

Secondly, they initiated the *ethical* theory of music. They developed the view commonly held in Greece that music is not only an amusement but also an incentive to do good[5] and maintained that rhythm and tonality affect man's moral attitude, influence his will by either paralysing or stimulating it, and may lead him away from normality towards madness, or, conversely, may soothe and remove psychological disturbances, and have therapeutic value. As the Greeks put it, they affect man's ethos.

The ethical interpretation of music, first formulated by the Pythagoreans, was developed by Damon† and Plato‡. From the very beginning there were two Pythagorean schools, the one treating music purely theoretically on equal terms with astronomy, the other concerned with its ethical influence. Plato supported the latter school, which may therefore be called the Pythagoreo-Platonic school.

The interpretation of music in ethical terms is easily explained. One reason was the Greeks' extraordinary sensitivity to music, a thing quite common among peoples in the early stages of cultural development. This had remarkable consequences in that musical theory showed greater concern with the moral than with the aesthetic effects of music, while the belief that music is constructed according to the same mathematical laws of harmony as the universe endowed Greek musical theory with a metaphysical and mystical bias. This partly metaphysical and partly moral and educational Pythagoreo-Platonic heritage survived into Hellenistic times. But so also did the Sophists' opposition to this theory. They held that music's only function is to give pleasure, and thus struck a serious blow against an art which claimed knowledge of the cosmos and the ability to improve men's minds. The ethico-metaphysical thesis and its critique were both perpetuated in Hellenistic times, but at the same time scholars from all the contemporary philosophical schools, notably the Peripatetic school, carried out specialized empirical musical studies free from metaphysical and ethical presuppositions.

4. THE *Problems*. This school was responsible for the *Problems*, which were once attributed to Aristotle himself.§ Though they are not his work, they are derived

---

* Cf. *op. cit.* by Frank and Schäfke.
† Cf. *op. cit.* by Schäfke and Koller.
‡ J. Regner, *Platos Musiktheorie*, Halle Univ. Thesis (1923).
§ C. Stumpf, "Die Pseudo-aristotelischen Probleme über Musik", *Abhandlungen der Berliner Akademie* (1896).

from him and employ his scientific method to answer specialized questions. At least eleven chapters of this work are concerned with musical theory and the questions which they elaborate are partly similar to those posed by modern aesthetics, though the solutions are traditional and typical of antiquity.

Thus, in *Problems 34, 35a* and *41* the question is asked, When are sounds in harmony and pleasing to the ear? The answer is, when they are in simple numerical relation. This was a traditional Pythagorean reply commonly accepted by the Greeks.

Problem 38 asks why rhythms, melodies and harmonies cause pleasure, and answers, that the pleasure they give is partly natural and innate, partly the result of familiarity, and partly has its source in number, stability, order and proportion, which are by nature pleasurable.[6] Here we meet a new doctrine of habit and familiarity together with the old Pythagorean doctrine that order and proportion are the sources of beauty and joy.

Problems 27 and *29* inquire how music, even if it is voiceless, can express character and give the answer that it can do so because in music we perceive movement, in movement we perceive action and in action character. This reply, too, reflects the old "ethical" interpretation of music.

Problems 33 and *37* ask why we find a low-pitched voice more pleasant than a high-pitched thin one and say that this is because we feel a thin high-pitched voice reflects a person's weakness. This too is an echo of the theory of "ethos" in music.

In *Problem 10* the question is asked why the human voice causes more pleasure than instruments and why this pleasure is diminished when the song is wordless. The answer is that this is because the pleasure of harmony by itself is enhanced when words are present by the pleasure of imitation. This reply is characteristically Aristotelian, for it introduces the idea of *mimesis* in an interpretation and this was peculiar to the Stagiryte.

Problems 5 and *40* inquire why we gain more pleasure from listening to a familiar song than we do from listening to an unfamiliar one. The answer is because there is pleasure in recognition and the recognition of a familiar song, of its melody and rhythm requires less effort. This observation is as old as Homer, but the explanatory reference to the "pleasure of recognition" introduces an Aristotelian idea.

All in all, the *Problems* show how widespread and permanent in Greece was the understanding of music evolved by the Pythagoreans, with its numerical interpretation of harmony and its doctrines of order, expression and ethos. However, these doctrines intermingled with certain ideas of Aristotle, notably his theory of imitation.

5. THEOPHRASTUS AND ARISTOXENUS. Theophrastus, Aristotle's brilliant pupil and a scholar who concerned himself even more with specialist and technical questions than his master, and whom Aristotle apparently chided for "excessive clarity", took considerable interest in aesthetics and art theory. In addition to his *Poetics* and monographs *On Style, On Comedy, On Humour* and *On Enthusiasm*, he wrote

the *Harmonics* and *On Music*. The surviving fragments of these musicological works tell us that he accounted for the effects of music in the three emotions which are aroused: sorrow, delight and enthusiasm. Music discharges these emotions and therefore prevents them from having negative effects. This shows that Theophrastus held to the theory of catharsis in music and the thesis of the moral effects of music. He retained the old Greek understanding of music, though in Aristotle's cautious formulation.

Aristoxenus of Tarentum, another of Aristotle's pupils, contributed even more to musical theory. Among his numerous works (Suidas lists 453 of his books) pride of place must be given to those concerned with musical theory. Three books of his *Harmonics* have survived, as have fragments dealing with music from the *Introduction to Harmonics* (in Cleonides) and of *Banqueting Miscellanies* (in Plutarch). His *Elements of Eurhythmics* is known from later transcriptions. The ancients were aware of his role in this field and called him "the musician". Cicero compared his achievement in the annals of music with that of Archimedes in mathematics. The historical information compiled by Aristoxenus makes him one of our chief sources on ancient music, while his own musical studies are still not obsolete even after two thousand years.

He was a pupil not only of Aristotle but also of Pythagorean mathematicians and experts in acoustics. He studied both the technical and the philosophical questions connected with music. He favoured the simple music of the past and praised the early musicians who "scorned polyphony and variety". He opposed the innovators and maintained that "we are like the inhabitants of Paestum, who were once Hellenes but have taken to barbarism and have become Romans". He maintained the traditional teaching about the ethos of music and about its moral, educational and therapeutic effects. He believed that "the old Hellenes were right to value the educational power of music".

6. THE PYTHAGOREAN AND ARISTOXENIAN TRENDS. But the novelty of Aristoxenus and his historical significance lie not so much in this as in his objective studies of music, including psychological studies. Their importance he recognized by starting from the premise that even more attention should be paid to the act of judgment than to the thing judged.[7]

He had to face two contending views on music, one of which said that music is moral power, while the other claimed that it merely "tickles the ear". The Pythagorean view was that music had immutable mathematical foundations, while Democritus and the Sophists claimed that it was a matter of the senses. Aristoxenus did not support either view in its entirety but drew some of his ideas from each. He included Pythagorean doctrines in his theory but he also emphasized the sensory elements of music. He wrote that so far as music is concerned, "accuracy of sense perception is an [almost] fundamental requirement"[8] and that apprehension of music depends on two things: sensation and memory.[9] Thus, musical theory was henceforth to contrast the Pythagorean with the Aristoxenian trends. Both favoured the "ethical" interpretation of music and the difference between them lay in that the approach of the first was metaphysical and mystical, associated musical harmony with the harmony of the cosmos and ascribed to music a special power and a unique ability to influence souls, whereas the Aristoxenian movement attempted a positivist, psychological and medical interpretation. The difference between the Pythagoreans and the followers of Aristoxenus lay not so much in the way they understood music but rather in the method they used to study it.

Following the spirit of the times, the majority of musical theorists henceforth supported Aristoxenus, although they also adopted an attitude of compromise towards the Pythagorean position. These included a number of Stoics, among whom the greatest interest in the theory of music was shown by Diogenes, known as the Babylonian. His work *On Music*, in which he extolled the power of music and its usefulness in worship and education, in war and in games, in action and in thought, and in which he stressed not only its moral but also its epistemological value, had for a time considerable success. The most important of the later writers of this movement was Aristides Quintilian, the author of *Three Books on Music*.*

7. THE STUDY OF ETHOS. An essential element in the whole theory of music, both in its Pythagorean and its Aristoxenian interpretation, was the ancient Greek study of "the ethos of music".[10] As it grew more and more detailed,† this study went beyond a general thesis about music's effect on character (cthos) to show various aspects of this effect, and in particular, to contrast its positive and negative effects. The music of each Greek tribe had a different mode: the Dorian was austere, the Ionian was mellifluous. Eastern music set in the Phrygian and the Lydian modes, which had gained a foothold in Greece, was very different from genuinely Greek music, especially Dorian music. For the Greeks the sharpest contrast lay between the austere Dorian music and the passionate, penetrating Phrygian music. Their modes were different. The one was deep and low-pitched (*hipata*), the other high-pitched (*neta*). One employed the cithara, the other the flute. They accompanied different cults, the Dorian being associated with the cult of Apollo and the Phrygian with the cult of Dionysus, Cybele and the dead. The one was native, the other exotic. Phrygian music was so different from what the Greeks were familiar with that its introduction came as a shock to them and was probably to some extent responsible for the rise of the whole theory about the varied ethos of music. The Greeks regarded their own traditional music as strengthening and soothing and the new foreign music as stimulating, exciting and orgiastic. The traditionalists, Plato in particular, ascribed a positive ethos to the former and a negative one to the latter. They con-

---

* *Aristides Quintilianus*, ed. A. Jahn.—The following are also well-preserved and important works on music produced in late antiquity: Plutarch's *De Musica* (*De la musique*, ed. H. Weil, and Th. Reinach, 1900) and Ptolemy's *Harmonica* (ed. J. During, 1930). — Interpretation of music in the final phase of antiquity is covered in G. Pietzsch's *Die Musik in Erzeihungs- und Bildungsideal des ausgehenden Altertums und frühen Mittelalters* (1932) and in Schäfke's book already mentioned.

† H. Abert, *Die Lehre vom Ethos in der griechischen Musik* (1899).

demned the Phrygian mode, confining their approval exclusively to the Dorian mode.

Between the two extremes the Greeks recognized many intermediate modes: the Aeolian epic mode (which, because of its proximity to the Dorian mode, they called the Hypodorian), the Ionian lyric mode (which, because of its proximity to the Phrygian mode, they called Hypophrygian), the Lydian mode, the Mixolydian mode, the Hypolydian mode and other modes as well. In an attempt to simplify this variety, Greek theoreticians distinguished three musical modes, two of them extreme and a third intermediate mode embracing all the remaining ones.

Philosophers supplied a moral and psychological interpretation for this multitude of modes. From this point of view Aristotle distinguished three types of modes: the ethical, the practical and the enthusiastic. He held that the "ethical" modes affect a man's whole ethos either by endowing him with ethical stability (as does the Dorian with its austerity) or by actually destroying it (as does the Mixolydian with its wistfulness, or the Ionian with its enervating spell). The "practical" modes arouse in man specific acts of will, while the "enthusiastic" ones, especially the Phrygian, lead man from his normal state into ecstasy and bring about emotional relief.

This threefold division of modes remained throughout the Hellenistic era although usually in different combinations and under different names. Aristides Quintilian distinguished three types of music:[11] 1. music with the "diastaltic ethos", characterized by grandeur, virility and heroism; 2. its opposite, music with the "systaltic ethos", devoid of manliness and giving rise to amorous and plaintive feelings; 3. the intermediate "hesycastic ethos", characterized by internal stability. In poetry the first "ethos" is suited to tragedy, the second to laments and the third to hymns and paeans.

The "ethical" analysis, which is the most peculiar feature of the Greek theory of music, originated among the Pythagoreans in the form of a metaphysical and mystical theory. Then, from the time of Damon and Plato, it became associated with ethical,[12] pedagogical and political[13] conclusions, which demanded the use of certain modes and the banning of others. Finally, in the hands of Aristotle and his pupils, it changed so much that it was reduced to being the phenomenology of the effects of music. Its claims had diminished, while its scientific value increased.

Despite the respect which the Greeks showed towards metaphysical and ethical theories of music, these did not go without criticism. Even the phenomenological interpretation of "ethos" provoked objections because it assumed that the "ethos" exists in the mode independent of the listener's attitude, and ascribed to sounds a definite power. There were also more cautious thinkers who denied music this power and maintained that all the attributes of the modes—the exaltation of the Dorian mode, the inspired fancifulness of the Phrygian mode, the sorrowful plaintiveness of the Lydian mode—were not to be found within them but rather, that they had been charged with these attributes by man himself in the course of a long process of evolution.

8. THE UTILITARIAN TREND: PHILODEMUS. This criticism had already begun in the renascence period of the fifth century. The Sophists and the Atomists would not accept the "ethos" theory. They offered instead quite a different theory that music is simply a pleasant combination of sounds and rhythms and not a psychagogic or ethical force. The earliest doubts about the psychagogic power of music are to be found in a preserved fragment known as the Hibeh papyrus.[14] The conflict between the two movements, which we may call the ethical and the utilitarian, developed into the fiercest controversy over the theory of music of the Hellenistic period, with the Sceptics and Epicureans acting as spokesmen of the utilitarian movement. Two learned works on the subject have reached us: one by the Epicurean Philodemus and the other by the Sceptic Sextus Empiricus, both of which we have already discussed. Their views and particularly those of Philodemus which diverge from the metaphysico-ethical tradition of the Greek theory of music, may be taken as characteristic of certain schools of thought. Although the view of a minority, they were nevertheless characteristic of the period.

Philodemus* launched a polemical attack 1. against the allegation that there existed a specific association between music and the soul. He stated bluntly that its effect on the soul is no different from that of culinary art;[15] 2. against its alleged association with the deity, since the states of ecstasy brought about through listening to music are easily explained; 3. against its alleged elemental moral effects and its ability to strengthen or weaken virtue; 4. against its ability to express or represent anything and characters in particular.

He argued that the stimulus of music, upon which the theory of musical "ethos" was constructed, was not by any means general and that it affected only people of a certain type, principally women and effeminate men. Moreover, it could be explained psychologically without reference to mystical attributes and without ascribing to music any special power. If we were to express Philodemus' ideas in modern language, we would say that he explained the effects of music as being the result of association of ideas. Reactions to music depend not only upon auditory sensations but also upon ideas associated with them, while these ideas are in turn dependent upon various incidental elements, the most significant being the poetry which accompanies the music. The inventors of the ethical theory of music confused musical effects with poetic effects, imagining the effects produced by words and thoughts to be effects of sounds.[16] The founders of Greek music, such as Terpander and Tyrtaeus, were poets rather than musicians. In particular, Philodemus explains the effects of religious music and the ecstasy it aroused as the result of certain ideas and associations. He thought that the noisy instruments used during ceremonies caused particular "connections of ideas".

---

* A. Rastagni, "Filodemo contra l'estetica classica" *Rivista di filologia classica* (1923–4).

Philodemus concluded that, when we take all this into account, it becomes clear that music neither has nor can have any moral functions because it has no special qualifications in this field. It has no metaphysical or epistemological significance, since all it does is to cater for pleasures in much the same way as food and drink. It can bring relaxation and joy, at best it can make work easier, but apart from this it is a luxury. This cannot be otherwise because it is only an entertainment, a game with a formalized content. Thus we see that the materialist Epicurean Philodemus and the idealist Plato had areas of agreement as well as disagreement in their views of art.

The "ethical" movement exhausted its potential very early. From the very beginning it laid stress on the moral advantages of music, to the neglect of its aesthetic values. Later only the opposing movement represented by Philodemus made any contribution towards the development of aesthetics, even though in the heat of controversy Philodemus was driven to extremes. Two philosophical schools, the Epicureans and the Sceptics, declared their allegiance to this new, more utilitarian interpretation of music, but the reaction against the "ethos" theory was not permanent. It was revived during the twilight of antiquity when there was a general swing back to religious, spiritualist and mystical ideas.

9. MIND VERSUS EAR. Historians of the Hellenistic theory of music distinguish other factions beside these two. They list the "canonists" (the Pythagoreans), the "harmonists" (the followers of Aristotle), the "ethicists" (the followers of Damon and Plato) and the "formalists". For them the Greek theory of music was divided by other opposing forces as well. Among the Pythagoreans themselves there were two groups, one of which stressed the ethical aspect of music, while the other concentrated on its mathematical implications.

But there was another more important set of contrasted questions, namely, whether our judgment of music is based on reason or on feeling and whether it involves calculation or is simply a question of beauty and the experience of pleasure. Already in the classical period the Pythagoreans supported the first view, claiming that music has a rational character, while the Sophists opposed them by stressing its irrational character. The rationalists regarded judgments of music as being objective, while the irrationalists maintained that these were subjective. In this particular instance Plato sided with the Sophists, and interpreted music as irrational and subjective.

Both views survived in Hellenistic times but were joined by a third which held that the reception of music does not depend either on the mind or on feeling but upon the sense impression of hearing. This was the position adopted by Aristoxenus and it was this, rather than his attitude to the "ethos" theory, that gave his school a distinct character. It was also adopted by the Stoics. The important distinction in the concept of impression, which has been discussed in the chapter on the aesthetics of the Stoics, made possible a better application of this concept in aesthetics. It was introduced quite early by the academician Speusippus[17] and developed by

Diogenes the Babylonian, a Stoic. They distinguished impressions from the feelings of pleasure and pain which accompany them and which are indeed subjective, although the impressions themselves are not. Further, they also distinguished two types of impression (we must again stress this point when talking about music). Some, like the impressions of hot and cold, are spontaneous, while others, like the impressions of harmony and disharmony, are the result of training education and learning. It is upon these educated impressions that music depends. Music has a sensory basis and yet it is rational, objective and may be a subject of study.

It is surprising to find the theory of Speusippus and Diogenes appearing among the Greeks, especially after Plato had drawn a sharp distinction between the mind and the senses and had expressed his conviction of the rationality of thought and the irrationality of sense impression. The theory was as novel and promising as it was controversial and provoked opposition from Philodemus. The Epicurean, thinking along conventional lines, would not accept the subtle distinctions drawn by the Stoics, but above all, he was dissatisfied with the idea of music being a rational activity. It has been said of the dispute between the Stoics' rational interpretation of music and its irrational interpretation by the Epicureans that it was the "last great debate in ancient aesthetics".

L. Texts on the Aesthetics of Music

PLUTARCH, De musica 1133b.

1. τὸ δ' ὅλον ἡ μὲν κατὰ Τέρπανδρον κιθαρῳδία καὶ μέχρι τῆς Φρύνιδος ἡλικίας παντελῶς ἁπλῆ τις οὖσα διετέλει· οὐ γὰρ ἐξῆν τὸ παλαιὸν οὕτω ποιεῖσθαι τὰς κιθαρῳδίας ὡς νῦν, οὐδὲ μεταφέρειν τὰς ἁρμονίας καὶ τοὺς ῥυθμούς· ἐν γὰρ τοῖς νόμοις ἑκάστῳ διετήρουν τὴν οἰκείαν τάσιν· διὸ καὶ ταύτης ἐπωνυμίαν εἶχον· νόμοι γὰρ προσηγορεύθησαν.

ARCHAIC MUSIC

1. On the whole, music for the cithara in the times of Terpander and up to the time of Phrynis had retained its simplicity, because in those days it was not permitted as it is now to change keys or rhythms in compositions. In each *nomos* the proper scale was retained right through. Hence their name: they were called *nomoi*, that is, laws.

PLUTARCH, De musica 1138b.

2. οἱ μὲν γὰρ νῦν φιλομελεῖς, οἱ δὲ τότε φιλόρρυθμοι.

RHYTHM AND MELODY

2. Present-day musicians are enamoured of melodies, their predecessors were enamoured of rhythms.

DIONYSIUS, OF HALICARNASSUS,
De comp. verb. 11 (Usener, Radermacher, 40).

ἡ ἀκοὴ τέρπεται μὲν τοῖς μέλεσιν ἄγεται δὲ τοῖς ῥυθμοῖς.

The ear delights in the melodies, is fascinated by the rhythms.

tr. W. R. Roberts

PLATO, Leges II 9, 664e.

τῇ δὲ τῆς κινήσεως τάξει ῥυθμὸς ὄνομα εἴη.

Now the order of motion is called rhythm.
tr. B. Jowett

PLATO, Leges II 1, 653e.

τὰ μὲν οὖν ἄλλα ζῶα οὐκ ἔχειν αἴσθησιν τῶν ἐν ταῖς κινήσεσι τάξεων οὐδὲ ἀταξιῶν, οἷς δὴ ῥυθμὸς ὄνομα καὶ ἁρμονία.

...the animals have no perception of order or disorder in their movements, that is, of rhythm and harmony, as they are called.
tr. B. Jowett

PLUTARCH, De musica 1135f.

ἡμεῖς δ' οὐκ ἄνθρωπόν τινα παρελάβομεν εὑρετὴν τῶν τῆς μουσικῆς ἀγαθῶν, ἀλλὰ τὸν πάσαις ταῖς ἀρεταῖς κεκοσμημένον θεὸν Ἀπόλλωνα.

I think that it is not to man that we owe the discovery of the benefits of music but to Apollo, the god most excellent in all respects.

ARISTIDES QUINTILIAN I 13 (Jahn, 20).

ῥυθμὸς τοίνυν καλεῖται τριχῶς· λέγεται γὰρ ἐπί τε τῶν ἀκινήτων σωμάτων (ὥς φαμεν εὔρυθμον ἀνδριάντα) κἀπὶ πάντων τῶν κινουμένων (οὕτως γάρ φαμέν εὐρύθμως τινὰ βαδίζειν) καὶ ἰδίως ἐπὶ φωνῆς.

RHYTHM

We talk of rhythms in three ways: in relation to static bodies (in this sense we talk of a rhythmic statue), in relation to all bodies in motion (in this sense we say that someone marches rhythmically), and in relation to the voice.

SEXTUS EMPIRICUS, Adv. mathem. VI 1.

3. Ἡ μουσικὴ λέγεται τριχῶς, καθ' ἕνα μὲν τρόπον ἐπιστήμη τις περὶ μελῳδίας καὶ φθόγγους καὶ ῥυθμοποιΐας καὶ τὰ παραπλήσια καταγιγνομένη πράγματα, καθὸ καὶ Ἀριστόξενον τὸν Σπινθάρου λέγομεν εἶναι μουσικόν. καθ' ἕτερον δὲ ἡ περὶ ὀργανικὴν ἐμπειρίαν, ὡς ὅταν τοὺς μὲν αὐλοῖς καὶ ψαλτηρίοις χρωμένους μουσικοὺς ὀνομάζωμεν, τὰς δὲ ψαλτρίας μουσικάς· ἀλλὰ κυρίως κατ' αὐτὰ τὰ σημαινόμενα καὶ παρὰ πολλοῖς λέγεται μουσική. καταχρηστικώτερον δὲ ἐνίοτε προσαγορεύειν εἰώθαμεν τῷ αὐτῷ ὀνόματι καὶ τὴν ἔν τινι πράγματι κατόρθωσιν. οὕτω γοῦν μεμουσωμένον τι ἔργον φαμέν, κἂν ζωγραφίας μέρος ὑπάρχῃ καὶ μεμουσῶσθαι τὸν ἐν τούτῳ κατορθώσαντα ζωγράφον.

THREEFOLD MEANING OF MUSIC

3. The term "music" is used in three senses; in one as a science dealing with melodies and notes and rhythm-making and similar things, in which sense we say that Aristoxenus, son of Spintharus, was a musician; in another sense it connotes instrumental skill, as when we describe those who use flutes and harps as musicians... It is with these significations that the term "music" is properly and generally used. But it is sometimes our habit to apply the same name in a loose sense to correctness in some performance. Thus we speak of a work as "musical", even though it be a piece of painting, and of the painter who has achieved therein correctness as "musical".
tr. R. G. Bury

PLUTARCH, De musica 1144f.

4. Πυθαγόρας δ' ὁ σεμνὸς ἀπεδοκίμαζε τὴν κρίσιν τῆς μουσικῆς τὴν διὰ τῆς αἰσθήσεως· νῷ γὰρ ληπτὴν τὴν ταύτης ἀρετὴν ἔφασκεν εἶναι.

MUSIC AND REASON

4. Worthy Pythagoras in his judgment about music rejected the testimony of experience; he said that the value of that art has to be apprehended with the mind.

PLUTARCH, De musica 1143f.

καθόλον μὲν οὖν εἰπεῖν ὁμοδρομεῖν δεῖ τήν τ' αἴσθησιν καὶ τὴν διάνοιαν ἐν τῇ κρίσει τῶν τῆς μουσικῆς μερῶν.

In short, in judging music impressions must go hand in hand with intelligence.

PLUTARCH, De musica 1142c.

Εἰ οὖν τις βούλεται μουσικῇ καλῶς καὶ κεκριμένως χρῆσθαι, τὸν ἀρχαῖον ἀπομιμείσθω τρόπον· ἀλλὰ μὴν καὶ τοῖς ἄλλοις αὐτὴν μαθήμασιν ἀναπληρούτω καὶ φιλοσοφίαν ἐπιστησάτω παιδαγωγόν· αὕτη γὰρ ἱκανὴ κρῖναι τὸ μουσικῇ πρέπον μέτρον καὶ τὸ χρήσιμον.

If you wish to cultivate music beautifully and nobly, you must imitate the ancient style; you must also supplement the study of music with the study of other disciplines and take philosophy as your guide, because only philosophy is capable of providing music with proper principles and utility.

SEXTUS EMPIRICUS
Adv. mathem. VI. 18.

5. Καθόλου γὰρ οὐ μόνον χαιρόντων ἐστὶν ἄκουσμα, ἀλλ' ἐν ὕμνοις καὶ εὐχαῖς καὶ θεῶν θυσίαις ἡ μουσική· διὰ δὲ τοῦτο καὶ ἐπὶ τὸν τῶν ἀγαθῶν ζῆλον τὴν διάνοιαν προτρέπεται.

MUSIC CONDUCIVE TO GOODNESS

5. [A wide-spread opinion which Sextus impugned] In sum, music is not only a sound of rejoicing, but is heard also in sacred hymns and feasts and sacrifices to the gods; and because of this it incites the mind to emulate the Good.

tr. R. G. Bury

PSEUDO-ARISTOTLE,
Problemata 920 b.29.

6. Διὰ τί ῥυθμῷ καὶ μέλει καὶ ὅλως ταῖς συμφωνίαις χαίρουσι πάντες; ἢ ὅτι ταῖς κατὰ φύσιν κινήσεσι χαίρομεν κατὰ φύσιν· σημεῖον δὲ τὸ τὰ παιδὶ εὐθὺς γενόμενα χαίρειν αὐτοῖς. διὰ δὲ τὸ ἔθος τρόποις μελῶν χαίρομεν. ῥυθμῷ δὲ χαίρομεν διὰ τὸ γνώριμον καὶ τεταγμένον ἀριθμὸν ἔχειν καὶ κινεῖν ἡμᾶς τεταγμένως· οἰκειοτέρα γὰρ ἡ τεταγμένη κίνησις φύσει τοῦ ἀτάκτου, ὥστε καὶ κατὰ φύσιν μᾶλλον... συμφωνίᾳ δὲ χαίρομεν, ὅτι κρᾶσίς ἐστι λόγον ἐχόντων ἐναντίων πρὸς ἄλληλα. ὁ μὲν οὖν λόγος τάξις, ὃ ἦν φύσει ἡδύ.

MUSIC AND PLEASURE

6. Why do all men delight in rhythm and melody and concords in general? It is because we naturally rejoice in natural movements. This is shown by the fact that children rejoice in them as soon as they are born. Now, we delight in the various types of melody for their moral character, but we delight in rhythm because it contains a familiar and ordered number and moves in a regular manner; for ordered movement is naturally more akin to us than disordered and is therefore more in accordance with nature... We delight in concord because it is the mingling of contraries which stand in proportion to one another. Proportion, then, is order which, as we have said, is naturally pleasant.

tr. W. R. Roberts

ARISTOXENUS, Harmonica 41
(Marquardt, 58).

7. διημαρτηκέναι δὲ συμβήσεται τἀληθοῦς ἐὰν τὸ μὲν κρῖνον μήτε πέρας μήτε κύριον ποιῶμεν τὸ δὲ κρινόμενον κύριόν τε καὶ πέρας.

SUBJECTIVE CONDITIONING OF JUDGMENT

7. We shall be sure to miss the truth unless we place the supreme and ultimate, not in the thing determined, but in the activity that determines.

tr. H. S. Macran

ARISTOXENUS, Harmonica 33
(Marquardt, 48).

8. τῷ δὲ μουσικῷ σχεδόν ἐστι ἀρχῆς ἔχουσα τάξιν ἡ τῆς αἰσθήσεως ἀκρίβεια.

ROLE OF SENSE IMPRESSION

8. But for the student of musical science, accuracy of sense perception is a fundamental requirement.

tr. H. S. Macran

ARISTOXENUS, Harmonica 38
(Marquardt, 56).

9. ἐκ δύο γὰρ τούτων ἡ τῆς μουσικῆς ξύνεσίς ἐστιν, αἰσθήσεώς τε καὶ μνήμης· αἰσθάνεσθαι μὲν γὰρ δεῖ τὸ γιγνόμενον, μνημονεύειν δὲ τὸ γεγονός.

IMPRESSIONS AND MEMORY

9. The apprehension of music depends on these two faculties, sense perception and memory: for we must perceive the sound that is present, and remember that which is past.

tr. H. S. Macran

SEXTUS EMPIRICUS,
Adv. mathem. VI 48.

10. ... τὶς μὲν μελῳδία σεμνά τινα καὶ ἀστεῖα ἐμποιεῖ τῇ ψυχῇ κινήματα, τὶς δὲ ταπεινότερα καὶ ἀγεννῆ. Καλεῖται δὲ κατὰ κοινὸν ἡ τοιουτότροπος μελῳδία τοῖς μουσικοῖς ἦθος ἀπὸ τοῦ ἤθους εἶναι ποιητική.

THE ETHOS OF MUSIC

10. ...a certain kind of melody produces in the soul stately and refined motions, another kind motions that are base and ignoble. Such melodies are usually called character by musicians because they form character.

THEOPHRASTUS, (Philodemus, De musica, Kemke, 37).

κεινεῖν ὅλως καὶ εὐρυθμίζειν τὰς ψυχὰς τὴν μουσικήν.

Music moves souls and provides them with rhythm.

DIOGENES THE BABYLONIAN
(Philodemus, De musica, Kemke, 8).

τὰ κατὰ τὰς ὀργὰς καὶ τὰ μεθ' ἡδονῆς καὶ λύπης ἐντυγχάνοντα κοινῶς, ἐπειδὴ τῶν οἰκείων διαθέσεων οὐκ ἔξωθεν, ἀλλ' ἐν ἡμῖν ἔχομεν τὰς αἰτίας· τῶν δὲ κοινῶν εἶναί τι καὶ τὴν μουσικήν· πάντας γὰρ Ἕλληνάς τε καὶ βαρβάρους αὐτῇ χρῆσθαι καὶ κατὰ πᾶσαν, ὡς εἰπεῖν, ἡλικίαν· ἤδη γὰρ πρὸ τοῦ λογισμὸν ἔχειν, καὶ σύνεσιν ἅπτεσθαι τὴν μουσικὴν δύναμιν παιδικῆς ᾗστινος οὖν ψυχῆς.

The experience of anger, pleasure and sadness is common because the tendency resides in us and is not something outside us. Music, too, belongs among these common experiences because both all the Greeks and the barbarians cultivate it in, we may say, all phases of life. For even before it attains to reason, every child's soul surrenders itself to the power of music.

PHILODEMUS, De musica (Kemke, 92).

κατανοήσαντας ἡμᾶς τἀναγεγραμμένα παρ' Ἡρακλείδῃ περὶ πρέποντος μέλους καὶ ἀπρεποῦς καὶ ἀρρένων καὶ μαλακῶν ἠθῶν καὶ πράξεων καὶ κρούσεων ἁρμοττουσῶν καὶ ἀναρμόστων τοῖς ὑποκειμένοις προσώποις οὐ μακρὰν ἀπηρτημένην τῆς φιλοσοφίας ἡγήσεσθαι τῷ πρὸς πλεῖστα ἐπὶ τοῦ βίου χρησιμεύειν τὴν μουσικὴν καὶ τὴν περὶ αὐτὴν φιλοτεχνίαν οἰκείως διατιθέναι πρὸς πλείους ἀρετάς, μᾶλλον δὲ καὶ πάσας.

When we read in Heracleides about suitable and unsuitable melody, about manly and weak characters, about deeds which are and are not in accord with the personalities of those who perform them, we will agree that music stands not far from philosophy thanks to the fact that it brings a lot of value into human life and that by taking an interest in it we shall be properly attuned to many and, perhaps, even to all the virtues.

ARISTIDES QUINTILIAN I 11
(Jahn, 19).

11. τρόποι δὲ μελοποιΐας γένει μὲν τρεῖς, νομικός, διθυραμβικός, τραγικός... ἤθει, ὡς φαμὲν τὴν μὲν συσταλτικήν. δι' ἧς πάθη λυπηρὰ κινοῦμεν, τὴν δὲ διασταλτικήν, δι' ἧς τὸν θυμὸν ἐξεγείρομεν, τὴν δὲ μέσην, δι' ἧς εἰς ἠρεμίαν τὴν ψυχὴν περιάγομεν·

ARISTIDES QUINTILIAN II 6
(Jahn, 43).

12. Οὔτε τῆς μουσικῆς αὔτε [sc. ἡ τέρψις] τέλος, ἀλλ' ἡ μὲν ψυχαγωγία κατὰ συμβεβηκός, σκόπος δὲ ὁ προκείμενος ἡ πρὸς ἀρετὴν ὠφέλεια.

DAMON (Plato, Respublica IV 424c).

13. οὐδαμοῦ κινοῦνται μουσικῆς τρόποι ἄνευ πολιτικῶν νόμων τῶν μεγίστων, ὥς φησί τε Δάμων καὶ ἐγὼ πείθομαι.

PAPYRUS OF HIBEH
(Crönert, Hermes, XLIV 504, 13).

14. λέγουσι δέ, ὡς τῶν μελῶν τὰ μὲν ἐγκρατεῖς τὰ δὲ φρονίμους, τὰ δὲ δικαίους, τὰ ἀνδρείους, τὰ δὲ δειλοὺς ποιεῖ. κακῶς εἰδότες, ὅτι οὔτε χρῶμα δειλοὺς οὔτε ἁρμονία ἂν ἀνδρείους ποιήσειεν τοὺς αὐτῇ χρωμένους.

PHILODEMUS, De musica (Kemke, 65).

15. οὐδὲ γὰρ μιμητικὸν ἡ μουσική, καθάπερ τινὲς ὀνειρώττουσιν, οὐδ' ὡς οὗτος, ὁμοιότητας ἠθῶν οὐ μιμητικὰς μὲν ἔχει, πάντως δὲ πάσας τῶν ἠθῶν ποιότητας ἐπιφαίνεται τοιαύτας ἐν αἷς ἐστι μεγαλοπρεπὲς καὶ ταπεινὸν καὶ ἀνδρῶδες καὶ ἄνανδρον καὶ κόσμιον καὶ θρασύ, μᾶλλον ἤπερ ἡ μαγειρική.

PHILODEMUS, De musica (Kemke, 95).

16. καί τοῖς διανοήμασιν, οὐ τοῖς μέλεσι καὶ ῥυθμοῖς ὠφελοῦσι.

---

11. There are three kinds of music: the nomic, the dythyrambic and the tragic... The first one contracts souls, it awakens sad feelings; the second expands them and thanks to it we are raised in spirits; while the third stands in the middle and thanks to it we lead souls into a state of peace.

ETHICAL AND POLITICAL EFFECTS OF MUSIC

12. The aim of music is not pleasure; it is incidentally a control over souls, but its proper aim is the service of virtue.

13. So Damon tells me, and I can quite believe him—he says that when modes of music change, the fundamental laws of the state always change with them.

tr. B. Jowett

CRITICISM OF THE "ETHOS" THEORY

14. It is claimed that some melodies induce restraint in people, that others induce sense, justice, bravery or cowardice. But those who say this judge wrongly, because neither can colour induce cowardice nor can harmony induce bravery in those who employ harmony.

15. Despite the nonsense talked by some, music is not an imitative art; nor is it true what he [Diogenes the Babylonian] says that although music does not mirror characters in imitative way, it does nevertheless reveal all the aspects of character which represent magnificence and baseness, heroism and cowardice, politeness and arrogance. Music does not bring this about in any greater measure than culinary art.

16. [Poems] are useful on account of their thoughts, not on account of their melodies and rhythms.

SPEUSIPPUS (in Sextus Empiricus Adv. mathem. VII 145).

17. Σπεύσιππος δὲ, ἐπεὶ τῶν πραγμάτων τὰ μὲν αἰσθητὰ τὰ δὲ νοητά, τῶν μὲν νοητῶν κριτήριον ἔλεξεν εἶναι τὸν ἐπιστημονικὸν λόγον, τῶν δὲ αἰσθητῶν τὴν ἐπιστημονικὴν δὲ αἴσθησιν· ἐπιστημονικὴν δὲ αἴσθησιν ὑπείληφε καθεστάναι τὴν μεταλαμβάνουσαν τῆς κατὰ τὸν λόγον ἀληθείας. ὥσπερ γὰρ οἱ τοῦ αὐλητοῦ ἢ ψάλτου δάκτυλοι τεχνικὴν μὲν εἶχον ἐνέργειαν, οὐκ ἐν αὐτοῖς δὲ προηγουμένως τελειουμένην, ἀλλὰ τῆς πρὸς τὸν λογισμὸν συνασκήσεως ἀπαρτιζομένην· καὶ ὡς ἡ τοῦ μουσικοῦ αἴσθησις ἐνάργειαν μὲν εἶχεν ἀντιληπτικὴν τοῦ τε ἡρμοσμένου καὶ τοῦ ἀναρμόστου, ταύτην δὲ οὐκ αὐτοφυῆ, ἀλλ' ἐκ λογισμοῦ περιγεγονυῖαν· οὕτω καὶ ἡ ἐπιστημονικὴ αἴσθησις φυσικῶς παρὰ τοῦ λόγου τῆς ἐπιστημονικῆς μεταλαμβάνει τριβῆς πρὸς ἀπλανῆ τῶν ὑποκειμένων διάγνωσιν.

NATURAL AND EDUCATED IMPRESSIONS

17. According to Speusippus, some things are perceived by the senses and others are perceived by the mind. He maintained that the measure of the former are educated impressions and the measure of the latter educated thoughts. He regarded as educated those impressions which partake of reasoned truth.

The fingers of a flute-player or a lute-player perform actions which have their origins not in themselves but in mental activity. In a similar way the impressions of a musician who in a faultless manner divides that which is harmonious from that which is not are derived not from nature but from thought. Educated impression benefits in a natural manner from the learned accomplishments [which the particular man possesses]: this accomplishment is based on reason and attains a faultless knowledge of the object.

8. Aesthetics of Poetry

(a) HELLENISTIC POETRY

1. HELLENISTIC LITERATURE. A variety of literary works was produced during the Hellenistic period. This production began in the first half of the third century B.C. with the didactic poems, epigrams, lyrics, elegies and hymns of Callimachus, the idylls of Theocritus and the realistic mimes of Herondas; later came romances and novels. The period was a long one and such eminent works as Plutarch's *Lives* and the essays of Lucian of Samosata were produced as late as the second century A.D. On the other hand, literary works of this period were not of such enduring significance as those of the previous age. It is true that Alexandria boasted of its Pleiad, the seven stars of its drama, but posterity has judged these stars differently and has forgotten them. However, one development of great significance took place at this time; the Greek language spread beyond Greece to dominate the world.

There had been a great change in the attitude of society toward poetry. It had ceased to be a matter of public concern. The direct link with society which the poet had enjoyed in the small city-states was no longer possible in great monarchies, vast countries and urban centres. It was no longer possible for the whole population to participate in producing and judging tragedy. Poetry ceased to be a ritual attracting the population as a whole and became the personal concern of a few individuals. Its character also changed, because the Greek merchants and traders who were now setting the tone in Alexandria and Antioch had more use for farce and cabaret than for tragedy.

The literature of the Hellenistic period had several characteristic features. Most significant was that its authors were also men of learning, who studied the theory of literature or philosophy. People therefore expected literature to be erudite and full of philosophical, historical and literary allusions. This was true even of lyric poetry. Hellenistic poetry was a learned art written for the learned; it sought inspiration in libraries. It was refined and it addressed itself to an exclusive audience. It was consciously selective and scorned the vulgar.

In Alexandria writers were called "grammarians". As has already been noted, the Latin term *litteratus* or "man of letters" was simply the Latin equivalent of the Greek "grammarian". This term embraced those who were engaged in writing literature, as well as those who theorized about it. It evolved in such a way, however, that for Sextus Empiricus it meant only literary theorists and philologists. Later, writers came to be called "philologists" in Alexandria and "critics" in Pergamum.

The whole of this literature was controlled by experts and guided by them. It was subjected to rules and obeyed laws. At an early stage treatises appeared on how to write and read works of literature. Literary theories and philology enjoyed a vogue equal to that of literature itself.

The second important feature of Hellenistic literature, in marked contrast to classical literature, was its pursuit of originality and its love of literary experimentation. Alexandrian literature relied on models, but it imitated literary forms which were rare and *recherchè*.

A third feature particularly evident in the visual arts, but apparent also in literature, was its baroque quality, that is, on the one hand, its concentration on richness at the expense of simplicity and, on the other, its pursuit of depth rather than clarity.

A fourth feature was realism, which appeared in the literature of the day no less prominently than in painting and sculpture. Realism and acute observation are so outstanding in the essays of Herondas that the great philologist Tadeusz Zieliński paradoxically regarded them as scientific papers rather than works of literature.

A fifth feature was the sober attitude of writers towards their works. "Thundering is the business of Zeus, not mine", wrote the poet Callimachus. This was, as another philologist has observed, "the abandonment of great, divine poetry in favour of poetry that was more human but also (according to Callimachus) more artistic".

A sixth feature of Hellenistic literature was its gradual relegation of poetry to a place below scientific writings. Hellenistic monarchs supported scientific work by founding huge centres of learning on an unprecedented scale, the most outstanding of these being the Royal Museum and the Library of Alexandria with its 700,000 rolls. These facilities were maintained with great pertinacity. When the Library was burned down in 47 B.C. it was replaced by the Pergamum collection, which had 200,000 rolls. When in turn this collection was destroyed, another library in Alexandria, the Serapeum, became the chief seat of Hellenistic learning.

Hellenistic institutions performed a significant service to literature. Accurate editions, prepared by Alexandrian grammarians, spread throughout the Greek and Roman world and became for thousands of years the basis of European civilization. It was this that prompted S. Reinach to call the third and second centuries B.C. "one of the greatest epochs of the human spirit", and U. von Wilamowitz went so far as to say of the third century, which created the basis of Hellenistic culture that "it was the apex of Hellenic culture and thereby of the ancient world". Eternal thoughts had been thought and eternal works of art had been created earlier, but it was only now that they acquired the power to dominate the world and to survive for centuries.

The great learned institutions of Hellenism, particularly the Library of Alexandria, owed their origin to the conviction that the great Greece of old had vanished and that the duty of her descendants lay in rescuing and preserving her heritage. The Library reflected an attitude which gave precedence to conservation and to a historical and philological research. It created the conditions for acquiring book-learning, erudition and an interest in antiquarianism. It contributed to the evolution of the learned specialists and inaugurated an era in which books exercised a dominating influence.

It also did a great deal for philology and for "grammar", as the specialized theory of literature was then called. To aesthetics in general, however, it contributed little. Neither did it contribute very much towards philosophy in general. Long before the tragic end of the learned collection in Alexandria, which took place in 390, when the patriarch Theophilus destroyed the Serapeum in the belief that it was a nest of paganism, the small and impoverished city of Athens with its schools of philosophy was an incomparably more important centre of aesthetic thought than Alexandria. It is against the background of Athens and later of Rome, and not Alexandria, that one should consider the creators of Hellenistic aesthetics.

2. ROMAN LITERATURE. In the early period of their history the Romans cared little for literature and produced no works of any significance until as late as the first century B.C. This period was, however, immediately followed by a golden age. It spanned the last years of the Republic and the beginning of the Empire, that is, the splendid final period of the Republic (80–42 B.C.), known as the age of Cicero, and the even more illustrious first years of the Empire (42 B.C.–14 A.D.), known as the Augustan Age. This was the classical phase of Roman literature (classical in all the meanings of the word; polished, balanced and possessing affinity with the archetypal classical period of the Age of Pericles). It was the Roman equivalent of Periclean Greece.

Apart from the ornate prose of Cicero himself, the Age of Cicero produced the writings of Caesar—an unsurpassed model of simple unadorned prose—the learned prose of Varro, "the most learned Roman", and the poem of Lucretius, the only successful philosophical poem after philosophers had turned to prose. But it was the Augustan Age which produced poets of whose excellence we are all aware. It was said of Virgil that he was sufficiently gifted not to expose himself to ridicule even when he aspired to challenge Homer. Roman poetic theory was inaugurated in the "golden age" of Roman poetry. Cicero was the leading aesthetician in Rome and the poet Horace was the author of an influential *Art of Poetry*. This poetic theory was based not only on ancient Greek literature, but also on the new Roman literature regarded by contemporaries as a model of perfection.

Like all classical periods, this one did not last long. Quintilian blamed writers of the time of Nero and Domitian for not equaling those of the reign of Augustus. The period that followed is known as the "Silver Age" of Roman literature. Historians normally date it from the death of Augustus to the year 130. The character of Roman literature changed to some extent, and it now resembled the literature of Alexandria. Poetry was not of particular significance, but literary, philosophical and, especially, scientific prose was of high quality and included the works of Tacitus and other historians, of lawyers, doctors and geographers. A comparatively large proportion of it was devoted to aesthetics, while the architect Vitruvius and the encyclopaedist Pliny also left valuable information about the history of aesthetics.

The closing phase of Roman literature was not distinguished. Eventually, indeed, the best writers were Christians, such as Minucius Felix and Tertullian. Creative literature declined, while "grammar" flourished and commentaries on earlier works multiplied.

The aesthetics of literature in the Hellenistic and Roman periods was discussed in such detail and so explicitly in theoretical formulations, that there is no need to search for it in the literary works themselves. There is no need to examine Cicero's speeches to discover his aesthetic theory, because he himself stated it in *The Orator*. Similarly, we do not have to search through Horace's poems, because his theory is formulated in his *Epistle to the Pisos*. The important question, however, is whether literary theory evolved from creative literature or the other way round, and whether, in any case, the two were in agreement. The literature of the time was marked by variety and ornamentation and these same qualities were recommended by theorists. Literature was decidedly technical in character and theorists advised the poet to perform exercises in order to master technique. The cult of form in poetry was matched by the formalistic strain in the works of theorists. On the other hand, however, the literature of the day, particularly in Alexandria, was a literature of grammarian intellectuals, whereas theory stressed the author's inspiration and the listeners' emotional response. Literature was full of abstraction and allegories, whereas theory demanded eye-witness accounts. The novel was naturalistic, although theory insisted that writers should take the Idea rather than Nature as their model. In short, there were, as is usually the case, various literary streams, some within the framework of theory, others outside it.

(b) POETICS

1. ANCIENT POETICS. The Hellenistic and Roman periods lack any comprehensive poetics such as that of Aristotle.* Horace's *Art of Poetry*† in his *Epistle to the Pisos*, composed in the years 19–20, A.D., is comparatively full, but it is an "eclogue", that is to say, it consists of a selection of themes. Rather than being a learned treatise, it is poetry about poetry and therefore full of poetic similes and licences of expression. Horace's formulas were not precise, but capable of surviving for centuries.

The lost work of Neoptolemus, on which (according to the testimony of Porphyry) Horace drew, was surely fuller and more precise. This Neoptolemus, who was at his prime in the third century, was scarcely younger than Aristotle and was probably a Peripatetic. He organized the problems of poetry into a system, becoming the forefather of Hellenistic poetry.

Theophrastus' manual *On Style* has survived only in quotations. Two later treatises on style by Dionysius of Halicarnassus and Demetrius‡ have come down to us complete. The former, who lived in the first century B.C. (60–5), the author of the treatise *On the Arrangement of Words*, was a prolific writer and an influential supporter of the Atticist trend. Demetrius, who was more or less his contemporary, was the author of another work on style entitled *On Expression*.

A sizable monograph called *On the Sublime*§ has also survived. It is considered to be the most beautiful book on style in Greek. In the Hellenistic dispute between the Atticist and the Asianist schools, which recommended simple and ornate styles respectively, the book *On the Sublime* supported the simple style. In accord with the spirit of times, it emphasized the sublime and the poetical inspiration. It is an anonymous book which was formerly attributed to Longinus. When this ascription was proved false, its author was renamed Pseudo-Longinus. The Polish scholar Sinko has suggested he should be called Anti-Caecilius, because his work is a polemic against the once famous and now lost treatise by Caecilius *On the Sublime*.

As has already been indicated, considerable fragments of *On Poetical Works* by Philodemus of Gadara, an Epicurean of the first century B.C., have been preserved in the rolls of Herculaneum. They give us information about the views on poetry not only of the Epicureans, but also of their adversaries.

Discussions on poetic theory are also to be found in ancient works on rhetoric by Cicero, Quintilian, Hermogenes, and the so-called Pseudo-Syrian. They also occasionally appear in philosophical works, for example, in the writings of Cicero, in the *Letters* of Seneca, in the treatises of Plutarch, Strabo, Maximus of Tyre,

---

* T. Sinko, *Trzy poetyki klasyczne* (1951).

† O. Immisch, "Horazens Epistel über die Dichtkunst", *Philologus*, Suppl., Bd. XXIV, 3 (1932).

‡ W. Madyda, *Trzy stylistyki greckie* (1953). W. Maykowska, "Dionizjos z Halikarnasu jako krytyk literacki", *Meander*, V, 6–7 (1950).

§ T. Sinko, *op. cit.*, p. XXVIII ff. W. Maykowska, "Anonima monografia o stylu artystycznym" (1926).

Sextus Empiricus and Hermogenes, in the speeches of Dion of Prusa and in the essays of Lucian.

To summarize: we possess fragments of third-century works by Theophrastus and Neoptolemus, which laid the foundations of Hellenistic poetics; most works in this field, however, date from the first century B.C. These include the works of Dionysius of Halicarnassus, Demetrius, Horace and Philodemus. The treatise *On the Sublime* is even later. Some of the poetic theories are in Greek, some in Latin. The most popular one is in Latin (by Horace), but the Greek works are earlier and more numerous.*

2. DEFINITION OF POETRY. In the Hellenistic period literary prose had already achieved a status almost equal to that of poetry. Both were classified as "literature", and "literary theory" (*grammatike*)[1] concerned itself both with the works of poets (*poietai*) and of prose-writers (*syngrapheis*) both with poetry (*poiemata*) and prose (*logoi*).[2]

For a long time in antiquity the concept of poetry, as distinguished from prose, remained indeterminate; Gorgias defined it as *rhythmic* speech and Aristotle as *imitative* speech. This duality survived into the Hellenistic period. Poetry was often defined in Aristotelian terms as "the imitation of life in words", from which followed the division of literature into imitative (that is, poetry in its strict sense) and non-imitative (that is, prose).[3] Poetry used to be contrasted with oratory on the ground that it was literature with a metrical structure, and it used to be contrasted with history on the ground that it was literature with fictional themes. It was thus distinguished either on the basis of form or on basis of content.

Both points of view, the one stressing form and the other stressing subject-matter, were united in the definition of Posidonius,[4] to which we have already referred. This assumed that a poem is a metrical and rhythmical speech (*lexis*), distinguished from prose by ornamentation. It thus recognized the formal criterion for poetry, i.e., metrical form. But Posidonius' definition added that "poetry is a poem full of meaning, representing things divine and human". It thus distinguished between a "poem" and "poetry", a poem being only different from prose by virtue of its form, while poetry must in addition possess significant meaning. Poetry must therefore fulfil two conditions. It must have both metrical form and significant meaning.

Earlier Greeks saw the purpose of poetry in teaching and in improving characters. "They called poetry propaedeutics of philosophy", as Strabo reports.[4a] This was much changed in Hellenistic centuries. Poetry was now supposed to give pleasure, but also to excite emotions.[5] The first demand was old, the other more recent, having been introduced by Aristotle and later gaining predominance. "Not enough

---

* The fullest information so far collected about Hellenistic poetics is in W. Madyda's *De arte poetica post Aristotelem exulta* (1948). — The present chapter in a slightly modified version has been published in English under the title "The Poetics of the Hellenistic Age" in the *Review of the Polish Academy of Sciences* (1957) — K. Svoboda, "Les idées esthétiques de Plutarque" in *Mélanges Bidez*.

is it for poems to have beauty: they must have charm, and lead the hearer's soul", wrote Horace.⁽⁵ᵃ⁾ This idea of the soul being guided by poetry was expressed earlier by Eratosthenes. It is natural that when verse charms, it also guides: but this guidance of souls (*psychagogia*) is not the same as their instruction. In late antiquity the question of whether poetry should instruct became highly disputed.[6] So did the matter of whether it should improve people's behaviour.

Poetry was the art of words. But so were history, philosophy and oratory. What was the difference between them and poetry?

3. POETRY AND HISTORY. The ancients were at first inclined to link poetry with history on the assumption that every human activity must seek truth, and this applied to poetry no less than to history. Later on, however, it was precisely in this connection that they noticed a difference between the two. They first drew up a formula for this difference in the first century B.C., and it was thereafter reiterated by many writers.[7] It distinguished true history, false history and fable, which are called in Latin *historia*, *argumentum* and *fabula* respectively. The juxtaposition ran as follows. "The legendary tale comprises events neither true nor probable, like those transmitted by tragedies. The historical narrative is an account of exploits actually performed but removed in time from the recollection of our age. Realistic narrative recounts imaginary events which yet could have occurred, like the plots of comedies". Poetry is included in two of the three categories: in fable and in untrue history. In the first case its subject-matter is impossible and in the second it is potentially realizable, but in both instances it is an invention, a fiction (*ficta res*). The difference between poetry and history may therefore be expressed in this way: the one deals with fictions, while the other deals with reality. History serves truth, whereas poetry can serve only pleasure, since it does not serve truth. This led Cicero to the conclusion that since history is directed towards truth and poetry almost exclusively directed towards pleasure, the laws governing history and the laws governing poetry must perforce be different.[8]

4. POETRY AND PHILOSOPHY. The ancients found the relation between poetry and philosophy more difficult to establish than the relation between poetry and history. It was so because they equated philosophy with the whole of science and knowledge except history, which they regarded as a chronicle and not a science. In early times poetry was given the same task as science: that of obtaining knowledge about gods and men. Before philosophy had developed, people looked to poetry for explanations about life and the world. With the advent of philosophy it was questioned whether poetry provided or could provide knowledge about the world. During the Hellenistic period, however, the enmity between poetry and philosophy already declined.

Two opposing views were now defended. The one brought poetry and knowledge together, while the other opposed them. On the one hand, the Epicureans condemned poetry for presenting things in a way different from science. Similarly, the Sceptics held that if any philosophy at all could be found in poetry it would be bad philosophy. On the other hand, the Stoic Posidonius placed poetry on an equal footing with philosophy, saying that it, too, "represents things divine and human". This formula was to be repeated by numerous authors, including Cicero, Seneca, Strabo, Plutarch and Maximus of Tyre. They regarded poetry and philosophy as two aspects of cognition. Although poetry was less advanced, it nevertheless constituted, together with philosophy, "one harmonious art". Poetry relied on verse form, but this, according to Strabo, was merely a means of attracting the masses. In other respects poetry and philosophy were one and the same.

It was characteristic of ancient thought to contrast poetry with history and to link it with philosophy. History was thought to deal with particular facts and philosophy with general laws. It was the latter discipline that Greeks considered to be closer to poetry. In their explanation of poetry, two very different ideas were put forward: that it creates fictions and that it seeks truth. When it was contrasted with history, the fictional aspect of poetry was stressed, whereas when it was likened to philosophy, its cognitive elements were emphasized.

5. POETRY AND ORATORY. The ancients were puzzled by the relation between poetry and oratory because they saw them as very similar and yet different.

A. Today the most natural basis for a distinction between poetry and oratory would appear to be that the former is written, while the latter is spoken. In antiquity, however, it had long been the custom for poetry to be spoken or sung, while the speeches of great speakers were not only delivered and heard but were also published and read.

B. The Greeks therefore employed another basis of distinction: they declared that the purpose of poetry was to please people and of oratory to guide them (*flectere*). However, the speeches of the ancients were also composed as works of art and in order to give pleasure. On the other hand, dramatic poetry, Athenian tragedy and particularly comedy aimed not only at pleasing, but also at arguing and persuading, at combating certain ideas and implanting others.

C. The third basis of the distinction was that poetry dealt with fictions while oratory was concerned with real social affairs. Poetry would thus appear to differ from oratory in the same way as it differed from history. The Romans did not, however, insist on this point because in fact their orators were trained in schools, where fictional subjects were used for the exercises (*declamationes*).

D. Finally, there appeared a fourth point of view: poetry is composition in metrical speech, and oratory is composition in prose. In his *Dialogue on Orators* Tacitus treated poetry as a kind of oratory and distinguished between rhetorical and poetical oratory, that is, oratory proper and poetry. The identification of oratory with literary prose had a historical justification because during the period from Gorgias to Isocrates speeches were the only form of artistic prose. The achievements of orators in artistic prose were later utilized by men of letters, and thus the principles of rhetoric were applied not only in oratory, but in almost all literary prose. As a result of this, rhetoric became the theory of prose in general. A division of roles was established: poetics became the aesthetics of poetry, and rhetoric became the aesthetics of literary prose. It was apparently Hermogenes who eventually curbed this arrogation of rhetoric: he claimed that neither political nor courtroom rhetoric had anything to do with literature proper. Therefore, while the whole of poetics fell within the sphere of aesthetics, only a section of rhetoric did.

6. POETRY AND TRUTH. The main problems of ancient poetics may be grouped under three headings: poetry's relation to *truth*, to the *good* and to *beauty*.

The earlier Greeks were convinced that truth is the main purpose of poetry; there cannot be any good poetry without it. A change occurred in the Hellenistic period: a conviction grew that poetry required something else besides truth, namely freedom and imagination. Therefore poets were entitled to employ fictions. And indeed, they employed them. "What is more of an invention (*fictum*) than a poem, a fable?", asked Cicero, and Pseudo-Longinus declared: "Poets' fantasies lean towards fables and go beyond all probability". Plutarch contrasted poetry with life, Lucian wrote that poetry stands in the same relation to history as freedom to truth. Eratosthenes wrote that poets may invent anything that is necessary to influence souls.

Sextus Empiricus was aware of the existence of both tendencies. He saw that some poets sought truth while others, on the contrary, invented fictions: they did so because they desired to dominate men's minds and this they could achieve through invention rather than through truth.[9]

Most ancients supposed that poetry contains *either* truth *or* freedom. In earlier times they were willing to deny its freedom in order not to deprive it of truth. But in later period they lost interest in poetic truth and were willing to relinquish it in order to retain freedom.

The conservative Stoics continued to search for truth in poetry and, for that reason, recommended its allegorical interpretation. But Hellenistic aestheticians of other schools thought it a mistake to look for truth in poetry. They were convinced that "one should neither judge poems according to their thought content nor seek information from them", as Eratosthenes wrote. In Philodemus we read that wise and true thoughts in a poem must not be regarded as its virtue.[10]

7. POETRY AND THE GOOD. The early attitude of the Greeks towards poetry was moralistic no less than intellectual. The Greeks thought that poetry can justify itself only when it supports virtue and the state, when it instructs, educates and improves men. Plato drew the most extreme conclusions from this view, by declaring that poetry was morally harmful. Hellenistic aestheticians, withdrawing partly from this position, doubted whether poetry was harmful, but neither were they convinced that it should be beneficial. Marcus Aurelius treated it as a school of life and Athenaeus as a means of frightening off evil. However, other views also emerged: Philodemus maintained it was impossible simultaneously to cater for people's enjoyment and their welfare. To be sure, "virtue is not an entertainment".[11] We read in Ovid: "Nothing is more useful than this art which has no use":[11a] it is useful, but has no moral use.

The dispute as to whether poetry should teach (*docere*) or entertain (*delectare*) was eventually solved by a compromise. Cicero expected poetry to provide both "necessary utility" (*utilitas necessaria*) and "unfettered joy" (*animi libera quaedam oblectatio*): life demands utility while joy comes from creative freedom. Horace, who was to some extent faithful to the old moralist view, wrote that poetry should "both teach and entertain" (*docere et delectare*). Another formula expressing his compromise stand was that a work of poetry should be both *utile* and *dulce*, that is to say, should provide utility as well as pleasure.[12]

The fundamental distinction here had already been drawn earlier by Theophrastus; he noted that there are two types of literature: *logos pros tous akroatas* and *logos pros pragma*, that is, literature which is interested mainly in the listener and literature interested exclusively in its object. In Hellenistic times it was realized that there is room for both categories. Literature of the first category should be judged according to its effects on human morality and condemned when these effects are detrimental. There is, however, also room for writing of the second category. Gradually the view prevailed that the first was more important.

Apart from the problem whether poetry produces good and evil, Hellenistic writers also considered whether it represents good and evil. In particular, they were concerned with the question whether poetry *ought* to represent the good and avoid evil. It became more and more usual to maintain that if poetry is to give a full picture of reality, it must represent the whole gamut of characters and customs, both good and bad, both virtues and vices, because, after all, men fall short of the ideal. According to a Plutarch or a Maximus of Tyre, poets would be wrong to present their heroes as models of virtue.

8. POETRY AND BEAUTY. While in Hellenistic poetry truth and moral goodness were less emphasized than in classical times, the role of beauty was increased. Still more attention, however, was devoted to the pleasant and pleasurable (*iucundum et suave*).

Even before Hellenistic times the ancients had distinguished in visual arts between objective beauty (*symmetria*) and beauty which is subjectively determined (*eurhythmia*). The distinction in Hellenistic poetics was similar though not identical: it distinguished between the beauty of the presented objects and the beauty of their presentation. In other words, in poetry a distinction was drawn between beauty stemming from nature and beauty introduced by art. It was also stressed that the beauty of poetry is mostly of the second type. The description of ugly things may also be enjoyed. Poetry does not so much imitate beauty as imitate beautifully: *how* it describes is more important than *what* it describes.

Secondly, the ancients distinguished between beauty appreciated by all in the same way, and individual beauty which depends on the person, the circumstances and the epoch. *Symmetria*, and even eurhythmy were understood as universal beauty, whereas suitability (*decorum*) was understood as an individual one. In Hellenistic times the latter began to acquire increasing significance. The concept of *decorum* became dominant in the understanding of poetry, while *symmetria* and eurhythmy continued to hold sway in sculpture. In order to be beautiful, declared Hermogenes, poetry ought to be proper and fitting.[13] Quintilian wrote: *Omnibus debetur suum decor*—each thing deserves its proper form, and Dionysius of Halicarnassus said that, along with melody, rhythm and change, there is a fourth most powerful and most important source from which speech draws its charm and beauty: the "appropriateness to the subject". Plutarch wrote that to represent beautifully means to represent suitably and this in turn means not only the representation of beautiful things in a beautiful way, but also the representation of ugly things in an ugly way. Hellenism continued to believe that the beauty of poetry depends on order, measure and conformity between parts; but it introduced some fresh ideas: that poetical beauty depends on grandeur, splendour and sublimity; and that it depends as well on decorativeness and variety. In his list of "the virtues of poetic expression" (or style), the Epicurean Philodemus included concrete, emphatic, concise, precise, clear and suitable expression. The list compiled by Diogenes the Babylonian and naming the five virtues—correctness of language, clarity, conciseness, appropriateness and distinction[14]—was almost identical.

Variety is the cause of satisfaction: *varietas delectat*, a phrase often used by Hellenistic writers. Plutarch wrote[15] that poetic art is various and polymorphous and added that simple things neither arouse feelings nor imagination. Hermogenes did not appreciate literature which is uniform and lacks variety. Hellenistic writers also saw the value in literature of what they called in Greek *enargeia* and in Latin *evidentia*.[16] Especially Hermogenes considered *evidentia* as the most important element in poetry.[17] Akin to this was the demand for clarity.[18] Hellenistic poetics also expected a literary work to arouse inner faith (*pistis*).

9. Problems in poetics. Problems in poetics were normally discussed in accordance with a pattern derived from Neoptolemus, who divided his treatise into three parts dealing successively with poetry, the poem and the poet (*poiesis, poiema* and *poietes*). The first part was concerned with poetry in general, the second with types of poetry, and the third with characteristics of poetry due to the poet's personality. This pattern was not confined to textbooks, the so-called "isagogues"; philologists have discovered it even in the apparently free arrangement of Horace's *Art of Poetry*. The pattern also appeared in a simplified form: Poetry and the Poet, more generally: Art and the Artist.

The historian of aesthetics is especially interested in such problems of Hellenistic poetics as Representation versus Imagination, Wisdom versus Enthusiasm, Intuition versus Rules, Nature versus Art, Sublimity versus Charm.

10. Representation versus imagination. The Hellenistic era witnessed a fundamental change in the attitude to the poet and to the artist in general: his role was now seen to be active. He was increasingly considered a creator, relying on his imagination rather than on the things he sought to represent. The Greeks of classical times paid little attention to poetic imagination, whereas in Hellenistic

times they recognized it as a fundamental element in poetry. They denoted it, even when writing in Latin, by the Stoic term *phantasia*[19] or called it as did Pseudo-Longinus, an ability to "create images".[20] They consciously contrasted it with imitation. Philostratus wrote that "*mimesis* represents things it has seen, while fantasy represents also things it has not seen". They made great play with the example of blind bards, and regarded Homer's blindness as a symbol and a proof that the imagination has greater power than the senses. Formerly, poetic works had been found interesting because they presented a picture of the world, now because they revealed the poet's soul.[21]

Seneca expressed the current opinion when he wrote that, in order to create a work of art, besides the four elements (the artist, his intention, the material and the shape he gives to the material), a fifth one is also required, namely, the model. However, it is immaterial whether this model is outside the artist, or whether he has invented the model himself and carries it inside him.[22] In earlier poetics it had been supposed that the model always came from the real world. The internal model was termed "image" (*eikon*) or, more frequently, "idea". The latter term was used by Cicero, who borrowed it from Plato, although he deprived it of the meaning it had had in Plato. Ideas were transferred from the outside world into the poet's imagination. Plutarch maintained that the idea in poet's mind is "pure, independent and infallible". Vitruvius wrote that an artist differs from a layman in that he knows his work in advance, because even before starting it, he has decided in his soul what its beauty, utility and *decorum* will be.

11. WISDOM VERSUS ENTHUSIASM. Hellenistic and Roman writers were agreed that thought is necessary in poetic composition. The Stoic Crates of Pergamum maintained that "only a sage is capable of evaluating poetic beauty without being led astray by the imprecisions of language". Cicero wrote that "in all the arts we require what in common speech is called prudence". Wisdom, Horace wrote, is the origin and source of good writing (*scribendi recte sapere est et principium, et fons*).[23]

On the other hand, wisdom alone will not help a poet if he lacks inspiration.[24] Latin as well as Greek writers used to describe the state of inspiration with the Greek word "enthusiasm" (*enthousiasmos*), which signified that it has a divine source. Some writers did indeed regard inspiration as supernatural, while others saw it only as the poet's inner tension and fancy which resembles a supernaturally induced state. Platonists ascribed it to divine action; Epicureans explained it in terms of natural causes. The former attached considerable importance to it, the latter emphasized rather thought and prudence, but by and large the thinkers of the age agreed that both elements are necessary.

Many Hellenistic writers thought of inspiration as a state of tension and excitement, even of possession and madness. But there were also those who held that an inspired poet must be calm in order to represent the anger of Achilles. Seneca was convinced that the artist achieves more when his emotions are artificial rather than authentic.

12. INTUITION VERSUS RULES. Earlier in Greece poetry was not included among the arts, because it was thought to be the subject of inspiration rather than rules. But a double change took place in Hellenistic times. First, it came to be acknowledged that poetry was subject to as many rules as the other arts. Pseudo-Longinus held[25] that even sublimity is subject to rules. Second, Hellenistic scholars noticed that the importance of rules in poetry and in art was not really so great as had formerly been supposed. *Intuitus*, Quintilian said, has more importance than technical rules. Dionysius of Halicarnassus wrote that artistic composition relies not on logical principles but upon the artist's imagination (*doxa*) and upon his ability to find the proper solution (*to kairon*).

The conviction emerged that, contrary to accepted practice, artistic rules could not be regarded as immutable. They were dependent on their time and circumstances and could not be employed mechanically. It is always necessary to "know how to use rules". Hellenistic age realized that works of art came first and that rules were later derived from them. "Verse preceded reflexions on verse". With Lucian each thing has its own beauty,[26] which is something no rule can encompass. Since rules have their limits, it follows that the poet has a margin of freedom.[27] The same holds good for readers. Ariston of Chios said that "there has to be a poetry to suit every taste"[28] and Pseudo-Longinus wrote: "Let each one enjoy whatever brings him pleasure".

Dionysius of Halicarnassus contrasted artistic production based on rules with the charm of spontaneous creation and on another occasion he contrasted it also with art produced by passion. Spontaneous and passionate art derives not from rules, but from a love of beauty.[29] The earlier thinkers had related rules to be observed in poetry with the view that the chief virtue of poetry is faultlessness. Now, on the contrary, it was said that greatness is more important than faultlessness. Pseudo-Longinus wrote that faultlessness merely escapes criticism, whereas greatness arouses admiration, and that great writers are far from being faultless[30]

13. THE INTELLECT VERSUS THE SENSES. The discussion as to whether rules or intuition are more important in poetry linked with a still more general one on the intellect versus the senses. In the works of the anonymous writer known as Pseudo-Syrianus anti-intellectualism acquired, so to speak, a vivid, Bergsonian character.[31] Our intellect (*logos*) can grasp only the elements of things, while only direct experience (*aisthesis*) can grasp the whole. The intellect is incapable of grasping things and forms directly. It can do this only symbolically (*symbolikos*), whereas the duty of the artist is to give not only a symbolical, but also a direct and concrete picture of things. Hellenism did not avoid symbols, but it was also sympathetic to direct representation of things through poetry and art.[32]

Is direct representation achieved by intuition or simply by the senses? The problem concerned the psychology of aesthetic experience as well as of artistic creation. It was a *locus communi* of ancient poetics that poetry affects the ear. Some writers thought with Pseudo-Longinus that the harmony of speech speaks "to the soul itself and not to the ear". Nevertheless, the development of Hellenistic poetics rather favoured the role of the ear (we shall return to this point in our discussion of the Hellenistic view on form and content in poetry). The Stoics produced arguments to justify a higher evaluation of the sensuous element. So especially did Diogenes the Babylonian, who distinguished the educated sensory perceptions from the common ones.

14. NATURE VERSUS ART. In addition to the four debating points of Hellenistic times already discussed (i.e., imitation versus fantasy, prudence versus enthusiasm, rules versus intuition, and the intellect versus the senses) there was a fifth one, namely, nature versus art. Here "nature" was synonymous with the poet's nature, with his natural talents. The question was asked whether the *talent* which nature has given the poet was more or less important than any *art* which he may learn. While in the first four debates sympathies were all very much on one side, in favour of fantasy, enthusiasm and intuition, in this instance a compromise was reached. Horace wrote:[33] "Often it is asked whether a praiseworthy poem be due to nature or to art. For my part I do not see of what avail is either study, when not enriched by Nature's vein, or native wit, if untrained".

Greater emphasis than in modern times was however placed upon the distinction in verse between nature and art. There were debates over whether the poet owed the mellifluousness of his verse and his good style to art or to sensitive ear. Neoptolemus and Philodemus agreed that a technically accomplished writer is not the same as a good poet.[34]

The compromise formula was usually more complex, i.e., not twofold but threefold: nature—practice—art (*physis—melete—techne*). In addition to nature (that is, the poet's natural talent) and art (that is, acquaintance with rules) account was taken of practice, that is, the writer's experience and training which allow him to make good use of his talent and his knowledge of art. A Hellenistic poem quoted by Stobaeus says that a poet needs acquaintance with the means available, creative passion, a feeling for the right place and the right time, competent criticism, a tidy mind, experience and wisdom. In this list "acquaintance with the means" stands for what is popularly known as art, and "creative passion" for what is known as the creator's nature. The so-called Anonym of Iamblichus wrote that the same type of man succeeds in science as in art: the scholar and the artist must be endowed by nature, but the rest depends on them, they must love beautiful things, must be fond of work, must have acquired their education early in life, and must be persevering in their work. Horace expressed himself in almost identical terms.

15. SUBLIMITY VERSUS CHARM. Of all the antitheses of Hellenistic aesthetics perhaps the most penetrating was that concerned with the conditions of the value of poetry. Here the conflict involved two concepts, *kalon* and *hedu*, that is, *beauty* and *pleasure*. The first described the work itself, the second its effect upon the recipient; the first represented the rational elements in poetry (*logikon*), and the other its irrational elements (*alogon*).

In Hellenistic times beauty became identified with *sublimity* and pleasure with *charm*. Dionysius of Halicarnassus wrote:[35] "Under 'charm' I class freshness, grace, euphony, sweetness, persuasiveness and all similar qualities; and under 'beauty' grandeur, impressiveness, solemnity, dignity, mellowness and the like". Sublimity ceased to be one of several aesthetic categories or one of many poetic styles, and became the supreme and only style. Horace regarded *pulcher* as synonymous with "sublime": *omnis poesis grandis*. Dionysius employed the word "beautiful" interchangeably with "great" and "sublime". Styles in poetry, as well as in oratory, came to be analysed from this point of view, the "dignified" being contrasted with the "unpretentious", and the "mean" style being placed between the two.[36]

The prevailing tendency was to combine beauty with pleasure. As Dionysius wrote, they are the objectives of every work of truth and art. When these objectives are achieved, then their purpose is fulfilled. To combine these two qualities is quite natural, for, as Dionysius also wrote, "the principles of a beautiful arrangement are no different from those of a pleasant one: the aim of both is noble melody, exalted rhythm, splendid variety and, always, suitability". Among Hellenistic writers the combination of these two qualities became a formula of excellence for every human artifact and especially for poetry.

16. FORM VERSUS CONTENT. Hellenistic aestheticians evolved concepts similar to the modern concepts of form and content: in poetry they distinguished between "speech" (*lexis*) and "thing" (*pragma*). The first concept corresponded to our "form" and the second to "content".[37]

Of the modern variants of the concept of form the earlier Greeks were already acquainted with two: (a) form in the sense of an arrangement of parts (this form they considered as the essence of beauty) and also (b) form in the sense of the manner in which things are presented, that is, *how* the poet expresses himself, as opposed to *what* he expresses.[38] Moreover, Hellenism developed a third conception of form: (c) that which is presented to the senses directly, versus the indirect, conceptualized and apprehended by thought: this was precisely the concept of form, which has come to play such an important role in modern times. Hellenistic poetics discussed the question whether the value of poetry lies in its direct linguistic form or in the conceptual contents, in words or in things.

Certain schools, like the Epicurean and the Stoic, in accordance with their assumptions deferred in poetry to sublime or useful content. The Platonic and Aristotelian traditions pointed in the same direction. Cato's *rem tene, verba sequentur* (if the subject is weighty, suitable words will appear) was the watchword.

But "formalists" also appeared. They denied that the purpose of poetry was to instruct people; they advised not to judge the poems with reference to their thought. They had been unknown before Hellenistic times and even when they did appear they formed a minority opposed to the dominant trend in poetics. We can see the origins of formalism in the Peripatetic Theophrastus, who argued that beautiful style depends on beautiful words. What we know of Hellenistic formalism is strikingly radical.

The writings of Theophrastus' followers have not survived, but we know of them from his opponent Philodemus. The names of the first formalists were Crates of Pergamum, Heracleodor and Andromenides. They belonged to the Stoic and Peripatetic schools and they appeared at the very beginning of the Hellenistic era, in the third century B.C. Crates maintained that good poems differ from bad by having a *pleasing sound*, while Heracleodor saw the difference in a *pleasing arrangement of sounds*[39] and held that the ear alone is sufficient to grasp a poetical work in full. All three agreed that the thought expressed in a poem has no influence on its effect.

The formalists argued that poetry was a matter wholly for the *ear*; such views were put forward in late Hellenistic and in Roman times. Even Cicero wrote that "the ears are ... marvellously skilful organs of discrimination" (*aurium item est admirabile ... artificiosumque iudicium*).[40] Quintilian thought that "the ears are best in judging" poetical composition (*optime ... iudicant aures*), while Dionysius of Halicarnassus said that "some sounds caress the ear, others irritate and embitter it, others soothe". Elsewhere he wrote: "Speech is necessarily beautiful if it contains beautiful words, and beautiful words consist of beautiful syllables and letters ... From the basic structure of letters are derived the varieties of speech in which human characters, passions, moods, actions and particularities are all revealed". Nevertheless, the relevant difference in these writers lay in their stress on the significance of form in poetry without denying the significance of its content. They valued form without being formalists. A formalist, aural interpretation of poetry was not by any means generally accepted in Hellenistic times. According to Philodemus, the view that "good composition is apprehended not by the mind but by a trained ear"[41] could not be taken seriously. At the other extreme, Pseudo-Longinus agreed with Philodemus: artistic composition speaks to the soul and not only to the ear.[42]

The conceptual apparatus of the ancients was more complex than the simple distinction of form and content. For example, the early Stoic Ariston of Chios employed a fourfold distinction: the thought expressed in a poetical work, the characters presented in it, its sounds and its composition. Both characters and thought belonged to what was later to be called "content" of a poetical work, and both sounds and composition belonged to what became known as "form".

17. CONVENTION VERSUS UNIVERSAL JUDGMENT. Finally, Hellenistic writers held differing views as to whether judgments of poetry were objective and universal. Some held that "in itself" and "by its nature" poetry is neither good not bad but only appears to be so to men.[43] Philodemus tells us about scholars who affirmed that all judgments about poetry are based on conventions and are never universally valid; he himself held a different view:[44] that literary criteria are conventional, but at the same time that they are universal.[45] Similarly, the author of the treatise *On the Sublime* was convinced that universally valid judgments in this sphere exist and, despite difference in customs, ways of life and predilections, men hold the same view about the same things.[46]

It was not denied that judgments of poetry rest on certain criteria, but the question was whether these criteria are rooted in experience, and so are generalizations of the sensations felt, or are independent of experience, have their source in the person making the judgment and are therefore conventions accepted by him. The Stoics favoured in this regard experience, whereas the principles of the Epicureans led them to treat the criteria of aesthetic judgments as conventions.

18. POETRY AND PAINTING. Few ancient apothegms on the theory of art are as famous and popular as Horace's dictum: *ut pictura poësis*—a poem is like a picture.[47] It must be remembered, however, that he was not stating a theory of poetry in this phrase, but simply making a comparison, that it was the pendant to a fairly platitudinous idea (different poems have to be read in different ways just as some pictures are viewed at a distance and others close to), that it was not intended to persuade poets to seek graphic, painterly effects, that the comparison was by no means Horace's invention but had been made earlier, notably by Aristotle, and that the habit favoured by the ancients of comparing poetry with painting is not evidence that they regarded these two arts as related: quite the contrary, they invariably thought them very far removed from each other; it is only modern art-theory that has brought them closer together, recommending not only poetry to model itself on painting (*ut pictura poësis*) but also painting to imitate poetry (*ut poësis pictura*). At least one classical author—Plutarch—disputed the analogy between poetry and painting: he saw a greater resemblance to the dance.[48]

In the theory of poetry Hellenism was concerned primarily with pitting fundamental points of view against each other and adjudicating between them; it paid less attention to detailed inquiry into concepts and issues. Nevertheless, there were some writers, like Sextus and Philodemus, who were also aware of this problem and called for more precise statement. Philodemus argued that vague talk about the "reproduction" of reality by poetry, about "ideas" in poetry, about "beauty" and "harmony" would not do, since these qualities were also to be found in prose, and that it was necessary to explain in detail what gave a work a poetic character and distinguished it from prose.

M. Texts on the Aesthetics of Poetry

DIONYSIUS THRAX, Ars grammatica 1, 629^b.

STUDY OF LITERATURE

1. Γραμματική ἐστιν ἐμπειρία τῶν παρὰ ποιηταῖς τε καὶ συγγραφεῦσιν ὡς ἐπὶ τὸ πολὺ λεγομένων. μέρη δὲ αὐτῆς ἐστιν ἕξ... ἕκτον κρίσις ποιημάτων, ὃ δὴ κάλλιστόν ἐστι πάντων τῶν ἐν τῇ τέχνῃ.

1. The study of literature is an experimental science concerning what in general is written by poets and prose-writers. It has six sections... the sixth is criticism of poetry and it is, of course, the most beautiful aspect of the discipline.

SEXTUS EMPIRICUS
Adv. mathem. I 57; 74; 84.

Διονύσιος μὲν οὖν ὁ Θρᾷξ... φησί «γραμματική ἐστιν ἐμπειρία ὡς ἐπὶ τὸ πλεῖστον τῶν παρὰ ποιηταῖς τε καὶ συγγραφεῦσι λεγομένων»... ⟨Ἀσκληπιάδης⟩ οὕτως ἀποδίδωσι τῆς γραμματικῆς τὴν ἔννοιαν· «ἡ δὲ γραμματική ἐστι τέχνη τῶν παρὰ ποιηταῖς καὶ συγγραφεῦσι λεγομένων»... Δημήτριος δὲ ὁ ἐπικαλούμενος Χλωρὸς καὶ ἄλλοι τινὲς τῶν γραμματικῶν οὕτως ὡρίσαντο «γραμματική ἐστι τέχνη τῶν παρὰ ποιηταῖς τε καὶ τῶν κατὰ τὴν κοινὴν συνήθειαν λέξεων εἴδησις».

Now Dionysius "the Thracian" says... "grammar" is mainly expertness regarding the language of poets and composers... [Asclepiades] presents the concept of Grammar in this form: "Grammar is the art dealing with the speech of poets and composers"... Demetrius, surnamed Chlorus, and certain other Grammarians have given this definition: "The Art of Grammar is knowledge of the forms of speech in the poets' and also those in common usage".

tr. R. G. Bury

PHILODEMUS, De poëm. V (Jensen, 21).

POETRY AND PROSE

2. καὶ γὰρ κατὰ τὸ εὖ τό τε εὐπρεπῶς ἅμα καὶ πειστικῶς πάντ' ἂν εἴη κοινὰ καὶ ποιημάτων καὶ λόγων καὶ τὰ πράγματα παρέχειν πάντων τῆς εἰκαστικῆς τρόπων οἰκεῖόν ἐστιν.

2. The demand for good, suitable and convincing presentation must on all accounts apply in equal measure to poetry and to prose. The fact that they represent reality is common to all representational arts.

SCHOLIA to DIONYSIUS THRAX
(Bekker, An. Gr. II 656).

PROBLEMS OF ART

ἰστέον δὲ ὅτι περὶ πᾶσαν τέχνην ὀκτώ τινα θεωρεῖται· εἰσὶ δὲ ταῦτα αἴτιον, ἀρχή, ἔννοια, ὕλη, μέρη, ἔργα, ὄργανα, τέλος.

One should know that in every art one examines eight things: namely, cause, principle, invention, material, parts, products, tools and the aim.

TRACTATUS COISLINIANUS. I
(Kaibel, 50).

TYPES OF POETRY

3. τῆς ποιήσεως
ἡ μὲν ἀμίμητος
ἱστορικὴ παιδευτική
ὑφηγητικὴ θεωρητική
ἡ δὲ μιμητή
τὸ μὲν ἀπαγγελτικόν, τὸ δὲ δραματικόν

3. Poetry of the first type is not imitative: it is either historical or educational and either in a practical or a theoretical guise. Poetry of the second type is imitative and it is either descriptive or dramatic.

POSIDONIUS (Laërt. Diog. VII 60).

DEFINITION OF POETRY

4. ποίημα δέ ἐστιν, ὥς ὁ Ποσειδώνιός φησιν ἐν τῇ περὶ λέξεως εἰσαγωγῇ, λέξις ἔμμετρος ἢ ἔρρυθμος μετὰ σκευῆς τὸ λογοειδὲς ἐκβεβηκυῖα... ποίησις δέ ἐστι σημαντικὸν ποίημα, μίμησιν περιέχον θείων καὶ ἀνθρωπείων.

4. As Posidonius says in the Introduction to the treatise *On expression*, a poem is metrical and rhythmic speech, which differs from prose on account of its embellishments... Poetry is work full of meaning which represents matters human and divine.

SCHOLIA to DIONYSIUS THRAX
(Bekker, An. Gr. II 649).

εἴπωμεν δὲ τὸν ὅρον τῆς τέχνης. οἱ μὲν Ἐπικούρειοι οὕτως ὁρίζονται τὴν τέχνην· Τέχνη ἐστὶ μέθοδος ἐνεργοῦσα τῷ βίῳ τὸ συμφέρον... ὁ δὲ Ἀριστοτέλης οὕτως· τέχνη ἐστὶν ἕξις ὁδοῦ τοῦ συμφέροντος ποιητική. ἕξις δ' ἐστὶ πρᾶγμα μόνιμον καὶ δυσκατάληπτον. οἱ δὲ Στωϊκοὶ λέγουσι· τέχνη ἐστὶ σύστημα ἐκ καταλήψεων ἐμπειρίᾳ συγγεγυμνασμένων πρός τι τέλος εὔχρηστον τῶν ἐν τῷ βίῳ·

DEFINITION OF ART

We give a definition of art. The Epicureans define it thus: art is a planned action producing that which is necessary to life. While Aristotle says this: art is a disposition to such an action as produces useful things. And disposition is something permanent and beyond the sphere of concepts. As for the Stoics, they say: art is a system of concepts produced jointly from experience and aiming at something useful in life.

STRABO, Geographica, I 2, 3

4a. οἱ παλαιοὶ φιλοσοφίαν τινὰ λέγουσι πρώτην τὴν ποιητικήν, εἰσάγουσαν εἰς τὸν βίον ἡμᾶς ἐκ νέων καὶ διδάσκουσαν ἤθη καὶ πάθη καὶ πράξεις μετὰ ἡδονῆς. οἱ ἡμέτεροι καὶ μόνον ποιητὴν ἔφασαν εἶναι σοφόν· διὰ τοῦτο καὶ τοὺς παῖδας αἱ τῶν Ἑλλήνων πόλεις πρώτιστα διὰ τῆς ποιητικῆς παιδεύουσιν οὐ ψυχαγωγίας χάριν δήπουθεν ψιλῆς, ἀλλὰ σωφρονισμοῦ· ὅπου γε καὶ οἱ μουσικοὶ ψάλλειν καὶ λυρίζειν καὶ αὐλεῖν διδάσκοντες μεταποιοῦνται τῆς ἀρετῆς ταύτης· παιδευτικοὶ γὰρ εἶναί φασι καὶ ἐπανορθωτικοὶ τῶν ἠθῶν· ταῦτα δ' οὐ μόνον παρὰ τῶν Πυθαγορείων ἀκούειν ἐστὶ λεγόντων, ἀλλὰ καὶ Ἀριστόξενος οὕτως ἀποφαίνεται, καὶ Ὅμηρος δὲ τοὺς ἀοιδοὺς σωφρονιστὰς εἴρηκε.

ART TEACHES AND EDUCATES

4a. The ancients assert, on the contrary, that poetry is a kind of elementary philosophy, which, taking us in our very boyhood, introduces us to the art of life and instructs us, with pleasure to ourselves, in character, emotions and actions. And our School goes still further and contends that the wise man alone is a poet. That is the reason why in Greece the various states educate the young, at the very beginning of their education, by means of poetry; not for the mere sake of entertainment, of course, but for the sake of moral discipline. Why, even the musicians, when they give instruction in singing, in lyre-playing, or in flute-playing, lay claims to this virtue, for they maintain that these studies tend to discipline and correct the character. You may hear this contention made not merely by the Pythagoreans, but Aristoxenus also declares the same thing. And Homer, too, has spoken of the bards as disciplinarians in morality...

tr. W. H. S. Jones

PLUTARCH, De aud. poët. 17a.

5. τοῦτο δὲ παντὶ δῆλον, ὅτι μυθοποίημα καὶ πλάσμα πρὸς ἡδονὴν καὶ ἔκπληξιν ἀκροατοῦ γέγονε.

AIM OF POETRY

5. But it is patent to everybody that this is a mythical fabrication which has been created to please or astound the hearer.

tr. F. C. Babbit

HORACE, De arte poëtica 99.

5a. Non satis est pulchra esse poëmata;
   dulcia sunto,
Et quocumque volent animum auditoris
   agunto.

5a. Not enough is it for poems to have beauty: they must have charm, and lead the hearer's soul where they will.

tr. H. R. Fairclough

ERATOSTHENES (Strabo I 2, 3 and 17).

6. ποιητὴν γὰρ, ἔφη, πάντα στοχάζεσ-θαι ψυχαγωγίας, οὐ διδασκαλίας. μὴ κρίνειν πρὸς τὴν διάνοιαν τὰ ποιήματα, μηδ' ἱστορίαν ἀπ' αὐτῶν ζητεῖν.

6. Eratosthenes contends that the aim of every poet is to entertain, not to instruct.
Eratosthenes bids us not to judge the poems with reference to their thought, nor yet to seek for history in them.

tr. H. L. Jones

RHETORICA AD HERENNIUM I 8, 13.

7. Fabula est, quae neque veras neque veri similes continet res, ut eae sunt, quae tragoediis traditae sunt. Historia est gesta res, sed ab aetatis nostrae memoriae remota. Argumentum est ficta res, quae tamen fieri potuit, velut argumenta comoediarum.

POETRY AND HISTORY

7. The legendary tale comprises events neither true nor probable, like those transmitted by tragedies. The historical narrative is an account of exploits actually performed but removed in time from the recollection of our age. Realistic narrative recounts imaginary events which yet could have occurred, like the plots of comedies.

tr. H. Caplan

The same in Cicero, De inv. I, 19–28.
CICERO, De legibus I 1, 5.

8. Q.: "Intellego te, frater, alias in historia leges observandas putare, alias in poëmate". M.: "Quippe cum in illa omnia ad veritatem, Quinte, referantur, in hoc ad delectationem pleraque".

8. Q.: As I understand it, then, my dear brother, you believe that different principles are to be followed in history and in poetry.
M.: Certainly, Quintus; for in history the standard by which everything is judged is the truth, while in poetry it is generally the pleasure one gives.

tr. C. W. Keyes

SEXTUS EMPIRICUS,
Adv. mathem. I 297.

9. οἱ μὲν γὰρ τοῦ ἀληθοῦς στοχάζονται, οἱ δὲ ἐκ παντὸς ψυχαγωγεῖν ἐθέλουσιν, ψυχαγωγεῖ δὲ μᾶλλον τὸ ψεῦδος ἢ τὸ ἀληθές.

POETRY AND TRUTH

9. [And the fact that the prose-writers rather than the poets show what is useful for life is easy to demonstrate.] For the former aim at the truth, but the latter seek by every means to attract the soul, and the false attracts more than the true.

tr. R. G. Bury

PSEUDO-LONGINUS,
De sublimitate XXII 1

ἡ τέχνη τέλειος, ἡνίκ' ἂν φύσις εἶναι δοκῇ, ἡ δ' αὖ φύσις ἐπιτυχής, ὅταν λανθάνουσαν περιέχῃ τὴν τέχνην.

ART AND NATURE

For art is then perfect when it seems to be nature and nature, again, is most effective when pervaded by the unseen presence of art.

tr. H. L. Havell

HERACLEODOR (?) (Philodemus, Vol. Herc. 2 IV 179).

10. τὸ ἀγαθὸν τοῦ ποιήματος οὐκ ἐν τῷ καλὰ διανοήματα συσκευάζειν ἢ σοφὸν ὑπάρχειν.

PHILODEMUS, De poëm. V (Jensen 51).

11. καὶ γὰρ καθὸ πόημα φυσικὸν οὐδὲν οὔτε λέξεως οὔτε διανοήματος ὠφέλημα παρασκευάζει.

Ibid., (Jensen, 7)
οὐκ ἔστι τέρπειν δι' ἀρετήν.

OVID, Ep. ex Ponto I. V. 53.

11a. Magis utile nil est artibus his, quae nil utilitatis habent.

HORACE, De arte poëtica 343.

12. Omne tulit punctum qui miscuit utile dulci,
Lectorem delectando pariterque monendo.

HERMOGENES, De ideis (Rabe 369).

13. τὸ πᾶσι τοῖς πεφυκόσι λόγου σῶμα ποιεῖν χρῆσθαι δύνασθαι δεόντως καὶ κατὰ καιρὸν ἡ ὄντως οὖσα δεινότης ἔμοιγε εἶναι δοκεῖ... δεινὸς χρῆσθαι πράγμασι λέγεται... ὁ εἰς δέον τοῖς παραπεσοῦσι πράγμασι χρώμενος οἷον ὕλῃ τινὶ οὖσι τῆς ὥσπερ τέχνης αὐτοῦ.

DIOGENES THE BABYLONIAN
(Diocles Magnes in Laërt. Diog. VII, 59).

14. ἀρεταὶ δὲ λόγου εἰσὶ πέντε· ἑλληνισμός, σαφήνεια, συντομία, πρέπον, κατασκευή. ... πρέπον δέ ἐστι λέξις οἰκεία τῷ πράγματι.

PLUTARCH, De aud. poët. 25 d.

15. μάλιστα μὲν ἡ ποιητικὴ τῷ ποικίλῳ χρῆται καὶ πολυτρόπῳ.

DIONYSIUS OF HALICARNASSUS
De Lysia 7.

16. ἔχει δὲ καὶ τὴν ἐνάργειαν πολλὴν ἡ Λυσίου λέξις. αὕτη δ' ἐστὶ δύναμίς τις

POETRY AND THOUGHT

10. It is no virtue in a poem to supply beautiful thoughts or to be wise.

POETRY AND UTILITY

11. By its very nature a poem presents no value either through its words or through its thought.

Virtue is not an entertainment.

UTILITY OF THE ARTS

11a. Nothing is more useful than this art which has no use.

tr. A. L. Wheeler

12. He has won every vote who has blended profit and pleasure, at once delighting and instructing the reader.

tr. H. R. Fairclough

ARTISTRY

13. What appears to me to be true artistry is the knowledge and ability to employ all figures of speech in the right manner and at the proper time... The one who employs the subject of his speech as though it were the material of his art is regarded as an outstanding speaker.

POETIC VIRTUES

14. There are five excellences of speech—pure Greek, lucidity, conciseness, appropriateness, distinction. ...appropriateness lies in a style akin to the subject.

tr. R. D. Hicks

VARIETY IN POETRY

15. But poetic art... chiefly... employs variety and diversity.

tr. F. C. Babbit

PALPABILITY IN POETRY

16. The speeches of Lysias have many visual qualities. This is a particular ability to bring

ὑπὸ τὰς αἰσθήσεις ἄγουσα τὰ λεγόμενα, γίγνεται δ' ἐκ τῆς τῶν παρακολουθούντων λήψεως.

before the senses the subject-matter of the speech; it arises thanks to a grasp of the properties of that object.

HERMOGENES, De ideis (Rabe, 390).

17. τὸ μέγιστον ποιήσεως μίμησιν ἐναργῆ καὶ πρέπουσαν τοῖς ὑποκειμένοις.

17. In poetry the most important thing is a representation that is visual and suited to the subject.

CICERO, De finibus III 5, 19.

18. Omne, quod de re bona dilucide dicitur, mihi praeclare dici videtur.

CLARITY IN POETRY

18. ...to my mind, any clear statement of an important topic possesses excellence of style.

tr. H. Rackham

QUINTILIAN, Inst. orat. VI 2, 29.

19. φαντασίας ... nos sane visiones appellemus, per quas imagines rerum absentium ita repraesentantur animo, ut eas cernere oculis ac praesentes habere videamur.

IMAGINATION

19. There are certain experiences [which the Greeks call] φαντασίας and the Romans visions, whereby things absent are presented to our imagination with such vividness that they seem actually to be before our very eyes.

tr. H. E. Butler

PSEUDO-LONGINUS
De sublimitate XV 1.

20. Ὄγκου καὶ μεγαληγορίας καὶ ἀγῶνος ἐπὶ τούτοις... καὶ αἱ φαντασίαι παρασκευαστικώταται. οὕτω γοῦν εἰδωλοποιίας αὐτὰς ἔνιοι λέγουσι· καλεῖται μὲν γὰρ κοινῶς φαντασία πᾶν τὸ ὁπωσοῦν ἐννόημα γεννητικὸν λόγου παριστάμενον· ἤδη δὲ τούτων κεκράτηκε τοὔνομα, ὅταν ἃ λέγεις ὑπ' ἐνθουσιασμοῦ καὶ πάθους βλέπειν δοκῇς καὶ ὑπ' ὄψιν τιθῇς τοῖς ἀκούουσιν. ὡς δ' ἕτερόν τι ἡ ῥητορικὴ φαντασία βούλεται καὶ ἕτερον ἡ παρὰ ποιηταῖς, οὐκ ἂν λάθοι σε, οὐδ' ὅτι τῆς μὲν ἐν ποιήσει τέλος ἐστὶν ἔκπληξις, τῆς δ' ἐν λόγοις ἐνάργεια... (8) τὰ μὲν παρὰ τοῖς ποιηταῖς μυθικωτέραν ἔχει τὴν ὑπερέκπτωσιν. ... καὶ πάντη τὸ πιστὸν ὑπεραίρουσαν, τῆς δὲ ῥητορικῆς φαντασίας κάλλιστον ἀεὶ τὸ ἔμπρακτον καὶ ἐναληθές.

20. Images, moreover, contribute greatly... to dignity, elevation and power as a pleader. In this sense some call them mental representations. In a general way the name of "image" or "imagination" is applied to every idea of the mind, in whatever form it presents itself. But at the present day the word is predominantly used in cases where, carried away by enthusiasm and passion, you think you see what you describe, and you place it before the eyes of your hearers. Further you will be aware of the fact that an image has one purpose with the orators and another with the poets, and that the design of the poetical image is enthralment, of the rhetorical—vivid description... Those which are found in the poets contain... a tendency to exaggeration in the way of the fabulous, and they transcend in every way the credible, but in oratorical imagery the best feature is always its reality and truth.

tr. W. R. Roberts

DIONYSIUS OF HALICARNASSUS, Ant. Roman. I 1, 3.

21. εἰκόνας εἶναι τῆς ἑκάστου ψυχῆς τοὺς λόγους.

SENECA, Epist. 65. 7.

22. Nihil autem ad rem pertinet, utrum foris exemplar habeat exemplar, ad quod referat oculos, an intus, quod ibi sibi ipse concepit et posuit; haec exemplaria rerum omnium deus intra se habet.

HORACE, De arte poëtica 309.

23. Scribendi recte sapere est et principium, et fons.

LUCIAN, Demosth. encom. 5.

24. πολλῆς δεῖ τῆς μανίας ἐπὶ τὰς ποιητικὰς ἰοῦσι θύρας. δεῖ γάρ τοι καὶ τοῖς καταλογάδην... ἐνθέου τινὸς ἐπιπνοίας, εἰ μέλλουσι μὴ ταπεινοὶ φανεῖσθαι καὶ φαύλης φροντίδος.

SENECA, De tranquil. animi 17, 10.

Nam sive Graeco poëtae credimus: "Aliquando et insanire iucundum est", sive Platoni: "Frustra poëticas fores compos sui pepulit", sive Aristoteli: "Nullum magnum ingenium sine mixtura dementiae fuit", non potest grande aliquid et super ceteros loqui nisi mota mens.

PSEUDO-LONGINUS, De sublim. II 1.

25. εἰ ἔστιν ὕψους τις... τέχνη, ἐπεί τινες ὅλως οἴονται διηπατῆσθαι τοὺς τὰ τοιαῦτα ἄγοντας εἰς τεχνικὰ παραγγέλματα. γεννᾶται γάρ, φησί, τὰ μεγαλοφυῆ καὶ οὐ διδακτὰ παραγίνεται... ἐγὼ δὲ ἐλεγχθήσεσθαι τοῦθ᾽ ἑτέρως ἔχον φημί... τὰς δὲ ποσότητας καὶ τὸν ἐφ᾽ ἑκάστου καιρόν, ἔτι δὲ τὴν ἀπλανεστάτην ἄσκησίν τε καὶ χρῆσιν ἱκανὴ παρο-

WORK OF ART AS PICTURE OF THE SOUL

21. A man's words are the images of his mind.

tr. E. Cary

INTERNAL AND EXTERNAL MODEL

22. But it doesn't matter whether he had his model without, to fix his eyes on, or within, a notion conceived and built up in his own brain. Such models of all things God has within Himself.

tr. E. P. Barker

POETRY AND WISDOM

23. Of good writing the source and fount is wisdom.

tr. H. R. Fairclough

INSPIRATION

24. A considerable touch of madness is required of him who would pass the gates of poetry. If you come to that, prose cannot do without some divine inspiration either, if it is not to be flat and common.

tr. H. W. Fowler and F. G. Fowler

For whether we believe with the Greek poet that "sometimes it is a pleasure also to rave", or with Plato that "the sane mind knocks in vain at the door of poetry", or with Aristotle that "no great genius has ever existed without some touch of madness"—be that as it may the lofty utterance that rises above the attempts of others is impossible unless the mind is excited.

tr. J. W. Basore

POETIC RULES

25. Whether there is such a thing as an art of the sublime, some hold that those are entirely in error who would bring such matters under the precepts of art. A lofty tone, says one, is innate and does not come by teaching... But I maintain that this will be found to be otherwise. ...but system can define limits and fitting seasons, and can also contribute the

ρίσαι καὶ συνενεγκεῖν ἡ μέθοδος, καὶ ὡς ἐπικινδυνότερα αὐτὰ ἐφ' αὑτῶν... ἐαθέντα, τὰ μεγάλα... δεῖ γὰρ αὐτοῖς, ὡς κέντρου πολλάκις, οὕτω δὲ καὶ χαλινοῦ.

safest rules for use and practice. Moreover, the expression of the sublime is more exposed to danger when it goes its own way... It is true that it often needs the spur, but it is also true that it often needs the curb.

tr. R. W. Roberts

LUCIAN, Historia quo modo conscribenda 16.

26. ἑκάστου γὰρ δὴ ἴδιόν τι καλόν ἐστιν· εἰ δὲ τοῦτο ἐναλλάξειας, ἀκαλλὲς τὸ αὐτὸ παρὰ τὴν χρῆσιν γίγνεται.

EVERY OBJECT HAS ITS BEAUTY

26. For each part has its own peculiar beauty, and if you alter that, you make it ugly and futile.

tr. K. Kilburn

HORACE, De arte poëtica 9.

27. Pictoribus atque poëtis
Quidlibet audendi semper fuit aequa potestas.

POETIC LICENCE

27. Painters and poets... have always had an equal right in hazarding.

tr. H. R. Fairclough

LUCIAN, Pro imag. 18.

παλαιὸς οὗτος ὁ λόγος ἀνευθύνους εἶναι καὶ ποιητὰς καὶ γραφέας.

It is an ancient saying... that poets and painters are not to be held accountable.

tr. A. M. Harmon

LUCIAN, Historia quo m. conscrib. 9.

ποιητικῆς μὲν καὶ ποιημάτων ἄλλαι ὑποσχέσεις καὶ κανόνες ἴδιοι, ἱστορίας δὲ ἄλλοι· ἐκεῖ μὲν γὰρ ἀκρατὴς ἡ ἐλευθερία καὶ νόμος εἷς· τὸ δόξαν τῷ ποιητῇ· ἔνθεος γὰρ καὶ κάτοχος ἐκ Μουσῶν.

History has aims and rules different from poetry and poems. In the case of the latter, liberty is absolute and there is one law—the will of the poet. Inspired and possessed by the muses as he is.

tr. K. Kilburn

ARISTON OF CHIOS (Philodemus, De poëm. V, Jensen 41).

28. πᾶσα γὰρ ἐξουσία πᾶσιν λελέχθω.

READER'S FREEDOM TO CHOOSE

28. There has to be a poetry to suit every taste.

DIONYSIUS OF HALICARNASSUS (De Dinarcho 7, Usener, Raderm. 307).

29. δύο τρόποι... μιμήσεως ὧν ὁ μὲν φυσικός τέ ἐστι καὶ ἐκ πολλῆς κατηχήσεως καὶ συντροφίας λαμβανόμενος, ὁ δὲ τούτῳ προσεχὴς ἐκ τῶν τῆς τέχνης παραγγελμάτων. ... πᾶσι τοῖς ἀρχετύποις αὐτοφυής τις ἐπιπρέπει χάρις καὶ ὥρα τοῖς δ' ἀπὸ τούτων κατασκευασμένοις, ἂν ἐπ' ἄκρον μιμήσεως ἔλθωσι, πρόσεστιν τι ὅμως τὸ ἐπιτετηδευμένον καὶ οὐκ ἐκ φύσεως ὑπάρχον, καὶ τούτῳ τῷ παραγγέλματι οὐ ῥήτορες μόνον ῥήτορας

CHARM OF ORIGINALITY

29. Of the methods of imitation one is natural and arises out of rich experience and a thorough acquaintance with the model; but there is also another one based on artistic rules... All original works display a certain innate charm, whereas in everything done in imitation of them, even where imitation is at its peak, there is something artificial and alien to nature. It is on the basis of this principle that not only orators judge other orators

διακρίνουσιν, ἀλλὰ καὶ ζωγράφοι τὰ Ἀπελλοῦ καὶ τῶν ἐκείνον μιμησαμένων καὶ πλάσται τὰ Πολυκλείτου καὶ γλυφεῖς τὰ Φειδίου.

DIONYSIUS OF HALICARNASSUS,
De imit. frg. 3 (Usener, Raderm. 2, 200).

μίμησίς ἐστιν ἐνέργεια διὰ τῶν θεωρημάτων ἐκματτομένη τὸ παράδειγμα. ζῆλος δέ ἐστιν ἐνέργεια ψυχῆς πρὸς θαῦμα τοῦ δοκοῦντος εἶναι καλοῦ κινουμένη.

PSEUDO-LONGINUS,
De sublim. XXXV 5.

30. εὐπόριστον μὲν ἀνθρώποις τὸ χρειῶδες ἢ καὶ ἀναγκαῖον, θαυμαστὸν δ' ὅμως ἀεὶ τὸ παράδοξον... τοῦ ἀναμαρτήτου πολὺ ἀφεστῶτες οἱ τηλικοῦτοι ὅμως πάντες εἰσὶν ἐπάνω τοῦ θνητοῦ... τὸ μὲν ἄπταιστον οὐ ψέγεται, τὸ μέγα δὲ καὶ θαυμάζεται... ἐπὶ μὲν τέχνης θαυμάζεται τὸ ἀκριβέστατον, ἐπὶ δὲ τῶν φυσικῶν ἔργων τὸ μέγεθος, φύσει δὲ λογικὸν ὁ ἄνθρωπος. κἀπὶ μὲν ἀνδριάντων ζητεῖται τὸ ὅμοιον ἀνθρώπῳ, ἐπὶ δὲ τοῦ λόγου τὸ ὑπεραῖρον... τὰ ἀνθρώπινα.

PSEUDO-SYRIANUS,
In Hermog. περὶ ἰδεῶν praefatio.

31. ὅλως τὸ τέλειον αἰσθήσει καὶ μόνῃ διαγινώσκεται· οὐ γὰρ ἂν δυνηθείη τις λόγος παραστῆσαι τὸ ὅλον ὡς ὅλον πλὴν εἰ μὴ συμβολικῶς· ἡ δὲ τοιαύτη γνῶσις οὐ καθάπτεται τῶν παρακολουθημάτων μή τί γε δὴ ὑποκειμένης οὐσίας... τὰς ἐξαλλαγὰς τῶν ἀτόμων καὶ τὴν ἀποτελουμένην ἐκ τῶν κατὰ μέρος μορφὴν αἰσθήσει καὶ μόνῃ καταλαμβάνομεν.

DIONYSIUS OF HALICARNASSUS,
De Dem. 50 (Usener, Raderm. 237).

32. κριτήριον ἄριστον ἡ ἄλογος αἴσθησις.

HORACE, De arte poëtica, 407.

33. Natura fieret laudabile carmen an arte, Quaesitum est. Ego nec studium sine divite vena.

but also painters distinguish the works of Apelles from those of his imitators and similarly sculptors distinguish the works of Polyclitus and carvers the works of Phidias.

ARDOUR

Imitation is an activity which with the aid of principles represents the original.

Ardour is an activity of the soul spurred by admiration for what seems beautiful.

FAULTLESSNESS AND GREATNESS IN POETRY

30. What is useful or necessary men regard as commonplace, while they reserve their admiration for that which is astounding... Though writers of this magnitude are far removed from faultlessness, they none the less all rise above what is mortal...; and while immunity from errors relieves from censure, it is grandeur that excites admiration. ...In art the utmost exactitude is admired, grandeur in the works of nature, and it is by nature that man is a being gifted with speech. In statues likeness to man is the quality required; in discourse we demand... that which transcends the human.
tr. W. R. Roberts

INTUITION

31. Generally speaking, a whole can be recognized only through direct impression, because no rational sentence could present the whole as a whole unless this were done symbolically. Such knowledge cannot grasp the properties of an object, much less so its essence... Individual differences and the form arising from the parts we can grasp only through direct impression.

32. The best test is an impression independent of the mind.

TALENT AND ART

33. Often it is asked whether a praiseworthy poem be due to nature or to art. For

Nec rude quid prosit video ingenium: alterius [sic
Altera poscit opem res et coniurat amice.

my part I do not see of what avail is either study, when not enriched by Nature's vein, or native wit, if untrained; so truly does each claim the other's aid and make with it a friendly league.

tr. H. R. Fairclough

PHILODEMUS, De poëm. V (Jensen 23).

34. τὸ διαφέρειν τὸν εὖ ποιοῦντα τοῦ ἀγαθοῦ ποιητοῦ δέχομαι.

34. I agree that he who can produce technically good poetry differs from a good poet.

QUINTILIAN, Inst. orat., II 17, 9.

Omnia, quae ars consummaverit, a natura initia (duxerunt)... Nec fabrica sit ars, casas enim primi illi sine arte fecerunt; nec musica, cantatur ac saltatur per omnes gentes aliquo modo.

NATURE AND ART

Everything which art has brought to perfection had its origin in nature... else too, architecture must not be considered an art, for the first generation of men built cottages without art; nor music, since singing and dancing, to some sort of tune, are practised among all nations.

tr. J. S. Watson

OVID, Met. III, 158.

Simulaverat artem
Ingenio natura suo.

But nature by her own cunning had imitated art.

tr. F. J. Miller

DIONYSIUS OF HALICARNASSUS,
De comp. verb. 11 (Usener, Raderm., 37).

35. ἐξ ὧν δ' οἶμαι γενήσεσθαι λέξιν ἡδεῖαν καὶ καλὴν τέτταρά ἐστι τὰ κυριώτατα ταῦτα καὶ κράτιστα, μέλος καὶ ῥυθμὸς καὶ μεταβολὴ καὶ τὸ παρακολουθοῦν τοῖς τρισὶ τούτοις πρέπον. Τάττω δὲ ὑπὸ μὲν τὴν ἡδονὴν τήν τε ὥραν καὶ τὴν χάριν καὶ τὴν εὐστομίαν καὶ τὴν γλυκύτητα καὶ τὸ πιθανὸν καὶ πάντα τὰ τοιαῦτα· ὑπὸ δὲ τὸ καλὸν τήν τε μεγαλοπρέπειαν καὶ τὸ βάρος καὶ τὴν σεμνολογίαν καὶ τὸ ἀξίωμα καὶ τὸν πίνον καὶ τὰ τούτοις ὅμοια. Ταυτὶ γάρ μοι δοκεῖ κυριώτατα εἶναι καὶ ὡσπερεὶ κεφάλαια τῶν ἄλλων ἐν ἑκατέρῳ. Ὧν μὲν οὖν στοχάζονται πάντες οἱ σπουδῇ γράφοντες μέτρον ἢ μέλος ἢ τὴν λεγομένην πεζὴν λέξιν, ταῦτ' ἐστὶ καὶ οὐκ οἶδ' εἴ τι παρὰ ταῦθ' ἕτερον.

PLEASURE AND BEAUTY

35. Among the sources of charm and beauty in style there are, I conceive, four which are paramount and essential—melody, rhythm, variety and the appropriateness demanded by these three. Under "charm" I class freshness, grace, euphony, sweetness, persuasiveness, and all similar qualities; and under "beauty" grandeur, impressiveness, solemnity, dignity, mellowness and the like. For these seem to me the most important—the main heads, so to speak, in either case. The aims set before themselves by all serious writers in epic, dramatic, or lyric poetry, or in the so-called "language of prose", are those specified, and I think these are all.

tr. W. R. Roberts

RHETORICA AD HERENNIUM IV 8, 11.

36. Sunt... tria genera, quae genera nos figuras appellamus, in quibus omnis oratio non vitiosa consumitur: unam gravem, alteram

THREE STYLES

36. There are... three kinds of style, called types, to which discourse, if faultless, confines itself: the first we call the Grand; the second,

mediocrem, tertiam attenuatam vocamus. Gravis est quae constat ex verborum gravium magna et ornata constructione; mediocris est quae constat ex humiliore, neque tamen ex infima et pervulgatissima verborum dignitate; attenuata est quae demissa est usque ad usitatissimam puri sermonis consuetudinem.

NEOPTOLEMUS (Philodemus, De poëm. V, Jensen, 25).

37. παραπλησίως ἀναγκαῖα τὴν τε λέξιν εἶναι καὶ τὰ πράγματα λόγον ἔχειν. πλεῖον ἰσχύειν ἐν ποιητικῇ τὸ πεποιημένον εἶναι τοῦ τὰ διανοήμαθ' ἔχειν πολυτελῆ.

DEMETRIUS, De eloc. 75.

38. δεῖ γὰρ οὐ τὰ λεγόμενα σκοπεῖν, ἀλλὰ πῶς λέγεται.

HERACLEODOR (?) (Philodemus, Vol. Herc². XI 165).

39. τὴν ἀρετὴν τοῦ ποιήματος ἐν εὐφωνίᾳ κεῖσθαι.

CICERO, De natura deorum II 58, 145.

40. Primum enim oculi in eis artibus, quarum iudicium est oculorum, in pictis, fictis caelatisque formis, in corporum etiam motione atque gestu multa cernunt subtilius: colorum etiam et figurarum tum venustatem atque ordinem et, ut ita dicam, decentiam oculi iudicant... Auriumque item est admirabile quoddam artificiosumque iudicium.

cf. HORACE, De arte poëtica 180.

Segnius inritant animos demissa per aurem,
Quam quae sunt oculis subiecta fidelibus et quae
Ipse sibi tradit spectator.

PHILODEMUS, De poëm. V (Jensen, 47).

41. ['Αρίστων] καταγελάστως δ' ἐπιτίθεται καὶ τὴν σπουδαῖαν σύνθεσιν οὐκ εἶναι λόγῳ καταληπτήν, ἀλλ' ἐκ τῆς κατὰ τὴν ἀκοὴν τριβῆς.

the Middle; the third, the Simple. The Grand type consists of a smooth and ornate arrangement of impressive words. The Middle Type consists of words of a lower, yet not of the lowest and most colloquial, class of words. The Simple type is brought down even to the most current idiom of standard speech.

tr. H. Caplan

FORM AND CONTENT

37. Verbal expression is just as indispensable as content. For poetry good craftsmanship is more significant than a rich content.

38. One should consider the manner of his discourse rather than the matter.

tr. G. M. A. Grube

JUDGMENT OF THE SENSES AND JUDGMENT OF REASON

39. The value of a poem lies in beautiful sound.

40. In the first place, our eyes have a finer perception of many things in the arts which appeal to the sense of sight—painting, modelling and sculpture—and also to bodily movements and gestures; since the eyes judge beauty and arrangement and, so to speak, propriety of colour and shape... The ears are likewise marvellously skilful organs of discrimination.

tr. H. Rackham

Stories which pass into the mind by the ear stir our thoughts less vividly than those brought before the faithful test of sight, which the spectator submits to himself.

tr. T. A. Moxon

41. [Ariston] is laughable when he goes on to say that good composition is apprehended not by the mind but by a trained ear.

PSEUDO-LONGINUS, De sublim. XXXIX 3.

42. τὴν σύνθεσιν, ἁρμονίαν τινὰ οὖσαν λόγων ἀνθρώποις ἐμφύτων καὶ τῆς ψυχῆς αὐτῆς, οὐχὶ τῆς ἀκοῆς μόνης ἐφαπτομένων.

42. Composition is a harmony of that language which is implanted by nature in man and which appeals not to the hearing only but to the soul itself.

tr. R. W. Roberts

SEXTUS EMPIRICUS Adv. mathem. II 56.

43. ἥ τε λέξις καθ' ἑαυτὴν οὔτε καλή ἐστιν οὔτε μοχθηρά.

UNIVERSALITY AND CONVENTIONS IN JUDGMENTS ABOUT POETRY

43. ...language of itself is neither good nor bad.

tr. R. G. Bury

PHILODEMUS, De poëm. V (Jensen, 53).

44. μίμησίς τις ἐν τοιαύτῃ κατασκευῇ... κοινὸν ἀποδώσει κρῖμα πᾶσιν.

44. Imitative art of a certain kind provides a basis for a common judgment for all.

PHILODEMUS, De poëm. V (Jensen, 51).

45. ἠλήθευον δὲ φυσικὸν ἀγαθὸν ἐν ποιήματι μηδὲν εἶναι λέγοντες... ἐψεύδοντο δὲ θέματα πάντα νομίζοντες εἶναι καὶ κρίσιν οὐχ ὑπάρχειν τῶν ἀστείων ἐπῶν καὶ φαύλων, ἀλλὰ παρ' ἄλλοις ἄλλην.

45. They were right when they said that there is nothing in a poem which is good by nature... On the other hand, they erred when they thought there are only literary conventions, that there are no general criteria and that everyone has his own criteria.

PSEUDO-LONGINUS, De sublim. VII 4.

46. καλὰ νόμιζε ὕψη καὶ ἀληθινὰ τὰ διὰ παντὸς ἀρέσκοντα καὶ πᾶσιν. ὅταν γὰρ τοῖς ἀπὸ διαφόρων ἐπιτηδευμάτων, βίων, ζήλων, ἡλικιῶν, λόγων, ἕν τι καὶ ταὐτόν ἅμα περὶ τῶν αὐτῶν ἅπασι δοκῇ, τόθ' ἡ ἐξ ἀσυμφώνων ὡς κρίσις καὶ συγκατάθεσις τὴν ἐπὶ τῷ θαυμαζομένῳ πίστιν ἰσχυρὰν λαμβάνει καὶ ἀναμφίλεκτον.

UNIVERSALITY IN JUDGMENTS ABOUT POETRY

46. Consider those examples of sublimity to be fine and genuine which please all and always. For when men of different pursuits, lives, ambitions, ages, languages hold identical views on one and the same subject, then that verdict which results, so to speak, from a concert of discordant elements makes our faith in the objects of admiration strong and unassailable.

tr. W. R. Roberts

HORACE, De arte poët. 361.

47. Ut pictura poësis: erit, quae, si pro-
[prius stes,
te capiat magis, et quaedam, si longius abstes;
haec amat obscurum, volet haec sub luce videri,
iudicis argutum quae non formidat acumen;
haec placuit semel, haec deciens repetita
[placebit.

POETRY AND PAINTING

47. A poem is like a picture: one strikes your fancy more, the nearer you stand; another, the farther away. This courts the shade, that will wish to be seen in the light, and dreads not the critic insight of the judge. This pleased but once; that, though ten times called for, will always please.

tr. H. R. Fairclough

PLUTARCH, Quaest. conviv. 748 A.

48. μεταθετέον τὸ Σιμωνίδειον ἀπὸ τῆς ζωγραφίας ἐπὶ τὴν ὄρχησιν· σιωπῶσαν καὶ φθεγγομένην ὄρχησιν πάλιν τὴν ποίησιν· ὅθεν εἶπεν οὔτε γραφικὴν εἶναι ποιητικῆς, οὔτε ποιητικὴν γραφικῆς, οὔτε χρῶνται τὸ παράπαν ἀλλήλαις· ὀρχηστικῇ δὲ καὶ ποιητικῇ κοινωνία πᾶσα καὶ μέθεξις ἀλλήλων ἐστί, καὶ μάλιστα [μιμούμεναι] περὶ τὸ τῶν ὑπορχημάτων γένος ἓν ἔργου ἀμφότεραι τὴν διὰ τῶν σχημάτων καὶ τῶν ὀνομάτων μίμησιν ἀποτελοῦσι.

POETRY AND THE DANCE

48. One can transfer Simonides' saying (cf. above, A 36) from painting to dancing and call dance silent poetry, and poetry articulate dance. There seems to be nothing of painting in poetry or of poetry in painting, nor does either art make any use whatsoever of the other, whereas dancing and poetry are fully associated and the one involves the other. Particularly is this so when they combine in that type of composition called "hyporchema", in which the two arts taken together effect a single work, a representation by means of poses and words.

tr. F. H. Sandbach

9. The Aesthetics of Rhetoric

1. RHETORIC. The ancients loved oratory and fine speech-making. They not only classed the rhetoricians' skill among the arts, but allowed it a place of distinction. They attached a special weight, greater than any bestowed by subsequent epochs, to the theory of oratory, namely rhetoric.* This was probably because they were conscious of the problems which this art raised, and sought its justification in theory. Their oratory was governed by rules and could therefore be regarded as an art in the wide Greek sense of the term; but it was less certain whether it could also be regarded as an art in the narrower sense, as a fine art like poetry. And if it could be so regarded, what distinguished it from the other arts of the word, since its purpose was neither imitation nor entertainment but persuasion and the achievement of an aim? Could it be distinguished by the task it had to perform? If the fact that it was live speech distinguished it, this would not accord with its function of persuading people, because persuasion can be conducted in writing. Was oratory distinguished by the fact that it served real life, while poetry lived on fictions, or by the fact that oratory was expressed in prose, whereas poetry was written in verse? The ancients asked these questions and argued how oratory should be defined and where its functions and its proper value should be sought.

2. GORGIAS. In democratic Greece, where every citizen had a voice in public affairs and there was therefore a constant need to persuade and captivate people, a theory of sound speech-making and persuasion was of considerable importance. This theory, called rhetoric, originated in Greater Greece in the fifth century B.C. Earlier still the Greeks already possessed distinguished speakers, but now theo-

---

* C. S. Baldwin, *Ancient Rhetoric and Poetics* (1924). W. R. Roberts, *Greek Rhetoric and Literary Criticism* (1928).

reticians also appeared on the scene to formulate in general terms effective methods of addressing people. In the classical era Athens became the centre of rhetoric.

The first outstanding figure in the history of rhetoric was Gorgias, the creator of the general theory of art which we have already discussed. This general theory of art was in fact Gorgias' generalization of his theory of oratory. He maintained that a good speaker in effect casts a spell on his listeners, as he creates illusions and is capable of making them believe what does not exist. He expanded this idea to include all art, which he regarded as a spell and a creation of delusion. He thus formulated the illusionist theory of art.

With regard to rhetoric he held the view that the business of a speaker is to affect his listeners and make an impression upon them. This he can do if he is able to fit his speech to the occasion, find suitable words for it and talk in an original, unexpected and arresting manner. The striking and arresting turns of phrase which Gorgias employed and recommended to others came to be known in the ancient world as "the phrases of Gorgias", We may formulate his view as follows: the ideal speaker is one who is an *ideal artist*. His oratory is then effective and spellbinding, persuades people to believe in what does not exist and even convinces them that the weak is strong and the strong weak.

The speeches of Gorgias, which implemented these principles, were the first pieces of Greek prose with a claim to art, a claim which until then had been confined to poetry. In his rhetoric Gorgias combined persuasion with entertainment and oratory (which the Greeks regarded as a political rather than an artistic matter) with art and literature. Gorgias' rhetoric played a pioneering role in the development of artistic prose and his admirers have compared his achievement in this field with that of Aeschylus in poetry.

3. ISOCRATES. In Athens rhetoric was taught mainly by the Sophists. They held that the rhetorician's task should be confined to finding a way of defending the cause entrusted to him without deliberating whether the cause were good or evil, whether he was defending truth or falsehood. As a professional speaker, he should consider his defence of the case regardless of what its merits might be. In other words, the Sophists interpreted the art of oratory formally: they held it to be concerned with form rather than content. They believed, however, that the form should be persuasive rather than beautiful, since the effectiveness of the speech was the prime consideration. This approach loosened the links between oratory and art, thereby strengthening those between oratory and logic.

Closely associated with the Sophists was Isocrates, equally famous as a speaker and a theorist of oratory, who initiated the second stage in the development of rhetoric. He regarded it primarily as a science, a skill and a question of familiarity with the rules of oratory. An accomplished speaker is one who knows the rules and is an *excellent theorist of oratory*. At the same time the science of the speaker carries no guarantee of certainty. According to the general philosophy of the Sophists, there can be no certain knowledge and nobody can venture beyond guesses and conjectures.

For Isocrates the primary role of oratory was the utilitarian one of persuasion, although it also had another: to give satisfaction to the listeners. This also indirectly serves to persuade. The beauty and splendour of speech arouse in the listeners not only pleasure, but also confidence in what the speaker has to say, so that, though its goal makes oratory a skill, the means it employs make it what we should today call a fine art. The same is equally true of poetry, but the style of oratory can and should be different from that of poetry: it must be prosaic, not poetic. Isocrates produced examples of such a style, which had influenced not only orators, but also historians and prose-writers in general. Oratory influenced literature, while rhetoric influenced the interpretation of literature. It influenced it no less than the rhetoric of Gorgias, though in a different spirit.

4. PLATO. Plato expressed a new and quite different attitude towards rhetoric. Living in the Athens of the fifth and fourth centuries B.C., he could not remain indifferent to rhetoric. Proof of his interest is given by his remarks in *Phaedrus* about the meanness of the written word compared with the power of the live, spoken word. But, devoted as he was to truth and morality, he could only regard as the embodiment of evil, immorality and perversity Gorgias' "turning the weak into the strong and the strong into the weak" and the formalism of the Sophists, who were prepared to defend any theses regardless of whether they were true. Neither could he agree with the relativism of Isocrates, who admitted that rhetoric relies on conjecture rather than knowledge. Thus, although Plato took an interest in rhetoric, he had no respect for it. His was the first dissident voice to be raised in Greece against over-estimation of rhetoric. In his arguments Plato did not question the artistic values of rhetoric, but he attempted to demonstrate how rhetoric threatened knowledge and ethics. He maintained that the ability to distinguish between truth and falsehood, between good and evil, was more necessary to the orator than acquaintance with the rules of speech-making. In other words, the orator stands in greater need of philosophy than of rhetoric, and it is the *perfect philosopher* who is the perfect orator.

5. ARISTOTLE. The attitude of Aristotle was different again. Unlike Plato, he did not condemn rhetoric and did not argue against it. Instead, he investigated the value of its particular assertions, prescriptions and rules. He made a compilation of those that were true and put this into a manual of rhetoric. It is possible that an earlier manual had been compiled by Polus, a pupil of Gorgias, but Aristotle's *Rhetoric* is the oldest preserved manual on the subject: it is the oldest and is, in its way, still unsurpassed.

Aristotle regarded oratory as an art; not an art for art's sake, but one having a definite aim: to act on people. It is, however, difficult to attain this end, because it depends not only on the orator, but also on the people he is addressing, and, therefore, the rules of rhetoric cannot be universal or necessary. Nevertheless, rhetoric has at its disposal some rules based on rational principles. People are convinced not by being spellbound, but by means of arguments and the skill with which arguments are used. Logic is the most important tool of oratory and it is the *perfect logician* who is the perfect orator.

Rhetoric depends less on ethics than on logic. Aristotle opposed Plato by arguing that moral considerations were the purpose of ethics, not of rhetoric. Rhetoric can and should serve the good, but it achieves this by emphasizing effective arguments rather than moral aims. The business of rhetoric is to ensure that the speech is persuasive, and the business of ethics to ensure that it is exalted. Aristotle used a similar approach in establishing the relationship between rhetoric and aesthetics: beauty cannot be the aim of oratory, since this aim is persuasion. Unlike Gorgias and Isocrates, he did not regard oratory as a fine art; however, it was in his *Rhetoric* that he included the theory of beautiful style, because, while beauty is not the aim of rhetoric, it is one of its means.

6. THEOPHRASTUS. All these conceptions of rhetoric (by Gorgias, Isocrates, Plato and Aristotle) were formulated in the classical era. The Hellenistic and Roman epochs, having retained the Greek interest in rhetoric, inherited and added to them. This interest was particularly keen in the School of Aristotle. From the surviving fragments written by Aristotle's brilliant pupil Theophrastus, and particularly from his treatise *On Style*, we know that he emphasized the musical values of speech. He was convinced that "beautiful words" which furnish pleasant aural sensations and evoke pleasing associations make a stronger appeal to the listeners' imagination. One could perhaps say of him that he believed the *perfect musician* to be the perfect orator.

Theophrastus' new device was to advise the orator to share his task with the listener: the orator has to suggest ideas, while the listener has to develop them. Theophrastus regarded the listener and the spectator from a very modern standpoint as one who co-operates with the orator and who is the co-author of a work of art.

7. TYPES OF ORATORY. From the time of Aristotle the writers used to tally the *virtues* of oratory. Theophrastus devoted a special treatise to them, which however has not survived. Hermogenes enumerated seven virtues: clarity, grandeur, beauty, energy, suiting mood, truth and suggestiveness. This was one of those theories having a general aesthetic significance which, however, arose within the specialized study of rhetoric.

Rhetoric also compiled the elements of oratory, and the types of oratory: it juxtaposed political and legal speeches, encouraging ("protreptics") and discouraging speeches ("apotreptics"). But it devoted the greatest attention, particularly in Rome, to the classification and compilation of rhetoric styles. The three most quoted styles, the analysis of which was ascribed to Theophrastus, were the sublime, the medium and the humble, or, in Ciceronian terminology, the serious style (*grave*), the moderate (*medium*) and the simple (*tenue*). Quintilian distinguished between *genus grande, subtile* and *floridum*. A later Roman rhetorician, Cornificius (c. 300 A.D.), distinguished *tria genera orationis*: *grave*, *mediocre* and *attenuatum*. Fortunatianus (c. 300 A.D.) called the first type *amplum*, *grande* or *sublime*, the second type *moderatum* or *medium*, the third *tenue* or *subtile*. There were many such classifications but they all resembled each other.

Cicero argued that there can be no single "universal type of oratory" fit for all subjects, listeners and times. Account must be taken of the audience (whether the listeners are the senate, the people or the judges), especially of the size of the audience, but also it must be taken of the speaker, of whether he speaks in time of war or of peace, during a ceremony or a holiday, whether the speech examines a case (*deliberatio*), presents an argument, apportions, praise or blame. Listeners' tastes vary and even depend on social status. Horace wrote that "those who own a stable, claim noble descent and possess a fortune will not present a wreath to a speaker who flatters the taste of bean sellers and chestnut buyers".

8. ASIANISM AND ATTICISM. Two contrasting styles, in particular, were distinguished in the Hellenistic era. They were called Asianism and Atticism. The first one was rich, flowery, loaded with effects and ornaments. It corresponded to the modern "baroque" style. To some extent it developed under the influence of the East, as the name it was given indicates. This name had a pejorative connotation to many Greek ears. Its opponents supported Atticism, a simpler, "classical" style, which was deemed to be the only style conforming to tradition and the spirit of the nation, although in fact examples of the rich style could also be found in the speeches of famous classical orators. The antagonism between these two styles was also apparent in poetics, but it was rhetoric that it affected most powerfully. There it was not merely a question of distinguishing between two styles, but also of deciding which was the more excellent. In the Hellenistic era, when the Greeks intermingled with the peoples of the East, the success of Asianism followed naturally, although Atticism too had conserved its supporters. At the turn of the second century one of these was Hermagoras of Temnos, a famous teacher of rhetoric, who for a time swung the balance in favour of Atticism. He condemned the reliance of the Asianists on intuition, and called for organized studies of rhetoric. He devised a *system* of rhetoric based on classical orators and theoreticians, particularly Aristotle. Because this system was based on school examples and tended to stabilize forms and laid stress on rules, it has been called by some historians the "scholastic" system. According to it, the best orator was the one who had most know-how, *savoir faire*.

9. CICERO. In Rome at least partial support for Asianism came from Cicero, who stood at the summit of Roman oratory and theory of oratory. He studied oratory in Greece and moulded himself on Greek tradition, but he owed a great deal to his native talent. His style was one of moderate Asianism and both his speeches and treatises on rhetoric demonstrate this. He wrote as many as six treatises on rhetoric, of which the most important are *De oratore* (55 B.C.) and the later *Orator ad Brutum* (46 B.C.). They had to be polemical in character because Atticism

too had distinguished supporters in Rome in the persons of Caesar and Brutus. Cicero injected new life into rhetoric, which was becoming sterile and scholastic. For one who attained pinnacles of success and fame through his oratory, it was something more than an art and a profession, it was a way of life. And it was a matter of moral concern, since an orator pronounces upon justice, truth, right and goodness All these things, which are of the greatest importance in a man's life, fall within the orator's sphere of activity. Cicero's position may be described thus: the perfect orator is the perfect human being.

Cicero regarded oratory as an art. The speaker resembles the poet, and their activities differ only in details, as the poet has to pay more attention to rhythm while the orator is concerned with the choice of words. Nevertheless, Cicero valued oratory more highly than poetry because poetry thrives on fictions and allows itself liberties (*licentia*). The poet merely wishes to please, while the orator wishes to demonstrate the truth. For Cicero the charms of poetry took second place to oratory, in which he found the greatest excellence, true philosophy, true morality and the highest art.

This admiration for oratory and the cult of rhetoric survived for some time after Cicero. Tacitus assigned to oratory, together with history, the highest place among the arts. Quintilian, the last great representative of Roman oratory* and the author of *De institutione oratoria*, spoke of oratory in superlatives and saw it as the highest and the all-embracing goal of education. His work, which codified the rules of oratory and gathered them into a system, marked the pinnacle of "scholastic" rhetoric.

It is noteworthy that Quintilian did not regard oratory as a "poietic" (productive), but as a "practical" activity, such as the dance, which leaves nothing behind it and exhausts itself in the process of being performed. It thus became a sort of art for art's sake. Mesmerized by the splendid techniques which rhetoric had developed during the centuries, later rhetoricians lost sight of the ends for which they had been devised.

The intensive cultivation of rhetoric led to the evolution during the Hellenistic era of numerous concepts, categories, and distinctions, some of which came to be applied to the theory of art in general. This period saw the formulation of the concept of composition (*compositio*) or structure (*structura*); it distinguished between the beauty of parts (*in singulis*) and of wholes (*in coniunctis*); it stressed a variety of aesthetic values, such as *latinitas, decorum, nitor* or *splendor* (in Sulpicius Victor), *copia* (plenitude) and *bonitas* (in Fortunatianus), *elegantia* and *dignitas* (in Cornificius).

10. THE ECLIPSE OF RHETORIC. Rome provided as good a stage for oratory as Greece. The *Lex Cincia* forbade advocates to charge fees so that their profession became honorary, thus further increasing its popularity. Orators were required

---

* J. Cousin, *Études sur Quintilien*, two vols. (1936).

in courts all over the Empire and their status was further raised by the fact that they were men of wide education. In the Rome of the Caesars oratory was the only organized higher study, foreshadowing later faculties of philosophy. It included, among other subjects, the study of law and the study of literature. During the Empire public teachers of rhetoric were called "Sophists", a designation similar to that of professor. The chairs of rhetoric were of two types: political rhetoric and sophist rhetoric, that is, practical and theoretical rhetoric. Though in this period rhetoric flourished, it was not marked by any progress. It acquired stability, became a kind of scholasticism and produced works of a merely compilatory character. Hermogenes of Tarsus, who lived under Marcus Aurelius, was the last to gain fame in Roman rhetoric; his role was that of historian and editor.

The history of rhetoric ends with the close of antiquity. Subsequent ages had nothing substantial to contribute. It remained a characteristic feature of antiquity, during which it had unfolded and realized all its possibilities. Among the ancients it was the subject of the most disparate evaluations from outright condemnation, as in Plato, to elevation above all human activities and works, as in Cicero. It assumed all styles ranging from classical Atticism to baroque Asianism and all interpretations from the purely ethical to the purely formal. It appeared as a branch of poetics, of ethics, of logic and of philosophy.

Later ages questioned virtually the whole of its basis, or more precisely, broke it up into sections and relegated these to different disciplines. What in rhetoric concerned persuasion was transferred to logic, what concerned argument to philosophy, and what concerned ornamentation to the theory of literature. Later ages ceased to see rhetoric as the proper place for the discussion of philosophy, morality, art and poetry, finding a better place for such discussions elsewhere. Those later ages distinguished the means whereby speech persuades and the means whereby it gratifies. These had not been sufficiently distinguished in antiquity. The means to gratify became a problem in aesthetics. Rhetoric was deprived of its tasks so thoroughly that nothing of it remained. Thus Renan could say that rhetoric was a mistake of the Greeks, and even their only mistake.

10. The Aesthetics of the Plastic Arts

(a) THE PLASTIC ARTS IN HELLENISTIC TIMES

1. CLASSICAL ART AND HELLENISTIC ART. Hellenistic art differed from classical art in subject-matter. It included the architecture of palaces, theatres, baths and stadiums but also religious art. The conquests of Alexander the Great were responsible for the creation of many new cities, and town planning emerged as an art. Portraits, landscapes, genre-painting and decorative compositions became the main types of painting. Among the social classes which had acquired huge fortunes and

lived in ostentatious luxury there arose a demand for decorative utensils, and artistic industry now gained greater importance.

It is more significant, however, that Hellenistic art, which could still draw upon the achievements made toward the end of the classical era, was now the expression of a different taste and its style was no longer classical. Sculptors imitated the energy and pathos of Scopas, the elaborate shapes and emotional force of Praxiteles and the illusionism and virtuosity of Lysippus. Painters acknowledged their affinity with the sophisticated proportions, colour schemes and portraiture of Apelles.

The novelty of Hellenistic art consisted primarily in its baroque quality, to use a modern term. It aimed at richness and monumentality, and at dynamism, pathos and expressiveness. The former qualities were found particularly in architecture, the latter chiefly in sculpture. The huge altar of Zeus and Hera in Pergamum (second century B.C.) and the melodramatic Laokoon (first century B.C.) are particularly well-known and typical monuments of Hellenistic baroque.

Symptomatic of the evolution of art from classicism to baroque was the disappearance of the Doric order, which had been so characteristic of the previous era, and the proliferation of the Ionic order, which became the architectural signature of the new era. At the turn of the third century the representative of the Ionic order was Hermogenes, who influenced the theory of art as well as art itself. Another order, called "Corinthian", evolved as a variant of the Ionic order and was even further removed from the Doric order. This did not occur, however, until the second half of the Hellenistic era. The first great building in Corinthian style was the second-century A.D. Olimpeion in Athens.

The novelty of Hellenistic art also lay in its variety of subject-matter and of types and styles. This was in marked contrast to the canonical, homogeneous art of the classical era. Consonant modern terminology may not only describe Hellenistic art as baroque but also as mannerism, as academic art, and even as rococo. Rococo qualities may be found, for instance, in the terracotta figurines of Tanagra. Hellenistic art produced both extremely naturalistic works and works completely devoid of realism. It demanded monumental art and at the same time had a weakness for bric-a-brac. Hellenistic art searched for new forms, but on occasion turned back toward classicism, even archaism. This happened in Pergamum in the middle of the first century B.C. The art of Alexandria was typically eclectic. This was a natural parallel to the Hellenistic *koine* in the Greek language.

The variety of Hellenistic art was not merely due to the long duration of the period; even in one single generation the large territory where Hellenistic art was found embraced most varied themes, forms and artistic movements. Art historians have often made invidious comparisons between classical and Hellenistic art, treating the latter as though it were inferior or even regarding it as a symptom of artistic decadence. In reality it was not a poorer version of classical art, but an art different from classicism, employing other means and having other aims. It did not achieve the perfection of classical art, but it showed achievements of which classical art could not boast.

2. ROMAN ARCHITECTURE. Already in the period of the Republic the Romans had revealed certain rather negative attitudes toward art, notably a lack of a deeper creative instinct, a readiness to rely on the achievements of others in art, eclecticism and utilitarianism. These symptoms were also characteristic of the Empire, but nevertheless certain positive features appeared. At the same time great opportunities arose, through which Roman art became more than a continuation of Hellenistic art and undertook new tasks, adopted new forms and made new achievements. Under the Republic art was poor compared with the art of the Diadochi states, but under the Caesars it already occupied a dominant position. In certain works it has never since been rivalled. Religious cults, from which Greek art had sprung, disappeared almost completely in Rome. Wars, triumphs and the desire for greatness and legends gave rise to new themes and artistic forms. Art was patronized by the imperial court as well as for a time during the first century by the landed aristocracy. It was then patronized by the middle classes under the Antonines in the second century and finally by the new military aristocracy in the third century.

The individuality and greatness of Rome were revealed primarily in its architecture, whose claim to distinction lies in the interiors rather than the façades, in civic buildings and private dwellings rather than in temples, and in techniques rather than architectonic forms. Basically, it retained Greek forms, giving prominence, however, to the Corinthian order, which was the most decorative of all. Its technical solutions were, however, bold and original. Arches, vaults and cupolas, now technically mastered as never before, made it possible for large areas to be covered, and the use of concrete enormously widened the scope of building. It was this fact that led Wickhoff to say that, in comparison with the Roman, Greek architecture was "child's play". Barrel vaults, which were already used in the days of the Republic, reached huge dimensions in such buildings as Domitian's palace on the Palatine (late first century A.D.) or Caracalla's Baths (third century A.D.). The new techniques made possible the construction of cupola-type buildings, beginning with the Pantheon, built in Hadrian's reign, in which the problems of constructing a cupola over a circular area were solved.

Thematically, Roman architecture was more varied than Greek architecture and has left us huge palaces (such as Diocletian's in Split) and small town and suburban villas; many-storied houses ranged in blocks and terraces (particularly at Ostia); forums, baths, colonnades, libraries, basilicas and theatres, ranging from such delicate constructions as the theatre at Orange to huge ones such as the Coliseum in Rome (80 A.D.). The Romans gave their theatres a new shape, different from that of Greek theatres. Although temples did not play the same role as they had in Greece, the Romans constructed some refined specimens, such as the Maison Carrée at Nîmes (16 A.D.) and the little round temple at Tivoli. The architecture of Rome included also such monumental tombs as those of Cecilia Metella and

Hadrian as well as monotonous but imposing triumphal arches. Furthermore, such utilitarian buildings in Rome as bridges and aqueducts, based on the arch, were, by their simplicity, purposefulness and monumentality, not insignificant works of art.

Naturally enough, during a period of over three centuries from the reign of Augustus to Constantine the Great, Roman art was subject to various fashions and changes. At certain times, for example under Hadrian, it had the characteristics of a state art, at others it came under oriental influences and adopted baroque pathos or a hieratic religious character. Over the huge territories of the Empire it displayed significant local features. In the south of France it was delicate and classical, in Asia Minor, in Palmyra and Baalbeck in flourishing first-century Syria, it was baroque and fused with oriental elements. However, both in general character and in particular forms, in the basic outlines of triumphal arches, theatres or basilicas, it remained remarkably constant and the weight of tradition proved stronger than the desire for change.

3. ROMAN PLASTIC ARTS. Roman sculpture was less independent than Roman architecture. It copied Greek statues and repeated their themes extensively, but, nevertheless, it had its own achievements. In realistic portraiture it surpassed anything that had been produced hitherto. The statue of Marcus Aurelius became the prototype of all subsequent equestran statues. It developed figurative bas-relief, particularly group scenes in the special "continuous style", which made it possible to depict simultaneously complex narratives, wars, conquests and triumphs. In contrast to Greek sculptors, the Romans concentrated primarily on bas-relief and, again unlike the Greeks, they put all their efforts into mastering drapery rather than the naked body. Their works had realistic features, but these were mingled in a characteristic way with conventional designs and formalized patterns.

The situation of painting was analogous. It was almost wholly devoted to decoration but in this respect was of high quality. Wall frescoes displayed great variety, as we can see at Pompeii. Mosaics enjoyed considerable vogue in Rome and were among the notable triumphs of Roman art. Superb reproductions in mosaic of animals and still-life subject vied with decorative mosaics. The artistic industry throve and never before had there been such vast supplies of gems and cameos.

The art of Hellenism and of the Roman Empire expressed an artistic attitude different from that of classical art in Greece and it prompted different aesthetic theories, favouring pluralism, freedom, originality, novelty, imagination and feeling.

4. VARIETY IN HELLENISTIC ART AND AESTHETICS. In contrast to the uniformity of classical art and culture, Hellenistic art and culture displayed diverse trends, as could scarcely have been otherwise during an age which lasted so long and over territories which were so vast and included so many centres. There were at least three dualities.

A. Baroque versus Romantic art. With the passage of centuries Hellenistic art moved increasingly further away from classical art in two different directions.

It moved towards greater richness, dynamism, fullness and fantasy and also towards an intensification of spiritual, emotional, irrational and transcendental elements. This duality made its appearance in art no less than in poetry. It appeared not only in the work of artists, but also in the theories of aestheticians. The aesthetics of Philostratus corresponded to the first type and championed sensuous baroque, while the aesthetics of Dion of Prusa supported spiritualist romanticism.

B. Attic versus Roman art.* In Hellenistic times there existed, chiefly in the original Greek territories, a conservative movement whose object was to preserve the old classical forms of art, i.e., forms that were harmonious, static, organic and yet idealized. Because of its historical sources and its geographical location, historians have designated this art "Attic". But another movement developed simultaneously which sought to break these age-old conventions and bring about greater liveliness and naturalness, and which favoured impressionism, the picturesque and the abandonment of restraints in composition. Earlier historians pointed to Alexandria as the centre of this art and, to distinguish it from Attic art, called it Alexandrian. However, it later came to be accepted that these new trends originated in Rome. This would explain why this art displayed clarity as well as freedom and impressionism. Just as there were two arts in the Hellenistic era, so also were there two aesthetics: the Attic and the Roman.

C. The art of Europe and the art of the East.† On several occasions ancient Greece came in contact with the art of the East and was influenced by it. In the earlier period it drew on Egyptian art and, in the days of Alexander and of the Diadochi, on Asiatic art. The Roman Empire, which stretched from Europe into Asia, provided a meeting ground for two different arts, which had not only different forms, but also different aesthetic bases. The art of Asia was characterized by greater spirituality and also by schematicism, both of which were alien to Greece. Asian art relied on the principle of rhythm as much as Greek art relied on organic structure. It did not fuse with Graeco-Roman art and did not influence it. As excavations have shown, particularly at Dura-Europos on the Euphrates, in some places the two kinds of art existed side by side. Asian art was cultivated by the Parthians and echoed the art of the Persians and perhaps even of more distant peoples of Asia. Since it did not influence Graeco-Roman art, it had no influence either on Greek or Roman aesthetics and there is no trace of it in any Hellenistic work on aesthetics. Nevertheless, it held the key to the future. It came to occupy a dominant position in the Christian era, in the Eastern Church and in Byzantium, and in the aesthetics of these periods.

---

* E. Strong, *Art in Ancient Rome,* two vols. (1929). E. A. Swift, *Roman Sources of Christian Art* (1951). Ch. R. Morey, *Early Christian Art* (1953).

† J. Strzygowski, *Orient oder Rom* (1901). A. Ainalov, *Ellenisticheskiye osnovy visantyiskogo iskusstva* (1900). J. H. Breadstead, *Oriental Forerunners of Byzantine Painting* (1924). F. Cumont, *Les fouilles de Doura-Europos*. M. Rostovtzeff, "Dura and the Problem of Parthian Art", *Yale Classical Studies,* V (1934). *Dura-Europos and its Art* (1938).

(b) THEORY OF ARCHITECTURE

1. THE ANCIENTS ON ARCHITECTURE. The ancients wrote a great deal about architecture. This applied particularly to architects themselves, especially the eminent and famous ones, who enjoyed describing the buildings they had raised. Thus Theodorus wrote about the temple of Hera on Samos, Chersiphron and Metagenes about the temple of Artemis at Ephesus, Ictinus and Carpion about the Athenian Parthenon, Hermogenes about the temple of Artemis in Magnesia, Pytheos and Satyrus about the Mausoleum in Halicarnassus. The same can be said about a great many others. We know this chiefly through Vitruvius. This literature, which had its origins in the classical era, consisted primarily of descriptions of buildings, but at least some of them must have included remarks of a more general, aesthetic character.

Apart from these descriptive works, there were also systematic textbooks of architecture, such as Philon's *On the Proportions of Sacred Buildings* (*De aedium sacrarum symmetriis*) and Silenus' *On the Proportions of Corinthian Buildings* (*De symmetriis Corinthiis*). Architects were in the habit of publishing their *praecepta symmetriarum*, that is, instructions for perfect proportions. The names of some authors of such works have survived: Nexaris, Theocides, Demophilus, Pollis, Leonidas, Silanion, Melampus, Sarnacus and Euphranor. These texts and the calculations they contained had certain points in common with the calculations of sculptors and painters because architectural proportions were derived in part from the proportions of the human body.

2. VITRUVIUS. None of these treatises on architecture has survived. All we have is the later *Ten Books on Architecture*, written in the first century A.D. by the Roman Marcus Vitruvius Pollion. This, the only fully extant ancient work on architecture, is, however, copious, inclusive, encyclopaedic and ranges over historical and aesthetic problems as well as technical questions. It is a late work, but is thereby the more informative; it is derivative and selective, but, as a result, it is all the more representative of the Hellenist conception of art. In his introduction to Book VII, Vitruvius lists previous writer-architects and declares that his Book contains everything from their works that was useful. Vitruvius* was primarily a practising engineer, but he also had a general liberal education, quoted freely from Lucretius and Cicero and took an interest in aesthetics. He may therefore be considered as a reliable authority on the aesthetics of ancient architecture.

3. DIVISION OF ARCHITECTURE. What the ancients called "architecture" actually consisted of the sum total of technical knowledge which included building (*aedificatio*), clock-making (*gnomonice*), the construction of machines (*machinatio*) and the building of ships (in Vitruvius' work only this last is missing). Building was divided into private and public, and the latter was in turn divided into buildings which served defence (*defensio*), worship (*religio*) and the requirements of public

---

* G. K. Lukomski, *I maestri della architettura classica da Vitruvio allo Scamozzi*, Milano 1933.

life (*opportunitas*). Tombs as well as temples and altars were included among structures of a religious character, while the *opportunitas* category included ports, squares with depots and basilicas, offices, conference halls, prisons, granaries, arsenals, theatres, amphitheatres, odeons, stadiums, hippodromes, gymnasiums, palaestras, baths, wells, cisterns and aqueducts. All this variety was a phenomenon characteristic of Hellenistico-Roman times in contrast to the early Greek period when architecture was in practice confined to temples.

4. THE ARCHITECT'S EDUCATION. Following ancient tradition, Virtruvius meant by "architecture" not so much the architect's tangible achievement, but rather the craft, skill and knowledge which enabled him to construct buildings. This consisted of the practical knowledge (*fabrica*) required by most building workers (*fabritektones*), and also of the purely theoretical knowledge (*ratiocinatio*) required by the foreman. The Greek word for "foreman" (*architekton*) has given the whole art of architecture its name.

According to an ancient opinion going back to Aristotle and even the Sophists, anybody practising an art should possess three things: inborn abilities (*natura*), knowledge (*doctrina*) and experience (*usus*). This applied also to architects, and the knowledge that Vitruvius demanded from them was extraordinarily extensive. They should not only have a thorough grasp of matters concerned strictly with building, but also of arithmetic, optics, history (necessary for the appreciation of architectural forms), medicine (to ensure that the buildings were hygienic), law, music (to ensure that the buildings had good acoustics), astronomy and geography (to ensure an adequate water supply to the site of the building). They had, moreover, to have a philosophical training because they had to be men of character and this could only be moulded by philosophy. "No work can come into being without faith and purity of aims".

An architect then, like any other technician, was expected to have both ability (*ingenium*) and training (*disciplina*), both practical knowledge (*opus*) and theoretical knowledge (*ratiocinatio*), both the knowledge which learned men in general possess (*commune cum omnibus doctis*) and personal experience. Thus, ancient theoreticians demanded considerable learning from an architect. Yet, in spite of this, they did not choose to include architecture among the liberal arts. Although he was a humanist, Cicero was typical of his age and regarded architects as ordinary *opifices*, that is labourers, as opposed to men of learning, *studiis excellentes*.

These details do not appear to have any connection with aesthetics and yet they show that the fine arts were linked with questions of technique and learning.

5. ELEMENTS OF ARCHITECTURAL COMPOSITION. According to Vitruvius, the architect had to make sure not only that his buildings had stability (*firmitas*) and purpose, that is usefulness (*utilitas*), but also beauty (*venustas*).[1] For this reason his arguments were aesthetic in character as well as technical. His aesthetic views are particularly noticeable in his discussion of architectural composition.

He distinguished as many as six elements of architectural construction:[2] *ordinatio*, *dispositio*, *symmetria*, *eurythmia*, *decor* and *distributio*. These terms have no precise equivalents in modern architectural theory; *ordinatio* may be tentatively rendered as "order", *dispositio* as "arrangement" (or rather, "proper arrangement"), *decor* as "suitability", *distributio* as the "economy" of a building. We have to retain the original Greek terms of *symmetria* and eurhythmy because no modern term conveys their special meaning. Vitruvius and other Romans also failed to find suitable Latin equivalents. *Non habet Latinum nomen symmetria*, writes Pliny. These two concepts had a general aesthetic application, whereas the remaining four were concerned specifically with architecture.

6. PROPORTION AND DISPOSITION. These six terms have for centuries caused historians and theorists of architecture the greatest difficulties. They form the most complete list of its kind in antiquity, not only in relation to architecture, but also to other arts. Yet the terms are ambiguous, the concepts lack precision and the definitions are muddled. We do not know whether Vitruvius devised this list, or whether it was in general use and merely accepted by him. It seems that the answer lies somewhere between these possibilities: the particular elements of good architecture were generally known. *Ordinatio* and *dispositio* were used in building technique, *distributio* in economics, *decor* in general philosophy and *symmetria* and *eurythmia* in aesthetics. What Vitruvius did was to combine them in one list. Such a compilation could not avoid conceptual inconsistencies, but rather than stress them the historian will do better to concentrate on what is valuable in the ideas bequeathed by Vitruvius.

A. By order (*ordinatio*) Vitruvius meant "a fully restrained arrangement of the particular parts of a building and the fixing of the proportions of the whole work". He meant by this a quantitative, a numerical relation of parts, but he also meant, though he did not say so clearly, arrangement and proportions which would ensure the building's strength and utility. In other words, he was concerned with proportions that would be suited to the building's utility but not to its visual effect.

B. By arrangement (*dispositio*) Vitruvius meant "the proper siting of a building's parts in such a way as to give it distinction and quality". This notion supplemented "order". It was concerned with the qualitative arrangement of the elements of projection and elevation, just as order was concerned with the quantitative arrangement. It, too, was a matter of suitability for the utility of the building.

C. The economy of a building (its *distributio*) was a means of ensuring that its shape was economical and its cost low, that it would be planned to fit the conditions of the site, the resources available and the demands of the commission. This element must certainly have been concerned exclusively with the building's utility and have had nothing to do with beauty and aesthetics. If it was a manifestation of beauty, then it was so only in the wide sense of decorousness employed in antiquity, but not in the sense of beauty directly perceived. The latter was covered by Vitruvius' three remaining elements.

7. SYMMETRIA AND EURHYTHMY. *D.* By *symmetria* the ancients meant a harmonious arrangement of parts, and this was the most fundamental concept of their aesthetics. It was not concerned with power or utility but with beauty. It was in this sense that Vitruvius employed the term. He said that "*symmetria* is the harmonious agreement arising out of the parts of the work itself". It was firstly an objective beauty that had its source in the building itself and not in the spectator's attitude. Secondly, it depended on rigid, mathematical proportion capable of being calculated on the basis of the "module", that is, the unit of measurement. The measurements of a whole temple could be worked out from the thickness of a column or a triglyph, just as Greek sculptors calculated the measurements of an ideally built man from the size of the face, a foot or a finger.

E. On the other hand, the ancients applied the term *eurythmia* to an arrangement of parts which, even if it did not contain objective *symmetria*, yet aroused a pleasant sensation in the spectator. The term took into account not only the requirements of beautiful things, but also the requirements of the spectator, and the proportions were chosen not only for their rightness, but for their capacity to appear and feel right to the spectator. They not only had to be ideal, they had to appear ideal. Vitruvius applied this panaesthetic concept to architecture. His definition was as follows: "Eurhythmy depends on the beautiful (*venusta*) shape (*species*) of the building and on the proper (*commodus*) appearance (*aspectus*) achieved by the arrangement (*compositio*) of its individual parts". It was thus a definition in terms of *species* and *aspectus*, which mean "shape" and "prospect" and represent the strictly visual element in architecture. The same applied to *venustas*, which also appears in the definition.

8. SUITABILITY AND ECONOMY. *F.* Vitruvius defined *decor* as *emendatus operis aspectus probatis rebus compositi cum auctoritate*, which may be translated as "the faultless appearance of a work which is achieved when the work is composed of parts that have stood the test of time and arouse respect". The term *decor* here meant the same as its adjectival form *decorum* employed by the Stoics and may be best translated as "suitability". At that time the term had not acquired its modern meaning and had nothing to do with decoration and ornamentation. Vitruvius argued that, in deciding whether or not a building was suitable, three considerations were involved: nature, tradition (*statio*) and custom (*consuetudo*). Nature itself decided for example what lighting is suitable: it demands that bedrooms should be facing south. But in more instances a building's suitability depends on human conventions. Thus tradition demands that Athene and Ares should have Doric temples, Aphrodite and the nymphs Corinthian temples, and Hera and Dionysus Ionic temples, since only these forms are considered suitable. Custom also demands that splendid interiors should be approached through ornamental vestibules and forbids the mixing of Doric and Ionian styles.

We can therefore discern an order and a deeper meaning in the six elements of architectural composition enumerated by Vitruvius. The first three are concerned with suitability and utility (but only indirectly, if at all, with beauty), and the last three are concerned exclusively with beauty. *Symmetria* in particular deals with the objective conditioning of beauty, eurhythmy with its psychological conditioning and *decor* with its social conditioning.

9. THE CONCEPTUAL APPARATUS OF VITRUVIUS. To a great extent Vitruvius' analysis of architecture lay within the technical field of Hellenistic aesthetics, as opposed to the humanist standpoint adopted by contemporary philosophers, poets, rhetoricians, and even painters and sculptors. In architecture, however, the problems were somewhat different. There was no dispute over whether form or content should take precedence, whereas both the social and optical problems of aesthetics were prominent.

The historian is interested not only in this group of six main concepts listed by Vitruvius, but also in the more numerous and, in some cases, even more general concepts which helped Vitruvius to define the six and without which a full picture of the conceptual apparatus of Hellenistic aesthetics cannot be gained. The most important of these denoted artistic virtues and values. If we are to ignore technical virtues such as power and utility, we are still left with three groups: namely optical, mathematical and social virtues.

The first group included concepts denoting that which pleases the eye, above all the two concepts of *aspectus* and *species* (prospect and shape), both essential to the aesthetics of the visual arts. An even more general concept denoting visual beauty was *venustas* (*symmetria* belonged to a different group), while *elegantia* was applied to a more precious type of visual beauty. In this group we may also include another concept used by Vitruvius, namely *effectus*, that is, the effect of a work on man.

The second group included the concepts of relation, number and measure, which decided of the success and the beauty of a work. The foremost concept was *proportio* and others included *commodulatio* (i.e., the employment of a single module, a single measure), *consensus membrorum* (agreement of parts among themselves), *convenientia* (suitability of parts), *compositio* (order), *conlocatio* (disposition) and *commoditas* (accordance). All the terms of this series are related, first through the common prefix *con-* (together). Some (*commodulatio, commoditas*) are derived from *modus*, one of whose meanings—and the meaning applied to it in architectural theory—was "measure". Just as the first group covered sensory qualities, so the second group dealt with rational ones. This duality is quite natural. Ancient theoreticians were aware that architecture pleases either because it gives the spectator direct, sensuous and visual satisfaction or because the spectator recognizes in it proper measures and successful solutions.

Vitruvius had yet a third group of concepts. These had a social character and pointed to the social conditioning of good architecture. They included such concepts as *probatio* (probation) and *auctoritas* (general approval). Just as the first group served mainly to define eurhythmy and the second to define *symmetria*, so this third group served to define the suitability and, to some extent, the economy of architecture.

Vitruvius applied his concepts to architecture, but the majority of them also had a wider application. *Mutatis mutandis*, the ancients applied them to sculpture and painting and even to music and rhetoric. Vitruvius himself drew parallels between architectural and rhetorical styles. In his chapter on harmony he compared architecture with music. He not only sought an analogy between architecture and other arts, but also with nature. He would compare works of architecture with human bodies and architectural styles with human forms: he regarded the Doric style as having masculine proportions (*virilis*), the Ionic as having womanly proportions (*muliebris*), and the Corinthian as having maidenly proportions (*virginalis*).

10. ARCHITECTURE AND THE HUMAN BODY. The similarity which Vitruvius discerned between architecture (and art as a whole) and nature, especially the human body, was something more than an analogy. It amounted to a dependence, because nature is a model for art.[3] This is so not only for painting or sculpture, but also for architecture, since we are concerned in architecture not with a model of appearances but one of proportions and structure. He wrote that in architecture "*symmetria* and good proportions should be strictly based upon the proportions of a well-built man". He assumed that all "the parts of the human body have fixed proportions" and insisted that "similarly the parts of a temple should have the most suitable proportions". "Since nature has so contrived the human body that its parts are proportional in relation to the whole frame, the principle of the ancients that buildings should also exhibit a relation between the parts and the whole appears just".

11. THE TRIUMPH OF EURHYTHMY. Among the problems raised by Vitruvius, the relation between *symmetria* and eurhythmy* seems particularly important for aesthetics in general. All the ancient theoreticians, no less than artists, admired *symmetria*, that is, geometric forms and arithmetical proportions, in which they saw perfection, beauty and the test of good art. They were, however, worried by the question of whether deviations from *symmetria* should be allowed in order to adjust forms and proportions to the needs of the spectator and his eyes, and in order to counteract the distortions of perspective. During the classical period this was for architects chiefly a practical question of how to build. Evidence from ruins suggests that they sometimes departed from *symmetria*.† In so doing, they accorded with the ideas of certain contemporary philosophers such as Democritus and Socrates, but displeased others, particularly Plato.

We have no direct knowledge of what classical theoreticians of architecture thought of these problems because their works have perished. Only in Vitruvius' *Ten Books* do we find an explicit statement on the attitude of the ancient theoret-

---

* J. A. Jolles, *Vitruvs Ästhetik*, Diss. (Freiburg, 1906).
† See above, p. 63 ff.

icians, and this reveals that Vitruvius cherished a Pythagoreo-Platonic admiration for mathematical forms and proportions. He presented the proportions of temples and theatres, of whole buildings and their details in numerical terms, and demonstrated mathematical methods of drawing diagrams, both of whole façades and of the helices of capitals and the depths of flutes in columns. He inherited these methods and these numbers from the tradition and practice of architects. He was not only a spokesman for the ideas of his own epoch, but also of an older tradition. From his books a historian can glean detailed information about earlier Greek canons.

Yet this advocate of *symmetria* also argued in favour of departing from it when the peculiarities of human sight so demanded and when there was a danger that *symmetria* would appear to the spectator as an absence of *symmetria*. Here too Vitruvius reverted to the practice and tradition of architects who tilted outward columns inwards, reinforcing them and placing them more closely together, and who introduced irregularities into buildings precisely in order to make them appear regular.

Vitruvius writes that, in order to create an impression of *symmetria*, one must in one place add (*adiectiones*) to the true *symmetria* and in another take away from it (*detractiones*). To make *symmetria* appear as what it truly is one must introduce into it certain deviations and attenuations (*temperaturae*).[4] Often such changes are unnecessary, namely, when we are able to view a thing clearly at close quarters, but at other times they cannot be avoided, particularly when the object under observation is placed high and at a distance. Vitruvius comments that "the higher the eye has to penetrate, the more difficult it is to pierce the density of air, and therefore, being tired by the journey it has had to travel it supplies the senses with incorrect measurements. For this reason it is necessary to include correctives in the proportional measurements of parts". And in another place he writes: "The eye seeks a pleasing view; if we do not satisfy it by using proper proportions and supplying additional correctives of the modules by adding where something appears missing, we shall present the spectator with an unpleasant view lacking in charm".

Clearly relying on the individual experiences of architects, Vitruvius adds: "All the parts which have to be placed above the capitals of columns, namely architraves, friezes, cornices, tympana, gables and acroteria should be tilted one-twelfth of their length at the front, because if we were to stand facing the frontal façade and drew two straight lines from the eye, one to the apex of the building and the other to its lowest point, the line leading to the apex would appear longer. The longer the line leading to the upper parts of a building, the further these appear to recede... But if we tilt these parts forward, then they will give us the appearance of being straight".

Since he regarded both *symmetria* and eurhythmy as indispensable, Vitruvius took a middle position in the dispute of "*symmetria* versus eurhythmy". He applied both principles, although he placed more emphasis on eurhythmy. *Symmetria* as a principle of mathematical calculation was for him an irreplaceable basis for artistic composition, but eurhythmy he regarded as its corrective, its means of improvement. It was a higher plane of composition. Vitruvius was not here stating a new idea, for others before him had uttered similar opinions, but since these earlier works have perished he is perforce our best source of information. Moreover, in presenting his case, he uses such felicitous expressions as *adiectiones, detractiones* and *temperaturae*.

Vitruvius was not alone in his views. The works of other theorists of architecture of Hellenistico-Roman times have not survived, but we have contemporary statements by the first-century B.C. mathematician Geminus, the engineer Philon, and the fifth-century A.D. Neo-Platonic philosopher and scholar, Proclus on the need to modify *symmetria* in order to achieve eurhythmy.

Geminus[5] wrote: "That part of optics known as perspective is concerned with how buildings should be drawn. Because things do not appear as they really are, the purpose of the study of perspective is not to find out how to represent actual proportions, but how to render them as they appear to be. The architect's aim is to give his work a harmonious appearance and to find within the limits of possibility ways of counteracting optical illusions; he seeks not any real smoothness and harmony, but what appear to be so to the eye". Proclus expressed himself similarly concerning painting.[6] He wrote that perspective is a skill by means of which the artist can present phenomena in such a manner that in his painting they will not seem distorted by distance and height.

Heron drew an emphatic contrast between *symmetria*—that which is objectively (*kata ousian*) or truly (*kat' aletheian*) proportional—and *eurhythmia*—that which seems proportional to the eye (*pros ten opsin*). The idea of such an opposition was undoubtedly of earlier origin (and was referred to in a previous chapter when discussing the aesthetics of earlier centuries), but Heron is the first writer to state it in such precise terms. He came down on the side of *eurhythmia*, as was only natural in his age, and so bade artists to take account of optical illusions (*apatai*) when carving or building and take pains to make their works seem proportional to the observer even if they were not so really.[7]

Despite the original all-embracing objectivism of the ancients, the idea now appeared that the arts were designed for the eye or the ear and that therefore account should be taken of how the eye and the ear receive sensations. There was nobody like Plato to oppose this point and agreement on it was reached in Hellenistic times. Vitruvius' views on this question were authoritative and typical of his age.

12. VITRUVIUS AND HELLENISTIC ARCHITECTURE. It has been a matter of concern for historians that the proportions of perfect architecture given by Vitruvius do not fully agree with the measurements of ancient ruins. This discrepancy was noticed as early as the fifteenth century by L. B. Alberti. Vitruvius was familiar with and admired tradition, but classical architecture was not for him, as it is for us, something closed, something to be looked at with admiration but from a distance. On the

contrary, it was something very much alive. None the less, he was already separated from it by several centuries and he therefore wished to modernize it, to blend the old with the new.* However, tastes had changed and antagonism had grown up between the two orders which had once developed side by side. Vitruvius liked the Ionic style but thought the Doric style old-fashioned and wished to modernize it. With this in mind he toyed with the idea of various diastyles and sistyles. These, however, remained unrealized projects. He dreamt of a "correct and faultless style", the dream of an epigone. His book contains, on the one hand, information about classical architecture and, on the other, a selection of the ideas of a classicist. The former tells us about early ancient art and the latter, because his ideas were not unique but were representative of the later Hellenistic style, tells us about more recent art. This Hellenistic style had found earlier and perfect expression in the buildings and writings of Hermogenes, an architect working in Asia Minor in the second century B.C. Vitruvius modelled his ideas upon the work of Hermogenes and owed most to his opinions.

But Hellenistic taste was not uniform. Using later terminology, we may say that is was partly baroque and partly classicist, though not classical. Vitruvius supported the classicist movement of his times and opposed the baroque. He criticized baroque buildings in the following terms: "Columns are being replaced by reeds, conchs with dressed-up flowers replace frontons, and candelabra are made to support the whole edifice. Shapes with human and animals' faces spring from behind stalks. All these are things which are not, cannot be and never were (*haec autem nec sunt, nec fieri possunt, nec fuerunt*). How can a reed support a roof, how can a candelabra carry a whole building? How can fully formed shapes spring from weak and frail stalks? Yet people look at these falsehoods without condemning them. They are, on the contrary, entertained by them and do not consider whether or not they are possible. Surely, a painting does not deserve approval if it does not resemble truth." All this criticism arose from a conviction that only that which agrees with reality and with understanding may be beautiful. That which has no justification (*sine ratione*) and does not correspond to nature ought not to find acceptance or a place in art. This was an expression of the rationalism of the classicist movement.

13. VITRUVIUS' AESTHETIC PRINCIPLES. One may summarize Vitruvius' aesthetic position as follows. 1. One of the cardinal concepts which he employed in discussing architecture was the concept of beauty. The aesthetic point of view had entered into the characterization and evaluation of art. 2. Vitruvius interpreted beauty so widely that it included not only that which delights the eye directly through proportion and colour but also that which delights by its purposefulness, suitability and utility, or, to use Latin terminology, by its *decorum, aptum* and *pulchrum*. His theory of architecture therefore preserved a balance between functional and purely formal beauty. 3. Vitruvius' aesthetic ideas were based on a belief in objective beauty con-

---

* C. J. Moe, *Numeri di Vitruvio* (1945).

ditioned by the laws of nature rather than by man's attitudes. He regarded a perfect temple as the product of natural laws rather than the work of an individual. The individual could discover those laws but not invent them. Nevertheless, he regarded as permissible, and even necessary, the correction of objective laws of beauty in the interest of the spectator's subjective requirements: eurhythmy had to supplement and correct symmetry. Here too Vitruvius achieved a compromise and a balance. For him beauty depended both upon objective measure and the subjective conditions of perception. This was a natural result of centuries of aesthetic exploration and discussion.

N. Texts on the Aesthetics of Architecture

VITRUVIUS, De archit. I 3, 2.

PERMANENCE, AIM, BEAUTY

1. Haec autem ita fieri debent, ut habeatur ratio firmitatis, utilitatis, venustatis... venustatis vero, cum fuerit operis species grata et elegans membrorumque commensus iustas habeat symmetriarum ratiocinationes.

1. When building, account should be taken of strength, utility, beauty... Beauty will be guaranteed when the appearance of the work is pleasing and elegant, and the scale of the constituent parts is justly calculated for symmetry.

tr. F. Granger

VITRUVIUS, De archit. I 2, 1-9.

ELEMENTS OF ARCHITECTURE

2. Architectura autem constat ex ordinatione, quae graece τάξις dicitur, et ex dispositione, hanc autem Graeci διάθεσιν vocitant et eurythmia et symmetria et decore et distributione, quae graece οίκνομία dicitur.

Ordinatio est [modica] membrorum operis [commoditas] separatim universeque proportionis ad symmetriam comparatio, haec componitur ex quantitate, quae graece ποσότης dicitur. quantitas autem est modulorum ex ipsius operis e singulisque membrorum partibus sumptio universi operis conveniens effectui.

Dispositio autem est rerum apta conlocatio elegansque compositionibus effectus operis cum qualitate... hae nascuntur ex cogitatione et inventione. cogitatio est cura studii plena et industriae vigilantiaeque effectus propositi cum voluptate. inventio autem est quaestionum obscurarum explicatio ratioque novae rei vigore mobili reperta. hae sunt terminationes dispositionum.

2. Now architecture consists of Order, which in Greek is called "taxis", and of Arrangement, which the Greeks name "diathesis", and of Proportion and Symmetry and Decor and Distribution which in Greek is called "oeconomia".

Order is the balanced adjustment of the details of the work separately, and, as to the whole, the arrangement of the proportion with a view to a symmetrical result. This is made up of Dimension, which in Greek is called "posotes". Now Dimension is the taking of modules from the parts of the work; and the suitable effect of the whole work arising from the several subdivisions of the parts.

Arrangement, however, is the fit assemblage of details, and, arising from this assemblage, the elegant effect of the work and its dimensions, along with a certain quality or character... [All these] arise from imagination and invention. Imagination rests upon the attention directed with minute and observant fervour to the charming effect proposed. Invention, however, is the solution of obscure problems;

Eurythmia est venusta species commodusque in compositionibus membrorum aspectus. haec efficitur, cum membra operis convenientis sunt altitudinis ad latitudinem, latitudinis ad longitudinem, et ad summam omnia respondent suae symmetriae.

Item symmetria est ex ipsius operis membris conveniens consensus ex partibusque separatis ad universae figurae speciem ratae partis responsus. uti in hominis corpore e cubito, pede, palma, digito ceterisque particulis symmetros est eurythmiae qualitas, sic est in operum perfectionibus. et primum in aedibus sacris aut e columnarum crassitudinibus aut triglypho aut etiam embatere... e membris invenitur symmetriarum ratiocinatio.

Decor autem est emendatus operis aspectus probatis rebus compositi cum auctoritate... is perficitur statione, quod graece θεματισμῷ dicitur, seu consuetudine aut natura.

Distributio autem est copiarum locique commoda dispensatio parcaque in operibus sumptus ratione temperatio... aliter urbanas domos oportere constitui videtur, aliter quibus ex possesionibus rusticis influunt fructus; non item feneratoribus, aliter beatis et delicatis; potentibus vero, quorum cogitationibus respublica gubernatur, ad usum conlocabuntur; et omnino faciendae sunt aptae omnibus personis aedificiorum distributiones.

the treatment of a new undertaking disclosed by an active intelligence. Such are the outlines of Arrangement.

Proportion implies a graceful semblance; the suitable display of details in their context. This is attained when the details of the work are of a height suitable to their breadth, of a breadth suitable to their length; in a word, when everything has a symmetrical correspondence.

Symmetry also is the appropriate harmony arising out of the details of the work itself; the correspondence of each given detail among the separate details to the form of the design as a whole. As in the human body, from cubit, foot, palm, inch and other small parts comes the symmetric quality of eurhythmy; so is it in the completed building. First, in sacred buildings, either from the thickness of columns, or a triglyph, or the module... so also the calculation of symmetries... is found from the details.

Decor demands the faultless ensemble of a work composed, in accordance with precedent, of approved details. It obeys convention, which in Greek is called "thematismos", or custom, or nature.

Distribution or Economy, however, is the suitable disposal of supplies and the site, and the thrifty and wise control of expense in the works... [It appears that] houses should be arranged in one way in towns; in another way for persons whose income arises from country estates; not the same for financiers; in another way for wealthy men of taste; for the powerful, however, by whose ideas the state is governed, there must be special adjustment to their habits. And generally, the distribution of buildings is to be adapted to the vocations of their owners.

tr. F. Granger

VITRUVIUS, De archit. III 1, 1–4, 9.

3. Aedium compositio constat ex symmetria, cuius rationem diligentissime architecti tenere debent. ea autem paritur a proportione, quae graece ἀναλογία dicitur. proportio est ratae partis membrorum in omni opere totiusque commodulatio, ex qua ratio efficitur symmetriarum. Namque non potest aedis ulla sine symme-

ARCHITECTURE AND THE HUMAN BODY

3. The planning of temples depends upon symmetry: and the method of this architects must diligently apprehend. It arises from proportion (which in Greek is called "analogia"). Proportion consists in taking a fixed module, in each case, both for the parts of a building and for the whole, by which the method of

tria atque proportione rationem habere compositionis, nisi uti hominis bene figurati membrorum habuerit exactam rationem. corpus enim hominis ita natura composuit, uti os capitis a mento ad frontem summam et radices imas capilli esset decimae partis, item manus pansa ab articulo ad extremum medium digitum tantundem, caput a mento ad summum verticem octavae, cum cervicibus imis ab summo pectore ad imas radices capillorum sextae, ⟨a medio pectore⟩ ad summum verticem quartae. ipsius autem oris altitudinis tertia est pars ab imo mento ad imas nares, nasum ab imis naribus ad finem medium superciliorum tantundem, ab ea fine ad imas radices capilli frons efficitur item tertiae partis, pes vero altitudinis corporis sextae, cubitum quartae, pectus item quartae. reliqua quoque membra suas habent commensus proportiones, quibus etiam antiqui pictores et statuarii nobiles usi magnas et infinitas laudes sunt adsecuti. similiter vero sacrarum aedium membra ad universam totius magnitudinis summam ex partibus singulis convenientissimum debent habere commensus responsum. item corporis centrum medium naturaliter est umbilicus. namque si homo conlocatus fuerit supinus manibus et pedibus pansis circinique conlocatum centrum in umbilico eius, circumagendo rotundationem utrarumque manuum et pedum digiti linea tangentur. non minus quemadmodum schema rotundationis in corpore efficitur, item quadrata designatio in eo invenietur. nam si a pedibus imis ad summum caput mensum erit aeque mensura relata fuerit ad manus pansas, invenietur eadem latitudo uti altitudo, quemadmodum areae, quae ad normam sunt quadratae. ergo si ita natura composuit corpus hominis, uti proportionibus membra ad summam figurationem eius respondeant, cum causa constituisse videntur antiqui, ut etiam in operum perfectionibus singulorum membrorum ad universam figurae speciem habeant commensus exactionem. igitur cum in omnibus operibus ordines traderent, maxime in aedibus deorum, ⟨quod eorum⟩ operum et laudes et culpae aeternae solent permanere.

symmetry is put into practice. For without symmetry and proportion no temple can have a regular plan; that is, it must have an exact proportion worked out after the fashion of the members of a finely-shaped human body. For Nature has so planned the human body that the face from the chin to the top of the forehead and the roots of the hair is a tenth part; also the palm of the hand from the wrist to the top of the middle finger is as much; the head from the chin to the crown, an eighth part; from the top of the breast with the bottom of the neck to the roots of the hair, a sixth part; from the middle of the breast to the crown, a fourth part; a third part of the height of the face is from the bottom of the chin to the bottom of the nostrils; the nose from the bottom of the nostrils to the line between the brows, as much; from that line to the roots of the hair, the forehead is given as the third part. The foot is a sixth of the height of the body; the cubit a quarter, the breast also a quarter. The other limbs also have their own proportionate measurements. And by using these, ancient painters and famous sculptors have attained great and unbounded distinction. In the like fashion the members of temples ought to have dimensions of their several parts answering suitably to the general sum of their whole magnitude. Now the navel is naturally the exact centre of the body. For if a man lies on his back with hands and feet outspread, and the centre of a circle is placed on his navel, his figure and toes will be touched by the circumference. Also a square will be found described within the figure, in the same way as a round figure is produced. For if we measure from the sole of the foot to the top of the head, and apply the measure to the outstretched hands, the breadth will be found equal to the height, just like sites which are squared by rule. Therefore, if Nature has planned the human body so that the members correspond in their proportions to its complete configuration, the ancients seem to have reason in determining that in the execution of their works they should observe an exact adjustment of the several members to the general pattern of the plan. Therefore, since in all their works they handed down orders, they did so especially

Ergo si convenit ex articulis hominis numerum inventum esse et ex membris separatis ad universam corporis speciem ratae partis commensus fieri responsum, relinquitur, ut suspiciamus eos, qui etiam aedes deorum inmortalium constituentes ita membra operum ordinaverunt, ut proportionibus et symmetriis separatae atque universae convenientes efficerentur eorum distributiones.

in building temples, the excellences and faults of which usually endure for ages.

Therefore, if it is agreed that number is found from the articulation of the body, and that there is a correspondence of the fixed ratio of the separate members to the general form of the body, it remains that we take up those writers who in planning the temples of the immortal gods so ordained the parts of the work that, by the help of proportion and symmetry, their several and general distribution is rendered congruous.

tr. F. Granger

VITRUVIUS, De archit., III 3, 12 et 13; III 5, 9; VI 2, 1.

OPTICAL CORRECTIVES

4. Angulares columnae crassiores faciendae sunt ex sua diametro quinquagesima parte, quod eae ab aere circumciduntur et graciliores videntur esse aspicientibus. ergo quod oculus fallit, ratiocinatione est exaequandum.

Haec autem propter altitudinis intervallum scandentis oculi species adiciuntur crassitudinibus temperaturae. venustates enim persequitur visus, cuius si non blandimur voluptati proportione et modulorum adiectionibus, uti quod fallitur temperatione adaugeatur, vastus et invenustus conspicientibus remittetur aspectus.

Quo altius enim scandit oculi species, non facile persecat aeris crebritatem; dilapsa itaque altitudinis spatio et viribus exuta incertam modulorum renuntiat sensibus quantitatem. quare semper adiciendum est rationis supplementum in symmetriarum membris, ut, cum fuerint aut altioribus locis opera aut etiam ipsa colossicotera, habeant magnitudinum rationem.

Nulla architecto maior cura esse debet, nisi uti proportionibus ratae partis habeant aedificia rationum exactiones. cum ergo constituta symmetriarum ratio fuerit et commensus ratiocinationibus explicati, tum etiam acuminis est proprium providere ad naturam loci aut usum aut speciem ⟨detractionibus aut⟩ adiectionibus temperaturas ⟨et⟩ efficere, cum de symme-

4. ...angle columns also must be made thicker by the fiftieth part of their diameter because they are cut into by the air and appear more slender to the spectators. Therefore, what the eye cheats us of, must be made up by calculation. It is on account of the variation in height that these adjustments are added to the diameters to meet the glance of the eye as it rises. For the sight follows gracious contours; and unless we flatter its pleasure, by proportionate alterations of the modules (so that by adjustment there is added the amount to which it suffers illusion), an uncouth and ungracious aspect will be presented to the spectators.

For the higher the glance of the eye rises, it pierces with the more difficulty the denseness of the air; therefore, it fails owing to the amount and power of the height, and reports to the senses the assemblage of an uncertain quantity of the modules. And so we must always add a supplement to the proportion in the case of the symmetrical parts, so that works which are either in higher positions or themselves more grandiose may have proportionate dimensions.

The architect's greatest care must be that his buildings should have their design determined by the proportions of a fixed unit. When, therefore, account has been taken of the symmetries of the design and the dimensions have been worked out by calculation, it is then the business of his skill to have regard to the nature of the site, either for use or

tria sit detractum aut adiectum, uti id videatur recte esse formatum in aspectuque nihil desideretur. alia enim ad manum species esse videtur, alia in excelso, non eadem in concluso, dissimilis in aperto, in quibus magni iudicii est opera, quid tandem sit faciundum. non enim veros videtur habere visus effectus, sed fallitur saepius iudicio ab eo mens.

beauty, to produce a proper balance by adjustment, adding or subtracting from the symmetry of the design, so that it may seem to be rightly planned and the elevation may lack nothing.

For one kind of appearance is seen near at hand; another, in a lofty building; yet another in a confined site; a different one in an open site. And it is the business of a fine judgment to determine exactly what is to be done in these cases. For the eye does not seem always to record true impressions and the mind is often thus led astray in its judgment.

tr. F. Granger

GEMINUS (?) (Damianus, R. Schöne, 28).

5. τὸ σκηνογραφικὸν τῆς ὀπτικῆς μέρος ζητεῖ πῶς προσήκει γράφειν τὰς εἰκόνας τῶν οἰκοδομημάτων. ἐπειδὴ γὰρ οὐχ οἷά ἐστι τὰ ὄντα, τοιαῦτα καὶ φαίνεται, σκοποῦσιν πῶς μὴ τοὺς ὑποκειμένους ῥυθμοὺς ἐπιδείξονται, ἀλλ' ὁποῖοι φανήσονται ἐξεργάσονται. τέλος δὲ τῷ ἀρχιτέκτονι τὸ πρὸς φαντασίαν εὔρυθμον ποιῆσαι τὸ ἔργον καὶ ὁπόσον ἐγχωρεῖ πρὸς τὰς τῆς ὄψεως ἀπάτας ἀλεξήματα ἀνευρίσκειν, οὐ τῆς κατ' ἀλήθειαν ἰσότητος ἢ εὐρυθμίας, ἀλλὰ τῆς πρὸς ὄψιν στοχαζομένῳ. οὕτω γοῦν τὸν μὲν κυλινδρικὸν κίονα, ἐπεὶ κατεαγότα ἔμελλε θεωρήσειν κατὰ μέσον πρὸς ὄψιν στενούμενον, εὐρύτερον κατὰ ταῦτα ποιεῖ· καὶ τὸν μὲν κύκλον ἔστιν ὅτε οὐ κύκλον γράφει, ἀλλ' ὀξυγωνίου κώνου τομήν, τὸ δὲ τετράγωνον προμηκέστερον, καὶ τοὺς πολλοὺς καὶ μεγέθει διαφέροντας κίονας ἐν ἄλλαις ἀναλαγίαις κατὰ πλῆθος καὶ μέγεθος. τοιοῦτος δ' ἐστὶ λόγος καὶ τῷ κολοσσοποιῷ διδοὺς τὴν φανησομένην τοῦ ἀποτελέσματος συμμετρίαν, ἵνα πρὸς τὴν ὄψιν εὔρυθμος εἴη, ἀλλὰ μὴ μάτην ἐργασθείη κατὰ τὴν οὐσίαν σύμμετρος, οὐ γὰρ οἷα ἐστὶ τὰ ἔργα, τοιαῦτα φαίνεται ἐν πολλῷ ἀναστήματι τιθέμενα.

FURTHER OPTICAL CORRECTIVES

5. That part of optics which is called perspective is concerned with how one should render likenesses of buildings. Because objects do not appear as they really are, one studies not how to render actual proportions, but how to represent them as they actually appear. The architect's aim is to give his work and to discover as far as possible ways of counteracting the illusions of sight; he aims not at real equality and harmony, but at such as they appear to the eye. So he designs a cylindrical column because the eye sees it as tapering towards the middle and because otherwise it would appear broken. And sometimes he draws the circle in the form of an ellipse and a square as an elongated oblong, and with many columns of varying lengths he varies the proportions according to their number and size. This same consideration shows the sculptor of giant statues what the proportions of his work will appear like when it is finished, so that it is harmonious to the eye and ear, and so that he does not vainly attempt to produce proportions which are objectively perfect, for works of art do not appear as they really are when they are placed high above.

PROCLUS, In Euclidis librum, Prol. I (Friedlein, 40).

6. πάλιν ὀπτικὴ καὶ κανονικὴ γεωμετρίας εἰσὶ καὶ ἀριθμητικῆς ἔκγονοι, ἡ μὲν... διαιρουμένη... εἴς τε τὴν ἰδίως καλουμένην ὀπτικήν, ἥτις τῶν ψευδῶς φαινομένων παρὰ τὰς ἀποστάσεις τῶν ὁρατῶν τὴν αἰτίαν ἀποδίδωσιν,

6. As for optics and the canon they are derived from geometry and arithmetic. The former consists of optics in the strict sense of the term and provides the reasons for such false appearances of distant objects as the

οἷον τῆς τῶν παραλλήλων συμπτώσεως ἢ τῆς τῶν τετραγώνων ὡς κύκλων θεωρίας, καὶ εἰς τὴν κατοπτρικὴν σύμπασαν τὴν περὶ τὰς ἀνακλάσεις τὰς παντοίας πραγματευομένην καὶ τῇ εἰκαστικῇ γνώσει συμπλεκομένην, καὶ τὴν λεγομένην σκηνογραφικὴν δεικνῦσαν, πῶς ἂν τὰ φαινόμενα μὴ ἄρυθμα ἢ ἄμορφα φαντάζοιτο ἐν ταῖς εἰκόσι· παρὰ τὰς ἀποστάσεις καὶ τὰ ὕψη τῶν γεγραμμένων.

merging of parallel lines or the turning of squares into circles; but it also consists of a whole study of reflection connected with knowledge through images, and of the so-called study of perspective which shows how phenomena may be presented in pictures without distortion of rhythm and of the figures represented even though the painted objects are far and high above.

HERON, Definitiones 135, 13 (Heiberg).

7. τοιοῦτος δ' ἐστὶ λόγος καὶ ὁ τῷ κολοσσοποιῷ διδοὺς τὴν φανησομένην τοῦ ἀποτελέσματος συμμετρίαν, ἵνα πρὸς τὴν ὄψιν εὔρυθμος εἴη, ἀλλὰ μὴ μάτην ἐργασθείη κατὰ οὐσίαν σύμμετρος. οὐ γὰρ, οἷά ἐστι τὰ ἔργα, τοιαῦτα φαίνεται ἐν πολλῷ ἀναστήματι τιθέμενα... ἐπειδὴ γὰρ οὐχ, οἷά ἐστι τὰ ὄντα, τοιαῦτα καὶ φαίνεται σκοποῦσιν, πῶς μὴ τοὺς ὑποκειμένους ῥυθμοὺς ἐπιδείξονται, ἀλλ' ὁποῖοι φανήσονται, ἐξεργάσονται. τέλος δὲ τῷ ἀρχιτέκτονι [το] πρὸς φαντασίαν εὔρυθμον ποιῆσαι τὸ ἔργον καὶ, ὁπόσον ἐγχωρεῖ. πρὸς τὰς τῆς ὄψεως ἀπάτας ἀλεξήματα ἀνευρίσκειν, οὐ τῆς κατ' ἀλήθειαν ἰσότητος ἢ εὐρυθμίας. ἀλλὰ τῆς πρὸς ὄψιν στοχαζομένῳ.

(cf. B 11)

7. Adhering to the same principle the creator of monumental statues achieves the proper arrangement of the parts of his work, taking account of the way the work will eventually be seen. It must appear beautiful to the eye and must not be spoiled through adherence to objective symmetry, for works seen from a great distance do not appear as they really are. Since then objects do not appear to spectators as they really are, they must be executed in accordance not with the proportions which they really possess but in accordance with proportions calculated in relation to the sight of the observer. The master's aim is to make the work beautiful to the eye and, as far as it is possible, to discover means leading to optical illusion; after all, he is concerned not with objective, but with optical propriety and harmony.

(c) THE THEORY OF PAINTING AND SCULPTURE

1. HELLENISTIC LITERATURE ON THE PLASTIC ARTS. In the literature of antiquity no book about painting and sculpture survives comparable to the poetics of Aristotle or Horace, the rhetoric of Quintilian, the treatise on harmony by Aristoxenus or Vitruvius' work on architecture. There are, however, plenty of works which inform us incidentally and indirectly as to what the ancients thought about the aesthetics of the plastic arts*. This information comes from various technical, historical, travel, literary and philosophical works.

A. Ancient artists like Xenocrates and Pasicles wrote treatises about painting and sculpture which were technical in character and resembled Vitruvius' work. None of these have survived, but they can be traced in the *Historia naturalis*, the

---

* As in the case of Hellenistic poetics, the most comprehensive collection of material concerning the Hellenistic theory of painting and sculpture is to be found in W. Madyda's book *De pulchritudine imaginum deorum quid auctores Graeci saec. II p. Chr. n. iudicaverint,* Archiwum Filol., Polish Academy of Sciences, 16 (1939).

huge encyclopaedic work of Pliny the Elder (first century A.D.), of which the 34th book contains information about sculpture in bronze, the 35th book about painting and the 36th book about sculpture in marble.*

B. Books on the plastic arts written by laymen differed in character from books written by artists, in that they concentrated mainly on the artist's personality and were written from an historical point of view. The older among them, such as the book by Duris of Samos written in the fourth century, have perished. However, the work of the Roman polymath Pliny has survived and is a mine of information about ancient art. This information is chiefly historical and purely factual, but there are incidental references to aesthetic problems of a general nature.

C. Information about ancient art is also available in one or two books about topography and travel. The *Guide to Hellas*, written in the second century A.D. by Pausanias the Periegite, is extant but it contains little about aesthetics.

D. The works of rhetoricians, poets, commentators and prose-writers contain important aesthetic information. Particularly so *The Life of Apollonius of Tyana*, written in 217 A.D. by Philostratus of Athens. Such writings often include descriptions of painting, sculpture and indeed whole galleries. We find such descriptions in Lucian of Samosata and the subject receives special attention in the *Pictures* (*Eikones*) by Philostratus II and Philostratus III, the nephew and the grandson of Philostratus I, and in the *Descriptions* (*Ekphraseis*) by Callistratus.

E. None of the Hellenistic philosophers devoted a separate work to the aesthetics of the visual arts, but their writings contain references to this subject. Treatises on the aesthetics of poetry, oratory and music sometimes allude to visual arts, and aesthetic theories are extended to include them.

Apart from Pliny and Philostratus, comparatively the most exhaustive information is available in Dion and Lucian. Dion of Prusa, "the golden-mouthed" (Chrysostom),† who lived at the turn of the first century A.D., a famous orator and learned philosopher, expounded his aesthetic ideas especially in his famous 12th "Olympic" oration of the year 105. Lucian of Samosata in Syria, an excellent and versatile writer of the second century A.D., touched upon aesthetic problems in various satirical and descriptive pieces.

Like a collection of tiny stones forming themselves into a big mosaic, these scattered fragments of information arrange themselves into an expansive and colourful picture of the Hellenistico-Roman aesthetics of the visual arts:‡ It should however be stressed that antiquity never evolved so wide a concept as that of the

---

* A. Kalkmann, *Die Quellen der Kunstgeschichte des Plinius* (1898).

† M. Valgimigli, *La critica letteraria di Dione Crisostomo* (1912). H. v. Arnim, *Leben und Werke des Dio von Prusa* (1898).

‡ B. Schweitzer, "Der bildende Künstler und der Begriff des Künstlerischen in der Antike". *Neue Heidelberger Jahrbücher*, N. F. (1925). "Mimesis und Phantasia", *Philologus*, vol. 89, 1934, E. Birmelin, "Die kunsttheoretischen Grundlagen in Philostrats «Apollonios»", *Philologus*, vol. 88 (1933). — But above all the book by W. Madyda cited above.

modern "visual arts", although in Hellenistic times painting and sculpture, that is, plane and three-dimensional art, were treated together. In contrast with the old Greek classification, which regarded bronze sculpture and sculpture in stone as two different arts, Philostratus used the term *plastike* to include modelling in clay, casting in metal and chiselling in stone, and regarded them all as one art.

2. POPULARITY OF THE VISUAL ARTS. In Hellenistico-Roman times the interest in visual arts was phenomenal and painting decorated market-places, palaces and galleries as well as temples. Works of art were shipped to Rome and sold for colossal sums. They had not only monetary value, but were also greatly admired. The island of Cnidos refused to sell the Aphrodite of Praxiteles, although the sum offered would have extinguished its national debt. The Aphrodite of Scopas was the subject of a religious cult. Tours to view Cnidian sculptures were organized. The discovery of a special technique by which paint could be made resistant to salt, wind and sun made it possible to cover ships with paintings. Paintings and sculptures were sought and purchased in huge quantities. In 58 A.D. Marcus Scaurus decorated a theatre stage with 3000 statues. Mucianus, who was a consul in the isle of Rhodes, maintained that despite thefts there were still 73,000 pieces of sculpture on the island, and at least as many in Athens, Olympia and Delphi. After the conquest of Achaea thousands of works of art were shipped to Rome as spoils of war. "He who does not love painting offends truth and wisdom", wrote Philostratus.

3. HELLENISTIC TASTE. The art which was valued in Hellenistic states and in Rome had certain defined features.

A. It was principally a naturalistic art. Pliny wrote that "for several generations faithful portraits have been the greatest ambition of art". It had set itself the task of creating an illusion of life. There was a popular story of the rivalry between Zeuxis and Parrhasius. Zeuxis painted a boy carrying grapes which birds tried to peck. But the painter himself was not pleased with the painting, saying that, had the boy been as successfully rendered as the grapes, the birds would have been frightened and flown away. Greeks and Romans displayed a boringly uniform admiration for statues which looked as if they "were alive", as if they "were real", as if they "were live bronze" (*aera quae vivunt*). The dog licking its wounds in the temple of Juno in Rome was so greatly valued for its unheard-of realism (*indiscreta similitudo*) that the temple's curators answered with their lives for any damage.

B. Contrary to what may be inferred from modern museums of antiquities, Hellenistic and Roman sculpture was not by any means confined solely to the human form. Its subjects were varied and to some extent complex. This was even more true of painting. Subject-matter and form were most prized when they were multifarious and varied. Both Dion and Plutarch condemned simple unadorned forms. Artists no longer shunned innovation, but, on the contrary, showed a particular liking for novelty. "Since novelty contributes to the increase of pleasure, we should not despise it, but rather pay attention to it". This view was quite different from the

Greek outlook in the early and the classical era. In this connection, the audacity (*audacia*) of invention was especially prized.

C. Also valued in works of art were movement, life and freedom. Quintilian wrote: "It is worthwhile to introduce certain changes in the accepted forms of art, indeed it is necessary to introduce them into facial expressions, aspects and poses depicted in paintings and sculpture because an erect body has least charm. With the frontal aspect of the face, arms hanging down and legs drawn closely together, the figure has a stiff appearance. Inclination and, if one may say so, movement, enliven the figure and round it off. That is why one does not always model hands in precisely the same way and why faces have a thousand expressions... Whoever criticizes Myron's Discobolus for not being a sufficiently simple piece of sculpture reveals himself as ignorant about art because it is singularity and difficulty which are especially praiseworthy".

D. Technical competence in workmanship was valued and many works of the period display a high degree of technical excellence. Works of art were prized for their distinction, exclusiveness and elegance. This last term made its first appearance at that time and was used by Vitruvius to describe works of good quality.

E. A certain number of contemporary patrons had a predilection for large size, for superhuman scale and colossi. The statue of the sun on Rhodes, in which the dimension of one finger was greater than that of a whole life-size statue, became one of the Seven Wonders of the World. There were people like Zenodorus, a contemporary of Vitruvius, who specialized in erecting colossi. Similarly, at least some consumers prized richness and sumptuousness. The Romans started the practice of gilding statues. Nero commanded Lysippus' statue of Alexander to be gilded, but though the statue gained in value it lost its appeal (*cum pretio periit gratia artis*, according to Pliny) and the gold had to be removed.

This predilection of the times for art that was naturalistic, illusionist, original, free, technically ingenious, elegant, colossal and rich was characteristic of a taste no longer classical but baroque. This taste did not, however, manifest itself very markedly in the general principles of contemporary aesthetics. It was less prominent in the theory of art than in art itself, since theory remained more conservative than practice and had to a large degree retained the principles of classicism.

But the most striking fact is that Hellenistic theory drew its examples and models not from contemporary but from classical art. Art produced after the reign of Alexander the Great was not mentioned and was treated as if it did not exist. Of earlier art it was said that "while the equipment was then more modest the results were better because now we take more interest in the value of the materials than in the talent of the artist". The public adored the new baroque art, while historians, specialists and connoisseurs preferred the old classical art. When they praised it, however, they stressed its vitality, variety and freedom—features which were characteristic of the new art. Despite their avowed conservatism, they could not ignore their own times. Generally speaking, no single, constant and over-all view marked

288   HELLENISTIC AESTHETICS

the Hellenistic era, because it stretched over a long period and had various centres. The Romans did not have a Greek mentality, and their emperors were not scholars.

4. TENDENCIES. Divergences in the Hellenistic view of art were also derived from the philosophical schools which were in conflict with one another and whose disparate trends were reflected in their theories of art.

A. The *moralist* tendency to subordinate art to morality had a tradition traceable to Plato. During Hellenistic times it was kept alive by the Stoics. It was a view held by certain philosophers but was not shared by artists or the wider circles of the intelligentsia. Despite completely different premises, similar conclusions were drawn from the *utilitarian* tendency, which likewise denied art any independent value. This tendency assumed that the value of art was in direct relation to its utility. Both Quintilian and Lucian defined art in terms of utility, and the Epicureans also came close to this view. But two other tendencies had greater significance than moralism and utilitarianism.

B. The Sceptics and some of the Epicureans adopted a *formalist* position. This had the support of two schools, and a section of the intellectual élite. It was, however, alien to the masses. It was successfully defended in the theory of music (by Sextus) and in the theory of poetry (by Philodemus). It had much fewer supporters in the theory of the visual arts, although one would have thought that these were equally susceptible to a sensuous or formalist interpretation. It did little to promote an understanding of the arts, but it had the merit of combatting muddled and mystical theories.

C. The *spiritualist* and *idealist* tendency carried great weight in the theory of the visual arts.[1] In one of its aspects it interpreted art in terms of religion and mysticism, seeing in it the inspiration of the gods. It was as extreme as formalism and represented the other pole of the artistic theory of the times. It grew in strength towards the end of antiquity and found expression in the works of Plutarch and even more strongly in Philon and Proclus.

However, the less extreme, *eclectic* form of spiritualism had a larger following. This probably first arose in the "Middle Academy" at Athens under Antiochus. From the poetics, in connection with which it had first appeared, it was extended to the theory of visual arts. It met with response in Rome and Alexandria. It had many Platonic elements, but the details of its arguments were to a considerable extent borrowed from the Peripatetics, and some of its concepts, like that of the imagination, were borrowed from the Stoics. This tendency laid stress on the ideal and spiritual elements in painting and sculpture, whereas previously such elements had been recognized only in poetry and music.

D. Finally, we may discern among writers on the visual arts some who did not subscribe to any theory, whether formalist or idealist, who eschewed syntheses and philosophy and who represented an *analytic* tendency. These, however, played a less important role than the extremist writers, either formalists or spiritualists.

Thus in Hellenistic ideas about art we see not merely differences, but also the greatest possible divergences. The representatives of the spiritualist movement, particularly those who stressed its religious aspect, regarded a work of art as a gift of the gods and something of a miracle, and wrote about it with religious unction, while the Sceptics and Epicureans could only find in it vain indulgence and a source of scandal. Hellenistic analyses of art undoubtedly made undisputed gains which ousted older biased and narrow views. At the same time, however, new and misguided notions appeared. One extreme view was negative and barren, the other mystical.

5. A FRESH VIEW OF THE ARTIST. Despite these great conflicts in the Hellenistic view of art, there were certain ideas about art and the artist to which the majority, including learned aestheticians, artists and connoisseurs, subscribed and which were therefore characteristic of the whole epoch. These most characteristic ideas were new and freshly formed and differed from those which had prevailed in previous epochs.* True, the two main assumptions held in the past, namely, that art relies on rules and on the imitation of reality, were not abandoned, for naturalistic art enjoyed enormous popularity. Vitruvius was not alone when he wrote that "paintings not resembling truth should not deserve admiration". Nevertheless, contrary views also appeared.

A. *Imagination* is essential to any artist's work.[2] It is no less important for a painter or a sculptor than for a poet. Philostratus wrote that "it is a wiser artist than imitation", which presents only what it has seen, whereas imagination also shows what has not been seen. Thought "paints and sculpts better than an artisan's craft". The praise of imagination was not by any means a call to art to abandon truth; quite the contrary, by being free to choose and weave together themes, it becomes more effective in rendering truth. Introduced by the Stoics and swiftly popularized, the concept of imagination began to supersede *mimesis* in the theory of art. However, the conflict between *mimesis* and "phantasy" arose only when "phantasy" was conceived as something passive. Plato had this view of it, but in Aristotle it had the elements of what the Hellenistic age was to call "imagination".

B. Thought, knowledge and *wisdom* are essential to the artist because he can and should present not only the surface of things, but also their deepest characteristics. Dion wrote that a good sculptor represents all the god's nature and power in the statue of the god, while Philostratus said that before Phidias sculpted Zeus, he must have given himself to the contemplation of the world, "together with the sky and the stars", since the statue demonstrated so great an understanding of the nature of the world. Such a view of the artist brought him close to the philosopher. The earlier Greeks had related the poet to the philosopher but had never done so in the case of painters and sculptors. Now, however, the sculptor Phidias was regarded as the "interpreter of truth". "The same wisdom which comes to the poet also determines the value of the art of painting because this art also contains wis-

---

* W. Tatarkiewicz, "Die spätantike Kunsttheorie", *Philologische Vorträge,* Wrocław, 1959.

dom." Dion maintained that man's idea of the divinity came not only from acquaintance with nature and from writers, but also from the work of painters and sculptors.[3]

C. *Idea* is essential to the artist. He creates according to the Idea he has in his mind.[4] Cicero wrote: "There is something perfect in forms and figures and the idea of this perfection is in our minds". Dion and Alcinous as well as Cicero argued that Phidias created Zeus not according to nature but according to an idea within him. To the question how an image of a god could appear in the human mind of Phidias, Dion's reply was: "As Phidias says, to imagine a god is inborn and necessary, the artist possesses the idea as a result of his resemblance to a god. It existed before him and he is merely its interpreter and teacher". This was one of the major alterations in views on art that occurred during antiquity.

The term "idea" itself and its original meaning were Platonic, but Hellenistic writers altered its meaning while retaining the term. According to Plato, idea was a reality existing outside man and the world, an eternal immutable reality beyond the reach of the senses but apprehended conceptually. In the eyes of Cicero, as we have already remarked, or of Dion, it was transformed from being the object of a concept to being the concept itself, and from being a transcendent idea to being an image in the artist's mind. Furthermore, it was transformed from an abstract concept into the kind of image that the artist uses. In Cicero it even lost the innate character it had had in Plato. Cicero thought it was derived from experience, saying that the phenomena which the artist sees impress their idea upon his mind. This was characteristic of the Stoics' way of thinking, not of Plato.

D. However important it may be for the artist to know the rules of art, these rules alone are not enough, because in addition he needs personal and above-average *talent*. The Hellenistic idea of a great artist was already close to the modern idea of genius.

A great artist has talents and a mind which set him apart from the generality of mankind. Even his eyes and his hands are different. When asked why he admired a picture by Zeuxis the painter Nicomachus replied: "You wouldn't have asked such a question if you had had my eyes". Dion regarded sculptors as "sages" and "divine" men. For Plato "divine men" were philosophers, poets and statesmen but never sculptors. Dion also asked the question, which was never asked before, whether Homer or Phidias was superior. From the old Greek point of view the superiority of the poet over the sculptor was axiomatic, since it was the superiority of a bard over the craftsman.

But even genius was not enough for Hellenistic writers to explain great art. They believed also that the artist needs inspiration. He creates in a state of "enthusiasm" and *inspiration*. Pausanias wrote that the work of a sculptor is as much the product of inspiration as the work of a poet. To many of those who now wrote about art, inspiration was not, as it had been for Democritus, a natural state but a supernatural state, an expression of the intervention of the gods. Callistratus held that "the hands of sculptors, when they are seized by the gift of a more divine inspiration, give utterance to creations that are possessed".[5] The same author says that when Scopas sculpted Dionysus he was full of that god. The concept of "creative madness", which Plato applied to poets, was now used in connection with painters and sculptors. In contemporary writings we constantly come across descriptions of apparitions visiting artist both in dreams and in their waking life. Strabo wrote that Phidias could not have created his Zeus had he not seen the god's true image and that, therefore, either he ascended to the god or the god descended to him. Pausanias sought a higher "wisdom" in the sculptures of Phidias and had no wish to measure the statue of Zeus because he was convinced that numbers would be incapable of explaining its powerful effect.[6] Divine origin was ascribed to some of the best statues. Mystico-religious writers wrote at length about divine inspiration and divine statues, and even Cicero in his speech against Verres mentioned a statue of Ceres which was said to have come from heaven.

E. In matters of art only the artist is the *legislator*. Great artists, Phidias in particular, were regarded not only as the creators of their own work, but also as legislators (*legum lator*) who influence the works and ideas of future generations. Cicero stated that we know the gods in the form which painters and sculptors have given them. Quintilian stated that Parrhasius was called the law-giver because others imitated his methods of portraying gods and men as if this were the one correct way of doing it.

The artist is also the *judge* in matters of art. In the quarrel between artists and laymen the artists gained the upper hand. Pliny the Younger wrote that all matters relating to art should be reserved exclusively to them,[7] while another writer thought that "the state of the arts would be happy if the artists themselves judged them". But the opposite view also had its supporters. Dionysius of Halicarnassus held that the layman (*idiotes*) as well as the artist should be heard, and Lucian was inclined to allow the layman a say if he were educated and a lover of beauty.[8]

In contrast with earlier times, in which interest had been solely in the artist's work and had ignored the artist completely, the later Greeks and the Romans also showed an interest in the artist's *personality*. In one of his characteristic pieces of information Pliny tells us that a certain artist's last paintings, which he had left unfinished, were admired and valued more than his finished works because in them the progress of the artist's thought could more clearly be seen (*ipsae cogitationes artificum spectantur*).[9]

F. The *social position* of the visual artist had improved, though at first this could only be said of the painter because deeply rooted prejudice made it difficult for the ancients to forgive the sculptor his heavy physical labour. These prejudices were only gradually shed and then only partially. This led to a transitional period when contradictory views were held of the artist. According to Plutarch, it was often possible to enjoy a work and hold the artist in contempt.[10] He thought that, even after seeing such masterpieces as Phidias' Olympian Zeus or Polyclytus' Argive Hera, no well-born youth would wish to be a Phidias or a Polyclitus; if the work is worthy of admiration, it does not follow that the artisan-producer is also admirable. Plutarch was by no means alone in his views; on the contrary, he represented the view of the majority. Some Hellenistic writers were already aware that a sculptor was something more than a craftsman, but most people still clung to the old view. Lucian wrote that we should go on bended knee before Phidias, Polyclitus and other great artists as we would before the gods whom they created, but he also wrote: "Let us even assume that you become a Phidias or a Polyclitus and that you create masterpieces... you will still be thought of as a craftsman and an artisan, and people will remind you that you earn your living by the work of your hands".

6. A FRESH VIEW OF WORKS OF ART. In Hellenistic times the attitude towards works of art underwent a change similar to that adopted towards the artist. They ceased to be regarded mimetically, intellectually and technically.

Antiquity possessed a pattern according to which a work of art was to be judged, or rather there were several patterns, because some philosophical schools saw more elements in art than others. According to Seneca's detailed analysis, the Stoics discerned two elements, the Aristotelians four, and the Platonists five.[11-11a] The Stoics divided art, as they divided nature, only into matter and effective cause: in the case of a statue the bronze is the matter and the artist is the cause. Aristotle discerned two further elements besides matter and effective cause. These were the form which the work is given and the purpose it serves. Plato discerned a fifth element: the idea or model. Seneca tells us that he distinguished that *from* which the work arose, that *through* which it is, that *which* it has become, *in accordance with what* it has been created, and *towards what* it aims. Thus for example a statue is made of a certain *material*, by an *artist*, possesses the *form* which he has given it, is executed in accordance with a certain *model* and aims at a certain *goal*. These patterns, particularly the more elaborate ones of Aristotle and Plato, made possible a new approach to works of art and instigated a retreat from a mimetic, intellectual and purely technical interpretation.

A. According to the new interpretation, a work of art was a *spiritual* product rather than merely a handicraft. Lucian observed that the Cnidian Venus was only a stone until the artist's mind transformed it into a goddess. Philostratus held that when Phidias sculpted Jove, "his mind was wiser than his hand". For this reason art was seen as something more than enjoyment and an embellishment of life: it gave proof of human dignity, an *argumentum humanitatis*. Dion maintained that it was by virtue of their art that the Greeks were superior to the barbarians.

B. A work of art is an *individual* work and not mass-produced. For that reason it is capable of both presenting and expressing individual experiences. Quintilian argued that painting is capable of penetrating the most intimate feelings and in this respect can go deeper than poetry. In contrast with the earlier Greeks, who interpreted art in purely objective terms and made its forms depend solely on the ends it was to serve, Hellenistic writers insisted on stressing its subjective elements and its dependence on man, the maker.

C. A work of art is a *free* work not depending on reality[12] and is autonomous. Callistratus argued that it rivals nature rather than imitates it. Lucian wrote that poetry has "boundless freedom and is subject to one law only: the poet's imagination". He would have said the same about the visual arts. Horace also said that painters have as much right to freedom as poets.

D. A work of art presents the invisible and spiritual through the visible. Dion Chrysostom discussed this at length in his twelfth *Olympian Oration* where he said that art presents the body in such a way that we might recognize in it the presence of the spirit. Mystical writers maintained that through human bodies the painter or the sculptor represented divinities; the forms of great works of art were "worthy of divine nature" and their beauty was supernatural.

E. These great works not only gladden the eye, they also force the mind to work.[13] They require a spectator who while in a state of contemplation will substitute thought for sight.[14] But in order to be able to admire them, contemplation, free time and peace are required.[15]

A work of art has a powerful effect. According to Callistratus, it renders man speechless and enslaves his senses. Dion wrote that works such as Phidias' Zeus gave "unequalled" delight and made it possible to forget everything terrible and hard in human life. In contrast with earlier authors who thought that art soothes and bridles the passions, Hellenistic writers inclined to the view that its effects are violent, stimulating and bewitching. Dion thought that "emotion" was essential to art and Callistratus wrote of the "miraculous" effects of art. Lucian used to say that when faced with great works the eyes cannot satiate themselves and men behave as if mad. As Dionysius said, it is feeling and sensory impression, rather than ratiocination, that is responsible for man's artistic experience. No one went further than Maximus of Tyre in demonstrating the effects of art and giving reasons for its esteem.

In the Hellenistic aesthetics the view arose that it is essential to art to express feelings. Earlier Greeks were convinced that dances and songs do so, but they were doubtful as to whether dances and songs are arts. Socrates thought that sculpture is able to represent feelings of the sculpted hero, but he did not mention that it might express the feelings of the sculptor. Now even Quintilian the orator stressed that not only his own art but also "mute" arts are expressive.[15a]

A man's attitude to art measures his worth. Philostratus said: "Whosoever scorns painting is unjust to truth... and to wisdom".[16] Although perishable, works of art are immortal[17] They collect and select whatever in the world is beautiful.[18] They not only represent bodies, but also express the soul and its music.[19] They not only delight the eye, but also teach it how to see.[20] They are the products not of accident but of conscious art, which creates beauty.[21]

The most fundamental assumptions of the classical view of art underwent change. Subjective eurhythmy became more important than *symmetria*. The new age decreed that beauty may reside not only in a complete work, but also in a fragment detached from the whole.[22] The concept of *mimesis*, of imitation, which had defined Greek art for so long, lost its significance and was replaced by *imagination*.

7. VISUAL ARTS AND POETRY. All these changes in the attitude to the visual arts brought them close to poetry and placed them on the same level. The question therefore arose what, despite their similarity, were the differences between the visual arts and poetry. In the past the question was seldom asked because the two activities appeared too distinct for a comparison even to be attempted. The fullest answer to this new question came from Dion Chrysostom, who detected four differences between the visual arts and poetry. 1. The sculptor creates an image which persists and does not resolve itself in time as a poem does. 2. Unlike the poet, the sculptor cannot express all thoughts directly,[23] but must work indirectly and rely on symbols.[24] 3. The sculptor has to wrestle with his material, which resists him and restricts his freedom.[25] 4. The eyes for which the sculptor creates are more difficult to persuade;[26] it is impossible to make them believe improbable things, whereas the ear may be deceived by the charm of words. Dion touched on the same problems as were to preoccupy Lessing 1500 years later. He brilliantly noticed the differences between poetry and sculpture but exaggerated them because he did not see that poetry also has recalcitrant material.

Dion considered that, for the reasons he had given, the sculptor's task was more difficult than the poet's. It was more difficult for Phidias than for Homer to represent divinity. It was also more difficult because sculpture had come into being later than poetry and had to take into account the ideas created by poetry. It was just poetry that limited the sculpture's freedom. Nevertheless, Dion said, Phidias had freed himself from the authority of Homer and had represented divinity as perfectly as a mortal being could. He had presented Zeus in divine majesty: in human form and yet unlike any human being. It is not difficult to trace in these arguments the influence of the idealistic philosophy of Plato and probably also of Posidonius.

8. THE VISUAL ARTS AND BEAUTY. The old Greek division of the arts into free arts and handicrafts remained in force. It was employed by Philostratus, although he gave it a slightly different basis when he wrote that the free arts require wisdom while handicrafts require only skill and diligence. But the principal change was that people began to classify the visual arts as liberal rather than servile. This occurred despite the prejudices that continued to surround painters and sculptors. Painting and sculpture now found themselves classed with philosophy, poetry and music. Philostratus justified this grouping on the grounds that truth is the main concern of all of these, whereas the purpose of handicrafts is utilitarian.

Philostratus was not alone in appreciating the arts in this way. Maximus of Tyre contrasted handicrafts with the visual arts, the latter having been regarded until quite recently by the Greeks themselves as nothing but handicrafts. Callistratus was also of the opinion that these arts are something more than mere products of the hands. Seneca (although he did not share this view) tells us that in his day the visual arts were classed among the liberal arts.

Painting and sculpture owed the raising of their status to the fact that attention for once was given to the beauty which they embody. Plutarch said that artists surpass craftsmen through their *art of beauty (kallitechnia)*.[27] He joined in one word something which the earlier Greeks did not join: art and beauty. He thus came close to the modern idea of fine arts. The Stoics (probably Posidonius) originated the view that nothing beautiful comes into being outside art. Lucian described art as a "particle of beauty". And *Charidemus*, a dialogue ascribed to him, contrasted the products of handicraft, whose purposes are utilitarian, with painting "whose aim is beauty".[28] Cicero and Quintilian were a little more conservative and said that art does not seek beauty, but nevertheless achieves it. Others, like Maximus of Tyre, maintained categorically that "the arts seek the greatest beauty". In early antiquity the attraction of art was thought to lie in faithful imitation of reality and in the skill of the work. Hellenistic writers substantiated this claim differently: for them the attraction of art was the outcome of imbuing matter with spirit, of imagination, intelligence, artistry and beauty. Plutarch wrote that nature endowed men with a love of beauty,[29] just as earlier writers had maintained that it endowed them with a love of imitating reality. Demetrius was criticized for preferring verisimilitude to beauty.

Hellenistic aestheticians sought beauty both in art and nature and found it difficult to decide which had the greater share of it. They saw that, on the one hand, the beauty of art is less than the beauty of nature, since it is itself only a mirror of nature. They saw, on the other hand, that it is greater, because the artist selects the beauty scattered throughout nature and makes good its shortcomings.

The concept of beauty, which was used by the early Greeks in a wide, not specifically aesthetic sense, changed its meaning in the Hellenistic period. Now Lucian equated beauty with charm and grace, symmetry and eurhythmy,[30] and Maximus of Tyre described it as charm, attraction, longing, agreeable mood and "everything that has a pleasant name".[31] Maximus praised the Greeks because they "recognized that the gods ought to be praised with whatever is most beautiful", and he understood that beauty is one of the reasons for which works of art are admired.[32] He realized that products of art are honoured not only on account of their utility, but also on account of their beauty.[33]

Some Hellenistic writers even exaggerated the sensory character of beauty and called "beautiful" every pleasure of the senses, including foods and perfumes.[34]

9. POLARITIES OF HELLENISTIC AESTHETICS. While classical writers usually occupied a middle position between two possible extremes, Hellenistic aestheticians took up one or the other extreme position. Some, chiefly the Sceptics and Epicureans, adopted a positivist or materialist attitude, while the Platonists adopted a spiritualist and religious attitude. These included writers like Plutarch, Dion and Maximus, whose

aesthetic writings have survived in larger fragments. The former tendency did not reappear until modern times, whereas the latter foreshadowed mediaeval aesthetics.

One of the problems typical of this religiously orientated final period of antiquity, and one which was the subject of totally conflicting solutions, was whether art should be connected with religion, or more precisely, whether art should represent the gods and create statues to portray them.[35] Some writers of antiquity, such as Varro and Seneca, deplored divine statues with human shapes. Others, from Posidonius to Maximus of Tyre, took the view that even if these statues could not be praised they should at least be tolerated because any other attitude to the divinity lay outside human possibilities. Dion of Prusa was full of enthusiasm for statues of divinities, Plotinus discerned a metaphysical basis for worshipping them, and Iamblichus thought that they were indeed "imbued with divinity". Antiquity had already embarked on the mediaeval dispute over the worship of images, and the two sides with their respective arguments were already represented, sides which were to enter into open conflict in the period of iconoclasm in eighth-century Byzantium.*

10. FOUR CHANGES. The changes which the theory of the visual arts underwent in the Hellenistic period had various sources and a varied character. Some were formal in character and led the ancients from a classical to a baroque position. This was a double evolution, involving a change from static to dynamic forms and a change from forms promoting harmony to forms promoting expression.

Other changes were social and political, replacing the modest, restrained and sparing forms of the democratic Athenian republic by the rich and monumental forms of the Roman empire.

Thirdly, there were ideological changes from the materialistic or semi-materialistic philosophies of the early Ionian philosophers and the Sophists to the idealist and religious philosophy of Plotinus and his contemporaries. Because it sought innate ideas and divine inspirations in the artist, this change, too, had its effect on art and its theory.

Finally, the fourth line of development was scientific in character, depending on the development of experience and analysis and showing itself in the perfecting of concepts. By this means correction of earlier biased and dogmatic theories was achieved, and in particular doubts were raised about the thesis that beauty depended exclusively upon an arrangement of parts. In contrast to the old purely objective conception of beauty, emphasis was laid on subjective and conventional elements.

---

* J. Geffcken, "Der Bilderstreit des heidnischen Altertums", *Archiv für Religionswissenschaft* XIX (1916–19).

O. Texts on the Aesthetics of the Plastic Arts

PLUTARCH, Pro pulchritudine 2.

1. Ἡ γοῦν τοῦ σώματος εὐμορφία ψυχῆς ἐστιν ἔργον σώματι χαριζομένης δόξαν εὐμορφίας. πεσέτω γοῦν θανάτῳ τὸ σῶμα καὶ τῆς ψυχῆς μετῳκισμένης... οὐδὲν ἔτι καταλείπεται τῶν ἐρασμίων.

SPIRITUALITY

1. Beauty of the body is the work of the soul which gives of itself beauty to the body. When the body succumbs to death and the soul goes elsewhere... nothing pleasant remains in the body.

PROCLUS, Comm. in Tim. 81 C.

καὶ ὁ πρὸς τὸ γεγονός τι ποιῶν, εἴπερ ὄντως ἀφορᾷ πρὸς ἐκεῖνο, δῆλον ὡς οὐ καλὸν ποιεῖ· αὐτὸ γὰρ ἐκεῖνο πλῆρές ἐστιν ἀνομοιότητος καὶ οὐκ ἔστι τὸ πρώτως καλόν· ὅθεν πολλῷ μᾶλλον ἀφεστήξεται τὸ πρὸς αὐτὸ γεγονὸς τοῦ κάλλους· ἐπεὶ καὶ ὁ Φειδίας ὁ τὸν Δία ποιήσας οὐ πρὸς γεγονὸς ἀπέβλεψεν, ἀλλ' εἰς ἔννοιαν ἀφίκετο τοῦ παρ' Ὁμήρῳ Διός· εἰ δὲ καὶ πρὸς αὐτὸν ἠδύνατο τὸν νοερὸν ἀνατείνεσθαι θεόν, δηλονότι κάλλιον ἂν ἀπετέλεσε τὸ οἰκεῖον ἔργον.

IDEALISTIC INTERPRETATION OF ART

He who creates in accordance with reality, assuming he is really looking at it, does not of course create beauty, for reality is full of disharmonies and is not the prime beauty. Therefore, that which arises modelled upon reality is the more removed from beauty. Phidias, too, executed the statue of Zeus not by observing reality but by contemplating Homer's Zeus, and if he could have reached to the god himself apprehended with the mind, he would of course have made his work the more beautiful.

PHILON, De opif. mundi 4.

οἷα δημιουργὸς ἀγαθὸς ἀποβλέπων εἰς τὸ παράδειγμα τὴν ἐκ λίθων καὶ ξύλων (sc. πόλιν) ἄρχεται κατασκευάζειν, ἑκάστη τῶν ἀσωμάτων ἰδεῶν τὰς σωματικὰς ἐξομοιῶν οὐσίας.

And like a good craftsman, he begins to build the city of stones and timber, keeping his eyes upon the pattern and making the visible and tangible objects correspond in each case to the incorporeal ideas.

tr. F. H. Colson and G. H. Whitaker

MAXIMUS OF TYRE, Or. XI 3 (Hobein, 130).

2. πάντα γὰρ τοιαῦτα ἀπορίᾳ ὄψεως καὶ ἀσθενείᾳ δηλώσεως καὶ γνώμης ἀμβλύτητι, ἐφ' ὅσον δύνανται ἕκαστοι ἐξαιρόμενοι τῇ φαντασίᾳ πρὸς τὸ κάλλιστον δοκοῦν ⟨καὶ γραφεῖς ἀπεργάζονται καὶ ἀγαλματοποιοὶ διαπλάττουσι καὶ ποιηταὶ αἰνίττονται⟩ καὶ φιλόσοφοι καταμαντεύονται.

IMAGINATION

2. In view of the difficulties encountered by sight, in view of the restricted means of verbal expression and of clouded thought, everyone tries, as far as he can, to be carried away by imagination and it is in accordance with the most beautiful model that painters paint the god, sculptors sculpt him, poets express him in similes, and philosophers talk oracularly about him.

PHILOSTRATUS THE YOUNGER, Imagines, Prooem. 6.

σκοποῦντι δὲ καὶ ξυγγένειάν τινα πρὸς ποιητικὴν ἔχειν ἡ τέχνη εὑρίσκεται καὶ κοινή τις ἀμφοῖν εἶναι φαντασία. θεῶν τε γὰρ πα-

IMAGINATION IN ART

If one reflects upon the matter, however, one finds that the art of painting has a certain kinship with poetry, and that an element of

ρουσίαν οἱ ποιηταὶ ἐς τὴν ἑαυτῶν σκηνὴν ἐσάγονται καὶ πάντα, ὅσα ὄγκου καὶ σεμνότητος καὶ ψυχαγωγίας ἔχεται, γραφική τε ὁμοίως, ἃ λέγειν οἱ ποιηταὶ ἔχουσι, ταῦτ' ἐν τῷ γράμματι σημαίνουσα.

imagination is common to both. For instance, the poets introduce the gods upon their stage as actually present, and with them all the accessories that make for dignity and grandeur and power to charm the mind; and so in like manner does the art of painting, indicating in the lines of the figures what the poets are able to describe in words.

tr. A. Fairbanks

PHILOSTRATUS, Vita Apoll. VI 19.

φαντασία... ταῦτα εἰργάσατο σοφωτέρα μιμήσεως δημιουργός· μίμησις μὲν γὰρ δημιουργήσει, ὃ εἶδεν, φαντασία δὲ καὶ ὃ μὴ εἶδεν, ὑποθήσεται γὰρ αὐτὸ πρὸς τὴν ἀναφορὰν τοῦ ὄντος, καὶ μίμησιν πολλάκις ἐκκρούει ἔκπληξις, φαντασίαν δὲ οὐδέν, χωρεῖ γὰρ ἀνέκπληκτος πρὸς ὃ αὐτὴ ὑπέθετο.

IMAGINATION IN IMITATION

Imagination wrought these works, a wiser and subtler artist by far than imitation; for imitation can only create as its handiwork what it has seen, but imagination equally what it has not seen; for it will conceive of its ideal with reference to the reality and imitation is often baffled by terror, but imagination by nothing; for it marches undismayed to the goal which it has itself laid down.

tr. F. C. Conybeare

DION CHRYSOSTOM, Or. XII 44.

3. τριῶν γὴ προκειμένων γενέσεων τῆς δαιμονίου παρ' ἀνθρώποις ὑπολήψεως ἐμφύτου, ποιητικῆς, νομικῆς, τετάρτην φῶμεν τὴν πλαστικήν τε καὶ δημιουργικὴν τῶν περὶ τὰ θεῖα ἀγάλματα καὶ τὰς εἰκόνας, λέγω δὲ γραφέων τε καὶ ἀνδριαντοποιῶν καὶ λιθοξόων καὶ παντὸς ἁπλῶς τοῦ καταξιώσαντος αὑτὸν ἀποφῆναι μιμητὴν διὰ τέχνης τῆς δαιμονίας φύσεως.

FOUR SOURCES

3. Now that we have set before us three sources of man's conception of the divine being, to wit, the innate, that derived from the poets, and that derived from the law-givers, let us name as the fourth that derived from the plastic art and the work of skilled craftsmen who make statues and likenesses of the gods—I mean painters and sculptors and masons who work in stone, in a word, everyone who has held himself worthy to come forward as a portrayer of the divine nature through the use of art.

tr. J. W. Cohoon

DION CHRYSOSTOM, Or. XII 71.

4. ἀνάγκη παραμένειν τῷ δημιουργῷ τὴν εἰκόνα ἐν τῇ ψυχῇ τὴν αὐτὴν ἀεὶ μέχρις ἂν ἐκτελέσῃ τὸ ἔργον, πολλάκις καὶ πολλοῖς ἔτεσι.

PICTURE IN THE ARTIST'S SOUL

4. The sculptor must keep the very same image in his mind continuously until he finishes his work, which often takes many years.

tr. J. W. Cohoon

ALCINOUS, Isagoga IX (Hermann, 163).

δεῖ τὸ παράδειγμα προυποκεῖσθαι· εἴτε καὶ μὴ εἴη ἔξω τὸ παράδειγμα παντὶ πάντως ἕκαστος ἐν αὑτῷ τὸ παράδειγμα ἴσχων τῶν τεχνιτῶν τὴν τούτου μορφὴν τῇ ὕλῃ περιτίθησιν.

The model must come before [the work of art]; even though it may not be embodied externally for everyone, it is undoubtedly true that every artist carries the model in himself and conveys its form into matter.

CALLISTRATUS, Descr. 2, 1.
(Schenkl-Reisch, 47).

5. οὐ ποιητῶν καὶ λογοποιῶν μόνον, ἐπιπνέονται τέχναι ἐπὶ τὰς γλώττας ἐκ θεῶν θειασμοῦ πεσόντος, ἀλλὰ καὶ τῶν δημιουργῶν αἱ χεῖρες θειοτέρων πνευμάτων ἐράνοις ληφθεῖσθαι κάτοχα καὶ μεστὰ μανίας προφητεύουσι τὰ ποιήματα.

INSPIRATION

5. It is not the art of poets and writers of prose alone that is inspired when divine power from the gods falls on their tongues, nay, the hands of sculptors also, when they are seized by the gift of a more divine inspiration, give utterance to creations that are possessed and full of madness.

tr. A. Fairbanks

PAUSANIAS, V 11, 9.

6. μέτρα δὲ τοῦ ἐν Ὀλυμπίᾳ Διὸς ἐς ὕψος τε καὶ εὖρος ἐπιστάμενος γεγραμμένα οὐκ ἐν ἐπαίνῳ θήσομαι τοὺς μετρήσαντας, ἐπεὶ καὶ τὰ εἰρημένα αὐτοῖς μέτρα πολύ τι ἀποδέοντά ἐστιν ἢ τοῖς ἰδοῦσι παρέστηκε ἐς τὸ ἄγαλμα δόξα.

MEASUREMENTS AND IMPRESSIONS

6. I know that the height and breadth of the Olympic Zeus have been measured and recorded; but I shall not praise those who made the measurements, for even their records will fall far short of the impression made by a sight of the image.

tr. W. H. S. Jones and H. A. Ormerod

PLINY THE YOUNGER, Epist. I 10, 4.

7. Ut enim de pictore, sculptore, fictore nisi artifex iudicare, ita nisi sapiens non potes perspicere sapientem.

ARTISTS AS ARBITERS IN ART

7. For as none but those who are skilled in painting, statuary or the plastic arts can form a right judgment of any master in those arts, so a man must himself have made great advances in philosophy, before he is capable of forming a just notion of a philosopher.

tr. W. Melnoth

LUCIAN, De domo 2.

8. οὐχ ὁ αὐτὸς περὶ τὰ θεάματα νόμος ἰδιώταις τε καὶ πεπαιδευμένοις.

CONNOISSEURS AND LAYMEN

8. In all that appeals to the eye, the same law does not hold for ordinary and for educated men.

tr. A. M. Harmon

QUINTILIAN, Institutio oratoria II 17, 42.

Docti rationem artis intelligunt, indocti voluptatem.

The learned appreciate the meaning of art, the ignorant appreciate its pleasures.

PLINY THE ELDER, Historia naturalis XXXV 145.

9. Illud vero perquam rarum ac memoria dignum est suprema opera artificium imperfectasque tabulas... in maiore admiratione esse quam perfecta, quippe in iis liniamenta reliqua ipsaeque cogitationes artificum spectantur atque in lenociniis commendationis dolor est manus, cum id ageret, exstinctae.

UNFINISHED WORK OF ART

9. It is also a very unusual and memorable fact that the last works of artists and their unfinished pictures... are more admired than those which they finished, because in them are seen the preliminary drawings left visible and the artist's actual thoughts and in the midst of approval's beguilement we feel regret that the artist's hand, while engaged in the work, was removed by death.

tr. H. Rackham

PLUTARCH, Vita Pericl. 153a.

10. ἡ δ' αὐτουργία τῶν ταπεινῶν τῆς εἰς τὰ καλὰ ῥᾳθυμίας μάρτυρα τὸν ἐν τοῖς ἀχρήστοις πόνον παρέχεται καθ' αὑτῆς καὶ οὐδεὶς εὐφυὴς νέος ἢ τὸν ἐν Πίσῃ θεασάμενος Δία γενέσθαι Φειδίας ἐπεθύμησεν ἢ τὴν Ἥραν τὴν ἐν Ἄργει Πολύκλειτος, οὐδ' Ἀνακρέων ἢ Φιλήμων ἢ Ἀρχίλοχος ἡσθεὶς αὐτῶν τοῖς ποιήμασιν. οὐ γὰρ ἀναγκαῖον, εἰ τέρπει τὸ ἔργον ὡς χαρίεν, ἄξιον σπουδῆς εἶναι τὸν εἰργασμένον.

THE ARTIST'S SOCIAL STANDING

10. Labour with one's own hands on lowly tasks gives witness, in the toil thus expended on useless things, to one's own indifference to higher things. No generous youth, from seeing the Zeus at Pisa or the Hera at Argos, longs to be Pheidias or Polycleitus; nor to be Anacreon or Philetas or Archilochus out of pleasure in their poems. For it does not of necessity follow that, if the work delights you with its grace, the one who wrought it is worthy of your esteem.

tr. B. Perrin

SENECA, Epist. 65, 2 sqq.

11. Dicunt... Stoici nostri duo esse in rerum natura, ex quibus omnia fiant, causam et materiam... Statua et materiam habuit, quae pateretur artificem, et artificem, qui materiae daret faciem. ergo in statua materia aes fuit, causa opifex... Aristoteles putat causam tribus modis dici: "prima" inquit "causa est ipsa materia, sine qua nihil potest effici; secunda opifex. tertia est forma, quae unicuique operi imponitur tamquam statuae"... "Quarta quoque" inquit "his accedit, propositum totius operis"...

His quintam Plato adicit exemplar, quam ipse ἰδέαν vocat: hoc est enim, ad quod respiciens artifex id, quod destinabat, effecit. nihil autem ad rem pertinet, utrum foris habeat exemplar, ad quod referat oculos, an intus, quod ibi ipse concepit et posuit...

Quinque ergo causae sunt, ut Plato dicit: id ex quo, id a quo, id in quo, id ad quod, id propter quod... Tamquam in statua... id ex quo aes est, id a quo artifex est, id in quo forma est, quae aptatur illi, id ad quod exemplar est, quod imitatur is, qui facit, id propter quod facientis propositum est, id quod ex istis est, ipsa statua est.

ELEMENTS OF A WORK OF ART

11. Our brethren of the Porch maintain... that there are in nature two principles from which all things are derived, cause and matter... Take a statue: it involved the presence, first, of matter for treatment by the artist, secondly, of an artist to give that matter shape. In the statue's case, in fact, bronze was the matter, the sculptor the cause... Aristotle thinks that the term "cause" admits of three applications. "The first cause", says he, "is the matter itself, for without it nothing can be made; the second's the creative hand; the third's the form with which every creation, like a statue, is endowed"... "To these three," he proceeds, "a fourth may be added, the end at which the whole work aims"... To these four causes Plato adds a fifth in the model—what he himself called "idea"; for it's this the artist contemplated as he carried out his intention. But it doesn't matter whether he had his model without, to fix his eyes on, or within, a notion conceived and built up in his own brain. ...There are accordingly five causes stated by Plato: the material, the efficient, the formal, the archetypal and the final... For example, to return to... the statue, the bronze is the material cause, the sculptor the efficient, the shape given to it the formal, the model copied by the maker, the archetypal, the end held in view by the maker, the final, the statue itself, the resultant of these several causes.

tr. E. P. Barker

PSEUDO-ARISTOTLE, De mundo 5 (in the Berlin Academy edition of Aristotle's works 396b 7).

11a. ἴσως δὲ καὶ τῶν ἐναντίων ἡ φύσις γλίχεται, καὶ ἐκ τούτων ἀποτελεῖ τὸ σύμφωνον ... ἔοικε δὲ καὶ ἡ τέχνη τὴν φύσιν μιμουμένη τοῦτο ποιεῖν· ζωγραφία μὲν γὰρ λευκῶν τε καὶ μελάνων ὠχρῶν τε καὶ ἐρυθρῶν χρωμάτων ἐγκερασαμένη φύσεις τὰς εἰκόνας τοῖς προηγουμένοις ἀπετέλεσε συμφώνως, μουσικὴ δὲ ὀξεῖς ἅμα καὶ βαρεῖς μακρούς τε καὶ βραχεῖς φθόγγους μίξασα ἐν διαφόροις φωναῖς μίαν ἀπετέλεσεν ἁρμονίαν, γραμματικὴ δὲ ἐκ φωνηέντων καὶ ἀφώνων γραμμάτων κρᾶσιν ποιησαμένη τὴν ὅλην τέχνην ἀπ' αὐτῶν συνεστήσατο. ταὐτὸ δὲ τοῦτο ἦν καὶ τὸ παρὰ τῷ σκοτεινῷ λεγόμενον Ἡρακλείτῳ.

11a. It may perhaps be that nature has a liking for contraries and evolves harmony out of them... The arts, too, apparently imitate nature in this respect. The art of painting by mingling in the picture the elements of black and white, yellow and red, achieves representations which correspond to the original object. Music, too, mingling together notes, high and low, short and prolonged, attains to a single harmony amid different voices; while writing, mingling vowels and consonants, composes of them all its art. The saying found in Heraclitus "the Obscure" was to the same effect.

tr. E. S. Forster

SUPERHUMAN BEAUTY OF ART

(Dion puts these words into Phidias' mouth)

DION CHRYSOSTOM, Or. XII 63.

12. τὸ δέ γε τῆς ἐμῆς ἐργασίας οὐκ ἄν τις οὐδὲ μανείς τινι ἀφομοιώσειεν θνητῷ, πρὸς κάλλος ἢ μέγεθος συνεξεταζόμενον.

12. But as to the product of my workmanship, nobody, not even an insane person, would liken it to any mortal man soever, if it be carefully examined from the point of view of a god's beauty or stature.

tr. J. W. Cohoon

SIGHT AND THOUGHT VIS-A-VIS WORKS OF ART

LUCIAN, De domo 6.

13. τούτου δὲ τοῦ οἴκου τὸ κάλλος... εὐφυοῦς θεατοῦ δεόμενον καὶ ὅτῳ μὴ ἐν τῇ ὄψει ἡ κρίσις, ἀλλά τις καὶ λογισμὸς ἐπακολουθεῖ τοῖς βλεπομένοις.

13. On the contrary, the beauty of this hall... wants a cultured man for a spectator who, instead of judging with his eyes, applies thought to what he sees.

tr. A. M. Harmon

LUCIAN, De domo 2.

14. ὅστις δὲ μετὰ παιδείας ὁρᾷ τὰ καλά, οὐκ ἄν, οἶμαι, ἀγαπήσειεν ὄψει μόνῃ καρπωσάμενος τὸ τερπνὸν οὐδ' ἂν ὑπομείναι ἄφωνος θεατὲς τοῦ κάλλους γενέσθαι, πειράσεται δὲ ὡς οἷόν τε καὶ ἐνδιατρῖψαι καὶ λόγῳ ἀμείψασθαι τὴν θέαν...

14. But when a man of culture beholds beautiful things, he will not be content, I am sure, to harvest their charm with his eyes alone, and will not endure to be a silent spectator of their beauty: he will do all he can to linger there and make some return for the spectacle in speech.

tr. A. M. Harmon

CONTEMPLATION

PLINY THE ELDER, Historia naturalis XXXVI 27.

15. Romae quidem multitudo operum et iam obliteratio ac magis officiorum negotio-

15. At Rome, indeed, the great number of works of art, and again their consequent ef-

rumque acervi omnes a contemplatione tamen abducunt, quoniam otiosorum et in magno loci silentio talis admiratio est.

facement from our memory, and, even more, the multitude of official functions and business activities must, after all, deter anyone from serious study, since the appreciation involved needs leisure and deep silence in our surroundings.

tr. D. E. Eichholz

QUINTILIAN, Inst. orat., XI, 3, 66.

15a. Saltatio frequenter sine voce intelligitur atque afficit, et ex vultu ingressuque perspicitur habitus animorum; et animalium quoque sermone carentium ira, laetitia, adulatio et oculis et quibusdam aliis corporis signis deprehenditur. Nec mirum, si ista, quae tamen in aliquo posita sunt motu, tantum in animis valent, cum pictura tacens opus et habitus semper eiusdem, sic in intimos penetret affectus, ut ipsam vim dicendi nonnunquam superare videatur... Decor quoque a gestu atque a motu venit.

EXPRESSION

15a. The movements of the dance are frequently full of meaning and appeal to the emotions without any aid from words. The temper of the mind can be inferred from the glance and gait, and even speechless animals show anger, joy, or the desire to please, by means of the eye and other physical indications. Nor is it wonderful that gesture which depends on various forms of movement should have such power, when pictures, which are silent and motionless, penetrate into our innermost feelings with such power that at times they seem more eloquent than language itself... Gesture and movement are also productive of grace.

tr. H. E. Butler

PHILOSTRATUS THE ELDER, Imagines, Prooem. 1.

16. ὅστις μὴ ἀσπάζεται τὴν ζωγραφίαν, ἀδικεῖ τὴν ἀλήθειαν, ἀδικεῖ δὲ καὶ σοφίαν.

IN PRAISE OF PAINTING

16. Whosoever scorns painting is unjust to truth; and he is also unjust to... wisdom.

tr. A. Fairbanks

PHILOSTRATUS, Dialexeis (Kayser, 366)

17. καὶ μὴ τὸν νόμον ἀφαιρώμεθα τὸν τοῦ ἀθανάτου λόγον, καὶ γὰρ εἰ καὶ φθαρτὰ ἐργάζεται, ἀλλ' ἀθάνατά γε αὐτὰ ποιεῖ, ὄνομα δ' αὐτῷ τέχνη.

IMMORTALITY OF WORKS OF ART

17. We must not deny a claim to immortality to human creation, because, although it creates objects which are subject to destruction, it yet causes them to be immortal. And the description of this creation is art.

MAXIMUS OF TYRE, Or. XVII 3 (Hobein, 211).

18. οἱ παντὸς παρ' ἑκάστου καλὸν συναγαγόντες, κατὰ τὴν τέχνην ἐκ διαφόρων σωμάτων ἀθροίσαντες εἰς μίμησιν μίαν, κάλλος ἓν ὑγιὲς καὶ ἄρτιον καὶ ἡρμοσμένον αὐτὸ αὑτῷ ἐξειργάσαντο καὶ γὰρ οὐκ ἂν εὕρες σῶμα ἀκριβὲς κατὰ ἀλήθειαν ἀγάλματι ὅμοιον· ὀρέγονται γὰρ αἱ τέχναι τοῦ καλλίστου·

ART GATHERS THE BEAUTY OF THE WORLD

18. Painters gather beauty from every detail of every human body, they collect them artistically from different bodies into one representation and in this manner they create one beauty which is healthy, fitting and internally harmonized. In reality you would never find a body precisely like a statue, since the arts aim at the greatest beauty.

CALLISTRATUS, Descr. 7, 1
(Schenkl-Reisch, 58).

19. ὁ ... χαλκὸς τῇ τέχνῃ συναπέτικτε τὸ κάλλος τῇ τοῦ σώματος ἀγλαΐᾳ τὸ μουσικὸν ἐπισημαίνων τῆς ψυχῆς.

ART AS EXPRESSION OF THE SOUL

19. The bronze joined with art to give birth to beauty, indicating by the splendour of the body the musical nature of the soul.
tr. A. Fairbanks

DIOGENES THE BABYLONIAN
(Philodemus, De musica, Kemke, 8).

20. τὸ δὲ καλῶς καὶ χρησίμως κινεῖσθαί τε καὶ ἠρεμεῖν τῷ σώματι τῆς γυμναστικῆς καὶ τὰς ἐπὶ τούτων τεταγμένας αἰσθήσεις κριτικὰς ποιεῖν· ὑπὸ δὲ τῆς γραφικῆς τὴν ὄψιν διδάσκεσθαι καλῶς κρίνειν πολλὰ τῶν ὁρατῶν.

ART TEACHES TO LOOK

20. The gymnastic art causes the body to move and be at rest beautifully and purposefully, and causes the senses to which these movements are subject to function accurately. The art of painting teaches the eye how to evaluate justly many of the things we see.

PLUTARCH, De placitis
philosophorum 879c.

21. οὐδὲν γὰρ τῶν καλῶν εἰκῇ καὶ ὡς ἔτυχε, ἀλλὰ μετά τινος τέχνης δημιουργούσης. καλὸς δ' ὁ κόσμος· δῆλον δ' ἐκ τοῦ σχήματος καὶ τοῦ χρώματος καὶ τοῦ μεγέθους καὶ τῆς περὶ τὸν κόσμον τῶν ἀστέρων ποικιλίας. σφαιροειδὴς δ' ὁ κόσμος· ὁ πάντων τῶν σχημάτων πρωτεύει.

BEAUTY IS NOT DUE TO ACCIDENT

21. Nothing beautiful comes about accidentally and without design, it comes about thanks to art which creates beauty. The world is beautiful, we can discern this from its shape, colour and size, and from the variety of stars which surround it. For the world is spherical, and this takes precedence over all other shapes.

PLINY THE YOUNGER, Epist. II 5, 11.

22. Si avulsum statuae caput aut membrum aliquod inspiceres, non tu quidem ex illo posses congruentiam aequalitatemque deprendere, posses tamen indicare, an id ipsum satis elegans esset... quia existimatur pars aliqua etiam sine ceteris esse perfecta.

BEAUTY OF A FRAGMENT

22. If you were to examine the detached head or any other part of a statue, though you could not thereby apprehend the harmony and just proportions of the entire figure, yet you would be able to judge of the elegancy of that particular member... it is supposed that beauties of particular parts may be seen without taking a view of the whole.
tr. W. Melnoth

DION CHRYSOSTOM, Or. XII 57.

23. ἐκείνων ⟨ποιητῶν⟩ μὲν δυναμένων εἰς πᾶσαν ἐπίνοιαν ἄγειν διὰ τῆς ποιήσεως, τῶν δὲ ἡμετέρων αὐτουργημάτων μόνην ταύτην ἱκανὴν ἐχόντων εἰκασίαν.

POETRY AND VISUAL ARTS

23. For they, the poets, were able through poetry to lead men to accept any sort of idea, whereas our aristic productions have only this one adequate standard of comparison.
tr. J. W. Cohoon

DION CHRYSOSTOM, Or. XII 65.

πλείστη μὲν οὖν ἐξουσία καὶ δύναμις ἀνθρώπῳ περὶ λόγον ἐνδίξασθαι τὸ παραστάν. ἡ δὲ τῶν ποιητῶν τέχνη μάλα αὐθάδης καὶ ἀνεπίληπτος.

Very great, indeed, is the ability and power of man to express in words any idea that comes into his mind. But the poet's art is exceedingly bold and not to be censured therefore.
tr. J. W. Cohoon

DION CHRYSOSTOM, Or. XII 59.

24. νοῦν γὰρ καὶ φρόνησιν αὐτὴν μὲν καθ' αὑτὴν οὔτε τις πλάστης οὔτε τις γραφεὺς εἰκάσαι δυνατὸς ἔσται· ἀθέατοι γὰρ τῶν τοιούτων καὶ ἀνιστόρητοι παντελῶς πάντες... ἐπ' αὐτὸ καταφεύγομεν, ἀνθρώπινον σῶμα ὡς ἀγγεῖον φρονήσεως καὶ λόγου θεῷ προσάπτοντες, ἐνδείᾳ καὶ ἀπορίᾳ παραδείγματος τῷ φανερῷ τε καὶ εἰκαστῷ τὸ ἀνείκαστον καὶ ἀφανὲς ἐνδείκνυσθαι ζητοῦντες, συμβόλου δυνάμει χρώμενοι.

24. For mind and intelligence in and of themselves no statuary or painter will ever be able to represent; for all men are utterly incapable of observing such attributes with their eyes or of learning of them by inquiry... Men fly to it for refuge, attributing to God a human body as a vessel to contain intelligence and rationality, in their lack of a better illustration, and in their perplexity seeking to indicate that which is invisible and unportrayable by means of something portrayable and visible, using the function of a symbol.

tr. J. W. Cohoon

DION CHRYSOSTOM, Or. XII 69; 70.

25. τὸ δὲ ἡμέτερον αὖ γένος, τὸ χειρωνακτικὸν καὶ δημιουργικόν, οὐδαμῇ ἐφικνεῖται τῆς τοιαύτης ἐλευθερίας, ἀλλὰ πρῶτον μὲν ὕλης προσδεόμεθα ... τὸ δέ γε ἡμέτερον τῆς τέχνης ἐπίπονον καὶ βραδὺ μόλις καὶ ⟨κατ'⟩ ὀλίγον προβαῖνον ἅτε οἶμαι πετρώδει καὶ στερεᾷ κάμνον ὕλῃ.

25. But our art, on the other hand, that which is dependent on the workman's hand and the artist's creative touch by no means attains to such freedom; first we need a material substance... But of our art the execution is laborious and slow, advancing with difficulty a step at a time, the reason being, no doubt, that it must work with a rock-like and hard material.

tr. J. W. Cohoon

DION CHRYSOSTOM, Or. XII 71.

26. καὶ δὴ τὸ λεγόμενον, ὡς ἔστιν ἀκοῆς πιστότερα ὄμματα, ἀληθὲς ἴσως· πολὺ γε μὴν δυσπειστότερα καὶ πλείονος δεόμενα ἐναργείας. ἡ μὲν γὰρ ὄψις αὐτοῖς τοῖς ὁρωμένοις συμβάλλει, τὴν δὲ ἀκοὴν οὐκ ἀδύνατον ἀναπτερῶσαι καὶ παραλογίσασθαι, μιμήματα εἰσπέμποντα γεγοητευμένα μέτροις καὶ ἤχοις. καὶ μὴν τά γε ἡμέτερα τῆς τέχνης ἀναγκαῖα μέτρα πλήθους τε πέρι καὶ μεγέθους, τοῖς δὲ ποιηταῖς ἔξεστι καὶ ταῦτα ἐφ' ὁποσονοῦν αὐξῆσαι.

26. Indeed, the popular saying that the eyes are more trustworthy than the ears is perhaps true, yet they are much harder to convince and demand much greater clearness; for while the eye agrees exactly with what it sees, it is not impossible to excite and cheat the ear by filling it with representations under the spell of metre and sound. Then again, while the measures of our art are enforced upon us by considerations of numbers and magnitude, the poets have the power to increase even these elements to any extent.

tr. J. W. Cohoon

PLUTARCH, Vita Pericl. 159 d.

27. ἀναβαινόντων δὲ τῶν ἔργων ὑπερηφάνων μὲν μεγέθει, μορφῇ δ' ἀμιμήτων καὶ χάριτι, τῶν δημιουργῶν ἁμιλλωμένων ὑπερβάλλεσθαι τὴν δημιουργίαν τῇ καλλιτεχνίᾳ.

KALLITECHNIA

27. So, then, the works arose, no less towering in their grandeur than inimitable in the grace of their outlines, since the workmen eagerly strove to surpass themselves in the beauty of their handicraft.

tr. B. Perrin

LUCIAN, Charidemus 25.

28. σχεδὸν δ' ὡς εἰπεῖν πάντων τῶν ἐν ἀνθρώποις ὥσπερ κοινὸν παράδειγμα τὸ κάλλος ἐστί... ἀλλὰ τί ταῦτα λέγω, ὧν τὸ κάλλος τέλος ἐστίν; ὧν γὰρ εἰς χρείαν ἥκομεν ἀναγκαίως, οὐκ ἐλλείπομεν οὐδὲν σπουδῆς εἰς ὅσον ἔξεστι κάλλιστα κατασκευάζειν.

καὶ σχεδὸν εἴ τις ἑκάστην ἐξετάζειν βούλεται τῶν τεχνῶν, εὑρήσει πάσας εἰς τὸ κάλλος ὁρώσας καὶ τούτου τυγχάνειν τοῦ παντὸς τιθεμένας.

PLUTARCH, Quaest. conviv. 673 E.

29. οὕτως ὁ ἄνθρωπος, γεγονὸς φιλότεχνος καὶ φιλόκαλος, πᾶν ἀποτέλεσμα καὶ πρᾶγμα νοῦ καὶ λόγου μετέχον ἀσπάζεσθαι καὶ ἀγαπᾶν πέφυκεν.

LUCIAN, De domo 5.

30. ἐκείνης γὰρ ἐν τῇ πολυτελείᾳ μόνῃ τὸ θαῦμα, τέχνη δὲ ἢ κάλλος ἢ τέρψις ἢ τὸ σύμμετρον ἢ τὸ εὔρυθμον οὐ συνείργαστο οὐ δὲ κατεμέμικτο τῷ χρυσῷ, ἀλλ' ἦν βαρβαρικὸν τὸ θέαμα... οὐ φιλόκαλοι γάρ, ἀλλὰ φιλόπλουτοί εἰσιν οἱ βάρβαροι.

MAXIMUS OF TYRE, Or. XXV 7
(Hobein, 305).

31. ἀνάγκη γὰρ παντὶ τῷ φύσει καλῷ συντετάχθαι χάριτας καὶ ὥραν καὶ πόθον καὶ εὐφροσύνην καὶ πάντα δὴ τὰ τερπνὰ ὀνόματα· οὕτω καὶ ὁ οὐρανὸς οὐ καλὸς μόνον, ἀλλὰ καὶ ἥδιστον θεαμάτων, καὶ θάλαττα πλεομένη καὶ λήϊα καρποτρόφα καὶ ὄρη δενδροτρόφα καὶ λειμῶνες ἀνθοῦντες.

MAXIMUS OF TYRE, Or. II 3
(Hobein, 20).

32. Ἀγαλμάτων δὲ οὐχ εἷς νόμος, οὐδὲ εἷς τρόπος, οὐδὲ τέχνη μία, οὐδὲ ὕλη μία· ἀλλὰ τὸ μὲν Ἑλληνικόν, τιμᾶν τοὺς θεοὺς ἐνόμισαν τῶν ἐν γῇ τοῖς καλλίστοις, ὕλῃ μὲν καθαρᾷ, μορφῇ δὲ ἀνθρωπίνῃ, τέχνῃ δὲ ἀκριβεῖ.

BEAUTY AS AN AIM

28. Beauty is something like a common model in almost all human affairs... Why should I be talking about matters whose aim is beauty? Surely we put all our efforts into making objects which serve us as necessities as beautiful as possible.

Almost everyone who wishes to examine the arts will conclude that they all gaze at beauty and wish to attain it at all costs.

NATURAL PREDILECTION FOR BEAUTY

29. In this way man, taking by nature a delight in art and beauty, loves and appreciates every artefact and activity which partakes of mind and thought.

SUMPTUOUSNESS AND BEAUTY

30. That [palace] was wonderful only on account of its cost; there was no craftsmanship or beauty or charm or symmetry or grace wrought into the gold or combined with it. The thing was barbarous... The barbarians are not beauty-lovers; they are money-lovers.

tr. A. M. Harmon

EFFECTS OF BEAUTY

31. For of necessity with each thing which is naturally beautiful are associated charm, attraction, longing, a pleasing atmosphere and everything that has a pleasant name. And so the sky not only is beautiful, but also presents the most pleasing sight, and similarly the sea across which one sails, fields yielding crops, tree-clad mountains and blooming meadows.

THE GREEKS WORSHIPPED GODS WITH BEAUTY

32. Statues are not subject to a single norm, are not all of the same kind, they are the product of more than one art and more than one material. The Greeks have recognized that the gods ought to be praised with whatever is most beautiful on earth: pure material, human shape and perfect art.

MAXIMUS OF TYRE, Or. II 9
(Hobein, 27).

33. Ὦ πολλῶν καὶ παντοδαπῶν ἀγαλμάτων· ὧν τὰ μὲν ὑπὸ τέχνης ἐγένετο, τὰ δὲ διὰ χρείαν ἠγαπήθη, τὰ δὲ δι' ὠφέλειαν ἐτιμήθη, τὰ δέ δι' ἔκπληξιν ἐθαυμάσθη, τὰ δὲ διὰ μέγεθος ἐθειάσθη, τὰ δὲ διὰ κάλλος ἐπῃνέθη.

WHY ARE STATUES RESPECTED?

33. How many and various are the statues! Some are the products of art, others have been accepted because of various needs, others have been honoured on account of their utility, others have been admired on account of their size, others still have been praised on account of their beauty.

PLUTARCH, Quaest. conviv. 704 e.

34. οὐ μὴν Ἀριστοξένῳ γε συμφέρομαι παντάπασι, ταύταις μόναις φάσκοντι ταῖς ἡδοναῖς τὸ «καλῶς» ἐπιλέγεσθαι. καὶ γὰρ ὄψα καλὰ καὶ μύρα καλοῦσι καὶ καλῶς γεγονέναι λέγουσι δειπνήσαντες ἡδέως καὶ πολυτελῶς.

THE RANGE OF BEAUTY

34. On the other hand, I do not agree completely with Aristoxenus' statement that the word "beautiful" is applied to the pleasures of these senses [i.e., hearing and sight] alone; for people call both foods and perfumes "beautiful" and say that it was a "beautiful" occasion when they have enjoyed a pleasant and sumptuous meal.

tr. F. H. Sandbach

MAXIMUS OF TYRE, Or. II 2 et 10
(Hobein, 20 et 28).

35. οὕτως ἀμέλε καὶ τῇ τοῦ θείου φύσει δεῖ μὲν οὐδὲν ἀγαλμάτων οὐδὲ ἱδρυμάτων, ἀλλὰ ἀσθενὲς ὂν κομιδῇ τὸ ἀνθρώπειον, καὶ διεστὸς τοῦ θείου... σημεῖα ταῦτα ἐμηχανήσατο, ἐν οἷς ἀποθήσεται τὰ τῶν θεῶν ὀνόματα καὶ τὰς φήμας αὐτῶν.

οἷς μὲν οὖν ἡ μνήμη ἔρρωται, καὶ δύνανται εὐθὺ τοῦ οὐρανοῦ ἀνατεινόμενοι τῇ ψυχῇ τῷ θείῳ ἐντυγχάνειν, οὐδὲν ἴσως δεῖ τούτοις ἀγαλμάτων· σπάνιον δὲ ἐν ἀνθρώποις τὸ τοιοῦτο γένος...

ὁ μὲν γὰρ θεός... κρείττων δὲ τοῦ χρόνου καὶ αἰῶνος καὶ πάσης ῥεούσης φύσεως, ἀνώνυμος νομοθέτῃ, καὶ ἄρρητος φωνῇ καὶ ἀόρατος ὀφθαλμοῖς· οὐκ ἔχοντες δὲ αὐτοῦ λαβεῖν τὴν οὐσίαν, ἐπερειδόμεθα φωναῖς καὶ ὀνόμασιν, καὶ ζῴοις καὶ τύποις χρυσοῦ καὶ ἐλέφαντος καὶ ἀργύρου, καὶ φυτοῖς, καὶ ποταμοῖς, καὶ κορυφαῖς, καὶ νάμασιν· ἐπιθυμοῦντες μὲν αὐτοῦ τῆς νοήσεως, ὑπὸ δὲ ἀσθενείας τὰ παρ' ἡμῶν καλὰ τῇ ἐκείνου φύσει ἐπονομάζοντες· αὐτὸ ἐκεῖνο τὸ τῶν ἐρώντων πάθος, οἷς ἥδιστον εἰς μὲν θέαμα οἱ τῶν παιδικῶν τύποι.

SHOULD THERE BE STATUES OF GODS?

35. It appears that, by nature, god does not need statues and symbols. But men, in their boundless weakness, removed from god as far as "earth from heaven", have invented these signs in order to deposit within them the names of, and their knowledge of, the gods.

But those who have good memory and with their souls rise to heaven, may come close to the divinity—those, perhaps, do not need statues at all, but they are rare among men...

There is a god... above time, eternity and the whole mutable nature, not susceptible to being named by the law-giver, expressed in language or beheld with the eye. Unable to grasp his essence, we seek support in words, names, animals, likenesses in gold, ivory and silver, in plants, rivers, mountain peaks and sources of rivers. We wish to embrace him in thought, but all our weakness allows us to do is to describe his nature in terms of what appears beautiful to us. We proceed like lovers for whom the images of beloved persons form the pleasantest sight.

11. Classification of the Arts

1. ART AND BEAUTY. The conceptual apparatus of aesthetics which Hellenism inherited from the classical era was geared to the general needs of philosophy rather than to the particular needs of aesthetics and it was therefore a burden which Hellenistic writers tried to shed. This applied, in particular, to the four concepts which have already been discussed several times.

A. The concept of beauty was so wide that it included not only the beauty of shapes, colours and sounds, but also of thoughts, virtues and actions. It included moral as well as aesthetic beauty. Hellenistic writers tried to narrow it down and to extract from it aesthetic beauty. When the Stoics defined beauty as a "proper arrangement of parts and pleasing colour", they had in mind this narrower conception of beauty.

B. The concept of art was so wide that it included "all skillful production performed in accordance with rules" regardless of whether it was a fine art or a handicraft. Attempts had already been made in classical times to confine art to the "imitative" arts, such as music and painting, and Hellenism moved further in that direction.

C. The concept of beauty and the concept of art were not linked. In definitions of beauty no reference would be made to art and in definitions of art no reference would be made to beauty. Hellenistic writers began to bring these concepts closer together until the conclusion was reached that for some arts "beauty is the goal".

D. The concept of art and the concept of poetry were not linked. Art was subject to rules, whereas poetry was regarded as a subject of inspiration and could not therefore be classed among the arts. Hellenistic writers brought these concepts closer together by recognizing that poetry is also subject to rules and that inspiration is indispensable in the other arts.

Ever since the ancients started meditating on the concept of art it had always been for them a skill depending on general rules and having a rational character. This remained so regardless of changes which occurred in the concept. For them irrational art, whether based on intuition or upon the imagination, was not art. The classic statement on the subject was made by Plato: "I do not call any irrational activity art".[1] But on the other hand, the ancients knew that only the principles of art were general and that its products were specific. This idea was neatly expressed by a later writer: "in every art the rules are universal but the products individual".[2]

In connection with these conceptual transformations, attempts were made to classify beauty and, even more, art. This had already begun with the Sophists, with Plato and Aristotle; and Hellenistic writers spared no efforts to provide a satisfactory classification. The matter was important in view of the extensiveness of the concept of art and the wide field of the arts which had to be categorized. Of special concern was the question whether the classification approached a distinction of the "fine arts" and whether these were different from handicrafts.*

2. CLASSIFICATION BY THE SOPHISTS. The Sophists divided the arts into those that are *useful* and those that *provide pleasure*,[3] in other words, into those that are essential to life and those that have entertainment value. In Hellenistic times this view became popular and more or less self-explanatory. But it did little to help solve the problem of how to isolate those arts which were of special interest to aesthetics. This was so even in its more sophisticated form which was suggested by Aristotle and formulated by Plutarch. Plutarch added to the useful and enjoyable arts those that are pursued on account of their *excellence*. It might have been thought that Plutarch's idea would have served as a basis for distinguishing the "fine arts" as those which seek excellence. However, the examples which Plutarch gives show that he did not have them in mind. He mentions mathematics and astronomy, but makes no reference either to sculpture or music.

3. THE CLASSIFICATIONS OF PLATO AND ARISTOTLE. Plato divided the arts in various ways. Some of his ideas, for example that the arts should be divided into those which (like music) are based on calculation and those which are based on simple experience were generally ignored. Two of his ideas, however, were accepted. One was that the difference among the arts depends on their relation to objects which they either exploit (as in hunting), or imitate (as in painting), or produce (as in architecture).[4] This differentiation† was the foundation of a threefold division of the arts and played a significant role in the ancients' treatment of the arts. The same may be said of another of Plato's attempts at dividing the arts, in which those arts which produced things (architecture) were distinguished from those which produced only images of things (painting). As far as Plato was concerned, the two divisions were similar: arts either produce things or imitate things by producing their images.

Aristotle reflected Plato's ideas and in a similar manner divided the arts into those which amplify nature and those which imitate her.[5] This division enabled him to include under the classification of "imitative" some, if not all, of the arts which in modern times are called "fine" arts. But he worked on a different assumption from the modern one. He based his division not on the grounds that these arts aspire to beauty, but that they "imitate", and because of this he gave aesthetic thought a different aspect from that which it has today.

4. GALEN'S CLASSIFICATION. The division of the arts into servile and liberal enjoyed great popularity both in the early period and in Hellenistic times. It was typically Greek but is best known in its Latin terminology of *artes vulgares* and *liberales*.[6] In this case the basis of division was the physical effort which some arts require and others do not. To the ancients this difference appeared immensely significant.

---

* W. Tatarkiewicz, "Art and Poetry, a Contribution to the History of Ancient Aesthetics", *Studia Philosophica* II (Lwów, 1938) and "Classification of Arts in Antiquity", *Journal of the History of Ideas* (1963). P. O. Kristeller, "The Modern System of Arts", *Journal of the History of Ideas* (1951).

† This classification by Plato is reported also by Laertius Diogenes, III 100.

Of all the ancient divisions of the arts this one most clearly depended on historical conditions and social relations. It was an expression of the ancient aristocratic social system and the attendant contempt for physical labour. This contempt found expression in the term *artes vulgares,* and Cicero went so far as to call physical arts "dirty" (*sordidae*). It was a division dictated by the Greek love of intellectual pursuits as well as by the ancients' dislike of physical toil.

It would be difficult to trace the originator of this old division, but we can name those who used and developed it. In the second century A.D. it was employed by Galen[7] among others, who called some arts *handicrafts* and other arts *intellectual.* He regarded the former as, of course, inferior to the latter. The only ones he included without qualification among the superior arts were rhetoric, geometry, arithmetic, dialectics, astronomy and grammar, i.e., all scholarly disciplines, none of which would today be considered an art. He included music in the group, but by music he meant music theory based on mathematics. He was not sure whether painting and sculpture should be included and wrote that "if one wishes" one may include them within the liberal arts. This classification by Galen once more indicates the difference between the ancient and the modern understanding of art.

In Hellenistic times there were certain doubts as to which arts should be regarded as liberal. Varro, for instance, tried to include architecture, but architecture could not retain this status because public opinion continued to relegate it to the crafts.

The Greeks also presented this division in a different form, by which the "handicrafts" retained their names and meanings, while the "liberal" or "intellectual" arts acquired new names and new characteristics. They were called the *encyclical* arts, that is, literally, those that formed a closed circle. Greek writers explained that this term was chosen "because the artist has to pass through all of them in order to introduce into his own art all that is useful to him in the other arts". In other words, they regarded them as "arts which belonged to general education". These normally included the sciences and the arts of music and rhetoric, but not visual arts.

Several variants and amplifications of this division were produced. The most outstanding example is the fourfold division presented by Seneca, who probably derived it from Posidonius.[8] The arts which he termed handicrafts were not different from those which he called servile, and those which he called "serving virtue" were no different from the liberal arts. But he mentioned arts "designed for education" (*pueriles*) and arts "for entertainment" (*ludicrae*) which "foster the pleasures of eye and ear". The twofold division now became fourfold, with the two new divisions close to those which were distinguished by the Sophists. This was in a sense a combination of the two great divisions, now the previous one-sidedness of the division was lost, but with it its original intention and coherence were lost also.

5. QUINTILIAN'S CLASSIFICATION. Another classification was evolved by Quintilian, a Roman rhetorician of the first century A.D.[9] Borrowing concepts which Aristotle had employed in another context he applied them to divide the arts into three groups.

The first one consisted of those arts which 1. depend on observation (*inspectio*), or in other words, on the discovery and evaluation of objects (*cognitio et aestimatio rerum*). These, however, do not require any action. Quintilian used the Greek term *theoretical* to designate them and gave astronomy as an example. Alongside these arts, there were those that 2. consist in action (*actus*) and exhaust themselves in action, leaving nothing behind (*ipso actu perficitur nihilque post actum operis relinquit*). These were given the Greek name *practical* and the dance was cited as an example. Finally, 3. there were those that left a product (*effectus*). These were the *poietic* arts, among which painting was included.

If we distinguish three elements in the arts, namely, skill, activity and product, we may say that Quintilian divided the arts in such a way that the first category contained only the first element, the next the first and the second, but only the last category contained all three. Because the first element was common to all the arts, the ancients regarded it as essential. Thus, the emphasis on skill enabled them to class the theoretical arts, i.e., the sciences, as arts in the full sense of the word, whereas in contemporary thought production and the artifact are essential and therefore "theoretical arts" are not included among the arts. Quintilian's division did not separate the "fine" arts from the rest. Some "fine arts" appeared in his second group and others in his third group.

This classification, which we know through Quintilian, is ascribed by Diogenes Laertius to Plato. This is strange for two reasons. Firstly, he describes Plato's classification as a classification of sciences rather than of arts, although at the same time he cites stone-masonry as an example of a "poietic" science and playing the flute as an example of a practical science. This can only be explained in terms of the fluid division between the arts and the sciences characteristic of ancient thinking. Secondly, Diogenes Laertius ascribes this classification to Plato, though there is no evidence for it in any of Plato's writings. This may be explained by the fact that the classification was employed in Plato's Academy and that therefore the doxographer linked it with the Academy's founder.

This trichotomy appears instead in Aristotle. But, in the first place, it has a different application (being used with reference to ways of life) and, moreover, has a different intention. By a "practical" activity the Stagirite meant not so much one which lacked a product as one which concentrated not upon the product, but upon the moral intention.

Dionysius Thrax noted a division of the arts into the *practical* and the *apotelestic*. This, however, is the same division as that of Quintilian with only one difference: it leaves out the theoretical arts and gives a different name to the poietic arts ("apotelestic" means "completed", "carried through to a finish"). R. Westphal, the music historian, who first drew attention almost a hundred years ago to Dionysius' division, gave it a different interpretation and said that apotelestic arts are those which emerge complete from the act of creation (as in the case of visual arts), whereas practical arts require an interpreter (as in the case of music). Westphal regarded this as the most important classification produced in antiquity because it achieved what other classifications failed to achieve: from among the arts (in the broad meaning of the term) it distinguished the fine arts, which he divided into the visual and the musical arts. This interpretation is not, however, authentic, since it imposes a modern cast upon an ancient thought. (It may be added that with Dionysius Thrax, the division was fourfold. It also included the "theoretical" arts and the "peripoietic" arts, i.e., those arts which simply make use of nature, such as fishing and hunting.)[10]

The grammarian Lucius Tarrhaeus (quoted by Dionysius) produced another variant of the classification. To the theoretical, practical and apotelesmatic arts he added the *organic* arts. These were arts which rely on *tools* or instruments, for example the art of playing the flute.[11] He thus divided Quintilian's "practical" arts into two: those requiring tools (which he called "organic") and those, like the dance, requiring no tools (which he called "practical").

6. CICERO'S CLASSIFICATION. Cicero usually relied on traditional classification of the arts: the liberal and the servile or the useful and the pleasurable. Occasionally, however, he referred to other classifications. Thus, taking the value of any art as the basis of classification, he would divide them into the highest (*artes maximae*), the middle (*artes mediocres*) and the lower (*minores*). The political and military arts he regarded as the highest; the intellectual arts headed by philosophy (*procreatrix et quasi parens omnium laudatarum artium*) and including poetry and oratory he classified in the middle, while in the lowest category he placed the remaining arts, that is, painting, sculpture, music, acting and athletics. The majority of the "fine" arts thus found themselves in the lowest category, and this affords further proof that the ancients did not value highly the arts at which they excelled.

Cicero outlined yet another classification into articulate and silent arts (*artes mutae*).[12] Poetry, oratory and music belonged to the first category, painting and sculpture to the second. He only mentioned this division, however, in passing and it neither gained acceptance nor exercised any influence in antiquity. It acquired great significance in the modern theory of art, however. It was made with reference to the arts of imitation or entertainment and it separated two significant groups of arts: the articulate and the visual.

7. THE CLASSIFICATION OF PLOTINUS. In the twilight of antiquity Plotinus once more attempted to classify the arts. He, too, classified them on the basis of the all-inclusive Greek meaning of the term. We shall refer to his classifications in the following chapter, which is devoted to his aesthetics, but we must anticipate here that in the 4th *Ennead* (IV, 4, 31) he divided the arts according to their tools, into those which rely on the *forces of nature*, and those which rely on their *own tools*. To these he added yet the third category of the psychagogic arts, which make use of *mental tools*.[13] This classification by Plotinus echoes Plato and Aristotle but also contains independent ideas.

Another classification appears in the 5th *Ennead* (V, 9, 11). It is probably the fullest of all those devised in antiquity and represents its last word on the subject of art.[14] Plotinus divided the arts into the *productive*, such as architecture, the *imitative*, such as painting, sculpture, the dance, pantomime and music, those *which aid nature*, such as agriculture and medicine, those which *improve human activity*, such as rhetoric, strategy, economics and the art of government, and the purely *intellectual* arts, such as geometry. Despite the significant part that beauty played in Plotinus' philosophy, he did not distinguish the "fine" arts as a particular type of art; they are to be found in three of the five types of art which he recognized.

8. SIX CLASSIFICATIONS. It may thus be stated that Graeco-Roman antiquity produced at least six classifications of the arts. The first, which originated with the Sophists, took as its basis the purpose of the arts and from this standpoint distinguished those that were "useful" from those that were "entertaining", or, to use slightly different terminology, those that were "necessary in life" from those that were "pleasurable".

The second classification, formulated by Plato and Aristotle, took as its basis the *relation of the arts to reality* and divided them into those which "create things" and those which "create images" or, in another version, into those which "complete nature" and those which "imitate her".

The third classification divided the arts according to the *activities*, mental or physical, required of the practitioner. The arts which demanded only mental activity were termed "liberal", while those requiring physical effort were termed "servile". Galen called the former "intellectual" arts and the latter "handicrafts". The true intention of these divisions was to separate the higher arts from the lower, and for this reason Cicero's division into the "highest", the "middle" and the "lower" arts may be regarded as related to it.

The fourth classification, recorded by Quintilian, took as its basis the *degree of realization* attainable in each of the arts, which were accordingly divided into the "theoretical", the "practical" and the "poietic". This classification had the merit of separating the sciences and of not mixing them with the productive arts.

The fifth, which originated with Cicero, divided the arts on the basis of the *physical material* which they employ. From this point of view the arts were divided into the articulate and the "mute".

The sixth, devised by Plotinus, divided the arts according to the *tools* which they employ.

The classification of Posidonius and Seneca was a combination of the third and the first classification and distinguished four types of arts which it called the "vulgar", the "entertaining", the "educative" and the "liberal". It was an eclectic classification without any unifying principle. The same applies to the fivefold classification of Plotinus, which is an amalgam of the first, second and fourth classifications. It is more nearly a collection of the most important types of art than a true classification.

Though Hellenistic writers took an intense interest in classifications of art, the most valuable were those which had been formulated earlier, i.e., chiefly the first three. Plutarch's classification had been prepared by Aristotle, as was the fourth classification.

The historical significance of these classifications, their diffusion and recognition in the ancient world were in each case very different. Only two of them, the first (made according to the artist's activity) became universal. The second (made according to the relation of the arts to reality) gained acceptance in learned circles but never spread beyond them.

It is remarkable that from the earliest times Greek arts fell into two large groups, the expressive, including poetry, music and the dance, and the contemplative, including sculpture and architecture. Yet in no ancient writer do we find a division of the arts into these two categories. The reason for this is that the ancients did not regard the expressive arts as arts. These appeared in their writings under the title of "poetry". The fundamental duality of Greek art found expression in the opposition of art and poetry.

9. "FINE" ARTS. None of these classifications helped to distinguish the "fine" arts, which are of special interest to aesthetics. The concepts of arts as "liberal", as "entertaining" or as "poietic" were both too wide and too narrow. Among the fine arts are to be found some that were liberal and some that were servile, some that were practical and some that were poietic. Therefore, this division could not be employed as a basis to separate the "fine" arts from the rest. The classification of the arts into productive and imitative might have proved more fruitful in this respect, but the uncertainty and lack of clarity inherent in the concept of "imitation" blurred this distinction.

The aesthetic arts could have been distinguished either because they contain beauty or because they contain an expression of human experiences. The first idea was alien to the Greeks of the classical era, the second one was familiar, but they did not apply it to the classification of the arts. Two other thoughts were adopted by the Hellenistic writers, however: that certain arts are guided by the imagination and by ideas. Both thoughts could have served as a basis for distinguishing the aesthetic arts; but this did not happen in antiquity.

Comparatively the greatest advance in the separation of the "fine" arts was made at the close of antiquity by Philostratus the Elder.[15] The idea which he presented (in his treatise *On Gymnastics*) was that there are two types of art. Some arts are handicrafts, others are something more and to this latter group he gave the name *sophia*. This term was originally applied by the Greeks to the gifts of both sages and of poets and artists, before it was confined to sages. Philostratus, however, widened the term again to include artists. There is no modern term which corresponds to this ancient idea and the closest we can come to it is perhaps "artistic skill". In this concept Philostratus included both sciences and those arts which we call "fine" arts. It might be imagined that his division into common arts and higher artistic skills was synonymous with the division into common and liberal arts. Yet his distinction was different, because the test for inclusion among the higher arts was not the negative one of absence of physical toil. He admitted that sculpture and the shaping of artistic objects in stone and metal were higher arts. The test was the positive one of a loftier and freer mental effort. In Philostratus the "fine" arts were still not covered by a single term and were still classed together [with skills, but this was for the first time in antiquity (indeed the only time, if the sources are to be trusted) that the "fine" arts were listed together in full and all included within the same concept.

10. THEORY OF THE ARTS. Music, poetry, oratory, painting, sculpture and architecture were in antiquity practised separately and each one had its own theory.

Each of these special theories posed different problems, but some had general application to all the arts. The theory of music was concerned with the dependence of subjective aesthetic experience on objective mathematical proportions: it was also concerned with the educative effect of music. The theory of architecture emphasized problems of artistic composition and artistic canons. The theory of painting and sculpture was concerned with the artist's psychology, with his creative or reproductive attitude to the world. Rhetoric succeeded in distinguishing between various styles and forms of artistic expression. But it was in poetics that the problems were most wide-ranging, for they touched on the question of artistic truth, the relation between form and content, of inspiration and skill and of intuition and rules. Poetics was concerned with the largest number of those problems which in later centuries were to become the subject of aesthetics. Cumulatively these special theories of the arts stood for one general theory, which did not exist.

P. Texts on the Classification of the Arts

PLATO, Gorg. 465 A.

1. ἐγὼ δὲ τέχνην οὐ καλῶ ὃ ἂν ᾖ ἄλογον πρᾶγμα.

1. And I do not call any irrational activity an art.

tr. B. Jowett

JOANNES DOXAPATRES, In Aphthoni Progymnasmata (H. Rabe, Prolegomenon Sylloge, 113)

2. πᾶσα... τέχνη τοὺς μὲν κανόνας ἔχει καθολικούς, τὰ δὲ ἀποτελέσματα μερικά.

2. In every art the rules are universal, but the products individual.

tr. J. C. B. Lowe

ANON, In Hermogenis De statibus (H. Rabe ib. 321).

DIVISION OF THE ARTS ACCORDING TO UTILITY AND PLEASURE

3. [ἑκάστη τέχνη] πρὸς τρία τέλη ἀφορᾷ, ἢ πρὸς τέρψιν ὡς γραφική, ἢ πρὸς χρήσιμον

3. [Each art] has [one of] three ends in view: either pleasure, like the art of drawing,

ὡς ἡ γεωργική, ἢ πρὸς τὰ συναμφότερα [ὡς ἡ μουσική]. τὸν γὰρ ἀγριαίνοντα θυμὸν ἡμεροῖ καὶ τόν πεπτωκότα ἀνεγείρει.

Cf. also Isocrates E 4 and Cicero K 10, above.

PLATO, Respublica 601 D.

4. See above: F 22 and 23.

PLATO, Sophista 219 A.

See above: F 23.
Similar classification is given in Laertius Diogenes, III 100.

ARISTOTLE, Physica 199 a 15.

5. See above: G 6.

SCHOLIA to DIONYSIUS THRAX
(Bekker, An. Gr. II 654).

6. ἔτι δὲ τῶν τεχνῶν αἱ μὲν εἰσι βάναυσοι, αἱ δὲ ἐγκύκλιοι. καὶ βάναυσοι μὲν, αἳ καὶ χειρωνακτικαὶ λέγονται, ὥσπερ ἡ χαλκευτικὴ καὶ τεκτονική. ...ἐγκύκλιοι δέ εἰσιν, ἃς ἔνιοι λογικὰς καλοῦσιν, οἷον ἀστρονομία, γεωμετρία, μουσική, φιλοσοφία, ἰατρική, γραμματική, ῥητορική. ἐγκυκλίους δὲ αὐτὰς καλοῦσιν, ὅτι τὸν τεχνίτην ⟨δεῖ⟩ διὰ πασῶν αὐτῶν ὁδεύσαντα, τὸ χρειῶδες ἀφ' ἑκάστης εἰς τὴν ἑαυτοῦ εἰσάγειν.

Similar classification is given by Cicero: see: K 9.

GALEN, Protrepticus 14
(Marquardt, 129).

7. διττῆς οὔσης διαφορᾶς τῆς πρώτης ἐν ταῖς τέχναις — ἔνιαι μὲν γὰρ αὐτῶν λογικαί τ' εἰσὶ καὶ σεμναί, τινὲς δ' εὐκαταφρόνητοι καὶ διὰ τῶν τοῦ σώματος πόνων, ἃς δὲ βαναύσους τε καὶ χειρωνακτικὰς ὀνομάζουσιν — ἄμεινον ἂν εἴη τοῦ προτέρου γένους τῶν τεχνῶν μετέρχεσθαί τινα. τὸ γάρ τοι δεύτερον γένος αὐτῶν ἀπολείπειν εἴωθε γηρῶντας τοὺς

or utility, like agriculture, or both [like music]. For it tames the wild spirit and rouses the fallen.

tr. J. C. B. Lowe

DIVISION OF THE ARTS ACCORDING TO THEIR PRODUCTIVE AND THEIR IMITATIVE FUNCTIONS

4. See above: Plato, F 22 and 23

ARTS DIVIDED INTO THOSE WHICH SUPPLEMENT AND THOSE WHICH IMITATE NATURE

5. See above: Aristotle, G 6.

ARTS DIVIDED INTO HANDICRAFTS AND ENCYCLICAL ARTS

6. Among the arts some are crafts, while others are "encyclical", i.e., forming part of general education. Crafts, which are also called "handicrafts", are such activities as metal working and building... The arts which form part of general education, are also called "mental" by some, and include such arts as astronomy, geometry, music, philosophy, medicine, grammar and oratory. They are given this name because the artist must work his way through all of them in order to pick out whatever he finds useful for his particular art.

(Note: Those arts which the Greeks considered to be part of general education they called "encyclical", i.e., "forming a circle", a circle of knowledge through which every educated person must pass.)

INTELLECTUAL ARTS AND HANDICRAFTS

7. There is a twofold difference between the arts, because some of them are mental and dignified, while others are despised and are the product of physical toil, and these latter we call crafts or handicrafts. For this reason it would be better if everyone applied himself to the first type of art because artists have to abandon the second type as they grow old.

τεχνίτας. εἰσὶ δ' ἐκ τοῦ προτέρου γένους ἰατρική τε καὶ ῥητορικὴ καὶ μουσική, γεωμετρία τε καὶ ἀριθμητικὴ καὶ λογιστικὴ καὶ ἀστρονομία καὶ γραμματικὴ καὶ νομική. πρόσθες δ' εἰ βούλει, ταύταις πλαστικήν τε καὶ γραφικήν· εἰ γὰρ καὶ διὰ τῶν χειρῶν ἐνεργοῦνται, ἀλλ' οὐκ ἰσχύος νεανικῆς δεῖται τὸ ἔργον αὐτῶν.

The first type includes medicine, oratory, music, geometry, arithmetic, logic, astronomy, grammar and law. You may, if you wish, also add sculpture and painting, for, though these last two arts require the use of hands, they do not demand great youthful strength.

POSIDONIUS (Seneca, Epist. 88, 21).

8. See above: J. 23.

THE FOURFOLD DIVISION ACCORDING TO THE STOICS

8. See above: J 23.

QUINTILIAN, Inst. orat. II 18, 1.

9. Quum sint autem artium aliae positae in inspectione, id est cognitione et aestimatione rerum, qualis est astrologia, nullum exigens actum, sed ipso rei, cuius studium habet, intellectu contenta, quae θεωρητικὴ vocatur; aliae in agendo, quarum in hoc finis est, et ipso actu perficitur, nihilque post actum operis relinquit quae πρακτικὴ dicitur, qualis saltatio est; aliae in effectu, quae operis, quod oculis subicitur, consummatione finem accipiunt, quam ποιητικὴν appellamus, qualis est pictura.

ARTS DIVIDED INTO THE THEORETICAL, THE PRACTICAL AND THE "POIETIC"

9. Some arts, however, are based on examination, that is to say, on the knowledge and proper appreciation of things, as, for instance, astronomy which demands no action, but is content to understand the subject of its study; such arts are called "theoretical". Others again are concerned with action: this is their end which once performed, nothing more remains to do: these arts we style "practical"; and dancing will provide us with an example. Thirdly, there are others, which consist in producing a certain result and achieve their purpose in the completion of a visible task; such we style "productive"; and painting may be quoted as an illustration.

tr. H. E. Butler

SCHOLIA to DIONYSIUS THRAX (Bekker, An. Gr. II 670).

"PERIPOIETIC ARTS"

10. τέτταρα δὲ εἴδη τεχνῶν εἰσί. τὰς μὲν γὰρ θεωρητικὰς καλοῦσι, τὰς δὲ πρακτικάς, τὰς δὲ ἀποτελεστικάς, τὰς δέ περιποιητικάς. καὶ θεωρητικὰς μὲν, ὧν τέλος ἐν θεωρίᾳ ἢ ἐν λόγῳ, ὡς ἐπὶ ἀστρονομίας καὶ ἀριθμητικῆς. τῆς μὲν γὰρ ἴδιόν ἐστι τὸ θεωρῆσαι τὰς ὑποστάσεις καὶ περιφορὰς τῶν ἄστρων, τῆς δὲ τὸ θεωρῆσαι τὴν τῶν ἀριθμῶν διαίρεσιν καὶ σύνθεσιν. πρακτικὰς δέ, ἅς τινας μετὰ τὴν πρᾶξιν οὐχ ὁρῶμεν ὑφισταμένας, ὡς ἐπὶ κιθαριστικῆς καὶ ὀρχηστικῆς· μετὰ γὰρ τὸ παύσασθαι τὸν κιθαρῳδὸν καὶ τὸν ὀρχηστὴν τοῦ ὀρχεῖσθαι καὶ κιθαρίζειν, οὐκέτι πρᾶξις ὑπολείπεται. ἀποτελεστικὰς δὲ λέγουσιν, ὧν τινῶν τὰ ἀποτελέσματα μετὰ τὴν πρᾶξιν ὁρῶνται, ὡς ἐπὶ τῆς ἀνδριαντο-

10. There are four types of art: some are called theoretical, some are called practical, others productive and causative. The ones called theoretical are those whose sole aim is rational enquiry, as in the case of astronomy and arithmetic: the first one is concerned with the substance and the orbits of the stars, and the second with analysis and synthesis of numbers. Practical ones are those which cease when the activity comes to an end, as is the case with lyre-playing and the dance: for the moment the lyre-player ceases to play or the dancer ceases to dance and play the lyre, there remains no residual product. Productive ones are those whose products we can see when the activity has ceased, as is the case with sculpture

ποιίας καὶ οἰκοδομικῆς. μετὰ γὰρ τὸ ἀποτελέσαι τὸν ἀνδριαντοποιὸν τὸν ἀνδριάντα καὶ τὸν οἰκοδόμον τὸ κτίσμα, μένει ὁ ἀνδριὰς καὶ τὸ κτισθέν. περιποιητικὰς δὲ καλοῦσι τὰς περιποίησιν δηλούσας, ὡς ἐπὶ τῆς ἁλιευτικῆς καὶ τῆς θηρευτικῆς.

and building, for when a sculptor has finished the statue and the builder has built the house, there remains a statue and a building. Finally, causative are those arts which acquire something and thus increase our possessions, as is the case with fishing and hunting.

SCHOLIA to DIONYSIUS THRAX
(Bekker, An. Gr. II 652).

11. φασὶ δὲ τῶν τεχνῶν διαφορὰς τέσσαρας εἶναι. λέγουσι γὰρ ὅτι τῶν τεχνῶν αἱ μέν εἰσι ποιητικαί, αἱ δὲ θεωρητικαί, αἱ δὲ πρακτικαί, αἱ δὲ μικταί. ...
... Λούκιος δὲ ὁ Ταρραῖος λέγει ὅτι τῆς τέχνης εἴδη τέσσαρα, ἀποτελεσματικόν, πρακτικόν, ὀργανικόν, θεωρηματικόν. καὶ ἀποτελεσματικαὶ μέν εἰσι τέχναι, ὅσαι εἰς συντέλειαν ἦσαν καὶ τὸ συμφέρον ἀπαρτίζουσι καὶ συμπεραίνουσι πᾶν τὸ κατασκευαζόμενον... ὀργανικὰ δὲ εἰσι ὅσαι δι' ὀργάνων συνεστήκασι.

ORGANIC ARTS

11. It is said that the arts differ among themselves in four ways, because some are productive [poietic], others are theoretical, practical and mixed.
...While Lucius Tarrhaeus says that there are four types of art: the productive, practical, organic and theoretical. The productive ones are those which produce something useful and take care to bring their products to a finished state... The organic are those which come about through the use of tools.
(Note: The term "productive art" (*apotelesmatike techne*) is derived from *telos* ("end"), and the term "organic art" is derived from *organon* ("tool").

CICERO, De Oratore III 7, 26.
12. See above: K 11.

DIVISION INTO VERBAL AND MUTE ARTS
12. See above: Cicero, K 11.

PLOTINUS IV 4, 31.
13. See below: R 21.

FIRST DIVISION ACCORDING TO PLOTINUS
13. See below: Plotinus, R 21

PLOTINUS V 9, 11.
14. See below: R 22.

SECOND DIVISION ACCORDING TO PLOTINUS
14. See below: Plotinus, R 22.

PHILOSTRATUS, De gymnastica 1 (261 k).

15. σοφίαν ἡγώμεθα καὶ τὰ τοιαῦτα μὲν οἷον φιλοσοφῆσαι καὶ εἰπεῖν ξὺν τέχνῃ ποιητικῆς τε ἅψασθαι καὶ μουσικῆς καὶ γεωμετρίας καὶ νὴ Δί' ἀστρονομίας, ὁπόση μὴ περιττή, σοφία δὲ καὶ τὸ κοσμῆσαι στρατιὰν καὶ ἔτι τὰ τοιαῦτα· ἰατρικὴ πᾶσα καὶ ζωγραφία καὶ πλάσται καὶ ἀγαλμάτων εἴδη καὶ κοῖλοι λίθοι καὶ κοῖλος σίδηρος. βάναυσοι δὲ ὁπόσαι, δεδόσθω μὲν αὐταῖς τέχνη, καθ' ἣ ὄργανόν τι καὶ σκεῦος ὀρθῶς ἀποτελεσθήσεται, σοφία δὲ ἐς ἐκείνας ἀποκείσθω μόνας, ἃς εἶπον.

ART AS CRAFT AND AS HANDICRAFT

15. We shall regard as art, on the one hand, such activities as philosophizing, artistic speech, the practice of poetry, music and geometry, and indeed astronomy as well when it does not go beyond practical requirements, and, on the other hand, arranging troops in formations and similar activities, and, in addition, the whole of medicine, painting, modelling and various types of sculpture, and stone and metal products. On the other hand, we regard as handicrafts those arts which can turn out a tool or a utensil; but only the first-named are truly artistic.

12. The Aesthetics of Plotinus

1. PLOTINUS AND PLATO. Hellenistic aesthetics produced many valuable ideas, but these were concerned with details rather than with general theory. At the close of the epoch, in the third century A.D., however, Plotinus exhibited a new aesthetics.* It was new both in its metaphysical foundations and in its empirical analysis of beauty.

Plotinus took up the most fundamental problems of aesthetics which had not been raised since the classical times. He had little in common with Hellenistic aestheticians; indeed, his thought derived to such an extent from Plato that he is rightly regarded as Plato's successor. His philosophy is called neo-Platonism. But Plato lived at the beginning of the classical period, while Plotinus lived at the close of the Hellenistic era. The six centuries which divided them had left their mark, and although Plotinus agreed with Plato, the differences between their philosophies are considerable.

Plotinus (born ca. 203, died 269–70) was both a very original philosopher and an erudite scholar. He came from Egypt and spent his youth in Alexandria, but at the age of forty he moved to Rome. Here his philosophy found supporters. It was a thoroughly personal philosophy, but in its spiritualism and transcedentalism it conformed to the spirit of the times.

Plotinus began to write at the age of fifty. He left 54 treatises, which were later arranged in six *Enneads*, that is, groups of nine, and it is under this title that they are known. They covered many subjects and were not composed systematically, but had a common underlying thought and expounded a uniform system. This system was idealistic, spiritualistic, and transcendental. Aesthetic problems occupied an important place in it,† more so than in former Greek system. *Enneads* I, 6 ("On beauty") and V, 8 ("On intellectual beauty") were particularly concerned with aesthetics. The *Enneads* disclose a development of Plotinus' ideas from a position comparatively close to traditional views to an independent one. His two main treatises on beauty are characteristic of his earlier thought.

It is a paradox that such an abstract and transcendental philosopher should have played such a significant role in the history of aesthetics and devoted so much thought to sensory beauty. He conceived this beauty of shapes and colours, however, as the reflection of different, more perfect supramundane beauty.

Both Plotinus and Plato contrasted two worlds: "this" world and the one "there", as Plotinus called them, or in other words, the imperfect material world of the senses in which we live and the perfect, spiritual world which is independent of our senses and which we can only approach through thought. The difference between the aesthetics of the two philosophers lay in the fact that Plotinus, notwithstanding

---

* E. Krakowski, *Une philosophie de l'amour et de la beauté* (Paris, 1929).

† E. de Keyser, *La signification de l'art dans les "Ennéades" de Plotin,* (Louvain, 1955). F. Bourbon di Petrella, *Il problema dell'arte e della bellezza in Plotino*, 1956. A. Plebe, "Origini e problemi dell'estetica antica", *Momenti e problemi di storia dell'estetica,* vol. I (1959), pp. 1–80.

his transsensory aspirations, highly appreciated sensory beauty. He saw in it the most perfect property of the sensory world, and even its only perfect property, because he thought it was one which proceeded directly from the ideal world.

2. DEFINITION OF BEAUTY. The traditional conception generally accepted in Greece defined beauty as *symmetria*, thus expressing the conviction that beauty depends on relation, measure, mathematical proportion and agreement of parts. This conception of beauty, introduced by the Pythagoreans, adopted by Plato and Aristotle, was centuries later still preserved by Cicero, who called beauty *apta figura membrorum*, and by Lucian, who explained it as "the unity and harmony of parts in relation to the whole".

Plotinus[1] rejected this definition for several reasons. He argued first that if beauty depended on *symmetria*, it would only appear in complex objects and would not be present in a particular colour or sound, nor be discernible in the sun, in light, in gold or in lightning. None of these has either multiplicity or diversity and yet they are among the most beautiful things. Secondly, he argued that the same face may appear either more or less beautiful depending on its expression. This would not be possible if beauty depended solely on proportion, because, despite changes in expression, the proportions of the face remain constant. Thirdly, he argued, that beauty cannot consist in accordance because there may also be accordance in evil and accordance is never beautiful in evil. His fourth argument was that the concept of *symmetria* may indeed be applied to material objects, but not to spiritual ones such as virtue, knowledge or a beautiful social system. Thus, the traditional definition of beauty can at best only apply to some beautiful objects but not to all.

With these arguments Plotinus attacked the basic tenet of ancient aesthetics that beauty depends on relationship and on the arrangement of parts. He regarded it as an axiom that some beautiful objects are simple, having no parts. From this he inferred that beauty cannot be a question of relationship; it must therefore be a *quality*. This was the first basic thesis of Plotinus' aesthetics.

3. INNER FORM. Plotinus thought that the beauty of some objects might depend on *symmetria*, i.e., on relations and proportions, but that these were merely the external manifestation of beauty and not its essence. The essence and source of beauty is not *symmetria* but that which reveals itself in *symmetria*, or, as Plotinus put it, which "illuminates"[2] *symmetria*. Beauty consists in unity and, he thought, there is no unity in matter; therefore matter cannot be the source of beauty. Thus, the source of beauty can only be spirit. This thesis that the source of beauty is spirit replaced in Plotinus the old thesis that its source is *symmetria*. As he put it, beauty is ultimately neither form nor colour nor magnitude, but the soul.[3] For a transcendental philosopher like Plotinus it was only natural to think that a soul can delight only in another soul. If sensory phenomena, colours and shapes, also delight us it is because the soul expresses itself in them. The analysis of sensory beauty proves that it is not purely sensory but includes intellectual elements.[4]

The common Greek concept of beauty embraced both sensory and intellectual beauty. Plato was interested only in intellectual beauty, and Hellenistic aestheticians in sensory beauty. The position of Plotinus was different from both. He saw in beauty an attribute of the sensory world which, however, reveals the intellectual world.[5] Bodies are beautiful, but they are so by virtue of the spirit.[6] In other words, the world of the senses is beautiful, but it is so through the ideal model (*archetypon*) of beauty.[7] Or again, external forms are beautiful, but the source of their beauty lies in their inner form (*to endon eidos*). If a building did not emerge from the mind of an architect, it would not have a beautiful shape. Neo-Platonic aesthetics assumed that external shape, *symmetria* and harmony have beauty but that it is a borrowed beauty which "shares" in the inner, spiritual, intellectual and ideal form.

It is easy to detect a certain ambiguity in Plotinus' concept of beauty: on the one hand it referred to a *psychic* image ("inner form") and on the other to an *ideal* image ("model"). But Plotinus quite deliberately did not differentiate between the two. He retained the old concept of beauty as that which arouses admiration, but also created the new concept of beauty as revelation of the spirit in matter.

Despite this ambiguity, certain characteristics of the Neo-Platonic concept are clear. First, beauty was held to reside not only in *symmetria*, that is, not solely in the arrangement of parts, but also in the parts themselves. Second, even if it does reside in *symmetria*, *symmetria* is not its source, but only its external manifestation. Matter is not in itself beautiful, but the spirit which reveals itself in it and which alone has unity, reason and form.[8]

Only a spirit can recognize a spirit; therefore only a spirit can grasp beauty. "Only the soul which has become beautiful can see beauty", but then "it perceives it at first sight". The eye must become similar to the contemplated object before it can contemplate it. The eye could never see the sun without becoming sun-like. Every human being, therefore, should become divine and beautiful if he wants to see goodness and beauty.[9]

Plotinus' aesthetics was spiritualistic, but it was not anthropocentric. In nature there are more spiritual and creative forces than in man. Only an artist who has completely mastered his art can create as nature does. Beauty in nature has the same source as it has in art: nature is beautiful because an idea shines through it; and likewise art is beautiful because the artist endows it with the idea. But nature possesses more beauty than does art: "A living creature even when it is ugly is more beautiful than a beautiful statue". Despite the changes which Plotinus introduced into aesthetics, the old Greek conviction of the superiority of nature over art had retained its force, although the justification for this was now different.[10]

4. BEAUTY AND ART. Plotinus' general position had far-reaching consequences for his theory of art:

A. When art represents the world of the senses, its subject is full of deficiencies and imperfections; however, art can have a different subject. The statue which the artist has sculpted or the temple which he has constructed may also be a *mirror of the spirit*; and only then does it have real value. This was true, Plotinus said, of the most highly valued statues and temples.[11] Although Plotinus took a special interest in painting and sculpture, he ranked music higher. He did so because he observed that music does not take bodily objects as its model and is concerned only with harmony and rhythm.

B. In Plotinus there developed an altered view of the function of the arts. Hitherto the majority of the Greeks and the Romans had thought that the function of the visual arts and the literary arts was representational. This mimetic doctrine was rejected in the spiritualistic philosophy of Plotinus, who wrote: "The arts do not simply copy visible objects, but reach out to principles of nature; the arts provide much themselves, for they can add where there is deficiency; they can do so since in themselves they possess beauty.[12,13]

C. Phidias sculpted his Zeus, Plotinus wrote, not in accordance with what he saw, but in the guise that Zeus would have appeared had he wished to reveal himself to us.[14]

Plotinus compared two blocks of stone, one in its natural state and the other shaped by the artist.[15] The latter did not originally possess this shape, it was the artist who possessed it and transferred it onto the stone. The shape of the stone is not imitated from nature, but is derived from the artist's idea. The beauty of the inner shape passed into the stone to the extent to which the stone was obedient to art.

Thus art comes about by virtue of the artist's *Idea*. Plotinus, however, understood the Idea differently from his Greek and Roman predecessors. For Plato the Idea was eternal and immutable, while for Plotinus it was the live idea of the artist. For Cicero the idea in the artist's mind was a psychological phenomenon, whereas for Plotinus it was a metaphysical one, being a reflection of the transcendent model.

With Plotinus the artist in one sense was creator, and in another sense he was not. He was creative in so far as he did not reproduce reality but the "inner shape" which he had in his mind. The inner shape is, however, not his creation but a reflection of an eternal model.

Plotinus recognized uniqueness in the work of the artist who interprets things in his own way.[16] On the other hand, in agreement with the traditional view, he regarded this work in a way as automatic. He was convinced that the artist succeeds through skill and that he reasons only when he meets a difficulty.[17]

Plotinus placed art between this world and the other. It is of *this* world because it represents real things and visible forms; but it is also of the other world because it springs from the artist's mind.[18] The works of a painter, Plotinus said, are usually contemplated quietly because of their attractive *symmetria* and order, but sometimes they shock the spectator because they remind him of the distant, eternal model behind him.[19]

D. Art is *knowledge*. Scientific knowledge consists of assertions and is based on observation and ratiocination. But there are two kinds of knowledge; it may consist either in assertions or in images; it may be reached either through ratiocination or by direct perception. Figurative and direct knowledge is the province of art; and "the wisdom of the gods and the blessed is expressed not in statements but in beautiful pictures". Through them men can attain an intellectual vision of the world and embrace its order; through them "the world becomes transparent to the mind".

E. Different arts have various aims: some represent reality and some are useful to people. Nevertheless, for such as the visual arts, music and poetry these are minimal aims since their proper function is the investment of things with spiritual shape and thereby the *creation of beauty*. Thus Plotinus' theory implied a kinship between art and beauty.[20] More than any earlier aesthetic theory, it considered beauty to be the first task, the value and the measure of art. This has been called "Plotinus' unsurpassable achievement". Today such an interpretation of art appears quite natural, but the history of aesthetics teaches us that in antiquity few would have accepted it. What is remarkable is that this interpretation was conceived by a metaphysician and spiritualist.

F. Plotinus outlined two classifications of the arts. The first divided the arts according to whether they employ their own tools or make use of the forces of nature.[21] The second ordered the arts according to their proximity to the "higher" spiritual world.[22] It distinguished five kinds of arts. Those which 1. produce physical objects, such as architecture, and which 2. improve nature, such as medicine; both have no connection with the spiritual world "there"; 3. imitative arts also generally lack this link but may have it if, as in the case of music, they concentrate on rhythm and harmony; the link is more likely to occur, in arts which 4. introduce beauty into human activities, as in rhetoric or politics, and particularly in those 5. concerned exclusively with the intellectual matters, such as geometry.

Though Plotinus concentrated on the world beyond, his speculations were combined with observations. So also was his division of the arts, which, although it was undertaken from a transcendent viewpoint, was the most detailed of those known in antiquity.

Plotinus' philosophy was based on the concepts of the *absolute* and of the *emanation*. The absolute radiates like light, and all the forms of reality have emanated from it; first the world of ideas, then the world of the souls, and finally the world of matter. Worlds are the more imperfect the further they are away from the absolute; but even the world of matter, which is furthest away, is an emanation of the absolute; and its beauty is the reflection of the absolute.

Man, who lives in this imperfect world, wishes to *return* to the higher worlds from which he has come. One of the paths leading there is art. As a result of this conviction Plotinus placed beauty and art at the very core of philosophy and made them an essential element of his philosophical system.

5. VIRTUES AND WEAKNESSES OF PLOTINUS' AESTHETICS. In Plotinus' aesthetics two aspects must be distinguished. On the one hand, there is his metaphysical con-

ception: vertiginous, abstract, transcendent and emanative, into which beauty and art have been incorporated. On the other hand, there are his aesthetic ideas which are independent of his metaphysics. The concept of beauty as a quality (and not as a relation between parts), the recognition of the intellectual element in sensory beauty, the admission of beauty as the proper object of art, the recognition of the imagistic character of art and of its direct, emotional impact:[23] these are Plotinus' aesthetic discoveries independent of his metaphysics.

There can be no doubt whatever that these ideas are important in the history of aesthetics. It was rather the metaphysical edifice which could and did invite criticism. Plotinus wrote: "He who looks at physical beauty should not lose himself in it, but should realize that it is only an image, a hint and a shadow, and should *flee* to that of which it is a reflection". Using his own term, we may say that his aesthetics is an *aesthetics of flight*; a flight from where? From the only beauty we know directly but which for Plotinus had become no more than a shadow. A flight towards what? Towards pure fiction, in the view of the historian hostile to metaphysical aesthetics. One historian even maintained that Plotinus did no more than duplicate the existing beauty and transfer its double into the world beyond. But historians who are favourable to Plotinus stress that his attempt to fit beauty into a metaphysical system showed considerable daring and is almost the only such attempt ever made.

6. A PROGRAMME FOR ART. The practical consequence of Plotinus' aesthetics was the creation of a programme for art essentially different from all that had gone before. In the case of painting, which was most amenable to his reforms, he worked out this programme in detail.

The most important points in his programme were these: (*a*) all that is the result of imperfection in the sense of sight must be avoided, i.e., diminution of size and the fading of colour (which is the consequence of seeing them from a distance), deformation (through perspective), and alterations in the appearance of things (produced by light and shade). Things must therefore be shown as the spectator sees them at close quarters, all together in the foreground, in the same full light, in their particular colours and with all the details clear. (*b*) According to Plotinus' theory, matter was mass and darkness, while the spirit was light, so that in order to reach beyond matter to the spirit, painting should avoid depth and shadows and represent only the luminous surface of things. It is essential, he wrote, that, "to perceive its true size, we must have it [the object] close at hand".[24] All depth is matter and is therefore dark. Only the light which illumines matter is form, which can be perceived by the mind. Essentially this was a Platonic programme, but it was more radical and more detailed.

The type of painting which would follow logically from Plotinus' aesthetics flourished in reality at the time. Excavations at Dura-Europos have shown that it existed as early as the first century A.D. (*a*) In representing objects, an attempt was made to eliminate the spectator and his incidental effect, so that the object revealed only its own permanent features. Each object was therefore represented in its true size, colour and shape, in a uniform full light without shadows, and upon a single plane without perspective. (*b*) The object so represented had no contact with its surroundings; it did not even touch the earth and appeared to be suspended in the air. (*c*) It was however represented meticulously, each detail being portrayed as it is seen when the attention is exclusively concentrated upon it. (*d*) This concentration on a single plane brought about the disappearance of depth. Bodies lost their mass and weight. And, although paintings represented real bodies, they did not reproduce the pattern and character of the real world. Instead, they turned the real world into a transparent shell for the spiritual world. (*e*) Further, real forms were replaced by schematic forms, and organic forms by geometric forms. The artist would make strenuous efforts to render reality faithfully in every detail, but in fact he would transform it and introduce a different order and rhythm into it. Thus, in the spirit of Plotinus, he would try to transcend material phenomena and to obtain "an inner vision and a deep union not with the sculpture but with the sculpted divinity". Thus "contemplation is not a spectacle, but another form of vision, namely ecstasy".[25]

Plotinus and his pupils did not, strangely enough, support the art which corresponded to their aesthetics. They supported the quite different traditional classic art, in which they saw a means of strengthening paganism and opposing Christianity. The Christians, on the contrary, developed an art akin to Plotinus, though they were hostile to him. They did not justify their spiritual art theoretically, but its justification was to be found in Plotinus. This is an example of historical parallelism, which is only partial, between aesthetic theories and artistic practice.

Plotinus' theory of art, particularly of painting, survived for centuries and became an essential element of mediaeval aesthetics. Echoes of it may be found already in the early Church Fathers; the chief link between Plotinus and the Middle Ages was the anonymous fifth century writer known as Pseudo-Dionysius. The art corresponding to Plotinus' theory, which was the negation of classical purely representational art, became for centuries the main current of Europe. Byzantine art, in particular, was a realization of Plotinus' programme, but Western art also had a similar basis.

In aesthetics, more clearly even than in other parts of his philosophy, Plotinus bridged two epochs: antiquity, in which he was born, and the Middle Ages, which he influenced. It is not easy to decide in which epoch he should be fitted. If one places him in the Middle Ages, he is torn from his roots; but if one places him in antiquity, he is torn from the fruits of his work. He succeeded Plato, but he was himself succeeded by Pseudo-Dionysius and the neo-Platonic current in scholastic aesthetics.

R. Texts from Plotinus

PLOTINUS I 6, 1.

1. Τὸ καλόν ἐστι μὲν ὄψει πλεῖστον, ἔστι δ' ἐν ἀκοαῖς κατά τε λόγων συνθέσεις καὶ ἐν μουσικῇ ἁπάσῃ· καὶ γὰρ μέλη καὶ ῥυθμοί εἰσι καλοί· ἔστι δὲ καὶ προιοῦσι πρὸς τὸ ἄνω ἀπὸ τῆς αἰσθήσεως καὶ ἐπιτηδεύματα καλὰ καὶ πράξεις καὶ ἕξεις καὶ ἐπιστῆμαί τε καὶ τὸ τῶν ἀρετῶν κάλλος. Εἰ δέ τι καὶ πρὸ τούτων, αὐτὸ δείξει. Τί οὖν δὴ τὸ πεποιηκὸς καὶ τὰ σώματα καλὰ φαντάζεσθαι καὶ τὴν ἀκοὴν ἐπινεύειν ταῖς φωναῖς, ὡς καλαί; Καὶ ὅσα ἐφεξῆς ψυχῆς ἔχεται, πῶς ποτε πάντα καλά; Καὶ ἆρά γε ἑνὶ καὶ τῷ αὐτῷ καλὰ τὰ πάντα, ἢ ἄλλο μὲν ἐν σώματι τὸ κάλλος, ἄλλο δὲ ἐν ἄλλῳ; Καὶ τίνα ποτὲ ταῦτα ἢ τοῦτο; Τὰ μὲν γὰρ οὐ παρ' αὐτῶν τῶν ὑποκειμένων καλά, οἷον τὰ σώματα, ἀλλὰ μεθέξει, τὰ δὲ κάλλη αὐτά, ὥσπερ ἀρετῆς ἡ φύσις. Σώματα μὲν γὰρ τὰ αὐτὰ ὁτὲ μὲν καλά, ὁτὲ δὲ οὐ καλὰ φαίνεται ὡς ἄλλου ὄντος τοῦ σώματα εἶναι, ἄλλου δὲ τοῦ καλά.

Τί οὖν ἐστι τοῦτο τὸ παρὸν τοῖς σώμασι; Πρῶτον γὰρ περὶ τούτου σκεπτέον. Τί οὖν ἐστιν, ὃ κινεῖ τὰς ὄψεις τῶν θεωμένων καὶ ἐπιστρέφει πρὸς αὐτὸ καὶ ἕλκει καὶ εὐφραίνεσθαι τῇ θέᾳ ποιεῖ; Τοῦτο γὰρ εὑρόντες τάχ' ἂν ἐπιβάθρᾳ αὐτῷ χρώμενοι καὶ τὰ ἄλλα θεασαίμεθα. Λέγεται μὲν δὴ παρὰ πάντων, ὡς εἰπεῖν, ὡς συμμετρία τῶν μερῶν πρὸς ἄλληλα καὶ πρὸς τὸ ὅλον τό τε τῆς εὐχροίας προστεθὲν τὸ πρὸς τὴν ὄψιν κάλλος ποιεῖ καὶ ἔστιν — αὐτοῖς καὶ ὅλως τοῖς ἄλλοις πᾶσι τὸ καλοῖς εἶναι τὸ συμμέτροις καὶ μεμετρημένοις ὑπάρχειν· οἷς ἁπλοῦν οὐδέν, μόνον δὲ τὸ σύνθετον ἐξ ἀνάγκης καλὸν ὑπάρξει· τό τε ὅλον ἔσται καλὸν αὐτοῖς, τὰ δὲ μέρη ἕκαστα οὐχ ἕξει παρ' ἑαυτῶν τὸ καλὰ εἶναι, πρὸς δὲ τὸ ὅλον συντελοῦντα, ἵνα καλὸν ᾖ· καίτοι δεῖ εἴπερ τὸ ὅλον, καὶ τὰ μέρη καλὰ εἶναι· οὐ γὰρ δὴ ἐξ αἰσχρῶν, ἀλλὰ πάντα κατειληφέναι τὸ κάλλος.

TYPES OF BEAUTY AND ITS ORIGIN

1. Beauty addresses itself chiefly to sight; but there is a beauty for the hearing too, as in certain combinations of words and in all kinds of music, for melodies and cadences are beautiful; and minds that lift themselves above the realm of sense to a higher order are aware of beauty in the conduct of life, in actions, in character, in the pursuits of the intellect; and there is the beauty of the virtues. What loftier beauty there may be yet our argument will bring to light.

What, then, is it that gives comeliness to material forms and draws the ear to the sweetness perceived in sounds, and what is the secret of the beauty that is in all that derives from soul?

Is there some One Principle from which all take their grace or is there a beauty peculiar to the embodied and another for the bodiless? Finally, one or many, what would such a principle be?

Consider that some things, material shapes, for instance, are gracious not by anything inherent but by something communicated, while others are lovely of themselves, as, for example, virtue. The same bodies appear sometimes beautiful, sometimes not; so that there is a good deal between being body and being beautiful.

What, then, is this something that shows itself in certain material forms? This is the natural beginning of our inquiry. What is it that attracts the eyes of those to whom a beautiful object is presented and calls them, lures them towards it; and fills them with joy at the sight? If we possess ourselves of this, we have at once a standpoint for a wider survey.

Almost everyone declares that the symmetry of parts towards each other and towards a whole, with, besides, a certain charm of colour, constitutes the beauty recognized by the eye, that in visible things, as indeed in all else, universally, the beautiful thing is essentially symmetrical, patterned. But think what this means. Only a compound can be beautiful, never anything devoid of parts; and only a whole; the several parts will have beauty not in themselves, but only as working together to give a comely total. Yet beauty in an aggregate demands beauty in details: it cannot be constructed out of ugliness; its law must run throughout.

tr. S. Mackenna

PLOTINUS VI 7, 22.

2. Διὸ καὶ ἐνταῦθα φατέον μᾶλλον τὸ κάλλος τὸ ἐπὶ τῇ συμμετρίᾳ ἐπιλαμπόμενον ἢ τὴν συμμετρίαν εἶναι καὶ τοῦτο εἶναι τὸ ἐράσμιον. ... τῶν ἀγαλμάτων δὲ τὰ ζωτικώτερα καλλίω κἂν συμμετρότερα τὰ ἕτερα ᾖ· καὶ αἰσχίων ζῶν καλλίων τοῦ ἐν ἀγάλματι καλοῦ; ἢ ὅτι τοδὶ ἐφετὸν μᾶλλον· τοῦτο δ' ὅτι ψυχὴν ἔχει· τοῦτο δ' ὅτι ἀγαθοειδέστερον.

PROPORTION AND RADIANCE

2. So here below, too, beauty, that which is really lovely, is what illuminates good proportions rather than the good proportions themselves... And are not statues more beautiful if they are more lifelike, even if others are better proportioned; and is not an ugly living man more beautiful than a beautiful statue? Yes, because the living is more desirable; and it is more desirable because it has soul; and it has soul because it has more the form of Good.

tr. A. H. Armstrong

PLOTINUS I 6, 6.

3. καὶ δὴ καὶ τὰ σώματα, ὅσα οὕτω λέγεται, ψυχὴ ἤδη ποιεῖ· ἅτε γὰρ θεῖον οὖσα καὶ οἷον μοῖρα τοῦ καλοῦ, ὧν ἂν ἐφάψεται καὶ κρατῇ, καλὰ ταῦτα, ὡς δυνατὸν αὐτοῖς μεταλαβεῖν, ποιεῖ.

BODILY BEAUTY CAUSED BY THE SOUL

3. After all, the soul is that which also makes bodies, which we call beautiful, beautiful. For it is something divine and seemingly a particle of beauty. So, whatever it touches, over whatever it gains control, that object becomes beautiful, so long as [that object which it does touch] can have a share in beauty.

PLOTINUS VI 3, 16.

4. τὸ καλὸν τὸ ἐν σώματι ἀσώματον· ἀλλ' ἀπέδομεν αὐτὸ αἰσθητὸν ὂν τοῖς περὶ σῶμα καὶ σώματος.

4. The beauty inherent in body is similarly bodiless: but it is subject to sense-perception and we have therefore assigned it to the order of things bound up with body and subordinate to it.

tr. C. Mackenna

PLOTINUS I 6,2.

5. τί δῆτά ἐστι τὸ ἐν τοῖς σώμασι καλὸν πρῶτον· ἔστι μὲν γάρ τι καὶ ἐπιβολῇ τῇ πρώτῃ αἰσθητὸν γινόμενον καὶ ἡ ψυχὴ ὥσπερ συνεῖσα λέγει καὶ ἐπιγνοῦσα ἀποδέχεται καὶ οἷον συναρμόττεται. πρὸς δὲ τὸ αἰσχρὸν προσβαλοῦσα ἀνίλλεται καὶ ἀρνεῖται καὶ ἀνανεύει ἀπ' αὐτοῦ οὐ συμφωνοῦσα καὶ ἀλλοτριουμένη. ... τίς οὖν ὁμοιότης τοῖς τῇδε πρὸς τὰ ἐκεῖ καλά; ... πῶς δὲ καλὰ κἀκεῖνα καὶ ταῦτα; μετοχῇ εἴδους φαμὲν ταῦτα.

BODILY BEAUTY CAUSED BY THE IDEA

5. What then is beautiful in bodies? There is beauty which is perceivable at first glance; the soul embraces and expresses it when it recognizes it and submits itself to it. But when its glance falls on something ugly, then it turns away from it; it shudders and turns itself away from it because the ugly does not suit it and is alien to it... But how is it possible for there to be a resemblance between beautiful objects here and beautiful objects there?...

And if there is a resemblance, how can both the objects here and those there be simultaneously beautiful? This happens, so we maintain, through the participation of ideas.

PLOTINUS I 6, 2.

6. ⟨εἶδος⟩ ὅταν δὲ ἕν τι καὶ ὁμοιομερὴς καταλάβῃ εἰς ὅλον δίδωσιν τὸ αὐτό οἷον ⟨εἰ⟩ ὁτὲ μὲν πάσῃ οἰκίᾳ μετὰ τῶν μερῶν, ὅτε δὲ ἑνὶ λίθῳ διδοίη τις φύσις τὸ κάλλος, τῇ δὲ ἡ τέχνη.

6. When [the Form] comes upon something that is one and composed of like parts, it gives the same gift to the whole; as sometimes art gives beauty to a whole house with its parts, and sometimes nature gives beauty to a single stone.

tr. A. H. Armstrong

PLOTINUS I 6, 3.

7. πῶς δὲ τὴν ἔξω οἰκίαν τῷ ἔνδον οἰκίας εἴδει ὁ οἰκοδομικὸς συναρμόσας καλὴν εἶναι λέγει; ἢ ὅτι ἔστι τὸ ἔξω, εἰ χωρίσειας τοὺς λίθους, τὸ ἔνδον εἶδος.

INTERNAL FORM

7. How can an architect adjust the external house to the internal idea of the house and claim that it is beautiful? Only thanks to the fact that the external house, once we abstract it from its stones, is precisely the internal idea.

PLOTINUS I 6, 2.

8. Αἰσχρὸν δὲ καὶ τὸ μὴ κρατηθὲν ὑπὸ μορφῆς καὶ λόγου οὐκ ἀνασχομένης τῆς ὕλης τὸ πάντῃ κατὰ τὸ εἶδος μορφοῦσθαι.

UGLINESS

8. ...every shapeless thing which is naturally capable of receiving shape and form is ugly and outside the divine *logos* as long as it has no share in *logos* and form.

tr. A. H. Armstrong

PLOTINUS I 6, 9.

9. τό γὰρ ὁρῶν πρὸς τὸ ὁρώμενον συγγενὲς καὶ ὅμοιον ποιησάμενον δεῖ ἐπιβάλλειν τῇ θέᾳ. οὐ γὰρ ἂν πώποτε εἶδεν ὀφθαλμὸς ἥλιον ἡλιοειδὴς μὴ γεγενημένος, οὐδὲ τὸ καλὸν ἂν ἴδοι ψυχὴ μὴ καλὴ γενομένη. γενέσθω δὴ πρῶτον θεοειδὴς πᾶς καὶ καλὸς πᾶς, εἰ μέλλει θεάσασθαι θεόν τε καὶ καλόν.

ONLY A BEAUTIFUL SOUL SEES BEAUTY

9. To any vision must be brought an eye adapted to what is to be seen and having some likeness to it. Never did eye see sun unless it had first become sunlike, and never can the soul have vision of the First Beauty unless itself be beautiful. Therefore, first let each become godlike and each beautiful who cares to see God and Beauty.

tr. C. Mackenna

PLOTINUS IV 3, 10.

10. τέχνη γὰρ ὑστέρα αὐτῆς καὶ μιμεῖται ἀμυδρὰ καὶ ἀσθενῆ ποιοῦσα μιμήματα, παίγνια ἄττα καὶ οὐ πολλοῦ ἄξια, μηχαναῖς πολλαῖς εἰς εἰδώλων φύσιν προσχρωμένη.

ART BENEATH NATURE

10. But art is of later origin than soul; it is an imitator, producing dim and feeble copies—toys, things of no great worth—and it is dependent upon all sorts of mechanism by which alone its images can be produced.

tr. C. Mackenna

PLOTINUS IV 3, 11.

11. Καί μοι δοκοῦσιν οἱ πάλαι σοφοί, ὅσοι ἐβουλήθησαν θεοὺς αὑταῖς παρεῖναι ἱερὰ καὶ ἀγάλματα ποιησάμενοι, εἰς τὴν τοῦ παντὸς φύσιν ἀπιδόντες... προσπαθὲς δὲ τὸ ὁπωσοῦν μιμηθέν, ὥσπερ κάτοπτρον ἁρπάσαι εἶδός τι δυνάμενον.

ART, A MIRROR OF THE IDEA

11. I think, therefore, that those ancient sages who sought to secure the presence of divine beings by the erection of shrines and statues showed insight into the Nature of the All... Something, reproducing it or representing it and serving like a mirror to catch an image of it.

tr. C. Mackenna

PLOTINUS V 8, 1.

12. εἰ δέ τις τὰς τέχνας ἀτιμάζει, ὅτι μιμούμεναι τὴν φύσιν ποιοῦσι, πρῶτον μὲν φατέον καὶ τὰς φύσεις μιμεῖσθαι ἄλλα· ἔπειτα δεῖ εἰδέναι, ὡς οὐχ ἁπλῶς τὸ ὁρώμενον μιμοῦνται, ἀλλ' ἀνατρέχουσιν ἐπὶ τοὺς λόγους, ἐξ ὧν ἡ φύσις· εἶτα καὶ ὅτι πολλὰ παρ' αὑτῶν ποιοῦσι. καὶ προστιθέασι γὰρ ὅτῳ τι ἐλλείπει, ὡς ἔχουσαι τὸ κάλλος.

IMITATION IN ART

12. ...if anyone despises the arts because they produce their works by imitating nature, we must tell him, first, that natural things are imitations too: and then he must know that the arts do not simply imitate what they see; they go back to the *logoi* from which nature derives; and also that they do a great deal by themselves: since they possess beauty, they make up what is defective in things.

tr. A. H. Armstrong

PLOTINUS VI 4, 10.

13. εἰ τὴν παρὰ τοῦ ζωγράφου εἰκόνα λέγοι τις, οὐ τὸ ἀρχέτυπον φήσομεν τὴν εἰκόνα πεποιηκέναι, ἀλλὰ τὸν ζωγράφον.

CREATIVITY IN ART

13. If we are reminded of an artist's picture, we observe that here the image was produced by the artist, not by his subject.

tr. C. Mackenna

PLOTINUS V 8, 1.

14. ὁ Φειδίας τὸν Δία πρὸς οὐδὲν αἰσθητὸν ποιήσας ἀλλὰ λαβὼν οἷος ἂν γένοιτο, εἰ ἡμῖν ὁ Ζεὺς δι' ὀμμάτων ἐθέλοι φανῆναι.

14. Phidias did not make his Zeus from any model perceived by the senses; he understood what Zeus would look like if he wanted to make himself visible.

tr. A. H. Armstrong

PLOTINUS V 8, 1.

15. κειμένων τοίνυν ἀλλήλων ἐγγύς, ἔστω δέ, εἰ βούλει, λίθων ἐν ὄγκῳ, τοῦ μὲν ἀρρυθμίστου καὶ τέχνης ἀμοίρου, τοῦ δὲ ἤδη τέχνῃ κεκρατημένου εἰς ἄγαλμα θεοῦ ἢ καί τινος ἀνθρώπου, θεοῦ μὲν Χάριτος ἤ τινος Μούσης, ἀνθρώπου δὲ μή τινος, ἀλλ' ὃν ἐκ πάντων καλῶν πεποίηκεν ἡ τέχνη, φανείη μὲν ἂν ὁ ὑπὸ τῆς τέχνης γεγενημένος εἰς εἴδους κάλλος καλὸς οὐ παρὰ τὸ εἶναι λίθος — ἦν γὰρ ἂν καὶ ὁ ἕτερος ὁμοίως καλὸς — ἀλλὰ παρὰ τοῦ εἴδους, ὃ ἐνῆκεν ἡ τέχνη. τοῦτο μὲν τοίνυν τὸ εἶδος οὐκ εἶχεν ἡ ὕλη, ἀλλ' ἦν ἐν τῷ ἐννοήσαντι καὶ πρὶν ἐλθεῖν εἰς τὸν λίθον·

TWO BLOCKS OF STONE

15. Let us suppose, if you like, a couple of great lumps of stone lying side by side, one shapeless and untouched by art, the other which has been already mastered by art and turned into a statue of a god or of a man, of a Grace or one of the Muses, and if of a man, not just of any man but of one whom art has made up out of every sort of beauty. The stone which has been brought to beauty of form by art will appear beautiful not because it is a stone (for then the other would be just as beautiful), but as a result of the form which art has put into it. Now the material did not

ἦν δ' ἐν τῷ δημιουργῷ οὐ καθ' ὅσον ὀφθαλμοὶ ἢ χεῖρες ἦσαν αὐτῷ, ἀλλ' ὅτι μετεῖχε τῆς τέχνης. ἦν ἄρα ἐν τῇ τέχνῃ τὸ κάλλος τοῦτο ἄμεινον πολλῷ· οὐ γὰρ ἐκεῖνο ἦλθεν εἰς τὸν λίθον τὸ ἐν τῇ τέχνῃ, ἀλλ' ἐκεῖνο μὲν μένει, ἄλλο δὲ ἀπ' ἐκείνης ἔλαττον ἐκείνου· καὶ οὐδὲ τοῦτο ἔμεινε καθαρὸν ἐν αὐτῷ, οὐδὲ οἷον ἐβούλετο, ἀλλ' ὅσον εἶξεν ὁ λίθος τῇ τέχνῃ.

have this form: it was in the man who thought it before it came into the stone. It was in the workman, not in so far as he had hands and eyes, but because he had some art in him. So this beauty was in the art, and it was far better there; for the beauty in the art did not come into the stone: it stays in the art, and another comes from it into the stone which is derived from it and less than it. And even this does not stay pure and as it wants to be in the stone, but is only there as far as the stone has submitted to the art.

tr. A. H. Armstrong

PLOTINUS V 7; 3, 7.

16. ὡς γὰρ ὁ τεχνίτης, κἂν ἀδιάφορα ποιῇ, δεῖ ὅμως τὸ ταὐτὸν διαφορᾷ λαμβάνειν λογικῇ, καθ' ἣν ἄλλο ποιήσει προσφέρων διάφορόν τι τῷ αὐτῷ.

UNIQUENESS OF A WORK OF ART

16. A craftsman, even in constructing an object identical with a model, must envisage that identity is a mental differentiation enabling him to make a second thing by bringing in some difference side by side with the identity.

tr. C. Mackenna

PLOTINUS IV 3, 18.

17. ὥσπερ καὶ ἐν ταῖς τέχναις λογισμὸς ἀποροῦσι τοῖς τεχνίταις, ὅταν δὲ μὴ χαλεπὸν ᾖ, κρατεῖ καὶ ἐργάζεται ἡ τέχνη.

ART AND RATIOCINATION

17. Craftsmen faced by a difficulty stop to consider; where there is no problem, their art works on by its own forthright power.

tr. C. Mackenna

PLOTINUS V 9; 11, 1–6.

18. τῶν δὴ τεχνῶν ὅσαι μιμητικαί, γραφικὴ μὲν καὶ ἀνδριαντοποιία, ὄρχησίς τε καὶ χειρονομία ἐνταῦθά που τὴν σύστασιν λαβοῦσαι αἰσθητῷ προσχρώμεναι παραδείγματι καὶ μιμούμεναι εἴδη τε καὶ κινήσεις τάς τε συμμετρίας ἃς ὁρῶσι μετατιθεῖσαι, οὐκ ἂν εἰκότως ἐκεῖ ἀνάγοιντο, εἰ μὴ τῷ ἀνθρώπου λόγῳ.

ART IS OF THIS WORLD

18. The imitative arts—painting, sculpture, dancing pantomimic gesturing—are largely earth-based; they follow models found in sense, since they copy forms and movements and reproduce seen symmetries; they cannot therefore be referred to that higher sphere except indirectly, through the Reason Principle in humanity.

tr. C. Mackenna

PLOTINUS II 9, 16.

19. Τίς γὰρ ἂν μουσικὸς ἀνὴρ εἴη ὃς τὴν ἐν νοητῷ ἁρμονίαν ἰδὼν οὐ κινήσεται τῆς ἐν φθόγγοις αἰσθητοῖς ἀκούων; Ἢ τίς γεωμετρίας καὶ ἀριθμῶν ἔμπειρος, ὃς τὸ σύμμετρον καὶ ἀνάλογον καὶ τεταγμένον ἰδὼν δι' ὀμμάτων οὐχ ἡσθήσεται; εἴπερ οὐχ ὁμοίως τὰ αὐτὰ βλέπουσιν οὐδὲ ἐν ταῖς γραφαῖς οἱ δι' ὀμμάτων τὰ τῆς τέχνης βλέποντες, ἀλλ' ἐπιγιγνώσκοντες μίμημα ἐν τῷ αἰσθητῷ τοῦ ἐν

TWOFOLD EFFECTS OF ART

19. For how could there be a musician who sees the melody in the realm of *Nous* and is not stirred when he hears the melody of sensible sounds? Or how could there be anyone skilled in geometry and the science of numbers who is not pleased when he sees right relation, proportion, and order with his bodily eyes? Of course, people do not look at the same things in the same way; some, when they are

νοήσει κειμένου οἷον θορυβοῦνται καὶ εἰς ἀνάμνησιν ἔρχονται τοῦ ἀληθοῦς· ἐξ οὗ δὴ πάθους καὶ κινοῦνται οἱ ἔρωτες.

looking at pictures, see the works of art with their eyes but recognize in them an imitation in the world of sense of the reality existing in *Nous*, and are excited by it and come to a recollection of the truth: this is the experience from which passionate loves arise.

tr. A. H. Armstrong

PLOTINUS III 8, 7.

20. καὶ ὅ γε κακὸς τεχνίτης ἔοικεν αἰσχρὰ εἴδη ποιοῦντι.

ART AND BEAUTY

20. In the end, the sorriest craftsman is still a maker of forms, ungracefully.

tr. C. Mackenna

PLOTINUS IV 4, 31.

21. τέχναι δὲ αἱ μὲν οἰκίαν ποιοῦσαι καὶ τὰ ἄλλα τεχνητὰ εἰς τοιοῦτον ἔληξαν· ἰατρικὴ δὲ καὶ γεωργία καὶ αἱ τοιαῦται ὑπηρετικαὶ καὶ βοήθειαν εἰς τὰ φύσει εἰσφερόμεναι, ὡς κατὰ φύσιν ἔχειν· ῥητορείαν δὲ καὶ μουσικὴν καὶ πᾶσαν ψυχαγωγίαν ἢ πρὸς τὸ βέλτιον ἢ πρὸς τὸ χεῖρον ἄγειν ἀλλοιούσας.

CLASSIFICATION OF THE ARTS

21. As for the arts: such as look to house-building and the like are exhausted when the object is achieved, there are again those—medicine, farming and other serviceable pursuits—which deal helpfully with natural products, seeking to bring them to natural efficiency; and there is a class—rhetoric, music and every other method of swaying mind or soul with their power of modifying for better or for worse.

tr. C. Mackenna

PLOTINUS V 9, 11.

22. τῶν δὲ τεχνῶν ὅσαι μιμητικαί, γραφικὴ μὲν καὶ ἀνδριαντοποιία, ὄρχησίς τε καὶ χειρονομία... καὶ μὴν καὶ μουσικὴ πᾶσα περὶ ἁρμονίαν ἔχουσα καὶ ῥυθμὸν τὰ νοήματα... ὅσαι δὲ ποιητικαὶ αἰσθητῶν τῶν κατὰ τέχνην, οἷον οἰκοδομικὴ καὶ τεκτονικὴ... γεωργία συλλαμβάνουσα αἰσθητῷ φυτῷ, ἰατρική τε τὴν ἐνταῦθα ὑγίειαν θεωροῦσα ἥ τε περὶ ἰσχὺν τὴν τῇδε καὶ εὐεξίαν ... ῥητορεία δὲ καὶ στρατηγία, οἰκονομία τε καὶ βασιλική, εἴ τινες αὐτῶν τὸ καλὸν κοινοῦσι ταῖς πράξεσιν ... γεωμετρία δὲ τῶν νοητῶν οὖσα.

22. The imitative arts—painting, sculpture, dancing, pantomimic gesturing... and music, since its thought is upon melody and harmony..., the crafts such as building and carpentry which give us matter in wrought forms...; so agriculture dealing with material growths; so medicine watching over physical health, so the art which aims at corporeal strength and well-being...; oratory and generalship, administration and sovereignty—under any forms in which their activities are associated with Good...; geometry, as a science of the intellectual entities.

tr. C. Mackenna

PLOTINUS I 6, 4.

23. ὥσπερ δὲ ἐπὶ τῶν τῆς αἰσθήσεως καλῶν οὐκ ἦν περὶ αὐτῶν λέγειν τοῖς μήτε ἑωρακόσι μήθ᾽ ὡς καλῶν ἀντειλημμένοις, οἷον εἴ τινες ἐξ ἀρχῆς τυφλοὶ γεγονότες, τὸν αὐτὸν τρόπον οὐδὲ περὶ κάλλους ἐπιτηδευμάτων εἰ μὴ τοῖς ἀποδεξαμένοις τὸ τῶν ἐπιτηδευμάτων

EXPERIENCE OF BEAUTY

23. As it is not for those to speak of the graceful forms of the material world who have never seen them or known their grace—men born blind, let us suppose—in the same way those must be silent upon the beauty of noble conduct and of learning and all that order,

καὶ ἐπιστημῶν καὶ τῶν ἄλλων τῶν τοιούτων κάλλος, οὐδὲ περὶ ἀρετῆς φέγγους τοῖς μηδὲ φαντασθεῖσιν, ὡς καλὸν τὸ τῆς δικαιοσύνης καὶ σωφροσύνης πρόσωπον, καὶ οὔτε ἕσπερος οὔτε ἑῷς οὕτω καλά. ἀλλὰ δεῖ ἰδόντας μὲν εἶναι, ᾧ ψυχὴ τὰ τοιαῦτα βλέπει, ἰδόντας δὲ ἡσθῆναι καὶ ἔκπληξιν λαβεῖν καὶ πτοηθῆναι πολλῷ μᾶλλον ἢ ἐν τοῖς πρόσθεν ἅτε ἀληθινῶν ἤδη ἐφαπτομένους· ταῦτα γὰρ δεῖ τὰ πάθη γενέσθαι περὶ τὸ ὅ τι ἂν ᾖ καλόν, θάμβος καὶ ἔκπληξιν ἡδεῖαν καὶ πόθον καὶ ἔρωτα καὶ πτόησιν μεθ' ἡδονῆς.

who have never cared for such things, nor may those tell of the splendour of virtue who have never known the face of Justice and of Moral Wisdom beautiful beyond the beauty of Evening and of Dawn.

Such vision is for those only who see with the soul's sight—and at the vision they will rejoice, and awe will fall upon them, and a trouble deeper than all the rest could ever stir, for now they are moving in the realm of Truth. This is the spirit that Beauty must ever induce, wonderment and a delicious trouble, longing and love, and a troubling that is all delight.

tr. C. Mackenna

PLOTINUS II 8, 1.

24. παρεῖναι οὖν δεῖ αὐτὸ καὶ πλησίον εἶναι, ἵνα γνωσθῇ ὅσον·... Ἐν ἀμφοτέροις κοινὸν τὸ ἧττον ὅ ἐστι· χρῶμα μὲν οὖν τὸ ἧττον ἀμυδρόν, μέγεθος δὲ τὸ ἧττον σμικρόν, καὶ ἑπόμενον, τῷ χρώματι τὸ μέγεθος ἀνὰ λόγον ἠλάττωται.

ADVICE TO PAINTERS

24. So that to perceive its true size, we must have it close at hand... There is the common fact of diminution. There is colour with its diminution, faintness; there is magnitude with its diminution, smallness: and magnitude follows colour diminishing stage by stage with it.

tr. C. Mackenna

PLOTINUS VI 9, 11.

25. τὸ ἔνδον θέαμα καὶ τὴν ἐκεῖ συνουσίαν πρὸς οὐκ ἄγαλμα οὐδ' εἰκόνα, ἀλλ' αὐτό· ... τὸ δὲ ἴσως ἦν οὐ θέαμα, ἀλλὰ ἄλλος τρόπος τοῦ ἰδεῖν, ἔκστασις.

CONTEMPLATION

25. The vision in the temple and the communion are achieved not with the statue, but with the divinity itself... Contemplation is not a spectacle, but another form of vision, namely ecstasy.

PLOTINUS V 1, 6.

δεῖ τοίνυν θεατὴν ἐκείνου ἐν τῷ εἴσω οἷον νεῷ ἐφ' ἑαυτοῦ ὄντος, μένοντος ἡσύχου ἐπέκεινα ἁπάντων, τὰ οἷον πρὸς τὰ ἔξω ἤδη ἀγάλματα ἑστῶτα... θεᾶσθαι.

In order to contemplate that god, one has to concentrate inwardly as though inside a temple and to remain silent above all matters of this world as though one were beholding statues.

13. An Assessment of Ancient Aesthetics

1. PERIODS OF PROGRESS AND PERIODS OF STAGNATION. The history of ancient aesthetics spans an era of almost a thousand years and is a chequered one. It saw times of tension which were full of discoveries and new ideas, but also periods of stagnation, marked only by the repetition of accepted ideas.

A. The fifth century B.C. in Athens marks the first period of intensive thinking about aesthetics. The Pythagoreans, the Sophists, Socrates and Plato establish the main concepts of aesthetics and the basis of its further development. Important aesthetic concepts continued to develop throughout the fourth century to the beginning of the third century. Aristotle's theory of art was framed in the fourth century and the first theories of Hellenism, the musicology of Theophrastus and Aristoxenus and the poetics of Neoptolemus, appeared at the turn of the fourth century.

B. The third and second centuries mostly reflected the thought of the preceding two great centuries. It was not until the first century B.C., again in Athens, that intensive study reappeared. New ideas developed both in general aesthetics and especially in more detailed theories of the arts. Some new and some eclectic solutions to aesthetic problems were worked out by the Stoic school under Panaetius and Posidonius, and by the Academy under Philon and Antiochus of Ascalon.

Greeks and Romans acquired a knowledge of aesthetics in those reputable Athenian schools, and for two centuries afterwards many authors, both in Greece and in Rome, devoted themselves to aesthetics with considerable success: Philodemus, Pseudo-Longinus, Hermogenes and Dion in Greece; and Cicero, Quintilian, Vitruvius, Pliny and Seneca in Rome.

C. There was not another period of extensive development in aesthetics until the third century A.D., the close of antiquity. Stress had now shifted from metaphysical concerns and from empirical and scientific sobriety to religious other-worldliness. It had shifted from the compromises of eclectic thinkers to the extreme aesthetics of Plotinus. Thus, the development of ancient aesthetics ended with a metaphysico-religious conception. But it would not be true to maintain that its whole development tended towards such a conclusion. Rather the tendencies of the final phase of antiquity were responsible for it. Ancient aesthetics ended with the system of Plotinus, but it cannot be said that this was the fulfilment of any long-term design. On the contrary, during the five centuries from Aristotle to Plotinus no system at all was developed, but only detailed studies.

2. THE VARIETY OF ANCIENT AESTHETICS. The Greek concept of beauty and art may appear monolithic when it is compared with the aesthetic concepts of other lands and other times. It was a classical concept: modelled upon the real, perceivable world, without the symbols or transcendence which at other times and in other places dominated the concepts of beauty and art. And yet, despite this fundamental unity, the aesthetic attitudes of the ancients exhibited considerable variety.

A. Ancient aesthetics developed its *own forms*, but it *borrowed* some as well. Very early Greek culture drew on established Eastern culture. Diodorus Siculus writes that the early Greek sculptors were similar to the Egyptians in regarding their art as *kataskeue*, that is, as the composition of a work of art out of parts in accordance with defined rules. Later the Greeks framed their own classical concept of art. But their retention of a borrowed idea gave their concept a dual cast.

B. Expressive and contemplative forms. The Greeks distinguished two types of arts: some arts, like music, they regarded as expressive, others, like sculpture, they regarded as contemplative. The difference between the two they thought to be so great that they could not find a common theory to embrace them all. It was only later that they evolved the idea that each art may serve both expression and contemplation and that each one can—to use Nietzsche's figurative terms—be both Dionysian and Apollonian.

C. Doric and Ionic forms. By giving the names Doric and Ionic to two different forms of their art, the Greeks showed that they connected them with two regional tribes. The differences between Doric and Ionic forms are known chiefly from architecture; the terms referred to two orders, two proportions, the one heavier and the other lighter. But the same duality existed throughout Greek art and culture. The Doric aspect represented the objective tendencies in their aesthetics, while the Ionic represented the subjective ones. It was the Doric community that conceived measure as a criterion of good art, while the Ionians found this criterion in the pleasure of the spectator. The Dorians continued to observe rules, the Ionians were quick to develop impressionistic tendencies. The former relied on *symmetria*, the latter on eurhythmy. The former leaned toward absolutism and rationalism, the latter towards relativism and empiricism. At first these different views represented the differing predilections of two tribes, but in time they both became part of the general Greek culture and appeared side by side as its two variants. Two streams polarized its culture, its art and aesthetics.

D. Hellenic and Hellenistic forms. The duality of Hellenic and Hellenistic attitude was a chronological one, marking earlier and later attitudes of the ancients toward beauty and art. Hellenic art was classical in the strictest sense of the word, while its "Hellenistic" counterpart partially departed from classicism, either toward what may be called the baroque or toward romanticism; that is, either toward greater richness and dynamism or toward sentiment and transcendentalism. Hellenistic aesthetics followed art in these directions but it did not immediately rid itself of Hellenic classicism. As a result, Hellenic and Hellenistic forms appeared side by side in the later antiquity.

3. ACCEPTED TRUTHS. Aesthetic theories of antiquity were not uniformly accepted. Some, such as the theory that beauty depends upon the relation of parts, won common acceptance. Others, however, caused extensive disputes. Among these were theories concerning the value of art. Still others underwent gradual development, such as those concerned with the autonomy of art. It might be added that certain aesthetic questions, such as the description of aesthetic experience, did not interest the ancients, and no theories concerning them were produced at all.

The proposition that beauty depends on the relation of parts was a kind of aesthetic axiom until the time of Plotinus. But the same is true of certain other propositions, such as the following: that beauty depends on number and measure; that beauty is an objective property of things and not a projection of subjective experience; that its essence is unity; that it is linked with goodness and truth; that beautiful wholes are formed of similar as well as opposite elements; that there is more beauty in nature than in art; or that intellectual beauty is superior to sensory beauty. There were as many commonly accepted propositions regarding the theory of art: that all arts are based on knowledge; that none is purely a handicraft; that they all demand mental ability; that they are subject to general laws; and that the works of such arts as painting or music represent the real world, but belong to a world of fiction.

4. THE GREAT DISCUSSIONS. While the ancients accepted single solutions to some aesthetic problems without admitting any alternatives, to others they gave differing solutions, and opinion was divided between them. Here there was not so much an evolution from one solution to another as a wavering between several solutions. This state of affairs prevailed in ancient aesthetics with regard to (a) fiction and truth, (b) creation and imitation, (c) beauty and suitability, and (d) the aim of art.

A. Fiction versus truth. The Greeks based their aesthetics on two axioms which could easily conflict. On the one hand they held that, since truth is required in every human activity, it must also be present in imitative arts. On the other hand, they saw the essential characteristic of these arts to be the use of fictions and the creation of illusions. Gorgias admired them because they produce powerful effects, although they are only fictions. Plato, on the contrary, held that their fictions are a betrayal of truth and a disgrace.

If at certain periods and in certain schools the tension between truth and fiction abated, this was the result of the ancients' specific understanding of truth. For them truth was not a faithful reiteration of the facts but rather a grasp of their essence. Therefore they could maintain that art is capable of truth even though it relies on fictions. Aristotle even regarded poetry as truer than history, since the latter describes individual human characters, while the former generalizes them.

B. Imitation versus creation. The ancients were convinced that the human mind is passive; and with such a view it was only natural to maintain that the artist draws his works not from within himself but from the external world. But because this idea was generally accepted, little was said about it. Stress was laid on less obvious properties of art, for example, its creation of fictions or its expression of the soul. For most Greeks the main function of the imitative arts was to imitate reality, but also to express the state of soul. The first function was representational, the second creative. Plato was the first to ascribe to art only one function: the function of imitation; Aristotle soon departed from that position.

During the Hellenistic period the concept of imitation (*mimesis*), which had been fundamental in classical aesthetics, was employed less and less. The representational element of the arts ceased to be considered important. Art was now thought of more consistently as projection of ideas, an expression of souls, a creation of fantasy. Hellenistic writers proposed "imagination" (for example Philostratus) or "ardour" or "charm" (for example Dionysius of Halicarnassus) as the more essential properties of the arts.

It was never doubted in antiquity that representation of reality is a necessary condition of these arts. However, ideas changed on the importance of this indispensable element. It had become significant during the classical era, but ceased to be so during the Hellenistic period. Plato originated the naturalistic theory of art, but other Greeks, by emphasizing measure and imagination in art, inaugurated trends in direct opposition to this theory. It may even be said that Plato himself, who through his theory of art (based on the concept of imitation) stimulated naturalism, on the other hand, through his theory of beauty (based on the Idea of beauty and measure) encouraged his followers to adopt an attitude hostile to naturalism.

C. Beauty versus suitability. The Greeks considered beauty as an universal property; they believed that whatever is beautiful in one thing is also beautiful in every other and that whatever appears beautiful to one person, is also beautiful to everyone else. It is in this light that they understood "harmony" and *symmetria*. This universalistic aesthetics, created by the Pythagorean philosophers, was taken over by Plato and evidently became widespread because it appealed to the Greek mind.

On the other hand, a characteristic feature of the Greek mind was the conviction that each thing has its suitable shape, and in different things this shape is different. Every activity has its suitable moment, which the Greeks called *kairos* and which even early poets, such as Hesiod and Theognis, described as "the best". The ancients were particularly concerned about "suitability" in which they saw both an ethical and an aesthetic norm; they stressed it in their theories of art, of poetry and oratory. Thus they valued both beauty and suitability; the universal beauty and the individual suitability. Or, to put it differently, they valued two kinds of beauty, the universal beauty of *symmetria* and the individual beauty of suitability. Gorgias would have said that there was no universal beauty, and Plato would have said that so-called individual beauty was not beauty at all. But in the mind of the average Greek both ideas of beauty probably co-existed.

The development of the arts among the Greeks moved from universal to individual forms. This is clear enough in the plastic arts, but the transition from Aeschylus to Euripides may also be regarded as a move from a universal to an individual conception. The theory of art moved parallel with the development of art. The idea of suitability became dominant; it was in particular developed in Athens by the Stoic school under Panaetius, while Cicero popularized it in Rome under the name of *decorum*. This concept, that is the concept of individual beauty, became typical of Hellenistico-Roman times, although the concept of *symmetria*, of universal beauty, never disappeared in antiquity. The two concepts were used separately. It remained for St. Augustine to set them against each other.

D. Utility versus pleasure. The aim of art was both an important and a controversial issue. The alternatives put forward by the Sophists were that the aim of art was either pleasure or utility. Before that, as we know from their poets, the early Greeks had been quite convinced that both utility and pleasure were the aim of art. They thought art was useful mainly because it preserved the memory of human deeds which would otherwise be forgotten.

But the Sophists, who interpreted utility in a practical, materialistic way, concluded that art is not useful; therefore its only aim is pleasure. This was the first turning point in the interpretation of the aims of art. The second one was determined by the Cynics. They adopted the Sophists' idea, but they were indifferent to pleasure and attached prime importance to utility. Thus they concluded that since art is not useful, it has no aim whatsoever. This conclusion had its adherents: it became the basis of Plato's demand that artists and poets should be removed from the ideal state. It survived in one offshoot of the Stoic school and it found its clearest expression among the Epicureans. The Epicureans were not faced with a choice between pleasure and utility because they saw utility only in pleasure, and at the same time denied that art really provides it. The Cynics held that art has no aim because it does not give pleasure. The Greek artists of the day created great art at the same time as some Greek philosophers were denying art any aim or value.

Other philosophers, however, realized that there was a hiatus in the Sophists' reasoning. The proper aim of art, in their view, was neither ordinary pleasure nor common utility, but the gratification of a particular human need of harmony, proportion, perfection and beauty. They believed further that this gratification is both useful and pleasurable. It was to these philosophers, rather than the Cynics or the Epicureans, that aesthetics owed most.

Yet other thinkers maintained that art, particularly music, is concerned not with pleasure or utility or even perfection of its product, but with a special psychic effect, a purging of the soul, a *katharsis*. This idea originated with the Pythagoreans, who gave it a religious and mystical colouring. Later philosophers, particularly Aristotle, treated it in a more positive, psychological and medical way. Plotinus, however, returned to a metaphysical interpretation.

5. THE DEVELOPMENT OF ANCIENT AESTHETICS. Throughout antiquity several aesthetic problems underwent gradual enrichment and evolution.

(*a*) From the earlier assumption that art must correspond to moral laws and truth there gradually evolved the opposite view, emphasizing the *autonomy* of art and beauty. The classical representatives of this view were Aristophanes in poetry, Damon in music, and Plato in philosophy. This new idea had been expressed first by Aristotle and it was stressed later by Hellenistic aestheticians, though the Epicureans and to some extent the Stoics clung to the heteronomous view of art.

(*b*) From the early assumption that art is subject to general laws emerged gradually its recognition as *individual* creation. The earlier view was held by Plato, while Aristotle, and even more emphatically Hellenistic writers, supported the later idea. Yet in their theories of music or architecture they never doubted the existence of universal laws in art.

(*c*) There was an evolution from the early assumption that there is one perfect beauty and one perfect form of art to the acceptance of various forms and many styles in art. This was a movement towards *pluralism*. Both in architecture and in oratory various styles were employed concurrently and Hellenistic aesthetic theory justified this multiplicity. From a simplicity which had originally been valued above everything else both art and its theory moved toward greater variety, richness and decorativeness.

(*d*) From the early view that the source and criterion of art resides in the mind, there came about a recognition of the equality and even of the superiority of the *senses*. This was foreign to Plato, but was accepted by Aristotle. However, the decisive step was taken by the Stoics, who came to the conclusion that men possess not only ordinary sensory impressions, but also "educated" ones, which are capable of grasping not only the sounds of music, for example, but also their harmonies and disharmonies. While early poetics assumed that poetry affected the intellect, later theories stressed the sensory effects of poetry, and it came to be believed that poetic beauty depends primarily on "euphony", i.e., on beautiful sound judged not by the mind but by the ear.

(*e*) From the assumption that art draws its models from the external world, the view developed that it draws chiefly upon *ideas* in the mind of the artist. We find this later view particularly in Cicero. Through Philostratus we find that *imagination* came to be recognized as essential to art.

(*f*) From the assumption that thinkers and philosophers had the final word in matters of art it was later thought that this right belongs primarily to the artists themselves. This idea was accompanied by the conviction that it is *enthusiasm* and not philosophy which gives birth to the most valuable works, even though Cicero still held reflection to be a condition of good art and Horace wrote that wisdom is the beginning and source of good literature.

(*g*) From the assumption that the supreme element in art is truth there developed the idea that in art "beauty is paramount". This idea, however, did not appear until the time of Plutarch, Lucian and Plotinus.

(*h*) The early Greeks were aware of differences among the arts themselves, rather than of their common properties. This was particularly so with the two extremes, poetry and the plastic arts. The poet Simonides contrasted them but also brought them close together by maintaining that poetry is articulate painting and painting is silent poetry. The Hellenistic ideas on art moved toward a further rapprochement between the two.

(*i*) The evolution of ancient aesthetics led toward a greater differentiation of its concepts. From the general and vague concept of beauty there emerged narrower concepts of "suitability", "sublimity", "charm" and "sensory beauty". Similarly, the field covered by the equally general and vague concept of art was broken down and classified in various ways. A development spanning several centuries improved aesthetic concepts and perfected their definitions. This was the case both with the concept of beauty itself, which was defined successively by Plato, Aristotle and the Stoics, and with more detailed concepts. Among the latter was that of poetry, which Gorgias, Aristotle and Posidonius tried in turn to define.

6. AESTHETIC CONCEPTS. The history of aesthetic concepts in antiquity is analogous to the history of aesthetic theories. Some crystallized early and survived through antiquity. This was the case with the concept of "art" as a production based on rules. Others grew in the course of centuries, as, for example, the concept of "suitability" or "imagination". Still others, such as the concept of "taste", had not become fixed even by the very end of the period and had not acquired the status they were to gain in modern times.

The aesthetic concepts of the ancients, particularly the most fundamental and most frequently used, may appear similar to modern concepts. This is erroneous. Modern language has adopted old terms, but these terms now have a different meaning. This is especially true of the leading terms "beauty" and "art" which were employed in antiquity in a wider, not purely aesthetic sense. This is also true of other fundamental terms such as "imitation" and "purging".

On the other hand, numerous other concepts, particularly those which appeared in the later centuries of antiquity, were similar to those of modern aesthetics. Among them were "fantasy", "idea", "symbol", "harmony", "contemplation" (Greek *thea, theoria*), "intuition", "composition" (or in Greek, *synthesis*) and "fiction", in which even the ancient terms themselves have survived in modern languages. But even where the actual terms were different the meanings were similar. The Greek terms *ergon* and *poiema* (literally "a work") meant a work of art; *deinotes* (literally "daring") meant artistry; *lexis* (literally "way of expression") meant style; *thema* (literally "establishment") meant literary convention; *apate* (literally "mistake") meant illusionistic art; *plasma* (literally "that which is moulded") meant the work of art; *krisis* (from which "criticism" is derived) meant artistic judgment; *aisthesis* (from which "aesthetics" itself is derived) meant direct sensation: *hyle* meant the material of a work of art, and *mythos* meant a plot. One meaning of the term *pragma* (literally "thing") was the content of a work of art. (*Epinoia* was the Greek word for inspiration, and *ekplexis* (literally "dizziness") referred to emotion. Greek aesthetic categories resemble those of modern times: examples are *hypsos* (sublimity) and *charis* (charm). Also the merits of art which the Greeks stressed have modern analogies, as, for example, *enargeia* (sensory evidence), *sapheneia* (clarity) and *poikilia* (variety). Eventually the Greeks also developed the concept of originality and creativity in art: *autophues* meant an original work. *Technites* and *demiourgos* were applied to any producers, while *sophos, architekton* and *poietes* signified creators. Greek vocabulary was precise enough to distinguish between a good poet (*agathos poietes*) and one who is good at writing verse (*eu poion*). There were separate terms for representation (*homoiosis*), imitation (*mimesis*) and portrayal (*apeikasia*). There were also precise terms to denote relativity and subjectivity. The Greeks even had terms for which it is difficult to find modern equivalents, such as the Platonic *orthotes* (rightness of a work of art), *psychagogia* (the acting on souls and leading them),

Vitruvius' *temperantiae* (optical adjustments necessary in art), and the distinction between *aisthesis autophues* and *epistemonike* (natural and acquired sensations). Perhaps the only important aesthetic term lacking in antiquity was precisely the term "aesthetic". The Greeks did not use the terms "aesthetic experience" or "aesthetic judgment". These are modern terms with Greek etymology. The Greeks lacked the term "aesthetic" because they lacked its corresponding concept. They approached this concept but did not reach it.

7. THE LEADING DOCTRINES OF THE ANCIENT AESTHETICS. *A*. The leading doctrine of the ancient theory of beauty was above all that of *proportion* (beauty consists in arrangement of parts) and *measure* (beauty consists in measure and number). It was introduced by the Pythagoreans and subsequently became an axiom for the majority of Greek aestheticians. From the fourth century, however, it had a rival in the doctrine of *eurhythmy*, i.e., of subjective harmony (beauty depends on how harmony is perceived by man). Both rival doctrines were later opposed by Plotinus' contention that beauty is not an arrangement of parts, but a quality. This idea, however, did not appear until the close of antiquity. Until the third century A.D., ancient aesthetics vacillated between the doctrines of proportion and measure and of eurhythmy.

From the beginning of Greek aesthetics, two complementary doctrines developed: that of beauty as dependent on unity, and Heraclitus' doctrine that beauty arises from opposed elements. Later two antagonistic doctrines appeared: that of aesthetic sensualism and hedonism (beauty has a sensory basis) and that of aesthetic spiritualism (beauty has a mental basis). The former had been known from the time of the Sophists, the latter from the time of Plato. Two parallel doctrines, initiated by the Sophists and Plato respectively, were those of relativism (beauty is relative) and of idealism (there is an absolute beauty).

The doctrine of functionalism (beauty depends on purposefulness and suitability), which was taken up by Socrates, later reappeared in a more cautious formulation as the doctrine of *decorum* (one of the aspects of beauty as suitability).

In discussions on the value of beauty there were three doctrines struggling against each other: the Epicurean doctrine (beauty is useless), the Platonic and Stoic moralist doctrine (if beauty has a value it can only be of a moral character), and the doctrine of the autonomy of beauty (the value of beauty lies in itself). This last doctrine is found in the aesthetics of Aristotle and of many Hellenistic writers.

B. The same doctrines were to some extent present in the ancient theory of *art*. There, too, the doctrines of measure were dominant, the doctrine of *symmetria* and eurhythmy were strongly opposed and the doctrine of autonomy fought the doctrine of moralism. But apart from these the theory of art has several doctrines of its own. Discussions of the origin of art made use of the doctrine of inspiration which had appeared in the early poets and also later both in Democritus and in Plato, but most predominantly in the Hellenistic writers. In discussions on the function of art the doctrine of Gorgias (the products of art are pure illusions having nothing to do with reality) later gave way to the very influential doctrine of imitation of reality through art. Another aspect of the relation of art to reality was contained in the doctrine of Socrates (by selecting elements from nature the artist produces wholes which are more perfect than those existing in nature).

In their apprehension of art the Greeks early produced the concept of *katharsis*, the "Orphic doctrine" which proclaimed that the effects of art consist of purifying and making men happy. They sought a criterion of good art in successful illusion, in successful imitation and idealization. But the doctrine of *orthotes*, that is, of rightness or the guarantee of the excellence of a work of art through its compatibility with universal laws, was the deepest and most durable. Our knowledge of this doctrine comes chiefly from Plato. The same doctrine was also present in music under the name of *nomos* and in the plastic arts under the term "canon". Both terms expressed a conviction that for each artistic theme there exists a universal and absolutely binding rule.

If, to conclude, we were to ask which of the significant aesthetic concepts of antiquity was the most significant and at the same time the most specifically Greek, the most unlike any current today, we would have to list *symmetria*, *mimesis* and *katharsis*. The concept of *symmetria* embodies the ancients' understanding of beauty, the concept of *mimesis* their understanding of art, while the concept of *katharsis* embodies their idea of the effects of beauty and art on man.

8. VIRTUES AND FAULTS. The divergences appearing in ancient aesthetics need not cause us any surprise. The problems were too complex for any proposed solution to be universally accepted. What is surprising is rather the consistency and permanence of the chief doctrines. Many of them were indeed dictated not by strictly aesthetic considerations, but by religious beliefs, social factors and philosophical theories. Greek aesthetics praised *orthotes* under the influence of classical art; the later praising of fantasy was under the influence of baroque art. Aesthetics recognized divine inspiration in art through religious influence. It condemned the plastic arts because of the special character of the Greek social system. It promoted scepticism or idealism not by reference to any intrinsic aesthetic justification, but because of certain philosophical trends and philosophical schools.

If there were negative, restrictive ideas in ancient aesthetics, these arose from those foreign to aesthetic point of view. So it was with Plato's moralistic interpretation of art; with Epicurean judgments based on purely utilitarian principles; and with mystical elements in the aesthetics of late antiquity. In all these cases, however, negative elements were compensated for by positive ones: in Plato by his aesthetic intuition and countless new ideas regarding beauty and art, in the Epicureans by a sober analysis of poetry and music, in Plotinus by his criticism of the traditional theory of beauty. Later ages adopted and retained much of ancient aesthetics; they retained its main questions of beauty and of art and also other major concepts and theories. The theory of the "unity" of a work of art and the theory of "imitation" of reality are prominent even in the most recent times. And it is said that not enough advantage is taken of the heritage of antiquity, that still more use should be made of its achievements.

NAME INDEX*

Abert H. 19, 216, 222
Acron Helenius, grammarian (2nd c.) 194
Aeschylus, tragic poet (525–456 B.C.) 18, 45, 46, 48, 94, 126, 335
Aëtius, doxographer (1st or 2nd c.) 94, 194, 196
Aglaophon, painter (5th c. B.C.) 205, 214
Agatharchus of Samos, painter (5th c. B.C.) 48, 94, 111
Ainalov A. 269
Alberti L. B. 3, 277
Alcaeus of Mytilene, lyric poet (b. *c.* 620 B.C.) 21
Alcidamas, rhetorician and sophist (4th c. B.C.) 97, 99, 104
Alcinous, Platonic, formerly regarded as the author of an *Exposition of Platonism* which is at present attributed to Albinus 290, 298
Alexander of Aphrodisias, commentator on Aristotle (early 3rd c.) 197
Alexis of Thurii, comic writer (*c.* 372–270 B.C.) 47
Anacreon of Teos, lyric poet (b. *c.* 570 B.C.) 20, 30, 32, 300
Anaxagoras of Clazomenae, philosopher (*c.* 500–*c.* 428 B.C.) 43, 94, 100, 111
Anaxenous, musician (2nd c.) 217
Andromenides, theoretician of literature (3rd c. B.C.) 246
Antigonus, theoretician of painting (1st c. B.C.), 173
Antiochus of Ascalon, philosopher (b. *c.* 130–120 B.C.) 173, 201, 204, 288, 332
Antiphanes of Athens, comic writer (*c.* 388–*c.* 311 B.C.) 47

Antiphilus, painter (4th–3rd c. B.C.) 74
Appelles of Colophon, painter (4th c. B.C.) 59, 205, 214, 266
Archilochus of Paros, poet (7th c. B.C.) 18, 20, 30, 32, 37, 300
Archimedes, mathematician (287–212 B.C.) 221
Aristides Quintilian, theoretician of music (probably 3rd or 4th c.) 16, 82, 87, 222, 223, 227, 230
Aristides of Thebes, painter (4th. c. B.C.) 74
Aristippus of Cyrene, philosopher (*c.* 435–355 B.C.) 102, 103, 109
Ariston of Chios, philosopher (3rd c. B.C.) 186, 193, 243, 246, 254
Aristophanes, comic writer (446–338 B.C.) 32, 47, 76, 77, 124, 126, 136
Aristotle of Stagira, philosopher (384–322 B.C.) 3, 4, 6, 48, 75, 79, 80, 85, 87–89, 97, 101, 138–166, 170, 172, 175, 188, 190, 201, 203–206, 219–221, 223, 225, 235, 236, 247, 249, 253, 261–263, 271, 284, 292, 300, 301, 307, 308, 310–313, 315, 319, 332, 334, 336–339
Aristoxenus of Tarentum, scientist and theoretician of music (4th c. B.C.) 82, 87, 174, 206, 218, 220–222, 225, 227–229, 249, 284, 306, 332
Armstrong A. H. 326–330
Arnim H. von (J. ab) 185, 197, 285
Astidamus, tragic poet (4th c. B.C.) 47
Athenaeus of Naucratis, philosopher (2nd and 3rd c.) 83, 176, 178, 179, 239
Atkins J. W. H. 45
Aucher J. B. 195
Augustine, St., of Hippo, (354–430) 5, 335

---

*Names of modern translators, editors and authors of commentaries are italicized.

NAME INDEX

Babbit F. C. 76, 197, 249, 251
Bailey C. 180
Baldwin C. S. 259
Banks J. 34
Baeumler A. 9
Barker E. 161–163
Barker E. P. 198–200, 253, 300
Basore J. W. 253
Baumgarten A. 4
Batteux Ch. 4
Bekker J. 248, 315–317
Bénard Ch. 10, 170
Benvenga C. 178
Bernays J. 10
Bignami E. 10
Birmelin E. 285
Bosanquet B. 9
Bourbon di Petrella F. 318
Bowra C. M. 37–40
Breadstead J. H. 269
Bruns I. 197
Bruyne E. de 9
Burckhardt J. 170
Burke E. 3
Bury R. G. 184, 185, 227, 228, 248, 250, 258
Butcher S. H. 10, 34, 157–160, 162, 163
Butler H. E. 252, 302
Bywater I. 10

Caecillius of Calacte, rhetorician (1st c. B.C.) 235
Callimachus, poet (*c.* 305–*c.* 240 B.C.) 231, 232
Callistratus, critic of art (3rd or 4th c.) 285, 290, 293, 294, 299, 303
Caplan H. 250, 257
Carcimus of Acragas, actor and tragic poet (4th c. B.C.) 47
Carpenter C. 10
Carpion, architect and writer on architecture (5th c. B.C.) 270
Carritt E. F. 9
Cary E. 253
Caskey L. D. 59, 60
Cassirer E. 9, 10
Catandella Q. 99
Cato, Censorius, Roman statesman (234–149 B.C.) 245
Chalcidius, commentator on Plato (4th c.) 200

Chambers F. P. 9
Chermiss H. F. 93
Chersiphron of Cnossos, architect and writer (4th c. B.C.) 270
Choisy A. 70
Chrysippus, Stoic philosopher (3rd c. B.C.) 77, 186, 188–191, 194–200
Cicero, Marcus Tullius, orator (106–43 B.C.) 90, 93, 94, 172–174, 176, 179, 186–191, 194–197, 199, 200–215, 217, 221, 233–235, 237, 240, 242, 246, 252, 257, 263–265, 270, 271, 290, 291, 295, 309, 311, 312, 315, 317, 319, 321, 332, 335, 337
Cleanthes of Assos, philosopher (331–232 B.C.) 186, 187, 191, 192, 198, 199
Cleisthenes, architect (5th c. B.C.) 42
Clement of Alexandria, Christian writer (2nd 3rd c.) 90, 94, 105, 199
Cleonides, musicologist (2nd c.) 221
Cockerell C. R. 68
Cohoon J. W. 298, 301, 303, 304
Colson F. H. 194, 297
Combarieu J. 9, 18
Conybeare F. C. 298
Cornforth F. M. 128, 132, 133, 135, 136–138, 157
Cornificius Quintus, Roman orator (1st c. B.C.) 262, 264
Cooke H. P. 162
Cooper L. 10
Cousin J. 264
Cramer J. A. 87, 106
Crates of Pergamon, Stoic philosopher (3rd and 2nd c. B.C.) 242, 246
Croce B. 3, 9
Crönert W. 230
Cumont F. 269

Damianus, author of a work on optics (4th c. B.C.?) 283
Damon of Athens, theoretician of music (5th c. B.C.) 83, 84, 219, 223, 225, 230, 336
Dehio G. 49
Delatte A. 17, 80
Demetrius Chlorus, hellenistic Scholar 248
Demetrius of Phalerum, theorist of poetry and rhetoric (*c.* 350–280 B.C.) 78, 235, 236, 257, 295

NAME INDEX

Democrates, orator (4th c. B.C.) 93, 95
Democritus of Abdera, philosopher (*c.* 460–370 B.C.) 2, 78, 79, 85, 89–95, 100, 111, 112, 120, 121, 139, 143, 167, 176, 177, 183, 221, 275, 290, 339
Demophilus, painter and sculptor (5th c. B.C.) 270
Demosthenes, orator (384–322 B.C.) 47
Deonna W. 43
Dewey J. D. 3
Diehl E. 37, 40
Diels H. 76–78, 86, 88, 89, 93–95, 105–107
Diocles of Magnesia, philosopher (1st c. B.C.) 199, 251
Diodorus Siculus of Agyrium, historian (b. *c.* 80 B.C.) 8, 63, 332
Diogenes the Babylonian, historian (*c.* 240–152 B.C.) 186, 193, 197, 200, 206, 222, 226, 229, 241, 244, 251, 303
Diogenes Laertius, doxographer (2nd and 3rd c.) 46, 77, 83, 88, 106, 115, 127, 153, 174, 179, 189, 196, 199, 248, 251, 308, 310, 315
Dion of Prusa, called Chrysostomus, orator (1st and 2nd c.) 269, 285, 286, 289, 290, 292–296, 298, 301, 303, 304
Dionysius of Colophon, painter (5th c. B.C.) 74, 142
Dionysius of Halicarnassus, rhetor and theoretician of literature (1st c. B.C.) 19, 190, 216, 226, 235, 236, 241, 243, 245, 246, 251, 253–256, 291, 293, 334
Dionysius Thrax, scientist (1st c. B.C.) 247–249, 310, 311, 315–317
Donaldson J. W. 68
Doxapatres Joannes, commentator on Hermogenes (11th c.) 314
Dresdner A. 9
Duris of Samos, historian and author of a treatise on the plastic arts (*c.* 340–*c.* 260 B.C.) 285

Egger E. 45
Eichholz D. E. 302
Einstein A. 9
Else G. F. 10
Empedocles, philosopher (*c.* 493–*c.* 433 B.C.) 85, 91, 92, 94

Ephorus of Cyme, historian (*c.* 405–330 B.C.) 108
Epicharmus, poet and philosopher (*c.* 550–460 B.C.) 46, 76, 98, 106, 111
Epictetus of Hierapolis, Stoic philosopher (*c.* A.D. 55–135) 100, 186, 187
Epicurus of Samos, philosopher (341–270 B.C.) 172, 174–180
Eratosthenes of Cyrene, scientist (*c.* 275–194 B.C.) 237, 239, 250
Euphranor, sculptor and painter (4th c. B.C.) 48, 58, 74, 75, 270
Euripides, tragic poet (480?–406? B.C.) 46, 47, 75, 76, 142, 190, 215, 335

Fairbanks A. 77, 298, 299, 302, 303
Fairclough H. R. 94, 249, 251, 253, 254, 256, 258
Falconer W. A. 94
Fechner G. Th. 3
Ficino Marsilio, Renaissance philosopher (1433–1499) 3
Fierens P. 43
Finke G. C. 201
Finley D. J. 89
Finsler G. 10, 155
Fischer Th. 49
Forster E. S. 164, 301
Fortunatianus Atilius, metrician (4th c.) 263, 264
Fowler F. G. 253
Fowler H. N. 128, 129, 131–135
Fowler H. W. 253
Frank E. 10, 219
Freeman K. 34, 76, 86, 88, 89, 93–95, 106, 107
Freese J. H. 158, 159, 165
Friedlein G. 283
Fyfe W. H. 164

Galen of Pergamum, physician and writer (129 –? 199) 55, 77, 189, 196, 206, 309, 312, 315
Geffcken J. 296
Geminus of Rhodes, mathematician (1st c. B.C.) 277, 283
Georgiades T. 17
Gerold Th. 216
Gevaërt F. A. 18, 216
Gilbert K. 9

344 NAME INDEX

Giovannoni G. 68
Goodyear W. H. 68
Gorgias of Leontini, rhetor and philosopher (*c.* 483–376 B.C.) 48, 96, 98–100, 105, 107, 111, 112, 121, 122, 139, 144, 190, 236, 238, 259, 261, 262, 334, 335, 339
Granger F. 94, 279–283
Grassi E. 10
Grube G. M. A. 10, 257
Gudeman A. 10, 155

Hackforth R. 132, 135
Hambidge J. 59, 60
Harmon A. M. 254, 299, 301, 305
Hauck G. 68
Hautecoeur L. 43
Havell H. L. 250
Hegel G. W. F. 3
Heiberg J. L. 284
Helmbold W. C. 93
Heracleodor, theorist of literature (3rd c. B.C.) 246, 251, 257
Heraclides Ponticus, grammarian (4th c. B.C.) 179, 206, 229
Heraclitus of Ephesus, philosopher (*c.* 535–475 B.C.) 78, 84, 85, 88–90, 107, 111, 121, 179, 188, 301, 339
Hermann C. F. 298
Hermagoras of Temnos, teacher of rhetoric (2nd and 1st c. B.C.) 263
Hermogenes, architect (*c.* 200 B.C.) 255, 266, 270, 278
Hermogenes of Tarsus (b. *c.* 150) 173, 235, 236, 239, 241, 251, 252, 265,
Herodotus, historian (489–425 B.C.) 47
Heron of Alexandria, scientist (2nd c. B.C.) 78, 277, 284
Herondas, mimographer (3rd c. B.C.) 231, 232
Hesiod of Ascra, poet (*c.* 700 B.C.) 9, 32–34, 37–40, 87, 98, 111, 126
Hicks R. D. 127, 165, 179, 196, 251
Hiller E. 87
Hippocrates, physician (b. *c.* 460 B.C.) 93, 106
Hippolytus, Christian writer (2nd and 3rd c.) 88, 89
Hobein H. 297, 302, 305, 306
Hoffer J. 68
Homer 9, 20–22, 30–37, 45, 59, 87, 98, 126, 179, 220, 234, 242, 249, 290, 294, 297

Horace, poet (65–8 B.C.) 90, 94, 100, 174, 175, 206, 234–237, 240, 242, 244, 245, 247, 249, 251, 253–255, 257, 258, 263, 284, 293
Hook L. van 106
House H. 10
Howard E. 99
Hubbell H. M. 210, 212, 213
Huber-Abramowicz E. 10
Hume D. 3

Iamblichus, philosopher (*c.* 250–325) 86, 87, 296
Ictinus, architect and writer on architecture (5th c. B.C.) 48, 270,
Immisch O. 235
Ingarden R. 10
Isocrates, orator (436–338 B.C.) 43, 47, 96, 97, 99, 105, 106, 238, 260–262, 315
Iversen E. 8

Jaeger W. 43
Jaffré F. 10
Jahn A. 87, 198, 222, 227, 230
Jan K. von 18, 216
Jander K. 83
Jebb R. C. 158–160, 163
Jenkins R. J. 68
Jensen Ch. 175, 199, 248, 251, 254, 256–258
Jolles J. A. 275
Jones H. L. 88, 250
Jones W. H. S. 77, 93, 107, 249, 299
Jowett B. 34, 76, 104, 128, 130, 227, 230, 314
Jucker H. 170

Kaibel G. 146, 248
Kalkmann A. 57, 285
Kant I. 3, 4
Kayser C. L. 302
Keilland E. C. 8
Kemke I. 95, 175, 199, 200, 229, 230, 303
Keyes C. W. 250
Keyser E. de 318
Kiesling T. 63
Kilburn K. 254
King J. E. 200, 207, 215
Koller H. 17, 219
Körte A. 43

NAME INDEX

Krakowski E. 318
Kranz W. 30
Kristeller P.O. 9, 26, 308
Krueger J. 10
Kuhn H. 9, 43

Lamb W. R. M. 127
Lanata G. 30
Lang A. 39
Lange J. 8
Leaf W. 34
Leonardo da Vinci 3
Leonidas, author of a treatise on architecture 270
Lepik-Kopaczyńska W. 51
Lepsius C. R. 8
Lessing G. E. 294
Lodge R. C. 10
Lowe J. C. B. 76, 105, 197, 199, 200, 314, 315
Lucian of Samosata, orator and writer (2nd c.) 168, 187, 206, 231, 239, 243, 253, 254, 285, 291–293, 295, 299, 301, 305, 319, 337
Lucretius, philosopher (95–55 B.C.) 173–177, 180, 233, 270
Lukomski G. K. 270
Lysippus, sculptor (4th c. B.C.) 75, 205, 214, 266, 287

Mackenna S. 326–331
Macran H. S. 228, 229
Madyda W. 235, 236, 284, 285
Marchant E. C. 109–111
Marcus Aurelius, Roman emperor and philosopher (121–180) 186, 193, 197, 217, 239, 265, 268
Marquardt P. 218, 228, 229, 315
Martin Th. H. 78
Maximus of Tyre, Platonic philosopher (c. 125–185) 176, 178, 206, 235, 238, 240, 293–297, 302, 305, 306
Maykowska W. 235
Metampus, author of a treatise on architecture 270
Melanippides, musician (5th c. B.C.) 216
Melikova-Tolstoi S. W. 99
Melnoth W. 299, 303
Menecrates, cithara player (1st c.) 217

Metagenes, architect and author of a work on the temple of Artemis at Ephesus 270
Mezzantini C. 10
Michałowski K. 8
Mikkola E. 96
Miller F. J. 256
Miller W. 207–209, 212, 215
Minucius Felix, Christian writer (3rd c.) 234
Moe C. J. 278
Montmoulin D. de 10
Moxon T. A. 257
Mössel E. 49
Müller E. 10
Müller I. 77, 196
Murely C. 10
Myers E. 34
Myron, sculptor (5th c. B.C.) 69, 205, 214, 287

Neubecker A. J. 178, 193,
Neoptolemus, theoretician of poetry (3rd c. B.C.) 235, 236, 241, 257, 332
Nexaris, author of a handbook of architecture 270
Nicias, painter (4th c. B.C.) 48, 74, 78
Nicomachus, mathematician) 1st c.) 86, 290
Niemojewski L. 62
Nietzsche F. 15, 333
Norlin G. 105, 106

Olympiodorus, commentator on Plato (5th and 6th c.) 198
Oppel H. 59
Onlick C. B. 179
Ormerod H. A. 299
Ovid, poet (43 B.C.–A.D. 18) 239, 251, 256

Pamphilus of Amphilopolis, painter (4th c. B.C.) 59, 74
Panaetius, Stoic philosopher (c. 185–109, B.C.) 173, 186, 193, 203, 206, 332, 335
Panofsky E. 8, 9, 55
Parrhasius, painter (5th c. B.C.) 48, 74, 101, 102, 108, 121, 286, 291,
Pasicles, artist and writer on art 284
Pasiteles, sculptor (1st c. B.C.) 173
Paton W. R. 108
Pausanias the Periegite, geographer (2nd c.) 285, 290, 291, 299,

Pauson, painter (4th c. B.C.) 142, 157
Pennethorne J. 68
Penrose F. C. 68
Perrin B. 300
Phidias, sculptor (5th c. B.C.) 6, 44, 63, 69, 139, 204, 211, 255, 289–294, 297, 300, 301, 321, 328
Philetas of Cos, poet, (b. *c.* 320 B.C.) 300
Philodemus of Gadara, philosopher (*c.* 110–*c.* 40/35 B.C.) 92, 95, 175, 177, 178, 186, 199, 200, 206, 224–226, 229, 230, 235, 236, 239, 241, 244, 246, 247, 248, 251, 254, 256–258, 288, 303, 332
Philolaus, philosopher (5th and 4th c. B.C.) 80, 86
Philon of Alexandria, philosopher (20 B.C.–A.D. 50) 187, 194, 195, 270, 288, 297, 332
Philon of Byzantium, mechanician (3rd c. B.C.) 277
Philon of Larissa, philosopher (160/59–80 B.C.) 186, 201
Philostrati, the Athenian, the Elder, and the Younger, critics of art (2nd and 3rd c. A.D.) 6, 48, 77, 191, 206, 242, 269, 285, 286, 289, 293, 294, 298, 302, 313, 314, 317, 334, 337
Phrynis of Mytilene, musician (5th c. B.C.) 216
Pietzsch G. 222
Pindar of Thebes, poet (522–442 B.C.) 17, 20, 21, 30, 32–34, 37, 40, 111
Plaistowe F. G. 76
Plato, philosopher (428–348 B.C.) 2–4, 6, 7, 48, 63, 75, 76, 79, 80, 84, 87–89, 91, 93, 96, 97, 100, 101, 104, 105, 112–139, 141, 143, 145, 147–149, 151, 154, 155, 167, 172, 175–177, 179, 181, 183, 186–188, 190, 200–206, 215, 216, 219, 222, 223, 225–227, 230, 239, 242, 253, 261, 262, 265, 275, 288–292, 294, 300, 307, 308, 310–312, 314, 315, 318–321, 331, 334–337, 339, 340
Plebe A. 10, 178, 318
Pliny the Elder, author of *Historia naturalis* (A.D. 23/4–79) 6, 59, 74, 169, 173, 174, 234, 285, 286, 299, 301, 302, 332
Pliny the Younger, author of *Letters* (62–113) 291, 299, 303
Plotinus, philosopher (205–270) 172, 173, 194, 206, 296, 311, 312, 317–332, 336, 337, 339, 340
Plutarch, historian and moralist (45–125)18–20, 22, 40, 76, 93, 107, 179, 191, 195, 197, 206, 216, 219, 221, 226–228, 231, 235, 236, 238–242, 247, 249, 259, 286, 288, 291, 292, 295, 297, 300, 303–306, 308, 313, 337
Pohlenz M. 99, 185, 189
Pollis, architect and author of a treatise on architecture (4th c. B.C.) 270
Polus of Agrigentum, pupil of Gorgias (4th c. B.C.) 261
Polybius, Greek historian (*c.* 210–125 B.C.) 100, 108
Polyclitus, sculptor (5th c. B.C.) 48, 54, 55, 58, 59, 69, 74, 75, 77, 139, 167, 205, 214, 255, 291, 292, 300
Polygnotus, painter (5th c. B.C.) 72, 139, 142
Porphyry, philosopher (232–304) 235
Posidonius of Apamea, philosopher (2nd and 1st c. B.C.) 173, 186, 188, 191, 192, 194, 198, 203, 206, 236, 237, 248, 294–296, 309, 312, 316, 332, 338
Praxiteles, sculptor (*c.* 350 B.C.) 102, 266, 286
Proclus, philosopher (5th c.) 277, 283, 288, 297
Protagoras of Abdera, philosopher (5th c. B.C.) 89, 96–99, 106, 107
Pseudo-Aristotle, Eclectic philosopher (1st c. B.C.) 89, 228, 301
Pseudo-Dionysius, or Pseudo-Areopagite, an anonymous Christian mystical writer (5th c.) 324
Pseudo-Longinus, literary critic (1st c.) 171, 235, 239, 242, 243, 246, 250, 252, 253, 255, 258, 332
Pseudo-Cyprianus, writer (5th c.?) 235, 243, 255
Pyrrhion, Sceptic philosopher (*c.* 376–286 B.C.) 180
Pythagoras of Rhegium, sculptor (5th c. B.C.) 77
Pythagoras of Samos, philosopher (570–497) B.C.) 59, 80, 83, 88, 91, 219, 227
Pytheos, architect and writer on architecture (4th c. B.C.) 270

Quintilian, orator (*c.* 35–95) 174, 187, 190, 191, 198, 201, 234, 235, 241, 243, 246, 252, 256, 262, 264, 284, 287, 288, 291–293, 295, 299, 302, 309–312, 316, 332

NAME INDEX

Rabe H. 251, 252, 314
Rackham H. 93, 158, 160, 162, 163, 166, 179, 195, 197, 208–211, 213, 214, 252, 257, 299
Radermacher L. 226, 254–256
Randall G. H. 197
Rastagni A. 178, 224
Read H. 9
Regner J. 219
Riemann H. 18
Reinach S. 233
Reinach Th. 222
Reisch E. 77, 299, 303
Renan E. 265
Roberts W. R. 78, 226, 228, 252, 254–256, 258, 259
Rodenwaldt G. 43
Rose H. 43
Ross W. D. 85, 87, 155, 156
Rostovtzeff M. 269

Saintsbury G. 9
Sandbach F.H. 259
Sappho, poetess (c. 620–580 B.C.) 20, 21, 30, 34, 40
Sarnacus, author of a treatise on architecture 270
Satyrus, architect and writer on architecture (4th c. B.C.) 270
Scaurus Marcus, Roman statesman (4th c. B.C.) 286
Schaerer R. 26
Schäffer W. 8
Schäfke R. 9, 219, 222
Schasler M. 9
Schenkl C. 77, 299, 303
Schlosser J. 9
Schubert O. 56
Schöne R. 283
Schuhl P. M. 10, 63
Schweitzer B. 10, 43, 285
Scopas of Paros, sculptor (4th c. B.C.) 102, 266, 286, 291
Seneca, philosopher (3 B.C.–A.D. 65) 171, 173, 174, 186, 187, 191–193, 198–200, 235, 238, 242, 253, 292, 295, 296, 300, 309, 312, 316, 332
Sextus Empiricus, philosopher (2nd c.) 86, 174, 180, 182–185, 187, 198, 218, 224, 227–229, 231, 232, 236, 239, 247, 248, 250, 258, 288

Shelley B. P. 131, 132
Silanion, author of a treatise on architecture 270
Silenus, architect and writer on architecture 48, 270
Simonides, poet (556–468 B.C.) 18, 33, 97, 98, 259, 337
Sinko T. 42, 235
Smith J. A. 155, 156
Snell B. 47
Socrates, philosopher (469–399 B.C.) 42, 47, 75, 79, 80, 89, 95, 98–104, 108–115, 121, 126, 129, 131, 142, 151, 167, 275, 293, 331, 339, 340
Solon, lawmaker and poet (7th and 6th c. B.C.) 21, 30, 32–34, 38, 39, 42
Sophocles, tragic poet (495–405 B.C.) 44, 46, 47, 69, 75, 97, 139, 142
Speusippus, philosopher (4th c. B.C.) 193, 225, 226, 231
Stead J. H. 269
Stefanini L. 10
Stobaeus, doxographer (5th c.) 86, 95, 107, 187, 189, 194, 244
Strabo, goegrapher (c. 63 B.C.–A.D. 19) 88, 217, 235, 236, 238, 291
Stratton G. M. 94
Strong E. 269
Stroux J. 43
Strzygowski J. 269
Stuliński J. 63
Stumpf C. 219
Suidas, lexicographer (10th c.) 221
Sulpicius Victor, Roman rhetor 264
Sutton E. W. 93
Svoboda K. 10, 30, 186, 201, 236
Swift E. A. 269

Tacitus, historian (c. 55–120) 22, 234, 238, 264
Tarrhaeus Lucius, grammarian (1st c.) 311, 317
Tatarkiewicz W. 10, 25, 26, 43, 289, 308
Taylor A. E. 128–130, 132, 133, 137, 138
Teichmüller G. 10
Terence, comic writer (c. 195–159 B.C.) 209
Terpander of Lesbos, musician and poet (c. 675 B.C.) 19, 216, 224, 226
Tertullian, philosopher (c.160–240) 234
Thaletas the Cretan, musician and poet (1st c). 19

Theocides, author of a work on architecture 270
Theodorus of Phokai, architect and writer on architecture (6th c. B.C.) 270
Theognis of Megara, poet (6th c. B.C.) 21, 34, 40, 97
Theocritus, poet (3rd c. B.C.) 231
Theon of Smyrna, mathematician (*c.* 130) 87
Theophilus of Antioch, Christian writer (2nd and 3rd c.) 233
Theophrastus, Peripatetic philosopher (*c.* 372–287 B.C.) 94, 220, 221, 229, 235, 236, 240, 245, 246, 262, 332
Thiersch A. 49
Thomas Aquinas, St., philosopher (1225–1274) 5
Thomson J. A. K. 156, 161, 164, 165
Thrasyllus of Alexandria, astrologer (1st c. B.C) 89
Thucydides, historian (*c.* 460–*c.* 400 B.C.) 39, 42, 47
Timotheus of Miletus, musician (5th and 4th c. B.C.) 216
Todd O. J. 110
Tredennick H. 156
Tyrataeus, poet and musician (7th c. B.C.) 224
Tzetzes Johannes, Byzantine polymath (12th c.) 63

Ugolini G. 47
Untersteiner M. 96
Usener H. 174, 226, 254–256
Utitz E. 10

Vaglimigli M. 285
Varro Marcus Terentius, scientist (117–26 B.C.) 22, 173, 296, 309
Venturi L. 9
Verdenius W. J. 10
Viollet-le-Duc E. E. 25
Virgil, poet (70–19 B.C.) 187, 234

Vitelo, medieval scientist (13th c.) 3
Vitruvius Pollio, architect (1st c. B.C.) 3, 49–51, 53, 55, 57, 58, 62, 63, 66, 68, 91, 94, 171, 173, 174, 234, 242, 270–284, 287, 289, 332

Wagner R. 216
Walter J. 10
Warrington J. 164
Warry J. G. 10
Watson J. S. 198, 208, 209, 211, 212, 214, 256
Watts N. H. 214
Weil H. 222
Westphal R. 18, 216, 310
Wheeler A. L. 251
Whitaker G. H. 297
Wickhoff F. 267
Wickstead P. H. 157
Wilamowitz–Moellendorf U. von 48, 233
Wolff O. 49

Xenocrates, theoretician of painting (4th c. B.C.) 173, 284
Xenophanes, philosopher (*c.* 570–480 B.C.) 97, 98, 105, 111
Xenophon, soldier and writer (*c.* 430–355 B.C.) 42, 100–102, 104, 108–111, 121

Younge C. D. 207, 208, 210, 211, 215

Zeller E. 10, 112, 139
Zeno, philosopher (335–263 B.C.) 187, 188, 191, 193, 195, 197, 198
Zenodorus, sculptor (1st c. B.C.) 287
Zeuxis, painter (5th c. B.C.) 72, 74, 102, 139, 142, 205, 210, 214, 286, 290
Zholtovski A. 73
Zieliński T. 16, 232
Zimmermann R. 9

SUBJECT INDEX *

AESTHETICS: subject, method, difficulties, **1–7**; turning points in its history, 7–9, 11, 139, 331, 332; and philosophy, 78–80; characteristics of ancient ae., 74, 75, 166, 167, 331–340; characteristics of Hellenistic ae., 171–174, 268, 269, 295, 296, 331–340; objectivism in, 81, 112, 116, 126, 150, 188–191, 194, 195, 240 (see also SYMMETRIA); subjectivism in, 99, 100, 112, 175, 240, 275–277 (see also EURHYTHMY); relativism in, 96–98, 105, 110, 112; moralism in, 113, 119, 124, 127, 172, 187, 188, 288; hedonism in, 90, 97, 115, 116, 172, 175, 339; functionalism in, 102, 103, 109, 110, 112, 115, 116, 272–274, 279, 280, 288, 339; formalism in, 177, 178, 245, 246, 288; pluralism in, 154, 205, 206, 241, 336, 337; principal concepts, **338, 339**

APATE: see ILLUSION IN ART

ARCHITECTURE: term, 27; Greek, 22, 23, 49–54, 63–69; canon in Greek, **49–54**, 62, 63, 68; Hellenistic and Roman, 265–268, 277, 278; theory, 48, 270–279; optical illusions, **63–71**, 78, **282–284**; place in the classification of the arts, 22, 26, 27, 308–310, 322, 330

ART: concept, 26, 96, 101, 112, **119, 120, 139–141**, 155, 156, 191, 192, 198, 203, 208, 249, 338; and beauty, 1, 26, 112, 119, 120, 123, 135, 139, 150, 152, 202, 295, 304, 321, 322, 330, 337; fine arts, 27, 112, 121, 122, 142, 154, 295, 303, 304, 308, 311, 313, 314; and poetry, 28, 40, 120, 121, 144, 145, 289, 290, 294, 303, 304 (see also CLASSIFICATION OF ARTS); and nature, 89, 93, 96, 97, 101, 102, 104, 123, 124, 137, 147, 156, 167, 177, 180, 203, 204, 210, 250, 293, 321, 322, 327, 339, 340; representational and imitative (mimetic), 75, **101, 102**, 108, 109, **121, 122**, 125, **132–134**, 135, 136, **141–155**, 157, 159, 163, 204, 241, 242, 308, 321, 322, 329 (see also MIMESIS, CLASSIFICATION OF ARTS); and truth, 30, 31, **123, 124**, 167, 204, 211, **334** (see also POETRY and truth); and artistic truth, 124, 148, 149, 193, 314; and pleasure, **90**, 97, 104, 105, 111, 123, 175, 176; and utility, 97, 123; and science, 156; criteria of good art, 123, 124, **149, 150**, 193; value, 124–126, 136, 137, 153, 165, 176, 178, 179, 182, 183, 200; effects and aim, 38, 82, 91, 97, 107, 123, 124, 145–148, 160, 161, 293, 322, 329, 330, 335, 336 (see also CATHARSIS); moral significance, see ETHOS, AUTONOMY OF ART

ARTIST: 32, 38, 59, **112**, 125, 133, 140, 141, 143, 145, 150, 163, 173, 199, 204, 241, 242, 260, **289–292**, 299, 300, 320, 321; sources of his creation, 120, 121, 129, 131, 132, 154; and idea, 129, 204, 205, 211, 212, 290, 299; 320–222; value, 33, 36, 152, 192, 199, 200, his social position, 217, 271, 291, 292, 295, 299; and artisan (craftsman), 26, 121, 150, 163, 292, 304; as arbiter in art, 291, 299. See also INSPIRATION, CREATION

AUTONOMY OF ART: 31, 124, 148, 149, 154, 162, 176, 191, 293, 336. See also ART

BEAUTY: concept, 1, 5, **25**, 29, 30, 34, 79, **97, 98,** 103, 104, **113, 114,** 118, 119, 127, 129, 150, 151, 188, 189, 196, 201, 202, 295, 319; kinds, 95, 102, 103, 119, 120, 127, 130, 131, 148, 202, 325, 326; value, 123, 150, 153, 165, 175, 176, 190, 191, 339; spiritual *vs.* physical, 95, 102, 112, 114, 118, 119, 120, 127, 128, 187, 194, 202, 206, 320, 326; sensory and intellectual criteria, 193, 200, 219, 225–

---

* Bold type is used to denote pages on which the given problem is given more specific consideration.

228, 231, 243, 244, 257, 258, 293, 301, 337; conditions, 77, 80, 81, 84, 86, 87, 95, 111, 116–119, 125, 151–153, 192, 193, 231, 333; aesthetic (artistic) and moral, 25, 34, 40, 92, 113, 119, 126, 127, 150, 151, 185–188, 194, 202, 333; and truth, 114, 115, 122, 123, 127, 334; and utility, rightness (suitability), 98, 102, 103, 109, 110, 115, 123, 124, 135, 163, 202, 207, 208, 335, 337; and pleasure, 40, 90, 93, 97, 115, 116, 118, 127, 150, 153, 175, 178, 179, 225, 228, 244, 245, 256, 305, 335, 336; theory of universal beauty (*pankalia*), 25, 80, 118, 123, 185, 194, 195, 307; of nature, 152, 188, 194–196, 203, 204, 209, 210, 333, 334; and art, 1, 26, 112, 119, 120, 123, 135, 139, 150, 152, 202, 295, 304, 321, 322, 330, 337; relativity and subjectiveness, **97, 98**, 103, 105, 106, 110, 111, 119, 127, 130, 131, 185, 338; objectiveness and absoluteness, 77, 81, 85–87, 103, 112, 116, 119, 127, 130, 131, 153, 191, 197, 202, 333, 339; in the sense of suitability (fittingness), 102, 103, 104, 109, 110, 115, 123, 124, 151, 152, 189, 190, 196, 197, 207, 334, 335. See also DECORUM, EURHYTHMY, HARMONY, SYMMETRIA

CANON, universal rules in art; 8, 19, 20, 24, 25, 29, **49–69**, 72, 74, 77, 167, 243, 274, 275, 314, 332, 340; in architecture, 49–54, 270, 272, 274, 275, 279–282, 284; in sculpture, **54–59**, 77; in the Greek vases, **59, 60**; in music, 216, 219, 220
CATEGORIES, AESTHETIC: see BEAUTY, CHARM, SUBLIMITY
CATHARSIS: concept, **16**; in music, 82, 83, 87, 88, 211, 221, 336, 340; in the plastic arts, 145–147; in tragedy, 145, 146
CHARIS: see CHARM
CHARM (*venustas, charis*): 25, 30, 32, 39, 152, 202, 244, **245**, 337, 338
CHOREIA: **15–17**, 45, 82
CLASSICISM: see STYLES
CLASSIFICATION OF ARTS: 26–28, 97, 119–123, 132, 141, 142, 145, 154, 157, 191, 198, 203, 208, 209, **307–317**, 322, 330
COMEDY: 47, 145; and truth, 100
COMPOSITION: see CONSTRUCTION
CONNOISSEUR OF ART: 199, 289, 291, 299, 337
CONSTRUCTION: 8, 15; composition, 51, 123, 158, 177, 178, 218, 243, 246, 257, 258, 264, 271, 272, 314, 338; constructive *vs.* expressive arts, see EXPRESSION
CONTEMPLATION (*theoria*): **29, 30, 83**, 88, 160, 161, 301, 302, 320, 324, 331–333, 338
CONTENTS: 98, 99, 118, 144, 160, 177, 178, 257, 286; in painting, 77; in poetry, 230; in music, 230; and form, 74, 98, 99, 102, 111, 178, 199, 236, 237, 239, 240, 245, 246, 250, 251, 257. See also FORM
CONVENTION IN ART: 97, 246, 247, 258
CREATION (creativity), artistic: **29**, 90, 91, 139, 140, 143, 145, 150, 167, 203–205, **241–244, 289–292**, 321, 322, 328, 329, 334, 335

DANCE: 18, 218
DECORUM: see SUITABILITY

ETHOS, ethical theory of music: 81, 82, 177, 178, 219, **221–224**; criticism of, 224, 225, **230**
EURHYTHMY: 26, 75, 103, 104, 294; in poetry, 240; in architecture, 272, 273, **275–277**, 280, 335. See also BEAUTY, SYMMETRIA
EXPERIENCE, AESTHETIC: 1, 2, 82, 112, **153, 154**, 188, 192, 193, 243
EXPRESSION, ARTISTIC: 102, 108, 109, 196, 302, 303; in Hellenistic art, 266; expressive *vs.* constructive art, 15–17, 312, 332, 333; in poetry and music 15–17, 21, 22; of soul in art, 102

FANTASY: see IMAGINATION
FICTIVENESS OF ART: 31, 33, 39, 45, 176, 204, 211, **237–239**, 250, 334, 338. See also IMAGINATION
FITTINGNESS: see SUITABILITY
FORM: 150; as arrangement of parts, 81, 117, 118, 151, 296; as opposed to contents, 74, 98, 99, 102, 112, 144, 178, 199, 236, 239, 241, **245, 246**, 249, 250, 262, 263; perfect, 116, 118; individual, 98, 153; in art *vs.* nature, 20. See also CONTENTS
FORMALISM: 95, 177, 178, 245, 246, 288. See also AESTHETICS
FUNCTIONALISM: 102, 103, 109, 110, 112, 115, 272, 279, 280, 288, 339. See also AESTHETICS

HARMONY: **80, 81**, 83–85, 85–87, 129, 150, 258, 338; of cosmos, 25, **81**, 86, 87, 183, 185;

SUBJECT INDEX

in the plastic arts, 280–301; in music, **81, 82,** 86, 183, 185, 220, 227

HEDONISM: 90, 97, 115, 172, 175, 339. See also AESTHETICS

IDEA, inner form: 114, **118, 119,** 125, **129, 130,** 155, 204, 205, 211, 212, 242, 253, 290, 292, 298, **319, 320,** 321, 327, 338

IDEALIZATION IN ART: 46, 72, 75, 77, **101, 102,** 111, 118, 123, 124, 142, 157, 158, 210, 290, 297, 340

ILLUSION IN ART (*apate*): 75, 91, 94, **99, 100,** 107, 108, 112, 122, 123, 125, 133, 134, 260, 339

IMAGINATION (fantasy): 25, **191,** 197, 239, **241,** 243, 252, 289, 297, 298

IMITATION: see MIMESIS

IMPRESSIONS: see SENSE IMPRESSIONS

INSPIRATION ("enthusiasm"): 24, 34, **90, 91,** 93, 94, 210, 211, **242,** 253, 290, 291, 299, 307, 339

INTELLECTUALISM, predominance of thought and reason in art: 46, 116, 193, 212, 213, 219, 227, 230, 239, **242–244,** 246, 257

INTUITION: 123, **243,** 255, 338

LITERATURE: 231–234; and art, 3–4; characteristics of Hellenic, **45–48;** characteristics of Hellenistic, **231–234;** theory, 214, 233, 234, 238, 239, 264; negative attitude towards its theory, 181, 182, 184, 185. See also POETRY, PROSE, COMEDY, TRAGEDY, RHETORIC

MANIA: see INSPIRATION

METHODOLOGY OF AESTHETICS: 206, 215, 228, 229, 274, 310, 314

MIMESIS, imitation of reality by art: **16, 17,** 77, 89, 101, 112, **121, 122,** 132–134, **141–144,** 157–159, 204–220, 237, 240, 248, 255, 289, 294, 334, 335, 340; limits of imitation by art, 136, 137

MODULE: 49–51, 55, 274, 279. See also CANON

MORALISM IN AESTHETICS: 113, 119, 123, 126, 172, 187, 188, 339. See also AESTHETICS

MUSIC: concept, 27, 28, **258, 259;** modes, 216, 221, 224, 230; rules, 81–84; canon (*nomos*), **19, 20,** 80–82; sources, 225, 226, effects, 36, 82, 87, 88, 108, 148, 220–224, 230; expressiveness, 18, 22, 82, 224; hedonistic effects, 92, 95, 228; moral aim, 223 (see also Ethos); value, 182, 183; social significance, 217; cognitive significance, 192, 224; and catharsis, 82, 83, 87, 88, 224; and form, 177, 178; and imitation, 224; and poetry, 18, 19, 224; and dance, 218. See also ETHOS, CATHARSIS, NOMOS

NATURE: see ART and nature, BEAUTY of nature

NOMOS: **19, 20,** 49, 80, 216, 219, 221, 337. See also CANON

NORM: see CANON

OBJECTIVISM IN AESTHETICS: 74, 80, 112, **116,** 126, 152, 188–191, 193, 240. See also AESTHETICS

ORATORY: see RHETORIC

ORTHOTES, rightness of a work of art in Plato: **123,** 135, 338, 340. See also SUITABILITY

PAINTING, CLASSICAL: 72, 73; perspective, 91, 92, 94; illusionist, 100; imitation of nature by, 138; and poetry, 40. See also PLASTIC ARTS, SCENOGRAPHY

PANKALIA: see BEAUTY, universal

PLASTIC ARTS: concept, 22, **26–28, 284–286,** 308, 310, 311, 313, 314; characteristics in the archaic period, 22–25; in the classical period, 48–75; in the Hellenistic period, 265–269, 284–288; classification, 15, 16, 26–28, 294, 295, 307–314 (see also CLASSIFICATION OF ARTS); theory, 48–75 (of architecture, 200–279; of painting and sculpture, 284–288); representational character, 101, 108, 109, **121, 122,** 132, 133, 141, 286; relation to nature, 69, 74, 101, 137, 286, 289, 301; subject, 77, 286, 287, 306; illusionism, 63, 75, 78, 99, 100, 133, 134; materials 292–304; rules, ratios, numerical proportions, 24, 25, **49–59,** 72, **77,** 274, 299; aim and effects, 104, 105, 121, 123, 279, 292, 293; theory of colour, 91, 92, 94; optical illusions and, their correction, 63–69, 91, 133, 134; conditions of creativity, 289–292, 297–299; and truth, 59, 286, 290; and beauty, 294–295, 306; and philosophy, 285; and poetry, 40, **294,** 303, 304; and social value 291, 292,

296, 300; negative evaluation, 124, 125, 171.
PLURALISM IN AESTHETICS: 154, **205**, **206**, 214 241, 251, **268**, **269**, 337
POETRY: concept, **28**, **29**, 192, 236, 237; archaic and classical, 15–17, 20–22; Hellenistic and Roman, 231–234; kinds, 247, 248; theory and rules, 30, **141–150**, 157–160, 192, **235–247**, 253, 254; source, 32, 34, 35, 37, 150, 163, 177; subject, 31, **32**, **33**, 34, 192, 237, 239, 240; aim and effects, 30, 32, 35, 36, 38, 76, 99, 100, 107, 108, 123, 124, 176, 177, 236, 237, 249, 250; value, 31, 33, 36, 39, 120, 136, 137, 190, 192, 199, 200, 250, 303; inspiration, 31, 34, 76, 93, 94, 120, 131, 132, 210, 211, 242, 243, 253; imagination in, 241, 242, 252; and truth, 31, 33, 37, 39, 99, 100, 126, 138, 142–144, 148, 149, 162, 176, 192, 199, 237, **239**, 250, 255, 289; and the good, 148, **239**, **240**; and beauty, 240, **241**, 251; and oratory, **238**, **239**, 261, 264; and prose, 106, 212, 236, **238**, **239**, 245, 246; and music, 121, 145, 215, 224; and the plastic arts, 29, 40, 120, 121, 144, 145, **294**, 303, 304; and philosophy, 21, 33, 88, 126, 138, 199, 237, 238
PREPON: see SUITABILITY
PROPORTION: as commensurability, see SYMMETRIA, HARMONY; as a definite numerical ratio, see CANON; golden section, 72, 73; and radiance, 326
PROSE: characteristics of Hellenic, 47, 48; characteristics of Hellenistic and Roman, 231, 234; and rhetoric, 259; and poetry, 238, 239, 259–261. See also LITERATURE

RELATIVISM IN AESTHETICS: 96, 97, 98, 105, 106, 110, 112
REPRESENTATION IN ART: see MIMESIS
RHETORIC (and oratory): theory and rules, 47, 48, 164, 165, 196, 260–263; styles, 245, 256, 257, 263; characteristics of Hellenistic 259–265; aim and effects, 259–261; and truth, 99, 149, 162, 203; and logic, 262; and civic morality, 263, 264; and poetry, 238, 239
RHYTHM: 75, 83, 104, 129, 145, 159, 226, 227, 284; in music and dance, 18, 19, 83; in poetry, 98
RIGHTNESS: see SUITABILITY

SCENOGRAPHY: 63, 75, 91, 100, 124, 276
SCEPTICISM IN AESTHETICS: 172, **180–185**. See also AESTHETICS
SCULPTURE, CLASSICAL: 27; characteristics of Hellenic, 23–24; characteristics of Hellenistic, 287, 288; numericall proportions, 8, 55–59, 72, 73, 77, 103. See also PLASTIC ARTS
SENSE, AESTHETIC: 193, **205**, 212, 213, 225, 226, 295
SENSE IMPRESSIONS: 175, 177, 193, **205**, 221, 222, 226, 229, 244–246; vs. intellectual, 231, **243**, **244**, 257, 258, **319**, **320**, 323, 324, 330, 331, 337, 338
STYLES; classical, 43, 44; classical vs. Hellenistic, 266, 269, 278; Doric vs. Ionic, 24, 41, 42, 75, 275, 278, **333**; in music, 222, 223; in poetry, 235, 241, 244, 245; in rhetoric, 245, 256, 257, 261, 263; triple — the grand, the middle, the simple, 256, 257
SUBJECTIVISM IN AESTHETICS: see AESTHETICS
SUBLIMITY: 119, 171, 235, 236, 241, 243, **245**, 253, 254, 337
SUITABILITY (decorum, prepon), fittingness, rightness, purposefulness of a work of art, 34, 98, 102, 103, 109, 110, 115–117, 123, 135, **189**, **190**, 196, 197, 207, 240, 241, **272–274**, 280, **335**. See also ORTHOTES, SYMMETRIA
SYMMETRIA (proportion): 26, 48, 75, 77, 81, 85–87, **116–118**, 128, 129, **151**, **152**, 164, 188–190, 194, 196, 240, **272–277**, 279, 280–282, 294, 319–321, 325, 326, 335, 339; and decorum, 189, 190. See HARMONY, EURHYTHMY, BEAUTY

TALENT: 99, 190; and education, 99, 166, 167, 210, 244, 255, 256, 290
TECHNE: 26, 139, 140. See also ART
THEORIA: see CONTEMPLATION
TRAGEDY: 27, 28, 145, **160**; characteristics in antiquity, 45–48, 159; origin, 45; theory, 46; subject, 145, 146; effects, 145–147; and truth, 45, 100, 107

UGLINESS, 85, 97, 105, 109, 110, 188, 196, 240, 241

VENUSTAS: see CHARM

DISCARDED BY
DARTMOUTH COLLEGE LIBRARY